A Pirate's Life

in the Golden Age of
PIRACY

Robert Jacob

Published by
DocUmeant Publishing
244 5th Avenue, Suite G-200
NY, NY 10001

646-233-4366

Copyright ©2020 Robert Jacob. All rights reserved

Limit of Liability and Disclaimer of Warranty: The design, content, editorial accuracy, and views expressed or implied in this work are those of the author.

No part of this publication may be reproduced, stored in a retrieval system, or transmitted in any way by any means—electronic, mechanical, photocopy, recording, or otherwise—without the prior permission of the copyright holder, except as provided by USA copyright law.

For permission contact the publisher at Publisher@DocUmeantPublishing.com

Editor: Philip S. Marks

Map and Woodplate Images provided by Barry Lawrence Rudman Antique Maps Inc. www.Raremaps.com

Cover Design by: Patti Knoles, www.virtualgraphicartsdepartment.com

Ship Illustrations by: Ginger Marks, www.DocUmeantDesigns.com

Layout & Design by: DocUmeant Designs, www.DocUmeantDesigns.com

Library of Congress Control Number: 2019947708

First Edition

6 7 8 9 10

Publisher's Cataloging-In-Publication Data

(Prepared by The Donohue Group, Inc.)

Names: Jacob, Robert, 1955-

Title: A pirate's life in the golden age of piracy / Robert Jacob.

Description: NY, NY : DocUmeant Publishing, [2020] | Includes bibliographical references and index.

Identifiers: ISBN 978-1-950075-09-6 pbk; 978-1-9378-0191-5 hc;

Subjects: LCSH: Piracy--History. | Pirates--History.

Classification: LCC G535 .J33 2018 | DDC 364.164--dc23

DEDICATION

This book is dedicated to the living historians and reenactors throughout the world who devote many thousands of selfless hours in the pursuit of accurately portraying history and keeping it a real and interactive experience for those who attend their events and visit their historic sites.

The vast majority of these devoted individuals do this simply for the love of history, without any monetary compensation whatsoever. Each of them often bears a tremendous financial expense for clothing and equipment which they purchase on their own in order to make their historical interpretation as accurate and real as possible. They keep history alive.

CONTENTS

Dedication III

Preface XIII

Part I: The "Golden Age" XVI

    Chapter 1: Let the Piracy Begin 1

    Chapter 2: Chipping Away at the Spanish Main 5

    Chapter 3: Birth of the Buccaneers 10

Part I.I: The Buccaneers 1640–1670 17

    Chapter 4: The Buccaneer Privateers 19

    Chapter 5: Jamaica 23

    Chapter 6: The Pirate King 27

    Chapter 7: Port Royal, Dung Hill of the Universe 30

    Chapter 8: Enter Henry Morgan 34

    Chapter 9: Policy Changes 37

    Chapter 10: Privateers of the Second Dutch War 40

    Chapter 11: Henry Morgan—King of the Privateers 45

    Chapter 12: Searle's Sack of St. Augustine 51

    Chapter 13: Morgan's Panama Campaign 53

    Chapter 14: Summing Up the Buccaneers 1640–1670 57

Part I.II: The Buccaneer Pirates 1670–1702 59
- Chapter 15: Sailing Under French Colors 61
- Chapter 16: Sir Henry Morgan 65
- Chapter 17: Changing Times 70
- Chapter 18: The Buccaneer Author 73
- Chapter 19: The Treaty that Changes the Caribbean 82
- Chapter 20: Dampier's Round the World Voyage 84
- Chapter 21: The Glorious Revolution of 1688 93
- Chapter 22: Piracy and Higher Education 95
- Chapter 23: Pirate Ports & Trade in North America 97
- Chapter 24: The Pirate Haven of St. Mary's 105
- Chapter 25: Tew and Every 108
- Chapter 26: Captain William Kidd 117
- Chapter 27: The Last Great Pirate of the Indian Ocean 124
- Chapter 28: The Last Hurrah for the French Privateers 128
- Chapter 29: Summing Up the Buccaneer Pirates 1670–1702 131
- Chapter 30: The War Almost Nobody Knows About 133

Part I.III: Pirates and Privateers of the War of 1702–1713 137
- Chapter 31: Woodes Rogers 139
- Chapter 32: Queen Anne's War 143
- Chapter 33: Summing Up Pirates and Privateers of the War of 1702–1713 149
- Chapter 34: The Book that Altered History 151

Part I.IV: The Pyrates 1714–1722 157
- Chapter 35: The Pyrates are Back 159
- Chapter 36: Henry Jennings, and a New Pyrate Port 165
- Chapter 37: Hornigold's Pyrates 170
- Chapter 38: Black Sam Bellamy On His Own 174
- Chapter 39: Blackbeard the Pyrate 177
- Chapter 40: The Unlikely Partnership 180
- Chapter 41: The Queen Anne's Revenge 185
- Chapter 42: The King's Proclamation 193

Chapter 43: From Honduras to Ocracoke 196

Chapter 44: Woodes Rogers and the Rebel with a Cause 205

Chapter 45: Blackbeard's Girlfriend 210

Chapter 46: Sugar, Mutiny, and the Pyrate Banyan 213

Chapter 47: The Royal James. 218

Chapter 48: The Death of Blackbeard 221

Chapter 49: Who Was the Real Blackbeard?. 228

Chapter 50: The Big Pyrate Ships of the African Waters 231

Chapter 51: To the African Waters 234

Chapter 52: The Troubled Partnership, Davis, La Buse, and Cocklyn 241

Chapter 53: William Snelgrave's Invaluable Account 244

Chapter 54: Partnership Dissolved and Davis' Death 250

Chapter 55: Roberts Takes Command. 255

Chapter 56: The Pyrate Fleet of Edward England 261

Chapter 57: Taylor and La Buse 265

Chapter 58: Roberts Starts Over Again 267

Chapter 59: Calico Jack Rackham, Anne Bonny, and Mary Read 275

Chapter 60: Roberts Vows Revenge 284

Chapter 61: The Last Great Pyrate. 288

Chapter 62: Summing Up the Pyrates 1714–1722. 296

Part II: A Pirate's Life 304

Chapter 63: The Pirate's Code 305

Chapter 64: The Captain's Authority. 316

Chapter 65: Tools of the Trade—Sailing Vessels. 321

Chapter 66: Tools of the Trade—Guns 329

Chapter 67: Tools of the Trade—Firelocks. 335

Chapter 68: Tools of the Trade—Edge Weapons 347

Chapter 69: Tools of the Trade—Navigation. 355

Chapter 70: The Black Flag of Death's Head 358

Chapter 71: Tactics. 362

Chapter 72: Treatment of Captives 369

Chapter 73: Pirate Booty. 373
Chapter 74: Coin of the Realm 375
Chapter 75: Buried Treasure 383
Chapter 76: Daily Life, How They Lived 389
Chapter 77: Talk Like a Pirate 397
Chapter 78: A Square Meal 399
Chapter 79: Native to the Old World or the New 403
Chapter 80: What to Eat With 421
Chapter 81: Textiles 424
Chapter 82: Fashion 430
Chapter 83: How Do I Look? 442

GLOSSARY 477
BIBLIOGRAPHY 477

TABLE OF FIGURES

Figure 1: The Caribbean 4
Figure 2: Hispaniola 8
Figure 3: First Settlements 9
Figure 4: Tortuga 13
Figure 5: French Hispaniola 21
Figure 6: Jamaica 1670 24
Figure 7: Maracaibo 49
Figure 8: Exq Buccaneers of America 1678 Book Cover 67
Figure 9: Ringrose Buccaneers of America 1685 Book Cover 77
Figure 10: Mid-Atlantic 80
Figure 11: Dampier's 1697 Book Cover 88
Figure 12: Dampier's Travels 90
Figure 13: Africa & Indian Ocean 107
Figure 14: Henry Every Flag 114
Figure 15: Thomas Tew Flag 114
Figure 16: 1690s Galley, Similar to the Adventure Galley 119
Figure 17: Captain Kidd's First Map 122
Figure 18: Captain Kidd's Second Map 123
Figure 19: General History of Pyrates Title Page, 1724 153
Figure 20: Jamaican Sloop, Similar to the Revenge 181
Figure 21: Queen Anne's Revenge 186
Figure 22: Blackbeard's Flag 188
Figure 23: Queen Anne's Revenge Route 189

Figure 24: Topsail Inlet and Ocracoke 200
Figure 25: Atlantic and West Africa 253
Figure 26: Roberts, First Flag 270
Figure 27: Roberts, Second Flag 270
Figure 28: Rackham's Flag 276
Figure 29: Jamaica in 1720 283
Figure 30: Roberts ABH AMH Flag 285
Figure 31: West African Trading Posts 289
Figure 32: A Ship of War, of the third-rate, With Rigging etc. at Anchor, from the 1728 Cyclopaedia, Volume 2 327
Figure 33: Doglock with Frizzen Closed 339
Figure 34: Doglock with Frizzen Open 339
Figure 35: 1670 Doglock Musket 339
Figure 36: Flintlock with Frizzen Closed 340
Figure 37: Flintlock with Frizzen Open 340
Figure 38: 1685 Flintlock Pistol 344
Figure 39: 1680 Small Sword 350
Figure 40: Late 17th Century Shell Guard Cutlass 352
Figure 41: Early 18th Century English Hanger 352
Figure 42: Henry Every Flag 359
Figure 43: Thomas Tew Flag 359
Figure 44: Rackham's Flag 361
Figure 45: Edward England Flag 361
Figure 46: Blackbeard's Flag 361
Figure 47: Stede Bonnet Flag 361
Figure 48: Roberts, First Flag 361
Figure 49: Kennedy Flag 361
Figure 50: Captain Kidd's First Map 388
Figure 51: Captain Kidd's Second Map 388
Figure 52: Whiskey Johnny 392
Figure 53: Haul on the Bowline 392
Figure 54: Bartholomew de Portuguese 443
Figure 55: Rock Brasilliano 443
Figure 56: Francois Lolonois 443
Figure 57: Henry Morgan's Attack on Porto Bello 443
Figure 58: Henry Morgan 443

Figure 59: Blackbeard, First Edition 1724 444

Figure 60: Blackbeard, Second Edition 1724 444

Figure 61: Blackbeard 1725 Edition 444

Figure 62: Bartholomew Roberts, Second Edition 1724 444

Figure 63: Anne Bonny and Mary Read, Second Edition 1724 444

Figure 64: Anne Bonny and Mary Read, Dutch Edition 1725 444

Figure 65: Blackbeard, 1734 Edition 445

Figure 66: Henry Every, 1725 Edition 445

Figure 67: Edward England, 1725 Edition 445

Figure 68: Jack Rackham, 1725 Edition 445

Figure 69: Henry Morgan, Charles Johnson Later Edition 446

Figure 70: Howell Davis, 1725 Edition 447

Figure 71: Charles Vane, 1725 Edition 447

Figure 72: Bartholomew Roberts, 1725 Edition 447

Figure 73: Stede Bonnet, 1725 Edition 447

PREFACE

With each decade, there seems to be one historical time period that grabs the imagination and attention of the public. Sometimes this is brought on by the anniversary of a significant historical event, like the bicentennial of the Revolutionary War in 1976. Sometimes the craze is sparked by a blockbuster motion picture. Western reenacting was extremely popular in the late 1990s after the release of Tombstone. Beginning around 2005, it seems to be pirates.

I am not a formally trained historian with years of experience researching facts in dusty archives and lonely corridors. I haven't spent dozens of years of my life studying history in higher institutions of learning. I am an officer in the United States Marine Corps who retired after serving for 31 years. But in addition to my military service, for most of my life I have been a historical reenactor; a person dedicated to living history interpretation. I'm not a paid historian, but rather an amateur with a passion for history and historical accuracy. Being so involved with living history has given me a unique perspective on historical events. It has provided me with a first-hand look into the lives of people from the time periods I have re-created. My research has revealed that lifestyles in historical times were often very different, and more interesting than what is commonly believed today. The lives of real pirates, as described accurately in this book, are revealing examples.

My youngest childhood memories involve fascination with different time periods and historical events. Since 1971, I have been heavily involved in historical re-enacting and living history interpretation of one time or another from the Renaissance through the late 19th Century. The French and Indian War was my first era. That soon led to the Revolutionary War. *Well, it had to.* The date was 1974 and the entire country was gearing up for the Bicentennial. No self-respecting reenactor could even begin to contemplate the idea of being left out of this momentous event. Back then, just about everything had to be handmade. With the exception of weapons and accoutrements, there were few vendors who manufactured clothing and other household articles.

As I portrayed each time period, I searched for someone, or some book, that would answer my questions. Things like, "What did they wear?" or "What did they eat?" And most importantly, "How did they think and behave?" There was very little written. Historians usually focus on the political, economic, and factual aspects of a person or era. That's important to be sure, but for a living historian there needs to be more. I'm talking about the little details concerning everyday life that put things into perspective. Occasionally, there would be some old sage in the group who gave me a smattering of information. Often the information I received at first was incorrect. So, I would spend much time and money obtaining an outfit, only to find out later that most of what I had was not historically accurate.

About ten years ago I became involved with piracy. Not as a practicing participant in robbery on the high seas or illegally copying DVDs, but as a historical interpreter, re-enacting the thrilling time of the "Golden Age" of piracy for the general public. The bookstores of the world have been flooded with numerous volumes on pirates over the past several years. But in researching this period, I found that most of the historical events described in many books written about pirate history were highly contradictory. Also, there is very little written about how they lived, the clothes they wore, the weapons they used, the food they ate, and their general lifestyle. Hard facts from contemporary documents concerning pirate history are scarce. After all, as a rule, they were a very secretive group. They seldom filed reports or kept logbooks. There is almost nothing about how they lived or what they thought. But the real problem comes from the fact that the literary market has been flooded with hundreds of books professing to be historically correct—but they aren't! Many modern works about pirates are simply re-writes of books written hundreds of years ago. It was assumed that these books are historically accurate simply because they were written at a time contemporary to the pirates themselves—but they weren't. Most authors of the day were more interested in writing best sellers than scholarly works of history.

In this book, I have sifted through these works and looked for consistencies and inconsistencies. I have also searched for actual documentation from the period, such as newspaper articles. My goal in writing this book is to help clear up some of the inconsistencies about pirates and to portray them in a more accurate light. During this discourse, I will discuss the politics that motivated them. We must get the history right before we can understand how they lived and what they thought. Also, I will delve into their lifestyle as I examine clothing and fashion, weapons and tactics, food, ships, and attitudes which I hope will open a window into how they lived and what they thought.

You will find that I devote a large part of this book to the lives of three notable individuals: Henry Morgan, Blackbeard, and "Black Bart" Roberts. This is because these three men truly define their times. They are the quintessential examples of pirates from two very different eras. Henry Morgan represents the ultimate privateer of the 17th century; Blackbeard represents the ultimate pirate of the 18th century; Roberts represents the perfect image of everything we think of when we speak of pirates and was the last great pirate of the golden age. These three men give us a unique insight into three very different lifestyles and motivations of the men who chose piracy during their lifetimes. Additionally, they are without a doubt the most famous pirates ever.

In my experience, many authors who write histories about pirates take on each pirate, one at a time. In other words, they give a detailed account on the life of one individual then move on to the next. This doesn't allow the reader to effectively understand how the actions of one individual affected the life of another. Also, it doesn't allow the reader to understand the sequence of relevant historical events as they unfolded. Conversely, I connect the dots between the lives of the men and events of the day. To the greatest extent possible, I choose to relay all the historical events in a chronological order and explain how one event caused or affected the next. This puts a unique perspective on the history of pirates and sheds light on the possible reasons and the motivations for their actions. To assist the reader in keeping track of the current political situation and state of war, which plays such a dynamic role on the motivations of government officials and pirates, I will insert notifications into the text informing the reader of the beginning of each officially declared war, as well as who was on whose side and the dates of the conflict.

I'd also like to add a word of caution to researchers who read contemporary English documents with regard to the precise year. This can often become quite confusing due to the English day of New Year. Prior to 1752 in England, the New Year began on March 25th, which was Lady Day. This means that in the official record, March 24, 1715 was followed by March 25, 1716. To add even more confusion on the issue, other countries like Scotland had already changed the first day of the year to January 1st back in the early 17th century. This can become a problem for researchers who read documents that give the date for an event based upon this system. For example, a date that was documented as having occurred in February 1719 would have actually occurred in 1720 by our calendar. Some historians deal with this phenomenon by ignoring it and giving the dates exactly as they were written; however, this causes a great deal of confusion among modern readers. Other historians give the date indicating both years. In the example above, the date would be February 1719/1720. To avoid confusion, I have chosen to convert all dates to our modern calendar, with New Year's Day occurring on January 1st of each year.

PART I: THE "GOLDEN AGE"

> *Its population consists of pirates, cut-throats, whores, and some of the vilest persons in the whole of the world.*

Chapter 1
Let the Piracy Begin

It's a sad but true commentary to say that the first human to build a boat was probably a merchant and the second was probably a pirate. Technically, a pirate is one who commits robbery at sea—well, on the water at any rate. I don't want to limit the definition to just seagoing craft; there certainly have been plenty of river pirates throughout history. However, I would like to keep this book focused on the more romanticized European pirates of the 17th and 18th centuries. This book is about the pirates who plundered the Spanish Main; the pirates of the Caribbean; the pirates who raided ships and settlements all along the eastern coast of North America. It also includes the European pirates who sailed the Pacific and Indian Oceans.

Many scholars and authors have identified this era by the phrase "The Golden Age of Piracy." The exact beginning and ending dates between historians don't always match, but generally this period covers the years from 1620 to 1730. I place the beginning date for my exposé on the golden age of piracy at 1640 with the rise of the buccaneers and the ending date at 1722 with the death of the last great pirate, John Roberts, sometimes called Bartholomew Roberts, or just Black Bart. I certainly don't want to imply that there weren't any pirates before or after this time period. This term is like saying the golden age of baseball was from 1900 to 1950 or the golden age of television was from 1955 to 1980. The "golden age" refers to the era when the institutions grew and became recognized. It's also a time when they developed all their customs, traditions, and even stereotypes.

For pirates, the period between 1640 and 1722 was when they became stylized and our perception of what we think of when we say "pirates" became defined. It's when the most famous pirates lived. However, for these pirates, the golden age was not a period of development and growth of just one style; it was a period of remarkable transition and change. As we shall see, the motivation, political support, and social acceptance for these "pirates" dramatically changed four times during the years that mark the golden age. Some of these changes were brought about by war, some by political treaties, and some were brought about by the riches a country could gain through colonization. Religious freedom and political oppression also played a significant part. Therefore, this golden age can be divided into four distinct sub categories, or periods; 1640–1670 The Buccaneer Privateers; 1670–1702 The Buccaneer Pirates; 1702–1713 The Privateers of Queen Anne's War; 1714–1722 The Pyrates. Before we get into action, we need a little background to set the stage. So, let's set sail for the early 17th century and begin our tour of the pirates of the golden age.

In order to fully understand how pirates were used in the political arena, we must first become familiar with *letters of marque* and understand the subtleties between a pirate and a privateer; there actually was a huge difference between the two. The victims wouldn't make any distinction at all, but for the individuals attacking and taking a prize, it meant the difference between acting within the law of your country and acting as a criminal. It's the difference between having friendly ports to return to and entering port in secrecy.

In the 16th, 17th, and early 18th centuries, it was just too expensive for most nations to maintain large naval fleets during peacetime. They did, of course, have some warships for protection of the major ports and to escort their kings and queens as they traveled abroad, but not enough to effectively wage a naval campaign. When war broke out, governments would have to rapidly expand their small peacetime navies into large wartime fleets. The best way to accomplish this was to hire one. Governments would issue letters of marque to any willing sea captain and crew, regardless of their nationality, giving them legal permission to attack any nation's ships that were listed in the letters. Those letters were also referred to as commissions. Captains and crewmen sailing under letters of marque were officially called "privateers." The French referred to them as "corsairs." A percentage of the profits would be paid back to the government that issued those letters. In England, 1/15th of the profits went to the King and 1/10th to the minister of state or governor who issued the letters or who was appointed to supervise such activity. From the mid-16th to the mid-18th century, England, France, and the Dutch Republic all used privateers as part of their official state policy. Between 1702 and 1714 during the War of the Spanish Succession, Queen Anne of England issued 128 privateer commissions through the port of Bristol alone.

Privateers were quite literally naval mercenaries. The ones being attacked always regarded them as pirates, but these men were generally thought of as heroes rather than outlaws by the governments that issued the letters.

They were brave naval warriors attacking the vicious enemy and bringing valuable revenue back to the local economy. During the American Revolution (1775–1783) the greatest naval hero of the United States was John Paul Jones. He is considered a hero of the Revolution and the father of the U.S. Navy. But to the British, he was simply a pirate and was referred to as such. Letters of marque were also issued by heads of state in peacetime. It was a profitable way to wage a cold war against your enemies and generate some revenue at the same time. Governors also issued letters of marque to local privateers as a routine way of protecting their colonies and shipping lanes. As the English, French, and Dutch began colonization in the Caribbean, the use of privateers was an absolute necessity.

Privateer crews were normally a mix of sailors and landsmen in the form of soldiers, craftsmen, adventurers, shop keepers, and musicians. Privateer commissions often limited the number of seamen who could be taken aboard to not more than half of the total crew. A privateer captain didn't need a ship full of sailors, he needed fighting men. Privateers only needed enough sailors to handle the ship, the rest were for boarding enemy ships or for attacking cities ashore. For example, in 1719 the English privateer, Captain Shelvocke, only had 20 sailors among his 101-man crew.

Recruiting privateer crews was often done about the same as recruiting for any other crew, by public advertising. Notices would be posted around the docks and taverns, coffee houses, and even in the newspapers. One newspaper ad read, "Captain Peter Lawrence is going a Privateering from Rhode Island in a good Sloop, about 60 Tons, six guns and 90 men for Canada and any Gentlemen of Sailors that are disposed to go shall be kindly entertained."

The use of privateers goes back hundreds of years before the 17th century and continued through the 19th century; but the period which begins around 1640 and ends in 1670, with the Treaty of Madrid, was truly unique in the annals of privateer history. It was a time when just about everyone sailing the seas looking for loot was a privateer and began with the Spanish persecution of the English, Dutch, and French colonists in the Caribbean who became the buccaneers.

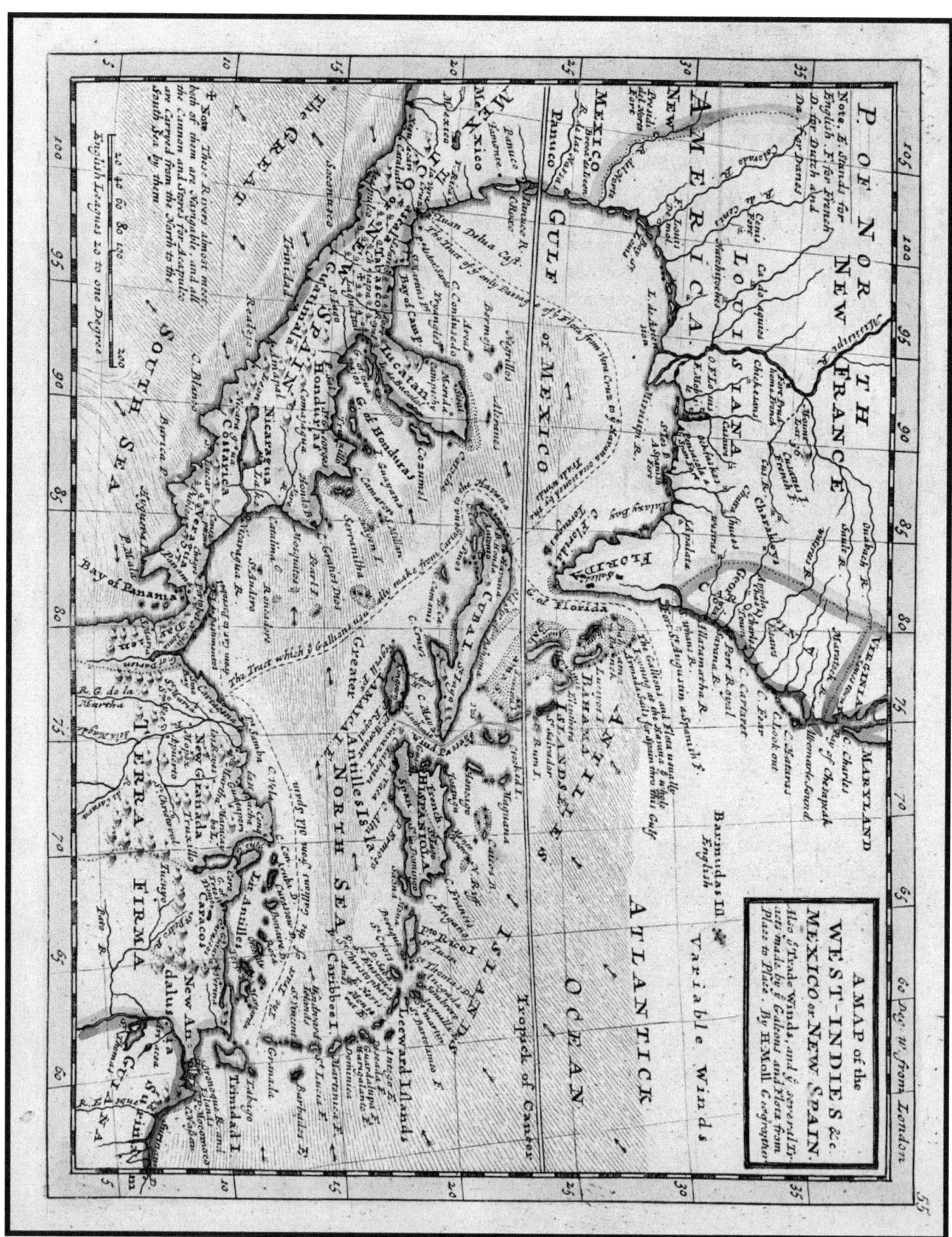

Figure 1: *The Caribbean*

Chapter 2
Chipping Away at the Spanish Main

Before we get into all the details of the pirates and buccaneers of the Caribbean, we must first understand why the Spanish were so hated by all the other European countries. The Treaty of Tordesillas signed by Spain and Portugal in 1497 drew an imaginary line around the world and granted Spain a total monopoly on trade west of that line in the Atlantic Ocean. The Spanish considered the Caribbean to be their own personal sea. Spanish colonization had already begun by Columbus on his second voyage in 1494.

By 1600, the Spanish had well-established colonies on Cuba, Hispaniola, Puerto Rico, Jamaica, Trinidad, and many of the smaller islands. They also ruled Mexico and all the territory between Mexico and Brazil, which was ruled by Portugal in accordance with the Treaty of Tordesillas. Spain had all the vast riches they took from the Inca and Aztec empires. In Europe, Spain was attempting to take over virtually every country possible and had been almost constantly at war with the rest of Europe since 1556, when the Dutch officially allied themselves with England and France against Spain. At sea, Dutch and English "pirates" began redirecting much of Spain's treasure stream to their own governments. The English called themselves "Sea Rovers" while the Dutch referred to themselves as "Sea Beggars." The Spanish called them "Pechelingues." These privateers took prizes wherever they could, in European waters as well as in the Caribbean and the Pacific. Throughout this period, all the waters north of the coast of South America, including the Caribbean, were referred to as the Spanish Main, meaning that these waters were mainly the exclusive property of Spain. The Spanish took a very strict view of any interlopers. In other words, no settlers allowed. Those who tried were met with immediate attack from the Spanish forces which resulted in either death or slavery.

1500–1550

The Spanish control the Caribbean with well-established colonies in Mexico and on Cuba, Hispaniola, Puerto Rico, Jamaica, Trinidad, and many of the smaller islands.

The Protestant Reformation played a major role in the colonization of the New World, especially for France. Martin Luther began the Protestant Reformation in 1517 and this new version of the Christian religion proceeded to sweep through Europe. In 1527 King Henry VIII began the Anglican Church in England, primarily to divorce his Catholic wife, Catherine of Aragon and marry Anne Boleyn. Then in the 1530s, a French scholar named Jean Calvin began the Calvinist movement, also known as Calvinism. His teachings rapidly spread thorough Europe. In Scotland, his philosophy became the Presbyterian Religion. In England, his followers were known as Puritans. Calvinism was embraced by the Dutch and Swiss whose rulers often converted from Catholicism. In France, his followers were known as Huguenots.

The Catholic French didn't take very kindly to this new form of religion. Between 1536 and 1560, France fluctuated between tolerance and oppression of the Huguenots. To make matters worse, more and more well-to-do Frenchmen were converting. By 1560, many French statesmen, merchants, and military leaders had become Huguenots. This was becoming a real problem for Catherine de Medici, who was ruling France for her ten-year-old son, King Charles IX. Her solution was to encourage the Huguenots to form colonies in the New World. By the early 17th century, the Spanish domination of the Caribbean islands and all the resources they offered was becoming increasingly annoying to the other European powers. To the rulers of France, sending the Huguenots to the Caribbean seemed a "win-win" for all. France got rid of the troublesome Huguenots while establishing a foothold in America, and the Huguenots got to leave France and enjoy religious freedom in their own colonies.

1564

French Huguenots establish a colony near present day Jacksonville, Florida, but it is destroyed a year later by the Spanish who establish a permanent settlement at Saint Augustine, Florida.

Jean Ribault led the first attempt by the French Huguenots to establish a colony in the Spanish territory in the New World. In 1562 his small party built a tiny settlement named Charlesfort near the coast of South Carolina located between the modern cities of Charleston, South Carolina and Savannah, Georgia. Today, the original site of Charlesfort is on the Marine Corps Recruit Depot, Parris Island. The first settlement failed due to starvation.

Ribault returned in 1564 and built a larger colony near present day Jacksonville, Florida. This colony was protected by a wooden star-shaped fort named Fort Caroline. However, the Spanish discovered the colony and destroyed it the following year. St. Augustine, Florida, the oldest city in the United States, was founded by the Spanish in 1565 in order to prevent further enemy settlements along the Florida coast. The English made the next attempt in 1587 with a substantial colony on Roanoke Island, part of the Outer Banks of North Carolina. The "Lost Colony" as it is called, disappeared without a trace a few years later.

Then, in 1607, the English finally established their first successful colony in the New World. Jamestown, named for King James I, was not just a settlement, but was strategically situated far enough away from the Spanish as not to draw their attention but close enough to their shipping lanes to serve as a base of naval operations if England wished to attack their fleets. But there still weren't any English, Dutch, or French settlements in the Caribbean.

Then, the Thirty Years' War (1618–1648) in Europe began and the situation for the Huguenots and other Protestant denominations became far worse. The war originally started over political control but rapidly became a war of religious persecution. In the 1620s the Huguenots began looking for places to settle in the Caribbean. As the 17th century progressed, King Louis XIV's Catholic government in France went from legal persecution to full scale slaughter in order to rid France of the Huguenots. This may explain why so many French Huguenots in the Caribbean often sided with the English or Dutch each time those nations fought France.

Meanwhile, after firmly establishing English settlements in Virginia and Massachusetts, the English decided to take a crack at the Spanish Main. The Lesser Antilles islands at the eastern end of the Caribbean seemed a good spot. They were out of the main Spanish shipping lanes and far from the large fortifications in Cuba. In 1623, Sir Thomas Warner led the first British colony in the West Indies which landed on Saint Kitts. The French government was on good terms with England during this period and wanted to get in on the action too. In 1625, the English willingly partitioned Saint Kitts giving half of the island to the French. This became the first French colony in the Caribbean. Also in 1625, English sailors began exploring Barbados and by 1627 the English had established a colony. The Dutch also wanted to get in on the action and established a small colony on Saint Maarten's (St. Martins) Island where they began a modest salt mining operation.

Located to the east of Cuba, the island of Hispaniola is among the largest islands in the Caribbean. Today, it contains the nations of the Dominican Republic and Haiti. It has rich and fertile soil, lush vegetation, and an ideal climate well-suited for agriculture. Named "La Espanola" or Spanish Island, by its discoverer, Christopher Columbus, the island is where his famous ship, the *Santa Maria*, ran aground and sank. Spanish colonization began in December 1492 with 1,300 settlers, making this the oldest European settlement in the New World. The capital city of San Domingo

1607

First permanent English settlement in the New World is established at Jamestown, Virginia.

1618–1648

Thirty Years' War in Europe begins over religious persecution.

1620

Plymouth colony is established by English pilgrims in New England.

1621

Philip IV (The Great) is crowned King of Spain

on the south side of the island dates back to 1496 and was officially established as the capital on August 5, 1498. It was the center of Spanish political authority in the Caribbean for hundreds of years.

Figure 2: *Hispaniola*

1620s

French, English, and Dutch begin small settlements in the Caribbean on Barbados, Hispaniola, Nevis, and Saint Kitts.

Thousands of Spanish settlers, plantation owners, slaves, and bureaucrats flocked to Hispaniola throughout the 16th century. However, they primarily settled on the eastern end where the farming was good or along the south coast close to the main shipping port and capital city of Santo Domingo. This left the vast interior, the western end, and the northern coast completely unoccupied. By the early 17th century, the jungles were filled with wild cattle and pigs that had escaped captivity over the years and had bred in the wild.

Even though San Domingo was the central point of the Spanish government in the Caribbean, the north side of Hispaniola seemed like an ideal place for the French and English settlers to establish a foothold in the Caribbean.

Beginning in 1625, some French Huguenots and a few English adventurers began arriving from Saint Kitts and settled on a tiny island off the northwest coast of Hispaniola. The island's name was Tortuga and they built a small sea port and town named Cayenne along the natural harbor on the south side of the island. Almost immediately after Cayenne was established, the English and French settlers began to migrate to the rich interior of Hispaniola. Tortuga was close enough to the north shore of Hispaniola for dugout canoes to be used to travel back and forth. Unlike the settlers on Nevis and St. Kitts, they were sharing their island with the enemy, the Spanish. The settlers on Hispaniola had to take every precaution not to be seen by the Spanish and remain extremely mobile just in case they were discovered. If they were found, they would have to get away quickly by disappearing into the vast woodlands.

Figure 3: *First Settlements*

The island of Nevis was colonized in 1628 by English settlers from Saint Kitts, which became the premier base for English and French expansion in the Caribbean over the next 10 years. Soon after, the English established settlements on Antigua, Montserrat, Anguilla, and Tortola. While the French established settlements on Martinique, the Guadeloupe Archipelago, and St. Barts. The Spanish attempted to stop this colonization, but every time they attacked a settlement, the settlers would disperse until the Spanish left.

Chapter 3
Birth of the Buccaneers

The English, French, and Dutch settlers had been settling in the Caribbean since 1623. Many of the English were adventurers and colonists sent by the King of England but many more of the English were religious dissenters escaping persecution back in England, like the Puritans of Massachusetts. Most of the French were Huguenots also escaping religious persecution in France. The Dutch, with far fewer numbers, were trying to establish colonies to help in trade or were refugees from the Thirty Years' War which devastated Holland and the surrounding nations.

Beginning in 1625, the English and French settlers on Tortuga and Hispaniola had developed into a uniquely different type of settler. Living under constant threat of Spanish attack, they had to remain extremely mobile in order to make a quick escape. Farming of any sort was totally out of the question because it took a lot of land and a lot of time. Large crops would be fairly easy for the Spanish to find and destroy. The settlers had to find another means of making a living, and they found it. As you may recall, for over 100 years, livestock had been escaping the Spanish settlements to the south and breeding in the wild.

The woodland of the interior was filled with cattle and pigs. It was a hunter's paradise. Hispaniola, like many of the islands in the Caribbean, was originally inhabited by the Tainos, an Arawak speaking people, believed to be originally from South America. Most of the Tainos had been killed by the Spanish or died from disease from European contact; however, there were a few left when the English and French settlers arrived. The Tainos had a very unique way of preparing meat. They wrapped the meat in wet leaves and placed it on a wooden platform over a very smoky, slow burning fire. In the Arawak language of the Tainos, that process was called "boucan" and the Arawak word for the dried meat it produced was "charqui," which was pronounced "jerky" in English. Today, we call this process "pulled" or "jerked" pork or beef. The settlers perfected this technique that they had learned from the Tainos and went into the meat processing business. Hence, those early hunters and cookers of meat were called "boucanniors" by the French and "boucaneers" by the English.

The French boucanniors and the English boucaneers worked together, hunting wild boar and cattle deep in the interior of Hispaniola, all the while evading the Spanish patrols. To sell their product, they established costal trading settlements and small ports on the western part of the island away from the Spanish sphere of influence. The Spanish continually attempted to capture or kill these interlopers. Occasionally, the Spanish were successful, but generally the boucanniors or boucaneers would simply disappear into the jungle and return after the Spanish left. Since their operations were illegal in the eyes of the Spanish authority, their customers tended to be smugglers and other settlers also operating outside of Spanish law. They would trade for the necessities of life including weapons, powder, shot, and of course, wine.

Their appearance would have been more like that of a mountain man from the American west during the 1820s. They were hunters and dressed as such. Contemporary accounts describe them as wearing coarse shirts and other clothing made mostly of animal skins. No fancy garments, just homemade clothing that is adapted and practical for travel in the jungle. This lifestyle required them to be heavily armed with muskets and assorted skinning knives. They had to be prepared to either hunt wild boar or defend themselves against Spanish patrols. **Additionally, they probably smelled horrible. Anyone who has spent time near a meat packing plant would testify to that.** According to a French clergyman, Abbe Jean Baptiste Du Tertre, "these are the butcher's vilest servants who have been eight days in the slaughterhouse without washing themselves."

By 1629, the Spanish had had enough. Not only were these settlers from enemy nations, they were heretics too. These English, French, and Dutch invaders were all predominantly Protestants. The task of driving these heretics out was given to one of Spain's ablest generals in the Thirty Years' War, Don Fadrique de Toledo. It was a Spanish "maximum effort" to rid the Caribbean of the heretics and foreigners once and for all. His first targets were the English and French settlements on the islands of Nevis and St. Kitts. He launched major military assaults on both colonies in 1629 and captured many of the settlers, but just as many managed to escape into the interior of the islands they were on or fled to other nearby islands. As soon as the Spanish left however, the escaped settlers simply returned and rebuilt their settlements. But many others decided to seek refuge and safety

1629

Don Fadrique de Toledo's Spanish forces attack all foreign settlements in the Caribbean.

on the tiny island of Tortuga, just off the northern coast of Hispaniola, which seemed to be a fairly defensible position.

Local Spanish attacks on the English and French settlers on Hispaniola had already intensified by 1629, causing many to flee to the safety of Tortuga. To the Spanish, it seemed that Tortuga was the last strongpoint of the Protestant invaders, so that's where Don Fadrique de Toledo's forces struck next. Don Fadrique de Toledo's forces arrived suddenly at Tortuga and he easily overran the port. As the Spanish assaulted the island, the English and French settlers fled to the mainland of Hispaniola and disappeared into the jungle. To prevent their return, the Spanish began to build fortifications on Tortuga but then decided to leave the island in pursuit of those settlers who had escaped to the mainland. For the Spanish, it was just too expensive to maintain troops on a remote island, especially if there was no one to fight. The Hispaniola operation eventually failed due to the vast territory and jungle-like terrain. Large-scale efforts to expel the English and French settlers on Hispaniola dramatically slowed to an occasional raid.

Even though Don Fadrique de Toledo's forces enjoyed some immediate success destroying settlements and rounding up prisoners, there was no permanence to his efforts. As soon as the Spanish forces left, the English, French, and Dutch settlers who escaped would return and rebuild. Overall, his campaign was a failure. Don Fadrique de Toledo did manage to achieve one thing, however. His attacks instilled a deep hatred for the Spanish among all the settlers. This hatred united them against the Spanish for the rest of the century.

The French boucanniors and the English boucaneers became organized into a resistance force. They decided to use their hunting skills against men instead of animals. In 1630, realizing that Tortuga was abandoned, the French boucanniors and the English boucaneers swiftly moved from the mainland back to reclaim their island. In a maximum effort to defend themselves, they completed the fortifications the Spanish had begun the previous year and made Tortuga their center of resistance and operations.

The most famous pirate port of all time, Tortuga has reached a legendary status within pirate lore, stories, novels, and Hollywood films. Despite this status, it's a real place and very deserving of its reputation. Tortuga is a tiny island at 12 miles long and 6 miles wide off the northwest shore of Hispaniola, close enough to row between the two islands. Like Hispaniola, the island was originally inhabited by the Tainos. First named Santa Ana by Columbus in 1493, the 17th century French named it Ile de La Tortue meaning Turtle Isle. This name eventually became Tortuga. In the four years prior to the Spanish attack of 1629, the French and English settlers had established a small port town called Cayenne on a natural harbor on the south side of the island. Although it probably was unimpressive at the time, it had a market that was used primarily to sell beef and pork. It was also a central trading spot for smugglers. But beginning in 1630, Tortuga began a rapid development into a major port with impressive fortifications.

The harbor of Cayenne on Tortuga was very close to the main Spanish shipping lane making it fairly easy to prey on small Spanish ships. The French boucanniors and the English boucaneers continued their resistance against the Spanish. Since offense is the best defense, they began taking the fight to the Spanish instead of just waiting for an attack to come. The more they fought back against the Spanish, the more, they realized that taking Spanish property was far more profitable than selling meat to the odd passerby. I'm sure that a certain amount of revenge for previous Spanish atrocities also played into the situation. Additionally, capturing Spanish shipping was undoubtedly a lot more fun.

Soon afterwards, Dutch adventurers began arriving to join the English and French. Their strength grew significantly and began a French/Dutch/English partnership against the Spanish that would dominate the Caribbean for the next 60 years. The hunters, processors, and sellers of pulled pork made the transition to a warrior culture that took ships at sea. French boucanniors and the English boucaneers were called buccaneers

1631

Tortuga established as a stronghold against Spanish attacks.

Figure 4: *Tortuga*

and forever afterwards, the word "buccaneer" would be synonymous with "pirate."

Meanwhile, Tortuga started a period of rapid growth with the beginning of the first plantations. Politically however, there was a sort of uneasy partnership between the English and French. Throughout the 1630s, the governors alternated between the Englishmen and the Frenchmen. In 1631, the first Governor was an Englishman, Captain Anthony Hilton. In 1633, the Dutch colony on St. Martin's was attacked by the Spanish and Dutch refugees began arriving in substantial numbers. In 1634, African slaves were brought in to help increase the production of tobacco on the plantations; however, this was a disaster as no one really wanted to control the slaves and soon they were in revolt. Continual arguing between the English and French made the situation worse.

1638

Louis XIV is crowned King of France.

Then, in 1634, the Spanish returned and sacked the town. Soon after, Dutch pirates took over the island and began using the port as a base for their operations. This ended the slave market and served to slow the growth of the plantations. It also ended the meat processing markets and Tortuga adopted a pirate-based economy. This meant taverns, brothels, nautical stores, and businesses to buy and sell all manner of captured merchandise. As a result, the English/French authorities not only allowed the buccaneers to come and go as they pleased, their presence was strongly encouraged.

By 1638, the English population had dwindled and a second Spanish attack in 1638 devastated the Island. The Spanish occupied the island for a short time, but eventually the French and Dutch re-organized and managed to drive the Spanish out. Once regaining control of Tortuga, they petitioned the Royal French Governor of Saint Christopher on the island of St. Kitts for help.

1640

Buccaneers from Tortuga begin raiding Spanish shipping.

Jean le Vasseur was officially appointed as the first Royal French Governor of Tortuga in 1640. He was an engineer as well as a politician and immediately began construction of a large and imposing stone fortress with 40 guns on a rocky hill overlooking the natural harbor. The fort was named Fort de Rocher and it commanded the entire city. Le Vasseur also issued letters of marque against the Spanish to all who applied. This act alone served to encourage buccaneers of all nations to flock to Tortuga. If that wasn't enough, in 1645 he imported 1,650 prostitutes to Tortuga in an attempt to bring harmony and control to the unruly pirates. At least that was his official story. From 1645 through the 1660s, Tortuga lived up to every elaborate description and portrayal in novels and in Hollywood films. It was a sea port filled with taverns, brothels, smugglers, and buccaneers. It was a no holds barred kind of town with a huge fortress on top of a hill to protect the pirates against the Spanish. It was a place where buccaneers could walk the streets and trade all their stolen booty for whatever they wanted free from worry of being arrested. It was a port with large buccaneer fleets in the harbor refitting for their next venture. In 1650, Tortuga was the buccaneer's haven. It was a pirate paradise that was totally unique from any other port in the world.

PART I.I
THE BUCCANEERS 1640–1670

> " You are hereby further authorized and required to land and attain any other place belonging to the Enemies. "

Chapter 4
The Buccaneer Privateers

This chapter, which I call "The Buccaneers," marks the first time period of the "Golden Age of Piracy." By 1640, the buccaneers had become a real force to be reckoned with in the Caribbean. They had an island stronghold on Tortuga that offered them a support system to obtain goods necessary to sustain their operations. And what they couldn't get in Tortuga, they took from the Spanish. But more importantly, the buccaneers were united against the Spanish. The deep hatred the original buccaneers had for the Spanish went back to the 1620s and still remained strong. Generally, the buccaneers didn't attack ships from non-Spanish nations. Since England, France, and the Dutch Republic were in a constant state of war with Spain, officially declared or otherwise, there were no complaints from them concerning the buccaneers' actions. **Most likely, they were secretly delighted.** The colonial governors of all three governments realized that this was a golden opportunity to bolster protection for their settlers and shipping lanes and challenge the vast resources of the Spanish at the same time. The settlements in the Lesser Antilles were left alone primarily because the Spanish had their hands full with the buccaneers of Tortuga. The buccaneers provided the balance of power that kept the Spanish occupied so their fledgling colonies could thrive.

The only drawback was that these buccaneers were pirates and were breaking the law. The royal officials might have asked, "How would it look back home if I was condoning piracy?" Well, that was an easy fix; make the actions of the buccaneers legal! As soon as Jean le Vasseur was appointed the Royal Governor of Tortuga, he began issuing letters of marque to just about everyone. This was the start of the era of the "Buccaneer Privateers." The buccaneers were already holding the Spanish in check and letters of marque were all they needed to justify their actions legally. The Spanish followed suit, issuing letters of marque against the other nationalities. To the Spanish, their privateers were a cost-effective way to enforce policy

1648

Thirty Years' War ends with the treaties of Osnabruck and Munster.

and prevent other nations from infringing on Spanish operations. To the English, Dutch, and French, the buccaneers were now an essential element of the colonization of the Caribbean and a vital part of national policy.

Throughout the 1640s, the buccaneers developed their own unique society, with rules, codes, and traditions. It was then that they became organized into the "Brethren of the Coast." No one knows if they actually called themselves Brethren of the Coast, but that's how they lived. Their rules were set down in prearranged agreements that they called "ship's articles." These ship's articles could be permanent for one particular ship or could be established before a particular venture. Before joining a crew, one would have to "sign articles." This was also a term used for reaching an agreement. Ship's articles could include anything from chain of command to treatment of prisoners. They would almost certainly establish rules for discipline and for the division of captured goods. Normally, the silver and gold taken in a buccaneer raid was divided among the crew according to the ship's articles; however, individual pirates were allowed to keep any jewelry, clothing, weapons, or other personally acquired booty they desired. This changed their appearance dramatically from that of the boucanniors. Now as buccaneers, pirates of the sea, they could have worn just about anything. Most likely, their clothing would have been a mix of practical nautical dress and stolen fancy clothing.

By 1650 the buccaneers of Tortuga were well-established and organized. Their success at privateering and piracy attracted more and more recruits. Escaped slaves, escaped prisoners, religious refugees, adventurers, and true pirates all wanted in on the action. Suddenly, around 1650, a new group of recruits flocked to Tortuga. The Thirty Years' War in Europe ended in 1648 and tens of thousands of soldiers were out of work. They migrated to the Caribbean looking for easy money using the only skill they had, warfare. This brought a whole new level of military expertise and weapons to the ranks of the buccaneers. Also, these ex-soldiers retained much of their uniform items and equipment. Above all, they would have been extremely well-armed. Their weapons were the first thing contemporary observers noted about their appearance.

As the size and skill of their crews grew, so did the boldness of their attacks. They acquired bigger ships, more arms, and better supplies and often banded together to form small fleets. The buccaneers were expanding all along the western end of Hispaniola. The small port of Petit Goave is ideally located on the mainland of Hispaniola on the north shore about 40 miles to the west of the modern city of Port-au-Prince. This port quickly became their second favorite port next to Tortuga. The French colonists and plantation owners were expanding their territory as well and making a serious attempt to establish the western end of Hispaniola as a bonafide French colony. It was the "golden age" for the buccaneers.

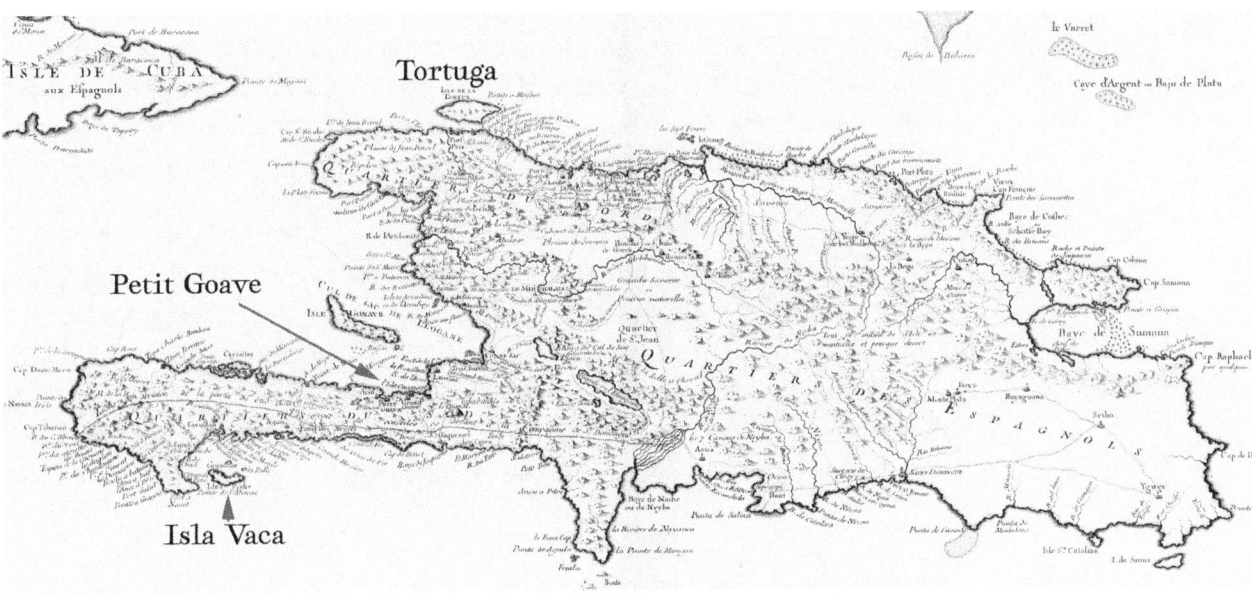

Figure 5: *French Hispaniola*

England's official interests in the Caribbean had diminished after the 1620s. Political issues at home took precedence. In 1646, Charles I was deposed in the first of three English Civil Wars. Two years later, the Thirty Years' War in Europe ended, and thousands of soldiers returned home which added to the volatile situation. Then, in 1649, Charles I was beheaded and his son, Charles, fled to France and then the Netherlands. Shortly afterwards, Oliver Cromwell became the ruler of England with the title of Lord Protector of the Commonwealth of England. For the first time in English history, there was no king on the English throne and the word "Royal" as in Royal Navy, was replaced with the word "Commonwealth." The new English government desperately needed money. The combination of supporting the Thirty Years' War and fighting civil wars at home had just about exhausted its resources.

At this same time, the Dutch Republic had established the largest maritime trading network in the world with merchant fleets trading all over the globe. Their trade in the Indian Ocean threatened the English East India Company's monopoly and the Dutch support for the recently executed Charles I of England made Cromwell uneasy. Additionally, because the French had supported Charles I in the recent English Civil War, Cromwell issued letters of marque against all French ships and any neutral ships carrying French goods. Using this excuse, Admiral George Ayscue captured 27 Dutch trading vessels that were trading with the English colony of Barbados and the Dutch declared war on England on July 8, 1652.

1642–1651

English Civil War

1649

Charles I of England executed—Oliver Cromwell becomes Parliamentary ruler of England.

Robert Jacob

1652–1654

The First Anglo/Dutch War—England against the Dutch Republic.

The war was fought entirely at sea with large naval engagements throughout European waters. In the Caribbean, the war was fought completely by privateers on both sides. English privateers completely dominated the efforts of the Dutch and inflicted serious damage on Dutch shipping. *This war must have created friction between the English and Dutch buccaneers, who joined opposite sides as privateers.* The Spanish saw this as an opportunity to finally drive out the buccaneers on Tortuga.

In February 1654, the Spanish launched a major amphibious expedition against Tortuga, which comprised of 700 troops and siege weapons. Tortuga fell to Spanish control once again. Not wishing to start a war with France, all the captured inhabitants of Tortuga were sent to France alive. But the Spanish occupation of Tortuga didn't last long and England and the Dutch signed a peace treaty on April 18, 1654.

Chapter 5
Jamaica

The war against the Dutch left England in even more desperate need of money. So, the Lord Protector of the Commonwealth of England, Oliver Cromwell, turned his attentions toward the Spanish Main. Taking a few of the ships from the Spanish treasure fleets would help fix the economy, temporarily, but Cromwell's real goal was to expand England's sugar production in the colonies of the Caribbean. Why sugar? Sugar was the cash crop of the day and worth a fortune. England needed a colony that produced sugar if it was going to get back on its feet. For the past 30 years, the English had maintained modest colonies along the outer islands of the Caribbean but had not really established any colony of great size. These colonies did contribute to the English economy, but sugarcane production was limited on these outer islands. In a bold move, Cromwell ordered his army to take Hispaniola, the jewel of the Spanish Caribbean.

In December 1654, an invasion force of 34 ships carrying 13,120 soldiers including 7,000 marines, 6,000 infantrymen, and 120 cavalry left England under the commands of General Venables and Admiral William Penn, who was the father of William Penn for whom the state of Pennsylvania is named. The strategic objective was the capital of Hispaniola, San Domingo. However, the Spanish were forewarned and withdrew almost all of the Spanish occupation forces on Tortuga to help in the defense of Hispaniola. Unaware of the Spanish preparation, Admiral Penn landed his forces away from any Spanish fortifications and began advancing toward the city. But the Spanish mobilized their defense force of about 2,400 and ambushed Penn's force, causing the entire English invasion force to flee back to the ships. Not wanting to return to England unsuccessful and face the wrath of Cromwell, Admiral Penn and General Venables decided to attack a smaller island, less likely to offer the kind of resistance that Hispaniola had offered. On May 10, 1655, Penn and his forces landed on Spanish held Jamaica and easily swept the tiny and poorly armed Spanish forces away.

1655

English forces under General Venables and Admiral William Penn captures Jamaica.

Jamaica was also originally inhabited by the Tainos who named the island "Xaymaca" meaning land of wood and water. Columbus landed there in 1494 on his second voyage and was marooned there for about a year in 1503 during his 4th voyage. A permanent settlement began in 1509 when Juan de Esquivel landed with a group of settlers. Because the Spanish had Hispaniola and Cuba, they didn't see much profit in developing the island of Jamaica. There was only one small Spanish city on the island, the city of Santiago de la Vega close to a deep natural harbor on the south side of the island. The English landed and made a swift assault on the city. Spanish resistance was very weak, and the city and island quickly fell to English authority. Santiago de la Vega, sometimes called Villa de la Vega, was renamed "Spanish Town" by the English, a name that it keeps to this day.

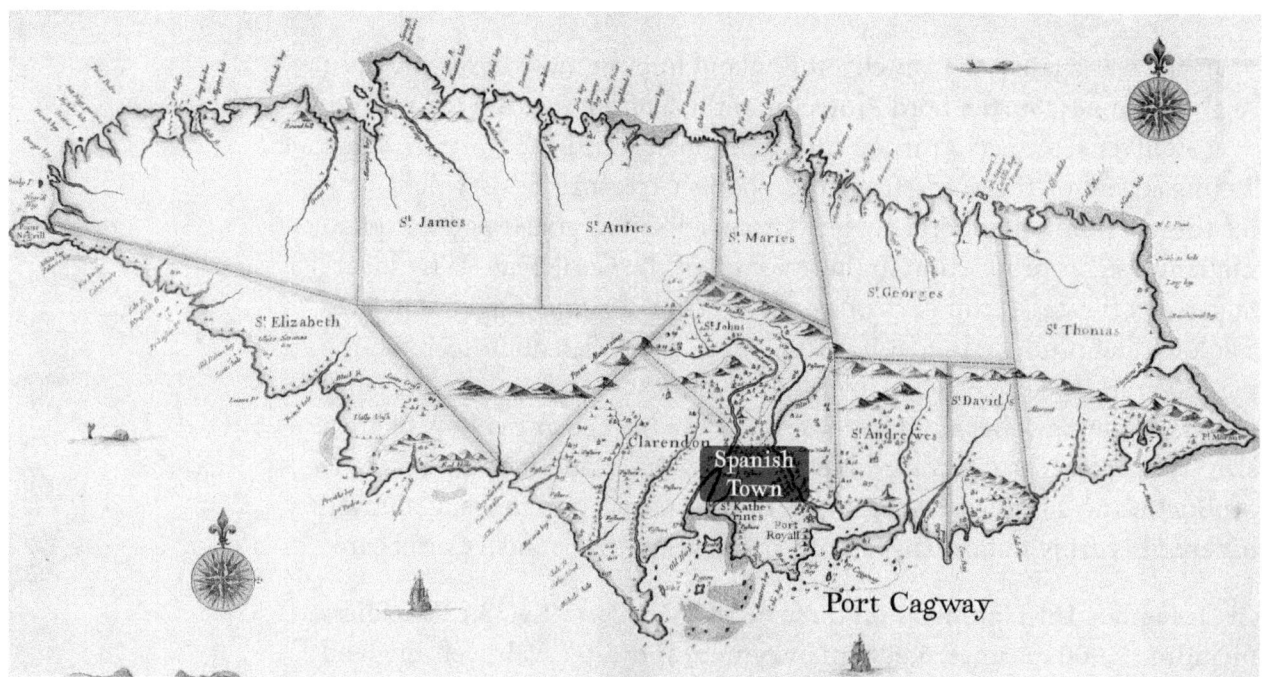

Figure 6: *Jamaica 1670*

1655—1660

1655-1660 The Anglo/Spanish War—England against Spain (France joins England in 1657).

Cromwell was determined to succeed in the Caribbean and he continued to send supplies, ships, and troops to support the Jamaican settlement against a Spanish counter attack. Time was of the essence as it was certain Spain would be quick to respond. To organize the colony and plan for its defense, Colonel Edward D'Oyley was appointed the first Governor of Jamaica. When the news of the English invasion reached Spain, the English act of aggression against Spanish territory in the Caribbean soon led to war which was declared in October 1655.

Spain and England were now officially at war. In January 1656, in an effort to defend Jamaica, the English sent a naval flotilla under the command of Subcommander Christopher Myngs, captain of the frigate *Marston Moor*.

However, a Spanish fleet didn't materialize and Myngs was soon ordered to return to England. On Jamaica, Spanish resistance continued on the island but on a very small scale. Most resistance was in the form of guerilla action from the Spaniards that fled into the mountains when the English first landed.

To supply the colony, the English constructed a port on a natural harbor on a large sand spit on the south-central coast of the island near Spanish Town. That port was ideally positioned to support large ships. Immediately afterwards, the construction of a fort was begun. It was situated at the tip of the sand spit separating the harbor from the Caribbean and commanded complete control of all access to the harbor through the narrow entrance. The fort was named Fort Cromwell in honor of Oliver Cromwell, Lord Protector of the Commonwealth of England. The tip of the sand spit was called Point Cagway and a small town developed next to the fort which was named Port Cagway.

Jamaica was well-situated to raid Spanish shipping and with all the loot that was coming in from the buccaneer raids in 1658 and 1659 Port Cagway began to grow rapidly. Its first inhabitants were mariners, merchants, craftsmen, and of course prostitutes. By 1659, two hundred houses, shops, and warehouses surrounded the fort. From modest beginnings, this port was destined to become one of the most famous and important ports in all of pirate history. A year later, Port Cagway was renamed Port Royal.

With a major Spanish counterattack looming, the new Governor of Jamaica, Colonel Edward D'Oyley decided to use the same defensive strategy that had worked so well against the Spanish at Tortuga. He used buccaneers to go on the offensive and his first Spanish target was Tortuga. Governor D'Oyley realized that Tortuga was virtually undefended since most of the Spanish troops were sent to Hispaniola. This was a terrific opportunity to regain control of the buccaneer stronghold and reorganize the buccaneer fleets against the Spanish. In 1656, he rounded up as many buccaneers as they could find and launched an invasion of Tortuga.

The Spanish defenders were easily overwhelmed, and Tortuga was once again under English rule, this time by the Governor of Jamaica. He immediately offered all buccaneers letters of marque and a safe haven in both Port Cagway and Tortuga. Most buccaneers moved to Port Cagway since Tortuga had been largely destroyed by the Spanish. It would take a while for Tortuga to bounce back. In European waters, General-at-Sea Robert Blake intercepted a Spanish treasure fleet in 1656. Then, in April 1657, Blake's English fleet completely destroyed the Spanish West Indies battle fleet in Santa Cruz harbor off the Canary Islands leaving all of the Spanish

1659

Port Cagway (later to be renamed Port Royal) established as a major English port on Jamaica.

1655—1656 & 1657—1661

Edward D'Oyley, Governor of Jamaica

1659

West side of Hispaniola officially deeded to France and named Saint Domingue.

treasure fleets virtually defenseless. This gave the buccaneers operating out of Port Cagway and Tortuga a distinct advantage as the bulk of the Spanish escorts for their treasure fleets were at the bottom of the ocean.

France and Spain had been fighting in Flanders for years and King Louis XIV of France saw this war as a golden opportunity to recover land lost to the Spanish. With the Treaty of Paris in March of 1657, France joined England as allies against Spain. Now that France and England were allies again, the two nations began to restore the relationship they had back in the 1620s when they divided St. Kitts into English and French sections.

Tortuga, of course, was of great interest to King Louis XIV of France and England gave Tortuga back to France in 1659, officially declaring Tortuga as a French possession. France then went on to develop a full-scale French colony on the west end of Hispaniola which they named Saint Domingue, no doubt named for Hispaniola's Spanish capital city of Santo Domingo. The English withdrew from Tortuga completely and the French and Dutch buccaneers returned.

Chapter 6
The Pirate King

Christopher Myngs was the clear leader of all buccaneer activity in the Caribbean from 1658 to 1665. He organized the buccaneers like never before, forming an incredibly large fleet. He was a daring and cunning captain whose remarkable accomplishments and superior leadership gave him the reputation of one of the most respected buccaneer captains of all time. Myngs not only held the buccaneers together, he molded them into highly-effective fighting teams. He also perfected the techniques and tactics of large-scale naval operations and amphibious assaults; that is to say, landing large amounts of infantry ashore and taking port cities from the landward side. He was given the title "The Pirate King." So why isn't he as famous as Henry Morgan or Blackbeard? The answer is simple. He was Captain Christopher Myngs of the Royal Navy, and by his death, Vice Admiral Sir Christopher Myngs. Pirates become famous only through the stories that authors write about them. Even if the books are highly inaccurate, the public learns their names through literature. In fact, it generally works out that the more inaccurate the story, the more famous the pirate becomes. Books about naval officers on assignment in the Caribbean can't compete with blood thirsty pirates in the Caribbean. Perhaps that's why Christopher Myngs' name remains virtually unknown.

1656

Christopher Myngs establishes buccaneer fleets from Jamaica.

As you may recall from Chapter 5, Sir Christopher Myngs was appointed captain of the frigate *Marston Moor* and was sent to Jamaica in 1656 to serve as the subcommander of their naval flotilla. His stay was brief, and he soon returned to England. By late 1657, a Spanish invasion of Jamaica was imminent and Myngs was ordered to return, arriving in February 1658 as the naval commander of the area. He returned with hundreds of ex-English soldiers fresh from the wars in Europe. The problem for Myngs was a serious lack of ships. He had plenty of men but precious few vessels, certainly not enough to fight the Spanish. As soon as he arrived, he recruited as many buccaneers as he could get. He skillfully combined the buccaneers with English soldiers to form the bulk of his force. This was the beginning of the large buccaneer fleets that sailed the Caribbean well-supported by the English government. Soon afterwards, buccaneers from all parts of the Caribbean flocked to Jamaica to get in on the action.

The Spanish counterattack came in February 1658 when 550 Spanish troops with artillery sailed from Vera Cruz and landed on Jamaica. They were met by Myngs with a force of 500 buccaneers. The Spanish were decimated by well-disciplined volley fire from the English ex-soldiers and the buccaneers and the Spanish surrendered in mass. Christopher Myngs was the hero of the day. Governor Colonel Edward D'Oyley of Jamaica was anxious to continue the privateer policy against Spain and encouraged Myngs to stay and further organize the buccaneer resistance. Myngs began to perfect his tactics of large amphibious forces consisting of those ex-soldiers and dozens of ships sailed by buccaneer crews from Tortuga. **One of the young staff officers present was said to have been Henry Morgan. This is undocumented, but documentation does show that Henry Morgan was named as one of Myngs' ship captains shortly afterwards.**

England and Spain were still "officially" at war. Myngs was not acting as an independent privateer; this was all part of the English economic strategy against the Spanish, although, a large portion of the loot Myngs took ended up in his possession and in the possession of his buccaneer partners. In 1658 and 1659, his fleet raided the coast of South America and plundered the cities of Tolu and Santa Maria in present-day Columbia and Cumana, Puerto Cavallo, and Coro in present-day Venezuela. With the help of Myngs and the buccaneer plunder, Cagway continued to grow. By 1659, two hundred houses, shops, and warehouses surrounded the fort. Nonetheless, Myngs' biggest haul was from the capture of the port of Coro where he took silver valued at a quarter of a million pounds off Spanish ships in the harbor. The shares were divided among the buccaneers with Myngs keeping a large portion for himself. As was the custom with the issuing of letters of marque, a portion of the profits must go to the official issuing those letters. In this case, Myngs neglected to give Governor D'Oyley his share and the governor charged him with embezzlement. Myngs was sent to England to stand trial.

As luck would have it, the date was 1660 and the English government had decided to restore Charles to the throne. **As you recall, Charles had been living in exile for 10 years since his father, King Charles I, was beheaded.** The English government had been ruled by Oliver Cromwell who took the title Lord Protector of the Commonwealth of England. However, when Cromwell died in 1658, the government almost fell apart and England was ready to restore the monarchy. In a real turn of irony, England's old enemy, Spain, actually helped Charles regain the throne. He promised Spain that if they helped him regain the throne, he would end the war between England and Spain and return all Spanish property in the Caribbean.

England was now ruled by King Charles II. This period in English history is called the "Restoration" and was a time of great confusion and disorganization in the English government. Think about it. Shifting from one government to another can be very challenging. One can only imagine how many things slipped through the cracks with court records in utter chaos. That was good news for Myngs, as all the evidence against him was somehow lost. On top of that, the governor of Jamaica had been appointed by the king's enemy, Oliver Cromwell, so how reliable could his charges be? King Charles II dropped the charges and Myngs was returned to the rank of Captain. Soon after, he was given command of a 40-gun warship, *Centurion*. This was just in the nick of time.

After becoming King of England, Charles II decided to renege on his promise to Spain and keep Jamaica as well as all the other English possessions in the Caribbean. The Spanish lodged formal protests and the cold war was on again. Just as before, King Charles II knew that privateers would be the only way to keep the Spanish at bay.

1660

King Charles II of England is restored to the throne.

Chapter 7
Port Royal, Dung Hill of the Universe

Actually, Port Royal really wasn't such a bad place. Most of the negative descriptions of Port Royal seem to come from people who have a dislike for prostitutes, drinking, and gambling. "The Sodom of the New World," was how one clergyman described Port Royal. He also stated, "Its population consists of pirates, cut-throats, whores, and some of the vilest persons in the whole of the world." Another account given by the captain of the William Galley described one particular tavern called Betty Ware's as a "noted house, as well as most of her neighbors, being notorious for their wickedness and nicknames, often called the fashioned dram cup upon a very lewd occasion." In Woodes Rogers' diary, Ned Ward called Port Royal the "Dunghill of the Universe" and commented on the exceptionally colorful nicknames of a few of the local ladies writing, "Unconscionable Nan, Salt Beef Peg, and Buttock-de-Clink Jenny whose swearing, drinking, and obscene talk are the principal qualifications that render them acceptable to male conversation." But in reality, I rather think of Port Royal as the Las Vegas of the day.

In 1660 after King Charles II was comfortably restored to the throne, any names or references to Oliver Cromwell or the old Commonwealth of England had to go. After all, Cromwell was the one who executed the King's father 11 years earlier and sent the king's family into exile. Port Cagway was renamed Port Royal and Fort Cromwell was renamed Fort Charles to honor the King and to honor the restoration of the royal bloodline. Additionally, a new governor was appointed, a pro-English and anti-Spanish governor named Lord Windsor. In its heyday, it was the largest English port in North America except for perhaps Boston. It was the capital of all English colonies in the Caribbean and the center of all English trade.

By 1660 Port Royal had become the New World's first real boom town. It was like San Francisco during the 1849 gold rush or the city of Las Vegas in the late 20th century. It was a place where anybody could earn a fortune in a short time. It was also a place where anyone could go broke in an even shorter time. There were over 6,000 local residents and one of every five buildings was a brothel, gambling house, or tavern. The population was extremely diverse. There were accounts of merchants who were Quakers, Papists, Puritans, Presbyterians, Jews, or, of course, Anglicans, practicing their religion openly alongside the free-wheeling buccaneers who frequented the port. The merchants had a friendly "Welcome to Port Royal" attitude toward buccaneers that had existed to some extent before, but dramatically increased with the new governor, Lord Windsor. He actively encouraged buccaneer ships in port and issued letters of marque to anyone who would sail against the Spanish.

But women, gambling, and liquor weren't the only businesses that flourished in Port Royal. Bills of export from London show that during the late 1600s, gun dealers in Port Royal were doing banner trade in flintlocks. That makes perfect sense. Every buccaneer wanted the finest weapons and flintlocks were the state of the art. Also, sugar plantations and large-scale mining operations, for things like gypsum and marble, began to spring up all over the island. That sparked the slave trade which also flourished throughout the period. It was also, without doubt, the center of all buccaneer activity after the decline of Tortuga. Christopher Myngs, Henry Morgan, Rock Brasiliano, Robert Searle (John Davis), Edward Mansfield, and many others all called Port Royal their home.

Thanks to the buccaneers, Port Royal had become the most important English port in the Americas, a mercantile center of the English Caribbean, with vast amounts of goods flowing in and out of its harbor as part of an expansive trade network. Port Royal was an ideal place for privateers to sell their captured cargo and to spend their money. The rich plantation owners were delighted to buy whatever cargo the privateers brought to port, exotic cloths from India, fancy jewelry from Spain, or even hard wood lumber from Mexico. Within a few years, the profits coming out of Port Royal would exceed the profits of all the other English colonies combined!

After gaining the king's favor and escaping the executioner in England, Christopher Myngs returned to Jamaica and quickly re-established his buccaneer partnerships and cultivated a network of loyal privateer captains. Using Port Royal as his base of operations, he enjoyed the full support of the new governor, Lord Windsor. However, there was one problem for the new governor, which was the question of loyalty among the hundreds of Commonwealth soldiers still living on Jamaica. The Commonwealth was

1660

Port Royal becomes the most profitable city in the New World.

the old political power established by Cromwell, but now, Charles II was on the throne. Windsor and Myngs found the solution by dangling profits their way. The thousands of soldiers on the island that had been loyal to Cromwell rapidly converted to the buccaneer way by the lure of the large profits they could earn.

With Port Royal as a base, Myngs quickly built a large buccaneer fleet. Among them were John Morris, David Martien, Robert Searle, and the king of the English buccaneers, Captain Edward Mansfield. Mansfield may have been Dutch due to the fact that his name occasionally appears as Mansvelt in contemporary documents, but other sources indicate that he was English. His original identity remains unknown, but by 1660, he had been a buccaneer captain sailing out of Tortuga for quite some time and was among the most respected of the buccaneers. Myngs appointed Mansfield his second in command.

1660s

Governors of Jamaica sponsor a privateer war against Spain.

In October 1662, using Port Royal as a base, Myngs led an assault force of 1,300 men and a dozen vessels on an attack of the city of Santiago, Cuba, in the heart of the Spanish Caribbean Empire. The buccaneers landed ashore at night to the east of the city and quickly overran and destroyed the infamous Castillo del Morro guarding the entrance to the Bay of Santiago. The town fell the next day. This was Myngs' first full scale buccaneer amphibious assault, one that would be repeated over and over again for the next 30 years. The tactics were simple. First, identify a rich Spanish port, then sail there with a large fleet of ships filled with soldiers, land on shore far away from the enemy fortifications, and attack using traditional European infantry tactics. He returned to Port Royal with a string of prize ships filled with Spanish plunder.

1663

Henry Morgan is first mentioned as captain of a small buccaneer fleet of 5 ships.

The 1662 raid on the city of Santiago, Cuba is far more significant to our story for another reason. The detailed records of that attack mentioned the names of two of Myngs' captains who were destined to become famous buccaneers. One of them became perhaps the most famous buccaneer of them all. He was a young and upcoming member of Myngs' officers who may have gotten his start as one of Mansfield's captains. His name was Henry Morgan. The other became a successful buccaneer in his own right and is today known as one of the buccaneers who sacked the Spanish city of Saint Augustine, Florida. His name was Robert Searle. I shall discuss both of them in detail a little later on.

By 1663, Myngs had over 1,400 buccaneers including some French and Dutch, all operating out of Port Royal. Myngs repeated his success with the raid on San Francisco de Campeche, Mexico in February 1663 and returned to Port Royal with a fleet of prize ships. However, Myngs was wounded in the attack and returned to England. His second in command, Captain Mansfield took over as the Admiral of the English privateer fleet at Port Royal. Two years later, Myngs was promoted to Vice Admiral and was knighted by the King Charles II, but he was killed in action fighting the Dutch Navy in a major four-day long sea battle off the English coast in 1666.

This was a time when large buccaneer fleets threatened Spanish cities throughout the Caribbean through well-planned and orchestrated amphibious assaults. These fleets required some port to serve as a supply base of operations before the assault and a place to sell the captured goods afterwards. By 1662, the French buccaneers had all returned to Tortuga and it was their port of choice, just as Port Royal was the English main port. The French buccaneer, Jean-David Nau, who went by the name of François L'Olonnais, used Tortuga as his base. Among the most successful of all the French buccaneers, he was given a Spanish prize vessel by the Governor of Tortuga in 1662. However, Tortuga's reign as the premier buccaneer port was about to decline. Most of the English buccaneers were now operating out of Port Royal and France was putting a maximum effort into supporting their new colony of Saint Domingue which was located on the west end of Hispaniola itself. The capital city of the colony was the newly established port of Petit Goave. It was a great sea port with far better access to Spanish shipping lanes than Tortuga. The buccaneer trade gradually began to shift over to Petit Goave.

By 1665 the French West India Company had taken possession of Tortuga and established Bertrand d'Ogeron as the new French governor. His goal was to turn Tortuga into an island of tobacco and sugar plantations rather than a buccaneer haven. Realizing that the Spanish were still a threat, Governor d'Ogeron continued to issue letters of marque to all the buccaneers as a form of defense against future attacks. Despite d'Ogeron's efforts to transform Tortuga away from a buccaneer base, it managed to hang on throughout the rest of the decade as a great place to recruit buccaneer crews and stage large operations on the surrounding islands.

1664

England captures many Dutch slave trading forts along West African coast and establish the English slave trade.

Chapter 8
Enter Henry Morgan

Much of what we know, or don't know, about Henry Morgan's early life and his personal conduct as a privateer came from a book published in Holland in 1678 entitled *De Americaensche Zee-Roovers (The American Sea Rovers)*. The work was written by Alexander O. Exquemelin who claimed to have been a buccaneer surgeon from Tortuga and a member of Henry Morgan's crew. Why I say "what we know or don't know" is because Exquemelin's description of Morgan is highly-flawed, historically. Many of the accounts are fairly correct when looking at the overall picture, but the book treats Morgan very unfairly; embellishing the events, inventing gruesome details, and making up facts to suit the author's depiction. The accuracy of Exquemelin's book was even called into question in the 17th century.

There is an enormous amount of documentation that proves Exquemelin's depiction of Henry Morgan to be far from the truth. Yet, this fictional version of the life of Henry Morgan is what most people believe, even today. Part of the reason for this is that so many modern authors writing books on pirates have assumed that this book, which was actually written during Morgan's lifetime, must be accurate. *The General History of Pyrates* written by Charles Johnson and published in 1724 is merely a rehash of what Exquemelin wrote. Morgan's real story is far different.

Scholars have narrowed Henry Morgan's birth to 1635 in one of two locations. He was either from Abergavenny, England or Llanrhymny, Wales. In either case, his family was Welch and he spent his childhood in Wales. He had two noteworthy uncles. One of his uncles, Edward Morgan, rose to the rank of Major General in Cromwell's army. His other uncle, Thomas Morgan, fought on the Royalist side as a Colonel. It wasn't uncommon for families to serve on opposing sides guaranteeing that whichever side won, the family name would survive.

Exquemelin writes that Morgan came to Barbados as an indentured servant. The documentary evidence which supports this assertion is a curious entry in the *Bristol Apprentice Books* which reads "Servants to Foreign Plantations: February 9, 1655, included Henry Morgan of Abergavenny, Labourer, Bound to Timothy Tounsend of Bristol, Cutler, for three years, to serve in Barbadoras on the like Condiciouns." But according to Henry Morgan himself, he arrived in the Caribbean as a junior officer with the army of General Venables in 1655. When Morgan read Exquemelin's book and the claim that Morgan had once been an indentured servant, he was outraged. Given that his uncles were both high ranking officers and uncle Edward eventually became Lieutenant Governor of Jamaica, I personally have a hard time believing the "indentured servant" version. **I believe that Henry Morgan was a junior officer under General Venables and arrived in Jamaica in 1655.**

According to Exquemelin, Morgan joined the buccaneers and made several voyages before obtaining his own ship. He made several raids along the Mexican coast near Campeche before joining Captain Edward Mansfield's buccaneer fleet which was part of Myngs' operation. Captain Henry Morgan is listed as a captain serving under Myngs on the 1662 Santiago, Cuba raid. After Myngs returned to England, Captain Mansfield became the number one English buccaneer sailing from Port Royal. Morgan teamed up with many other buccaneer captains, most of whom sailed with Myngs. One of these captains was John Morris.

By December 1663, Morgan was captain of a small buccaneer fleet of five ships. Henry's uncle, Colonel Edward Morgan, had just arrived in Jamaica as the new lieutenant governor and commanding officer of all military on the island. Nonetheless, Henry wasn't there to meet him because he was away sailing under letters of marque issued by Lord Windsor, attacking Spanish cities.

Together as partners, Morgan and Morris raided Spanish shipping and various ports all along Mexico's Yucatan peninsula. The first major port to fall was Villahermosa in the province of Tabasco. Morgan and Morris landed their buccaneers at the mouth of the Grijalva River far from any resistance. Then, they marched 50 miles upriver to take the city completely by surprise. When they returned to the coast, Morgan and his men discovered that the Spanish navy had captured their ships. The buccaneers managed to overpower a few troops and escaped in two Spanish trading pinnaces and four Indian canoes. They made their way south, looting as they went, until they reached Trujillo in present day Honduras. There, they boarded a ship at anchor and sailed to the San Juan River. Not wanting to quit while they were ahead, Morgan decided to repeat his amphibious tactics once again. The buccaneers were safely landed ashore and marched 100 miles upriver to Lake Nicaragua where they took the city of Granada completely by surprise.

This was Morgan's style. As a rule, he didn't take ships at sea; Morgan landed large troop formations away from the enemy's fortifications and marched overland to attack cities using the latest European siege tactics. Most of his buccaneers were ex-soldiers from the Thirty Years' War who came to the Caribbean looking to get rich. The tradesmen, sailors, and escaped servants who joined his ranks were trained as infantrymen, to advance in disciplined ranks, to fire by volley, and to march in platoon formation. During this two-year voyage, Morgan used the same infantry tactics employed by Myngs. Infantry of the day advanced in neatly formed ranks, marching in step to drums and displaying flags to identify their units. Exquemelin certainly described it that way, writing that Morgan's buccaneers attacking with "drums beating and colors flying." However, that's difficult when traveling through the jungles of the Yucatan Peninsula. It may have happened a few times.

Morgan returned to Port Royal in November 1665 a hero and a wealthy man. He was now recognized as one of the top buccaneer captains among the Brethren of the Coast. He was also a very well-respected citizen among the planters and government officials. Because his letters of marque were legally issued by Lord Windsor and Henry was out of touch with the world, there were no legal problems with the new pro-Spanish policy. Henry bought a sugar plantation and married his cousin Elizabeth, the daughter of his recently deceased uncle, Colonel Edward Morgan, the former Lieutenant Governor. By the end of his life, Morgan accumulated three sugar plantations, one at Port Maria on the northeastern coast, one in what was called Morgan's Valley in Clarendon Parish along the Rio Minho River, and a 4,000-acre plantation near Lucea in Hanover Parish on the northwestern shore, just west of Montego Bay. Sir Thomas Modyford, the Governor of Jamaica, became good friends and political allies with Henry. They shared the same anti-Spanish views.

Chapter 9
Policy Changes

England was trying to corner the West African trade by 1664. However, the Dutch were already well-established there with many trading posts along the West African coast. To force a war, England began issuing letters of marque against Dutch shipping to privateers, mostly in the Caribbean. But a new war with the Dutch Republic would be costly and fighting the Spanish too would be impossible for England to manage. Several pro-Spanish advisors to the King urged Charles II to negotiate peace treaties with Spain. However, if England was to have any success with Spain, King Charles II would first have to put a stop to English privateering against Spanish ships in the Caribbean. The first step was to replace Governor Lord Windsor of Jamaica, who was a big supporter of the buccaneer raids and full-scale operations against the Spanish. He was replaced by Sir Thomas Modyford, who brought a new Lieutenant Governor along with him, Colonel Edward Morgan, the uncle of the young and upcoming privateer, Henry Morgan.

When Sir Thomas Modyford left England to assume his position as Governor of Jamaica, he was directed by King Charles II to discourage buccaneer raids against the Spanish and to encourage raids against the Dutch. Modyford arrived in Jamaica in June 1664 and began to initiate these new policies. At first, the buccaneers and merchants of Jamaica probably thought that this was just a small gesture to calm the political situation back in Europe, but that nothing had really changed. Yet, just as Modyford was assuming his position, Spain began applying new pressure on King Charles II to put an immediate stop to all English raids against Spanish property. On June 15, 1664 King Charles II wrote a letter to Modyford with a new set of instructions which didn't arrive in Jamaica until a few months later. This letter stated, "His Majesty cannot sufficiently express his dissatisfaction at the daily complaints of violence and depredation." Modyford was "again strictly commanded not only to forbid the

1664–1671

Sir Thomas Modyford was the Governor of Jamaica.

prosecution of such violence for the future, but to inflict condign punishment upon offenders, and to have the entire restitution and satisfaction made to the sufferers." In effect, Modyford was ordered to recall all letters of marque against the Spanish, return all captured Spanish property, and he was forbidden to allow any further English raids against the Spanish.

Like his predecessor, Lord Windsor, Governor Modyford realized that the only way to defend Jamaica from Spanish attacks was to keep the Spanish on the defensive through the use of privateer raids. He personally disagreed with King Charles II's pro-Spanish position. Many modern accounts of Governor Modyford's actions state that he ignored the King's wishes and continued to issue letters of marque against the Spanish, perhaps for personal profit, but this is totally untrue. Most of the original correspondences between Charles II and Modyford still exist. The records show that Modyford followed orders. At first, Modyford reluctantly rescinded all letters against the Spanish and began arresting privateers and confiscating their prize ships and loot which was returned to the Spanish authorities.

This created a tremendous shock wave among the merchants and tavern keepers of Port Royal whose livelihood was suddenly threatened. First of all, a very large part of Port Royal's revenue was from Spanish prizes taken by English privateers. Secondly, without letters of marque, all the buccaneer trade would go the French at Tortuga or Petit Goave. It was also a shock to all the privateers who considered Port Royal as their home port. Modyford encouraged the privateers to attack the Dutch, and many did, but many others refused. The Dutch and English buccaneers were the brethren of the coast. Many had been partners at one time or another.

Even though Modyford recalled all letters of marque against the Spanish, Spain still refused to recognize the English right to Jamaica as well as all their other settlements in the Caribbean. Additionally, they continued to attack English ships on sight. For the English in the Caribbean, the Spanish were still the real enemies and posed the main threat. The English privateers wanted to continue taking Spanish prizes to keep their colonies safe. The French on Tortuga and Petit Goave were still issuing letters of marque against the Spanish, so many English privateers quietly left Port Royal and returned to Tortuga as their home port.

The first buccaneer to find himself in trouble over the new policy of King Charles II was Robert Searle. One of Sir Christopher Myngs' protégées, Robert Searle was also known as John Davis. Perhaps he used this alias from time to time because he often found himself in trouble with Governor Modyford, who once took his privateering commission away and, on another occasion even had him arrested. So far, no record of his early life has been found, but it is very likely that he was the brother of Daniel Searle, who was the Governor of Barbados in the 1650s. During that time, Modyford lived on Barbados and a bitter political rivalry existed between Modyford and Daniel Searle. As mentioned earlier, Searle first appears in the historic record when he is named as one of Myngs' captains in the accounts of the Santiago raid in October 1662. Searle must have been with Myngs for some time before that because he was given command of the 8-gun sloop, the *Cagway*. This, of course, was the original name of the city of Port Royal before King Charles II was restored to the throne. The *Cagway* was the largest of four Spanish vessels captured by Myngs as he returned from his attack of Santa Marta and Tolu in Columbia in 1659.

Captain Searle was successfully operating as a privateer with letters of marque from the old Governor of Jamaica during the summer of 1664. He took two very rich Spanish prizes off Cuba and brought them to Port Royal to sell the cargo, divide the profits with his crew, and pay the English government their share in accordance to his commission. Most of the cargo had already been sold when King Charles II's letter ending attacks against the Spanish arrived at Jamaica. As Governor Modyford read the King's letter, he could glance toward the dock and see the sight of two recently captured Spanish vessels being looted by Searle and his crew. It was instantly clear to Modyford that this would be the first test case and Robert Searle had to be made an example of. An emergency meeting of the Council of Jamaica was called and the King's letter and the situation with Searle were debated.

The decision of the Council was that the Governor of Cuba should be informed and that the Spanish vessels and all the treasure and cargo be immediately returned to the Spanish authorities. They also resolved to declare anyone a pirate who took Spanish prizes in the future and to take Captain Searle's commission from him and to confiscate his rudder (navigational charts) and all his sails. This is stated in one of Modyford's letters:

> "On reading the King's letter of June 15 last, commanding restitution of captured ships and goods to the Spaniards: ordered that the ship and bark brought in by Captain Searle of the Port Royal be seized and restored to that nation, and also all specie that can be found; that notice thereof be sent to the Governor of Havana; that persons making any further attempts of violence and depredation upon the Spaniard be looked upon as pirates and rebels; and that Captain Searle's commission be taken from him, and his rudder and sails taken ashore for security."

Chapter 10
Privateers of the Second Dutch War

As King Charles II was patching relations with Spain, he was still trying to start a war against the Dutch. To really get things going, he sent English invasion fleets to Africa and North America. The first fleet successfully captured the Dutch West African trading posts along the West African coast. The second fleet landed on June 24, 1664 and easily took the Dutch's largest colony in North America, New Netherland, whose capital was on the island of Manhattan. The English renamed the possession New York. The Dutch retaliated by attacking English shipping wherever they could. War was declared on March 4, 1665.

1665–1667

Second Anglo/Dutch War - England against The Dutch Republic and France (France changes sides at the end).

In Europe, the war was fought primarily at sea with large naval engagements. Beginning on June 1, 1666 the longest naval engagements in history began near Dunkirk. Lasting four days and included 79 English ships and 84 Dutch ships. It was during that battle that Admiral Sir Christopher Myngs was killed. In the Caribbean, that war was waged entirely with privateer fleets. This must have created many problems for the buccaneers who had been united against the Spanish. It was common for the crew of one ship to be comprised of men who were English, French, and Dutch. This undoubtedly divided some of the buccaneer crews along nationalistic lines. Now they had to decide which way to go. In some cases, I imagine those buccaneers who had been adversaries or just didn't like one another used this as a perfect excuse to attack a fellow buccaneer. But in other cases, buccaneers had to choose between friendship and patriotism. It appears that most chose patriotism. Over 200 Dutch ships were taken by English privateers in the Caribbean alone and the Dutch privateers retaliated. Still, Dutch privateer raids weren't just restricted to the Caribbean, in 1667 Dutch raiders sailed up James River in Virginia and captured an English tobacco fleet near the colony's capital city, James Town.

As the Dutch war got under way, Governor Modyford needed as many privateers as he could get. Robert Searle's ship, rudder (navigational charts) and sails were returned to him and he joined an expedition under the command of the Colonel Edward Morgan, the new Lieutenant Governor of Jamaica and the uncle and Father-in-law of Henry Morgan. Edward Morgan's force consisted of nine vessels with 650 men and in March or April of 1666 they sailed from Port Royal to attack the Dutch islands of Saint Eustatius and Saba. Modyford described the force of "chiefly reformed privateers, scare a planter amongst them, being resolute fellows and well-armed with fusils and pistols." Unfortunately for Edward Morgan, he died of heat stroke during the assault. Arguments over who would assume command caused the force to split up and Searle sailed away with his new partner, Captain Stedman.

In the spring of 1667, Searle and Stedman in their two vessels with a force of about 80 men attacked the Dutch island of Tobago, close to Trinidad. They were very successful and completely sacked the entire island. This was most unfortunate for Lord Willoughby, Governor of Barbados, who had planned an expeditionary raid of Tobago himself. His force arrived three days after Searle and Stedman, only to find that everything of value had already been safely loaded onto their two vessels. Lord Willoughby demanded possession of the island and the goods in the king's name. After some debate, Searle and Lord Willoughby agreed that Searle and Stedman could keep their loot as long as they sold it in Barbados. However, Governor Modyford wasn't so forgiving. After hearing of Searle's exploits, he felt that Searle should be punished for this disrespect toward Lord Willoughby. This was the second time that Searle angered Governor Modyford.

Meanwhile, back at Port Royal, Mansfield was named admiral of the fleet and Morgan was his vice admiral. They built a buccaneer fleet of 15 ships and 600 men. Letters of marque were issued and orders were given to attack the Dutch settlement of Curaçao. They left Port Royal in January 1666 with Admiral Mansfield in command and Vice Admiral Henry Morgan as his second. On the way to Curaçao, there was some trouble with the crew. The usual buccaneer crews who accompanied Morgan and the other privateer captains were made up of two groups. They were a mix of the ex-English soldiers on Jamaica and the French-Dutch buccaneers from Tortuga. That must have made for some interesting crews, since England, France, and the Dutch Republic were constantly going to war against each other. At any rate, there was some resistance to attack Curaçao. Perhaps it was the Dutch crewmembers feeling somewhat loyal to their mother country. Perhaps the crew just felt that there wasn't enough treasure in to make the venture profitable. The buccaneers weren't in this for territorial gain. Anyway, the crew voted to take another city, preferably Spanish. They would be doing this without letters of marque and against the king's new policy. Dissatisfied with how things seemed to be going, some of the crew left and returned to port, but enough remained to continue the venture.

By April 1666 they were off Costa Rica. Their plan was to attack Cartago, but the Spanish were too well prepared and the plan seemed too risky. They decided on a small island port of Santa Catalina off the coast of Columbia. The island was well protected by several Spanish forts, but Morgan's attack was so effective that the Spanish were unable to form a defense and the town surrendered. The island was renamed Providence and the English attempted to start a new settlement. Mansfield's plan was to build another pirate haven, like Tortuga. Governor Modyford's brother, Sir James Modyford, who happened to be along on this venture, was even made the governor. Many buccaneers remained in the city while Morgan and Mansfield sailed for Port Royal. The island never really got going however, and it was soon abandoned, returning to the control of the Spanish. When Mansfield and Morgan returned to Port Royal, there were no apparent consequences for their actions attacking the Spanish against the king's policy. Shortly after that, Edward Mansfield died. Some say he was caught and killed by the Spanish; some say he died of illness. At any rate, by the end of 1666, Henry Morgan was Admiral of the fleet, and undisputed king of the privateers. Oh, and if that wasn't enough, Morgan was also promoted to Colonel of the Port Royal Militia.

France began the war by halfheartedly supporting the Dutch against the English and many French buccaneers began attacking English shipping. But King Louis XIV of France still wanted to regain the territory France had previously lost to Spain in the Spanish Netherlands (modern-day Belgium). King Charles II of England saw this as a chance to get France's help and win against the Dutch, so he offered to assist France regain their territory if they abandoned their support for the Dutch and became English allies. In early 1667, King Louis XIV signed a treaty with England and switched sides. Many French and Dutch buccaneers were undoubtedly confused when France decided to change alliances right in the middle of the war.

François L'Olonnais, the French buccaneer, joined forces with the Dutch buccaneers on Tortuga just before France switched sides. They set sail with a fleet of 8 ships and 600 men bound for the Antilles where they planned to attack the English settlements. In July, as they were sailing to their target, L'Olonnais' fleet intercepted a vessel that informed him that

France was now on England's side, so the French and Dutch buccaneers went their separate ways.

L'Olonnais took his French buccaneers and went after the very wealthy Spanish port of Maracaibo instead. L'Olonnais' real name was Jean Davis Nau and he had been a very successful buccaneer since the early 1660s. Apparently he had a very deep hatred for the Spanish. One story tells that early in his buccaneer career, his entire crew was massacred by the Spanish and he escaped by smearing blood all over himself and playing dead. All accounts about L'Olonnais speak of his brutality and extremely harsh treatment of his captives, especially the Spanish ones. For L'Olonnais, it seems that revenge against the Spanish was his motivation, along with a healthy profit.

No one had ever taken a large port like this. If he could pull it off, he would be extremely wealthy. On the way, he took a Spanish merchant ship carrying cocoa beans, gemstones, and 40,000 pieces of eight. He arrived at Maracaibo during the late summer of 1667. The port city of Maracaibo lies slightly inland at the mouth of a very large lake, Lake Maracaibo, in modern Venezuela. Its natural harbor had made it an important Spanish port since 1574 but to get there, ships had to travel through a narrow and difficult shallow channel that wound around sandbars and tiny islands. Nevertheless, a good pilot who was familiar with the channel would have no difficulty guiding large ships into the harbor. This channel was protected by a fort of poorly constructed earthworks and 16 guns. The Spanish felt it adequate for the protection of the city. In the 17th century, goods and treasure from all over South America were brought to Maracaibo by mule throughout the year and stored in warehouses. Every now and then, Spanish ships would arrive and load the cargo aboard for transport to Havana and eventually to Spain. Imagine the vast riches that would be in the warehouses at any given time awaiting the arrival of the next ships.

Upon reaching the entrance to the channel, L'Olonnais got around the old Spanish fort by simply landed a large force of men ashore and taking the fort from land. Then, they sailed their ships through the channel and pillaged the city. Many of the citizens hid their valuables and fled into the jungle, but they were tracked down by L'Olonnais' men and tortured until the revealed where their valuables were hidden. It had been written that L'Olonnais was a master torturer who used techniques like slicing portions of flesh off his victims or burning them alive. He also would tie a knotted rope around the victim's head and tighten it until their eyes were forced out. Once L'Olonnais had completely sacked Maracaibo, he sailed down to the southeast side of the lake and pillaged the sister city of Gibraltar, wiped out the Spanish garrison, and massacred about 500 Spanish soldiers.

1667

French buccaneer, François L'Olonnais, takes Maracaibo.

L'Olonnais had taken over 260,000 pieces of eight in addition to goods like gems, silverware, silks, and cattle. A single share given to a crewman amounted to more than 100 pieces of eight.

According to Exquemelin, after the Maracaibo operation, L'Olonnais plundered Puerto Cavello, which is probably Puerto Cortez in modern Honduras, then the inland city of San Pedro, which was off the Yucatan coast, and captured a large Spanish ship of 42 guns. Arguing over where to go next, L'Olonnais buccaneer fleet split up, giving L'Olonnais command of the captured Spanish ship. But his ship ran aground a short time later near Cabo Gracias a Dios which is on the border of modern Honduras and Nicaragua. Stranded there for about six months, they built long boats from the wreck of the Spanish ship and sailed along the coast toward Cartagena. As they reached the Gulf of Darien, which lies between the modern countries of Panama and Columbia, they were captured by natives and eaten. In the words of Exquemelin, "L'Olonnais was hacked to pieces and roasted limb by limb."

Back in England, King Charles II's pro-Spanish policy had to change. France and Spain were bitter enemies and France only joined the English side to put pressure on Spain. As part of the deal with the French, King Charles II had to resume some sort of attacks against the Spanish. Additionally, for the past several years, King Charles II and his government missed receiving their percentage of Spanish loot taken by English privateers. Their share was always 1/15th directly to the King and 1/10th to the minister of state. Modyford wrote the king and made a strong argument to resume the issuing of letters of marque against the Spanish. King Charles II gave his permission to issue letters against the Spanish on a limited basis, but to attack ships only, no ports. As far as Modyford was concerned, the king's policy against issuing letters of marque against the Spanish was gone and all anti-Spanish letters of marque could once again be issued freely. Modyford made a political victory against the King's advisors and had made political enemies among the pro-Spanish members of the English court.

The war ended shortly afterwards. It really wasn't good for the economy of anyone. By the time France switched sides, the economy of both England and the Dutch Republic had been destroyed, as well as their fleets. Neither side had gained anything except disaster. England and France were now allies, but France's focus was against the Spanish. King Charles II had had enough and signed The Treaty of Breda on July 31, 1667 ending the war. The English kept New Netherland, which they renamed New York, and the Dutch retained control over Pulau Run and the valuable sugar plantations of Suriname. Other than that, everything stayed exactly the way it was before the war.

Chapter 11
Henry Morgan–King of the Privateers

Back at Port Royal, Henry Morgan was rapidly emerging as not only one of the principal players in the Caribbean, but perhaps one of the most famous larger-than-life figures of all time. He was very well connected politically and close friends with Governor Modyford. He also had enormous experience as a buccaneer and was destined to become the next Pirate King. It was the spring of 1667 and France was now allied with England against the Dutch. Additionally, England's policy toward the Spanish had changed. As soon as Governor Modyford got permission to again issue letters of marque against the Spanish, Henry Morgan was first in line. Governor Modyford gave Morgan a commission to attack Cuba which in part read, "To Admiral Henry Morgan Esq. Greeting. Whereas the Queen Regent of Spain hath by her Royal Shadula dated at Madrid the 20th of April 1669 Commanded her respective Governours in the Indies to publish and make War against our Sovereign Lord the King in these Parts. And Whereas Don Pedro Bayona de Villa Nueva... out of the great confidence I have in the good conduct courage and fidelity of you the said Henry Morgan ...to use your best endeavours to surprise take sink disperse and destroy all the enemies ships or vessels which shall come within your view and also for preventing the intended Invasion against this place you are hereby further authorised and required in the case that you and your Officers in your Judgement find it possible or feasable to land and attain the said Town of St. Jago de Cuba or any other place belonging to the Enemies."

Morgan originally wanted to take Havana, but he didn't have enough men. Finally, Morgan decided on the Cuban city of Puerto Principe. For that operation, Morgan would need the finest crew he could get. After recruiting as many soldiers, townsmen, and buccaneers he could get

1667

Henry Morgan now King of the Buccaneers has full support of Governor Modyford.

on Jamaica, he sailed to the French port of Tortuga. In a touch of irony, while L'Olonnais was sailing to attack English settlements in the Antilles, unaware of the new alliances, Morgan was at Tortuga recruiting French buccaneers to fight the Spanish. Henry Morgan had been a regular patron of Tortuga for many years and often used it as a staging area as well as a place to recruit additional crew members for his operations.

Morgan's recruiting methods were quite unusual for the day. Most captains sent word around and waited for crews to come to them. Not Morgan. Instead of sending out a flyer or something, Morgan sought out his crewmen in all the local pirate hangouts. Morgan would sail to buccaneer ports like Tortuga and actively recruit from the most daring crews. When he arrived at the ports, he was dressed as flamboyantly as possible, sometimes in red silk outfits with lots of fancy gold and jewels. This made Morgan appear extremely successful to the other crews and attracted a large selection of the most qualified privateers, all wanting to join Morgan's crew. With 10 ships and 500 men, Morgan sailed for Cuba. On the way to Cuba, a storm brought Morgan's fleet to the southern shore, on the other side of the island. Morgan decided to re-provision his ship with food and water. He met a French buccaneer crew from Tortuga that had been caught in the storm too. They joined forces and the attack was on. The Spanish had been warned, however, and most of the valuables had been hidden away from the port. Morgan only netted about 50,000 pieces of eight, not enough to pay his large crew and turn a profit. Some say that the French portion of the group didn't get along with Morgan and his Englishmen. It was even reported that there was an actual duel between two members of the two crews. Some say that the French believed Morgan got more than the 50,000 pieces of eight and that he cheated them out of their share. At any rate, the French returned to Tortuga in disgust.

The war between the Dutch and the English was over, but that didn't change anything for Henry Morgan. After all, the Spanish were still the real threat and he had letters of marque against the Spanish. Morgan's tactics were always the same. He would sail a large fleet close to a wealthy city then land his infantry ashore and take the city from the land. He would loot the city and demand a ransom for the safe return of the citizens, then return to Port Royal to sell all captured merchandise and divide the silver and gold among the crew. By 1668, Morgan was an extremely wealthy and well-respected citizen of Port Royal. He was the governor's best friend, a plantation owner, the Colonel of the militia, and the Admiral of the privateer fleet. He was no pirate; he was a pillar of the community. He was also the most successful privateer of his day. However, after the failed operation in Cuba, he still owed a large sum of money to the buccaneer crews who accompanied him. In July 1668 Morgan decided to take the third most important Spanish city in the Caribbean, Portobelo.

Located on the northern coast at the center of the Isthmus of Panama, Portobelo was considered the center of Spanish trade in the Americas, so it contained warehouses of the goods and valuables of many wealthy merchants. It was also extremely well protected by three Spanish forts. True to style and tactics, Morgan anchored his fleet far away from the fortifications at the small port of Puerto do Naos where there was a river that led to the main objective. After "questioning" a Spanish prisoner, he devised a plan of attack. Traveling by foot along the river bank with two of his long boats, called pinnaces, following close by, he quietly advanced up the river to the south side of the city. In a lightning fast assault, he took the first fort and then the second. The third fort surrendered, and the city was his. The Spanish fleet counterattacked, but Morgan was ready. He set an ambush at a narrow passage and the much larger Spanish fleet with 3,000 troops withdrew. Morgan's buccaneers occupied and looted the city for 14 days, clearing over 150,000 pieces of eight in coin and goods. Then, they demanded a ransom of 100,000 pieces of eight for the safe return of the city and the people. With the ransom, the Spanish governor sent Morgan an emerald ring and requested that he not attack Panama again. They returned to Port Royal with a fortune, over 250,000 pieces of eight. Morgan was the hero of the day and even wealthier than before. As a reward, Morgan was presented with an English warship of 34 guns, the *Oxford*. But his next venture wouldn't be so easy.

1597

Portobelo, on the north coast of Panama, established.

Henry Morgan's Portobelo raid in 1668 alone produced plunder worth 75,000 English pounds, more than seven times the annual value of the island's sugar exports. Many shop keepers and artisans wanted to get in on the profits too. It was common to find regular citizens signing articles and joining the buccaneer crews for one or two short ventures. Of the 300 townsfolk who joined Morgan on the Portobelo raid, the individual share was 60 pounds each, three times their normal annual wage. It was a wealthy city of merchants, artisans, ships' captains, slaves, and, of course, buccaneers, who gave it its 'wickedest city in the world' reputation.

The *Oxford* was an English warship of 34 guns given to Port Royal for protection. It was natural to give command of the ship to the Admiral of Port Royal's fleet, Henry Morgan. In October of 1668, Morgan began gathering his fleet. In the usual buccaneer fashion, they anchored off a small island to do a bit of recruiting, organize the crew, sign articles, plan the attack, and throw a party. **One just can't begin an expedition without a party, can one?** Morgan chose Isla Vaca, a small island just southwest of Hispaniola. The English call this island Cow Island and it had been used by buccaneer crews before and was a known rendezvous point. It was conveniently located between Tortuga and the main Spanish shipping lanes. By January 1669, several French buccaneer crews had rendezvoused with Morgan and joined his fleet, which now consisted of 11 ships and 900 men. They had decided on Cartagena as their next objective. This was an exceptionally wealthy city because it was the staging port for all the gold that was transported over the mountains from Peru. With the arrangements finished and the target identified, the crew naturally turned to the next event in their daily planners, the massive crew party. No one really knows how it happened, but somehow the powder magazine ignited and the ship blew up. Perhaps a drunken crewman lit his pipe in a place where he shouldn't have been smoking. Over 300 crewmen were killed, only ten of the ship's crew survived the enormous blast. Remarkably, Henry Morgan was one of them. He was rescued from the water a short time afterwards.

With one less ship and a smaller total force of men, Morgan sailed for Cartagena. It was a rough passage. From their position, they had to sail into the wind for almost the entire journey. This exhausted his men, having to work the lines and rigging 24 hours a day. It also put a strain on the structure of his ships. For one reason or another, by March 1669, Morgan's force had diminished to about 500 men. This was too small to take on a well-fortified city like Cartagena, so an alternate plan was proposed. A year and a half earlier, the French buccaneer, L'Olonnais, had successfully taken Maracaibo and made off with a large haul. Some of Morgan's French buccaneers had accompanied L'Olonnais on that raid and one of the French buccaneer captains assured Morgan that he could lead them through to the town. They discussed it and Morgan agreed; the next objective would be the town of Maracaibo, in the modern country of Venezuela.

Reaching the town, however, was a difficult task. As mentioned earlier, Maracaibo is located at the mouth of Lake Maracaibo where it flows into the Gulf of Venezuela and eventually, the Caribbean. In order to get to the town, ships had to navigate through a narrow and shallow channel that wound around sandbars and tiny islands. The French captain who suggested the target claimed that he could direct the ships safely through it. What he didn't know was that the entrance harbor had changed since he was there in 1667. L'Olonnais' men easily overpowered the earthwork fort that the Spanish thought was sufficient protection, so they decided to upgrade their defenses with a large and well-built fort at the channel's narrowest point.

When Morgan's fleet reached that point, cannon fire from the fort kept them from continuing to the city. The master tactician, Morgan halted his ships and landed his men on the beach. Once nightfall arrived, Morgan and his men quietly assaulted the fort. There was no resistance, as the Spanish troops fled and left a slow-burning explosive charge as a trap for Morgan's men. He disarmed the fuse and looted all the supplies. Then, he ordered his men to take the city by using small vessels and canoes. Navigating the difficult channel was just too slow for his large ships. But the town was alerted and much of the gold and silver was effectively hidden away. Morgan loaded the large ships with as much provisions and booty as he could find and then navigated through the narrow channel into the lake and attacked the nearby town of Gibraltar. But at Gibraltar he found the same thing; most items of real value were hidden in the jungle. After eight unsuccessful weeks in the Lagoon of Maracaibo he decided to return to Port Royal.

On the morning of May 1, 1669, Morgan's fleet approached the narrow inlet which was the only channel that led back to the Gulf of Venezuela. Suddenly, Morgan spotted three Spanish men-o-war waiting in ambush. Commanded by Vice Admiral Don Alonso del Campo y Espinosa, the ships were the 48-gun *Magdalen*, the *Santa Louisa*, and the *Marquesa*. This was a desperate situation for Morgan and his men. They first had to get past these three large warships, then navigate the narrow

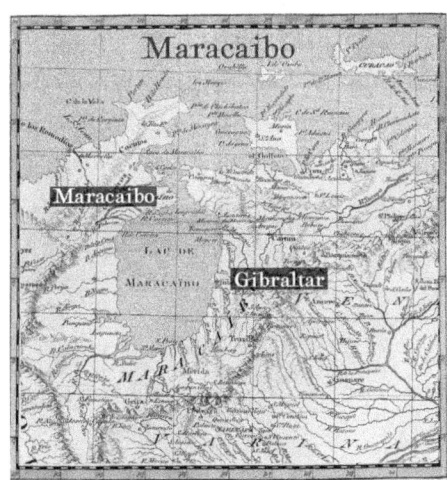

Figure 7: *Maracaibo*

channel past the Spanish fort. Morgan's plan was bold and highly imaginative. It was a brilliant combination of aggressiveness and deception. He took his largest ship, the *Satisfaction*, and staged explosives in hollowed out logs all about the deck. He dressed the explosives in clothes to look like crewmen standing about. Then, with only 12 men on board, they sailed the *Satisfaction* toward the *Magdalena*. The 12 buccaneers used grappling hooks to snare *Magdalen's* rigging, and then lit the fuses to the charges and jumped overboard. The *Satisfaction* blew up and the *Magdalen* burned and sank. The second Spanish ship, *Santa Louisa*, ran aground in the action and Morgan's ships overwhelmed and captured the *Marquesa* intact, which he kept as his flag ship. Vice Admiral Don Alfonso managed to escape the fire and made it to the fort. They were now at a stalemate. Morgan controlled the town and the ships, but the Spanish still controlled the only escape.

While Morgan and Don Alfonso negotiated over a ransom for the citizens of Maracaibo, Morgan's men salvaged 15,000 pieces of eight from the sunken Spanish warship. A ransom of 20,000 pieces of eight was finally agreed upon and Morgan was paid. But that still left Morgan with the problem of how to get past the Spanish fort. Morgan met this challenge with the same brilliance and cleverness. He tricked the Spanish into thinking he was going to attack the fort from land. All day long, his men would row ashore in his many small pinnaces. The pinnaces would return to the ships for the next load of men. However, his men just hid in the bottom of the pinnaces on the return trip and sat up again while rowing to the beach. In this way, it appeared that he had a huge force of men ashore, when in fact, he had very few. At night, the deceptive crewmen made as much noise as possible, pretending to be drunk and rowdy. The Spanish prepared for a land attack and moved all their cannon to defend the landward side of the fort. No guns now faced the water. In the wee hours of the next morning, the crew quietly returned to their ships and the fleet silently floated through the channel with the morning tide. On May 17, 1669, the cunning master returned to Port Royal aboard the *Marquesa*. He used his enormous profits to buy land in an undeveloped part of Clarendon Parish, Jamaica, which he named Morgan's Valley and built his second sugar plantation, close to the Rio Minho River.

Chapter 12
Searle's Sack of St. Augustine

Some accounts say that Searle decided to attack the Spanish city of Saint Augustine in retaliation for the Spanish attack on the English colony on New Providence, in the Bahamas. This is doubtful because the Spanish attacked the colony in 1664; four years before the date that Searle decided to sack Saint Augustine. A more believable account tells us that Searle may have learned that the treasury of Saint Augustine was filled with a large amount of silver bars recently recovered from a Spanish shipwreck from a former French surgeon named Pedro Piques who was a passenger on a Spanish brigantine that Searle took. At any rate, in May of 1668, Searle was in command of a fleet of four vessels and set his sights on Saint Augustine. Shortly before that, Searle was on his ship, the *Cagway*, cruising off the coast of Cuba with letters of marque from Governor Modyford. He had another vessel with him, perhaps it was his partner Steadman, but this is only speculation. The two privateers took two Spanish vessels, a ship bound for Vera Cruz and a brigantine bound for Havana.

On the morning of May 28, 1668, the fleet arrived at Saint Augustine. Searle kept his two English made vessels out of sight and entered the harbor with the two Spanish vessels he had captured. The Spanish soldiers manning the guns of the fort were not alarmed, thinking the two vessels to be Spanish merchant vessels coming into port. The two vessels dropped anchor and waited for night. The harbor pilot rowed out to greet them and was told by one of the Spanish speaking buccaneers that they were merchants from Mexico. The pilot returned to shore reassured that they were legitimate Spanish merchants. No one in the town or at the fort was suspicious. Around midnight, the other two vessels sailed past the fort's guns and quietly slipped into the harbor. However, they were spotted by Corporal Miguel de Monzón, who happened to be out in the harbor fishing. Realizing they were English privateers,

1668

Robert Searle sacks St. Augustine, Florida.

Monzón frantically rowed ashore under fire from Searle's men. Wounded twice, he managed to make it to shore and alert the Spanish authorities. This didn't matter, because Searle's buccaneers swarmed ashore and ran through the streets looting everything. Anyone who resisted was shot. Some made it to the fort for protection, including Governor Francisco de la Guerra de la Vega, while others escaped into the surrounding forest. It was over very quickly. About 60 Spanish townsfolk were killed and about 70 were taken prisoner, nearly half the entire population. Searle then turned his attack toward the fort, but after a halfhearted attempt to capture it, decided it wasn't worth the risk. In the morning, he exchanged his prisoners for firewood and provisions, then, he burned the city to the ground and sailed away. The buccaneers only lost 11 men and another 19 injured. The loot amounted to 133 silver marks, 760 yards of canvas for sails, twenty-five pounds of candles, and untold amounts of valuable jewelry and other personal items that they found. They also rescued Henry Woodward, an English surgeon who was living in the town after being captured by the Spanish several months earlier. It is believed that after his rescue, Woodward served as a surgeon aboard several privateer vessels and eventually settled in Charles Town, South Carolina.

Searle had letters of marque to attack shipping, but he clearly exceeded his authority when he took a Spanish port. Fearing that Governor Modyford would again be upset with his actions, Searle decided to quietly return to Jamaica and put in at Port Morant, which was just outside of the Governor's legal jurisdiction, until he could be sure of the governor's disposition. It was a good call, because Governor Modyford became furious when he learned of Searle's sacking of Saint Augustine. Eventually Governor Modyford was informed of his arrival and on March 18, 1670 he wrote, "There arrived also at Port Morant the Cagway, Captain Searle, with 70 stout men, who hearing that I was much incensed against him for that action of St. Augustine, went to Macarry Bay and there rides out of [my] command. I will use the best ways to apprehend him, without driving his men to despair."

When Searle finally came ashore within jurisdiction of the governor, he was arrested. Governor Modyford wrote the English authorities stating that Searle was still in the custody of Jamaica's Provost Marshal, awaiting trial and asked them what they wanted done with Searle and his men, but after several months without answer, Searle was released and his vessel, the *Cagway*, was returned to him. It seems that the governor needed Searle and his men to assist in one of the greatest privateer ventures ever planned. Henry Morgan was planning the taking of Panama.

Chapter 13
Morgan's Panama Campaign

As Henry Morgan sat on the veranda of his plantation sipping on a cool mojito he began thinking of his next venture. It would have to be an immense undertaking, since Maracaibo didn't prove to be as successful as he had hoped. England and Spain were still at a kind of cold war; at least, that's what everyone in Jamaica believed.

It was the summer of 1670 and the Treaty of Madrid had just been signed which ended hostilities between England and Spain, but the news of the Treaty hadn't reached the Caribbean yet. Morgan obtained his letters of marque from Modyford and left for Tortuga, accompanied by his old comrade, Robert Searle. They arrived on September 2, 1670. In Tortuga, Morgan began to add to his fleet. He already had about 1000 men he had brought with him from Jamaica. On Tortuga, he recruited another 800 French and Dutch buccaneers and late in 1670 Morgan left Tortuga for Spanish waters with a fleet of 36 vessels and 1846 men. The largest ship had 22 guns while the smallest had only four. This would be Morgan's greatest venture and the largest buccaneer fleet ever to sail the Spanish Main.

A mojito is a drink made with rum, lime juice, mint, and sugar. In the interest of historic accuracy, here is no documentation that Morgan ever had a mojito or that mojitos even existed in 1670, I just added that bit simply for dramatic impact.

Following buccaneer tradition, the fleet stopped at a rendezvous spot to discuss the articles of the venture and decide on a target. The spot was a leeward side of Cape Tiburon on the south western tip of Hispaniola. The terms of the articles were very generous, giving extra bonuses for wounds, etc. A target was finally agreed upon. It was the richest city in the Caribbean, a city that hadn't been attacked since Francis Drake sacked it in 1586, the crown jewel in the Spanish Main, the City of Panama. Just to get there would be a difficult undertaking as the city lay on the southern side of the Isthmus of Panama on the Pacific side.

Beginning his careful amphibious operation on December 15, 1670, Morgan first landed on the tiny island of Old Providence. From there he

Sir Francis Drake was a privateer for Queen Elizabeth I and lived from 1540 to 1596.

1670

Henry Morgan takes Panama.

launched his expedition landing on the Isthmus of Panama on December 27, 1670. Moving up the Chagres River and crossing to the Pacific side, Morgan led a well-organized attack of six ranks of infantry with both flanks supported by 200 cavalry. The Spanish were keeping a herd of "attack cattle" close by that they intended to stampede into the buccaneer ranks. That tactic was used often in the 16th century but was getting predictable by 1670. Morgan's left flank was commanded by a Dutch buccaneer named Laurens Prins. During the battle, he enveloped the Spanish right flank and seized a hill that controlled the battlefield. Prins' men opened fire from the hill which caused the cattle to stampede into the Spanish ranks instead. As Morgan's main force of buccaneers opened fire, the Spanish suffered heavy casualties and the rest of the troops routed. Panama fell, and Morgan had taken an estimated 400,000 pieces of eight.

After Panama was captured, Morgan gave the vitally important task of securing the port to his old comrade, Robert Searle. He was ordered to capture any vessel attempting to leave the port. Upon reaching the shore, Searle's men found a Spanish barque, the *Fasca*, which had been intentionally grounded and set on fire during the attack to prevent the English from capturing it. But Searle's men managed to put out the fire and refloat the vessel. In a few days, Searle managed to capture three other Spanish vessels. With his small flotilla, Searle cruised the offshore islands of Perico, Taboga, Tobogilla, and Otoque where they took many prisoners and valuable property. Unfortunately, that included a large amount of Peruvian wine and by evening all Searle's men were drunk, too drunk to notice the large Spanish galleon approaching nearby. It was the *Santissima Trinidad*, heavily laden with gold, silver, pearls, jewels, and other most valuable goods. The galleon had been in port when Morgan attacked Panama and was ordered to flee to another port, but the captain decided to simply put to sea and return to Panama after the English privateers left.

The captain of the Spanish galleon, Don Francisco de Peralta, saw Searle's barque but assumed it was just another Spanish vessel that had escaped the attack of the city. The galleon anchored nearby and a small party of seven men was sent ashore in a row boat to get fresh water. Some of Searle's men accidentally ran into the Spanish shore party, captured them, and brought them to Searle. Under threat of torture, the prisoners told Searle of the nearby location of their galleon. Additionally, they told Searle that the galleon was armed with only seven guns and about a dozen muskets.

Realizing that this incredibly rich prize was theirs for the taking, Searle quickly ordered his men to set sail, but they were all still too drunk to respond, so Searle decided to wait for morning. Suspicious when his men didn't return, De Peralta set sail and escaped in the night. When Morgan learned that Searle had let this rich prize slip through his fingers, he was outraged. Searle was bitterly reprimanded, and Morgan never trusted him again. After returning from Panama, Searle left Morgan's company and began operating in the Gulf of Campeche. Several years later, according to William Dampier, he was killed in a duel with one of his men on a tiny island at the northern end of the Gulf, still known as Searle's Key.

Even though Spain and England were not formally at war, a pseudo state of war existed between the two countries in the Caribbean since the mid-1620s, when the English first began to settle there. From the onset, the Spanish had waged a vicious campaign against all other settlers, attacking their ships and settlements enslaving the crews and colonists. The straw that broke the camel's back was the taking of Jamaica in 1655. Spain refused to recognize England's possession of Jamaica and constantly tried to destroy English shipping. The English protected their ships and ports with the use of privateers and aggressively waged war against the Spanish in the form of privateer attacks on Spanish ports and ships.

By 1670, Spain was low on money. The continuous wars in Europe were a tremendous drain on the Spanish economy and the constant English attacks on the South American and Mexican gold the Spanish depended on was just too much. The English also wanted to make peace and have Spain recognize their colonies in the Caribbean as legitimate. In July 1670, England and Spain signed the Treaty of Madrid. Under the terms of the treaty, Spain formally recognized all English possessions in the Caribbean to include Jamaica and the Cayman Islands. The English also had complete freedom of all shipping lanes. In return, the English agreed not to attack any more Spanish ships or ports. This one document would drastically change the operations of the buccaneers and effectively end the era of the large privateer fleets; but not just yet.

The Treaty of Madrid in 1670 officially ended English privateering in the Caribbean. Buccaneering had been the principal revenue for Port Royal and Tortuga. Now this had to change. Governor Modyford had actively supported privateering for six years arguing against the king's policies at times and making political enemies among the English ministers who were seeking a Spanish alliance. When the news of Morgan's attack on Panama reached Spain, it caused a major diplomatic incident. The English crown had to take immediate action in order to avoid another war. England needed a scapegoat and Modyford was tailor made. Sir Thomas Lynch was appointed the new governor of Jamaica and Modyford was arrested and sent to back England. Governor Lynch also had orders to arrest Morgan, but that proved difficult.

1670

Treaty of Madrid ended hostilities between England and Spain.

Robert Jacob

**1663–1664 &
1671–1674**

Sir Thomas Lynch, Governor of Jamaica

In April 1671, Morgan returned to a hero's welcome and the city council gave him a vote of thanks. The new governor, Sir Thomas Lynch, was in a difficult situation. Morgan was a national hero to the citizens of Jamaica and he had the support of the city council. Arresting Morgan would certainly cause a public riot. But the incident had created too much controversy and one year later; on April 4, 1672, Henry Morgan was finally arrested and taken back to England on the frigate *Welcome* to stand trial for piracy. Again, Morgan was treated like a hero upon his landing in London but was detained as a prisoner of the state anyway.

Chapter 14
Summing Up the Buccaneers 1640-1670

The era of the buccaneers began with the early colonization in the Caribbean by English, French, and Dutch settlers. Fierce attacks by the Spanish, both privateers and regular navy, led to organized resistance that quickly developed into cooperation in piracy between the English, French, and Dutch buccaneers devoted to fighting against the Spanish. With Tortuga as their base of operations, the buccaneers developed a pirate culture that was very similar to all the portrayals in modern books and film. They became the "Brethren of the Coast." As the years passed, their strength and reputation grew. They began to take larger and larger ships. Their partnerships led to the formation of buccaneer fleets and the huge influx of ex-soldiers from the 30 Years' War in Europe added greatly to their ranks. The buccaneers were well supported by the English, French, and Dutch governments, and letters of marque legitimized their actions.

Port Royal and Tortuga emerged as large ports filled with taverns, brothels, and everything else a pirate would need. But these weren't lawless pirate towns; they were the official seats of government. These early New World ports were also huge centers of commerce where all manner of goods were traded and plantation owners sold their crops. It was an ideal place for privateer crews to sell their captured merchandise. Buccaneers walked the streets, free and unafraid. After all, they weren't criminals; they were welcomed customers and military heroes. Some of the buccaneers were respected shop keepers, business owners, and craftsmen themselves. They spent their money in the taverns and provided the money that the towns' economies were based upon. The privateer captains became leading town citizens and plantation owners. Some of them were actually officers in the army or navy. They were given large warships to protect the community.

Large buccaneer fleets and huge amphibious assault forces ravaged Spanish cities. Many of these fleets were well sponsored by the governments they served. Privateers were used in the Caribbean as the regular standing navy and in European waters. The privateers waged large-scale war against shipping and trade, all on the orders of the crown. Their ships varied greatly in size and composition, but it was not unusual to see large buccaneer warships of 30 to 40 guns.

Their crews consisted of mostly soldiers with a few sailors to handle the ship. Their appearance would have been a mix of fancy clothing taken from prize vessels, nautical clothing used onboard as a matter of practicality, and contemporary military uniforms with the customary military boots. However, leather sandals also were worn. By the late 1660s, buccaneers looked more like land soldiers than sailors. With each raid, the captured clothing contributed greatly to their eclectic appearance. Also, they all would have been well-armed and provisioned when conducting a raid and also when on shore leave. The fact that they were exceptionally well-armed ashore is the first thing many contemporary observers mention. Even though the towns had some sort of law, they didn't have a police force. It was every man for himself when they went ashore. Contemporary accounts mention a buccaneer named Rock Brasiliano who would "scour the streets of Port Royal with a sword, dismembering anyone who crossed his path." If a buccaneer wanted to keep his money, he had to be prepared to fight for it. The Treaty of Madrid in 1670 put an end to large-scale state-sponsored piracy in the Caribbean and the Pacific. It also put an end to buccaneers being well-respected citizens. The buccaneers would have to become true pirates, at least for a little while.

PART I.II
THE BUCCANEER PIRATES 1670–1702

> Whereas we are informed, that Capt. Thomas Tew and other subjects of New-York have associated themselves with wicked and ill-disposed persons, and commit many and great piracies.

Chapter 15
Sailing Under French Colors

Relationships between buccaneers were complicated. In the rapidly changing political environment of the 17th century, your best friend on one venture might be your enemy on the next. Most of the time however, it was everyone against Spain. Even when the English and the Dutch were at war with each other, they'd soon be allies again and attacking their old common enemy, the Spanish. Buccaneers were used to sailing under their own country's flag because they represented that country due to their letters of marque. But now, England and Spain were at peace and all English buccaneers would have to sail under another country's flag if they wanted to attack Spanish ships. For the French and Dutch, it was business as usual. The French hadn't signed any treaty and Tortuga remained a port where not many questions were asked and the buccaneers could come and go as they pleased, sell their captured merchandise, and have a good time. Many of the English buccaneers from Port Royal who still wanted to pursue a career as a pirate relocated to the French ports and received French letters or marque. These letters weren't recognized by the English crown, so if they were caught, they were tried as pirates. English buccaneers like John Coxton and Edmond Cook flew under French colors. This was a time where the English buccaneers sailed not as privateers, but as pirates, at least from their own country's perspective. It was a time when the English privateers at Port Royal either turned pirate and left Jamaica or turned pirate hunter and sailed for the English government. It was a time when buccaneer captains sailed on their own without large-scale support from their nations. It was a time when Petit Goave became the center of the buccaneer's world.

The French port of Petit Goave had emerged as a better spot than Tortuga by 1670. As you may recall from the previous chapter, Tortuga had been controlled by the French West India Company since 1665 and the new governor, Bertrand d'Ogeron, was more interested in developing the tobacco and sugar plantations than supporting buccaneers. Petit Goave, on the other hand, had far more to offer. Located about 40 miles west of present-day Port-au-Prince on the north shore of the long peninsula that creates the Port-au-Prince Bay, it was much closer to the main shipping lanes and the harbor was naturally protected from storms. France had officially declared their half of Hispaniola a French colony named Saint Domingue and named Petit Goave as the new capital. The governor of Saint Domingue from 1676 to 1681 was Jacques Pouancey. He moved his house and office to Petit Goave as well as his military commanders. This new port had far more to offer, especially since the Governor actively encouraged buccaneering and issued letters of marque to everyone. He knew that for the past 30 years, the best defense against Spanish attacks was the buccaneers' raids against Spanish shipping and ports. This kept the Spanish occupied and off balance. It was a strategy that the French had used successfully at Tortuga and the English had used successfully at Port Royal. The English buccaneers who left Port Royal, now sailed out of Petit Goave for France, and themselves.

Charles II of England was still livid with the Dutch over the loss of his fleet in the last war five years earlier and King Louis XIV of France still wanted to regain the territory in the Netherlands that he had lost. This territory, known as Belgium today, was then called either the Spanish Netherlands or Flanders and was the main center of armed conflict for France from the 16th through the 18th century. Charles II wanted to get another war started, so in 1672 the English fleet attacked a Dutch convoy in the English Channel. France saw this as an opportunity to get back some territory in the Netherlands and declared war on the Dutch Republic on April 6, 1672. The English declared war on the Dutch the next day. Soon after, Spain allied with the Dutch Republic, hoping to re-establish its holding in the Spanish Netherlands.

1672–1678

Third Anglo/Dutch War—France and England against the Dutch and Spain.

There were significant infantry engagements throughout Europe as well as major naval engagements and amphibious operations during this war. But it was the alliances that created many problems for the close-knit Brethren of the Coast. The Dutch buccaneers who loathed the Spanish for years were now fighting on the same side. The French buccaneers, who had been partners with the Dutch, were now enemies. It wasn't much of a problem for the English who were used to being both allies and enemies with the Dutch and the French.

On Christmas Day 1672, Dutch naval forces took St Helena off the coast of Africa in the Atlantic, which was the English East India Company's re-provisioning station. However, the English managed to retake it in May 1673 without loss of life. In 1673, an English privateer named Thomas Peche entered the Pacific and raided Dutch shipping around the Philippines with a flagship of 44 guns, and 2 frigates of 18 guns each. The Dutch attacked in North America and retook New York as well as French possessions in Arcadia. The French Arcadians fled to what would become New Orleans and were eventually called Cajuns. Things weren't going well for the English. In previous conflicts, England had effectively used privateering as a means of waging war, but now, the Dutch privateers managed to capture the bulk of the prizes taking over 550 English merchant ships and over 2,800 total allied vessels. England had enough and signed a treaty with the Dutch restoring all holdings to pre-war conditions, retaking possession of New York. The French continued to fight the Dutch however, gaining significant territory in the Netherlands.

Michel de Grammont Le Chevalier arrived in the Caribbean sometime in the early 1670s. He had been in the French navy and was now a buccaneer captain with his own vessel sailing out of Petit Goave. After taking a Dutch vessel without the proper letters of marque, he had to remain in port for fear of being tried as a pirate. Once France and the Dutch Republic went to war, Grammont was free to acquire letters of marque and resume privateering. Grammont formed a small fleet and joined a French naval force under the command of the Comte d'Estrees. They attacked the Dutch island of Curacao in 1678, but after most of the French ships accidentally ran aground Grammont left with his force of six ships and 700 men and proceeded to raid the Spanish coast, after taking what they could from the French wrecks, of course. They decided to attack Lake Maracaibo as L'Olonnais had done 11 years before. In June 1678 he repeated L'Olonnais' attack plan, taking San Carlos and Gibraltar on the shore and then inland to Trujillo. The Spanish defended the town of Trujillo with 350 troops and a gun battery, but Grammont circled behind the town using captured horses and easily took it. By December 1678 they were laden with treasure and returned to Petit Goave. In May 1680 he attacked Caracas with 600 men, but the 2,000 Spanish defenders managed to contain the buccaneers inside a small captured fort and Grammont was seriously wounded.

Another of these famous French buccaneers was actually a Dutchman named Laurens Cornelis Boudewijn de Graaf. It is unclear why he sailed for France and not the Dutch. De Graaf served in the Spanish navy for three years before deserting in the West Indies in the mid-1670s. He joined a French buccaneer crew at Samana Bay, Hispaniola. Even though Samana Bay was located in Spanish territory it was a bit too far for the Spanish authorities to control. Saint Domingue's Governor Pouncay noted De Graaf's actions writing that he had captured a small bark, then a ship, then a bigger ship, and so on until he commanded a 28-gun warship named *Tigre* that he took from the Spanish navy in 1679. By this time, he was the leader of the Samana Bay buccaneers and taking prizes all around Hispaniola and the leeward passage.

The famous French buccaneer, Grammont, joined with De Graaf and another Dutch buccaneer named Nikolaas Van Hoorn. De Graaf had recently taken a Spanish 30-gun warship, *Francesca* in the Mona Passage off Puerto Rico which was carrying the annual pay for the Spanish troops in Havana. The three captains with their crews of over 1,300 men attacked Veracruz. Grammont used the same type of military tactics that Morgan used, standard 17th century infantry formations firing in volley. He ordered his buccaneers to bring as many firearms as they could carry. When he attacked the Spanish, he overwhelmed them with superior firepower. This was especially effective because the Spanish were mostly using outdated matchlocks. With most governments the best and most modern weapons went to the crack troops in Europe and the colonial militia were provisioned with the old stuff still in the armor's inventory.

Chapter 16
Sir Henry Morgan

Meanwhile, back at Port Royal, things weren't going well for Governor Sir Thomas Lynch and the local population. The loss of revenue from the privateers heavily impacted the economy. And now, England was at war with the Dutch and Port Royal was a prime target. Actually, things were going pretty badly for the English all over the Caribbean. Settlements were being attacked and destroyed everywhere. As for Henry Morgan, he had been a prisoner in London since his arrest in 1672. However, it wasn't as bad as it sounds. Morgan was free to walk about the city as long as he returned to his quarters for the evening. He spent most of his time in taverns drinking and telling amazing stories about his bravery and accomplishments. But the sly Morgan was doing far more than that, he was quietly forging political alliances and making friends in hopes of generating support for his release.

With the desperate situation in the Caribbean, King Charles II needed expert advice on how to defend his settlements. There just wasn't anyone in London who King Charles II could turn to for expert advice with the depth of understanding and experience needed in dealing with these matters. Except for one man. His name was Henry Morgan. In July 1673, some of the king's advisors who knew of Morgan, or perhaps had even met him at a tavern, persuaded King Charles II to seek Morgan's advice. At last, this was Morgan's golden opportunity. Morgan wrote a detailed letter advising the king on exactly what to do. His written reply so impressed King Charles II that Morgan was pardoned a short time later and his advice was taken.

Governor Lynch was fired and a new governor appointed, Lord Vaughn. Then, in December 1675, Henry Morgan was knighted by King Charles II and appointed Lieutenant Governor of Jamaica. He returned to Port Royal a hero on March 6, 1676. Imagine how awkward the moment was as Lt. Governor Sir Henry Morgan formally relieved Lynch of his responsibilities.

1675

Henry Morgan knighted and appointed Governor of Jamaica.

As you might remember, Lynch was the one who had Morgan arrested five years earlier. It must have been a very sweet victory for Morgan. One day, a condemned prisoner, the next, Lieutenant Governor. He might have attributed this to the luck of the Irish, but Henry Morgan was Welsh. As acting governor, the former privateer, Sir Henry Morgan, was also a wealthy plantation owner. He shifted the economy toward slaves, sugar, and raw materials. The buccaneer trade was still viable, but much more subdued. With a new anti-piracy policy, Morgan formed many of his old buccaneer friends into fleets of pirate hunters, to help track down and stop other pirates still operating in the Caribbean. Of course, one supposes the cargo and money recovered from many of the captured pirate ships wound up in the hands of wealthy merchants and government officials back in Port Royal. Between 1675 and 1680, the city of Port Royal continued to see annual profits of over 750,000 pieces of eight from buccaneers alone.

However, Sir Henry's life was about to take an unexpected turn. The aforementioned book published in Holland in 1678, *De Americaensche Zee-Roovers* put a black mark on Morgan's reputation which remains to this very day. This book seems to be the prime source of what we know, or don't know, about the life of Henry Morgan since it was published. Stories of his early life and his personal conduct as a privateer all came from this one book.

It was written by Alexander O. Exquemelin who claimed to have been a buccaneer surgeon from Tortuga and was supposedly a surgeon with one of Morgan's privateer fleets. This is highly doubtful as Morgan kept very accurate records of all his officers and Exquemelin's name does not appear anywhere among Morgan's log books. However, from the detail of Morgan's activities described in his book, we can suppose that Exquemelin probably was among Morgan's crew at one time.

The book was an instant best-seller. Why I said "what we know or don't know" is because Exquemelin's description of the actions of Morgan and even the events about Morgan himself are deeply flawed historically. When it comes to the overall big picture and things like dates, and the number of troops Morgan had, the accounts are fairly correct. However, when it comes to Morgan himself, the book treats Morgan very unfairly. Exquemelin greatly embellished the factual events, inventing gruesome details and making up facts to suit the author's depiction. The accuracy of Exquemelin's book was even called into question in the 17th century.

The book paints Morgan as a drunkard, a lout, and an unscrupulous cheat, even to his own men. Exquemelin accuses him of committing terrible atrocities to his prisoners, torturing them in horrible ways which were

Figure 8: *Exq Buccaneers of America 1678 Book Cover*

carefully described in extensive detail. He also has Morgan raping many of his women captives and using priests and nuns as human shields during his assault on the city of Portobelo. He depicts Morgan as burning the City of Panama, when in fact, he didn't. Exquemelin went so far as to reinvent Morgan's past, writing that he first came to the Caribbean as a lowly indentured servant and worked his way up through the buccaneer ranks becoming the most brutal and evil captain of them all. We know this is nonsense. Morgan's ancestry is well-documented. Additionally, Morgan was promoted to Colonel of the Guard and Captain of the Sea by the Governor of Jamaica. To the English settlers throughout the Caribbean, Henry Morgan was a national hero.

There is an enormous amount of documentation that proves Exquemelin's depiction of Henry Morgan to be far from the truth. So, why would Exquemelin get it so inaccurate? First, this book was written to be decidedly anti-English. Exquemelin was of either French or Dutch heritage and wrote the book at a time when England was at war with the Dutch. The book was even published in Holland. Anything negative about the English including books that describe their evil atrocities would go down pretty well with the Dutch, whether they were accurate or not. Secondly, there was probably bad blood between the two of them from the time when they served together. How accurate would a modern publication about a modern president be if the book was written by a political adversary? But most importantly, he was writing a best-seller, not a work of historical fact. Of course, there were going to be stories added and facts distorted. That's what writing a best-seller is all about. For Exquemelin, the decision to paint Henry Morgan as a scoundrel was a sound decision, both politically and financially.

After reading the English translation in 1684, Henry Morgan was outraged. His reputation suffered severely. In a curious turn of events, what seemed to have bothered Morgan the most was that part about him being an indentured servant. So, Morgan did exactly what one would expect a blood thirsty and vicious privateer to do. Morgan sued the publishers for libel in the English courts. Morgan won his lawsuit and was awarded over 400 pounds sterling in damages. Also, a new and far more accurate edition was published telling the story the way it was according to Morgan's log books and other English eye witness accounts. When Morgan died of illness on August 25, 1688 the old edition resurfaced and all of Morgan's blood thirsty and cruel deeds were back in print. After all, it was a far better seller—and still is. It is that original edition that is still in print today, although the language is modernized a bit. Yet, this fictional version of the life of Henry Morgan is what most people believe. Part of the reason for this is that so many authors of pirate books since the 18th century have assumed that *De Americaensche Zee-Roovers* is historical fact because it was written during Morgan's lifetime, and therefore must be accurate. Even *The General History of Pyrates* written by Charles Johnson and published in 1724, which is merely a rehash of what Exquemelin wrote, assumed those facts to be correct. I shall discuss Johnson's book in far more detail a little later on.

Chapter 17
Changing Times

New laws were passed by the English Parliament in 1680 that forbade Englishmen from sailing under the colors of any foreign nation. This dealt a major legal blow to the English buccaneers sailing out of Tortuga and Petit Goave. More and more, buccaneers were now pirates, not privateers. This gradual transition began in 1670 and by 1680 the conversion was complete. It was during this period when the hero privateers of the last decade were looked upon with scorn—as criminals. With government support gone and former buccaneers sailing the seas as pirate hunters in the employ of one government or another, many buccaneers turned to attacking plantations, small business operations, or anything that seemed profitable. Times were tough. Buccaneer ports like Tortuga and Petit Goave were suffering from an economic slump. With no wars in Europe, the English, Dutch, and French buccaneers banded together again just like the old days.

By 1685 Port Royal had grown into the center of trade and sugar exportation. In the late 1670s, Lieutenant Governor Sir Henry Morgan organized most of the English buccaneers into small fleets of pirate hunters and had chased all the other buccaneers out of Port Royal. Many relocated to the French port city of Petit Goave, the capital of the French colony of Saint Domingue on the Island of Hispaniola. In the early 1680s, the French hadn't yet cracked down on the buccaneers like the English had. The French governors on Petit Goave were still issuing letters of marque even though they weren't supposed to. This would be the center of all buccaneer activity for a few more years. Because it was better located it became the hub of all buccaneer activity in the Caribbean. As for the once famous buccaneer port of Tortuga, it slipped into obscurity never to recover. By 1700 Tortuga was a ghost town. There was almost no commerce. All the buccaneers, brothels, and taverns were gone and only the ruins of the old fort, which had guarded the port for almost 60 years, remained.

All the major European powers had been trading in the Far East since the beginning of the 17th century. The riches that could be imported from India, China, and Malaysia were enormous. Among the most valuable products were cotton, silk, and spices. France, England, and the Dutch Republic all established companies that specialized in trade in the Indian Ocean. These companies had fleets of large merchant ships traveling to and from India on a regular basis and were known as East India Trading Companies. Permanent stations were set up on islands and coastal ports to re-supply the merchant ships (called merchantmen) on the return voyage home.

In 1652, the Dutch East India Company established a large station just north of the Cape of Good Hope at Table Bay. This eventually became Cape Town. Bourbon Island, (now called Reunion Island) located east of Madagascar in the Indian Ocean, was established as a station for the French East India Company in 1655. And in 1659, the English East India Company established a station on Saint Helena Island in the middle of the South Atlantic between modern Brazil and Angola. This is the same island where Emperor Napoleon was imprisoned after the battle of Waterloo in 1815 and where he died in 1821. Saint Helena was ideally located for ships returning to England from the Indian Ocean. English ships would stop there to replenish their food and water supply as well as make any repairs to their ships that were needed. As a result, the island was loaded with livestock and covered with farmland. It was a naval store service station.

The Spanish didn't need to establish an East India Trading Company because they already had a system to obtain the wealth of the Far East. Spain established a colony in the Philippines in 1542 and had a major port at Manila by 1579. Hundreds of ships from China and elsewhere in the Far East traded with the Spanish at Manila each year. From 1565 until the early 19th century, these exceptionally valuable cargoes were sent to Spain by what became called Manila Galleons. Once a year, two galleons loaded with silk, spices, porcelain, ivory, lacquer ware, gold, pearls, and jewels, would sail from Manila to Acapulco. From there, the cargo would be taken overland across Mexico to Vera Cruse and then on to Spain with the treasure fleet. The capture of a Manila Galleon was the dream of any pirate. The Pacific and Indian Oceans were certainly rich targets for pirates and that's where the buccaneers went next.

During the 1680s, the far-off waters of the Pacific and Indian Oceans began to look better and better to the buccaneers of the Caribbean. The anti-piracy policies of England and France were a major factor, but another was the fact that taking Spanish prizes just wasn't as profitable as it had been. Spain had learned a hard lesson over the years and was making a greater effort to protect Spanish property. The major Spanish cities were now guarded by regular soldiers with modern weapons, not poorly armed militia, and the treasure fleets were better organized and protected. Additionally, French and English plantations were beginning to turn a sizeable profit without the risk of getting run through with a cutlass or taking a bullet in your chest. Many of the successful privateers of the last decade, like Henry Morgan, were now sitting on the verandas of their sugar plantations instead of raiding Spanish ports. However, this wasn't true in the Far East. The riches coming out of Manila, China, India, and Persia were staggering.

The two most common ways to get to the Indian Ocean from the east coast of America were to either sail across the Atlantic and around Africa or to sail around Cape Horn at the tip of South America and cross the Pacific. For pirates, crossing the Atlantic wasn't a bad option but there were few ports where pirates could re-provision along the way and even fewer unprotected merchant ships to take as prizes. Sailing around Cape Horn and across the Pacific was a very risky way to get to the Indian Ocean because it was a very long journey and rounding the cape was extremely dangerous due to the severe cold and constant storms. However, there was another option open to pirates. Simply cross the Isthmus of Panama on foot and steal new ships anchored in the Pacific side. The last option seemed the most favorable to a group of buccaneers and in 1680 that's exactly what William Dampier and his buccaneer friends did.

Chapter 18
The Buccaneer Author

William Dampier provides us with more invaluable information about the golden age than any other person. Not because he was a famous buccaneer captain, he wasn't. His career as a buccaneer was that of a common crewmember. It is because he was an author. When it comes to the study of buccaneers of the 17th century, his writings are invaluable. Unlike all the other books written in his day, Dampier's book was a brilliant work of science. He described in detail all the flora and fauna he encountered throughout his voyage around the world. He was the first author to describe the Galapagos Island and Australia. He also gave detailed descriptions of the natives, their culture, and their food. This is his story.

Anxious to see the world, at age 17 William Dampier became apprentice to a ship's master on a vessel that traveled from France to Newfoundland. Well-educated, he was born on September 5, 1651 in East Coker, Yeovil, England. He was sent to school as a child and studied Latin, arithmetic, and science. At 19 years of age, he signed on to a vessel that traveled to the Java Islands in Indonesia. When the Third Dutch War broke out in 1672, Dampier joined the Royal Navy and served under Sir Edward Spragge in the first two engagements of the war. But Dampier became ill and was sent home to recover, ending his naval career. Back home, a wealthy entrepreneur named Colonel Hillier became aware of the promising young man and hired him to manage his plantation, which was located 16 miles from Spanish Town, Jamaica.

This job brought William Dampier to the Caribbean and opened the door for the intelligent, inquisitive, and adventurous youth to make a significant contribution to the world of science and to our knowledge of buccaneers in the late 17th century. Six months after managing Hillier's plantation, Dampier switched jobs and managed the plantation belonging to Captain

Robert Jacob

1679

William Dampier begins his pirate career and crosses Panama

Heming, which was located on Jamaica's north shore in St. Ann's Parish. But the sea always seemed to be in the blood of William Dampier and shortly after taking this second job, he left to work as a sailor on a merchant vessel sailing throughout the Caribbean. This didn't last long either, and between 1675 and 1678, Dampier worked in the logging business on the Bay of Campeche. He eventually made enough money to return to England in August 1678. He lived in London for a brief time, just long enough to marry a woman named Judith.

Leaving his wife back in England, Dampier returned to Jamaica in April 1679. He wanted to buy a small estate in Dorsetshire, England and he knew that Jamaica was the place to make some quick cash. By the end of 1679, Dampier had made enough money for the purchase and prepared the documents to buy the estate. However, Dampier couldn't resist the opportunity to take part in just one more sailing venture and he accepted an invitation from a Jamaican merchant named Mr. Hobby to participate in a trading voyage to the Mosquito Shore, the eastern coast of modern Nicaragua. As Mr. Hobby's vessels gathered at Negril Bay on the west end of Jamaica, fate suddenly intervened. By coincidence, a buccaneer fleet of 9 vessels, 7 English and 2 French, happened to be anchored there too. Under the command of Captain John Coxon, the other captains were Richard Sawkins, Bartholomew Sharp, Peter Harris, Edmund Cook, Watling, Wright, Tristian, and Archemboe. Promises of quick riches sailing with the buccaneers overwhelmed Mr. Hobby's crew and they all left him to sign on with the buccaneers. William Dampier remained loyal to Hobby for a few days, but eventually he too decided to become a buccaneer.

It is uncertain precisely which captain Dampier signed articles with, but it was most likely Captain Edmund Cook. This conclusion is based upon two facts. Firstly, Dampier remained loyal to Cook months later when the coalition broke up. And secondly, Cook's navigator and later his quartermaster was Edward Davis and the lives of the three men, Edmund Cook, Edward Davis, and William Dampier, are deeply intertwined over the next several years. Not much is known about Cook prior to 1679 when Dampier first met him. Dampier describes Cook as "an English Native of St. Christopher's'... as we call all born of European Parents in the West Indies. He was a sensible Man, and had been some Years a Privateer."

The buccaneer fleet was commanded by Captain Coxon and consisted of nine vessels; two of them were French, with a total of 477 men. Hoping to repeat the success of Henry Morgan, the buccaneers attacked the wealthy Spanish port of Portobelo and easily overwhelmed the merger defenders netting about 100,000 pieces of eight. As their vessels lay at anchor, the buccaneers celebrated and divided their spoils. Quietly and mysteriously, they were approached by a band of Miskitos, the local natives indigenous to the northern shore of Panama. The Miskitos had long been oppressed by the Spanish and welcomed opportunities to attack them, so they offered to guide the buccaneers across the Isthmus of Panama and help them attack the rich Spanish cities on the west coast. When reading the original work, Dampier writes, "The Isthmus of Darien" because in the 17th century that is what the English called the Isthmus of Panama. This was William Dampier's first trip across the isthmus and his first close association with local natives. He became fascinated with the local plants, animals, geography, and native culture.

Miskitos are a group of Native Americans from Central America and Honduras and are a totally separate culture from the Tainos of the Caribbean. Their name comes from "Miskitu" which is what they called themselves and has nothing to do with the insect. In Dampier's book, he spelled their name "Mosquitos."

Crossing the Isthmus of Panama was very dangerous. If they were unsuccessful on the Pacific side, they might not be able to cross back, especially if pursued by angry Spanish soldiers. The two French buccaneer captains declined the offer to cross over to the Pacific and left the coalition, but the rest accepted. The buccaneers left their vessels under guard anchored off Portobelo and began the march across the Isthmus of Panama. After the French pulled out of the operation, the buccaneer force that crossed the Isthmus of Panama consisted of 331 men, among them was Basil Ringrose, who became a friend of Dampier's and later wrote and published his own account of the buccaneer raids in the Pacific.

The Miskitos were excellent guides and provided everything the buccaneers needed. It only took ten days to cross. The first town they captured was Santa Maria, which was located up the San Miguel River close to the Bay of Panama. The Spanish used this town to pan for gold dust, but the buccaneers found nothing of value. Arriving at the coast of the Bay of Panama, the Miskitos provided 35 canoes to the buccaneers so they could raid Spanish shipping. However, the current was too strong and the canoes were scattered. Dampier was in a group of only five canoes holding just 68 buccaneers when they came across five great ships and three large barks anchored off the Island of Perico, less than five miles due south of the City of Panama. Following traditional buccaneer tactics, they attacked the Spanish barks from their canoes and a fierce hand to hand battle ensued. When it was all over, 61 of 86 Spaniards were killed while only 18 buccaneers were killed and another 22 wounded. They were soon rejoined by the other buccaneers and now with a large crew and eight vessels, they could begin taking prizes at sea.

It seemed that the operation would be a big success, but things began to unravel rather quickly. Buccaneer crews normally experienced a tenuous relationship while working together, but the rivalry and mistrust on this expedition exceeded anything anyone had experienced. In just a few weeks the entire situation began to boil over. In May 1680, quarrels and disagreements among the captains and their crews let to turmoil and eventual mutiny. Captain Coxon was the first to leave taking his 70-man crew with him. Captain Sawkins was elected to replace him as the new overall commander, but he was killed soon afterwards in a poorly planned attack on the city of Puebla Nova, which was on the island of Coiba west of the Bay of Panama. Captain Sharp was elected as the succeeding commander, but Captain Edmund Cook and his buccaneers mutinied and refused to follow him. A compromise was reached with Captain Sharp in charge and Captain Cook as his second in command. But this arrangement didn't last long either.

Off Guayaquil, the buccaneer fleet took a Spanish bark and then they took the nearby city of La Serena. When the Spanish refused to pay any ransom, the buccaneers burned La Serena to the ground. Afterwards, the fleet sailed to Juan Fernandez Island, where they anchored and discussed what to do next. Juan Fernandez Island is located 360 miles west of Chile and became famous as the island of Robinson Crusoe in the novel by Daniel Defoe. Some of the buccaneers wanted to sail around Cape Horn and return home, while others wanted to remain in the Pacific. During the heated discussion, Captain Sharp was voted out of office as overall commander and Captain Watling was elected the new Commodore. On January 14, 1681 the buccaneer fleet sailed south to the coastal town of Arica, on the border between Peru and Chile. Unfortunately, it was too well fortified and the attack was another dismal failure. Captain Watling, his quartermaster, and 18 other buccaneers were killed and Captain Sharp was re-elected as the fleet commodore, much to the dismay of those who refused to follow him.

This internal strife was just too much for the buccaneers, so they decided to split forces. Captain Sharp took one group and Captain Edmund Cook took the other. Dampier went with Cook and apparently Basil Ringrose remained with Sharp. There is no record of the size of the group that stayed with Sharp, but Dampier records the size of Cook's group as 44 white buccaneers, 3 Miskitos, and 5 black slaves. It took 23 days for the 52 men to cross back over the Isthmus of Panama.

Sharp and his men, including Ringrose, returned to the Caribbean. Ringrose separated from Sharp and sailed to Antigua arriving on January 30, 1681 then sailed on to England arriving on March 26, 1681. Like Dampier, Basil Ringrose also kept a detailed journal during the entire expedition and he was eventually asked by the English government to give them information about the Spanish ports and operations in the Pacific and to help interpret some captured Spanish maps. This information was far more than just map making, it was valuable military intelligence. His maps were compiled into a book entitled "The South Sea Waggoner" but it remained filed away until it was finally published in 1992. Four years later, in 1684, Basil Ringrose wrote and published a book entitled *Bucaniers of America* in which Cook is mentioned numerous times in events that occurred prior to this split but is not mentioned at all afterwards. However, by the publishing date, Ringrose had already left England aboard the *Cygnet* as one of Captain Swan's crewmen and headed back to the west coast of Central America in the Pacific.

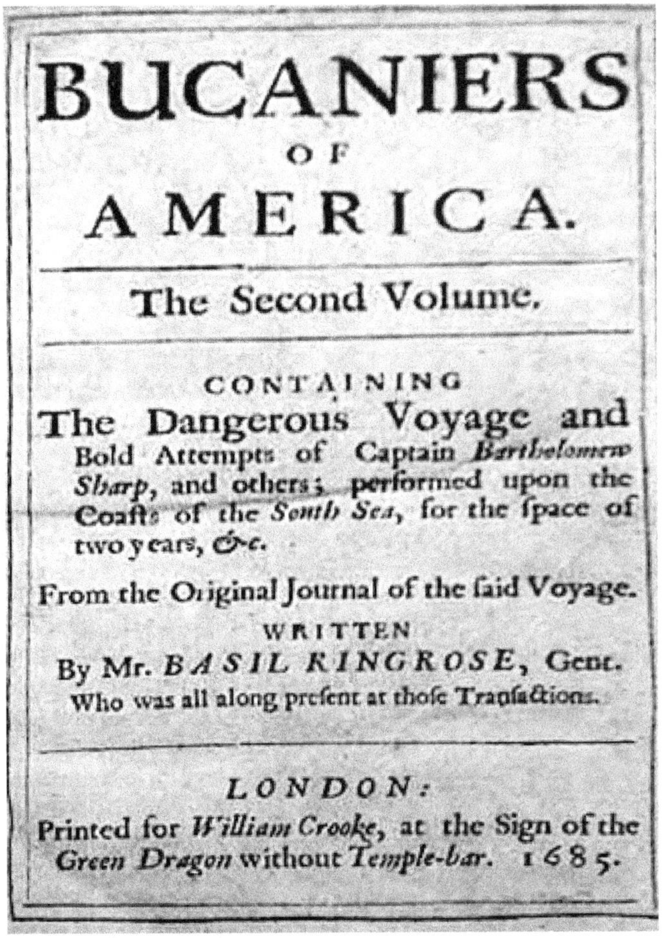

BUCANIERS
OF
AMERICA.

The Second Volume.

CONTAINING
The Dangerous Voyage and Bold Attempts of Captain *Bartholomew Sharp*, and others; performed upon the Coaſts of the *South Sea*, for the ſpace of two years, &c.

From the Original Journal of the ſaid Voyage.

WRITTEN
By Mr. *BASIL RINGROSE*, Gent.
Who was all along preſent at thoſe Tranſactions.

LONDON:
Printed for *William Crooke*, at the Sign of the *Green Dragon* without *Temple-bar*. 1685.

Figure 9: *Ringrose Buccaneers of America 1685 Book Cover*

Meanwhile, Captain Cook and his buccaneers reached Portobelo on May 24, 1681 and sighted the masts of a ship anchored nearby. It was Captain Tristian's ship. He was one of the French captains who refused to make the trip across Panama and was still sailing in the waters near Portobelo. The buccaneers had no option other than to sign on as crewmembers aboard the French ship. Tristan's vessel sailed to Springer's Key in the Samballoes Islands, now called San Blas Islands off the Caribbean coast of Panama. They rendezvoused with eight other buccaneer vessels. One of the vessels was captained by John Coxen who had returned from the Pacific with his 70 men the previous year and reclaimed his old vessel. Captain Cook accepted the lower position of quartermaster aboard the Dutch buccaneer vessel commanded by Captain Janke Willems. Cook's quartermaster, Edward Davis also signed on as a crewman. Dampier spells his name "Yankes" in his book. Dampier gives the following description of the vessels, their nationalities, and their captains:

English Coxen: 10 gun - 100 men

Payne: 10 gun - 100 men

Wright: 4 gun - 40 men

Williams: small barcolongo

Eng/D/Fr Yankes: 4 gun - 60 men

French Archemboe: 8 gun - 40 men
Tucker: 6 gun - 70 men
Rose: small barcolongo

Over the next several months, the ships scattered to search for prizes, often meeting occasionally on one island or another. During this time, the French vessel commanded by Captain Archemboe was in great need of additional crewmembers, so Dampier and a few other English buccaneers were transferred over. They hated serving aboard the French vessel. Dampier wrote, "Indeed we found no Cause to dislike the Captain; but his French Seamen were the saddest Creatures that ever I was among; for tho' we had bad Weather that requir'd many Hands aloft, yet the biggest part of them never stirr'd out of the Hammocks, but to eat or ease themselves."

Captain William Wright, commanding the small English vessel of four guns, engaged a small Spanish vessel of 30 men and fought a one hour running battle before the Spanish vessel finally yielded. Captain Wright took the prize to a small island to loot her and was later joined by the French vessel commanded by Archemboe. As the two crews socialized on the beach, Dampier and the other English crewmen from Archemboe's command secretly urged Captain Wright to give the Spanish vessel to them. Their real motivation was to escape from the French ship and they saw Captain Wright as their best opportunity. But Wright was very hesitant. He was one of the old Tortuga buccaneers and had long been friends with the French buccaneers. Additionally, he was now a resident of Petit Goave and on very good terms with the French governor who provided him with letters of marque. He didn't want to offend any French buccaneers by taking some of their crewmen away. However, when Dampier and his friends said they would leave with some of their Miskito friends rather than remain onboard the French vessel, Wright consented. Over the next several months, Dampier sailed aboard the Spanish vessel alongside of Captain Wright, taking many prizes. But in June 1682 about 20 English buccaneers including Dampier decided to leave Wright's company aboard one of the recently captured prize vessels. The parting was a friendly one and Dampier and the other buccaneers sailed to Virginia, arriving in July 1682.

Most of them, including Dampier, stopped at the largest seaport in the colony of Virginia, Elizabeth City. The name of this port city was changed to the City of Hampton in 1706, which is the city's name today. In Dampier's book, published in 1697, he gives absolutely no explanation or reason why he and the others decided to leave the company of buccaneers and sail to Virginia. But Dampier wasn't writing an autobiography in his book, he was writing a scientific book on natural history and his personal life just didn't seem important. Dampier remained in Virginia for 13 months and again, he tells his readers nothing of his experiences there except to say, "That country is so well known to our Nation that I shall say nothing of it, nor shall I detain the Reader with the Story of my own Affairs, and the trouble that befell me...."

As mentioned earlier, Captain Edmond Cook and his quartermaster, Edward Davis, were forced out of necessity to take lower positions aboard the Dutch vessel commanded by Captain Yanky Willems during the buccaneer rendezvous on Springer's Key. His crew was comprised of French, Dutch, and English buccaneers. Willems had a close association with Captain Wright during the time that Dampier was aboard as a crewman, but the two buccaneer captains had a falling out. Even though Yanky Willems himself was Dutch, he had strong ties to the French.

The trouble began in 1683 when Captain Willems took a Spanish vessel and gave command to his new quartermaster, Edmond Cook. That was customary. When a second vessel was added to a buccaneer fleet, the quartermaster who captured that vessel normally became the new captain. Cook named his old comrade Edward Davis as his quartermaster. After the capture, they sailed to Isle de Vaca to refit the vessel. Located just off the southern coast of Hispaniola at the eastern tip, Isle de Vaca had long been a favorite buccaneer rendezvous and was used by Henry Morgan regularly. Now, it was part of the French colony of San Domingue and was a safe haven for French buccaneers operating under letters of marque issued by the French colony's governor. They were soon joined by several more vessels belonging to both English and French buccaneers including Captain Tristan's vessel.

As the crews sat on the beach discussing recent events and captured prizes, the French buccaneers became incensed when they learned that Captain Willems had given command of the captured Spanish vessel to the Englishman, Captain Cook. Whether it was due to personal jealousy or animosity toward the English in general, the French buccaneers decided to take the Spanish ship away from Cook and keep it for themselves. Not satisfied with just the one vessel, the French buccaneers decided to take all of the other English vessels as well. The entire English contingent were taken prisoners, including the ones who belonged to the crews of French captains. They also took all their arms and valuables.

Captain Tristan sailed away with eight or ten English prisoners onboard including Davis and Cook and left the rest of the Englishmen marooned on the island. Tristan sailed to the French capital of Petit Goave where the

French governor would be able to legitimize his actions. While anchored at port, Tristan and most of their French crewmen went ashore, leaving only a small contingent onboard to guard the prisoners. Then, as if written for a Hollywood movie, the English buccaneers managed to overpower the guards and capture the vessel. Captain Cook took command and he forced the French crewmen ashore. They quickly set sail and escaped the harbor.

Safely at sea, they sailed back to Isle de Vaca and rescued the other Englishmen. With a good vessel and a full crew, Cook captured a French merchantman laden with wine and then another well-armed French ship, both of which the English kept. The French buccaneers were now bitter enemies of Cook and his crew. They realized that they couldn't remain in the Caribbean, so they decided to try the waters of the Pacific in search of prizes. But first, the vessels would have to be careened and fitted out for the long voyage. Worried that the French would find them, Cook had to find a safe and pirate-friendly location far away from the Caribbean. With three vessels, the largest carrying 18 guns, the English buccaneers under command of Captain Edmund Cook sailed north to the long-established pirate rendezvous of Accomack, Virginia.

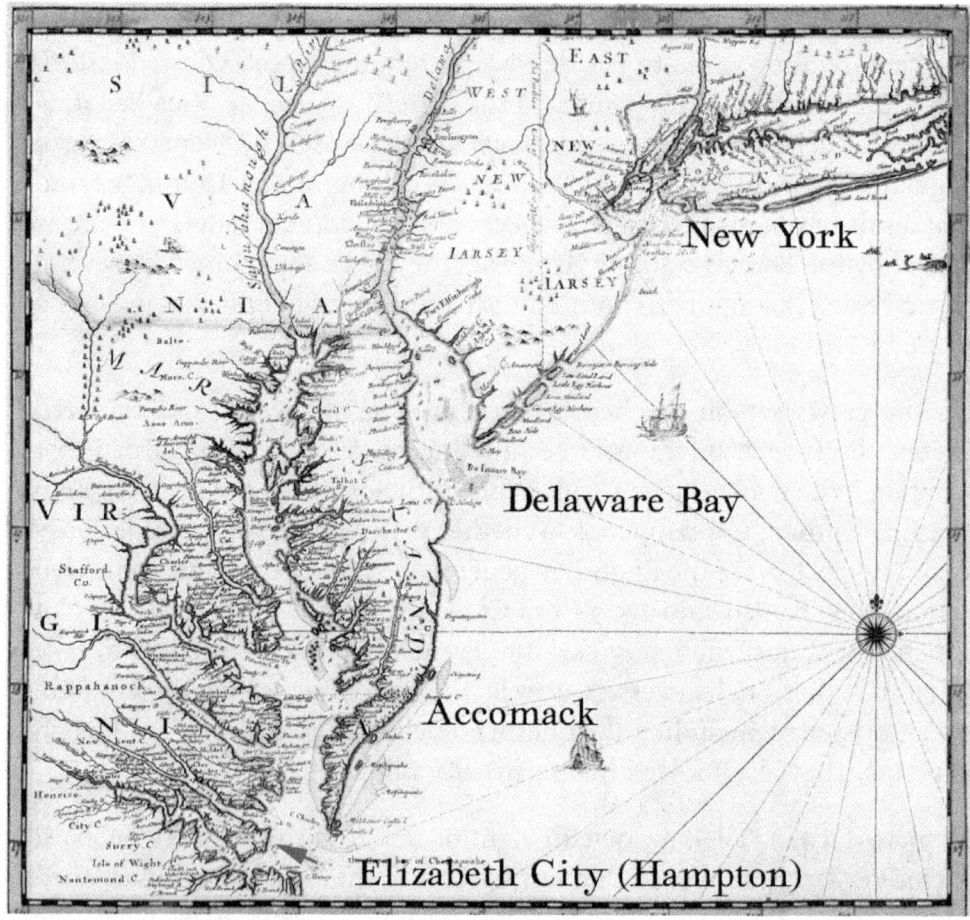

Figure 10: *Mid-Atlantic*

Located along an isolated stretch of beach on the Atlantic coast of the eastern shore of Virginia south of the Maryland border, Accomack was an ideal place to careen pirate vessels. In the 17th and 18th centuries, it was located a long way from any big city and the influence of government authorities and the locals welcomed all visiting ships that brought trade goods whether they were pirates or not. It had long been known as a pirate-friendly spot where they could refit and careen their vessels in safety on the wide beaches. While in Virginia, Cook and Davis were re-united with their old shipmates from the Panama expedition, including William Dampier. They had been living in Elizabeth City, Virginia for the past 13 months after leaving Captain Wright's group back in the Caribbean.

It is not known if Dampier and his friends heard that his old buccaneer shipmates were at Accomack or if Cook sought out Dampier and his friends, knowing that they were living close by. Perhaps Dampier and his friends may have even already been waiting at Accomack in hopes of joining any buccaneer vessel that stopped for careening. Regardless of how Cook and Dampier were reunited, he and his friend eagerly signed on as crewmen aboard Captain Cook's 18-gun vessel named the *Revenge*. Now seaworthy and well stocked for a long voyage, they sailed away from the Virginia coast on August 23, 1683. This would be no ordinary voyage to the Pacific; however, it would be a voyage around the world.

Chapter 19
The Treaty that Changes the Caribbean

1683-1684

War of the Reunions—France against Spain

While Captain Cook and William Dampier were sailing to the Pacific, war broke out on November 26, 1683 between France and Spain over the same territorial disputes. Not that it made much of a difference to the governor of Petit Goave, but this new war once again allowed letters of marque be legally issued against Spain. Grammont, De Graaf, and Van Hoorn were among the first to receive letters of marque to continue their Spanish plundering. But this war was a very short one and it ended in 1684 when the powers in Europe signed the Treaty of Ratisbon. This treaty contained new anti-piracy laws that put an end to state-sponsored piracy in the Caribbean. The French government back in Europe demanded that their local governors in the Caribbean put a stop to the indiscriminate issuing of letters of marque.

1684

Treaty of Ratisbon establishes new anti-piracy laws and limits state-sponsored piracy in the Caribbean

This was unfortunate for Grammont, De Graaf, and Van Hoorn. Their letters were recalled before they had taken anything of importance. The buccaneer captains rendezvoused on the Cuban Isle of Pinos to decide what to do. They decided to continue against the Spanish even without valid letters of marque. In 1685, they took Campeche, Mexico and held the city for ransom, but burned the city after three months as the Spanish refused to pay. The three-way partnership didn't last however, and during the Campeche attack De Graaf and Van Hoorn argued over treatment of prisoners. They fought a duel and De Graaf won, killing Van Hoorn. On the way back to Saint Domingue, De Graaf became separated and was attacked by two large Spanish warships. After exchanging broadsides all day long, De Graaf managed to slip away during the night. The next year De Graaf found himself operating without Grammont and without letters of marque. Along with 500 buccaneers, De Graaf attacked the city of Tihosuco on the Yucatan Peninsula. But things were getting too risky for buccaneers with the French government finally cracking down on piracy. De Graaf decided to retire as a buccaneer and became the military commander to the governor of Saint Domingue in his old port of Petit Goave. Years later, De Graaf left the Caribbean and took part in the 1699 expedition that secured Louisiana for France.

Chapter 20
Dampier's Round the World Voyage

The short war between France and Spain had no effect on Captain Cook or William Dampier, as their route kept them away from Caribbean and European waters. After leaving Virginia, they sailed across the Atlantic to the Cape Verde Islands. This seems out of the way, but when one considers trade winds and currents, the best way to get to the southern tip of South America from Virginia is to sail to the Cape Verde Islands first. Once there, Cook attacked a Danish ship of 36 guns and kept it for his own vessel. Cook knew that his mid-sized vessel would not be large enough for the long voyage to the Pacific. The ship was renamed the *Batchelor's Delight*. Dampier didn't write anything about the taking of this ship in his book for good reason. In the late 17th century, it was perfectly acceptable to the people back home in English for a privateer to take a Spanish town or vessel, after all, the Spanish were still the natural enemies of the English. But the Danes were strong allies of England, so for Dampier to admit to participating in the capture of a Danish ship would have been very poor judgment indeed.

1684–1691

William Dampier's round the world voyage

Crossing the Atlantic without incident, on January 28, 1684 they anchored off Sibbel de Wards Island, now called the Falkland Islands, to take on fresh water. There they met another English vessel that had stopped for the same purpose. Commanded by Captain Eaton, the vessel was the *Nicholas*. Cook and Eaton decided to become partners in their ventures in the Pacific and sailed through the Straits of Magellan in February 1684. They arrived at Juan Fernandez Island on March 22, 1684. Dampier had been there 2 years earlier and was very surprised when he met several of the Miskitos Indians who had guided them on the Panama expedition. They had been stranded there in January 1682 when the buccaneers elected Captain Watling as their Commodore and sailed away to take more prizes. Later on, in 1704,

Alexander Selkirk was marooned on this island and was helped by one of the Miskitos Indians who was left there by Captain Sharp in 1682. His story inspired the novel, *Robinson Crusoe*, and the Moskito Indian became the character named Friday.

During the month of May 1684, they took 4 Spanish prizes off the coast of Peru and then sailed to the Galapagos Islands, arriving on 31 May 1684. They brought three of the prize vessels with them, planning on keeping one or two of the best ones. The buccaneers traveled throughout the islands for a month, during which time, Dampier amassed an impressive amount of scientific observations. Dampier's writings about these unique islands inspired naturalists for the next 200 years. They left the Galapagos in June 1684 in three ships, the *Batchelor's Delight*, the *Nicholas*, and one of the Spanish prizes they decided to keep. The small fleet sailed toward the main coast and first reached land in early July 1684 at Cabo Blanco, located at the southern tip of the western side of the Gulf of Nicoya in Costa Rica. The crew was greatly saddened at the death of their trusted Captain, Edmund Cook. He died at sea after an illness he contracted over 3 months earlier. His quartermaster and longtime friend, Edward Davis, was named as the new captain.

"Robinson Crusoe" by Daniel Defoe was published on April 25, 1719

After burying Captain Cook and taking on fresh supplies, it is widely believed that Davis sailed to Cocos Island, an uninhabited island off Costa Rica, where he buried a large amount of treasure. This seems very likely, as there were absolutely no friendly ports where the buccaneers could spend their money or sell their cargo in the Pacific. English buccaneers taking prizes in that part of the world had to keep everything they had taken onboard their vessels until they returned to the Atlantic or the Caribbean, where they could put into an English or French port and sell their goods. Eventually, the ship's hold would become full. When that happened, there were only two choices: sail back toward home or bury the cargo on an isolated island and come back for it later with more ships.

Leaving the waters of Costa Rica on July 20, 1684, the three ships sailed north up the coast to the town of Ria Lexa, (named Realejo today) located on Corinto Bay, Nicaragua. Primarily inhabited by natives with a few Spanish officials and friars, Ria Lexa was a beautiful town near a picturesque volcano. The buccaneers negotiated for supplies with the townsfolk and careened their vessels, but didn't really make any profit from their stay since there really wasn't anything of value in the town. But they did discover that the town's Spanish officials had been alerted to their presence one month earlier. This concerned Captain Eaton who decided to sail to safer waters. Davis and Eaton parted company on September 2, 1684, much to the regret of Davis who felt they really needed Eaton and his ship to continue taking prizes. On September 20, 1684, Davis's ship dropped anchor off the Island of Plata, a fairly large island about 30 miles west of the coast of Ecuador south of Manta. The buccaneers used Plata as a base of operations over the next several months. Captain Eaton coincidently arrived at the island and had reconsidered the partnership and wanted to join forces again. However, Davis' crew had become somewhat unreasonable about the partnership and demanded that Eaton's crew shouldn't continue to receive equal shares. Eaton and his ship left for good.

Still anchored at Plata, they spotted a 16-gun ship and a small bark approaching. The date was October 2, 1684. Captain Swan was commander of the *Cygnet* and the bark was commanded by Captain Peter Harris. He was the nephew of the Captain Peter Harris who was killed on the Panama expedition three years earlier. But there was a member of Captain Swan's crew who Dampier knew very well. It was Basil Ringrose, his old friend from the Panama expedition. As you recall, Ringrose had remained with Sharp after Dampier left with Cook. Perhaps upon their reunion, Ringrose told his friend about his publications. His success at writing may have inspired Dampier to write his own book when he returned to England.

Their vessels careened and seaworthy, Captains Davis and Swan sailed south and arrived on November 2, 1684 at the town of Payta, Peru. In a classic amphibious operation that Henry Morgan would have been proud of, they paddled ashore in canoes and took the town with a rapid assault. However, the assault was far easier than planned. The town had been warned and was totally abandoned. Davis burned the town to the ground and also burned the small bark commanded by Harris. Apparently, it was a very poor sailing vessel and would have slowed them down. By early December 1684, they had reached Guayaquil, the largest Spanish city in the area. Once again, they used amphibious tactics and came ashore in canoes and one small bark, silently approaching to within one mile of the city. Suddenly, a musket shot rang out and torches were lit all throughout the city. The buccaneers realized that the Spanish had again been alerted. Fearing a trap, the buccaneers eventually called off the attack and their hopes for a really successful raid ended in failure. Over the next two months the only prize vessels they managed to take were of minimal value.

In late February 1685, they sailed to Taboga Island, just a few miles south of the City of Panama. While at anchor, they saw a group of 28 canoes paddling directly toward them. At first they were alarmed, but they soon realized that it was a group of buccaneers who had recently crossed the Isthmus of Panama (Darien) and were searching for a Spanish vessel to capture. Since the success of the 1681 expedition, just about everyone in the Caribbean was making the trip across Panama to raid in the Pacific.

Dampier wrote, "the Isthmus of Darien was now become a common Road for Privateers to pass between the North and South Seas at their Pleasure." The buccaneers were welcomed by Davis and Swan. There were 200 French and 80 English buccaneers under the command of the French captain Francois Gronet. Then, another group of 180 English buccaneers emerged from the jungle and joined Davis and Swan. More and more buccaneers joined their ranks over the next several weeks, some with captured vessels of various types. By March 30, 1685, they had a force of 8 vessels and 930 men. They all returned to Taboga to resupply with fresh water.

While hunting fowl on nearby Otoque Island, they accidentally intercepted a Spanish currier carrying letters telling of a treasure fleet that would be sailing from Lima to Panama. The taking of a really big prize had so far eluded them. This was their chance. They sailed to Pacheque Island, one of what is now called the Archipelago De Las Perlas in the middle of the Gulf of Panama, to wait. The sails of the treasure fleet appeared on the horizon on May 28, 1685. The Spanish fleet consisted of 14 vessels, including 6 ships mounting 48 guns, 40 guns, 36 guns, 24 guns, 18 guns, and 8 guns. There were 2 fireships brought along for protection and 6 small vessels with only small arms aboard. If attacked by an enemy fleet, the fireships would be set on fire and sailed into the enemy, with the crew escaping in canoes just before the ship hit. The English fleet consisted of only two well-armed ships, Davis' 36-gun *Batchelor's Delight* with 156 men and Swan's 16-gun *Cygnet* with 140 men. All the other vessels were small and carried no guns, only small arms. They included a bark with 110 commanded by Captain Townley, a bark with 308 French men commanded by Captain Gronet, a bark with 100 men commanded by Captain Harris, a bark with 36 men commanded by Captain Branly, another bark with 80 men, and a small bark they rigged as a fireship.

As the buccaneers sailed out to intercept the treasure fleet, the French Captain Gronet decided not to join in. They pursued the fleet all day, only firing an occasional shot. As night fell, all the vessels dropped anchor. The buccaneers thought they knew where the main Spanish ships were anchored by their lights, but the Spanish had fooled them and rigged lights on the small vessels to look like the big ones. When dawn came, the buccaneers found that the Spanish had gained the weather gage and was bearing down on them under full sail. Now, it was the buccaneers' turn to run. The Spanish chased them in a running battle all around the Gulf of Panama and back to Pacheque Island by evening, but eventually broke contact and sailed away. Back on the island, the buccaneers all decided that Captain Gronet and his French crew were cowards and ordered them to leave their group.

Disappointment over the escape of the treasure fleet was followed by more setbacks and failed operations. In August 1685, the buccaneers attacked the city of Leon 20 miles upcountry from the coast of Nicaragua. They were met by a defending Spanish force of 200 Spanish cavalry, and 500 infantry. But a few well aimed shots killed the Spanish officers and the rest of the defenders fled the city. However, they found little of value and after waiting several days for the Spanish to pay a ransom, they burned the city to the ground and left. Upon return to Ria Lexa, they found the town abandoned. They managed to find some flour and stayed there until 24 August 1685 when they burned the town and sailed away empty handed.

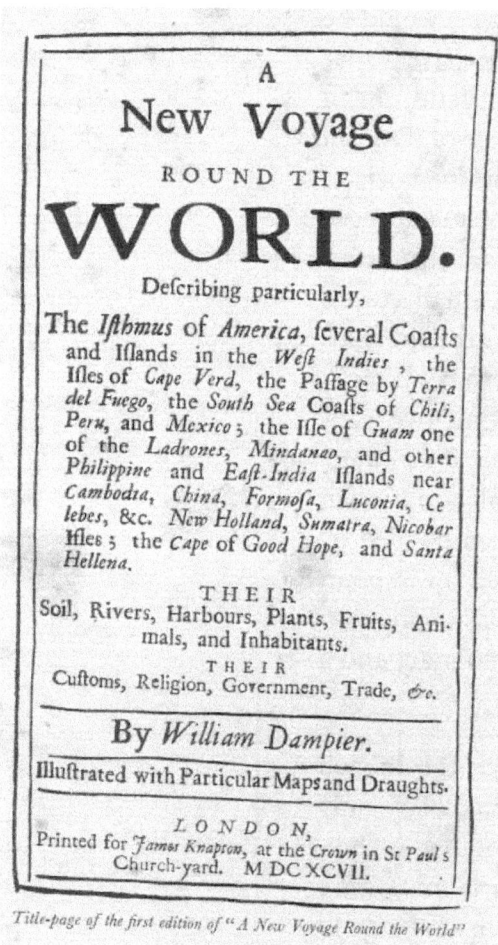

Figure 11: *Dampier's 1697 Book Cover*

The lack of success disheartened Captain Davis and he decided to sail south in search of richer pickings. Captain Swan believed that sailing north to Mexico might offer better prospects. The two captains decided to part company on August 25, 1685. Dampier had been friends with Davis for many years and was a loyal member of his crew, but he was enticed by the prospect of seeing new places, so he chose to go with Swan. Captain Townley and his bark also stayed with Swan, all the others sailed with Davis. For over 4 months, Captain Swan in the *Cygnet* accompanied Captain Townley and his bark, along with two small tenders, cruising the waters off Acapulco with little success. On January 7, 1686, Townley parted company too. Traveling north, by February 19, 1686, they were in desperate need of provisions, so they attacked the Spanish town of Santa Pecaque, located inland somewhere between the Mexican coast and the city of Compostella. The town was taken without resistance and the needed provisions, mostly corn, were seized. Swan had the supplies loaded onto pack horses and ordered a party of 50 buccaneers to take the supplies back to the ship. Just a little way outside the town limits, the buccaneers were ambushed by Spanish soldiers. Swan heard the shooting and rushed to their aid with about 50 remaining buccaneers, but found that they had all been killed. Among the dead was Dampier's old friend, Basil Ringrose.

Their bad luck continued. Sailing north up the Gulf of California, they didn't see a single prize. On March 8, 1686, they anchored near a small island on the west side of the Gulf and held a conference. Their decision was to sail to the East Indies. They remained on the island for a short while, careening and stocking up on water and provisions. Their force was down to 200 men and only 2 vessels, the *Cygnet* and a bark, probably one of the tenders mentioned before. They sailed south, reaching Cabo Corrientes on March 31, 1686, then turned west across the Pacific.

The Ladrone Islands were their first destination (now called the Mariana Islands). They reached Guam on May 21, 1686, staying only 12 days to re-provision. Mindanao in the Philippines was their next stop. The buccaneers found Mindanao a delightful change at first. The locals were friendly and Captain Swan made friends with the Sultan. The bark they had was riddled with worms, so the crew sank it. They spent 6 months ashore at Mindanao. During this time, Captain Swan was becoming more and more brutal and tyrannical toward his crew. Finally, on January 13, 1687, most of the crew mutinied. They elected John Read as their new captain and left Swan and 36 of his men on the beach as they sailed away on the *Cygnet*. From there, they sailed to Manila, Pulo Condore, Formosa, Celebes, and the north coast of Australia. Through all these travels, the buccaneers only managed to take a few prizes of little value. Even though Dampier wasn't having any success as a pirate, he continued to keep his journal and filled it with exceptionally valuable scientific observations and descriptions. This journal was a thoroughly detailed and scientifically organized chronicle describing every encounter, names of captains, ships, and crewmembers, and prizes taken. As a general rule, pirates don't normally keep records of all their adventures that could later be used against them in a trial. But Dampier didn't stop there. He also made a detailed description of every new plant and animal he encountered. He listed each location with latitude and longitude. He described the culture, dress, and food of the native peoples he met. For a man with no formal training in scientific observation, he did a remarkable job.

They finally reached Nicobar, a large island in the Bay of Bengal about 250 miles west of Thailand. By now, Dampier was disgusted with the whole situation. Under Captain Read's leadership, Dampier writes that the crew had become "drunken quarrelsome and unruly." While still at Nicobar Island, Dampier and 7 others took a small boat and escaped on May 15, 1688. The party included Mr. Hall, the ship's surgeon, an Englishman named Ambrose, 4 Malayans, and a Portuguese. They sailed to south to the English East India station at Achin, on the northern tip of Sumatra. Over the next three years, William Dampier waited for an opportunity to return to England. He kept busy occasionally signing on as a sailor making local trips for the East India Company. Eventually, he got passage on the Defiance and arrived back in England on September 16, 1691.

When he arrived, he began the process of turning his detailed journal into a book, which was finally published in 1697 and titled *A New Voyage Round the World*. Today, it is still in print but entitled *Memoirs of a*

Robert Jacob

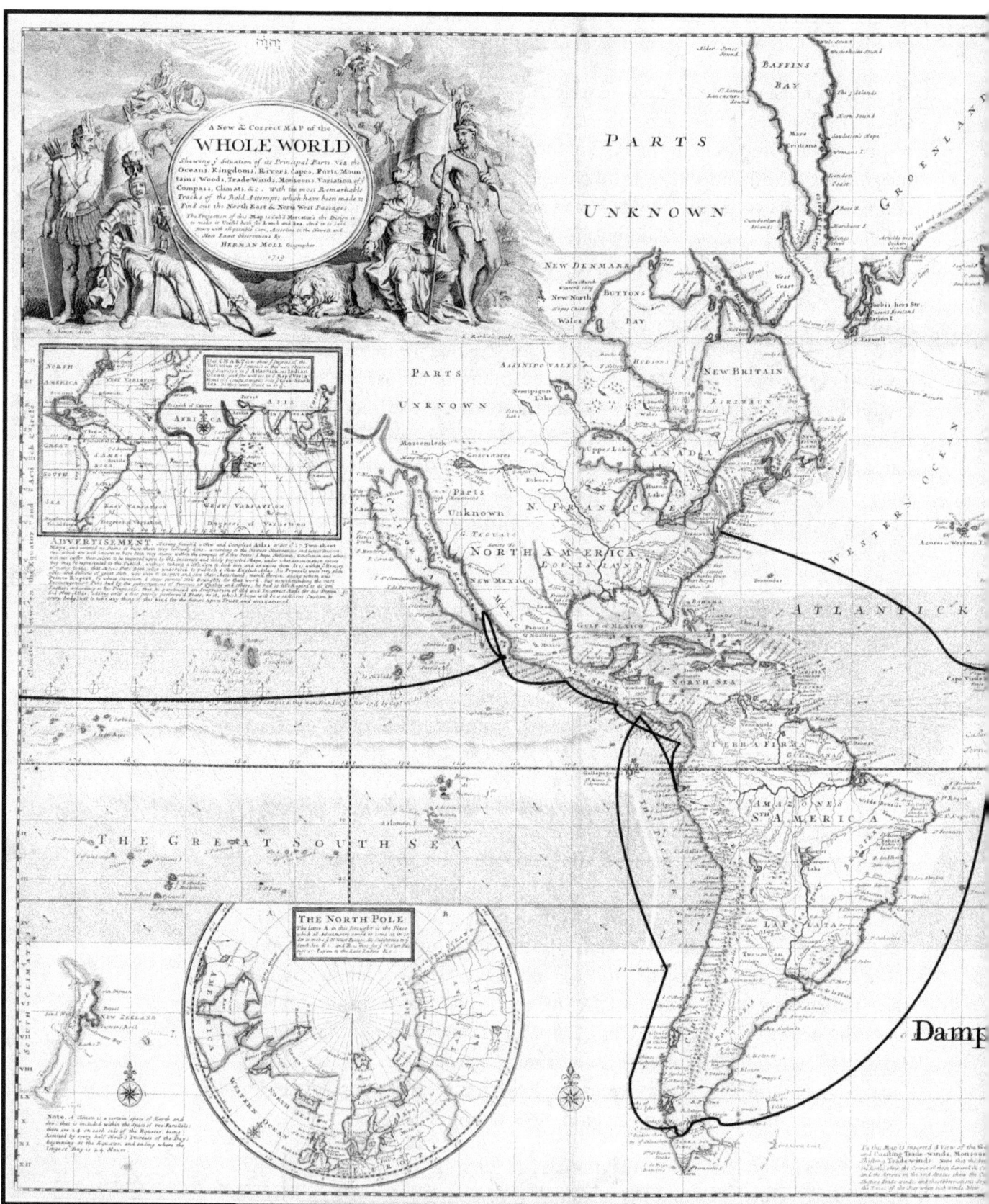

Figure 12:
Dampier's Travels

A Pirate's Life in the Golden Age of Piracy

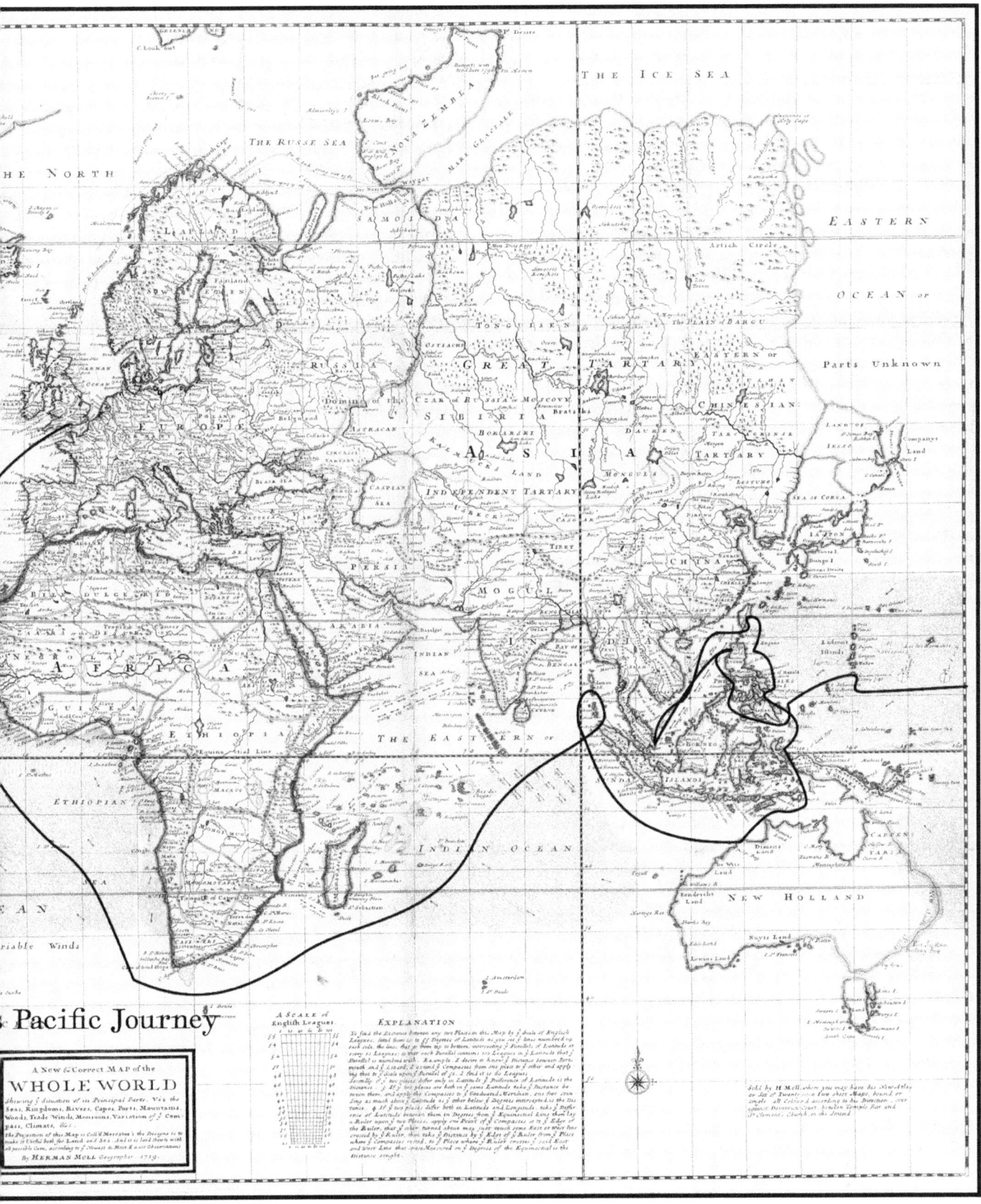

Pacific Journey

Buccaneer. Much of modern-day pirate research comes from this book. Unlike Exquemelin who had written a gory best seller about pirate atrocities, Dampier's work was detailed and highly scientific. He was the first to describe the Galapagos Islands in writing. One might think that after reading all about Dampier's confessed pirate crimes, the government authorities would have arrested him and thrown him into prison. But no! The book became a best seller. Not just with the coffee table crowd, but with the scientific community as well. This book had everything a reader in the late 17th century could want. It had adventure, pirating, exploration, and science. Dampier became a celebrity, a world-renowned naturalist, and college lecturer. A few years after his book was published, the English government promoted him to the rank of captain in the Royal Navy and gave him command of HMS *Roebuck*. He was commissioned to sail back to the Pacific and continue his amazing discoveries, but Dampier wasn't successful as a captain and after many difficulties his ship sank on February 21, 1701 in Clarence Bay, near Ascension Island. He was court martialed upon his return to England and dismissed from the Navy. After his dismissal, he wrote a second book entitled A Voyage to New Holland. There will be more on William Dampier in a future chapter.

Chapter 21
The Glorious Revolution of 1688

The buccaneers were now all pirates, taking prizes illegally with no government support, since 1685 when all the European nations agreed to put a stop to privateering. However, they were still in business, just on a much lower and quieter scale. But this end to privateering only lasted a few years as a new war enabled privateering to flourish once again. The War of the Grand Alliance was sometimes called the Nine Years' War, and in the Americas, it was known as King William's War. It began once again over French claims to territory in the Netherlands. Battles were primarily fought in Europe; however, it rapidly encompassed theatres in Ireland, North America, and the Caribbean.

Soon after fighting began in the Netherlands, the English Parliament saw an opportunity to get rid of their present ruler, King James II. James was Charles II's brother and had been ruling since Charles' death in 1685. However, James II had been a very unpopular king, and he had recently converted to Catholicism, which concerned the English government as well as their citizens. In 1688 he had a son, also named James Stuart. This made the situation intolerable to the English people as there was a Catholic heir to the throne. So, they looked upon the war in Europe as a means of getting rid of James.

It just so happened that William of Orange, the ruler of the Dutch Republic, was both the nephew and the son-in-law to James II and he was a protestant. So, the English Parliament covertly invited William to come to England and become king. In what is called the "Glorious Revolution" William landed in England on November 5, 1688 and was welcomed with open arms. On February 13, 1689 William was crowned King of England, and his wife, Mary, was crowned Queen. After all, she was the daughter of James II. For the first time in history, England had a king and a queen with

1688

King James II of England is deposed and flees to France.

1689

William of Orange and his wife Mary are crowned King and Queen of England.

1689–1697

War of the Grand Alliance—England, Dutch Republic, Holy Roman Empire, and Spain against France.

equal authority to rule. William and Mary were now King William III & Queen Mary II, King and Queen of England.

James and his infant son fled to France. This started a civil war in Scotland and Ireland, first because there were a lot of Catholics in Scotland and Ireland and second, because James was also the King of Scotland. He was a Scot himself, James Stuart. The Stuarts had been ruling both England and Scotland since 1603, when Queen Elizabeth died without any children. From their point of view, England may have had the right to kick out their king and put William on the throne, but not to replace the king of Scotland too. This revolt was known as the Jacobite revolt as Jacob is Latin for James. The Jacobites would play a large part in this war as well as in wars in the next century. They would also have a tremendous impact on the pirates of the early 18th century.

Meanwhile, France and the Dutch were on the verge of war again over territory in the Netherlands. When William of Orange became the King of England, France openly supported the old King James II and his infant son. Soon, everything blew up and the War of the Grand Alliance was on. On May 17, 1689 France went to war with just about every other nation in Europe. For the first time in well over 100 years, England and Spain were on the same side.

Privateering operations were revived in Port Royal. The new war authorized the issue of letters of marque. This time, however, Spain was allied with England and the Dutch Republic. But privateering wasn't like it was in the old days. The "Brethren of the Coast" had been torn apart by all the recent wars between the English, Dutch, and French. Now, the hated enemy Spain was allies with the Dutch and English. The camaraderie that had existed among the buccaneers was gone. Privateering was more of an individual endeavor rather than a group effort. The large buccaneer fleets were non-existent. Additionally, the Royal Navies were taking a more active role, restricting the privateers to smaller things. Now, privateers were limited to supporting the military objectives of the government. In many cases, privateers were actually assigned to accompany regular naval forces. As the war went on, more and more of these privateers found that piracy was more profitable. Many chose to venture away from the control of the naval forces in the Caribbean and seek prizes elsewhere—like the Pacific or Indian Oceans.

Chapter 22
Piracy and Higher Education

The moonlight glistened on the dark and quiet waters of Lynnhaven Bay as a mysterious small rowboat carrying four men suspiciously slipped through the water. Suddenly out of the darkness, HMS *Deptford* appeared and changed course directly toward the tiny vessel. The *Deptford* was an English warship assigned to patrol the waters of Virginia in search of smugglers or pirates. Her Captain, Simon Rowe, didn't think that this row boat looked right. It was 1688 and the Glorious Revolution had just begun. No telling who might be about late at night, but they probably were up to no good. The *Deptford* came along side and Captain Rowe ordered the boat to heave to. The men aboard were John Hinson, Lionel Delawafer, Edward Davis, and his slave, Peter Cloise. Yes, this is the same Edward Davis who accompanied William Dampier from Panama to the Pacific and eventually took command as Captain Edward Davis of the *Batchelor's Delight* and parted company in August 1685.

When HMS *Deptford's* crew searched the small boat, they found several chests filled with gold coins and silver plate valued somewhere between £5,000 and £6,000. The five men were immediately arrested as suspected pirates and taken to the capital city of Jamestown for questioning. At first, they denied any involvement with piracy and they told the Virginia Governor, Francis Howard, that they had acquired this fortune through honest trading in the Caribbean and that they intended to settle in Virginia. However, Peter Cloise told the governor that they were pirates and had just left the Caribbean after taking several Spanish ships and towns. While in jail, Hinson, Davis, and Delawafer learned that the king had recently issued a proclamation offering a pardon for all pirates, as he needed them for his war against the French. So, they admitted to being pirates and immediately petitioned for a pardon, as was allowed under the law. They also petitioned for the return of their loot.

Lynnhaven Bay is just off the Virginia shoreline to the north of what would later be known as Virginia Beach.

The local authorities argued over what to do. Some felt that they had been apprehended before the proclamation was known and should be tried. Then, even if they were released under the proclamation, what should become of their stolen loot? It was definitely a complicated issue. Prior to the 18th century, Englishmen could not be tried for piracy in the colonies; they had to be taken back to England. And so, Davis, Hinson, and Delawafer were sent to England along with their fortune. At the same time, Dr. James Blair of Virginia, a very important lawyer, Reverend, and Commissary of Virginia, was in London attempting to gather financial support for a proposed school in the Virginia colony. Welcoming this opportunity, the pirates hired Blair as their attorney. On March 10, 1692 the accused pirates appeared before the King's Privy Council and Blair managed to get them off with a full pardon. Additionally, all of the loot they had at the time of their arrest was returned to them with two conditions. Their release was dependent on the pirates making a generous donation to Blair's college fund. Dr. Blair was paid a personal fee of £300 for his services and the pirates made a sizeable donation of one fourth of their treasure. Blair returned to Virginia and used the pirate loot to fund a college he named for the King and Queen of England, the College of William and Mary.

Chapter 23
Pirate Ports & Trade in North America

One must keep in mind that pirates have to sell their stolen cargo in order to make a profit. If all you are after is gold or silver, then there's no need to sell anything, but much of the cargo taken at sea wasn't gold or silver. Some of the most profitable prizes included cotton and silk from India, porcelain from China, jewelry from anywhere, and spices from the East Indies. Quite often, these items brought greater riches than gold. Even routine shipments of lumber, tar, iron, and other products necessary for building plantations could turn a nice profit. Privateers never had any trouble disposing of their stolen cargo. They simply returned to their homeport where they got their letters of marque or some other port that was in alliance with their government. Once in port, they sold their cargo to the local law-abiding merchants and split the profits with the government officials who had given them the letters of marque in the first place.

Pirates, on the other hand, had to avoid the government authorities and find local merchants who were willing to purchase stolen goods. After 1670 privateering was greatly restricted in the Caribbean and many former privateers turned to piracy. For them, finding the best markets for their stolen cargo was vital for success. **This seems like a daunting task where stealth and secrecy would be essential. In reality, the English Navigation Acts made this a lot easier than one might think.** The Navigation Acts were a series of English laws that greatly restricted foreign trade, especially in the colonies. Essentially, all of the merchandise imported to English colonies in America had to come from England.

The merchants back in England felt threatened by the Dutch and other foreign traders who were importing fabulous goods from the Far East, like silk and cotton. The English merchants couldn't compete with such products. It was especially bad in the colonies. From a Dutch merchant's perspective there were hundreds of planters in the colonies with very limited access to European goods, planters who had a great deal of money and were willing to pay exorbitant prices for all sorts of exotic things. Additionally, those planters all had valuable crops they wished to sell. So, they loaded up their ships with cargos of spices and cloth in the East Indies and headed for the Americas, where they could get a lot more for their merchandise from the English tobacco and sugar planters than from the buyers back in Europe. Then, they purchased their tobacco or sugarcane and returned to Europe with an enormous profit. The problem for the English was that this cut out the English shipping merchants completely.

The English solution was to restrict foreign trade and in 1651, the first Navigation Act was passed. It was re-confirmed by King Charles II in 1660 and expanded in 1663 to include the "important staple principle" which required that all foreign goods be shipped to the American colonies through English ports. The result of this Act was that foreign goods were almost cut off from ever reaching English colonial ports. And the few foreign goods that did reach the colonies were the leftovers that the merchants back home in England didn't want. Additionally, with only one source of importation, English goods took far longer to reach the colonies and without competition the prices skyrocketed. By the 1680s the plantations began to turn enormous profits and the owners all wanted to build English style mansions, furnish them with the finest items, and wear the latest fashions. Merchants throughout the colonies could make a fortune if only they could get their hands on more luxury items. Doing business with pirates was the answer.

Trading with pirates in Port Royal was out of the question by 1688. Ironically, it was Henry Morgan, as Lieutenant Governor of Jamaica, who put an end to it. Port Royal was now a city focused on plantations and mining and had between 6,500 and 7,000 inhabitants and over 2,000 buildings, densely packed into 51 acres. Most of these buildings were large brick structures and some were even four stories tall. Five forts now defended the harbor. Also, 213 ships visited Port Royal that year, while 226 ships made port in all of New England. The War of the Grand Alliance in 1669 brought some of the privateers back to Port Royal, but the city's success as a buccaneer port was short lived.

For the French, Petit Goave, the capital of the French colony of Saint Domingue returned as the center of all French privateer activity. Tortuga was still used to launch a few more buccaneer raids, like Vera Cruz in 1683 and Campeche in 1686, but the port was definitely in decline as a pirate base. By 1690 Tortuga no longer saw buccaneer fleets at anchor. There were no more pirates walking the streets. Tortuga was just another sleepy little port and had all but disappeared from the buccaneer's memory. Petit Goave was the French port the English and Spanish had to worry about and in 1691 the Spanish invaded. The city was defended almost entirely by buccaneers. De Graaf was still military commander and the new governor, Jean-Baptiste Ducasse, was a former buccaneer himself.

Shocking and sudden devastation came to Port Royal on June 7, 1692 when a tremendous earthquake totally destroyed the city. The actual city of Port Royal and the defending forts were built on a sand strip that encircled the harbor. During the earthquake, almost the entire sand strip liquefied and almost everything sank into the harbor in about two minutes. Parts of Fort Charles were all that remained. The city of Port Royal was rebuilt along the new shoreline, but on a much smaller scale. It was now just a small merchant port with a few official government buildings that served the sitting colonial governor. Today, it's the city of Kingston. The Treaty of Ryswick in 1697 formalized the French occupation which had existed for the past 60 years, and Spain acknowledged France's title to the western third of Hispaniola, modern-day Haiti. By 1700 Petit Goave had become just a small government office in the backwater of the Caribbean.

As things got tough in the Caribbean, buccaneer pirates looked for new ports to sell their goods and enjoy a pleasurable evening of drinking, gambling, and cavorting. The newly settled Carolina coast was their first stop. Settlers first arrived in Carolina in 1670 and needed just about everything from cloth to furniture. They also needed rum, sugar, exotic foods, and weapons. Pirates could deliver all of these goods at cheaper prices than the English merchants back home.

By 1680, pirates were well-established all along the Carolina coast and were welcomed by the local merchants. In Charles Town, Carolina (modern-day Charleston, South Carolina) trade with pirates was rampant. What began as a small settlement on the west bank of the Ashley River had grown so rapidly that it had to be relocated in 1681 to its present location. By 1685 it was the largest port on the southern coast. The newly built rice and indigo plantations were very profitable, making Charles Town a rich city.

In the mid-1680s the Carolina government attempted to stamp out trade with pirates but found that there wasn't a single statute against trade with pirates on the books. A few laws were passed and pirate trade slowed down for a short time. Then in the early 1690s, the anti-pirate laws expired. Former pirates wishing to set up shop and merchants who didn't mind trading with pirates for a nice profit flocked to Charles Town. At that time

1692

Port Royal destroyed by a tremendous earthquake.

1670

English establish a colony in South Carolina.

anyone with £10 could vote and merchants friendly to pirates had plenty of money—so did the rich plantation owners who bought their stolen goods. As a result, all laws that passed were in favor of those who traded with pirates. A 1692 law granted complete indemnity to all pirates and they commonly walked the Charles Town streets in total safety. Elsewhere along the Carolina coast, the vast wilderness and unattended beaches were ideal for the small-time pirates. They could easily smuggle rum or sell stolen nautical goods to local fishermen with few questions asked.

Other hotbeds of pirate trade were New York and Rhode Island. These ports were settled by Puritans and other religious groups who weren't exactly supportive of the English crown. In New England in the late 17th century, piracy was looked upon as a boost to the local economy and a way to reduce unemployment. From the very beginning, the settlers in New England were considered outcasts by English society. Unlike the settlers in Virginia and Carolina who were predominantly members of the Church of England and had been given royal land grants, the New Englanders were Puritans, Quakers, Presbyterians, and other Non-Anglican religions, which were known in England during the 17th and 18th centuries as "dissenters." In other words, the dissenters were members of any protestant religion other than the Church of England. As such, by law, they couldn't hold public office, meet for worship in groups of more than five people, be an officer in the military or navy, get a degree from any university or college, or even vote. The dissenters began leaving England in the 1620s to start a new way of life based upon their religious convictions. Some went to the Caribbean, but most settled in what would be known as New England.

For a while, under parliamentary rule, (1649–1660) they had a bit more freedom, but with the restoration of King Charles II in 1660 laws like the Clarendon Code and the Test Act restricted the dissenter's freedom even more. After the Glorious Revolution of 1689, the Act of Toleration softened things a bit as far as freedom to meet publicly, but they still were third class citizens until the 19th century. In the colonies, their rights went unrecognized in Parliament. This, of course, caused significant resentment for English policy and eventually led to the American Revolution of 1775. Many of the New Englanders didn't feel obligated to follow English laws, especially when they were contrary to the needs of their colony.

The government of Massachusetts never really accepted piracy on the principle that it was immoral and protested against the "pirate-friendly" governments of the neighboring colonies. But for the rest of the colonies, piracy was viewed as a way to help the economy. As far as the merchants of Rhode Island and New York were concerned, these pirates weren't robbing New England ships, they were taking French and Indian prizes far off in some foreign waters. The pirates returned with valuable goods that the people throughout New England wanted, and in many cases, desperately needed. This included weapons, cloth, porcelain, and of course, gold and silver. Rhode Island was especially fond of pirates. Thomas Tew, a native of Newport, Rhode Island, was considered a hero when he returned from the Indian Ocean with riches that he took from the Mogul's ship. New York was also pirate-friendly in the 1690s. Tew became good friends with the governor, Colonel Benjamin Fletcher. Along with Tew, New York was home to his pirate partners John Ireland, Thomas Wake, and William Mace.

Eventually, the acceptance of pirates came to an end and Governor Fletcher was removed from office. A letter written by his replacement, Lord Bellomont, gives one an idea of the level of acceptance pirates enjoyed in the colonies of New York and Rhode Island prior to 1698. On May 8, 1698 Lord Bellomont wrote a letter to the Lords of Trade saying, "I find that those Pirates that have given the greatest disturbance in the East Indies and the Red Sea, have either been fitted out from New York or Rhode Island, and manned from New York. . . . It is likewise evident that Tew, Glover and Hore had commissions granted them by Governor Fletcher when none of them had any ship or vessel in Col. Fletcher's government, yet they had commissions and were permitted to raise men in New York and design [inform the] public of their being bound for the Red Sea. And Captain Tew, that had been before a most notorious Pirate (complained of by the East India Company), on his return from the Indies with great riches, made a visit to New York, where (although a man of most mean and infamous character) he was received and caressed [praised] by Col. Fletcher, dined and supped often with him and appeared publicly in his coach with him, and they exchanged presents, as gold watches, etc., with one another. All this is known to most of the city." During the 1690s pirates freely walked the streets of New York and Rhode Island with almost a celebrity status.

The thought of the tiny town of Marcus Hook as a pirate-friendly port comes as a surprise to most people. Today, Marcus Hook is a small port surrounded by oil refineries on the west bank of the Delaware River about 20 miles south of Philadelphia. It looked much different 400 years ago. The land between what is now Dover Delaware and Philadelphia was originally settled by Sweden in 1637 then taken by the Dutch in 1655 and added to their colony of New Netherlands, which was located in modern New York. A small port developed on the Delaware River that the Dutch named "Marrites Hoeck." The English took possession in 1664 as part of the Second Anglo-Dutch war but really didn't do anything with the colony until 1682. During that time, the land was still occupied by a mixture of Swedes and Dutch.

1692–1697

Colonel Benjamin Fletcher, Governor of New York

1698–1701

Richard Coote, 1st Earl of Bellomont, Governor of New York, Massachusetts, and New Hampshire

1680

William Penn establishes the colony of Pennsylvania, primarily inhabited by Quakers.

William Penn was a Quaker and the son of Admiral Sir William Penn, the admiral that invaded Jamaica in 1655. This was a real problem for his Anglican family as well as the King. He spent a lot of time under arrest for one religious offense or another, but always managed to obtain a release because his father was exceptionally well connected. In 1674, Penn's father died and left him a fortune. By the late 1670s, he had already purchased vast tracts of land in what is now New Jersey. But by 1680 the English were becoming less tolerant of the Quakers and something had to be done.

Penn managed to convince King Charles II that if he were given a large colony in North America, he could lead all the Quakers out of England in one fell swoop. To Penn's surprise, the King agreed and granted him about half of the former Dutch territory. The new colony was named in his honor, Pennsylvania, and included modern Pennsylvania and Delaware. By 1682 the city of Philadelphia was founded and settlers of all religions began flocking there. But there was already a well-established port just four miles away. A name change was in order and the former Dutch port of "Marrites Hoeck" was anglicized to Marcus Hook. By the 1690s, it was one of the largest trading ports in the colony with over 100 houses.

Just like the colonists in New England, the Pennsylvanian colonists didn't have any real loyalty to the crown of England. They were mostly Quakers and some left over Dutch and Swedes. Additionally, the economically savvy Quakers felt no moral obligation to abide by English trade laws. Quakers were very business-minded people as a general rule and pursued any opportunity to make a profit. Even though the Quakers didn't approve of piracy and drunkenness, they knew how to attract business.

According to local tradition, the business minded Quakers freely traded with pyrates at Marcus Hook as long as they remained on a street named Discord Lane which was named for the temporary discord that the pirate visitors brought to the community. Clearly shown on a 1701 map of the city, Discord Lane was a short street that began near the docks and ran about two blocks into the town. Today, that street is called Second Street. Contemporary accounts described this street as a place where pirates could indulge in noisy conduct and revel in a deep cup of strong drink. They also describe pirates walking the streets with their pockets full of gold. Apparently, pirates continued to visit Marcus Hook throughout the early 18th century. At the very least, we know that Blackbeard was in Marcus Hook in August 1718 when the Governor of Pennsylvania issued a warrant for his arrest.

Virginia was the one colony that maintained strong ties to England and the crown. Most of the landholders in Virginia received their land grants directly from the King and the leadership was Anglican churchmen and royal subjects. The citizens of mainland Virginia had always been against piracy and generally met pirates with strong legal force. Established in 1609, the port of Elizabeth City was the oldest port in Virginia. Its name was changed to the City of Hampton in 1706. Located at the entrance of Virginia's Hampton Roads, it was the closest major port to the colony's capital, James Town, situated just about 30 miles up the James River. Elizabeth City was the location for The Royal Customs House as well as the central headquarters of all English Royal Naval activity along the entire North American coast. Even with this strong governmental presence, pirates still visited Elizabeth City because it was a major seaport with lots of taverns. There are many local stories of pirates walking the streets of Elizabeth City in the 1690s. These pirates had to maintain a very low profile. In fact, during the late 17th century many pirates regularly visited the Hampton Roads area. The proof comes from numerous records of their arrests and their subsequent trials.

Accomack, Virginia was another matter. It's located along an isolated stretch of Virginia's Atlantic shoreline, about 20 miles south of the Maryland border. In the 17th century Accomack was a long way from the governor or any official authorities who were hundreds of miles away at the colony's capital city of James Town or at the Royal Customs House and naval forces at Elizabeth City. The locals welcomed all visiting ships bringing trade goods, whether they were pirates or not.

Accomack had long been known as a pirate-friendly place where they could stop and careen their vessels on the wide beaches in safety.

This can be very dangerous for a pirate. If found by either the authorities or other unfriendly pirates, there is no opportunity for them to sail away.

For this reason, pirates tended to careen their vessels on remote and secluded beaches, far away from the shipping lanes and ports. Accomack was ideal. It was far from the busy waters of the Caribbean, where government naval forces and unfriendly pirates were always on the lookout for helpless buccaneers careening on the beach. Also, the locals were always delighted to see pirates arrive and welcomed them with open arms. Being so isolated, the locals couldn't get many goods from England like cloth, sugar, or jewelry. They greatly benefited from access to both the practical and exotic trade goods the pirates brought—especially since they were tax free. Also, the pirates paid well for the supplies that the locals sold, like food, sail cloth, and lumber. The locals wanted to keep this prate trade going as long as possible, so they kept quiet about pirate activity and ensured the pirates were left alone to finish their careening. As you recall,

Careening is a process of pulling your vessel up out of the water and cleaning off the barnacles and other growth from below the waterline. If you don't keep your vessel clean, it will sail slower and slower, not a good thing for a merchant or a pirate. Also, the careening process gives the crew the opportunity to repair or replace damaged planking that causes leaks and can lead to the sinking of the vessel. Pirates normally had to careen their vessels on a beach. Yes, they would have to pull the entire ship up on the sand.

William Dampier joined Captain Cook's crew at Accomack in 1683 and it was still a favorite pirate stop for careening far away from the Caribbean during the early 1700s when Blackbeard careened his vessel there. There is no way of telling how long Accomack remained a pirate-friendly port, perhaps all the way through the 18th century and even into the 19th.

Chapter 24
The Pirate Haven of St. Mary's

At the end of the 17th century, the Caribbean was becoming less and less profitable to privateers and pirates alike. Also, pirate-friendly ports in the Caribbean were becoming scarce. Before the 1690s the Indian Ocean was not a practical hunting ground for most pirates based in the Caribbean. It was on the other side of the world. It took a long time to get there and a long time to return. There were no pirate-friendly ports to resupply and refit vessels while sailing the waters or for the long trip home. However, beginning in about 1680 a few European pirates began sailing to the Indian Ocean anyway. Most were unsuccessful. A base of operations was desperately needed and there were no pirate-friendly ports like Tortuga or Port Royal. In fact, there really weren't any safe ports at all along the African coast. The very large island of Madagascar off the south eastern side of Africa was ideally located. The local inhabitants were accommodating, especially the women. For many years, sailors who had been shipwrecked on the island settled down with native wives. Additionally, a few small French and English colonies had been established, so there were places where pirates could purchase supplies. Some of the settlers, like Robert Drury, who wrote a book about his adventures, decided that piracy was a better way of life and joined the crews. As is the case everywhere, when there is a need for something, all it takes is one enterprising individual to capitalize on that need. In this case, it was an ex-buccaneer from Jamaica named Adam Baldridge. This base would make piracy in the Indian Ocean practical. Of all the pirates who chose to ply their trade in those far off waters, there would be four who really distinguished themselves. Of the four, the first three had lives and careers that intertwined. For this reason, I shall tell you their stories as they happened, trying to stay in chronological order as much as possible.

Charged with murder, Adam Baldridge had to make a quick escape in 1685, so he fled and wandered about until he arrived on the island of Nosy

1690

Adam Baldridge establishes a pirate base on Saint Mary's Island, Macassar.

Boraha, in the early 1690s. Nosy Boraha is a small island 12 miles off the northeast coast of Madagascar. It's called St. Mary's by the English and St. Marie's by the French. Baldridge understood the need for a pirate port in the Indian Ocean and at that time there wasn't one. St. Mary's seemed perfect. It was close to the shipping lanes but far away from any threatening government and had good weather. Baldridge began building the perfect pirate port. First, he built a stronghold overlooking the harbor to protect any guests from attack. As far as pirates were concerned, this was going to be a neutral port. Then, he built warehouses and began importing all sorts of naval stores and supplies. There were also facilities for careening which had to be done on all ships from time to time to keep them watertight and minimize marine growth. This new pirate base on St. Mary's offered a good, safe port where pirates could careen their vessels without fear of attack. But St. Mary's offered more than just a safe place to careen. It had good food, liquor, and friendly women. Visitors could relax and engage in all the pleasurable activities their hearts desired while their vessel was being worked on.

Baldridge's settlement rapidly had become a popular haven for all pirates in the Madagascar waters. He lived an extravagant life on the island, which included his own harem of island girls. This port on Madagascar allowed the development of what was called the Pirate Round. Pirates would leave ports in New York, New England, or the Bahamas and sail across the Atlantic, rounding Africa and stopping at Madagascar to careen their vessels and re-provision with fresh water and local food. When they were refreshed and refitted, the pirates would sail northeast to take valuable Indian prizes coming from India or Yemen. If the pirates were well enough armed, they might try to take merchant ships from any of the East India Companies known as East Indiamen. On the return trip, the pirates would stop off at Madagascar once again. In some cases, depending on the time of year, they would have to wait for the turning of the monsoon wind. The pirate accredited with first spreading the word about Baldridge's port was Thomas Tew of New York.

1691

Piracy in the Indian Ocean greatly increases due to Baldridge's base.

Later publications claim that an immense pirate base called Libertalia existed, with strong fortifications and births for docking dozens of large pirate ships. Libertalia was supposedly the center of all pirate activity in the Indian Ocean. Located on the large island of Madagascar, it was a pirate-built stronghold with a pirate government and everything one needed to sail the ocean in search of loot. The problem is that it never existed beyond the imagination of Charles Johnson, the author of the 1724 publication *A General History of Pyrates*. A description of Libertalia appears in one of the later editions of that book. Shortly after the imaginary port first appeared in print, the legend somehow gained the status of fact. There are no other accounts or descriptions of Libertalia in any contemporary documentation and there are no ruins or local legends of a pirate city to be found anywhere on the island. Perhaps the legend of Libertalia was merely a greatly exaggerated description of a real pirate base of the waters of Madagascar, Adam Baldridge's pirate port on St. Mary's Island.

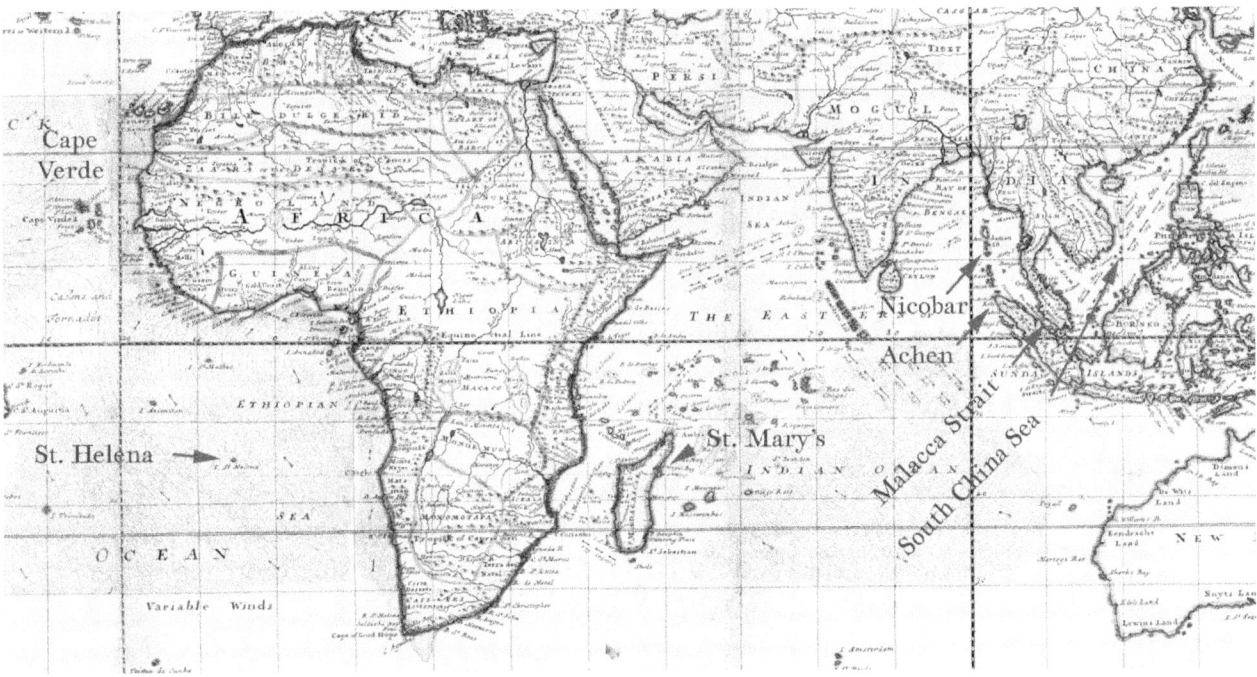

Figure 13: *Africa & Indian Ocean*

Chapter 25
Tew and Every

Among the first pirates to really exploit the opportunities of the Indian Ocean was Thomas Tew. However, Tew wasn't the typical pirate of his day. Similar to Henry Morgan, Tew was a family man with financial and political backing from the governor of a colony. Like most pirates, not much is known about his early life. Some sources say he was either the son or possibly the grandson of Richard Tew and Mary Clarke, who settled in Rhode Island in 1640. It is also possible that Thomas was a nephew. Regardless of his exact relationship to Richard, there is no doubt that Thomas Tew was from Rhode Island. In the 1680s he may have been a pirate operating near Jamaica. In a 1694 letter to the Council for Trade and Plantations, John Groves wrote about Tew stating, "The name of the master of the sloop was Thomas Tue, whom I had known living in Jamaica twelve years before." This reference places Tew in Jamaica in 1682. Also, Tew was good friends—and possibly partners—with New York's Governor Fletcher. After Tew's death, as they were gathering evidence against Governor Fletcher for his association with Tew, the King's council stated that "it was a thing notoriously known to everyone that he (Tew) had before then been a pirate." Tew's home was in Newport Rhode Island where he lived with his wife and two daughters. In 1694, Thomas Tew and his family attended a social function hosted by Governor Fletcher where it was reported that "his wife and daughters dressed in fine silks."

1693

Thomas Tew begins his pirate career off Africa.

The well-documented part of the life of Thomas Tew begins when he arrived in Bermuda in 1692. He went into partnership with Thomas Hall, Richard Gilbert, John Dickenson, Colonel Anthony White, and William Outerbridge who were all members of the governor's council. Together, they purchased the 70-ton sloop named the *Amity* and obtained letters of marque from Governor Richier of Bermuda to attack French vessels near the Gambia River in West Africa. When Tew left Bermuda, he was accompanied by another privateer vessel commanded by Captain George

Drew, however, this vessel sprung a mast in a storm and they lost sight of each other. At some point, Tew and his crewmembers decided to change their destination and go for the more valuable prizes of the Indian Ocean. It was now the summer of 1693 and Tew's sloop *Amity* had reached the Strait of Babelmandeb, at the entrance to the Red Sea. They spotted a merchantman headed from India to Arabia. Even though this ship had 300 soldiers aboard, Tew attacked anyway and easily took the ship without the loss of any of his crewmembers. After taking only one Indian merchant ship, the crew decided to head back home since the prize was an exceptionally wealthy one worth over £100,000 in gold, silver, ivory, spices, silk, and gems.

Before returning to the American colonies, Tew desperately needed a place to careen his sloop and to refit and stock up on supplies for the long trip home. Somehow he heard of the new "pirate-friendly" port on St. Mary's and decided to stop. Nobody really knew too much about it yet; it had just opened. It was far better than Tew had hoped for. It was absolutely ideal. In fact, Tew's quartermaster and 23 crewmembers decided to stay. After arriving back in America, Tew and his crewmen were so impressed with the accommodations of this luxury pirate port that they told everyone they met about it. Positive word of mouth is just what a starting business needs and soon almost every pirate and privateer in the Indian Ocean were stopping there, especially those from New York. Just five years later, Baldridge had to flee the island and return to America because the local king found out he was involved in the slave trade. But from 1693 to 1697, Adam Baldridge was a rich and powerful man.

Thomas Tew returned to Newport in April 1694 with riches beyond belief. After crossing the Atlantic, Tew tried to return to Bermuda, but a storm took him off course, so he decided to sail home to Newport, Rhode Island. Each member of Tew's crew received between £1,200 and £3,000 and Tew's captain's share came to about £8,000. After settling with the crew, Tew paid his backers in Bermuda 14 times the amount they had invested in giving him the *Amity*. But more importantly, shops all throughout New England were instantly stocked with all sorts of exotic merchandise like jewels, silks, and china. They even brought back Arabian coins. The colonists of New England had never seen anything like it. Everyone knew that Tew had obtained his riches through piracy, but that really didn't matter. After all, they weren't English; they weren't even Christians.

In 1694, Tew befriended the governor of New York, Colonel Benjamin Fletcher. The governor knew the wealth that pirates could bring to a community and he wanted to share in the profits. Tew and his family often traveled to New York as guests of the governor where Governor Fletcher entertained him and drove him about in his coach, though Tew publicly declared that he would "...make another voyage to the Red Sea and make New York his port of return...." For a brief moment, Thomas Tew was a rich man and a celebrity among New York society. A few years later, after Tew was denounced as a pirate and Fletcher was disgraced, Fletcher's successor, the Earl of Bellomont, wrote that, "He (Tew) had brought his spoil to Rhode Island and his crew dispersed in Boston where they shewed themselves publicly." As mentioned in Chapter 23, Bellomont also wrote a letter to the Lords of Trade on May 8, 1698 stating, "Captain Tew, that had been before a most notorious Pirate (complained of by the East India Company), on his return from the Indies with great riches, made a visit to New York, where (although a man of most mean and infamous character) he was received and praised by Col. Fletcher, dined and supped often with him and appeared publicly in his coach with him, and they exchanged presents, as gold watches, etc., with one another. All this is known to most of the city." It is apparent that Tew had found a new financial backer and political ally, Governor Fletcher, who gave him his letters of marque on November 8, 1694 to attack French shipping.

Tew fitted out his sloop *Amity* back in Newport and made no secret of the fact that he intended to return to the Red Sea. In a letter to the Council of Trade and Plantations, John Groves wrote, "I was travelling from New England to New York, when I saw three small ships, a sloop, a brigantine and a barque, fitting out at Rhode Island. The name of the master of the sloop was Thomas Tew, whom I had known living in Jamaica twelve years before. He was free in discourse with me and declared that he was last year in the Red Sea, that he had taken a rich ship belonging to the Mogul and had received for his owner's dividend and his sloop's twelve thousand odd hundred pounds, while his men had received upwards of a thousand pounds each. When I returned to Boston there was another barque of about thirty tons ready to sail and join Tew on the same account." Tew set sail in the *Amity* with a crew of about 40. Soon after, he was joined by Captain Want who commanded a brigantine and by Captain Wake who commanded a small vessel fitted out at Boston. Captain Want had accompanied Tew on a voyage in 1692 and had already spent his share of the loot in Rhode Island and Pennsylvania. Some sources say that a fourth ship commanded by Captain Glover and funded by New York merchants also joined Tew's fleet.

It is very interesting to note that Governor Fletcher was also good friends with William Kidd, the famous pirate we shall discuss a little later on. No one can say for certain, but Kidd and Tew must have met each other at some point during the year of 1694. The governor often held large social gatherings and both Tew and Kidd were known guests at some of these events. It is also interesting to speculate on the possibility that Tew and Kidd may have even planned to sail together. No one knows, of course, but in early 1695, Thomas Tew was on his way back to the Indian Ocean and William Kidd was seeking financial backers for an Indian Ocean expedition of his own.

Meanwhile, another major figure in the history of pirates was about to make his appearance in the Indian Ocean. His name was Henry Every, also known as "Long Ben." HMS *Rupert* was an English ship of the line under the command of Captain Francis Wheeler. 1689 was a year of considerable naval action in the War of the Grand Alliance and the *Rupert* helped capture a large enemy French fleet. One midshipman in that engagement gained promotion to Chief First Mate. In the summer of 1690, this Chief First Mate was invited to join Captain Wheeler on a new ship, HMS *Albemarle*. This Chief First Mate was Henry Every, one of the most successful pirates ever to sail the seas. Nothing is really known about Every prior to 1689. There are several biographies written about him in the early 18th century, but they don't offer any real information that can be verified about Every's early life. One such biography was written in 1709 by a Dutch author, van Broeck, who claims to have been one of Every's captives, but most scholars today believe the book to be mostly a work of fiction. Subsequent works like Daniel Defoe's 1720 book, "The King of Pirates" have made reference to the earlier 1709 work, but don't offer any real information that can be verified about Every's early life either. All accounts have narrowed his birth to sometime in the mid to late 1650s and that he came from England, perhaps Plymouth. Some have speculated that his birth name was actually Benjamin Bridgeman, especially since his nickname was "Long Ben," but this has yet to be proven.

By the early 1690s Every left the Royal Navy and according to Peter Henry Bruce, a West Indian merchant, he entered the illegal slave trade operating out of the Bahamas under the protection of Governor Cadwallader Jones. Captain Thomas Philips, an agent of the Royal African Company, describes the ease at taking slaves on the west African coast due to "tricks play'd them by such blades as Long Ben, alias Every." Captain Phillips wrote about Every several times alluding to him as a slave trader operating under a commission from Issac Richier, who was an unpopular Bermudian governor known to associate with criminals. In any event, all accounts describe Every as a dedicated family man who sent the greatest part of his earnings home to support his wife and children.

In early 1694, Every had signed on as first mate with a group of English privateers who had agreed to work for the Spanish. The Nine Years' War against France was still going on and Spain was England's ally. Fighting in

1694

Henry Every begins his pirate career off Africa.

the Caribbean had depleted Spanish resources. To make matters worse, French buccaneers had recently sunk a Spanish treasure fleet. The mission of the English privateers was to take arms and ammunition to the Spanish troops in the Caribbean and salvage as much of the sunken treasure as possible. Every's ship was provided by the Spanish and was the 46-gun *Charles II*, named for King Charles II of Spain, not the King Charles II of England who died nine years before. The other English ships were the *Dove*, the *James*, and the *Seventh Son*. The entire expedition was funded by several London based investors led by Sir James Houblon, who hoped to share in the finder's fee for the recovery of the sunken treasure. However, due to inefficient Spanish bureaucracy, the small fleet was stuck in the Spanish port of Coruna for eight months awaiting their commissions.

While in port, the crew wasn't paid a penny. Also, the Spanish treated them more like prisoners than privateer allies. They were kept ashore in a contained area and not allowed to go into the town or anywhere else for that matter. They couldn't spend what little money they had, nor could they send any money home to their families. To make matters worse, their Captains didn't really do anything to help. It was a desperate situation that led to mutiny with Every as their leader. In May of 1694, Every and 36 men boarded and took control of the *Charles II*. After receiving fire from the *James*, they escaped to open sea. Captain Gibson and the crew on board during the mutiny were given the option to either join the pirates or be safely set ashore. In true pirate fashion, the *Charles II* was renamed. Every's ship was now called the *Fancy*, and they sailed for the Indian Ocean. The first prizes that Every and his pirates took were three English merchantmen captured off the Cape Verde islands near the west coast of Africa. Then in October 1694 near the island of Principe, further south along the west coast of Africa, Captain Every and the *Fancy* took two Danish privateer ships. Of the captured Danish crewmembers, 17 of them decided to join Every's ship.

As Henry Every sailed toward the southern tip of Africa aboard his 46-gun Spanish warship, the *Fancy*, Thomas Tew was preparing to leave New York aboard the *Amity* and repeat the success of his last voyage. By November 1694, Tew was on his way. As Tew was approaching the west coast of Africa, Every reached Madagascar and restocked at Adam Baldridge's post. Soon afterwards, Every beached the *Fancy* on the Island of Johanna in the Comoro Islands which lie to the west of Madagascar half way between the north tip and the east coast of Africa. There, the *Fancy* was careened and the crew cut away much of the superstructure to improve speed and fighting space. Many pirates modified their captured merchant ships this way, making them more suitable for pursuit and boarding. With these modifications, the *Fancy* became one of the fastest ships then sailing in the

Indian Ocean. Soon after returning to the sea, Every took a French pirate ship and managed to recruit some of the crew. He now had 150 men. By August 1695, the *Fancy* had reached the Strait of Mandeb at the entrance of the Red Sea.

Meanwhile, Tew and the three other privateer captains weren't too keen on following the limitations on prize ships listed in their letters of marque given them by Governor Fletcher of New York. What they were planning was nothing short of piracy. They were after the riches of the Indian Mughals. **In reality, Governor Fletcher had probably had this in mind all along, but you can't put that sort of thing in writing.** Tew's fleet of four vessels reached Liparu Island at the mouth of the Red Sea in June 1695 and waited for a prize ship to pass by. Two months later, they spotted a large 46-gun Spanish privateer approaching. As she got nearer, they realized that it wasn't Spanish at all, it was an English pirate ship. Indeed, it was the *Fancy*, commanded by Captain Henry Every. As was customary with buccaneers of all nationalities, they anchored close by and socialized. During the festivities, they decided to join forces and become partners.

These two pirate captains made one of the most important contributions to the art of pirating during their brief partnership. They developed the pirate flag. Before 1694, pirates used a plain red flag that meant "no quarter." The French buccaneers often called this plain red flag the "Jolie Rouge" which means "Happy Red" as in, "Raise the happy red flag." The English buccaneers called it the "Jolly Roger."

No one can be certain, but according to tradition, it is believed that Henry Every wanted to distinguish himself and added a white skull and cross bones to his plain red flag. When Thomas Tew joined Every, he wanted a new flag too and added a white arm wielding a sword to his red flag. Soon after, Every and Tew changed the red colored background of their flags to black, which was the flag of death. Perhaps they thought black was more menacing or perhaps they felt that the red flag of "no quarter" was inappropriate, since they planned on letting the prize crew go unharmed anyway after they took what they wanted. Below are their two flags, the first pirate flags recorded.

1695

Tew and Every become pirate partners in the Indian Ocean.

Figure 14: *Henry Every Flag*

Figure 15: *Thomas Tew Flag*

The Mughal Convoy attacked

The Mughal convoy, bound for India, was one of the richest prizes on the seas. This particular year, it included the *Fateh Muhammed* and the *Ganj-i-Sawai*, carrying an enormously valuable cargo, many harem women, and presumably the Mughal's daughter as well. Captain Tew sighted the convoy and positioned the *Amity* for the attack. The *Fateh Muhammed* fought back, but resistance was fierce and the attack was called off when Thomas Tew was killed in the battle. Then the *Fancy* attacked. Weakened by the previous battle and seeing *Fancy's* 46 guns, the *Fateh Muhammed* surrendered. The rest of the convoy scattered and most of the other ships got away, but Every managed to track down the richest one of all, the *Ganj-i-Sawai*. After a fierce three-hour sea battle, one of Every's broadsides brought down the main mast and the pirates were able to board. After another two-hour fight, the pirates finally won. This time, the prisoners were treated very harshly. Most were tortured and killed. Some women were killed or committed suicide, the rest of the women were taken onboard the *Fancy* for the crew and kept. Once the looting and raping was complete, the male survivors were allowed to sail back to India. The pirates treated the Indians so brutally that it bothered many of the English for several years after. This is corroborated by the dispositions of the members of Every's crew who were captured by English authorities. One of the captured men, John Sparkes, testified that "the inhuman treatment and merciless tortures inflicted on the poor Indians and their women still affected his soul," and that, while apparently unremorseful for his acts of piracy, he was most repentant for the "horrid barbarities he had committed, though only on the bodies of the heathen."

The *Ganj-i-Sawai* was among the richest prizes ever taken. The haul included 500,000 gold and silver coins plus many valuable jewels. Some accounts say Every and his crew sailed away in the faster *Fancy* before settling with his pirate partners. Other accounts say the five ships made port at the island of Bourbon and split the loot according to their articles. As France and England were still at war, this port was a good spot to avoid the English authorities. Either way, Every divided the profits and returned to the Caribbean. When he arrived at the Dutch colony of Saint Thomas in what is now the Virgin Islands, each crew member is said to have received over £1,000 which was more than a sailor could earn in a lifetime. Every's share was three times that amount.

Bourbon is a small French island in the Indian Ocean east of Madagascar. It was established in 1642 as a re-provisioning station for the French East India Company.

By now, news of Every's actions had caused a major diplomatic incident and embarrassment for the English government. It was so serious that there was some doubt that the East India Company's trade privileges would remain in force. The enormous profits from the East India Company kept the English economy going. This really was the biggest calamity ever caused a government by the actions of a pirate. So, the English crown offer a large reward for the capture of Every and any of his crew and an international manhunt began. In March 1696 Every and his crew returned to their old home port of Nassau on the island of New Providence in the Bahamas.

Every was friends with the governor, Nicholas Trott, and he knew he would be safe, at least for a little while.

The town of Nassau in the Bahamas would grow to be the next great pirate port, but that was 20 years away.

In 1696, Nassau was an extremely remote port with a sparse population, no taverns, and no women. The crew was understandably restless. Additionally, Governor Nicholas Trott knew it was only a matter of time before the English authorities realized that he was hiding his friend, Every. As the English closed in, Trott told the authorities where Every and his men were. However, Trott also warned Every in enough time for him to escape with all but 12 of his men. Every returned to England on the sloop *Isaac* and 24 of his men were eventually caught in England. However, Henry Every, or Long Ben as he was known, was never seen again. Legend has it that he bought a manor house in Ireland and retired a wealthy man. **If true, sometimes piracy does pay.**

After the news of Thomas Tew reached the King of England, it was clear that Governor Fletcher of New York was implicated with pirates. The Council of Trade and Plantations wrote a letter of complaint to Governor Fletcher on February 1, 1697 that states, ". . . Further complaints have been made, especially from Jamaica, as to the entertainment of pirates in several places, and the King has given orders to the Governors of all Colonies to prevent the sheltering of pirates under the severest penalties.... By information given lately at the trial of several of Every's crew, your Government is named as a place of protection to such villains, and your favour to Captain Tew given as an instance of it." Additionally, one of the King's counselors made the point that Tew was a known pirate stating, "it was a thing notoriously known to everyone that he had before then been a pirate." Fletcher was relieved from his office in what was called a decommissioning on April 2, 1698. His replacement was Richard Coote, Earl of Bellomont, who was about to become one of the principal backers of William Kidd's Indian Ocean expedition.

Chapter 26
Captain William Kidd

Among the most famous pirates of all time was Captain William Kidd. Just like so many other historic figures of the period, very little is known about his early life. Largely these accounts are based upon incorrect information. Most recent scholarship believes William Kidd was born in 1654 in Scotland, perhaps near Dundee. At some point before 1689, he most likely settled in New York. The first actual record of Kidd is in 1689 as a member of a privateer crew sailing the Caribbean, where he was made captain of a captured French ship and sailed to into port on Nevis Island. Kidd was appointed Captain and renamed his ship, the *Blessed William*. In December 1689, the *Blessed William* was part of the Royal Navy Squadron that attacked the French town at Marie Galante. Kidd's share was £2,000. Shortly afterwards, Kidd's crew refused to go out after French warships, thinking it too dangerous. Kidd was very angry with his men. While still in port at Nevis, his crew, led by Robert Culliford, stole the *Blessed William* along with Kidd's money. Kidd was given a sloop, the *Antigua*, to command and he returned to New York where he assisted the new governor, Colonel Henry Sloughter, in putting down a local rebellion. Kidd was now a well-respected member of the community. On May 16, 1691 he married Sarah Ort, daughter of a wealthy businessman, and settled down to a life of luxury. In 1692 a new governor was appointed—Colonel Benjamin Fletcher. Kidd and Fletcher became good friends. By April of 1694, William Kidd was a pillar in the community, but the ambitious Kidd wanted more. He undoubtedly met Thomas Tew at one of the many social events sponsored by the governor and tales of Tew's success may have contributed to Kidd's decision to return to sea as a privateer.

William Kidd began planning his own trip to the Indian Ocean after Thomas Tew left New York in November 1694. It took him over a year to arrange the support to get the financial backing he needed. Eventually, Kidd arrived in London with his partner, Robert Livingston who introduced

1689

Kidd and the Blessed William

1696

Captain William Kidd and the *Adventure Galley*

Galleys could pursue an enemy in light wind or even directly into the wind. The design of their hulls also made them fairly fast.

him to Richard Coote, the Earl of Bellomont. Together, they soon found other backers and were ready to present their plan to the King of England, William III. What they proposed was fairly simple and very beneficial to the crown. King William III agreed. Captain Kidd was given a brand-new warship, the *Adventure Galley* and a King's commission which the King signed on January 26, 1696. This commission basically instructed Kidd to do three things: sail to the Indian Ocean to protect the English India merchantmen returning to England, serve as a privateer and attack all French ships he encountered and seize their cargo, and search out and destroy all pirate vessels operating in the Indian Ocean. For this last part of the assignment, Kidd was instructed to arrest the pirates if possible and bring their stolen booty back to the crown. He even got the King to mention specific pirates in the commission by name, "full power and authority to apprehend, seize, and take into your custody as well the said Capt. Thomas Too, John Ireland, Capt. Thomas Wake and Capt. Wm. Maze or Mace, as all such pirates." (Note the spelling of his name in the original document, "Too.")

I find it most curious that Thomas Tew is listed in the commission. Tew was a friend of Governor Fletcher, who was also a friend of Kidd's. I find it even more curious that Tew's partner, Thomas Wake, was also listed. This is speculation on my part, but based upon Kidd's actions after sailing, I believe that William Kidd and Thomas Tew planned this operation together along with Kidd's original backer, Robert Livingston. Kidd needed financial backing, a ship, and a commission in order to get in on some of the loot coming out of India. A King's commission would be even better. So, I believe that Kidd and Tew and the other pirates sailed to the Indian Ocean and thus, created a serious threat to the English East India Company's India merchantman. Kidd and Livingston then convinced Earl Belmont and the King to finance the whole thing, guaranteeing safe passage for the India merchantman and a sizeable profit from recovered pirate booty and French cargos. Of course, Kidd had no way of knowing that Thomas Tew had been killed five months before while taking the Mughal's ship at the mouth of the Red Sea or that Henry Every was already on his way back to England with a fabulous treasure.

Captain William Kidd set sail in the *Adventure Galley*, a fast and highly maneuverable galley armed with 34 guns, on February 27, 1696. Kidd's galley had been built just months before and was ideal for this kind of mission. His first stop was New York to recruit more crew. On September 6, 1696 Kidd left New York and by February 1697 made port at the island of Mehila in the Comoros Islands, which are located between the east coast of African and the northwest tip of Madagascar in the Indian Ocean. By now, Kidd was in a very bad situation. Many of his crewmembers were dead from fever, his ship was in bad need of careening and general repairs, he was almost out of food, and he still hadn't taken a single prize. To make matters worse, his delay in New York looking for additional crew put him almost a year behind schedule. His crew, especially the ones he recruited from New York, began to continually talk of turning pirate, even if that meant mutiny.

Eventually, his galley was repaired and re-provisioned and by April 1697, William Kidd was waiting at the mouth of the Red Sea for a prize. For the next nine months, the *Adventure Galley*'s bad luck continued, only taking a few meager prizes. They kept only one vessel, a French prize named the *Rouparelle* which Kidd renamed the *November*. Then, in February 1698, Kidd hit the jackpot. The *Quedagh Merchant* was a 500-ton Armenian merchant ship laden with gold, jewels, silver, silks, sugar, and guns. The *Adventure Galley* overtook and seized the *Quedagh Merchant* and kept it. This included the cargo worth an estimated £400,000. The taking of the *Quedagh Merchant* was easy but justifying the prize to the King would prove to be far more difficult. The ship was owned by Indian merchants who were in partnership with the English East India Company.

Figure 16: *1690s Galley, Similar to the Adventure Galley*

1698

Captain Kidd takes *Quedagh Merchant*

Additionally, the ship was carrying a Persian cargo, crewed by Arabs, and commanded by an English Captain named Wright. None of these nations were listed in his commission. The only legal loophole Kidd had was that the ship was sailing under a French pass. After all, England and France were at war, weren't they? And Kidd had a privateer's commission to take French ships; didn't he? The problem for Kidd was that it wasn't a French ship; it only had a French pass. Another problem was that England and France had been at peace for a year, although Kidd didn't know it.

Kidd's three vessels, the *Adventure Galley*, the *Quedagh Merchant*, and the *November (Rouparelle)*, reached St. Mary's on April 1, 1698 to prepare for the voyage home. Upon arrival, he met his old shipmate, Robert Culliford, who stole his ship and his money back in 1689 when they were sailing the Caribbean out of Nevis Island. He was now the pirate captain of the frigate, *Mocha*. Later in Kidd's court testimony, he claimed that Culliford attacked his three ships and his crew deserted. Then, after a fierce personal battle between Kidd and Culliford, Kidd was subdued and the pirates ransacked his ships, taking the guns, small arms, and cables, and burned the ship, *November*. However, there is absolutely no mention of the enormous wealth that Kidd had taken. Culliford and Kidd remained on St. Mary's together for another six weeks, along with their ships and crewmen without any further incident. During that time, Kidd claimed the *Adventure Galley* sank in the harbor due to excessive leaking from the long voyage and he had to burn her. Kidd sailed the *Quedagh Merchant* to the Caribbean and returned to New York in a sloop.

There are many things about this story that just don't add up. How did Culliford manage to take Kidd's 34-gun *Adventure Galley* with his smaller vessel? Why was Kidd allowed to keep his loot? Why did they all seem to get along for six weeks afterwards? Why did Kidd allow his *Adventure Galley* to sink? Some modern scholars suggest a different version. Kidd's crew wanted to continue pirating in the rich waters of the Indian Ocean but Kidd needed to return to England and his backers, so he made port at the Baldridge's settlement on St. Mary's where his crew could join other ships and he could get a new crew who wanted to return home. Kidd had no hard feelings against his old shipmate, Culliford; in fact, he was delighted to see him. Many of Kidd's crew joined Culliford and Kidd actually sold him the *Adventure Galley*. Shortly before, Culliford's frigate, *Mocha*, had been severely damaged in a skirmish with the British ship *Dorrill* in the Malacca Straits and most likely would not be easily repaired. Both ships were badly in need of careening and maintenance which would have taken the six weeks they remained in port together.

At some point, Kidd buried part of his treasure somewhere in what he called the "Indies." This refers to one of the islands of the China Sea near modern-day Vietnam. Upon his return to England, Kidd would have to pay a percentage of the total loot to his backers and the King. But the backers wouldn't know about any loot that was buried prior to his return, so Kidd wouldn't have to share it. Kidd believed that he could simply return for it later. He left the Indian Ocean on November 15, 1698. About that same time, news of Kidd's piracy reached London and made front page headlines. Some members of Parliament used this to discredit Kidd's backers, which turned into an enormous political scandal. Kidd was an international criminal, guilty even before arrested. Stories of his fabulous wealth were told in every tavern and port throughout England, and all of the colonies. The Royal Navy was dispatched to arrest him. Meanwhile, Kidd sailed toward the Caribbean in the *Quedagh Merchant,* totally unaware of his predicament.

Kidd was shocked to learn of his situation when he arrived back in the Caribbean making port in Anguilla in April 1699. Confident that he could clear his name in court, Kidd sailed the *Quedagh Merchant* to Catalina Island, a tiny island off the south east coast of Hispaniola. He obtained sloop named the *Antonio* from one of his old buccaneer friends, Captain Boulton, and transferred most of the loot aboard. Kidd sailed back to New York in the sloop, leaving the *Quedagh Merchant* behind with a portion of the loot and a few of his crew to guard it. Of course, as soon as Captain Kidd sailed out of view, the crewmen took all the loot and scuttled the ship. The wreck was actually discovered 70 feet off shore in 2007.

Positive that his main backer, Bellomont, would help clear him, Kidd sailed to New York to visit his wife, Sara. While there, he buried part of the treasure around Long Island, Block Island, and Gardner's Island as insurance, then sailed to Boston to meet with Bellomont. While on this way to Boston, his old partner, Robert Livingston, double crossed Kidd and racing ahead of him and insisted that Kidd be arrested as a pirate carrying stolen loot. When Kidd arrived in Boston, he was shocked at his arrest. He was also shocked that his trusted partner, Bellomont, wasn't interested in hearing anything Kidd had to say. As a staunch supporter of the King, Bellomont wanted to protect the King's reputation as well as his own from this political scandal.

After his arrest in Boston, Kidd was sent to London and imprisoned at Newgate. Over the next several months, Kidd continually talked about the treasure that he buried in New York and the "Indies" which can only mean an island in the Indian Ocean. He tried to use this as a bargaining chip to obtain his release, but it didn't work. Bellomont was able to recover loot

1701

Captain Kidd was executed on mud flats of the Thames River.

buried on Garner's Island worth £20,000. Many of Kidd's crew were also arrested and most turned state's evidence against him. Kidd was found guilty and executed on May 23, 1701 on the mud flats of the Thames at Execution Dock along with Darby Mullins, the only one of Kidd's crew who remained loyal to him. Two of his crewmen, Churchill and Howe, were eventually released and returned to America where they uncovered their buried share of the treasure, valued at £1,500, and £700 respectively. Today, that would be worth ten times that amount. So what of the treasure buried in New York, the Indies, and possibly elsewhere? Many treasure maps have mysteriously turned up, but so far, no treasure has been recovered. I will discuss these maps later on in this book.

Between 1929 and 1934, four treasure maps were found and sold to a rich pirate enthusiast living in London named Palmer. Of the four maps, two may be authentic. The first three of these maps were found by the London antique dealer, Hill Carter and sold to Palmer.

According to one theory, the first authentic map was found by Carter in 1929 in a secret compartment of a small chest Carter purchased from a woman named Pamela Hardy. Apparently, the chest came into her family when the great grandson of Kidd's boatswain on the Adventure Galley sold the chest to Palmer's great grand uncle. Carter copied the map twice and hid the forgeries in an 18th century bureau and the Hardy chest which he sold to Palmer. Later on, Carter hid the genuine map in the false bottom of another small chest he got from a man named Dan Morgan who claimed to be a descendant of one of Captain Kidd's jailers at Newgate

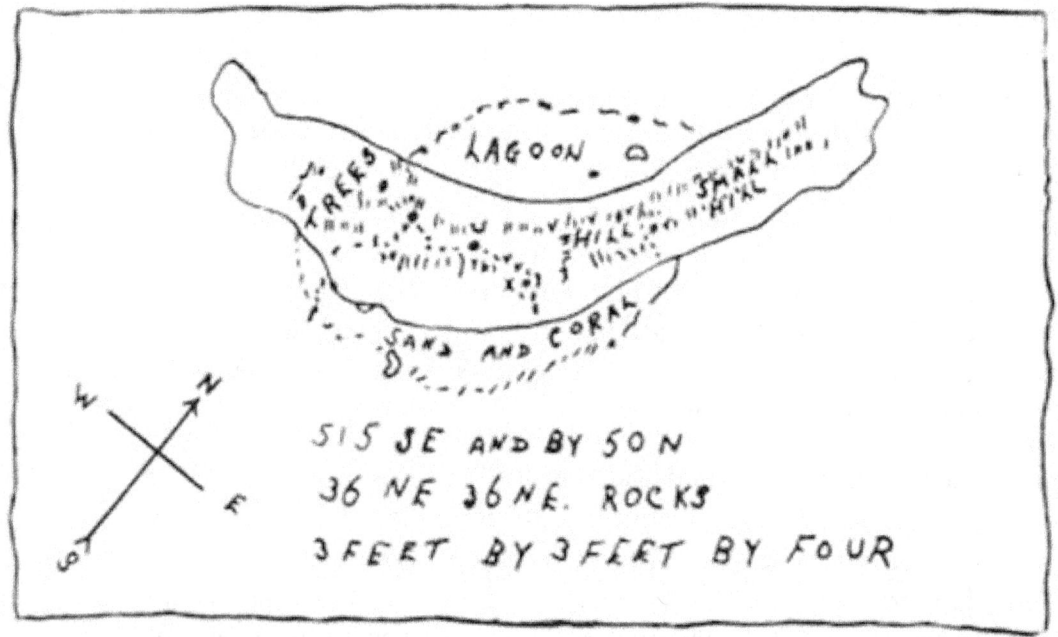

Figure 17: *Captain Kidd's First Map*

Prison who got the chest from Kidd. The second genuine map looks very much like the first. It was also found in the false bottom of a small chest with the inscription "𝔚𝔦𝔩𝔩𝔦𝔞𝔪 𝔞𝔫𝔡 𝔖𝔞𝔯𝔞𝔥 𝔎𝔦𝔡𝔡 ~ 𝔗𝔥𝔢𝔦𝔯 𝔅𝔬𝔵 ~ 1699." The box was also purchased by Palmer and has a traceable history back to a man who lived in America in the early 18th century. The maps were supposedly tested and found to be authentic, but the report and all other proof have disappeared. The maps went into private ownership after Palmer died and remain unavailable to examination or even viewing. Modern researchers believe that they have located the island indicated on the map, but it is within Vietnamese waters and is therefore not accessible.

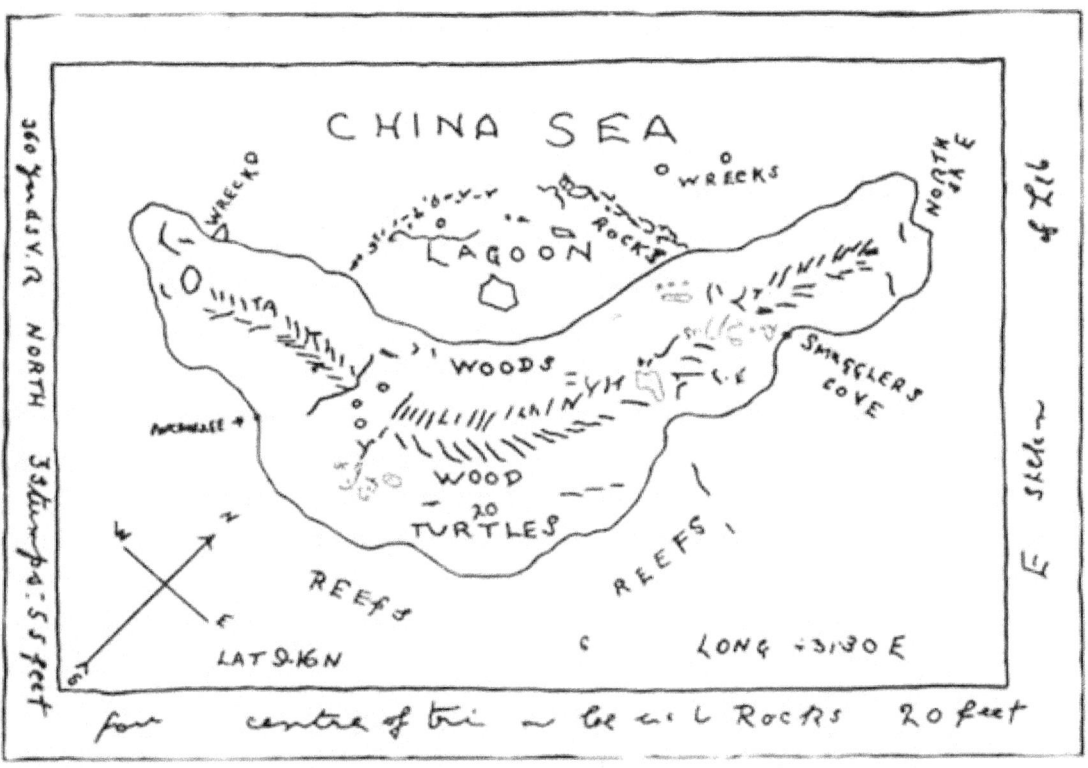

Figure 18: *Captain Kidd's Second Map*

Chapter 27
The Last Great Pirate of the Indian Ocean

After the success of Thomas Tew, Henry Every, and William Kidd, it was clear that the Indian Ocean was the place for a pirate to go. Well, success probably isn't the correct word as Tew was killed during an attack and Kidd was executed, but they were successful in taking prizes of enormous value and that's what counts. There was one problem. The real profits came from taking an East Indiamen, which was a very large and well-armed merchant ship belonging to any one of the East India companies operating at the time. That meant that the pirates would need big ships too, or at least a fleet strong enough to take down the wealthy ships. This eliminated the small-time pirate from the list of those who might be successful. Additionally, the pirate captains of the Indian Ocean had to be bold and aggressive.

George Booth was one of those pirates who was bold and aggressive enough to become a successful pirate captain. He actually had been coming to the Indian Ocean for quite some time as a crewmember and served as a gunner on the pirate ship *Pelican* in 1696 and as a gunner on the *Dolphin* in 1699. It was on the *Dolphin* that he got his break, although it didn't seem to be a break at the time. It was September 1699 and the *Dolphin* was tied up at the settlement on St. Mary's when a squadron of British Royal Naval vessels appeared. After the Captain Kidd incident, the English were anxious to stamp out piracy in the Indian Ocean and the settlement on St. Mary's seemed like a good place to start. Before they opened fire, the English kindly offered instant pardons for any pirates who wished to accept. Some did, but Booth and a few others didn't. They set fire to the *Dolphin* and escaped in stolen boats to nearby Madagascar. Booth and the others managed to capture a French merchant ship in port by pretending to be slave traders and came aboard to discuss business with ten of his crew. At some point, Booth gave the signal and his men overpowered the French crew and took the ship. Booth was naturally elected captain.

John Bowen was another of those bold and aggressive pirate captains. His story is somewhat different than Booth's. John Bowen was originally from Bermuda and was a ship's officer on an English merchant ship sailing from the Carolinas when he was captured and taken prisoner by French pirates. While on board, they took him across the Atlantic and rounded the Cape of Good Hope. But the French pirate ship ran aground near Elesa, which is slightly west of the southernmost tip of Madagascar. Bowen and a few others escaped and made their way to St. Augustin on the south western side of Madagascar. Eighteen months later, Bowen decided that becoming a pirate was the only way he was ever going to get home. He signed on with Captain Read's pirate crew as a sailing master. At some point along the way, John Bowen and George Booth met and Bowen decided to become a member of Booth's crew. They headed for the East Indies to hunt for prizes, but their first one would prove to be a bit unusual.

This account of George Booth's capture of the *Speaker* comes from a book entitled *The Pirates Own Book* published by Applewood Books in Bedford, Massachusetts in 1837. It appears to be accurate.

George Booth takes the *Speaker* off Madagascar.

"Returning to the waters on the west side of Madagascar, Booth spotted a smaller pirate vessel which was commanded by Captain White. They decided to join forces and begin to build a fleet. As they lay at anchor just off shore discussing the details of their new partnership, they spotted a very large man o'war approaching, or so they thought. It was the *Speaker* which had originally been built as a French ship of the line with 54 guns, but it had been captured by the English and reconfigured as a slave ship. Now it only had a few guns on board, but Booth and his crew didn't know that. The two pirate vessels made sail and approached the *Speaker*, not quite sure what to expect. The young and inexperienced captain of the *Speaker* fired a broadside which sent the two pirate ships into a panic. They were too near to shore to maneuver effectively and the wind was so light that steering was difficult. Captain White's vessel sailed into a mangrove swamp and a stump broke through the hull, sinking her in a short time. Booth's French ship also ran aground but onto a soft sandbar. The ship floated free when the tide came in. As for the *Speaker*, they sailed past shouting insults at the pirates and fired a few more times at the vessels and at the pirates ashore.

> The *Speaker* was in these waters to trade for slaves with the local tribal king. Firing at other ships and at the shoreline is the kind of thing that made the locals suspicious and reluctant to trade. So, when

the *Speaker* made anchor, they were met with a delegation from the local king asking them to leave. The *Speaker*'s captain apologized and said it was all a mistake. He said that they were just saluting the other vessels and his stupid gunner accidentally fired live shot. The apology was accepted and the captain sent his purser ashore with some trade goods to close the deal. As soon as the purser got ashore, one of Booth's men approached him and took him on board Booth's ship. Booth told the purser that they weren't pirates at all and that the captain of the *Speaker* had no right to shoot at them and would have to pay for damages. Eventually the purser was convinced and everyone met on shore. The local king threw a feast to celebrate the day's trading. Crews for all three vessels were there enjoying the oxen laden with rice and the local liquor called toke. This put the *Speaker*'s crew at ease."

A few days later, Captain Booth invited the *Speaker*'s captain to a barbecue dinner on shore and he accepted. At dinner, the captain didn't notice that Booth had left early. After dinner, John Bowen drew his pistols and told the *Speaker*'s captain that he was a prisoner. Meanwhile, Booth was leading a boarding party of 24 men over to take the *Speaker*. Most the crewmen were ashore enjoying the barbecue and Booth was easily able to take the ship without firing a shot or even spilling any blood. The *Speaker*'s crewmen were allowed to sail away on the old French ship and Captain Booth was now in command of a 54-gun warship. **Well, he actually didn't have the guns yet, but that was about to change.** At St. Augustine Bay, they met another pirate ship, the *Alexander,* commanded by Captain James. His ship had seen better days, so his crew joined Booth and came aboard the *Speaker*. They brought with them the guns Booth needed. He now had a 54-gun ship with a pirate crew of 240. Booth stopped at Zanzibar for supplies. He was going back to the East Indies and this time with the ship he wanted. It seemed that things were finally going well for George Booth. Zanzibar was currently under Arab administration and the principal export was slaves. Upon his arrival, the governor invited Booth and some of his men to dinner, but it was a deception. It is unknown if the governor knew they were pirates or just wanted to take their ship and goods. The Zanzibar officials were a pretty unscrupulous lot. Either way, as Booth and his men entered the governor's house, the doors closed and Booth and 14 of his men were killed. Arabs at the docks rushed the pirates who were waiting at the longboat. Some managed to escape back to their ship. John Bowen was elected as the new ships captain and his first order was to destroy the governor's house with gunfire from his ship.

As the new captain of the *Speaker*, John Bowen was initially successful. In the last half of 1701, Bowen took prizes in the Indian Ocean worth over £100,000. Bowen traded much of the captured good in local ports. Unfortunately, the *Speaker* ran aground late in 1701 near the Island of Mauritius, which is a fairly large island, a little over 100 miles east of Reunion Island and over 700 miles east of Madagascar. Building up again from scratch, Bowen was able to purchase a sloop named the *Content* and started all over again. In 1702 they took another sloop, the *Speedy Return*, and now had two vessels. Eventually, the *Content* became unfit to sail and was burned, with all crew coming aboard the *Speedy Return*. Bowen eventually came across a pirate ship of 36 guns, the *Prosperous*, commanded by Thomas Howard, who had been one of Bowden's crewmembers on the *Speaker*. In late December 1702, the two pirate captains joined forces. In August 1703 they took the East Indiaman, *Pembroke*, near the Comoros Island located halfway between the northern tip of Madagascar and Africa. Traveling north to the Red Sea, they took another large merchant ship named the *Defiant*. This was a 56-gun ship, the kind of ship pirates dreamed of taking. Both the *Speedy Return* and the *Prosperous* were abandoned and Captain John Bowden was now captain of the *Defiant* with a very large pirate crew. Now that Bowden had the perfect pirate ship, it's very strange that he disappeared from history. One account says that he died of some unidentified illness and is buried on Reunion Island and another account says that he simply retired with his loot and lived on Madagascar. In either event, his replacement on the *Defiant*, Nathaniel North, also fades into obscurity.

This was just about the end of the English pirates of the Indian Ocean. Their main support base of operations, Baldridge's pirate base on St. Mary's, had been destroyed by the English Royal Navy in 1699. A few pirates managed to remain in business for a year or two, but the large English pirate ships of the Indian Ocean were history.

Chapter 28
The Last Hurrah for the French Privateers

As the War of the Grand Alliance was coming to a close, it was the French privateers who seemed to control the waters of the Caribbean and even along the Atlantic coast of North America up to Virginia. England and Spain had reduced their use of privateers significantly, but France's encouragement of privateers continued in full force. In 1694 the French privateers, including De Graaf and Ducasse, raided Jamaica with minimal success. While Captain Kidd was sailing the Indian Ocean looking for a rich prize to take, the final French buccaneer raid of the War of the Grand Alliance occurred—the attack on Cartagena.

1697

The Treaty of Ryswick ended the war and firmly established French, Dutch, and English colonies in the Caribbean.

The long war had taken a terrible toll on France's resources and by 1696, France's treasury was exhausted. French Admiral Bernard Desjean, the Baron de Pointis, had been a key naval commander in the Caribbean throughout the war and he convinced King Louis XIV to authorize a daring raid on the richest Spanish city in the Spanish Main. A large fleet of seven regular French navy warships under command of Admiral Baron de Pointis arrived at Petit Goave in March 1697. He recruited three more buccaneer ships, and one month later his combined fleet of 10 ships with 1200 soldiers and 650 buccaneers attacked the wealthy Spanish city of Cartagena. The Spanish fortifications had deteriorated significantly over the years and the French easily overran the defenses and plundered the city. De Pointis divided the captured loot according to French naval regulations, where officers get a far greater share than sailors. This greatly angered the buccaneers. After de Pointis' fleet left, the buccaneers, who felt like they had been cheated, returned to Cartagena and sacked the city again. This time, their conduct and treatment of prisoners wasn't restricted by the regular French authorities, and torture and rape became the order of the day. The Treaty of Ryswick in 1697 formalized the end of the war and also the end of privateering—at least until the next war.

Pirates in Virginia

One doesn't normally think of pirates attacking ships along the Virginia coast and in the Chesapeake Bay, but there were actually numerous pirates in those waters. Virginia was one of the richest and largest tobacco producing colonies at the time with hundreds of plantations along all the rivers flowing into the Chesapeake Bay. Merchant ships from England were continually arriving, loaded with valuables that would be sold to the rich Virginia tobacco planters. As previously discussed, there was also the major seaport of Elizabeth City, located near the mouth of the James River. As mentioned earlier in this book, the city was renamed Hampton in 1706. This port had lots of taverns where sailors or pirates could go to relax. What made Virginia especially enticing was that narrow entrance to the Chesapeake Bay, less than 20 miles wide, between Cape Henry (present day Virginia Beach) and Cape Charles at the southern tip of the Eastern Shore. Once in the bay, the rivers leading from the bay right up to the plantations were very wide and deep, allowing large ships to easily navigate their waters. Pirates could choose between waiting near Cape Charles to ambush ships passing through between the capes or sailing into the bay and attacking plantations directly.

During the second Anglo/Dutch War in 1667, two Dutch privateers entered the James River and captured a Virginian tobacco fleet. Also, in July 1699, the *Providence Frigate,* a 26-gun English pirate ship under command of Captain John James, attacked a British flyboat named the *Maryland Merchant* off Cape Henry, Virginia. The *Essex Prize,* a Royal Navy patrol ship, just happened to be nearby and came to the rescue of the small merchant vessel. The *Providence Frigate* let loose a broadside that crippled the *Essex Prize*, then proceeded to capture and loot the *Maryland Merchant.* After the crew was finished, they defiantly came ashore in the Virginia port of Elizabeth City where they were seen walking the streets with gold chains about their necks. They even bragged about having taken treasure worth over several million pounds sterling and told the terrified citizens that they were former members of Captain Kidd's crew.

Next, it was the French buccaneer Captain Louis Guiattar's turn to raid the Chesapeake Bay. Commanding a ship of 20 guns named *La Paix* with a crew of 150 men, Guittar entered the bay on April 28, 1700. He boldly took five ships, burning two of them, setting one adrift, and keeping the other two as prizes. Afterwards, he anchored his three ships in Lynnhaven Bay, just north of the shoreline that is today known as Virginia Beach, Virginia, approximately where the Chesapeake Bay bridge tunnel is located.

A Royal Navy ship of 32 guns, the HMS *Shoreham,* under command of Captain William Passenger, sailed from the King Street docks in Elizabeth City, which was the headquarters of the Royal Navy in Virginia. It was 10:00 P.M. and Captain Passenger was preparing for a dawn attack when he sighted a rowboat pulling alongside. Much to his surprise, it was the Governor of Virginia, Francis Nicholson. He insisted on participating in the action. The *Shoreham* attacked the pirate fleet at 7:00 A.M. with the governor standing on the quarterdeck firing his pistols. They fought for over 10 hours in a classic naval battle with one broadside after another. At times the ships were only 20 or 30 yards apart. The *Shoreham* lost her main mast and the *La Paix* lost her rudder and ran aground. After the battle, it was determined that the *Shoreham* fired 1,671 shots and used 30 barrels of gunpowder. Of Guittar's 150 pirates, 26 were killed in the battle and 124 were taken prisoner. The English casualties were four killed and many wounded. Of the 124 pirates captured, 111 were taken to London for execution and the others were executed in Elizabeth City.

Chapter 29
Summing Up the Buccaneer Pirates 1670-1702

This era began exactly where the last era left off, with large buccaneer fleets sailing the Caribbean filled with ex-soldiers. But the privateer commissions soon became very restrictive and far less profitable. Many buccaneer privateers became buccaneer pirates while others became pirate hunters. Plantations were becoming more profitable and merchant ships more plentiful and the need for privateer merchandise and money began to diminish. The huge pirate ports of Tortuga, Port Royal, and Petit Goave began to fade away or even turn hostile toward the buccaneer pirates.

The constant wars in Europe added to the confusion; your friend on one venture is your enemy on the next. A stronger royal naval presence in the Caribbean made things worse for the privateers in conducting raids. It meant that there was far less opportunity for profits, as they would have to share a large portion of the prize with the naval commanders. Also, they had to follow orders from some royal admiral. The amphibious assaults that the buccaneers had been so famous for were now seldom done. And for the buccaneer pirates, the stepped-up naval protection for merchant fleets meant that prizes were harder to come by and even harder to take.

More and more, the buccaneers began to leave the troubled waters of the Caribbean. Some entered the vast Pacific and Indian Oceans and others tried their hand at taking prizes along the North American coast. For a short time, the waters of Madagascar became the center of pirate activity, but this too rapidly faded. The pirate port of St. Mary's had begun to decline after its founder, Adam Baldrige, was forced to flee. Then in 1699 warships from the English Royal Navy closed the pirate port for good.

Support for pirates still existed among the citizens and merchants all along the Atlantic coast of North America until the end of the 17th century. For local merchants, the need for goods and money far outweighed the way in which they obtained them. Corrupt government officials cavorted freely with pirates and sponsored their ventures. Pirates freely traded in the streets of ports like Charles Town, Marcus Hook, Newport, and New York. In many ports, there were very few laws to stop them. In Carolina, a 1699 pirate attack on the rice fleet out of Charles Town began to sway public opinion about pirates. The anti-piracy laws that had routinely been defeated by the Charles Town councilmen were finally passed in 1700. Soon, anti-piracy laws were being passed everywhere throughout English North America.

Just at the end of the 17th century, everything changed. Public opinion swayed against the pirates and the trial and execution of Captain Kidd sent strong repercussions through the continent. New laws were passed and government officials were replaced. The character of the men themselves began to change. Before, they were soldiers, adventurers, officers serving their King, and honest citizens looking to make a quick profit. Now, they were criminals operating outside the law. Many of them were recruited from captured merchant vessels, so they were seamen, not soldiers. Their appearance would have been a little more sailor-like. They still would have been armed to the teeth with every manner of weapon available, but the military uniform look was gone. Their clothing would have been a mix of practical nautical garments and fancy stolen landsman clothes. Many pirates like Dampier, remained loyal to their King and only attacked foreign prizes, but many others took whatever vessel they found. Pirates of this era dressed and conducted themselves a little more like the way in which pirates are portrayed in novels and movies. By 1700, to be a pirate meant that you were a criminal operating under a death sentence. The coming of the 18th century rapidly turned the tables on pirate operations. The pirates were all gone. Well, at least for a couple of years.

Chapter 30
The War Almost Nobody Knows About

Almost no one has heard about the War of the Spanish Succession. When was the last time you watched a movie or read a book that was set during The War of the Spanish Succession? There aren't even any documentaries about that war. The fact is that between 1702 and 1713, all of Europe was engaged in the first major war that encompassed almost the entire world. It all began with King Charles II of Spain. **Don't confuse him with King Charles II of England; they are two totally different kings.** King Charles II of Spain was the product of severe inbreeding. He was mentally deficient and incapable of reproducing. One look at his portrait makes you feel really sorry for his wife. As the Spanish court realized that King Charles II would never leave an heir, they began looking for a likely candidate. After much political debate, it basically came down to two individuals, Archduke Charles of Austria and Philip, Duke of Anjou.

The Archduke Charles was the son of Leopold I, ruler of the Holy Roman Empire which is modern-day Austria, Germany and much of Eastern Europe. His claim to the throne was through his father, Leopold I, who was the cousin of the Spanish king on the king's mother's side.

Philip, Duke of Anjou was the grandson of King Louis XIV of France, who was also the cousin of the Spanish king on the king's father's side. Eventually, the Spanish decided that Philip had a stronger claim and would become the next Spanish king when King Charles II died. And in November 1700, that's exactly what happened; Charles died and Philip was crowned as King Philip V of Spain. However, there had been a lot of territorial agreements, deals, and treaties that went along with the acceptance of Philip as the new Spanish king. One of those deals was that Austria would get back a great

1700

King Charles II of Spain dies without an heir which leads to the War of the Spanish Succession.

1702–1713

War of the Spanish Succession—England, Dutch Republic, Holy Roman Empire against Spain and France

amount of territory that had been taken by the Spanish over the past 200 years. This territory included parts of Italy and the Spanish Netherlands, modern-day Belgium. However, after he became king, Philip V decided to renege on the agreement and keep all the disputed territory for Spain. This greatly upset Leopold I of the Holy Roman Empire and his ally, England. Further negotiations broke down and in 1702, Archduke Charles claimed the title of King of Spain and war was declared with England, the Dutch Republic, and the Holy Roman Empire on one side and France and Spain on the other.

England was very involved in the process because much of the disputed territory was in the Netherlands, and King William III of England was also ruler of the Dutch Republic. King Louis XVI of France never officially recognized William & Mary as the rightful rulers of England. Louis still considered the former King James II as the rightful King of England and had given him sanctuary in France after he was deposed in 1688. To complicate the situation, James died in 1701 just before the start of the war. Upon his death, King Louis XIV of France formally recognized James's son, James Edward Stuart, as the rightful King of England. This greatly angered the English and compelled them to declare war against France. James Edward Stuart will forever be known as the "Old Pretender" to the throne of England. His attempts to gain the throne had a significant impact on English politics during the first half of the 18th century. As you shall see in the following section of this book, The Pyrates, it also had an enormous impact on the course of piracy after 1715.

Duke of Marlborough and Major Land Engagements

Certainly, the main effort during this war was in Europe, not the waters of America. The European countryside experienced huge armies marching through and destroying cities, crops, and villages. Most of the large-scale infantry campaigns centered in Italy, Spain, France, Germany, and the infamous Spanish Netherlands. For the English, the hero of the war was their general, the Duke of Marlborough, who won stunning victories in 1706 at the Battles of Ramillies and Turin, 1708 at the Battle of Oudenarde, and 1709 at the Battle of Malplaquet which was the bloodiest of the war. In 1711, Marlborough was replaced by the Duke of Ormond, who had been a rising star in the English military. By 1711, Ormond was appointed Colonel of the 1st Regiment of the Foot Guards, Commander in Chief of all British forces, and Captain General. Under his leadership, the British forces moved into the Netherlands and eventually took possession of Ghent and Burges.

The navies of all participants were heavily involved too. At sea, major naval engagements took place, but only at the first few years of the war. One of the first engagements occurred in the Caribbean. In early 1702, just before war was declared, the English sent a fleet of seven ships under the command of Admiral John Benbow to prevent the French from taking the Spanish treasure fleet that was about to sail from Cuba. At that time, no one was sure which side Spain would be on and England didn't want France to get the financial help the Spanish treasure fleet would offer. In August 1702, the French and English fleets battled it out with no clear victor. Admiral Benbow's leg was severely wounded by chain shot and he died later at Port Royal, Jamaica. Later in 1702, the French fleet was overwhelmed at the Battle of Vigo Bay, Spain and in 1704 a naval engagement of over 100 ships took place near Malaga, Spain. This wound up being a stalemate with the French/Spanish navies claiming victory but the Dutch/English navies gaining the strategic advantage. Large naval battles were too costly, and after 1704 battles at sea were limited to small engagement and the use of smaller privateer fleets.

The Admiral Benbow Inn in Robert Louis Stevenson's novel Treasure Island is named in his honor.

PART I.III
PIRATES AND PRIVATEERS OF THE WAR OF 1702–1713

> When close aboard each other, we gave her several broadsides . . . we shot a little ahead of them and played them so warmly, that she soon struck her colors.

Chapter 31
Woodes Rogers

For the pirates of the world, the opportunity to become a legal privateer had returned. Immediately at the start of the war, pardons for all pirates were offered on both sides and letters of marque against the enemy were issued to anyone with a ship and a crew. These privateers were generally sailors, not soldiers like the last century. Many were captains and officers on merchant ships who became privateers either out of patriotism or economic necessity. Others were simple sailors caught in a struggle for survival and still others were true pirates who took advantage of the situation. A few of these pirates continued to operate illegally and ignore their letters of marque by attacking friendly ships as well as enemy ships. Those who were caught were hung. The English government realized that privateers sailing the Pacific could possibly generate some much-needed revenue by taking Spanish prizes. During the war, 128 privateer commissions were issued by the English crown through the port of Bristol alone. For the next 12 years, it would have seemed like old times again except that there were no real professional privateers left. The experienced privateers of the 1680s were mostly retired or dead. The men who accepted privateer commissions were either merchants looking to recoup their losses or small-time pirates looking to improve their situation. The Spanish and French privateers generally sailed along with regular naval forces as part of their operations while the English privateers generally operated independently or in small groups of two of three ships. This was a far different kind of war than the one just ten years before. However, there were a few privateers that emerged who could stand up to the likes of the old buccaneers. Men like William Dampier and Woodes Rogers.

The remarkable accomplishments of William Dampier, buccaneer, pirate, navigator, naturalist, and bestselling author now seemed far more important to the war effort. His vast knowledge of the pacific and his experience as a buccaneer seemed ideal. Since publishing his book, Dampier had been

> 128 privateer commissions were issued by the English crown through the port of Bristol alone.

living well on the profits and giving lectures to a host of naturalists. Prior to the war, the English admiralty wanted to give him command of a ship and carry on the good work. Sure, he was a pirate, but that really didn't seem to bother the citizens of London or the admiralty. In 1699, he was given command of a ship with orders to explore Australia. His mission failed miserably due to his lack of leadership and he was court-martialed. After all, Dampier had never actually been a captain before. However, in 1703, with the war raging, he was again given a second chance and was named Captain of the *St. George*, a ship of 26 guns and a crew of 120 men. Dampier had orders to "Proceed in a warlike manner" against the enemy in the Pacific. Dampier was accompanied by the *Cinque-Ports* commanded by Captain Stradling. This was a galley of 16 guns and 63 men. After entering the Pacific, they sailed up the coast of South America and stopped at the old buccaneer base of Taboga Island to refit and repair their ships. This island had served as a buccaneer base in the Pacific for many years. Dampier was there 20 years earlier and the island was well known to him. While on Taboga, the two captains argued and split company, with Stradling sailing south. A short time later, Stradling got into an argument with one of his crewmen who insisted that their ship was unseaworthy. The crewman's name was Alexander Selkirk and the hot-tempered Captain Stradling decided to maroon him for insubordination. He was marooned on Juan Fernandez Island which is located 360 miles off the coast of Chile. Unfortunately for Captain Stradling, Selkirk was correct. A few months later, the *Cinque-Ports* sank and Stradling was caught by the Spanish and thrown in prison.

Taboga Island is a small island about 15 miles off the coast, south of Panama City.

After the separation, Dampier took several prizes and kept a small sloop which he renamed the *Dragon*. Soon after, the *Dragon* took a 40 Ton bark loaded with sugar, wine, and brandy, but it had become unseaworthy and was abandoned. In February 1705 Dampier's ship, the *St. George*, was severely crippled while trying to take a large Spanish Galleon. Dampier limped to Amapala Bay, just off the Pacific coast of modern Honduras. While repairing the ship, many of the crew mutinied and departed in a bark they had recently captured. Realizing that the *St. George* was too badly damaged to make the long voyage home, Dampier and his remaining crew captured another small bark and returned to England by sailing west across the Pacific Ocean and around Africa. They arrived back in England in 1707.

Even though Dampier's venture was unprofitable, his return attracted the attention of a few rich Bristol investors. The costly war had devastated the English economy, especially the shipping industry in Bristol. The French and Spanish had privateers too, and they were extremely successful in taking English ships in the Atlantic. In 1708, Dampier arranged for a group of merchants to finance two privateering ships under command of Woodes Rogers, a Bristol sea captain of good reputation. The ships were the *Duke*, a ship of 36 guns, and the *Duchess*, a ship of 26 guns. Dampier accompanied Rogers as the chief pilot. Although Rogers had never been a privateer, he was an experienced sea captain and a good leader with tremendous bravery. Rogers and Dampier planned to take one of the extremely wealthy Spanish Manila Galleons sailing from the Philippines to Acapulco. With the financial backing arranged, they received their commission from the Lord High Admiralty to wage war against the Spanish and French.

After rounding Cape Horn in January 1709, they stopped at Juan Fernandez Island to refit and re-provision. Upon arrival, they were surprised to find Alexander Selkirk alive and well. As you may recall, he had been marooned on Juan Fernandez Island by Captain Stradling four years earlier. Additionally, he had a companion, one of the Miskitos Indians who was left there by Captain Sharp in 1682. Selkirk was taken aboard and eventually returned to England aboard Rogers' ship. The remarkable story of Selkirk's marooning attracted the attention of the famous author and pirate enthusiast, Daniel Defoe. He fictionalized Selkirk's story in the immortal classic, *Robinson Crusoe* and the Moskito Indian became the character named Friday.

APRIL 1709

Woodes Rogers takes Guayaquil.

Over the next several months, they cruised the Chilean coast, taking a good number of Spanish and French prizes. Then, in April 1709 Rogers conducted the first privateer amphibious assault on a city in over ten years. It was the city of Guayaquil on the coast of Ecuador. Although later publicized in England as an enormous success, in reality the venture turned out to be a failure. Just as Rogers secured the city, there was an outbreak of yellow fever and Rogers was forced to leave before receiving the ransom he had demanded. By September 1709 Rogers had kept two prizes and increased his fleet to four vessels. But the prize Rogers really wanted was one of the Manila Galleons that sailed from the Philippines to Mexico each year, loaded with pearls and other fabulously wealthy cargo from the Orient.

The richest prize of the Spanish Pacific, taking any of the Manila Galleons would make the trip exceptionally profitable. Rogers knew that the only way to capture one was to wait in ambush close to Acapulco. Unfortunately for Rogers and his fleet, he waited there for several months in the baking sun with absolutely no ship in sight. Then, on December 22, 1709 just as he was about to give up and return a failure, one of his crew spotted a large ship on the horizon. It was the *La Encarnacion,* one of the two Manila Galleons they were waiting. After a running battle with frequent broadsides that lasted all night, the Spanish galleon struck her colors. Rogers later wrote:

> "But to our great and joyful surprise, about 9 a clock, the man at the mast head cried out he saw a sail. …We immediately hoisted our ensign and bore away after her. . . . it was the ship we so impatiently waited for . . . the Nostra Seniora do la Incarnacion Disenganio . . . I ordered a large kettle of chocolat to be made for the ship's company, having no liquor to give them. When close aboard each other, we gave her several broadsides . . . we shot a little ahead of them and played them so warmly, that she soon struck her colors."

Neither ship was severely damaged. The Spanish lost 25 men and the English only had one casualty, Rogers himself, who had part of his jaw shot off by a musket ball. The prize was worth 2,000,000 pieces of eight. Two days later, they faced the second and much larger Manila Galleon, the *Nuestra Senora de Begona*. She had 40 guns and 40 perriers (swivel guns). The second galleon was too well-armed to take and after a considerable battle, the attack was broken off with 34 English killed. Rogers kept the captured galleon and re-named it the *Batchelor*. After repairing and provisioning on San Lucas Bay on the Mexican coast, Rogers and his men sailed across the Pacific and returned to England in October 1711 with over £170,000 gross profits from his venture. Dampier later died in London in 1715. Rogers became the governor of the Bahamas in 1718 and launched one of the most successful anti-pirate campaigns of the early 18th century.

Chapter 32
Queen Anne's War

In America, the War for the Spanish Succession was called Queen Anne's War. Queen Anne was crowned in 1702, just as the war was getting under way. Her sister, Queen Mary II, had died back in 1694 and when King William III died in 1702 Anne became the ruler of England. Anne was the youngest daughter of old King James II. At the time of her crowning, there was a small push to put her half-brother James Edward Stuart on the throne as king, but he was Catholic and Anne wasn't. She was the one they chose. Queen Anne was well liked by the English people and was a very good ruler. Under her influence, the army and navy became modernized, making England among the most powerful nations of the 18th century. Queen Anne also passed the Union Act of 1707, officially joining England and Scotland as one nation. After 1707, the word "Britain" and "British" began to be used, rather than "England" or "English," and the empire became officially known as the British Empire.

To the colonists in America, the war was far off in Europe and the meaning, purpose, and political goals were unclear. As far as they were concerned, Queen Anne had declared war on the French and Spanish once again and that was that. In the colonies, the war was far more obscure than in Europe. In the northern waters, French privateers constantly threatened New England ports. In the south, privateer fleets occasionally attacked major ports.

In 1702, the very first year of the war, a small Spanish invasion fleet attacked Charles Town, Carolina and a few of the outlying settlements, but they were unable to do any significant damage. In retaliation, 500 militiamen and 300 supportive Indians attacked the Spanish city of St. Augustine, Florida. They were unable to take the main fortress, but they did manage to burn the city. Fighting in New England began in 1703 and mostly involved ground warfare between local English militia and French Canadians with

April 1702

Queen Anne crowned as Queen of England.

April 1707

Acts of Union officially brings Scotland and England together under one ruler.

Palmetto trees are native to the North American coastline along the Gulf Coast and up the Atlantic to North Carolina.

Native Americans like the Iroquois Confederacy siding with the English and the Abenakis and Caughnawagas fighting for the French.

In 1707, a large combined Spanish and French force from Havana attacked Charles Town again, but they were defeated. One interesting aspect of the city's defense was the protective walls made of palmetto logs which have wood that is fairly soft and fibrous. This was ideal for use as defensive walls because the attackers' cannon shot seemed to merely bounce off.

New York was among the first American colonies to get back into the privateering business. In the last decade, pirates sailing out of New York had been extremely profitable for the local merchants and they all saw an opportunity to make money. However, tolerance of piracy in the New England area came to an abrupt halt after the scandal with William Kidd in 1699. Now, just three years later, pirates had an opportunity to legally get back into the game and they jumped at the chance. In the first year of the war over 20 privateer vessels sailed from the harbor of New York. Among the most famous and successful privateer was the brave and daring Regnier Tongrelow and his New York galley. Over the next several years, he became a local hero to the people of New York. Tongrelow had a reputation for attacking much bigger ships and always coming out on top. He brought back much wealth to the merchants and his heroic accounts were even printed in the local press, the News Letter. Other successful privateers were Tom Penniston and Nat Burches, both associates of Tongrelow who often accompanied him. While ashore, the privateers frequented the taverns along the waterfront. There was one favorite in particular, a long roofed, low porched tavern owned by Benjamin Kierstede. As one would expect, the privateers soon became drunk and rowdy. Fights among the men often broke out, much to the dismay of the local citizens, but business was business, so their disreputable conduct was accepted.

April 1703

John Quelch begins his pirate career off Brazil.

Unlike the colonies of New York and Rhode Island, pirates never enjoyed the support of the local politicians in the colony of Massachusetts. But now, there was a war to win and Massachusetts began offering privateer commissions. One of the captains who sought a career as a privateer was Captain Daniel Plowman. In 1703, he obtained letters of marque from Governor Joseph Dudley of Massachusetts to attack French and Spanish ships. They left Marblehead, near Boston, in 1703 aboard his ship, the *Charles*. The only problem was that their captain, Daniel Plowman, had been locked in his cabin. While still in port, his crew decided it was more profitable to be pirates, so they quietly mutinied and elected John Quelch as their new captain. Once at sea, Plowman was killed and tossed overboard. They sailed south and took nine Portuguese ships off the coast of Brazil. The cargo's value was estimated at over £10,000 and consisted of large amounts of Brazilian sugar, weapons, hides, cloth, gold dust, and coins. Ten months later, they returned to Marblehead, but apparently, a few of the pirates had hidden some of their loot before arriving in port. Legend tells that Quelch's men hid their treasure on Star Island just off the New Hampshire coast. Over 100 years later, gold coins from that period were found hidden in a stone wall on the island.

When the crew of about 45 pirates landed in Marblehead, they scattered with their booty, but apparently they weren't too careful, spending their money and talking about their stolen cargo. Word of the pirates spread fast and within a week, ten members of the crew including Quelch were arrested. The others managed to disappear into obscurity. Prior to 1700 all pirates who were captured in any of the English colonies had to be taken to England to stand trial. It was a matter of jurisdiction. But at the dawn of the 18th century, newly passed English laws allowed local authorities in the colonies to try anyone suspected of piracy and to execute those who were found guilty. John Quelch and his crew would be the first. Of the ten pirates who were caught, three of them turned Queen's evidence and testified against their captain. Consequently, these three were released. A fourth pirate was released because he was only 13 years old. The other six, including Quelch, became the first pirates tried and executed in an English colony. They were hanged on Friday, June 30, 1704.

As was traditional with 18th century English law, those who committed crimes at sea had to be punished at sea. So, Quelch and his mates were executed at sea—well sort of. They were hanged below the high-water mark, on land that was exposed at low tide. That's the way it was for all pirate executions in the early 18th century. There were three basic choices. Pirates could be hung from a yardarm of a ship, hung on the docks above the water, like William Kidd, or hung on a portable gallows that could be wheeled out onto the soggy mud below the high water mark during low tide. They supposed that technically, the land exposed by "low tide" qualified as part of the sea.

By 1705 the coastline of New England had become infested by French privateers. Governor Dudley of Massachusetts and New Hampshire ordered a nightly patrol along the New Hampshire seashore from Hampton northward to Rendezvous Point. He also increased the militia and appointed a man named Lt. Colonel Hilton to impress men for this purpose. Several large forts had been constructed along the coastline and Lt. Colonel Hamilton needed men to fire the guns and defend against a possible French landing.

In the southern hemisphere, French privateers attacked Rio de Janeiro several times in 1710 and 1711. Brazil was a Portuguese colony and was allied with the English. In the Caribbean waters, a French naval expedition under command of Admiral Jacques Cassard raided British-held Montserrat and several Dutch colonial outposts, including St. Eustatius, Suriname, and Curacao in 1712.

One of the French privateer ships participating in naval operations in the Atlantic and Caribbean during the war seemed to be just another ordinary privateer vessel, but this ship, named *La Concorde*, was destined to become perhaps the most famous pirate ship of them all. The ship's known history begins with owner Rene Montaudoin. He sent his 300-ton vessel on a privateering mission under command of Captain Le Roux on July 21, 1710 from the Loire River, France. Le Roux first operated off the west coast of Africa and by February 1711, he had taken a few small Dutch prizes. La Concorde then sailed for Martinique for routine careening and repairs. *La Concorde* spent the spring and summer of 1711 capturing English costal vessels in the Caribbean waters. After the war was over, *La Concorde* was converted into a slave ship and routinely traveled between Africa and Martinique. It was on one of those trips in 1717 that La Concorde was taken by the famous pirate, Blackbeard and converted into a pirate ship named the Queen Anne's Revenge.

> Martinique is a French colony on an island in the eastern part of the Caribbean.

The British Royal Navy was also very active in the waters of Bermuda and the Caribbean during the war. Not with large naval operations as in European waters, but with English warships patrolling the waters taking enemy prizes and assisting friendly privateers. The captain of one such patrol ship was Captain George Cammock. He commanded HMS *Monck*, a fouth-rate ship of the line which mounted between 46 and 60 guns. In April 1712, Cammock took the French privateer, *Salamander*, which had 16 guns and 150 men. Captain George Cammock didn't know it at the time, but he was forging relationships with privateers who would become very prominent pirates just a few years later. As for the English privateers of the Caribbean, they were operating out of Port Royal, just as in the glory days of the past, but on a much smaller scale. Port Royal never really recovered after the 1692 earthquake and the forts and waterfront taverns were all but gone.

A few of these privateers went on to become famous pirates. Among them were Henry Jennings, Charles Vane, and the master of all English privateers of the day, Benjamin Hornigold. Very little is known about these men during Queen Anne's War, just that they were privateers, but much is known about them in the years to come.

Nassau is the name of the main city and port on the Island of New Providence, which in turn is in the island group called the Bahamas. In many references, you will read "New Providence" more often than the city of Nassau. Since Nassau was the only city on New Providence, they actually mean about the same thing and one must consider them interchangeable. The first European settlers in the Bahamas were English Puritans from Bermuda who settled on Eleuthera Island in 1648. Others soon arrived from Virginia and New England, but the colony struggled and many settlers returned in the 1650s. The remaining settlers founded communities on Harbor Island and Saint George's Cay, now called Spanish Wells, at the north end of on Eleuthera Island. There were about 20 families living in the Bahamas by 1670. New Providence was first settled in 1666 by a small group of farmers from Bermuda with almost 500 people living on the island by 1670. At that time administration of the island fell under the authority of the Proprietors of Carolina along with all the other islands in the Bahamas. Originally the settlement was just a series of small farms. However, Spanish ships coming through the Florida Straits kept wrecking on the tiny islands, so the Bahamians soon went into the salvage business. The Spanish objected and in 1684, burned the colonies on New Providence and Eleuthera Island. The English settlers slowly moved back in meager groups. In 1666 the town of Charles Town was founded and in 1695 the town was renamed Nassau in honor of the city in Holland where King William III was originally from.

Between 1690 and 1697 during the war with Spain and France, English privateers used Nassau as a base. It is perfectly located for all sorts of pirate action. Because of the favorable currents and wind, the only efficient way that ships could leave the Caribbean and sail to Europe was through the Florida Straits. That meant that every treasure ship, merchant ship, and every other sort of vessel would pass through a narrow channel with lots of tiny islands from which to lay in ambush. However, at that time, Nassau was nothing to brag about. It was just a place to stop and wait for French ships. In 1697 after the war was over, a small community of settlers began to arrive and some privateers remained on the island as pirates, but on a very small scale.

The Florida Straits is a strait located between the Florida including the Keys and the east coast and Cuba and the Bahama Islands and follows the Florida current to begin the Gulf Stream.

During Queen Anne's War, in 1703, a combined force aboard two frigates which was comprised of French privateers and Spanish soldiers invaded the small English colony of New Providence and totally overwhelmed the 250 English residents to capture the town. In the attack, over 100 citizens were killed and the 22 guns at the small fort were seized. They returned to Cuba a few days later with 13 captured vessels and about 100 prisoners, including the island's governor, Ellis Lightwood. The Proprietors of Carolina gave up on governing the Bahamas, as it was now almost

APRIL 1707

English privateers begin using Nassau as a base.

1713

Treaty of Utrecht ends the war—King Philip V remains king of Spain.

destroyed and not readily defendable against future attacks. The Spanish and French again invaded Nassau in 1706 and totally sacked the town leaving only 27 families living in small huts.

Things began to pick up for Nassau after 1707 when English privateers began arriving in large numbers. The war was at its height and Port Royal was too far away from the action. It was close to the main shipping lanes and the waters around the town were too shallow for large warships. By the war's end in 1713, an estimated 200 families of settlers and 1,000 privateers called Nassau their home. This doesn't compare to Tortuga or Port Royal of the 1660s, but for 1713 it was the biggest privateer port in the Caribbean. In just a few years, however, it would get a lot bigger.

The War for the Spanish Succession (Queen Anne's War) ended in 1713 with the signing of the Treaty of Utrecht. King Philip V kept the Spanish crown, most of the territory went back to pre-war status, and the English were permitted to sell up to 500 tons of merchandise to merchants in Spanish ports in the Caribbean. This limit was ignored however, and Vera Cruz and Portobelo became a monopoly for English trade. But what was more important was that the economies of all the major European powers were disasters. The war had drained everyone's resources. At the same time, it had produced a large number of privateers who were now out of business. For the first time in 12 years, there was no war and consequently no letters of marque to be had. For many of them, privateering was the only life they knew. Many of them counted on another war breaking out soon where they could return to legal privateering. For the professional privateer of the time, piracy was a way to make a living and stay in practice between wars. The only trick was to not get caught. Actually, there was another trick. Where could the pirates make port? Pirates needed to put in somewhere to sell their booty and to spend their money on the things pirates like to spend their money on, mostly strong drink and loose women. Nassau seemed to be the answer to their problem. Technically, no government claimed jurisdiction over the island since the Proprietors of Carolina relinquished control in 1707. With no official government and ideally situated for taking prizes, pirates flocked to the port of Nassau. However, in 1714, Nassau was still a fairly small operation. There were only a few small taverns and even fewer women. That was about to change.

Chapter 33
Summing Up Pirates and Privateers of the War of 1702-1713

This period marked a significant swing in public opinion toward pirates and privateers. At the beginning of the 18th century, there were no privateers. Most nations saw the need for the establishment of large professional standing navies and the use of privateers was diminishing. As for pirates, the Captain Kidd incident had dramatically turned public opinion away from any acceptance of pirates, at least for the most part. However, when the war started, the need for privateers returned. But it was far different than before. Privateers were far more controlled. They either served alongside the regular navy, operated under very restrictive orders, or operated on a very small scale. The Henry Morgan type of independent buccaneer who did what he wanted and struck with large-scale operations was almost extinct. Also, a clear separation between privateer and pirate was established. It was far more difficult to slip between one or the other. During this period, you were simply one or the other.

The anti-piracy trend that had begun in 1700 continued and intensified and by the war's end, local laws were toughened and piracy was no longer tolerated by local merchants in most of the major ports. Pirates were now looked upon as unpatriotic criminals. Privateers were still welcome in most of the ports, but they didn't receive the "hero like" fervor from the local merchants that they had enjoyed in the 17th century. Their celebrating and carousing was now viewed as poor behavior. New York and a few other ports welcomed privateers but restricted them to a few streets where their celebrating was controlled. Pirate havens like Tortuga had completely vanished. Nassau was still hanging on a bit in 1713, but on a very small scale.

The dress and physical appearance of these privateers or pirates would have been a bit more subdued than in the last century. Privateers were working for the king under stricter regulations than in the past century. Everything they looted had to be turned over to their backers and the crown at the end of the voyage and a share would be paid to each crewman according to law. They weren't as free to keep the personal goods they looted, such as clothing and finery, as did the crews of Captain Morgan. For those who were true pirates, they tended to remain very much in the background. They would try to fit in with everyone else and secretly sell their stolen goods. There are no famous pirates from this era. In fact, one hears very little about pirates from 1700 to 1715.

Another curious transition had been occurring over this period. In the days of Henry Morgan, whether they were privateers, buccaneers, or pirates, most of the members of the crew were not sailors, they were ex-soldiers, shop keepers, or anything else. Ships of the 17th century only kept enough sailors on board to work the vessel. Port Royal, Tortuga, and many other ports served as recruiting centers where anyone seeking a fortune could sign on as a privateer. By the 18th century things were very different. Privateer and pirate crews were almost entirely comprised of men of the sea. Perhaps this was due to the limitation of pirate-friendly ports where soldiers and landsmen could join crews. Crewmembers could only be recruited at sea, resulting in a crew of all sailors. With the close of the War for the Spanish Succession, there were no governments issuing letters of marque and many privateers turned to piracy. The stage was set perfectly for the last era of the golden age, "The Pyrates."

Chapter 34
The Book that Altered History

It's ironic how historians can be so discriminating when it comes to recent theories and research, but place 100% confidence and trust in the accuracy of one document written hundreds of years ago. That seems to be the case with most authors and researchers of pirate histories. What is the document of which I speak? It's the celebrated "General History of Pyrates" written by Captain Charles Johnson and first published in 1724. For almost 300 years most historians, authors, researchers, teachers, lecturers, and greeting card writers have relied almost completely on this one source. And why not? After all, it was a contemporary book, written by someone who claimed to have firsthand knowledge of each and every pyrate he wrote about. Let's examine this book a little closer to see how reliable it actually is.

Before we continue, I must explain the use of the letter 'Y' when spelling of the word 'pyrate.' Throughout this entire section of the book, I have chosen this spelling because that's how the word was spelled in the hundreds of English publications of the time as well as in Charles Johnson's book. In a small way, this spelling pays tribute to the authors of the time period.

England had become obsessed with pyrates in the early years of the 18th century, especially in Europe. There were lots of best sellers about pyrates, thousands of news articles about pyrate crimes and arrests, and even a great number of plays written and produced about pyrates. It's sort of like the "gangster craze" of the 1920s and 30s or the "cowboy craze" in the 1960s. No wonder Charles Johnson wanted to write a book about pyrates. Nothing is known about the real identity of Captain Johnsonfor certain. Some modern researchers believe he was actually the celebrated author, Daniel Defoe, who was fascinated with pyrates and authored several fictional books on the subject, the most famous being his novel, Robinson Crusoe, published in 1719. But it is far more likely that Johnson was actually Nathaniel Mist, the writer and publisher of the London tabloid, *Weekly Journal*. Mist was a former sailor and was also fascinated with pyrates. He printed over 100 stories about pyrates in his tabloid between 1717 and 1724 and ran the first promotional advertisement for the book on May 9, 1724, a week before the book came out. Additionally, the book was registered under Nathaniel Mist's name with "His Majesty's Stationers" Company on June 24, 1724

Unfortunately, many historians over the past 290 years have hailed this work as the absolute and definitive last word on the subject. Most books written between 1800 and the late 20th century do little to challenge the writings of Johnson. His historical details and events have been repeated so many times that they have achieved the status of fact. However, a few modern historians have now begun to question the accuracy of book. Many of the facts don't hold up under the simplest of examinations. What many historians didn't consider was that Johnson wasn't writing a work of historical significance, he was writing a best-seller.

The first edition titled A *General History of the Robberies and Murders of the Most Notorious Pyrates* was published in May 14, 1724. It did well, but not quite well enough. A few months later a second edition was released. Most of the content remained the same, it was just reordered a little bit. This new version was titled *A General History of the Pyrates: From Their First Rise and Settlement in the Island of Providence, To the Present Time, With the Remarkable Actions and Adventures of the Two Female Pyrates Mary Read and Anne Bonny*. That's quite a title. Notice how the lady pyrates are now in bold print right on the cover page. That did the trick. This second edition, still in print today, is filled with lots of gory stories of torture, rape, murder, amazing adventures, just about everything the public wanted to read about these scoundrels of the sea. Many of these accounts were total fabrications.

The strongest example of how one of these fabrications not only achieved the status of fact but was further embellished by modern historians is the account of the marriage habits of Blackbeard. The first edition doesn't mention anything about Blackbeard's love affairs, but the second edition has him married 14 times with, "about a dozen might be still living." Johnson continues with details of his 14th wife, just 16 years old and married to Blackbeard by none other than the Governor of North Carolina himself. But it gets even better. "After he had lain all night, it was his custom to invite five or six of his brutal companions to come ashore and he would force her to prostitute herself to them all, one after another, before his

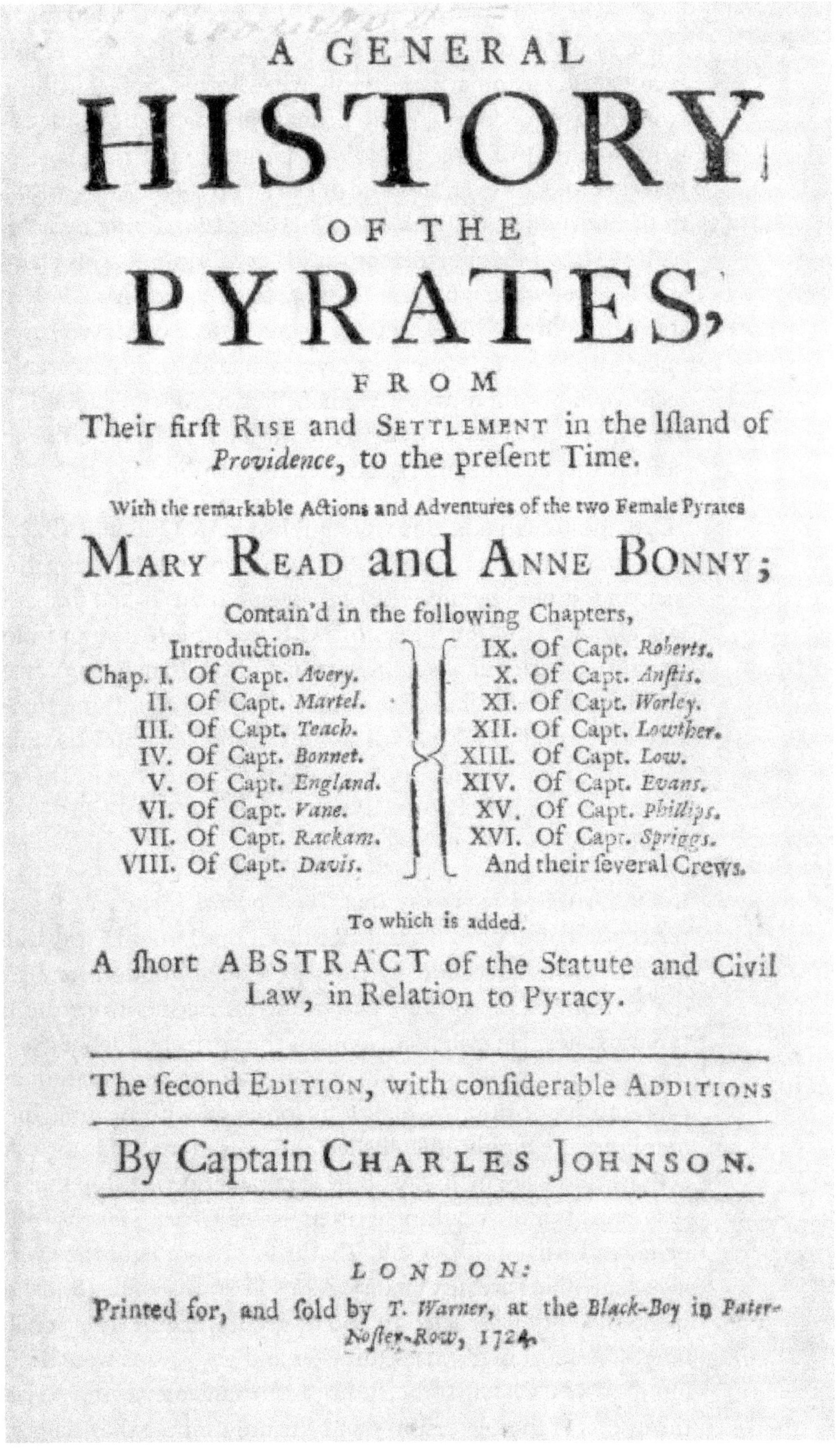

A GENERAL
HISTORY
OF THE
PYRATES,
FROM

Their first RISE and SETTLEMENT in the Island of *Providence*, to the present Time.

With the remarkable Actions and Adventures of the two Female Pyrates

MARY READ and ANNE BONNY;

Contain'd in the following Chapters,

Introduction.
Chap. I. Of Capt. *Avery*.
II. Of Capt. *Martel*.
III. Of Capt. *Teach*.
IV. Of Capt. *Bonnet*.
V. Of Capt. *England*.
VI. Of Capt. *Vane*.
VII. Of Capt. *Rackam*.
VIII. Of Capt. *Davis*.
IX. Of Capt. *Roberts*.
X. Of Capt. *Anstis*.
XI. Of Capt. *Worley*.
XII. Of Capt. *Lowther*.
XIII. Of Capt. *Low*.
XIV. Of Capt. *Evans*.
XV. Of Capt. *Phillips*.
XVI. Of Capt. *Spriggs*.
And their several Crews.

To which is added.

A short ABSTRACT of the Statute and Civil Law, in Relation to Pyracy.

The second EDITION, with considerable ADDITIONS

By Captain CHARLES JOHNSON.

LONDON:
Printed for, and sold by *T. Warner*, at the *Black-Boy* in *Pater-Noster-Row*, 1724.

Figure 19: *General History of Pyrates Title Page, 1724*

face." Wow, that's pretty racy stuff. The problem is that it never happened. There is no record or account that Blackbeard was ever married much less that he customarily gave his wives to his crew. Furthermore, all the North Carolina court records from that time period still exist and there is no mention of Governor Eden performing a marriage ceremony for Blackbeard. However, this tale doesn't stop there. Author Robert Lee adds to the story in his 1974 book, *Blackbeard the Pirate* by actually giving a name to this 14th wife, the name of Mary Ormond. This claim is based on a 1947 letter written by Ada S. Bragg to a relative, Mrs. E. P. White, which states that Mrs. White is the great-great niece of Mary Ormond who was married to Edward Teach, known as Blackbeard. A search of the actual records shows there was a woman named Mary Ormond, but she lived long after Blackbeard's death. Today, many websites and even historians portray this fictional marriage to Mary Ormond as fact.

Third and fourth editions were published in 1725 and 1728, respectively. This fourth edition included a second volume covering the exploits of many additional pyrates who had been left out of the first editions. There was also a 1725 Dutch version with even more sex and bloodshed and far more tantalizing visual depictions of the female pyrates. After all, the Dutch publishers allowed far more of that sort of thing than the conservative British. Just take a look at the difference in how the English portray Mary Read and Anne Bonny as opposed to the Dutch. These illustrations can be seen in the chapter "Pirate Appearance in Prints" toward the end of this book.

In all fairness, I won't say that *The General History of Pyrates* is a complete work of fiction. Charles Johnson, or Daniel Defoe, did a moderate amount of research, mostly from published London newspaper articles, books from other authors, and a few transcripts from the trials of captured pyrates. He also read some of the correspondences sent to London from governors and other officials. But all this information still left many gaps and suppositions which Johnson filled with his imagination. Added to this are the highly embellished and sensationalized stories of the deeds, actions, and even dialogue of these pyrates aboard ship that crept into the second edition. Everything written in *The General History of Pyrates* must be taken with a grain of salt. That is to say, some of the events are actual facts and others are just fantasy. As a sole source of historical research, this work must not be trusted in and of itself. Imagine if our civilizations suffered some sort of immense disaster and all records were destroyed. Three hundred years later, some future historians are trying to piece together the events of the 21st century and the only source they have is a work that blends fact and fiction.

Unlike the scenario above, we are fortunate enough to be able to check many of Johnson's events against source documents and records that still exist. As you read other modern books on pirates, you will come across many discrepancies or things that just don't make sense. In many cases, these things can be traced directly back to *The General History of Pyrates.*

We also have the ability to interpret the motivations and relationships among these pyrates in light of the political events of the day. In 1724, no author would dare to delve into a political discussion that disagreed with the official government position and suggest a political motivation for piracy. For the 18th century British government, pyrates were simply criminals and that's that. Suggesting political alternatives in print was the sort of thing that got you arrested. This restriction on discussing politics in print was one of the things that sparked the American Revolution in 1776. Now that I have shed some light on the accounts and events described by Charles Johnson in his book, we are free to examine the facts a little closer and even look at some of the possible political motivations and reasons for becoming a pyrate in the first place.

PART I.IV
THE PYRATES 1714-1722

> " Damnation, to you then, you cowardly puppies. We will give no quarter, nor take none. Mr. Morton, prepare your guns and fire when ready. Give them a taste of our hospitality. "

Chapter 35
The Pyrates are Back

The reasons that many privateers turned to piracy may be far more complex than previously suggested by Johnson and many other authors. To set the scene, the War of the Spanish Succession had been over for a year. No major nations were issuing letters of marque and the privateers were out of business. They had to become pyrates or go into some other enterprise. Many of them may have turned to piracy just to keep their ships and crews intact in hopes that another war would start soon and they could become privateers again. But that doesn't explain why we see far more honest seamen turning to piracy than ever before. If we don't include privateers, the number of true pyrates during this period far exceeds the number of true pyrates in any other period. A good question is why? What happened in 1715 to propel these men and women into piracy? The answer comes in two parts because two major events occurred that would hurl the seas into a whole new era of piracy.

The first of these major events was the civil war in England over the crowning of George Ludwig as King George I of England in 1714. In order to fully understand the impact of this event, I must once again go over the royal family of the House of Stuarts. Scotland had been ruled by the Stuarts for hundreds of years. When Queen Elizabeth Tudor died in 1603 without an heir, James VI of Scotland inherited the English throne and became James I of England. He was Elizabeth's cousin and a direct decedent of King Henry VII. But James also retained the throne of Scotland as did his decedents. In 1685, his grandson became King James II of England and King James VII of Scotland simultaneously. However, the English Parliament deposed James in 1688 primarily because he had converted to Catholicism. William and Mary then became King and Queen of England, Scotland, and Ireland. They were selected because William was James' nephew and Mary was his daughter. But as far as the people of Scotland and Ireland were concerned, James was still their king, even though he

1714

Queen Anne dies without heir—George Ludwig is crowned King George I of England.

was deposed in England. They argued that the English had no right to remove James from their throne, so they revolted. This revolt was known as the "Jacobite Rebellion" because Jacob is Latin for James. Everyone who supported James in this revolution was called a "Jacobite." The revolt was eventually put down and James fled to France with his infant son, James Edward Stuart, who became known as "The Pretender" and sometimes "The Pretender across the sea."

James II was living in exile when he died in 1701 and his 13-year-old son, James the Pretender, became a legitimate heir to the English and Scottish thrones in the eyes of his supporters. They hoped that when King William III died, the young James would become king. But young James was a Catholic like his father, so in 1701, just before King William III died, the English Parliament passed The Act of Settlement, which forbids a Catholic from becoming king of England. So, when King William III died in 1702 Anne Stuart was chosen to rule instead. Anne was a good choice because she was the second daughter of James II and the older half-sister of James the Pretender. Additionally, she was a member of the Church of England and not a Catholic. The English people accepted her as did the people of Scotland. During her reign, the Union Act was passed, officially joining England and Scotland as one nation. That's when they stopped calling the two nations England and Scotland and began calling them Great Britain. When you included Ireland and all the English colonies, it was called The British Empire. However, when Queen Anne died in August of 1714 with no living children, the stage was set for civil war.

James the Pretender was still living in France. In fact, he hadn't lived in England since he was an infant. Since English law forbade a Catholic from becoming king, a search went out for the next King of England. Because of the Union Act, the English didn't feel it necessary to consult the Scottish government, who also had a significant interest in who their king would be. The English decided upon George Ludwig, ruler of Hanover in what is now modern Germany. George was the great grandson of King James I of England through James' daughter Elizabeth. It was quite a stretch, but he was the only suitable heir that Parliament could find. He had never been to England and didn't even speak English, but now, George I was the King of Great Britain. King George I immediately instituted extensive policy changes that excluded all members of the Tory party from royal favor. Many successful and important military leaders and statesmen, like the Duke of Ormond, found themselves out of a job. This sent shock waves through the government as well as the military and created a division among party lines. Many royal officials and military leaders felt that James Edward Stuart was the right choice to sit on the throne, even if he was a Catholic. Others, who had originally supported George, began to have second thoughts. Some pretended to remain loyal while they secretly supported the Jacobite cause, while others actively joined the rebel forces gathering in Scotland and Ireland. Some of those high-ranking officials and military and naval leaders actually left England and joined the Spanish or French forces. This list included the Duke of Ormond, Captain General of the British Army, and Admiral George Cammock of the British Royal Navy.

By 1715, Scotland and Ireland were in revolt and a civil war raged. This was called the second Jacobite Revolution, and was an extremely important event that significantly influenced the motivations of many English pyrates from 1715 to the early 1720s. This event provided a highly charged political reason for men to turn to piracy as well as the usual reason, enormous wealth. A few political leaders actually saw piracy as a lucrative means to raise funds for the revolt. Others loyal to James decided to join the fight against the forces of King George I in any way they could. For the privateers of the last war who now sided with James the Pretender, piracy was the natural course of action. It may explain why some very respectable citizens suddenly became pyrates. Keep all this in mind when we enter the world of Edward Teach, Stede Bonnet, Charles Vane, Edward England, Howell Davis, and a few others.

1715

Jacobite revolution in Scotland and Ireland

The second major event occurred in 1715. This was the sinking of an enormous Spanish treasure fleet just off the coast of Florida. Since the mid-1500s, all the gold and silver that was mined in Peru, Bolivia, and Ecuador was taken to Panama and all the treasure from the Spanish possessions in the Pacific was brought to Acapulco by a dozen or so Manila Galleons each year. All this treasure was then transported across the Isthmus of Panama by mule caravan to either Portobelo, Cartagena, or Veracruz.

Additionally, the gold from Mexico along with cocoa and other valuable products were also taken by mule to Veracruz. Periodically, all of this tremendous wealth was loaded onto ships at Portobelo, Cartagena, and Veracruz and taken to Havana, Cuba, where officials would carefully record the exact amounts and box the treasure for shipment back to Spain. When all this bureaucracy was complete, the treasure would be loaded onto a fleet of large ships called the "treasure fleet." Once a year, this Spanish treasure fleet would sail from Cuba to Spain, timed precisely to miss the hurricane season. However, the War for the Spanish Succession changed all that. In 1702, just as the war was beginning, the English fleet attacked Vero Bay, Spain, as the treasure fleet was arriving. Many ships were sunk and captured. Then in 1708, the English attacked Cartagena and sunk part of that year's treasure fleet. These events forced Spain to stop all shipments until the war was over.

The long war took a terrible toll on the financial resources of the Spanish Empire, especially since their regular treasure shipments had been postponed. The end of the war began to wind down in 1713 and hostilities stopped a full year before the Treaty of Utrecht officially ended the war in 1714. This left the Caribbean filled with ex-privateers turned pyrate, so the Spanish decided to hold their fleet in port for a while longer. But the gold, silver, and other riches continued to arrive in Cuba on schedule. After years of waiting, the amount of treasure in the Havana warehouses was enormous. In addition to gold and silver, there were large amounts of porcelain, ivory, and silk from the Philippines, as well as an impressive assortment of pearls, emeralds, and other jewels. Spain was now in desperate need of funds, so the decision to send the treasure fleet was made, regardless of the risk. The job of command went to General Don Antonio de Echevers.

Normally, the fleet would sail from Havana in March, long before the hurricane season; however, this year was different. Delay after delay caused the fleet to sail well into the middle of the summer. First, the mule trains that brought the treasure over the Isthmus of Panama were slower than usual, causing the initial sailing date to be pushed back to April 11, 1715. The next delay was caused when a sudden storm hit Veracruz on March 28, 1715 damaging the ships that were about to sail for Havana. It took over five weeks to make repairs. This included the only French ship in the fleet, the *Griffon*. She was a 70-gun a French warship that had been sent to Veracruz to bring back 48,801 pieces of eight that the Spanish owed the French government for the loan of two warships in the recent war. The captain, Antoine d'Aire, wanted to leave much earlier but the Spanish governor ordered him to travel with the Spanish treasure fleet for safety. This greatly angered d'Aire and he made a formal protest, but the Spanish ignored his plea. Once all the ships were assembled at Havana, the treasure had to be recorded and boxed which pushed the departure date back even further. All this greatly annoyed General Don Antonio de Echevers but there was nothing he could do. With the King of Spain demanding his treasure, the fleet would have to sail late, well into the hurricane season.

By the end of July 1715, the treasure fleet was finally ready to sail with General Don Antonio de Echevers in command. Second in command was Captain General Don Juan Esteban de Ubilla. Eleven of the heavily laden ships were Spanish, including the flagship. They included the *Capitana*, the *Almiranta*, the *Nuestra Senora de la Conception*, the *San Miguel*, the *El Ciervo*, and six other ships. With the French ship *Griffon* reluctantly tagging along; the total number of ships in the fleet was twelve. The wealth was enormous. The *Capitana* alone carried 1,300 chests of coins plus gold bard, jewels, pearls, and porcelain china. The official estimation of the entire treasure carried on the fleet totaled over 15,000,000 pieces of eight. This, of course, was only the official count. In addition to the officers and crew, the treasure fleet was carrying hundreds of passengers back to Spain, many of whom were exceptionally wealthy. There is no way of knowing how much wealth was brought on board as personal property of these passengers. Also, there is no way of telling how much contraband jewels and pearls were being smuggled aboard the treasure fleet by officials not wanting to share a percentage of the value with the crown. On July 24, 1715 the Spanish treasure fleet left Havana.

The Spanish ships were less maneuverable than the French warship, *Griffon*, which was originally an English ship named the *Hampton Court* before the French captured her during the war. Captain d'Aire was anxious to get home and annoyed with the slower Spanish ships, so he ordered the *Griffon* to pull away and sailed through the straits well ahead of the rest of the fleet. Then, at 4 A.M. on July 31, 1715 the 11 Spanish ships were hit by a tremendous hurricane. Confined in the Florida straits with no room to maneuver, the ships were dashed about by fierce waves and blown westward to the shallow banks. Only the French ship, *Griffon*, escaped because she was so far ahead that the hurricane completely missed her and arrived safely in France unaware of the fate of the rest of the fleet. As for the 11 Spanish treasure ships, the hurricane drove every one of them onto the shallow Florida banks and destroyed them all.

July 1715

Spanish treasure fleet sinks off the Florida coast.

The ships went down along a 100-mile stretch that ranged from Fort Lauderdale on the southern end to the San Sebastian Inlet, about 16 miles north of Vero Beach at the northern end. Over 700 sailors and passengers died in the storm but many survived and made it to shore where they set up a large survivors' camp on a barrier island just south of what is now the San Sebastian Inlet. Apparently, much of the treasure was carried on the lead ships that sank at the northern end of long line of ships, so as soon as the survivors were rescued, a salvage camp arose on the same spot and a major salvage operation began to recover the sunken treasure. Since all the ships sank in relatively shallow water, much of the treasure could be recovered by divers, so the Spanish hired South American pearl divers to work the sites. Soon, huge amounts of recovered treasure began accumulating at the salvage camp, under guard of only 60 Spanish soldiers.

News of the sinking of the Spanish treasure fleet spread rapidly throughout the Caribbean and the entire eastern seaboard. Hundreds of opportunists began planning ways to loot the Spanish shipwrecks. Even English government officials were supporting and encouraging the looting of the Spanish wrecks. Governor Spotswood of Virginia wrote a letter to King George I of Great Britain saying, "There is advice of considerable events in

1711–1716

Lord Archibald Hamilton, born in Scotland, was a Naval Captain in the last war and Governor of Jamaica.

these parts that a Spanish Plate Fleet, richly laden, consisting of eleven sail ... are cast away in the Gulf of Florida ... I think it is my duty to inform his Majesty of this accident which may be improved to the advantage of his Majesty's subjects by encouraging them to attempt the recovery of some of the immense wealth."

This sparked an international race to the Florida coast by everyone who could sail a ship or row a boat. But for most, they arrived too late. A former privateer by the name of Henry Jennings beat them all. Acting quickly, the Governor of Jamaica, Archibald Hamilton, gave Jennings secret orders to attack the Spanish salvage camp and obtain as much treasure as he could. The reason for the secrecy was that Governor Hamilton was not planning on sending the profits he realized from the looting of the Spanish treasure fleet back to Great Britain. He wasn't planning on keeping the profits for himself either. He was in fact secretly planning on using the profits from the Spanish treasure fleet to establish a pyrate base in the Caribbean that could be used to raise money in support of the Jacobite revolution against King George I. Governor Hamilton was a Jacobite.

Chapter 36
Henry Jennings, and a New Pyrate Port

In order to have a major political or military movement in this world, you need four things, a sizeable work force, strong motivation, a place to gather, and financial backing. The end of the War of the Spanish Succession left the Caribbean with lots of unemployed privateers looking for work. This provided the work force. The unrest in Great Britain over the crowning of King George I provided the strong motivation, or at least the pretense for those who just wanted an excuse to loot ships. The old privateer port of Nassau provided the place to gather, once it was fixed up a bit of course. The only thing that was missing was the money. In 1714, shortly after George became King of Great Britain, he appointed Lord Archibald Hamilton Governor of Jamaica. This wasn't a very good decision on the part of King George I. It seems the new governor was a supporter of James Edward Stuart; Lord Archibald Hamilton was a Jacobite.

Almost immediately after assuming his position, he began to think of ways to support the revolt. His plan was to recruit the local privateers recently turned pyrate and use them to generate the financial support he needed for his Jacobite friends in Scotland. As the governor, he might be able to devise a way to legally issue letters of marque to the pyrates and secretly send the profits to Scotland. Hamilton made friends with a local land owner and former privateer named Henry Jennings, who had earned a large sum of money as a privateer in the recent war and used his profits to buy a modest amount of real-estate on Jamaica. Jennings may or may not have been a Jacobite, but he was an opportunist. Just as they were forming their plans, the startling news of the sinking of the Spanish treasure fleet reached them. It was the answer to their prayers. There was certainly enough loot in Florida to get a revolution going. Governor Hamilton rapidly responded and on November 21, 1715 he secretly commissioned Jennings to attack the Spanish treasure fleet salvage camp.

Jennings and the Treasure Fleet

Needless to say, Jennings jumped at the chance. He and his partner, John Wills, sailed their sloops to Florida. Jennings's sloop *Bersheba* had 8 guns and 80 men, and Wills's sloop *Eagle* had 12 guns and 100 men. On December 27, 1715, in the early morning light, just as the sun began to peek over the horizon, one hundred fifty well-armed men calmly walked up to the Spanish salvage camp with their weapons drawn. The Spanish must have been astonished and somewhat confused. Spain was at peace with everyone. The commanding officer approached Jennings and politely asked if their nations were at war again. Jennings answered no, they were there to fish the wrecks. Objections from the commander fell on deaf ears. Jennings even ignored an offer of 25,000 pieces of eight if they left immediately. The Spanish watched helplessly as Jenning's men looted the camp of 120,000 pieces of eight. On their way back to Jamaica, the pirates took a Spanish merchant ship with a large amount of silver, plus a valuable cargo of Indigo, which they sold when they returned to Jamaica. Estimations as to the value of the treasure taken vary greatly, but it is believed to be about 300,000 pieces of eight. No other raids on the salvage camp occurred. The Spanish finished up their salvage operations and left Florida in April 1716. The treasure hunters who arrived afterwards only found small amounts of loot that had either been overlooked by the Spanish or that occasionally washed up on the beach.

1716

Henry Jennings establishes Nassau as a base for pirates.

Hamilton intended to use the money Jennings had taken to build and establish a new pyrate base in the Caribbean, a base like Tortuga of the old buccaneer days, a base where pyrates could gather and plan ventures against all flags. Once the docks and ships' supply stores were in place, taverns and brothels would be built where hundreds of pyrates would spend their money. Like most successful developers, he realized that the real profits don't come from taking prizes at sea; they came from taking the money away from the pyrates who took the prizes at sea. The profits would then be sent to Scotland to help fund the Jacobite revolt. Jennings suggested the perfect spot for this new base, Nassau. Privateers in the last war had been using Nassau as a center of operations for many years and some of them were still living there. Its location was ideal for raiding the shipping lanes and no royal government had any authority over the island.

Soon after, Jennings arrived in Nassau with the loot from the Spanish treasure fleet and began building the pyrate port. He opened a series of taverns and imported lots of prostitutes. The town took off like a rocket, all just like Hamilton had planned. Except that Jennings didn't want to share the profits with Governor Hamilton or anyone else. Hamilton now realized that Jennings was out of control and that he wouldn't see a shilling of any profits from the Nassau operations. Governor Hamilton declared Jennings a pyrate, but it was too late. Word of Hamilton's involvement reached England and Hamilton was arrested in March 1716. He was sent back to London to stand trial. However, the times being what they were, Hamilton managed to obtain his release and returned to politics, remaining in England. He had a very successful career until his death in 1754, never having taken part in any more Jacobite revolts.

Henry Jennings had succeeded in building the last great pyrate port by March 1716. It was the main base of operations for all pyrates operating in the Caribbean. The town was filled with taverns that Jennings built and prostitutes who he had imported from colonies throughout the Caribbean. It also had just about anything else a pyrate would need. On top of that, there was no government. English authority was absolutely nonexistent. The pyrates did as they pleased. The peaceful inhabitants who were living there before the pyrate invasion could do nothing to stop them. If they protested, the pyrates burned their homes or worse. Pyrates from Jamaica were arriving in droves.

Among the pyrates at Nassau, a man named Thomas Barrow declared himself governor and vowed to make it the second St. Mary's, Madagascar. However, most of these pyrates were still relatively loyal to Britain and only focused on French and Spanish prizes. Many refused to attack English shipping unless attacked first. In the same 1716 account of Nassau mentioned above, resident John Vickers wrote:

"[They] committ great disorders in that Island, plundering the inhabitants, burning their houses, and ravishing their wives. One Thomas Barrow formerly mate of a Jamaica brigantine which run away some time ago with a Spanish marquiss's money and effects, is the chief of them and gives out that he only waits for a vessel to go out a pirating, that he is Governor of Providence and will make it a second Madagascar, and expects 5 or 600 men more from Jamaica sloops to join in the settling of Providence, and to make war on the French and Spaniards, but for the English, they don't intend to meddle with them, unless they are first attack'd by them . . ."

Captain Musson's Report

Now, the only thing missing was fortifications against attack. They rebuilt the old fort and mounted sufficient guns to thwart off any enemies. They also kept a captured Spanish ship with 32 guns in the harbor as a guard ship. Captain Thomas Walker, former Deputy Governor of New

Providence, remained on the island until the pyrates forced him to flee to South Carolina. In his report, he wrote:

> "The pirates daly increse to Providence and haveing began to mount ye guns in ye Fort for there defence and seeking ye oppertunity to kill mee because I was against their illegall and unwarrantable practices and by no means would consent to their mounting of guns in ye Fort upon such accots. I was thereupon forced with my wife and family to acquitt ye Island to my great exPence and damage and ye latter part of June last arrived safe to this Province (South Carolina) where I remaine, etc."

By March 1717 the deputy governor of South Carolina, Robert Daniel, wanted to stop the pyrate activity in the Bahamas. He sent an armed merchant vessel under command of Captain Mathew Musson to root out the pyrates. I believe this was more of an intelligence gathering mission rather than one of search and destroy. Certainly, Captain Musson didn't have the firepower to effectively attack the pyrate stronghold. At any rate, Hornigold learned of Captain Musson's mission and attacked his ship with five pyrate vessels and a combined crew of about 350 men. In order to escape, Musson ran his ship aground on Cat Cay. Hornigold broke off the attack and did not pursue. Eventually, Captain Musson made it to Harbour Island and gathered valuable intelligence on the pyrate activity. When he returned to the Carolinas he made a report to the Board of Trade dated July 5, 1717 in which he wrote:

> ". . .they had taken a Spanish ship of 32 gunns, which they kept in the harbour for a guardship. Ye greatest part of the inhabitants of Providence are. already gone into other adjacent islands to secure themselves from ye pirates, who frequently plunder them. Most of the ships and vessels taken by them they burn and destroy when brought into the harbour and oblidge the menn to take on with them. . . . there are severall more pirates than he can now give an accot. of that are both to windward and to leward of Providence that may ere this be expected to rendevous there he being apprehensive that unless the Governmt. fortify this place the pirates will to protect themselves."

From these accounts, it appears that Nassau had indeed become the last great pyrate port. Not nearly as grand or inspiring as Port Royal or Tortuga in their day, but by the standards of 1716, Nassau was the only pyrate haven in the world.

Chapter 37
Hornigold's Pyrates

Benjamin Hornigold is a name that most people would not recognize, but in reality, he was the king of the pyrates in the Caribbean from 1715 to 1718. Little is known about his early life except that he was certainly a successful privateer in Queen Anne's War and used Nassau as his home port. After the privateer commissions expired in 1713, he remained on Nassau as one of the leaders. He turned pyrate and continued to take Spanish and French prizes as if the war was still going on. In early 1714 there were reports of Hornigold and his men attacking merchant vessels using small sailing canoes and a sloop. In another account, he captured two Cuban vessels and took 46,000 pieces of eight. During this time, Hornigold operated out of both Jamaica and Nassau. In 1715, Hornigold went into partnership with John Cockram who had a little settlement on Harbor Island, less than a day's sail from Nassau. Cockram was in the business of selling stolen merchandise to legitimate businessmen in the colonies. In other words, Cockram was a nautical "fence." By November 1715, Hornigold was sailing a 6-gun Jamaica sloop named *Mary* with a crew of 140.

It seems there was always bad blood between Benjamin Hornigold and Henry Jennings. One might even say there were bitter rivals. They certainly knew each other for a long time. Both were privateers in the last war, both sailed out of Jamaica, and both decided to make Nassau their base. In November 1715, Hornigold captured a Spanish sloop loaded with dry goods and sugar and returned to Nassau to sell the cargo, but in classic pyrate fashion, Jennings managed to take the prize away from Hornigold. In January 1716, he captured a much larger Spanish sloop off the coast of Florida and kept it. Upon return to Nassau, he fitted it out as a pyrate vessel and renamed it the *Benjamin*.

> "Fitting out" is a term which meant to prepare a vessel for the next voyage. For pyrates, it also included all manner of modifications, such as changing the rigging, removing the superstructure to decrease weight and increase speed, adding more guns.

His old Jamaica sloop *Mary* was apparently returned to its rightful owner, a man named Golding. The Spanish sloop *Benjamin* held a crew of 200 pyrates, and Hornigold was ready to return to sea aboard his new vessel.

Much of what we know about Hornigold and Nassau at that time comes from an account written by John Vickers, a non-pyrate resident of Nassau who eventually fled to Virginia. He wrote:

1716

Ben Hornigold is leader of pirates in the Caribbean including Bellamy, La Buse, and Teach.

> "In Nov. last Benjamin Hornigold arrived at Providence in the sloop *Mary* of Jamaica, belonging to Augustine Golding, which Hornigold took upon the Spanish coast, and soon after the taking of the said sloop, he took a Spanish sloop loaded with dry goods and sugar, which cargo he disposed of at Providence, but the Spanish sloop was taken from him by Capt. Jennings of the sloop *Bathsheba* of Jamaica.
>
> "In January Hornigold sailed from Providence in the said sloop *Mary*, having on board 140 men, 6 guns and 8 pattararas [swivel guns], and soon after returned with another Spanish sloop, which he took on the coast of Florida. After he had fitted the said sloop at Providence, he sent Golding's sloop back to Jamaica to be returned to the owners: and in March last sailed from Providence in the said Spanish sloop, having on board near 200 men, but whither bound deponent knoweth not."

Throughout all his operations, Benjamin Hornigold always remained loyal to Great Britain and refused to take ships from England or her allies. An article in the Boston News Letter of May 1716 stated that Hornigold captured a French ship and informed the master that "they never consented to the Articles of Peace with the French or Spaniards" and that "they meddle not with the English or Dutch." Perhaps he was somewhat patriotic or perhaps he thought if he were caught, he might be able to negotiate a pardon if he only took ships that belonged to nations that were formerly enemies of the crown.

Meanwhile, a new pyrate was about to enter the role of Hornigold's close associates. This was the famous pyrate, Black Samuel Bellamy. A year earlier, he was an honest merchant sailor from Massachusetts. Believed to have been born in Devonshire, England in 1689, Bellamy had relocated to Massachusetts by 1715 and was in love with Maria Hallett, a 15-year-old resident of Cape Cod. Local legend has it that Maria's parents objected to a marriage until Bellamy had more money. When the news of the Spanish treasure fleet's wreck reached New England, it seemed like a terrific opportunity to get wealthy overnight. Everyone was talking about it, but very few actually had the bravery, or stupidity, to chase a hollow dream of wealth and prosperity by traveling over 1,000 miles to the Florida coast. Bellamy was among the few hopeful men who did just that. He managed to get financial backing from his friend, Paulsgrave Williams. They purchased a small vessel and sailed for Florida along with a crew of several other treasure seeking sailors. But they arrived too late. Jennings had already taken most of the treasure and the Spanish were far better prepared to defend what was left. Not wanting to return to Cape Cod empty handed, Bellamy decided to turn pyrate and Williams became his quartermaster.

Bellamy and his small band of pyrates were operating in the Gulf of Honduras and made a small raid near Portobelo in March of 1716. The following month while sailing north, Bellamy sighted another pyrate vessel commanded by Henry Jennings. After a brief meeting, the two captains decided to join forces. It was a very short association, however. Just off the coast of Cuba, they attacked the French frigate, *Sainte Marie*. The French crew fought back, but they were soon overwhelmed and the pyrates took about 30,000 pieces of eight. Jennings killed more than 20 Frenchmen and then went on to attack and burn an English merchant sloop. Perhaps there was something in Jennings' conduct during the attack that bothered Bellamy or perhaps Bellamy saw something in Jennings that he didn't trust. At any rate, having been partners for only a few days, Bellamy quietly sailed away with the entire haul, leaving Jennings in a rage. Bellamy then sought refuge with Ben Hornigold, the privateer master. As Hornigold and Jennings were virtual enemies in all things, Hornigold gladly took Bellamy's vessel on as part of his fleet.

Soon after joining Hornigold, they took a French sloop, the *Marianne*, off the west end of Cuba and in a surprising decision, Hornigold gave command of the *Marianne* to Bellamy. The newest member of the crew, Bellamy had very little experience as a pyrate captain. One can only suppose that Hornigold must have been very impressed with Bellamy's natural leadership. Just a few days later, the French pyrate sloop *Postillion*, with a crew of 70, approached Hornigold and requested to join in partnership. The *Postillion* was commanded by the Olivier Le Vasseur, who had two nicknames, "La Buse" which is French for "The Buzzard" and "La Bouche" which is French for "The Mouth." Both nicknames are used interchangeably to describe Le Vasseur in many publications. Hornigold's small pyrate flotilla now included his great sloop *Benjamin*, Bellamy's sloop *Marianne*, and La Buse's sloop *Postillion*. La Buse will play a prominent role in the careers of several pyrates in the years to come. Another member of Hornigold's flotilla was a pyrate who was destined to become the most famous of them all, Edward Teach also known as Blackbeard.

No documentation has been found thus far that identifies Edward Teach as a member of Hornigold's flotilla in the spring of 1716. His presence with Hornigold is supposition. However, Edward Teach is mentioned along with Hornigold as a captain of a sloop of 6 guns and 70 men in a report made by Captain Mathew Musson almost one year later. Additionally, Hornigold and Teach are mentioned together as partners in many reports and accounts throughout the year of 1717. From those observations, it seems very likely that Teach and Bellamy also knew each other and were possibly close friends.

Under Hornigold's leadership, the flotilla had taken 41 prizes in only a few months. But this was all about to change. On May 16, 1716 the flotilla was sailing north of Hispaniola when they sighted an English ship carrying logwood. Hornigold remained true to his convictions and refused to attack the English ship, but Le Vasseur had no such conviction and neither did Sam Bellamy. They attacked together. It took them about ten days to loot the ship. As the English prize ship was looted, the crew of all three sloops discussed and debated their futures sailing under a leader who refused to take English ships. After all, they weren't privateers, they were pyrates. After a peaceful vote, the crew elected Sam Bellamy as their new captain. Hornigold along with 26 loyal hands was allowed to peacefully leave aboard one of the prize sloops they had. It is assumed that Edward Teach was among those who left with Hornigold.

Chapter 38
Black Sam Bellamy On His Own

FEBRUARY 1717

Sam Bellamy takes the slave ship Whydah.

Bold and courageous, Samuel Bellamy was rapidly becoming the most successful pyrate of his day. By now, he was known as Black Sam. He always treated captive crews well, giving each man the chance to join his crew and many did. Bellamy and his crew considered themselves more like "Robin Hood and his Merry Men." In fact, they even called themselves that. Just like the buccaneers of the olden days, Bellamy's pyrates lived by a code of conduct with rules and articles. They were also an "equal opportunity employer." A large percentage of their crewmen were former black slaves. Even though Bellamy was now a pyrate, he always remembered his main purpose, which was to earn enough money to marry Maria Hallett back on Cape Cod. To really rake in the big bucks, he had to take big prizes. So, Bellamy was always on the lookout for larger ships. But to take large ships, one has to have a large ship. Bellamy needed to up-scale his operations.

In September 1716 Bellamy and La Buse attempted to take a French ship of 44 guns just off Puerto Rico. After an hour-long battle, they broke off the attack with little loss on either side. By November 1716 they were operating out of St. Croix. In the ensuing months, they took over a dozen prizes in Leeward Islands. Then, Bellamy got his bigger ship, the square-rigged ship, *Sultana*. Williams becomes captain of *Marianne*. By January 1717 Bellamy, Williams, and La Buse were sailing south toward Venezuela. Reaching Blanquilla Island, north of Margarita, La Buse and his crew decided to seek their fortune separately. It was a friendly parting and several years later, Williams would again sail with La Buse off the coast of Africa. Bellamy and Williams returned to the waters of St. Croix.

Then, suddenly in February 1717 Bellamy spotted the ship he had been waiting for. It was a 28-gun slave galley named the *Whydah*. True to form, after taking the *Whydah* he allowed the captured crew to safely sail away in his old ship, the *Sultana*. Slave ships made the best pyrate ships. First, they were built to be fast. Slaves began to die quickly in the horrible conditions below decks, so a fast ship was essential if you wanted to make a profit. Secondly, there was a lot of space below decks for your large pyrate crew to occupy. There was also a lot of room to store captured goods. And lastly, slave ships were normally fairly well-armed. The *Whydah* was now the most powerful pyrate ship in the Caribbean and Bellamy was the number one pyrate.

Bellamy had been tremendously successful and each of his crewmembers had a sack of treasure weighing over 50 pounds. With the wealth he needed for the marriage, Bellamy decided to return to Cape Cod. Sailing from the Caribbean, they took several ships along the way to include a galley-built snow, the *Anne*, taken off the Virginia capes and two other prizes taken that same day. A snow is a two-masted vessel, larger than a sloop. However, his luck was about to run out. The *Whydah* arrived at Cape Cod on April 26, 1717. That evening, a tremendous nor'easter hit the coast and the *Whydah* was blown onto a sandbar. Helpless in the fierce storm, at 15 minutes after midnight, the mast snapped and pulled the *Whydah* over on her side and then down into the dark and stormy water. Bellamy and 144 members of his 146-man crew drowned. Two crewmen managed to struggle to shore but they were arrested in the morning. Just south of the *Whydah*, the *Marianne* also sank with only seven survivors, who were also arrested.

Of the nine pyrates captured and tried for piracy, six were executed, one black crewmember was sold into slavery, and two pled "not guilty" at their trial claiming they had been forced into piracy. In English law, those who could prove they had been forced to join the pyrate crew might get an acquittal. Among pyrates, it was the custom of the day to allow any crew members of a captured ship to join their pyrate crew willingly. All others were either allowed to sail away in which ever ship the pyrates didn't keep or were safety put ashore somewhere. However, individuals who possessed special skills like ship's carpenters, surgeons, and musicians, were often forced to become pyrates. At least, that's what the *Whydah's* carpenter, Thomas Davis claimed, along with one other. They were believed and released.

The story of the *Whydah* doesn't end there. When the ship went down in 1717, it sank intact with all hands, weapons, gold, jewelry, and personal belongings of the crew. It also sank just 500 feet off shore and in only 30 feet of water. For 267 years, the *Whydah* rested there peacefully. Through the remarkable efforts of a team of underwater researchers led by Barry Clifford, the wreck site of the *Whydah* was discovered. Since then,

APRIL 1717

The Whydah sinks off Cape Cod.

thousands of valuable artifacts have been recovered. Many of them are on display in museums and traveling expeditions. Thanks to the tremendous efforts of Barry and his team, the modern world has learned a lot about the lifestyle of early 18th century pyrates.

Chapter 39
Blackbeard the Pyrate

❝ . . . that five pirates made ye harbour of Providence their place of rendevous vizt. Horngold, a sloop with 10 guns and about 80 men; Jennings, a sloop with 10 guns and 100 men; Burgiss, a sloop with 8 guns and about 80 men; White, in a small vessell with 30 men and small armes; Thatch, a sloop 6 gunns and about 70 men." This was the first time that the name of Edward Teach appears in any official record, even though it was spelled "Thatch."

This excerpt was part of a report written by Captain Mathew Musson and submitted to the deputy governor of South Carolina in 1717. As mentioned earlier, Musson was sent to gather information on the pyrate activity in the Bahamas. He was on Harbour Island in March of 1717 when he identified Edward Teach as the captain of a 6-gun sloop with a crew of 70 men. He also placed Edward Teach in the company of Benjamin Hornigold. Due to his prominence as the quintessential and most notorious pyrate of them all, he is perhaps the pyrate who has been the most misrepresented in the annals of history.

Captain Edward Teach, or Blackbeard as he is known, is without question the most famous pyrate of all time. There are actually several spellings of his name used in the early 18th century. "Teach" was how his name was spelled in an article that appeared in the Boston Newsletter in 1717. Recent research indicates that "Thache" is probably the more correct spelling based upon family records from Jamaica and England. It was probably pronounced "Tay-Ch" which would account for the variations. Johnson chose the spelling of "Thatch" in his first edition and "Teach" in all subsequent editions. The 2nd edition spelling of "Teach" has influenced authors and historians ever since. I will use "Teach" for convenience, even though "Thache" is most likelihood the proper spelling. In addition to the dozens of books that have been written about him, Blackbeard has been portrayed more times in films and television shows than any other figure from the "Golden Age of Piracy." Blackbeard is not only the most famous pyrate in history, he is also among the most mysterious. Almost nothing is known about his life before he emerged as Captain of the *Revenge* in September 1717. Just 14 months later, he was killed. Everything we know about this iconic figure comes from this brief time period. There are really no hard facts about his early life, only summation and speculation. To cloud his history even more, there have been so many stories and books written about Blackbeard that it is very difficult to separate truth from fiction. Let's start with his name and birthplace.

According to Charles Johnson's 1st edition, Teach was born in 1680 in Jamaica, but subsequent editions of his book places his birth in the English seaport of Bristol. After that, Johnson writes that he served as a privateer sailing out of Jamaica in the war. In 1900, Thomas T. Upshur wrote that Teach originally came from Accomack, Virginia. This too is unlikely. However, Blackbeard was known to have careened his vessel on the beach at Accomack and it is my guess that the local legend of that event may have been stretched by the author into something more. In his book, "Annals of Philadelphia and Pennsylvania," published in 1842, John F. Watson suggested that his real name was Edward Drummond and that he was from Scotland, but again there is no evidence and no historian gives any weight to that claim today. There is documented evidence from 1717 that suggests he may have been from Philadelphia or at least lived there for a time. As we shall see a little later on, one account printed in the Boston News Letter describes him as "one Teach, who Formerly Sail'd Mate out of this Port (Philadelphia)." But that could mean he only had visited the port several times in the years before becoming a pyrate.

1716

Teach with Hornigold

Some modern researchers have found several highly intriguing church records from St. Catherine's Cathedral in Spanish Town, Jamaica and from Stonehouse, Gloucestershire, England that tracks the Thache family's migration from England to Jamaica in the late 17th century. By 1699, a sea Captain named Edward Thache lived in Jamaica with his wife Elizabeth, son Edward, and daughter Elizabeth. His wife Elizabeth died that year and Edward remarried to a woman named Lucretia six months later. Edward Sr. died in 1706 and his son, who was serving aboard HMS *Winsor*, inherited everything. A fascinating document exists that was drafted aboard the *Winsor* in 1707 that clearly states Edward Thache Jr. decided to turn his inheritance over to his father's second wife and their three young children. If Edward Thache Jr. was Blackbeard, then Johnson was correct. Blackbeard was born in Gloucestershire, England, just 40 miles from Bristol, sailed with his family from Bristol to Jamaica as a youth, then joined the Royal

Navy and served in the war. However, there is a somewhat controversial idea put forth that suggests Blackbeard was really named Edward Beard and that he was from the North Carolina town of Bath.

It is widely believed that Teach was a member of Benjamin Hornigold's crew throughout 1716. If so, Teach was with Hornigold when Sam Bellay joined Hornigold and was given command of the *Marianne*. Teach also may have been one of the 26 men who sailed with Hornigold back to Nassau after Hornigold was voted out of command and replaced by Bellamy. As mentioned earlier, Teach enters the official record in March of 1717 when Musson mentions that he was in command of a small 6-gun sloop. With Nassau as their home port, Teach was sailing with Hornigold, who had a sloop named the *Adventure*. South of Cuba, they took a Spanish vessel out of Havana carrying 120 barrels of flour. Off Portobelo, Hornigold and Teach took the sloop named the *Bonnet*, which Hornigold kept for himself and gave the *Adventure* to Teach. South of Jamaica while returning to Nassau, they took one more sloop, the *Revenge*. Teach and Hornigold then sailed north along the Carolina coast and took a Spanish ship from Madeira that was on its way to Charleston, South Carolina, "out of which they got plunder of considerable value," according to a contemporary account.

From there, they may have careened their vessels at Accomack, which is about 20 miles south of the Maryland border on the Atlantic side of Virginia's eastern shore. As mentioned before, careening is a process of pulling your vessel out of the water up on to a large beach and scraping off all the barnacles and seaweed attached to the hull. For decades, Accomack had been used by pyrates as a place where they careened their vessels in safety. Captain Cook and William Dampier careened their vessel at Accomack in 1683. The locals benefited too, as they traded with the pyrates for valuable goods and were most likely well paid for their assistance and silence. One point of curiosity, there is a tiny inlet in the county of Accomack that is named for Blackbeard, but no one is certain how or when it got its name. From Accomack, Teach and Hornigold made an uneventful voyage back to Nassau.

Chapter 40
The Unlikely Partnership

The most curious, controversial, and mysterious part of the Blackbeard saga is his meeting and association with Major Stede Bonnet, the "Gentleman Pyrate." Historians gave him that name because he came from a well-to-do family. Getting to the truth of this relationship could explain much about the life and motivation of Edward Teach as well that of Stede Bonnet. We know that Bonnet was born on Barbados around 1688 to a moderately wealthy family. He inherited the family estate after his father's death in 1694 and married Mary Allamby in 1709. Bonnet was a well-respected landowner, family man, and a Major in the local militia. Suddenly, in the summer of 1717, with absolutely no experience as a sea captain, Bonnet bought a 12-gun Jamaica sloop named the *Revenge*, hired a crew of sailors, and went to sea as a pyrate. His unexpected behavior has been explained away by historians like Charles Johnson by simply saying he was having marital problems or he wanted to have some adventure and try something new. Those explanations seem highly unlikely. There has to be something more, something deeper, perhaps something like a deep political reason that highly motivated Bonnet toward piracy.

The next part of the story is even more astounding. Just a few months after setting sail from Barbados, Edward Teach was suddenly the captain of the *Revenge* and Bonnet was aboard without any authority. How did this happen? Several modern historians suggest that the two must have met in the summer of 1717 somewhere, either sailing the waters of the Caribbean or while in some unnamed port. The two instantly became friends and since Bonnet didn't know much about sailing, he relinquished command of his newly purchased sloop to Teach. To me, this explanation always sounded ludicrous. Frankly, people don't act that way—especially pyrates. Bonnet wouldn't spend all his money for a pyrate sloop only to give it over to someone he had just met. Other authors have suggested that Teach was invited on board as a friend and nautical advisor, but because of Bonnet's lack of experience at sea, Teach took over command against Bonnet's wishes. There has to be something more to this.

A report given by Captain Codd and published in the *Boston News Letter* in November 1717 gives some insight into their relationship. Captain Codd's ship was taken by Teach in October 1717 and he was held captive onboard the *Revenge* for a short time while his ship was being looted.

". . . a Pirate Sloop called Revenge, of 12 Guns 150 Men, Commanded by one Teach . . . On board the Pirate Sloop is Major Bennet, but has no Command, he walks about in his Morning Gown, and then to his Books, of which he has a good Library on Board, he was not well of his wounds that he received by attacking of a Spanish Man of War, which kill'd and wounded 30–40 Men. After which putting into Providence, the place of Rendevouze for the Pirates, they put the afore said Capt. Teach on board for this Cruise."

From this account, Edward Teach was clearly in command of the *Revenge* while Bonnet remained onboard with no apparent authority. It also tells us that Teach joined the *Revenge* in Nassau after Bonnet was wounded in a recent attack. Of course, this might be just what they told Captain Codd and the truth may lie elsewhere.

Bonnet's battle with the Spanish man o' war most likely took place in August 1717 while he was fishing the treasure fleet wrecks off the coast of Florida. Captain Codd was told about the attack by one of the pyrate crewmembers or even perhaps by Bonnet himself. After his release, Captain Codd relayed the account of the battle along with the details of his own ship's capture. No other record of this alleged attack exists. A man o' war is a large and well-armed naval ship, designed to fight in naval engagements.

Figure 20: *Jamaican Sloop, Similar to the Revenge*

A pyrate would not attack a man o' war especially with a 12-gun sloop; they would be totally outgunned. A more realistic explanation seems to be that it was a made-up story told to impress Captain Codd or to explain Bonnet's injury and lack of command.

According to Captain Codd's account, Edward Teach came aboard as captain of the *Revenge* in Nassau, probably in September of 1717. There is compelling evidence that Teach may have lived on Barbados as a child and may have actually been friends with a young Stede Bonnet. If true, this would explain a lot. Stede Bonnet was a Major in the army and a plantation owner with no experience at sea. He wouldn't fare very well as a pyrate ship's captain, yet he purchased a sloop and set out to sea. On the other hand, if Bonnet knew of his old friend, Teach, who was already a pyrate ship's captain with an abundance of experience as a sailor and navigator, Bonnet might have sought him out to command his sloop. This is supported by the evidence that Bonnet's crew aboard the *Revenge* were not entirely those he hired on Barbados. At least some of them were actually Teach's men, like William Howard, who was one of Teach's closest associates and was with him at the end of his career. There is no documentary proof found, as of yet, but I believe the two old friends signed articles in Nassau that summer of 1717 and Teach assumed command of the *Revenge*.

October 1717

Blackbeard and Bonnet take 17 prizes off Cape Charles, Cape May, and Long Island.

Still, that doesn't answer the question of why Stede Bonnet turned to piracy in the first place. What would motivate an honest Major and land owner to want to become a pyrate? Perhaps he was politically motivated and that decision had something to do with the revolt in Great Britain over King George I. If Stede Bonnet supported James Edward Stuart in his quest to claim the throne of Great Britain, he might have taken to piracy as part of that revolt. If so, that would explain a great deal. **There are clues to this which I will reveal later on. But for now, Edward Teach is captain of the Revenge and is about to establish himself as the most notorious pyrate in history.**

Sailing north along the coast in late September 1717, Teach and Bonnet aboard the sloop *Revenge* took the English sloop *Betty* off Cape Charles, Virginia. After looting all valuables aboard, the sloop was sunk. However, the crew was permitted to escape unharmed. An account of this incident can be found in the original charge sheet for Blackbeard's quartermaster, William Howard, who was arrested in Virginia one year later. Then, in October of 1717, Teach and Bonnet went on a ship taking spree like none before. They sailed to Cape May, which is the primary entrance to the port of Philadelphia, Pennsylvania, and took 9 prizes. Shipping came to a standstill. Apparently, Thatch had already acquired the nickname of "Blackbeard." An account of the pirate's actions was recorded in a letter written on October 23, 1717, by Jonathan Dickinson, the Mayor of Philadelphia. In that letter, Dickinson names the leader of the pirates raiding vessels off Philadelphia as "One Capan Tatch All[ia]s Bla[ck]beard." From there, he traveled to Long Island, where he took another 7 prizes. Not only was Teach taking cargo, coins, and valuables, he was building his own pyrate fleet. The first vessel he kept was a snow named the *Sea Nymph*. The second was a great sloop of 12 guns the pyrates had taken from Captain Sipkins. Shortly afterwards, Teach took a smaller Bermuda sloop commanded by Captain Goelet. Apparently, Teach thought this was a better vessel than the *Sea Nymph*, so he decided to keep the sloop and allow the captured crew to sail away onboard the other vessel. After several days of attacking and looting, Teach now had three ships in his fleet: Bonnet's original 12-gun Jamaica sloop *Revenge*, the 12-gun great sloop, and the 8-gun Bermuda sloop. Many details of Teach's exploits at Cape May were reported in the *Boston News Letter*, the most widely circulated newspaper of the day.

Of all the factual information learned from the *Boston News Letter's* articles, there is one fascinating bit of information that gives us insight into Teach's past. This brief comment is, "Commanded by one Teach, who Formerly Sail'd Mate out of this Port" which of course refers to Philadelphia. Edward Teach must have sailed into Philadelphia before 1717, either as an honest merchant or as a beginning pyrate. Remember, Marcus Hook? It was just 20 miles downriver from Philadelphia and was a well-known pyrate trading center. Perhaps Teach traded there earlier in his career. Later in this chapter, I shall discuss a local legend that tells of Edward Teach in love with a woman who lived in Marcus Hook.

After leaving Cape May and Long Island, some contemporary accounts tell us that Teach and his flotilla of three sloops were joined by his old friend and mentor, Benjamin Hornigold, now sailing a larger vessel of 30 guns, the *Ranger*. Together, they took a ship off the Virginia Capes. Further east, they took two more ships, the *Pritchard* and a ship from London. Two more articles from the *Boston News Letter* provide some details. One article from October 18, 1717, reads, "Pritchard from St. Lucie, who on the 18th of October in Lat. 36 and 45 was taken by Capt. Teach, in Compa, with whom was Capt. Hornygold, they took from him about 8 Cask Sugar and most of their cloaths at the same time, they took a Ship from London for Virginia, out of which they took something and let them go." The second article dated December 10, 1717 reads, "We are told from Maryland that a Ship from London was arrived there, who about fourteen days ago was taken off the Capes of Virginia by Teach & Hornigold, that took out of him a New Suit of Sailes and Rigging."

The dates for both of these attacks mentioned in the articles must be incorrect. Numerous reports chronicled in The *Boston News-Letter* and letters mentioning Blackbeard that were written by officials in Philadelphia clearly place Blackbeard in the Delaware River and along the shore of Long Island in October and early November 1717. He couldn't have been off the Virginia shoreline on the 18th of October. Since Blackbeard couldn't have been in two places at once, there must be an explanation for this discrepancy. Perhaps Hornigold and Blackbeard took those vessels months earlier on their way to Accomack, but Teach wasn't well known and Hornigold was yesterday's news. After Teach's spectacular assault on the Delaware Capes, his actions became a much bigger story, and the Boston Newsletter ran them as recent articles. In any event, in November 1717, Blackbeard sailed south towards Martinique. He had two sloops, the *Revenge* and the great sloop that was taken off Long Island. Apparently, Goelet's 8-gun Bermuda sloop either sank or was abandoned. It is also important to note that Ben Hornigold's name was never again mentioned in association with Teach in the historical record.

Chapter 41
The Queen Anne's Revenge

The bright white sails of a three-masted frigate set against the deep blue sky must have looked beautiful to the crews of Teach's two sloops as they rapidly approached. It was November 17, 1717 and they were cruising 60 miles east of Martinique on Latitude 14/27. The only vessels remaining in the pyrate's possession were Teach's Jamaican sloop *Revenge* armed with 12 guns and carrying 120 men and the great sloop armed with 8 guns and carrying 80 men. Teach needed a larger ship if he was going to be as successful as Sam Bellamy. He needed a slave ship, just like Bellamy had. Teach had rounded the east side of St. Johns and was sailing south in hopes of taking a few French vessels near their colony of Martinique when he hit the jackpot. I am certain that Teach couldn't believe his luck. Totally by chance, they had found the perfect pyrate vessel, the slave ship *La Concorde*.

A fairly large and fast sailing frigate, *La Concorde* was serving as a French slave ship in 1717. There is documentary evidence that *La Concorde* was a 26-gun French privateer ship between July 1710 and November 1711 taking English, Dutch, and Portuguese prizes off the west coast of Africa and in the Caribbean during the War of the Spanish Succession. Before that, some researchers suggest that *La Concorde* may have been an English merchant ship, the *Concorde,* and had been captured by the French sometime before 1710 and converted to a privateer ship. One contemporary account of the ship from the time it was commanded by Teach described the ship as "Dutch built." This has caused modern historians to believe that it was originally a Dutch flute. That conclusion is most likely incorrect. Dutch flutes were built for commerce, with a bulging hull that carried more cargo than most other ships, but that also made them slower, not a good thing for a slave ship.

NOVEMBER 1717

Blackbeard takes La Concorde and renames it the Queen Anne's Revenge.

Dutch and English shipbuilding techniques were similar, at that time, and the observer may have simply been mistaken. It is also possible that the French may have modified the ship to hold more cargo, giving the ship the appearance of being a Dutch flute. Whatever the ship's true history, in November 1717 *La Concorde* was a slave ship sailing from the African coast and armed with only 14 guns. As with Sam Bellamy and his slave ship *Whydah*, the most desirable vessel a pyrate could have was a slave ship because, as noted previously, they were fast and had plenty of room for pyrates and captured loot.

La Concorde was traveling from Africa to Martinique, among the largest French ports in this part of the Caribbean, when Teach's sloops found her. The two pyrate sloops prepared for battle as they came along side, but surprisingly there was none. The French captain, Pierre Dosset, offered little resistance and Edward Teach easily took *La Concorde*. In addition to being the ideal pyrate ship, Teach found gold dust, silver, jewels and 455 slaves onboard. The French crew was allowed to leave in the small Bermuda sloop— they sailed to Martinique. Below is an excerpt from a

Figure 21: *Queen Anne's Revenge conception painted by Sharon Glaze*

letter from Charles Mesnier, Intendant of Martinique, in which he relays Captain Pierre Dosset's account:

> ". . . last 28 November, being within 60 miles from here [Marinique] at 14 degrees 27 minutes north latitude, having been attacked by two boats of English pirates, one of 12 and the other of 8 guns armed with 250 men controlled by Edouard Titche English . . ."

Before we continue, I must take a moment to explain the difference in dates. Most books use November 17th as the date Edward Teach took the Queen Anne's Revenge. That's because the English and the French were using different calendars at that time. Most nations in Europe and North Africa had used the Julian calendar since the days of Roman rule. However, that calendar wasn't accurate. In 1582, Pope Gregory XIII promulgated the use of a more accurate calendar known as the Gregorian calendar. Most Roman Catholic countries soon adopted the Gregorian calendar while Greece, Russia and most protestant countries continued to use the Julian calendar. By 1717, the Julian calendar was 11 days behind the Gregorian calendar. Great Brittan, including the American colonies, didn't adopt the Gregorian calendar until September 1752 when Wednesday, September 2 was followed by Thursday, September 14. By the mid-1750s, all of Western Europe was using the Gregorian calendar. This explains the English date for the taking of the Queen Anne's Revenge as November 17, 1717 and the French the date of November 28th.

Teach then sailed his prize ship and the *Revenge* to Bequia Island, just south of St. Vincent where the process of converting the slave ship *La Concorde* into a pyrate ship began. That normally entailed removing most of the cabins below decks which made the ship lighter and offered more space for birthing. Modifications were also made to the rigging and to anything else that would improve speed. Then, more guns were brought onboard. Contemporary reports differ as to the exact number of guns on the pyrate ship, but it was generally between 26 and 40. Powerful and imposing, *La Concorde* had been transformed into the *Queen Anne's Revenge*, the strongest pyrate ship afloat and Edward Teach was now the greatest pyrate captain in the Caribbean.

As a name for a pyrate ship, the *Queen Anne's Revenge* is unique. It gives us tremendous insight into the political motivations of Edward Teach and his crew, which is surprisingly overlooked by most historians. Queen Anne was the last of the Stuart monarchs in England and the half-sister to James Edward Stuart. When she died in 1714 and King George I was crowned, a revolt broke out in Scotland and England. Known as "The Pretender" and sometimes "The Pretender Across the Sea," James Edward Stuart was living in exile in France. His supporters, known as "Jacobites," believed him to be the rightful King of England. Queen Anne was well liked by everyone and it is easy to imagine the Jacobites believing that she would have wanted her half-brother to have been named king instead of George I. The naming of his ship, the *Queen Anne's Revenge*, strongly indicates that Teach was a Jacobite, loyal to the England of Queen Anne's reign, but seeking revenge against the England of King George I. Supportive evidence of this is documented through numerous accounts and statements of Edward Teach's pyrate associates including Stede Bonnet.

Meant to intimidate a potential prize ship, all pyrates flew their own distinctive flags in the 18th century. They were normally black with some sort of white skull, skeleton, or figure carrying weapons of some kind. The distinctive nature would also serve to allow other pyrates to recognize their friends or rivals at sea. Although contemporary accounts about Teach's unique flag are not specific, in the late 20th century, Blackbeard's flag has come to be described as having a skeleton holding an hour glass in one hand, as if to say your time is running out, and a spear stabbing a bleeding heart in the other. This exact flag is precisely described in an account dated October 20, 1717 by French captain named Jean Dubois, whose ship was taken by two pyrate sloops off the north side of Hispaniola.

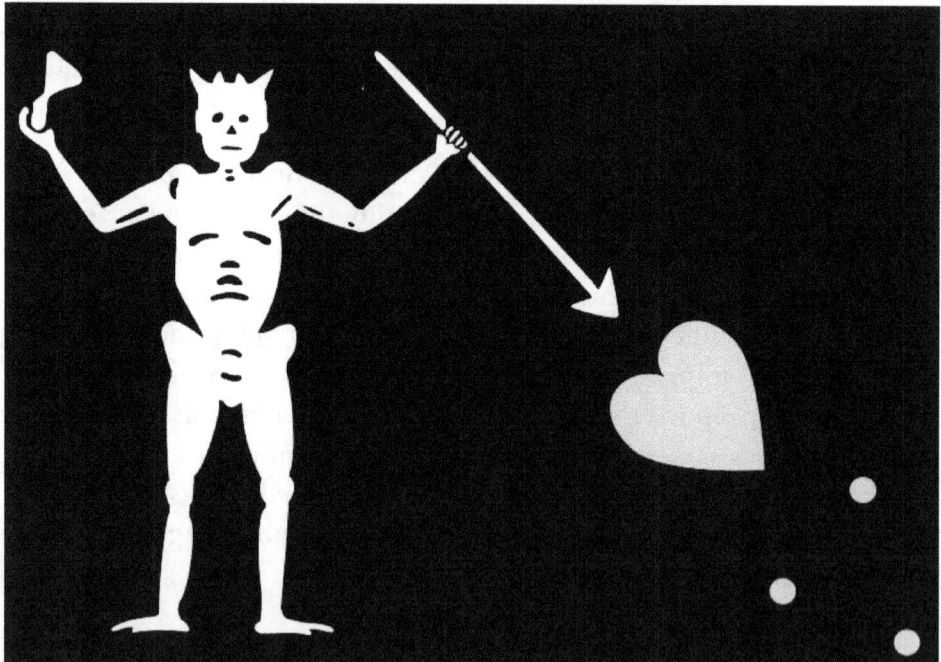

Figure 22: *Blackbeard's Flag*

The first action the *Queen Anne's Revenge* had as a pyrate ship was the taking of a Boston ship, the *Great Allen*. It was late November 1717 and Teach and his fleet left Bequia Isle and sailed north to pass St. Vincent and St. Lucia on the westward side of the islands. Somewhere along that route,

Teach came upon the *Great Allen*, commanded by Captain Taylor. After whipping the captain to make him reveal where he had hidden the silver and gold, Teach burned the *Great Allen* to the waterline and the ship sank. However, the entire crew and the captain were safely put ashore. This is the only report of Teach mistreating any of his captives. Normally, the crew of the prize vessel was well treated. Teach would gamble with them and usually got them drunk, but no harm came to them except for the headache they had the next morning. But this ship was different—perhaps because it was from Boston.

Some historians have suggested that Teach held a special grudge against ships from Massachusetts, because of the recent execution of Sam Bellamy's crew. Sam Bellamy was one of Teach's former companions and probably his friend when they sailed together under the command of Hornigold and when Bellamy's ship went down off Cape Cod, seven of the nine surviving crewmembers were executed. The following is an excerpt of the report that appeared in the *Boston News Letter*:

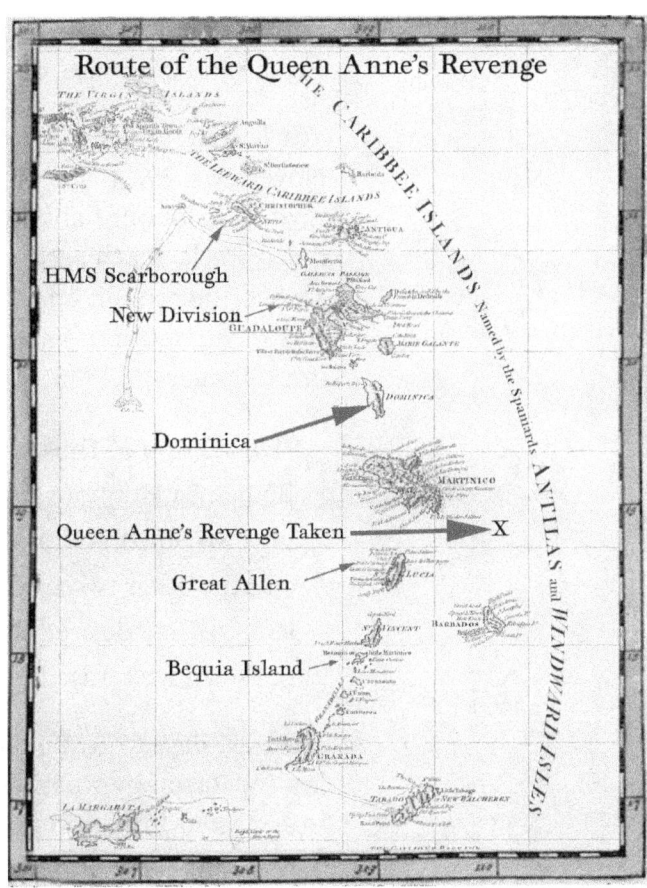

Figure 23: *Queen Anne's Revenge Route*

> "That in November Last . . . a great Ship from Boston, was taken at or near St. Lucia or St. Vincent, by Capt. Teach the Pirate in a French Ship of 32 Guns, a Briganteen of 10 Guns, and a Sloop of 12 Guns, his Consort, Capt. Taylor they put 24 hours in Irons, and Whipt him, in order to make him confess what Money he had on board, burnt his Ship, put his Men on Shore at Martinico"

That report made a very curious mention of a third pyrate vessel in the group, a brigantine of 10 guns. It clearly identified the *Queen Anne's Revenge* as "a French ship" and the *Revenge* as "a sloop of 12 guns," but what was that other vessel? Brigantines have two masts and sloops have only one. Therefore, it couldn't be the Bermuda sloop that was given to the French crew of *La Concorde* or the great sloop they took off Cape May. It couldn't have been with Teach when he took *La Concorde* or it would have been mentioned by the French captain. The origin of this brigantine remains unclear, but it was accompanying Teach when he was sighted by Benjamin Hobhouse, captain of the *Montserrat Merchant*.

Teach and his three vessels approached the *Montserrat Merchant* on November 29, 1717. Apparently Teach pretended to be friendly and invited Hobhouse aboard in an attempt to hold him for ransom, but it didn't work. Teach accidentally left his pyrate flag flying on the stern which alerted the captain and they quickly sailed away unharmed. The incident was recounted in a letter written by Governor Hamilton of Jamaica and dated January 6, 1718:

> "Deposition of Thos. Knight, belonging to the Mountserrat Merchant, Benjamin Hobhouse, commander, 30th Nov. 1717. On 29th Nov., seeing two ships and a sloop, and thinking one did belong to Bristol, and the other two to Guinea, he went in the long-boat to enquire for letters. They desired us to come on board, but seeing Death Head in the stern we refused it etc."

The next day, an Antiguan sloop, the *New Division*, captained by Richard Joy, was taken by what was described as two pyrate ships and a sloop. The two-masted brigantine could have been described as a ship. Apparently one of the sailors from the *New Division* decided to join the pyrate crew, after which, the rest of the crew were permitted to sail away in their sloop. That incident was also recounted in the letter of Governor Hamilton of Jamaica and dated January 6, 1718:

> "Deposition of Richard Joy, Master of the sloop New Division of Antigua, 30th Nov. 1717. This morning he was taken by two pirate ships and a sloop who said they belonged to Barbados and enquired what vessels were along shoar. They restored him to his sloop etc., keeping one of his men."

HMS *Scarborough*

Shortly afterwards, one of the most astounding battles that never happened— didn't occur. Read that statement a second time and allow me to explain. According to Charles Johnson as written in the *Grand History of Pyrates*, and hundreds of subsequent publications, Edward Teach on the *Queen Anne's Revenge* engaged, and did battle with, the *Scarborough*, a 32-gun 5th rate English frigate of the Royal Navy, west of Nevis Island. The account of this incredulous battle first appeared in Charles Johnson's second edition—the one that added a great deal of fabrications to boost sales. The trouble is, it never happened! No pyrate would ever attack a ship of the Royal Navy. Even though the *Queen Anne's Revenge* is reported to have 40 guns, most of those guns were probably small deck mounted guns. Additionally, at that time pyrate crews actually weren't very good fighters. They preyed on poorly armed merchant vessels and used intimidation to capture their prizes. They seldom had to actually fight anyone. On the other hand, the crew of a ship of the Royal Navy was trained to fight, they had very good gunners who could easily hit a moving ship at a farther distance than the untrained gunners aboard the average pyrate sloop.

But what if they accidentally met in the darkness and Teach had to fight in order to get away? That sounds plausible except for the fact that the log book of the *Scarborough* makes no mention of the incident. Captain Hume did make a note in the log of hearing of a pyrate ship operating in the nearby waters and that this ship took a French sugar merchant ship near St. Christopher, but the logs make no mention about any engagements. It is certain that in early December 1717, Teach on the *Queen Anne's Revenge* took a French sugar merchant ship near the island of St. Christopher and the *Scarborough* heard about it.

Sailing west, off Crab Island just south of Puerto Rico, Teach took the sloop *Margaret* on December 5, 1717. The ship's captain, Henry Bostock, was taken hostage for about eight hours while his sloop was looted of his "cargo of cattle, hogs, arms, books, and instruments," according to Bostock. It's difficult to say if "instruments" refers to navigational or musical instruments, because both musicians and their instruments were highly valued by pyrates. Two of the crewmen from the Margaret were forced to join the pyrates and a third went willingly. Captain Bostock's sloop was returned to him and he was permitted to sail on along with the remainder of his crew.

Henry Bostock gave a deposition that was included in a letter written by Governor Hamilton of Jamaica, dated January 6, 1718.

> "Deposition of Henry Bostock, master of the sloop *Margaret* of St. Christophers, 19th Dec., 1717. On 5th Dec., off Crab Island, he met a large ship and a sloop. He was ordered on board and Capt. Tach took his cargo of cattle and hogs, his arms books and instrument. The ship, Dutch built, was a French Guinea man, 36 guns mounted and 300 men. They did not abuse him or his men, but forced two to stay and one Robert Bibby voluntarily took on with them."

However, this deposition proved to be far more important to the story of Edward Teach than simply the details of the capture of the *Margaret*.

The first item of interest contained in this deposition is the comment that the *Queen Anne's Revenge* is "Dutch built." As mentioned earlier, it is most likely that the ship was built in England and modified in France and that Bostock was simply mistaken. Secondly, there is no mention of a third ship, so apparently the brigantine was no longer sailing with Teach. Further on in his deposition, Bostock cleared up any remaining question about the story of the battle with the *Scarborough*. He mentions that the pyrates talked about seeing a Royal Navy Ship-O-The-Line near Nevis, but they managed to slip away without being seen. However, Bostock's deposition included one fact about Edward Teach that no previous person had officially reported. Henry Bostock described Edward Teach as having a large black beard. From that moment on, Edward Teach would forever be known as Blackbeard.

With the vessels badly in need of repair, Blackbeard, as he shall now be called, sailed around Hispaniola and up to Samana Cay, a tiny island located between Turks and Caicos Islands and the Bahamas. There is no record of Blackbeard's activities from mid-December 1717 to March 1718, so we must conclude that he was careening and repairing his vessels. One thing is for certain, he didn't go to visit Governor Eden in North Carolina to ask for a pardon as some histories alleged. He was most likely lying on a beach drinking rum while his vessels were being repaired. As for the pardon that some Blackbeard biographers are referring to is the King's Proclamation of 1717, it is very unlikely that Blackbeard even knew of this proclamation.

Chapter 42
The King's Proclamation

Astounding news reached Nassau on February 23, 1718 when HMS *Phenix* sailed into port. Onboard was a government representative who had a King's Proclamation and was authorized to grant pardons to all pyrates on the spot.

By the KING,

A PROCLAMATION

GEORGE R.

hereas we have received information, that several Persons, Subjects of Great Britain, have, since the 24th Day of June, in the Year of our Lord, 1715, committed divers Pyracies and Robberies upon the High-Seas, in the West Indies, or adjoyning to our Plantations, which hath and may Occassion great Damage to the Merchants of Great Britain, and others trading unto those Parts; and tho' we have appointed such a Force as we judge sufficient for suppressing the

said Pyrates, yet the more effectually to put an End to the same, we have thought fit, by and with the Advice of our Privy Council, to Issue this our Royal Proclamation; the said Pyrates, shall on, or before, the 5th of September, in the year of our Lord 1718, surrender him or themselves, to one of our Principal Secretaries of State in Great Britain or Ireland, or to any Governor or Deputy Governor of any of our Plantations beyond the Seas; every such Pyratee and Pyrates so surrendering him, or themselves, as aforesaid, shall have our gracious Pardon, of, and for such, his or their Pyracy, or Piracies, by him or them committed, before the fifth of January next ensuing. And we do hereby strictly charge and command all our Admirals, Captains, and other Officers at Sea, and all our Governors and Commanders of any Forts, Castles, or other Places in our Plantations, and all other our Officers Civil and Military, to seize and take such of the Pyrates, who shall refuse or neglect to surrender themselves accordingly.

And we do hereby further declare, that in Case any Person or Persons, on, or after, the 6th day of September, 1718, shall discover or seize, or cause or procure to be discovered or seized, any one or more of the said Pyrates, so refusing or neglecting to surrender themselves as aforesaid, so as they may be brought to Justice, and convicted of the said Offence, such Person or Persons, so making such Discovery or Seizure, or causing or procuring such Discovery or Seizure to be made, shall have and receive as a Reward for the same, viz. for every Commander of any private Ship or Vessel, the Sum of 100 l. for every Lieutenant, Master, Boatswain, Carpenter and Gunner, the sum of 40 l. for every inferior officer, the Sum of 30. and for every private Man the Sum of 20 l. And if any Person or persons, belong to, and being Part of the Crew, of any Pyrat Ship or Vessel, so as he or they be brought to Justice, and be convicted of the said Offence, such Person or Persons, as a Reward for the same, shall receive for every such Commander, the Sum of 200 l. which said Sums, the Lord Treasurer, or the Commissioners of our Treasury for the time being, are hereby required, and desired to pay accordingly.

Given at our Court, at Hampton-Court, the fifth Day of September 1717, in the fourth Year of our Reign.
George R.

God save the King

The lives of many former privateers who were loyal to England but had become pyrates out of necessity, were instantly changed. It was quite apparent that Great Britain and Spain were moving toward war again in the summer of 1717 and that King Georg's advisors knew that Great Britain would need privateers to help boost up their navy. That was unfortunate, because the Royal Navy had just spent the past few years getting rid of as many former privateers as they could. The only solution was to offer a royal pardon to all eligible pyrates. The King's Proclamation, issued on September 5, 1717, offered a full pardon to every pyrate who met certain conditions. These pardons were issued by a Principal Secretary of State in Great Britain or Ireland or any Governor or Deputy Governor of any colony. Since most of the English pyrates called Nassau their home port, that's where King George I and British Government decided to concentrate their efforts.

However, there were a couple of stipulations. To be eligible for the pardon, all acts of piracy had to have been committed between June 24, 1715 and January 5, 1718. Any pyrates who committed piratical acts after January 5th were automatically ineligible whether they knew about the proclamation or not. It was understood that any pyrate who learned of the proclamation and did not immediately seek out a Governor or Deputy Governor to accept the pardon also became ineligible. Additionally, individuals had to accept the pardon by September 5, 1718, one full year from the original date of issue.

The term "plantations" in the original document means colonies.

Benjamin Hornigold was one of the first to accept the king's pardon and was of great assistance in convincing many other pyrates to accept as well. Over the next two days, a total of 209 pyrates accepted the pardon and received certificates of protection. Henry Jennings, developer of the pyrate port of Nassau, accepted the pardon, sold his interests, and sailed to Bermuda where he bought a large plantation and retired a wealthy man. For those stubborn individuals who didn't attempt to obtain a pardon, a reward was offered to anyone who brought them in. This was intended to encourage a sort of pyrate bounty hunter. Since the news of the King's Proclamation didn't reach the Americas until February 1718, it is very unlikely that Blackbeard sailed to North Carolina in January 1718 and accepted the pardon from the governor as some of his biographers claim.

Chapter 43
From Honduras to Ocracoke

By March 1718, Blackbeard and his two vessels were active again, sailing south into the Bay of Honduras. At some point, Blackbeard gave command of the *Revenge* to one of his most trusted crewmembers, Richards, whose first name is unknown. Just off the Turneffe Islands at the north end of the bay, Richards on the *Revenge,* took an 80-ton sloop named the *Adventure*. The sloop was captained by David Herriot who was taken on board the *Queen Anne's Revenge* along with the rest of his crew. At first, they were captives, but eventually they all decided to join Blackbeard's crew. The *Adventure* was kept, and Blackbeard gave command of this third vessel in his flotilla to another one of his long-time crewmembers, Hezekiah Hands, who is incorrectly identified as Israel Hands in many publications. Those two sloops were sent out together ahead of the *Queen Anne's Revenge* to look for prizes.

Further south in the Bay, Richards on the *Revenge* and Hands in the *Adventure* took four more sloops. When the captain of one sloop protested, Richards burned the sloop but allowed the crewmembers to get away. On April 9, 1718 at the southeast end of the Bay of Honduras, just past the port of Puerto Cortez, the two sloops spotted a large merchant ship, the *Protestant Caesar*. They raced behind the ship in hot pursuit for hours, but the *Revenge* and the *Adventure* were too slow to catch the valuable vessel. Quickly closing on the sloops from behind was the *Queen Anne's Revenge*, which eventually overtook the sloops and closed the distance with the *Protestant Caesar*. As Blackbeard's menacing pyrate ship approached the merchant vessel, the crew realized they couldn't outsail the faster ship, so they all jumped overboard and swam to shore. Blackbeard soon pulled alongside the abandoned merchant ship, looted her, and then burned her as a warning.

The Queen Anne's Revenge Sails to Nassau

With sufficient plunder, Blackbeard's flotilla headed back home to Nassau. On the way, they passed the Isla de la Bahia which is part of the Roatan Islands. As a source of fresh water, these islands had been a well-used rendezvous spot for buccaneers since the days of Henry Morgan. From there, they took a small turtler off the Caymans then went ashore for provisions. Blackbeard continued around the west side of Cuba and through the Florida Straits, taking one more small Spanish sloop of eight guns before reaching Nassau. That sloop was destined to become the sloop where Blackbeard would make his last stand less than eight months later. Blackbeard and his fleet arrived at Nassau in late April 1718. His fleet was described in a letter from the Lt. Governor of Bermuda dated May 31, 1718, "... one Tatch with whom is Major Bonnett of Barbados in a ship of 36 guns and 300 men, also in company with them a sloop of 12 guns and 115 men, and two other ships, in all which, it is computed there are 700 men or thereabt..."

Soon after his arrival, Blackbeard and his crew learned about the Royal Proclamation and the offer for pardon from many of the former pyrates who had already accepted it. **This probably included Blackbeard's old captain, trusted friend, and mentor, Benjamin Hornigold. It is not known if Hornigold was in port at the time, but if he was, he certainly would have met his old friend.** Blackbeard also would have learned that all his acts of piracy that he had committed after January 5, 1718 made him ineligible for the pardon. **Of course, that only would be true if the government official issuing the pardon knew Blackbeard had committed them.** All he needed to do was to find a friendly governor that was unaware of his recent acts. However, what Blackbeard did next was totally unexpected.

Four sailing vessels innocently approached the bustling harbor of Charles Town and, as usual, the pilot boat went out to meet them. However, these vessels weren't there to engage in honest trade, they were Blackbeard's pyrate vessels. The largest, richest, and most sophisticated port between Cuba and Philadelphia, the South Carolina city of Charles Town, spelled Charleston today, was a busy seaport filled with homes, taverns, churches, merchants, and shops. During the last decade of the 17th century, the port had been "pyrate-friendly," but that definitely was not the case in 1718. With its close proximity to the sea and minimal coastal defenses, Charles Town was a prime target for pyrates.

On May 22, 1718 Blackbeard began his siege and blockaded the harbor. He captured and looted eight to ten vessels, beginning with the pilot sloop that was sent out to escort the *Queen Anne's Revenge* into port. Of the

MAY 1718

Blackbeard blockades Charles Town, South Carolina.

following excerpts, the first two were extracted from several letters written by eyewitness accounts and the third is from a letter from Governor Johnson dated June 18, 1718:

> "... as he was just proceeding from the barr was unfortunately taken by two pirates, one a large French ship mounted with 40 guns and the other a sloop mounted with 12 guns with two other sloopes for their tenders having in all about 300 men all English the ship is commanded by one Theach and the sloop by one Richards ... Richards and another person master of one of their tenders to towne with a message to send them a chest of medicines ... Richards and his men were parading themselves up and down the principal streets, and their imprudent behavior aroused the indignation of the people to the highest pitch. They were protected by fear of a broadside ashore.
> ... about 14 days ago 4 sail of them appeared in sight of the Town tooke our pilot boat and afterwards 8 or 9 sail wth several of the best inhabitants of this place on board and then sent me word if I did not imediately send them a chest of medicines they would put every prisoner to death ... This company is commanded by one Teach alias Blackbeard has a ship of 40 od guns under him and 3 sloopes tenders besides and are in all above 400 men."

All in all, he took nine prisoners including an important merchant, Samuel Wragg, and held them for ransom. In addition to the spices, gold, and trade goods they had already taken from the prize vessels, Blackbeard demanded a chest of medicine from Governor Robert Johnson. This has puzzled historians for nearly 300 years. No one is absolutely certain what was meant by "a chest of medicine" or what kind of medicine it was. Some have suggested that the medicine was needed to cure venereal disease among the crew—but that is supposition. Unless new documents are miraculously discovered that clearly identify exactly what was given to Blackbeard, the true nature of the medicine shall remain anyone's guess.

Of interest is after Captain Richards of the *Revenge* and some of the crewmen came ashore to deliver the ransom message, they terrorized the residents with no fear of reprisal. They walked the streets and exhibited what was described as "imprudent behavior" and did pretty much as they pleased. There is no report of them actually hurting anyone, but I'm certain they frightened everyone and made a significant impact on the lives of the townsfolk. Eventually, the governor decided to grant Blackbeard's request and sent the mysterious chest of medicine over to the *Queen Anne's Revenge*. Afterwards, Blackbeard and his fleet quietly departed.

Fish Town was well named. Today, it is the quaint and beautiful town of Beaufort, North Carolina, but in 1718 it was a tiny fishing village of wooden shacks and a few well-built homes. It faces an isolated inlet on the Atlantic just west of Cape Lookout. The waters of the inlet were very tricky to navigate. Shifting sand bars were everywhere and the changing channels made the water's depth unpredictable to everyone except the locals. Dozens of small fishing vessels would have always been present to some degree. This inlet was called Topsail Inlet in the 18th century, which should not be confused with the modern-day Topsail Inlet that lies further south.

June 1718

Queen Anne's Revenge sinks.

The tranquility of the normal fishing operations was suddenly disrupted when a large and well-armed ship approached with three sloops in escort. The fishermen must have been astounded at the sight. Ships of that size just didn't sail those waters, let alone a pyrate flotilla. Pyrates had never come to Fish Town before. But what happened next was even more astonishing. As the *Queen Anne's Revenge* quietly navigated through the inlet, the imposing three-masted pyrate ship ran aground. The next morning while presumably attempting to assist the grounded ship, the sloop *Adventure*, under the command of one of Blackbeard's most trusted friends, Hezekiah Hands, also ran aground. Both vessels were eventually lost, but for quite some time, they rested exposed on the sand bar.

A pyrate ship running aground was big news and the story spread rapidly throughout the southern colonies. Within a month the news had reached Hampton, Virginia, and attracted the attention of the royal naval authorities. The event was mentioned in a letter from Captain Ellis Brand of HMS *Lyme* to the Lords of Admiralty dated July 12, 1718, "On the 10th of June or thereabouts a large pyrate Ship of forty Guns with three Sloops in her company came upon the coast of North Carolina ware they endeavour'd To goe in to a harbour, call'd Topsail Inlett, the Ship Stuck upon the barr att the entrance of the harbour and is lost; as is one of the sloops . . ."

Details about the pyrate command structure and a description of the sinking of the two vessels were described in a disposition given by David Herriot in 1719:

". . . they arrived at Topsail Inlet in North Carolina, having then under their Command the said Ship *Queen Anne's Revenge,* the Sloop commanded by Richards, this Deponent's Sloop, commanded by one Capt. Hands, one of the said Pirate Crew, and a small empty Sloop which they found near the Havana . . . the said Thatch's Ship *Queen Anne's Revenge* run a-ground off of the Bar of Topsail-Inlet, and the said Thatch sent his quartermaster to command this Deponent's Sloop to come to his Assistance; but She run a-ground likewise about Gun-Shot from the said Thatch . . . Thatch's Ship and this Deponent's Sloop were wreck'd;"

As you may recall, Herriot joined Blackbeard's group when his sloop, *Adventure*, was taken off the Turneffe Islands three months before the *Queen Anne's Revenge* and his sloop ran aground.

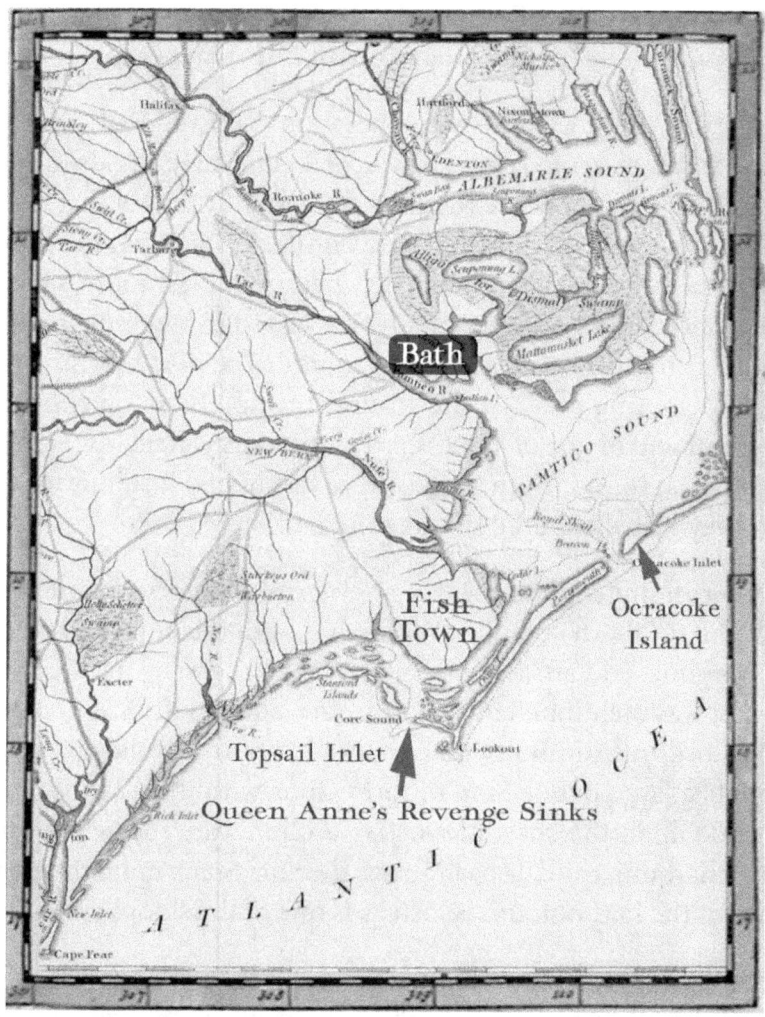

Figure 24: *Topsail Inlet and Ocracoke*

Since both vessels had sunk in shallow water, a massive salvage operation was possible. The crew had plenty of time to unload all the valuables and personal affects. Local legend maintains that Blackbeard stayed at a small house while the salvage operations were going on. It is likely that this legend is true. Now called "Hammock House" because it was constructed on a raised area known as a hammock, the house dates to 1709 or earlier. In the early 18th century, the two-story house was an easily recognizable landmark in the town that could be seen from the sea outside the inlet.

Because of this, it was used as a navigational aid for ships entering Topsail Inlet. Its location actually appears on navigational charts from the period. Local legend contends that Blackbeard stayed at Hammock House while supervising salvage operations, but this is unlikely. He was too busy dealing with the pirates who were loyal to Stede Bonnet.

But there is one big question which still remains. Was the grounding of the *Queen Anne's Revenge* intentional? This question has been debated for hundreds of years. The argument for "no" has always been that Blackbeard had no reason to destroy his fleet at the height of his success. Supporters of this view suppose that he entered the inlet hoping to re-provision his supplies and thought Fish Town looked like a safe spot. Blackbeard had no idea that the waters were so tricky to navigate and while trying to enter this little port, he struck a sandbar. This idea seems unlikely when closely examined. Topsail Inlet is filled with sandbars, small islands, tricky channels, and marshes. All of this means that a large ship would have an extremely difficult time making port—even if the water was deep enough. Any experienced sailor could tell this with just one glance. Also, there was the possibility of being attacked by vessels from Charles Town or even the Royal Navy. His ship could easily be spotted and trapped with no escape. Then there was the town itself. No taverns, no wealthy merchants, very few women, and exceptionally limited supplies. It's just not a good choice for a pyrate to make port.

The argument for "yes" has always been that there would be absolutely no reason for Blackbeard to enter Topsail Inlet unless he intended to ground his ship all along. The pyrates had just left Charles Town where they had taken all the provisions they needed. There was nothing in Fish Town to loot, and the tiny village had nothing to offer a large pyrate crew. Additionally, many of Bonnet's crew, such as David Herriot, Ignatius Pell, and William Scott, all testified at their trial that the sinking of the *Queen Anne's Revenge* was intentional. Herriot said, "It was generally believed the said Thatch run his Vessel a-ground on purpose to break up the Companies, and to secure what Moneys and Effects he had got for himself . . ." If you subscribe to the "Yes" option, Blackbeard's actions make perfect sense. First, he wanted to downscale so he didn't have to split his fortune with so many pyrates. Second, he intended to take the King's Pardon. This would be impossible if the *Queen Anne's Revenge* was still sailing about. **Between the two arguments, I think the choice of 'yes' is the correct one because that's exactly what Blackbeard did.**

There were about 300 pyrates with Blackbeard when he blockaded Charles Town according to the eyewitness accounts. After the *Queen Anne's Revenge* sank, only about 100 pyrates remained. There was no contemporary

1705–1722

Bath was the unofficial capital of North Carolina.

report or mention of any wrongdoing by Blackbeard concerning these 200 pyrates, so perhaps they were simply put ashore somewhere and peacefully left the crew with their share. After the sinking of the *Queen Anne's Revenge* and the *Adventure*, the pyrates had only two vessels left, Stede Bonnet's original sloop *Revenge* and the small Spanish sloop they took off Havana a few months earlier. Blackbeard renamed the small Spanish sloop the *Adventure* and sailed away in it with 40 of his most trusted pyrates. It seems that pyrates often named their sloops the *Adventure*. Confusing, isn't it?

The partnership between Blackbeard and Stede Bonnet was definitely over. Their parting was not a friendly one. Bonnet obtained a small boat and sailed to Bath and received a pardon from Governor Eden. Meanwhile, Blackbeard and five of his men boarded the *Revenge* with weapons drawn and managed to capture the sloop. Once the *Revenge* was under Blackbeard's control, he ordered fourteen of the men on the *Revenge* to join him. Perhaps those fourteen were secretly on Blackbeard's side all along. He also took all of their money, small arms, and provisions. Afterward, everyone was put on board Blackbeard's sloop *Adventure* and the *Revenge* was abandoned. They all sailed away from Topsail Inlet through the shallow channel that runs northeast between the barrier islands and the main shore, eventually arriving at a small island where Blackbeard put the remaining twenty-five of Bonnet's pirates ashore and marooned them. Blackbeard sailed away and out of sight.

Two-and-a-half days later, Bonnet returned from Bath on his boat. He had been successful and had a certificate given to him by Governor Eden, pardoning him for his piratical crimes. His men called to him from their island, and he put his boat ashore. They were all desperate to be rescued. They told Bonnet of Blackbeard's unexpected attack and that the *Revenge* was still at Topsail Inlet. As they climbed aboard Bonnet's boat, he explained to them that he intended to sail to St. Thomas and obtain letters of marque, which would legally allow him to take Spanish Vessels. This is consistent throughout the testimony of Bonnet's crew at their trial. John Carman said, "I would not have went on board, but Maj. Bonnet shewed me the Act of Grace." This "Act of Grace" was in reference to Bonnet's certificate. William Morrison said, "Capt. Thatch had run the Sloop ashore, and Maj. Bonnet went up to the Governor for the Act of Grace; and when he returned, he told me I might go to St. Thomas's." Ignatius Pell stated it best by saying, "Maj. Bonnet came with the Boat, and told us, as we were on a Maroon Island, that he was going to St. Thomas's to get a Commission from the Emperor to go against the Spaniards a Privateering..."

According to Herriot's 1719 deposition, the *Revenge* was re-named the *Royal James* and all the remaining pyrates left together in the two sloops. However, it isn't exactly clear how Blackbeard wound up with the Spanish sloop *Adventure*, or how Bonnet assumed command of the *Royal James*. Herriot stated, "and the said Thatch and all the other Sloop's Companies went on board the Revenge, afterwards called the Royal James, and on board the other Sloop they found empty off the Havana . . ." Teach and Bonnet had parted company forever. Stede Bonnet decided to continue on as a pyrate and was on his own as captain for the first time in his career.

After leaving Fish Town, Blackbeard sailed northeast to the Island of Ocracoke. These pyrates established a camp on the southwestern side of the island which they used as a small base of operations. Ocracoke was an absolutely ideal spot for a pyrate base. About ten miles long and one-quarter-mile wide, Ocracoke Island is part of a 200-mile long string of narrow barrier islands known as the Outer Banks which stretch from Virginia past Topsail Inlet, North Carolina. Today, Ocracoke is a charming tourist destination with restaurants, bed and breakfasts, and a Blackbeard museum. But in the early 18th century, it was an isolated and uninhabited island located near the main shipping lanes.

Pamlico Sound is the large body of water between those barrier islands and the mainland of North Carolina. In the early 18th century, all the ports in North Carolina were along two important rivers, the Neuse and the Pamlico, which flowed into the sound from the west. Literally every vessel traveling to and from any of the ports of North Carolina and the Atlantic Ocean had to sail near Ocracoke Island as the only entrance to Pamlico Sound was through the narrow channel that ran between Ocracoke Island and Portsmouth Island. That entrance was very difficult to navigate due to the shifting sandbars and shallow water. Large vessels with deep drafts couldn't make it through at all and smaller vessels had to slow down to navigate the channel. From July to November 1718, every vessel that passed through did so under the watchful eyes of Blackbeard's pyrates. If they were enemy vessels, the pyrates would have time to get away. If they were prize vessels, they'd be easy to take.

But another reason why Ocracoke Island was ideal for a base was that the island had the only freshwater well within 30 miles. Today, visitors can still see an old well called Teach's Hole, located about 2,000 feet south of the light house in a thicket close to an old slough. It was supposedly a place where local sailors in the early 18th century replenished their water supply before heading out to sea. As the only source of freshwater on the island, Blackbeard's camp must have been located within walking distance, just north of the slough.

1713–1722

Governor Charles Eden, 2nd Governor of North Carolina

In June 1718, while 15 of his men were building a base on Ocracoke, Blackbeard and the remainder of his crewmen sailed northwest across Pamlico Sound and up the Pamlico River to the small port town of Bath. That was the home of Governor Charles Eden and the capital of North Carolina. Upon arrival, Blackbeard—the notorious pyrate who had just blockaded Charles Town—went directly to the house of Tobias Knight, the attorney general and secretary of the colony, and requested a royal pardon for himself and all of his men in accordance with the King's Proclamation. Without a moment of hesitation, Tobias Knight forwarded his request to Governor Charles Eden who gladly gave it to them.

Why would Governor Eden grant the pardon to Blackbeard and his pyrates? In order to qualify for the pardon, a pyrate couldn't have committed any acts of piracy after January 5, 1718. Blackbeard had just come from Charles Town where he had taken 8 vessels, held some of the city's citizens as hostages, blockaded the port, and terrorized the city. These recent actions clearly disqualified him. There can be only one of three explanations for Governor Eden's actions, all of which have been debated in publications for about 300 years. The first explanation is that Governor Eden didn't know about the recent deeds of Blackbeard and his pyrates. This is very unlikely because Blackbeard's blockade of Charles Town about one month earlier had made national news. The second explanation is that Blackbeard intimidated the governor and forced him to grant the pardons against his will. This is also highly unlikely since Blackbeard only had 35 men with him and just a small sloop.

However, the third explanation makes the most sense and I think is the most likely. Tobias Knight, the governor's secretary, and Blackbeard were already good friends. I shall provide supportive evidence of this claim later in chapter 49. I believe that Blackbeard knew Tobias Knight long before he began his career as a pyrate and that he counted on Knight's support, perhaps as far back as April 1718 when he arrived in Nassau and first learned about the pardon.

After being pardoned, some of these supposedly fierce and blood-thirsty pyrates settled down to peaceful and quiet lives as law-abiding citizens in Bath. Some of the others went to Pennsylvania and perhaps used their share of the loot to build farms. Blackbeard himself, according to local legend, careened his sloop on Plum Point, which was just downstream from the town of Bath and across the creek from the house of Tobias Knight. However, he didn't build a house on the property because he didn't have time.

Chapter 44
Woodes Rogers and the Rebel with a Cause

The normal tranquility of the pyrate port of Nassau, if one could call it that, was broken the evening of July 21, 1718 when the Royal Navy warship, HMS *Rose*, quietly slipped into the harbor and dropped anchor. The pyrates must have been shocked at the sight and the news spread quickly. The flotilla from England had finally arrived. Commanding this flotilla was the new governor of the province, Woodes Rogers. He was an ideal choice as governor of the pyrate haven. He was the most experienced and respected privateer from the last war with Spain. He was considered to be one of them and he understood how the pyrates thought. He may have even been friends with some of the pyrates at Nassau. Also, he was very well-connected politically in England. The day after the pardon went into effect, Woodes Rogers was officially appointed "Captain General and Governor in Chief" of the Colony of Nassau. He knew that it would take several months to prepare his expedition, so he sent HMS *Phenix* to Nassau four months earlier to deliver the news with a King's Pardon. Each of the pyrates of Nassau began to realize that the days of their lawless pyrate port and unrestrained lifestyle were over. Each would have to choose between the life of a lawful citizen or a hunted pyrate with a price on his head.

Of all the pyrates who absolutely refused to accept the King's Pardon, Charles Vane and his crew of about 90 pyrates were the most notorious. Upon the arrival of HMS *Rose*, ahead of the rest of Rogers fleet, Vane and his crew realized that the king's authority had finally arrived and they decided to escape the port rather than be forced into taking the King's Pardon. With only a small six-gun Bermuda sloop at their disposal, Vane and his men took a French-built 22-gun ship and set it afire. The burning ship was then sent directly toward the *Rose* as a diversion. The fire ship actually had little effect as the crew of the *Rose* simply cut the anchor cable and the ship maneuvered out of the way. Failing to escape that evening, Vane was desperate to get out the next morning.

That morning came with the arrival of six more Royal Navy vessels, including the flagship, *Delicia* and another Royal Navy warship, HMS *Milford*. Aboard were 100 soldiers, 130 new colonists, a large amount of supplies, and religious pamphlets to hand out to the pyrates. As the remainder of the Rogers fleet entered the harbor, Vane and his crew set sail in their Bermuda sloop, the *Ranger* with their pyrate flag waving in the wind. They safely sailed past the burning fire ship and shot their way through Roger's fleet and then out to the open sea. Two sloops were sent after Vane, but they couldn't catch him. A detailed account of Vane's escape was contained in a letter Rogers wrote in October 1718:

". . . Charles Vane who command'd the pirates . . . finding it impossible to escape us, he with about 90 men fled away in a sloop wearing the black flag, and fir'd guns of defiance when they perceiv'd their sloop out say I'd . . ."

Woodes Rogers stepped ashore at Nassau on the morning of July 22, 1718 and assumed his position as Governor. He immediately began accepting pardons. Among the first to accept was Benjamin Hornigold. He was followed by 208 others. But there were still many pyrates like Charles Vane who hadn't yet accepted the King's Pardon, either because they were at sea or they were in remote ports where the news of the King's Pardon hadn't reached or because they absolutely refused to accept any pardon from King George I. These pyrates must have been motivated by political reasons—pyrates who supported the Jacobite cause. Hornigold provided the solution to this problem. Among all the ex-pyrates, Benjamin Hornigold was the man Woodes Rogers could trust the most. Hornigold was assigned as chief pyrate hunter for the King. Send a pyrate to catch a pyrate. It worked for Henry Morgan back at Port Royal in the 1670s.

Hornigold was the perfect choice. First, he had remained as loyal to Great Britain as one could during those times. Secondly, he was the pyrate king. He had the knowledge, leadership, experience, and reputation to organize a pyrate hunting fleet and he immediately began recruiting all the ex-pyrates he could. Ben Hornigold proved better than expected. His legendary status as the king of the privateers helped him organize a formidable pyrate hunting fleet. His loyalty to the King and to Rogers was very divisive among the ex-pyrates which seemed to assist Woodes Rogers in establishing power. In a letter Rogers wrote, ". . . Capt. Hornygold having proved honest, and disobliged his old friends by seazing this vessel it devides the people here and makes me stronger then[than] I expected."

1718

Charles Vane operates in the Caribbean.

After shooting his way out of Nassau, Vane set up a temporary base on Abaco Island, north of New Providence. Soon afterwards, Vane captured a small sloop and kept it as a consort vessel. He gave command of this consort sloop to his quartermaster, a man named Yates, and Jack Rackham was promoted to quartermaster of the *Ranger*. Soon after he shot his way out of Nassau Charles Vane had become the most well-known of the pyrates who actively defied King George's authority and became the prime adversary and threat to all of the repatriated ex-pyrates of Nassau. Vane was public enemy number one and Hornigold's prime task was catching him. However, Charles Vane managed to elude him.

The anticipated war with Spain was finally a reality. Even though war wasn't officially declared until December 1718, the war against Spain was in full force by August. On August 11, 1718 a major naval engagement between English and Spanish war fleets took place off the coast of Sicily. The ex-pyrates of Nassau who had accepted the King's Pardon could now acquire letters of marque and become privateers, but not Charles Vane.

The first question one has when discussing Charlie Vane is why did he refuse the King's Pardon and shoot his way out of Nassau? Even if Vane had no intention of giving up piracy, he could have easily pretended to accept the pardon and sail out of Nassau unhindered with his 22-gun ship. A pyrate who cares nothing for honesty certainly wouldn't have hesitated to take advantage of the situation. Once at sea, he could have plundered as he liked. But Vane not only refused, he made his refusal known to everyone. He risked everything by fighting his way through the British fleet in the harbor of Nassau. That type of behavior seems more consistent with the actions of a highly principled man making a strong politically statement. His actions are easily understandable if Charles Vane and his crew were Jacobites and supporters of James Edward Stuart and thoroughly opposed to the rule of King George I.

Accepting the King's Pardon included swearing loyalty and allegiance to George I, which would have been totally unacceptable to staunch Jacobites. It would have gone against their personal and political principles, even though they were pyrates. Jacobites would have looked upon Woodes Rogers as an enemy, the agent of a false king. Fighting their way out of port as they did might have appealed to them as an opportunity to show up King George's forces. As we have seen, Governor George Hamilton started Nassau in the first place as a resource to generate funds to finance the Jacobite rebellion back in Scotland. Henry Jennings was his partner and Vane was one of Jennings' original crewmembers. But there is more compelling evidence that Vane was a Jacobite long before Woodes Rogers came to Nassau. This evidence involves Admiral George Cammock.

1718–1720

War of the Quadruple Alliance—England, France, Holy Roman Empire, and the Dutch Republic against Spain

Admiral George Cammock

A celebrated naval hero throughout the War of the Spanish Succession, Admiral George Cammock was a highly successful officer in the English Royal Navy with an exceptionally splendid record. In April 1712 George Cammock was a captain and sailed the Atlantic under orders to pursue and attack French privateers. On the 28th he took the 16-gun French privateer, *Salamander*. On the following day, he came upon three merchant galleys that originally had been English but were previously captured by the French. Captain Cammock managed to re-capture them totally intact. He escorted the galleys to the English port of Crookhaven. However, they had been pursued by a large French privateer of 40 guns, the *Count Giraldin*, commanded by Captain du Pre. Realizing that the galleys, and indeed the port, was in great danger, Cammock moved ten guns ashore and hastily constructed gun placements creating two-gun batteries on each side of the harbor. When the French ship arrived, Captain du Pre, decided it was better just to sail away. However, Cammock quickly loaded his guns back on board and took off in pursuit of the French ship. With the weather gage in his favor, Cammock overtook the French ship and captured her at sea. However, when Queen Anne died in 1714 and King George I came to the throne, Cammock so protested the event that he was dismissed from the Royal Navy. He became a Jacobite, swearing to put James on the throne. Finding no support in England, he resigned his commission in the English Royal Navy and accepted assignment as an admiral in the Spanish Navy. He later commanded Spanish forces in battle against the very country that he had once loved.

What does this have to do with Charles Vane you ask? When Cammock was commanding naval forces in the Atlantic in the last war, it is possible that Vane may have been one of the privateers who served under his command. During the War of the Spanish Succession, privateers were often assigned to support Royal Naval operations, although very few records have survived. As of yet, there are no records that specifically tie Vane to Cammock during those years; however, there is evidence that Vane knew Cammock. For the Jacobites, the year of 1717 was a grim one. Their revolution had been effectively ended in England and Scotland two years earlier. Their main supporters were scattered throughout France and Spain. The only other supporters they had were a few bands of pyrates sailing the Caribbean. In that year, Charles Vane wrote a letter to Admiral George Cammock and stated that that if France pledges allegiance to James, that Cammock should come to Nassau to lead a fleet of pyrate ships against the forces of King George I. It does not seem likely that a pyrate would write such a letter to someone he had never met. Additionally, when added to Vane's association with Governor Hamilton, and his associations with other pyrates—who I also believe to be Jacobites, pyrates like Edward Teach and Stede Bonnet—I believe the conclusion that Vane was a true Jacobite is inescapable.

However, Charles Vane's behavior was more like the way that pyrates are portrayed in books and film rather than an honorable supporter of a noble cause. He was a very disagreeable fellow, cruel and cold-hearted, and was one of the few pyrates during this era that reportedly tortured and killed his captives. In May 1718 the captains of two plundered sloops made a report of Vane's piracy to the Governor of Bermuda that tells of him torturing and killing three captives within a few hours. There are many other reports of Vane torturing captives in order to get them to reveal hidden loot aboard their vessels. There are also reports of him killing captives who surrendered to him. Additionally, there are accounts that he was cruel to his own crew as well, sometime cheating them out of their share and even having a few of the whipped by the Boatswain for misconduct. This is extremely rare among pyrates. Among most pyrates of this period, captains were elected by the crew and they retained authority only as long as the crew was satisfied. A dissatisfied crew would quickly lead to a new captain. It was only a matter of time before Vane's crew mutinied.

But what of Benjamin Hornigold? He never did capture Charles Vane. Hornigold did capture the pyrate John Auger and twelve others. Over the next year Hornigold is mentioned several times in dispatches, all touting his success. Then, suddenly, his name was never mentioned again in the official record. The only account of Hornigold after 1719 came from the unreliable Charles Johnson who wrote, "Captain Hornigold, another of the famous pirates, was cast away upon rocks, a great way from land, and perished, but five of his men got into a canoe and were saved." It is believed that the great privateer legend died in a hurricane somewhere off the coast of Mexico in 1719. The death of Benjamin Hornigold marked the beginning of the end of the privateers.

Chapter 45
Blackbeard's Girlfriend

Blackbeard was married 14 times with, "about a dozen might be still living." His 14th wife was a 16-year-old girl he married shortly after he received the pardon from Governor Eden and bought his property in Bath, North Carolina. Governor Eden even performed the ceremony. That night, "after he had lain all night, it was his custom to invite five or six of his brutal companions to come ashore and he would force her to prostitute herself to them all, one after another, before his face." This account was first written by Charles Johnson and has been retold and embellished in so many subsequent biographies that it acquired the status of fact. In reality, none of that ever happened. There is no record or account that Blackbeard was ever married, much less 14 times, or that he customarily gave his wives to his crew. Further, all the North Carolina court records from that period still exist and there is no mention of Governor Eden performing a marriage ceremony for Blackbeard.

Author Robert Lee added the name of Mary Ormond to the story in his 1974 book, *Blackbeard the Pirate*. This claim is based on a 1947 letter written by Ada S. Bragg to a relative, Mrs. E. P. White, which stated that Mrs. White was the great-great niece of Mary Ormond who was married to Edward Teach, known as Blackbeard. A search of the actual records showed that there was a woman named Mary Ormond, but she lived long after Blackbeard's death. Today, websites and even some historians believe this fictional marriage to Mary Ormond to be fact. The real story is far more intriguing.

Discord Lane

Philadelphia was already a major metropolitan city and port in 1718. As we learned from an article in the *Boston News Letter*, Blackbeard had ties to Philadelphia, "Commanded by one Teach, who Formerly Sail'd Mate out of this Port" meaning Philadelphia. As discussed earlier, just 20 miles downriver from Philadelphia, the small port of Marcus Hook had been a well-known pyrate trading port since the 1690s. Clearly shown on a 1706 map of the city, a street named Discord Lane was named for the temporary discord that the pyrate visitors brought to the community. It was the only place in town where a pyrate could buy liquor and indulge in noisy conduct. Local legend contends that Blackbeard had visited that port regularly and was in love with a woman who lived there.

The book *Annals of Philadelphia* by John F. Watson was published in 1842, at a time when people still told and retold stories. Included in this book are many accounts and oral traditions from the local community and the grandchildren of people who claim they actually knew Blackbeard. They tell us that "Blackbeard used to revel at Margaret's house." *Margaret* refers to a Swedish woman who lived in a small house near Discord Lane, which appears on a 300-year-old map of the area. The house still stands today and has been confirmed by experts to date to the early 18th century.

John F. Watson's book also tells of an oral tradition that a Mr. & Mrs. Coats often told their grandchildren stories of Blackbeard, the tall mariner who was known by Philadelphia's early residence to frequent an inn close to their store at 77 High Street, always with his sword by his side. Also, when Blackbeard came to town, he paid for the goods he bought. Coats said, "He bought freely and paid well. He was careful to give no direct offence to any of the settlements where they wished to be regarded as visitors and purchasers."

We are certain that Blackbeard visited Marcus Hook in August of 1718, because records show that Governor William Keith of Pennsylvania issued a warrant for Blackbeard's arrest. The only reason for Blackbeard's visit to Marcus Hook that makes any sense in the days following his acceptance of the King's Pardon is that he went there to visit his girlfriend, the mysterious Swedish woman named Margaret.

While Blackbeard enjoyed the company of his lady friend at Marcus Hook, his quartermaster, William Howard, was being arrested in Norfolk, a major seaport in Virginia. Howard had brought two slaves with him and had about £50 in coin (about $10,000 in modern currency). That amount of wealth attracted attention and soon he was recognized. The government of Virginia didn't accept the pardon granted him by Governor Eden of North Carolina and Howard was arrested based on the acts of piracy he committed after the January 5, 1718 deadline. He was going to be defended by a very prominent local attorney, John Holloway, but the governor decided to convict him without a formal trial and he was placed in the Gaol (jail).

Part of the original Gaol still exists in Williamsburg and has been restored by the Colonial Williamsburg Foundation to appear exactly the way it looked at the time of William Howard's imprisonment.

Chapter 46
Sugar, Mutiny, and the Pyrate Banyan

Two French merchant ships loaded with sugar, cocoa, and various other valuables quietly sailed along the blue waters near Bermuda. They had nothing to fear. Most of the pyrates from Nassau were now all privateers sailing under English letters of marque in the war against Spain. Bermuda was a long-established English colony with a well-respected governor and honest citizens. Since France and Great Britain were allies, no English privateer would have dared to attack a French ship. That's exactly what the French captains must have thought. They were wrong. As the merchant ships made their way across the ocean, a small but well-armed sloop approached. This was no ordinary sloop; this was a pyrate sloop with a highly experienced pyrate crew. With little warning, the black flag went up and the two merchant ships were forced to surrender or be fired upon. Perhaps there was a short battle, perhaps not, but eventually the merchant ships heaved to, took in sail, and surrendered. At one point, the captain of the pyrate sloop finally came aboard the French merchant ship. Armed to the teeth, he was an imposing figure who could frighten anyone with a simple glance. He was the pyrate captain of the sloop *Adventure* and his name was Blackbeard.

It is interesting to note Blackbeard's actions in the months that transpired before the capture of the two French sugar merchant vessels. Blackbeard and his crew of 40 had accepted the King's Pardon from Governor Eden of North Carolina in June 1718, over a month before Woodes Rogers' arrival in Nassau. His crew had spent time building a small base on Ocracoke Island. He visited his girlfriend in Marcus Hook, Pennsylvania. And he had purchased property in the town of Bath. But now, Blackbeard was back in action. True to form, he didn't harm any of the crew. He simply loaded all the cargo from both vessels onto the larger of the two and let the captured French crew sail away unharmed in the smaller vessel. The pyrates aboard the *Adventure* escorted the larger captured ship to their base at Ocracoke Island, arriving on September 1, 1718.

Their arrival was witnessed by Isaac Freeman, the captain of a small local sloop. Freeman was quoted in the *Boston News Letter*.

"Teach the Pirate has brought in a Ship to Ockrycoke Inlet and Uncig'd her, and suffers no man to go on board except a Doctor to cure his wounded men."

This statement indicates that there may have been at least some fighting involved with the capture of the two French ships, but the men may have received their wounds from accidents loading the cargo or other non-aggressive means. There also could have been illness among the crew of some kind. At any rate, the merchant ship was tied next to the pyrates' camp on Ocracoke and unloaded cargo, as well as other ship's items, were spread all over the beach.

From Ocracoke, Blackbeard traveled to Bath, the capital of the colony, in a small boat. He visited Tobias Knight, who was Chief Justice and Customs Inspector. Blackbeard claimed that he had found the French ship abandoned and the cargo was his free and clear according to salvage laws. Governor Charles Eden and Tobias Knight both agreed. Blackbeard was given possession of all goods, as well as the ship. Over the next six weeks Blackbeard made several trips between Ocracoke and Bath, generally to visit Tobias Knight. One of those visits took place on October 10, 1718 when a portion of the cargo was brought to Bath. Later, 20 barrels of cargo were found in the possession of Tobias Knight. This is certainly more evidence that Blackbeard knew both men long before turning to piracy.

September 1718

Vane blockades Charles Town

While Blackbeard was taking the two French sugar merchantmen, Charles Vane was attacking the shipping near Charles Town, repeating to a lesser degree what Blackbeard had done just a few months earlier. Vane took between eight and twelve vessels at the entrance of the harbor (accounts vary on the number) during the first week of September 1718. One of the ships he took was a 12-gun brigantine from Africa that was carrying 90 slaves. He kept the brigantine and renamed it the *Ranger*. Apparently, all of Vane's vessels were named the *Ranger*. Governor Robert Johnson of South Carolina was outraged by this second pyrate attack of the most important city in the colony, so he commissioned Colonel William Rhett to find and destroy Vane's flotilla. Rhett was given two sloops, the *Henry* and the *Sea Nymph*, both fitted out for battle with eight guns each and a total of 130 men. Five days after the pyrate attacks began Colonel Rhett sailed out of Charles Town, but Vane had vanished.

Vane's days as a captain were numbered. His harsh treatment of his own crewmen, and his constant demand for total obedience, created a great deal of dissention among his crew and was worrying some of his officers. Captain Yates had been Vane's quartermaster but was recently given command of a small sloop they had taken. During the siege of Charles Town Yates decided that he had had enough. After Vane's small fleet left Charles Town, Yates and his crew of 15 pyrates quietly sailed away one night in the darkness. But they didn't go empty handed. They managed to take a large portion of the loot and the 90 captured slaves with them. Vane was furious but there was nothing he could do. Yates was gone and his remaining crewmen were becoming more and more restless.

After the Charles Town attacks and Yates' desertion, Vane was in need of a friend. He sailed north to Blackbeard's base at Ocracoke and requested a meeting with the famous captain. The two crews joined together in what was called a pyrate Banyan which was a sort of gathering involving lots of food, drink, and general camaraderie. It was a gathering where pyrates might form partnerships and plan ventures. In pyrate terms, it was an opportunity to reach an accord and sign articles.

Since both Blackbeard and Vane had made Nassau their home port, it is very likely that they were old friends, or at the very least, that they knew each other. If they hadn't previously met, it didn't seem to make a difference. Their association provides us with just one more clue that Blackbeard was a Jacobite. Vane certainly was, and wouldn't freely associate with anyone who wasn't. For an entire week, during the month of October 1718, Blackbeard and his crew of 25 men enjoyed a pyrate Banyan with Charles Vane and his crew of 90 on the Island of Ocracoke. The members of both crews drank wine, rum, and brandy from ceramic jugs and feasted on fresh barbecued beef, pork, lamb, bluefish, turtles, and shellfish stew. No one knows any of the details of their visit or what they discussed, but when Vane sailed off, it was under friendly circumstances. This particular pyrate Banyan, however, had an enormous impact on the colonies of Virginia and North Carolina and subsequently changed world perception of pyrates to this day.

Blackbeard was virtually unknown to the English colonies until he took 20 prizes off Cape May in 1717. Even then, no one really knew very much about him. However, when Blackbeard blockaded Charles Town, the English authorities, as well as the entire population of the English colonies, began to take notice. But at the apparent height of his pyrate career, Blackbeard and his crew accepted the King's Pardon and were living peacefully in North Carolina. Many politicians in the colonies were furious with Governor Eden when they found out that he had granted Blackbeard the

King's Pardon. To make matters worse, just two months later Blackbeard broke his pledge and took two French merchant vessels. Then, there was Charles Vane who also attacked shipping at Charles Town. At that time, Vane was more notorious than Blackbeard. After all, just three months earlier Vane had shot his way out of Nassau and past the seven ships of the Royal Navy. News that Blackbeard and Vane were both at Ocracoke soon reached Virginia and alarmed everyone. By October 1718 Vane and Blackbeard had become the most well-known and notorious pyrates of the North American coast. They must have feared that these two pyrate captains were forming some sort of partnership. It was especially alarming because the authorities in North Carolina were apparently doing nothing to stop it. The news of this Banyan rapidly caused a plan to be put in motion that led to the death of Blackbeard.

November 1718

Vane's crew mutinies and elects Jack Rackham as their captain.

As for Vane, after leaving Ocracoke on his brigantine, *Ranger*, with his old Bermuda sloop alongside as a consort sloop, Vane sailed to the Windward Passage between Cuba and Florida. In November 1718, they spotted a large ship. It looked like easy pickings. As Vane's sloops approached, they hoisted their pyrate flags, fully expecting the ship to heave to and surrender. Instead, they got a full broadside which totally shocked them. This was no merchant vessel; it was a French man o' war.

The crew wanted to continue the attack. If successful, that man o' war would have made a terrific pyrate ship. Imagine a ship built as a man o' war with a pyrate crew flying the black flag. However, Vane always preferred to take easy prizes and often refused to attack well-armed vessels. This particular case was no exception, so Vane ordered his vessels to break contact and sail away. This was the final straw for the crew. They mutinied and elected the quartermaster, Jack Rackham as their new captain. Calico Jack Rackham, as he was called, had been with Vane for several years and was now beginning a pyrate career of his own. He kept the brigantine and Vane with a few loyal crew members were allowed to leave in the same small sloop they had used to shoot their way out of Nassau several months earlier.

Starting all over again, Vane managed to take a few more prizes until February 1719 when he encountered a fierce storm in the Bay of Honduras. His sloop ran aground on a small uninhabited island, most of his crew drowned, and Charles Vane was marooned. When a ship finally sailed by, Vane hailed the ship from shore. However, this ship was commanded by Captain Holford, a former pyrate who had taken the King's Pardon and knew Vane personally. Knowing Vane's reputation for ruthlessness, Captain Holford refused to take the marooned pyrate on board.

Vane was eventually rescued by another merchant vessel but as fate would have it, his luck had run out. In an odd turn of circumstances, the merchant vessel that rescued Vane spotted Captain Holford's ship at sea. In a gesture of friendship, the merchant ship's captain politely invited Captain Holford onboard for a few drinks. As Captain Holford stepped over the ship's rail, he immediately recognized Charles Vane and alerted the merchant ship's captain as to Vane's true identity. Vane was immediately taken to Holford's ship and put in irons. Holford then sailed to Jamaica where Vane was turned over to the authorities. Charles Vane was tried and hanged for piracy on March 22, 1720. His body was hung from a gibbet on Gun Cay, at the mouth of Port Royal Harbor as a warning to all pyrates.

Chapter 47
The Royal James

NOVEMBER 1718

Stede Bonnet and the *Royal James*.

What of Stede Bonnet? As mentioned earlier, according to Herriot's 1719 deposition, Bonnet took his original sloop, *Adventure*, and re-named it the *Royal James* when he parted company with Blackbeard in June of 1718. That event once again gives us remarkable insight into the political motivation of Blackbeard, Bonnet, and perhaps most of the crewmen. Re-naming the sloop the *Royal James* was a direct reference to James Edward Stuart, the Pretender to the Throne. That was yet another clear indication that Blackbeard and Stede Bonnet were Jacobite supporters, or at the very least, wanted to appear so.

Stede Bonnet was sailing on his own as captain of his sloop for the first time without Blackbeard's assistance. He appointed David Herriot as his sailing master and named Robert Tucker as his quartermaster and in July 1718, he sailed out as a pyrate in search of prizes. Bonnet chose deception as his tactic. He approached merchant vessels and introduced himself as Captain Thomas and pretended to offer trade. Once invited on board, his pyrate crew suddenly assaulted the vessels and overwhelmed the surprised crew. But after using that tactic twice, he returned to the usual approach of raising the pyrate flag and terrorizing the prize ship right from the start of the pursuit. The *Royal James* sailed north to the Delaware Bay and took 11 more prizes. He kept the last two sloops, *Francis* and *Fortune*, along with some the prize ship's crew who voluntarily joined his crew. By August 1, 1718, Bonnet had a flotilla of three sloops, but the *Royal James* was badly in need of careening. They sailed to Cape Fear, an isolated spot on the southern coast of North Carolina close to the city of Wilmington. Bonnet and his men were in hope of careening their vessels in secrecy. Their choice was a poor one.

Charles Town had recently been attacked by pyrates under the command of Charles Vane and the Governor of South Carolina, Robert Johnson, wanted all pyrates stamped out. He commissioned Colonel William Rhett to seek out and destroy all pyrates near the colony. Rhett was given two sloops, the *Henry* and the *Sea Nymph,* both fitted out for battle with eight guns each. He also had a total of 130 men divided between the two sloops. Rhett's sloops sailed out of Charles Town to look for Vane, but he missed him. Then, Colonel Rhett heard of some pyrates near Cape Fear. He thought it might be Vane, but it was actually Stede Bonnet. On September 26, 1718 Colonel Rhett appeared at the mouth of the Cape Fear with his two sloops. Rhett was aboard his sloop *Henry*, which ran aground as they entered the river. Bonnet mistook the sloops for merchant vessels and sent three canoes over to the sloops to capture them. As the canoes approached their crew recognized that these were well-armed sloops of war, not merchant sloops. They quickly returned to warn Bonnet.

Bonnet had 46 pyrates scattered among his three sloops, but they were all brought aboard the *Royal James* during the night in order to make a quick getaway the next morning. At daybreak on September 27, 1718, the *Royal James* slowly sailed directly toward Rhett's sloops. All three opened fire at about the same time. Rhett divided his forces and tried to attack Bonnet on both sides, but as Bonnet maneuvered to sail past them, all three sloops ran aground. Over the next five or six hours the three sloops remained motionless firing volleys at each other with little progress. The pyrates continued to shout challenges to the Charles Town forces, daring them to come aboard and fight hand-to-hand. Bonnet himself showed great courage patrolling the deck with a pistol drawn and threatening to kill any pyrate who fled or refused to fight. Eventually the rising tide lifted Rhett's two sloops free while the *Royal James* remained grounded. Realizing that defeat was near, Bonnet ordered his sloop to be blown up, but the crew refused and accepted capture. Bonnet lost twelve men in the battle while killing 10 and wounding 14 of Rhett's crew. Colonel Rhett returned to Charles Town on October 3, 1718 with the captured pyrates.

The majority of the pyrates were held in the town provost dungeon. Much of the original structure still remains today as a museum called The Old Exchange Building and Provost Dungeon, located in the oldest part of modern Charleston, South Carolina. However, Bonnet, his boatswain, Ignatius Pell, and his sailing master, David Herriot were separated and held in the provost marshal's house. On October 24th Bonnet and Herriot managed to escape and an offer of £700 bounty was placed on their heads. Bonnet and Herriot joined company with a slave and an Indian. The four men stole a small boat and made for the north shore of Charles Town harbor, but the winds and lack of supplies forced them to land on Sullivan's Island. Eventually, a posse found them and opened fire killing Herriot and wounding the slave and the Indian. Bonnet surrendered and was returned

September 1718

Stede Bonnet captured off Cape Fear, North Carolina.

to Charles Town, this time held in the dungeon. At his trial, he was only charged with two counts of piracy, the taking of the *Francis* and *Fortune* in the Delaware Bay. That's all the prosecution really needed to hang them as pyrates. Among the witnesses who testified against Bonnet and his crew were the two former captains of the *Francis* and *Fortune*. Ignatius Pell, the boatswain on the *Royal James*, turned King's Evidence against Bonnet in return for a full pardon. Many other members of Bonnet's crew reluctantly testified against him too in hopes of a lighter sentence.

Bonnet pled "not guilty" and claimed that the others had forced him to be a pyrate. He claimed that even though he was the captain, he could do nothing with his crew. He conducted his own defense, cross-examining the witnesses to little avail, and calling character witnesses. Judge Trott made a long and damning summation of the evidence and the jury delivered a guilty verdict. Bonnet was sentenced to death. While awaiting his execution, Bonnet wrote a lengthy and somewhat whimpering letter to Governor Johnson begging for mercy, but that didn't work either. Bonnet was ultimately hanged below the waterline at White Point in Charles Town on December 10, 1718. As mentioned before, pyrates had to either be hanged at sea, on the docks, or below the high tide waterline due to the rather strange 18th century English legal jurisdiction that required criminals who committed crimes at sea had to be executed at sea, or at least over the sea somewhere.

Chapter 48
The Death of Blackbeard

Governor Alexander Spotswood of Virginia happened to be a member of the opposite political party from that of Governor Eden of North Carolina. Just as today, any politician would jump at the chance to involve an opponent in a scandal, Governor Eden provided his political opponents with the grandest scandal of them all, collusion with a pyrate. First, Eden had granted pardons to Blackbeard and his crew knowing that they must have committed acts of piracy after the deadline. Secondly, he accepted Blackbeard's story about the captured French ship. And finally, he did nothing after the reports reached him of the pyrate Banyan between Blackbeard and Vane on Ocracoke.

Of course, Governor Spotswood didn't really have authority to go into North Carolina, so any military operation into the neighboring colony would be tricky. The citizens of Virginia couldn't march down and invade another colony. That sort of thing just wasn't done. He conferred with Captain Ellis Brand and Captain George Gordon, both senior naval officers in the Royal Navy and stationed at Hampton, Virginia, headquarters for the Royal Navy in North America. Captain Brand commanded HMS *Lyme*, a fifth-rate 32-gun Ship-O-The-Line and Captain George Gordon commanded a larger ship in port, HMS *Pearl*, a fourth-rate 42-gun Ship-O-The-Line.

After what must have been some serious debate, a plan was formalized. That plan involved a coordinated land and sea effort, both originating at Hampton.

For the naval part of the operation, Captains Brand and Gordon knew their large ships had too much draft to navigate the shallow waters of Pamlico Sound, so they hired two local sloops, the *Jane* and the *Ranger*. Overall command of naval operation was given to one of Gordon's Lieutenants, Lt.

Robert Maynard, who took command of the *Jane* with 25 men from the *Lyme* aboard. The *Ranger* was commanded by a Midshipman named Mr. Hyde with 35 men from the *Pearl* aboard. A few civilian pilots and sailors who were familiar with the waters around Pamlico Sound went along too. Lieutenant Robert Maynard was the most passed over officer in the Royal Navy. No one can say for sure, but it is my belief that Maynard was given command because he was expendable if the operation blew up politically. They were operating out of their jurisdiction.

Ellis Brand's Route

For the land part of the operation, Captain Brand personally traveled overland from Hampton, Virginia to Bath, North Carolina. According to one author writing his history in 2007, Brand was accompanied by 200 men. But according to Captain George Gordon, who wrote a letter to the Admiralty on September 14, 1721, Brand was only accompanied by his servant and a single gentleman. Gordon wrote, "Capt. Brand who went by land with a single gentleman, and a servant to apprehend Thatch with the assistance of the Gentlemen of that country who were weary of that rogues insolence: being informed of his being on shoare often then on board."

Traveling with just one servant was in keeping with the low-profile nature of this operation. Governor Spotswood didn't know how this would come out and he probably didn't want to risk censure if it went badly. On Friday, November 21, 1718 Brand arrived at Queen Anne Creek, now the town of Edenton, North Carolina. He was met by three North Carolina representatives who were expecting him, Colonel Edward Mosely, Colonel Maurice Moore, and Captain Jeremiah Vail. However, these men weren't there to stop Brand; they were there to ensure his success. It seems that they were of the same political party as Governor Spotswood and wanted Governor Eden removed.

Maynard's Route

As Ellis Brand was traveling overland and Lt. Maynard was preparing to set sail, Blackbeard himself was having some unexpected difficulty. Blackbeard's sloop *Adventure* ran aground on Brant Island Shoal at the mouth of the Neuse River on the same day that Lt. Maynard left Hampton, November 17, 1718. That shoal had been a menace to navigation for many years and still is today. The Neuse River is one of the rivers that flow into Pamlico Sound from the interior of North Carolina and Brant Island Shoal lies just below the surface of the water near the point where the river enters Pamlico Sound, about 15 miles due west from Ocracoke. But what was Blackbeard doing on the Neuse River?

The small port town of Oriental was located near Pamlico Sound on the northern bank of the Neuse about three or four miles upstream of Brant Island Shoal. A charming sailing community, Oriental still exists at the exact same location today. Apparently, Blackbeard had been sailing from Oriental to his base on Ocracoke. Local legend and contemporary accounts lead us to the possibility that Blackbeard had a sister who lived in Oriental. Perhaps he stopped by for some biscuits and a spot of rum.

Whatever the reason for Blackbeard's trip up the Neuse River, the *Adventure* was stuck on the shoal and couldn't get free without the assistance of another ship. Apparently, Blackbeard was stranded there for quite some time. Captains on other vessels that passed by recognized Blackbeard. Maynard was searching in waters on the west side of the Outer Banks near Roanoke inlet when he encountered a passing vessel that had spotted Blackbeard stuck on the shoal a few days before and told Maynard the tale. Maynard headed directly for Brant Island Shoal and his destiny.

In the meantime, another merchant sloop captained by Samuel Odell saw the *Adventure* stranded on the shoal and decided to help. The *Adventure* was finally pulled free. Blackbeard was a man who showed gratitude and he invited Captain Odell to join his men for a little celebration. By nightfall, the *Adventure* was moored next to the large French merchant ship at Blackbeard's base on Ocracoke and Samuel Odell was aboard enjoying the festivities. At some point, Blackbeard was joined by two visitors from the town of Bath, James Robins and a slave named Caesar. Robins had been sent to Ocracoke to deliver a hand-written message from Tobias Knight. Later on, that letter would have an enormous impact on Knight's life and tell us much about the relationship between these two men. There were now 21 men aboard the *Adventure*, including the three guests.

As Maynard's sloops approached Brant Island Shoal, his crew saw no trace of the *Adventure*. Maynard assumed that Blackbeard and his pyrates must have sailed to Ocracoke, so Maynard changed course. Maynard's sloops arrived at Ocracoke on the evening of November 21, 1718 and dropped anchor. The beacon light positioned to mark the entrance of the channel burned brightly. Across the channel, Maynard could see Blackbeard's sloop *Adventure* at anchor next to the French merchant ship. If Blackbeard saw the two sloops dropping anchor he wouldn't have been alarmed. The channel was dangerous to navigate at night and vessels arriving at dusk would often drop anchor to wait for the morning light to continue their journey. The water and wind were dead calm and the only sound Maynard's crew may have heard was the sound of Blackbeard's crew partying into the late hours of the night. For the more than 60 men onboard the *Jane* and *Ranger*,

November 1718

Blackbeard is killed at Ocracoke

it was an evening of great anticipation. As for Blackbeard and many of his crewmen, it was the last night of their lives.

The sea and wind remained calm as the sun peaked over the horizon. Maynard's sloops quietly prepared for action. Some of what we know comes from the eye witness account of Humphrey Johnson, whose trading sloop happened to be nearby as the battle took place. His report was written in the *Boston News Letter*. The rest of the information comes from Maynard's own account which was also printed in the *Boston News Letter* and from Maynard's report to the Admiralty. We also have the reports of Captain Ellis Brand and Captain George Gordon which were made to the Admiralty afterwards. Brand and Gordon weren't at the battle, but they spoke with Maynard and many of his men just days afterwards, so their reports must have been fairly accurate.

At about 9:00 in the morning, the *Jane* and *Ranger* raised their sails, but there was no wind to move the sloops. Oars were run out and the two sloops slowly rowed across the channel and closed the distance with the *Adventure*. At some point, Blackbeard realized that the two sloops weren't heading for the open sea; they were heading directly for him. He roused his crew and began to get underway. He cut his anchor cable and raised his jib sail. As the two sloops approached, the *Jane* and the *Ranger* both ran aground. Both sloops heaved ballast overboard to lighten them. During that time, Blackbeard and Maynard supposedly had their famous dialogue.

Blackbeard begins with, "Damn you for villains, who are you? And whence came you? Leave us alone and we shall meddle not with you." Maynard's reply was, "It is you we want and we will have you, dead or alive, else it will cost us our life." Blackbeard's reply was, "Damnation, to you then, you cowardly puppies. We will give no quarter, nor take none. Mr. Morton, prepare your guns and fire when ready. Give them a taste of our hospitality."

This verbal exchange was published in the *Boston News Letter* at the time, and bits and pieces of these words appear in various reports and statements made by Maynard himself. It may not have been exactly what was said, but it was close. About that time, the wind began to freshen and the sails gently flapped in the breeze. The *Ranger* worked free of the sand and began to head directly towards the *Adventure* with the intent to board. As the *Ranger* neared, the crew opened fire with small arms. A very lucky shot hit the *Adventure's* fore halyard—the line that raises the jib sail—and the sail fell to the deck, reducing the *Adventure's* ability to steer. Suddenly, the thunderous sound of guns being fired was heard, and the air filled with grayish smoke. Blackbeard's master gunner, Phillip Morton, had let loose a broadside directly at the *Ranger*, killing two on deck. The *Ranger* turned away as the *Adventure* also began to move under sail.

The *Jane* was still struggling to row across the sandbar but was slowly closing the distance with the *Adventure*. Unable to effectively steer in the light wind without a jib, the *Adventure* was forced into a small inlet, known today as "Teach's Hole." As the *Jane* came alongside to board, the *Adventure* fired a full broadside, killing six men and wounding ten. Maynard ordered all men below deck. According to Gordon's report, the pilot and a midshipman remained above deck to steer the sloop. Other reports have Maynard remaining at the helm, but this is very unlikely. The *Jane* collided with the *Adventure* and Blackbeard and some of his crew swept over the side rail and onto the *Jane*. Maynard and his men sprang from below deck and a desperate hand-to-hand battle began. It was reported that Blackbeard and Maynard directly fought each other with cutlasses. Details of the battle are all speculative, as Maynard didn't offer any details. One unsubstantiated and sensational version printed in newspapers of the day describes one of Maynard's men wielding his sword and making a deep cut to Blackbeard's neck. In the story, Blackbeard said, "Well done lad." The sailor replied, "If it be not well done I'll do it better," and made a second stroke that severed Blackbeard's head from his body. Afterwards, the *Ranger* came alongside from the north and attacked the *Adventure*. It was soon all over.

Of the 21 people aboard the *Adventure*, 11 were dead and one more died of his wounds soon thereafter. These pyrates were Edward Teach (Blackbeard), Thomas Miller (the acting quartermaster), Philip Morton (gunner), Garret Gibbons (boatswain), Owen Roberts (ship's carpenter), John Philips, John Husk, Joseph Curtice, Joseph Brooks Senior, Nathaniel Jackson, and two others whose names are unknown. The others were arrested and taken to Williamsburg, the new capital of Virginia, to stand trial. Their names were James Blake, Thomas Gates, James White, Richard Stiles, Richard Greensail, John Carnes, Caesar (slave), Samuel Odell (visiting captain), and James Robbins (townsman). Blackbeard's head hung from the *Jane's* bowsprit and was taken back to Hampton where it was placed on a pole at the harbor's entrance as a warning to other pyrates. It is interesting to note that of the 21 men with Blackbeard, six of them were of black African descent. They were James Blake, Thomas Gates, James White, Richard Stiles, Caesar, and one of the unknown pyrates. These were Blackbeard's most trusted pyrates and his closest friends. Clearly, Edward Teach did not succumb to the racial prejudice of his day.

Meanwhile, Ellis Brand and his North Carolina supporters reached Bath and arrested six of Blackbeard's known crewmembers who were in town. Their names were John Martin, Joseph Brooks Jr., Stephen Daniel, John

Giles, Edward Salter, and Hezekiah Hands, who had been one of Blackbeard's most trusted pyrates. These six pyrates were also taken to Williamsburg to stand trial. During Brand's investigation in Bath, 20 barrels from the French merchant ship were found on the property of Tobias Knight, the Chief Justice. As mentioned before, this cargo was delivered to them back in October. Additionally, the curious letter that had been written by Knight and delivered by James Robins just before that battle was removed from the *Adventure* shortly after the battle. Tobias Knight wrote:

> 17 November, 1718
>
> My Friend
>
> If this finds you yet in harbour I would have you make the best of your way up as soon as possible your affairs will let you. I have something more to say to you than at present I can write; the bearer will tell you the end of our Indian Warr, and Ganet can tell you in part what I have to say to you, so refers you in some measure to him. I really think these three men are heartily sorry at their difference with you and will be very willing to ask your pardon; If I may advise, be friends again, its better than falling out among your selves. I expect the Governor this night or tomorrow, who I believe would be likewise glad to see you before you goe, I have not time to add save my hearty respects to you, and am your real friend.
>
> And Servant
>
> T. Knight

Tobias Knight vigorously defended himself at the council meeting held on May 27, 1719. As a result of Knight's brilliant defense and the lack of any real evidence against him, all charges were dismissed. Unfortunately, Knight died shortly afterwards of a prolonged illness. Governor Eden, who was never formally accused of implication with Blackbeard, remained a highly respected governor until he died of yellow fever in 1722. The other 16 suspected pyrates include the nine men who Maynard had arrested at Ocracoke, the six men who Brand had arrested in Bath, and William Howard, Blackbeard's former quartermaster, who had been arrested back in August. Samuel Odell and James Robins were acquitted as it was proven that they were not pyrates, just visitors. Two pirates were hanged in Hampton shortly after they were brought back from Ocracoke. Four were hanged in Williamsburg, not for piracy, but for robbery charges which stemmed from an alleged attack of a man in Bath, which supposedly occurred in September 1718. The rest were all released. In December 1718, King George issued another proclamation extending the date the pyrates had to accept the pardon. All of them were then eligible for a pardon. This included the black man named Caesar. This is contrary to what is written in the *General History of Pyrates*. Charles Johnson correctly recounts the acquittal of Samuel Odell and the pardoning of Caesar and Israel Hands, but Johnson writes that all the others were executed.

Chapter 49
Who Was the Real Blackbeard?

So how does one interpret the facts about Blackbeard? Most people including historians think of Blackbeard in simple terms. He was a pyrate and that's that. Most stories paint Blackbeard as one of the fiercest, most dangerous, and blood thirsty of them all. But after examining all the facts, a totally different narrative begins to emerge. Like so many other pyrates of his time, Blackbeard was most probably a Jacobite. His primary motivation for piracy was therefore politics rather than mere profit. Strong indications of this were the naming of two of his vessels after Stuart rulers. The *Queen Anne's Revenge* was named for Queen Anne, the last of the Stuart monarchs in England and the *Royal James* was obviously named for James Edward Stuart, the pretender to the throne and the catalyst of the Jacobite revolt. There was also his close association with Stede Bonnet and Charles Vane, both of whom also seem to have been Jacobites. Perhaps Blackbeard originally intended to contribute his stolen loot to the cause or perhaps it was simply a matter of justifying his actions against English ships. We shall never know the truth, but the evidence is exceptionally intriguing.

Nevertheless, how does one explain the quickly developing friendships among Stede Bonnet, Governor Charles Eden, and Chief Justice Tobias Knight? The only logical conclusion is that Blackbeard knew all three before he began his career as a pyrate. The most obvious proof of this is the letter Knight wrote to him shortly before his death. Then, there is his quick and easy pardon given by Governor Eden in June 1718. And why did his crew settle in the small rural town of Bath after they split up their loot? Blackbeard researcher Kevin Duffus has uncovered compelling evidence about Blackbeard that provides plausible answers to these questions. This is all laid out in his book, *The Last Days of Black Beard*. If he is correct, the truth about Blackbeard is far different from what is generally assumed.

Duffus' evidence points to Blackbeard really being named Edward Beard, the son of James Beard who owned a plot of land next to Charles Eden. If true, Blackbeard would have lived in Bath before turning to piracy. That would also explain his friendship with both Governor Eden and Tobias Knight. When he went to sea, he took a core of loyal crewmembers from his hometown, Bath. These are the ones who remained with him after sinking the *Queen Anne's Revenge*. A good example is Blackbeard's quartermaster, William Howard, whose apparent grandfather is mentioned in North Carolina records of 1663 and his father is mentioned in 1703 when he purchased 320 acres east of Bath. That would also explain the acceptance of the pyrates when the returned to Bath in July 1718 to settle. Prior to living in Bath, Edward Beard (Blackbeard) may have lived on Barbados at the same time as Stede Bonnet, giving them the opportunity to become friends.

But what about the compelling evidence that Edward Teach was from Jamaica and had served aboard HMS *Winsor*? To make this case stronger, in the 1720s, Cox Thache, Edward's half brother living on Jamaica, even claimed to be the brother of the famous pyrate, Blackbeard. If the theory that Blackbeard was actually Edward Beard is correct, then the name of Edward Teach is an alias chosen to hide his true identity. **This is highly speculative, but what if Edward Thache and Edward Beard actually knew each other. They were both seamen at a time when many seamen often sailed together. And what if Edward Thache died at sea while sailing with Edward Beard? His name would make the ideal alias, a real person with a history who couldn't contest the use of his name. This probably controversial view supports both lists of facts.**

How did Blackbeard get his name? We know that he had grown a large and fierce looking beard as part of his pyrate image. All eyewitness descriptions mention his beard. It is interesting to note that many pyrates of the day were nicknamed "Black." This was most likely related to the black flags they flew. Samuel Bellamy was called Black Sam. Bartholomew Roberts was called "Black Bart." Perhaps some of the crew who knew his real identity thought it a marvelous play on words to give him the name Black Beard.

And where did all the stories about Blackbeard's cruelty come from? Charles Johnson is the main source. He had Blackbeard doing battle with HMS *Scarborough* even though there is no mention of this in the logbooks of the *Scarborough*. Johnson wrote that Blackbeard killed and tortured many prisoners and even several members his crew, although the official statements of his former captives make no mention of any of these blood curdling deeds. In fact, there is no evidence to prove that Blackbeard ever killed anyone until his last battle in November of 1718. Johnson writes that Blackbeard had many wives, often giving his women to the crew when he tired of them. Again, there are no reports or statements that support this. They certainly didn't take any women from the vessels they captured or there would have been statements made by the victims and their families. As for marrying ladies while in port, Blackbeard had no opportunity to take women from shore. Between the time Blackbeard parted company with Ben Hornigold and the sinking of the *Queen Anne's Revenge*, the only real port Blackbeard visited was Nassau and he was only there once. After June 1718 there is no account of Blackbeard doing harm to any women in Bath or any other port he visited.

Why then, was Johnson so wrong? The answer may not be so simple. The *General History of Pyrates* was written as a best-seller, not a factual work of historical truth, but political propaganda may have contributed to these stories. Blackbeard certainly deserved the reputation of a pyrate who blockaded Cape May and Charlestown, but that wasn't enough for the political machine of the Governor Spotswood of Virginia. As you may recall, he ordered an illegal expedition into North Carolina that resulted in the death of Blackbeard and caused great political and legal difficulties for the North Carolina governor and chief justice. This was simply the age-old story of one political party against another. Their weapons were scandalous accusations and sensational news articles. Blackbeard's association with Governor Eden provided the fuel for the scandal. But after the expedition was over, Blackbeard had to appear to the public as the most vicious and villainous pyrate who ever lived. Not only did that serve to justify the expedition, but it really put the last nail in the coffin of any government official he associated with.

Chapter 50
The Big Pyrate Ships of the African Waters

Within the Caribbean and coastal North America, sloops were the number one choice for local commerce. After the glory days of Henry Every and Captain Kidd, most pyrates used sloops. This was not by choice, but by necessity, because sloops were the only vessels that most pyrates could get their hands on. Sloops were by far the most commonly used vessels on the seas and were relatively easy to capture when compared to large well-armed ships. Basically, a sloop was a one-masted vessel about 50 to 80 feet in length. There was room onboard for a pyrate crew of about 90 men. Smaller sloops could mount six guns, three on each side. Larger sloops could carry up to 14 guns. Fast and easy to sail, sloops had a shallow draft, making them very useful for sailing in the waters close to shore and in coastal rivers that were too shallow for larger ships. Sloops were also seaworthy and could easily cross large bodies of water, and even oceans. However, there were still plenty of big ships sailing about, mainly between Africa and America or between Europe and India. But big ships are expensive and unless you are a merchant with a very large cargo or who plans on shipping goods across an ocean, a sloop will do just fine.

Unless they happened to be exceptionally lucky, pyrates normally started out using a sloop and the most common means of procuring one was to steal it. However, there are many drawbacks to using a sloop as a pyrate ship. The limitation of space is a major drawback. The larger the pyrate crew, the easier it was to intimidate your potential prize ship, and sloops could only carry about 80 or 90 pyrates. There was also limited space for your captured cargo. Pyrates just didn't take silver and gold; they took cotton, silk, logwood, sugar, cocoa, and anything else they could sell in a pyrate-friendly port. Food and water were also a concern. A pyrate crew of 90 required a lot of space for provisions. There was certainly enough space on a sloop with a large crew for short trips lasting a week or two, but traveling across the ocean in a sloop was difficult unless you had a smaller crew or several sloops traveling in a fleet. Another drawback was defense. There was always the chance that a pyrate vessel would run into a Royal Navy warship, a pyrate hunter, or even an unfriendly pyrate. In that case, it would have been necessary to shoot it out to avoid capture. When it came to battle at sea, the more guns you had, the better. As for prize ships, many larger merchant ships carried between 40 or even 50 guns. For a pyrate, it was exceptionally challenging to take a big ship with a small one.

Ambitious pyrates always sought bigger prize ships because that's where they found the most loot. Of course, pyrates did manage to take larger ships with their sloops, but it was far easier and safer to take smaller ones. For small-time pyrates who were content with taking only small prizes, using a sloop was just fine. But for those few pyrates who possessed ambition, motivation, and a strong desire for riches, a sloop just wouldn't do. These pyrates had to upscale to larger ships. Examples of this can be seen throughout the golden age. In the 1680s, De Graaf first captured a small bark, then a ship, then a bigger one, and continued until he captured and commanded the *Tigre*, a 28-gun warship that he had taken from the Spanish Navy. Another notable example was Sam Bellamy, who started off with the sloop *Marianne*, and then got a square-rigged ship, *Sultana*, and finally captained the 28-gun galley, *Whydah*. Blackbeard is the most famous example, starting off with a small 6-gun sloop, then the 12-gun sloop, *Revenge*, and finally the 40-gun ship, *Queen Anne's Revenge*.

Another reason to upscale to a larger vessel was the rich plunder that could be found in the waters of Africa and the Indian Ocean. Piracy in the Caribbean became less and less profitable and more and more dangerous. Due to new anti-piracy laws and a change in public attitude, pyrate-friendly ports in the West Indies and coastal North America had all but vanished by 1720. Royal Navy warships were increasingly numerous and governments were employing pyrate hunters to seek out pyrates throughout the Caribbean. Africa and the Indian Ocean now seemed a better place for a pyrate to get a lot of loot. Slave ships usually also carried gold, and the ports along the African coast were increasingly wealthy due to the lucrative trade in slaves. In the Indian Ocean, the riches that could be taken from China, Arabia, and India were beyond imagination. To effectively plunder the waters of Africa and the Indian Ocean, a pyrate would eventually need a big ship. They needed a ship that had enough space for provisions, crew, and loot over long voyages. Also, if they planned on taking on the big ships of the East India Company, they needed a ship that could mount at least

30 guns. Our pyrate story now shifts from the Caribbean to the waters off Africa and focuses on the exploits of a group of pyrates whose lives and careers often intertwine. These pyrates all began their careers as pyrates in the Caribbean.

Chapter 51
To the African Waters

July 1718

Edward England begins his pirate career in the Caribbean.

Jasper Seagar was an honest seaman and mate on a merchant sloop sailing between Jamaica and New Providence when he was taken captive by pyrate Christopher Winter in 1717. He was most likely originally from Ireland. It was usually the custom among pyrates to offer all their captives the opportunity to join the pyrate crew. Many did, including Jasper Seagar. A name change was called for to protect him should he decide to return to the life of an honest seaman, so Jasper Seagar became Edward England. I shall refer to him as 'Edward' to avoid any confusion with his last name and that of the country of England. Charles Johnson writes that Edward was Charles Vane's quartermaster for a short time in 1718, just before Woodes Rogers arrived in Nassau on July 22, 1718. This may be true or not, but Edward undoubtedly knew Vane as they were both in Nassau when Rogers arrived that August. As you know, Charles Vane refused the King's Pardon and shot his way out of Nassau. There are two versions of Edward's course of action. One account tells of Edward and his crew accepting the King's Pardon and leaving Nassau soon afterwards, but immediately returning to piracy. The other account has Edward following Charles Vane's lead and refusing the King's Pardon, slipping away quietly in a sloop he had stolen. In either event, Edward and his small pyrate crew were sailing on an eastward heading toward Africa in late July of 1718.

Soon after leaving Nassau, Edward's pyrate sloop took the merchant snow *Cadogan*, which was sailing from Sierra Leone in West Africa and bound for Barbados. The captain of the *Cadogan* was a man named Skinner and having his snow taken by Edward England's crew was of particularly bad luck for him. By total coincidence, Captain Skinner had previously been the captain of some of Edward England's pyrate crewmembers who harbored tremendous hatred for him. Apparently, Captain Skinner was a tyrannical captain who may have even cheated his crew out of their pay, so when the pyrates recognized him, they saw their chance for revenge and Edward could do nothing to stop them. Skinner was tortured and finally killed. This was unusual for Edward, as he was among the kindest pyrate captains with regard to treatment of all of his prisoners. Even Charles Johnson, who tended to invent stories of pyrate brutality, wrote of Edward's kindness. He treated each captive with the utmost courtesy. But in the case of Captain Skinner, Edward's crew could not be controlled.

The chief mate of the *Cadogan* was a highly experienced seaman who literally grew up on a vessel at sea. His name was Howell Davis. After looting the *Cadogan*, Edward asked Howell Davis if he wanted to join the pyrate crew. According to Charles Johnson, Davis' reply and following exchange between Edward and Davis was this:

> "I would sooner be shot than sign the pyrates' articles. Upon which England, pleased with his bravery, sent him and the rest of the men on board the snow, appointing him captain. He also gave him a written paper sealed up, with orders to open it when he should come to a certain latitude . . . The paper contained a generous deed of gift of the ship and cargo to Davis and the crew, ordering him to go to Brazil, dispose of the lading to the best advantage and make a fair and equal divide with the rest."

That being said, Captain Edward England gave the *Cadogan* back to Davis. This wasn't at all unusual. Prize vessels that weren't kept by the pyrates were normally returned to the captain after looting, but since they had killed the captain, they turned command over to Davis.

Edward sailed on and took prizes in the waters of the Azores and Cape Verde Islands. Always hoping to get a bigger ship, Edward finally got his chance. Early in 1719 Edward captured a ship named the *Pearl* and kept it for himself. The prize crew was allowed to sail away in his old sloop. The *Pearl* was renamed the *Royal James*. As with Blackbeard and Stede Bonnet's sloop, the name *Royal James* is in direct reference to James Edward Stuart, the exiled son of the deposed king of England, who one day hoped to claim the throne of England. Was Edward a Jacobite? His friend Charles Vane certainly was. As we shall see, most of the English pyrates in Edward England's association openly showed support for James on a recurring basis. Many of their vessels would be named for James. Additionally, after they were released, some of their captives reported to the authorities that the pyrates would often drink to his health.

Meanwhile, Davis sailed across the Atlantic aboard the *Cadogan* and put in at Barbados. We will never know if Davis actually received a letter from Edward instructing him to sail to Brazil. His stop at Barbados may have

December 1718

Howell Davis begins his pirate career in the Caribbean.

been just to take on supplies. However, upon landing, his crew told the authorities that Davis had suggested to them that they turn to piracy, but they had refused. Howell Davis was arrested and was held for three months in the local gaol (the 18th century term for jail). But with no evidence of him actually committing any crime, he was released.

Known as "The Cavalier Prince of Pyrates," Howell Davis was intelligent and charismatic. He became one of the most daring and inventive pyrates of his day and an ideal model for all future fiction writers of novels, comic books, and Hollywood movies. He was the epitome of what a pyrate should be. Originally from the town of Milford in Pembrokeshire, Wales, Howell Davis was literally raised at sea. He was a highly experienced navigator, skilled sailing master, and a dynamic and strong leader, which made him the perfect pyrate captain.

Davis managed to get to Nassau where he hoped to sign on as a mate aboard some vessel. However, word of his arrest for piracy followed him and no one would sign him on in a leadership position. Woodes Rogers gave him a chance as an ordinary seaman aboard the *Buck*, one of three sloops that Rogers had commissioned to trade with the Spanish and French, but that's not what Davis wanted. There is no way to know exactly when he decided to become a pyrate. Perhaps it was onboard the *Cadogan* watching Edward England loot the vessel or perhaps it was while sailing to Barbados as his crew had testified. It may have been when he was locked up in prison, or perhaps it was when he arrived at the ex-pyrate port of Nassau. Regardless of when his decision was made, by December 1718 Howell Davis had decided that piracy was his course. Rogers' three merchant sloops, the *Buck*, the *Mumvil Trader*, and the *Samuel* were anchored just off Martinique and were loaded with goods. Davis convinced five of the *Buck*'s crew to turn to piracy. They seized the *Buck*, and the *Mumvil Trader* and prepared to set out to sea.

These other pyrates were Walter Kennedy, Dennis Topping, Thomas Anstis, Christopher Moody, and William Magness. More members of the two crews joined in and Davis was quickly elected captain. With a crew of about 35, the pyrates transferred everything of value from the *Mumvil Trader* over to the *Buck* and sailed into the vast sea. According to Charles Johnson, Davis drafted articles for his crew to sign and made a stirring speech, "the sum of which was a declaration of war against the whole world." It seems that in Howell Davis' case, his personal motivation for turning to piracy was more along the lines of what we expect from pyrates, the motivation of revenge and greed.

There is no way of knowing for sure, but one likes to imagine Howell Davis as a handsome and dashing pyrate captain. His cunning and bravery were certainly well documented. So was his kindness to all of his captives. Highly intelligent, he used deception whenever possible. If a Hollywood movie producer made a film that accurately depicted the adventures of Howell Davis—exactly the way they actually happened—most of the moviegoers would scoff and complain about how that pyrate film went too far and was totally unbelievable. For example, soon after setting sail from Martinique in the sloop *Buck*, he spotted a large French ship just north of Hispaniola. However, the ship was very slow and only mounted ten guns. Davis was easily able to overtake the ship and board without a struggle. While Davis and his pyrates were strolling the decks of the captured ship trying to decide the best way to transfer the loot over to their sloop, one of the pyrates spotted another French ship in the distance. But this one mounted 24 guns and had a crew of 60 men.

Davis knew that he didn't have the men or the firepower to take this larger French prize, so he devised a marvelously cunning plan. He hoisted his pyrate flag on the French ship and gave swords to all the French prisoners. Then, he ordered them to wave the swords about and shout. This gave the impression that this large ship was actually a pyrate ship. Leaving enough of his crew onboard the French ship to ensure cooperation from the frightened prisoners, he boarded the *Buck*, raised his pyrate flag, and sailed directly to the large French prize. As the *Buck* reached hailing distance, the French captain ordered his gunner to a fire a warning across the bow of the pyrate sloop, but Davis heard the command and shouted over to the French captain that his master gunner on the big pyrate ship would kill everyone if they didn't surrender immediately. The French captain saw the other ship approaching with what appeared to be a crew of bloodthirsty pyrates on deck waving swords. The deception worked. The French captain believed that there were two pyrate vessels headed his way, so he surrendered without further resistance.

Continuing on aboard the *Buck*, Davis took a ship out of Philadelphia and several other smaller prizes. He needed a larger crew, so he forced some of the crewmembers from the captured vessels to sign articles and become pyrates. Davis didn't like forcing men to join his crew and only did so when absolutely necessary. By now, Davis' sloop was badly in need of careening, so they sailed to Coxon's Hole on the east coast of Cuba. The *Buck* was safely careened and provisioned with boucan and fresh water. Captain Davis now had a crew of about 60 men.

One of the rarest and most unique pyrate command structures of any of the pyrate crews, Captain Howell Davis ran his ship more like a

January 1719

Davis sails to Africa.

government rather than a simple democracy. Davis had a close circle of advisors called his "House of Lords" which included Walter Kennedy, his gunner Henry Dennis, his quartermaster John Taylor and several other ship's officers. Aboard Davis' ship, the entire crew didn't vote on decisions like other pyrate crews, only the members the House of Lords did. Among most other pyrate crews, the captains had no special privileges or authority except during battle. The captains even slept among the crew. But that was not the case on Davis' ships. The members of the House of Lords had special privileges far beyond the rest of the crew. They could walk on the quarterdeck any time they pleased, which was off limits for the others. They also could speak directly with the captain anytime they chose. When addressing them, crew and lords alike would use the title of "Lord." For example, "Good day me Lord Williams" or "What does Your Lordship think?" The members of the House of Lords were the ones who accompanied the Captain on all shore parties to conduct business. The rest of the crew members belonged to the "House of Commons" and didn't make decisions for the ship's operations. However, their interests were recognized. If the House of Commons felt that the House of Lords had made a poor decision, the House of Commons could call for a popular vote of the entire crew.

By January 1719 the Caribbean just didn't seem as profitable as before, so Davis decided to leave the Caribbean and return to the familiar waters of West Africa. The *Buck* made the crossing easily and put in to the port of Sao Nicolau on the Cape Verde Islands. The Portuguese had ruled these islands since the early 17th century and were used as staging areas for their massive slave trade. Slaves would be captured in Africa and marched in chains to one of a dozen or more ports on the African coast. Then, they would be loaded into smaller vessels, like sloops or brigantines, and taken to the Cape Verde Islands. The slaves would be held there until a big slave ship arrived which would take them to the Americas, the great majority to Brazil and the Caribbean. When Davis arrived at Sao Nicolau, he hoisted a British flag knowing that Great Britain and Portugal were allies in the war against Spain. Upon seeing the British flag, the governor assumed that Davis was a British privateer. Davis and his crew were most welcome in port, remaining there for five weeks. During that time, the wealthy pyrate crew spent their money to purchase everything they wanted and the Portuguese merchants were delighted to accommodate them.

Back at sea, Davis hunted the waters off Maio Island, one of the Cape Verde Islands located at the southeast end of the chain. Beginning in February 1719 Davis took seven Dutch and English vessels and the ranks of his pyrate crew increased. Suddenly, Davis saw his opportunity to get a big ship. It was a two-masted merchant brigantine that mounted 26 guns, and Davis took it. There are differing accounts as to the name Davis gave this ship. In some histories written in the 18th century, Davis named his brigantine the *Saint James*, but later accounts say the brigantine was either named *King James* or *Royal James*. This actually makes a huge difference politically.

During the 18th century, England was constantly dealing with the possibility of a Jacobite revolt. The largest was in 1745. Whereas Jacobite supporters would rally to the name of "King James" or "Royal James," there would be no anti-English statement made with the name of "Saint James." As with so many other pyrates during that time, it appears that Davis may have been a Jacobite supporter. At the very least, he pretended to be for the sake of some of his crew and to anger the English authorities.

The west coast of Africa was teeming with wealth, mostly from the slave trade. There were dozens of warlords all dealing in the slave trade. Each had a territory in the interior that was staked out and controlled. Many of the warlords were of Portuguese decent, some were Moroccan, and others were pure West African. Most slaves were captured in the interior by the slavers employed by one of these warlords and then marched to one of several slave ports along the coast, all competing against each other to corner the slave trade market. Operating in the midst of these warlords and rival ports was the Royal Africa Company, started by Charles I of England back in the 1660s. With the threat from neighboring warlords and rival nations, these costal slave ports were usually very well fortified to prevent attack. One of those Royal Africa Company ports was on a small island at the mouth of the Gambia River. In reality, the Gambia River post was more like a castle than a port. And it was fabulously wealthy, since the slave trade was big business. Howell Davis decided to take a piece of the profits. The question was how? This wasn't a ship; it was a fortress with many guns, so Davis devised a plan.

Davis carefully navigated the *Royal James* and the *Buck* up the Gambia River and landed at the Royal Africa Company's port on February 23, 1719. Davis and his lords came ashore dressed in the finest clothes they had. Since he had taken many vessels, including the two French merchant ships, he had a huge wardrobe of fancy clothes to choose from. He played the role of a rich merchant from Liverpool who was somewhat of a "dandy." Davis told the governor of his terrifying experience at sea when he was chased by pyrates near the Senegal coast. He continued that he was too frightened to return to that part of the ocean, so he decided just to buy some slaves and sail back to England. The sympathetic governor consoled Davis and invited him to dinner as an honored guest. Perhaps the governor saw an opportunity to make some sales. The governor generously gave

Davis a personal tour of the castle, but for Davis, this was an opportunity to scout out the fortress. Davis noted every guard, every entry, and every passageway. He quickly developed a plan to take the castle that night. At the end of the tour, Davis informed the governor that he needed to return to his ship to get ready for the evening's festivities. Once aboard, Davis briefed his crew on the plan, which went like this. The merchant sloop laying at anchor in the harbor would have to be taken first, to prevent their crew from warning anyone. That could easily be accomplished by only a few men. Then, Davis explained the best way for an attack force to get into the castle. About 20 heavily armed pyrates would remain on the ship and wait for the signal to attack. That signal was the lowering of the flag that flew above the castle. With the crew ready to go, Davis and a few of his well-dressed men, with weapons hidden under their coats, went ashore and attended the governor's dinner. They were poised to attack when Davis fired his pistol.

Dressed in his finest ruffles and finery, Davis was welcomed personally by the governor. As they spoke, Davis' men carefully positioned themselves near all the guards. Suddenly, Davis drew a pistol and pointed it directly at the governor. Davis may have even smiled and said something like, "Don't be alarmed, governor, it's our turn to entertain you." Davis drew a second pistol and fired it. His pyrates sprang into action. They pulled out their weapons and subdued all the guards in only a few seconds. The governor, the guests, and all of the guards were locked in a room. Davis ordered the flag above the castle to be struck. With that signal, the 20 pyrates rushed ashore and took the entire fortress with no bloodshed. Davis' crew spent the next day partying, shooting off the castle's guns, drinking everything they could find, and looting the castle. Afterwards, they destroyed the fortifications. This was important if they wanted to sail away from the fort without receiving fire. The crew was given £2,000 in gold as ransom and looted large amounts of ivory and gold bars.

Chapter 52
The Troubled Partnership, Davis, La Buse, and Cocklyn

Two days later, with the smoking fortress still in sight, Davis' crew suddenly spotted a 14-gun sloop sailing directly toward them. It appeared that the sloop was going to attack. As soon as Davis ordered his men to go to quarters (take their battle positions) the other vessel raised a black pyrate flag. Davis ordered his black pyrate flag to be raised also. When the captain of the other sloop saw Davis' flag, he ordered his sloop to come alongside without firing. The other pyrate sloop's captain was none other than the French pyrate, Olivier Le Vasseur, nicknamed La Buse (the Buzzard). He was the same French pyrate captain who had sailed with Benjamin Hornigold, Sam Bellamy, and Edward Teach two years earlier. Captain La Buse apologized for the attack saying that he had no idea he was attacking fellow pyrates. The two crews spent the next week partying together.

On March 7, 1719 Davis and La Buse sailed out of the Gambia River to hunt for prizes in the waters off Sierra Leone. At the mouth of the river they spotted a ship that was also flying a black pyrate flag. It was Edward England on the *Royal James*. Howell Davis remembered the kindness Edward had shown him when the *Cadogan* was taken and suggested that they all join forces. After all, Edward England was the man responsible for launching Howell Davis' pyrate career. But Edward refused and sailed on. Soon after, Davis and La Buse arrived at Sierra Leone and spotted a tall galley and another vessel at anchor. That galley looked like a good prize to take. Firing a broadside to attract the attention of the galley, Davis and La Buse raised their pyrate black flags, but to their surprise, the galley also raised a black pyrate flag. They soon recognized this galley as the *Mourroon*, the pyrate ship of Captain Thomas Cocklyn and the other vessel was the *Two Friends*.

March 1719

Davis, La Buse, Cocklyn form partnership.

A vicious and violent man, Captain Cocklyn had a reputation as one of those pyrate captains who actually enjoyed torturing his captives. He would force many members of the prize crew to join his pyrate crew, often whipping them into submission. He was even cruel to his own men. Cocklyn had been operating in these waters for several weeks and had recently taken two vessels. One was the *Edward and Steed* which was allowed to sail on after being looted, but the other was the *Two Friends* which he kept as a possible replacement for the aging *Mourroon*. At first, Davis was hesitant about signing articles with a third captain; too many pyrates can spoil the hunting waters. But La Buse and Cocklyn were old friends and La Buse managed to persuade Davis to give the partnership a try.

Christopher Moody, one of the original members of Davis' crew, was very uneasy about these new partnerships. Before he met Howell Davis, Moody had been a pyrate captain in the Caribbean and La Buse and Cocklyn were both members of his crew. In fact, that was when La Buse and Cocklyn first became friends. Captain Moody didn't get along with Cocklyn and actually suspected him of mutiny, so Moody looked for an opportunity to get rid of Cocklyn without causing conflict among the rest of his crew. The opportunity came when they took a galley named the *Mourroon*, which was badly damaged and unable to get underway. He named Cocklyn the captain of the galley, but as soon as Cocklyn and a few of his loyal shipmates were on board, Moody quickly sailed away and left Cocklyn on the disabled galley far behind. Cocklyn eventually repaired the galley and was still the captain of the *Mourroon* when they met in off the West African coast.

Moody had concerns about La Buse too. Shortly after he left Cocklyn standing on the deck of a badly damaged galley, La Buse led a mutiny and took command of Moody's vessel. Eventually, Moody made it to Nassau, but without a vessel and without any money, he was badly in need of a job. Out of desperation, he signed on as a regular crewman aboard the *Buck*, one of the three merchant sloops that belonged to Woodes Rogers. That was the same sloop that Howell Davis joined. Moody assisted Davis in taking the sloop and had remained loyal to Davis ever since. But now, Moody was sailing with Captain Cocklyn who he suspected of mutiny and Captain La Buse who actually did mutiny.

Davis had never met Cocklyn before, but Christopher Moody certainly warned him about Cocklyn's bad character. Shortly after Davis first stepped aboard Cocklyn's galley, one of Cocklyn's crew told Davis of an incident that had happened just the day before. Apparently, a pyrate named William Hall, who was one of Cocklyn's crewmembers who had been forced to join them, was given an order to release the foretop sail. He climbed up into the shrouds as ordered, but he moved too slowly for Cocklyn, so his boatswain shot him with a pistol, then climbed up the shrouds and hacked him with his cutlass. The poor sailor's body fell into the sea. Upon hearing that tale, Davis became angry and drew his cutlass at Cocklyn, shouting that he was a fool. But La Buse intervened and tempers cooled. Howell Davis was a fair man who always treated his crew and captives well. He was now in the company of a cruel captain who killed and tortured crew and captives alike. The three captains remained uneasy partners for about two months.

Bence Island at the entrance of Tagrin Bay in Sierra Leone was the location for another of the Royal African Company's forts. That location was renamed Freetown in 1781 and today it's Sierra Leone's capital city. Davis hoped he could repeat the success he had had at the Gambia River post so Davis and La Buse sailed for the fort in March 1719 while Cocklyn remained behind preparing the *Two Friends* as a pyrate vessel. But this time, the fort was warned and ready for them. Davis wanted to wait for Cocklyn, but La Buse sailed ahead and received fire from the fort's guns. Some shots tore through the mainsail while others landed in the sea near enough to spray water over the deck. La Buse made a quick retreat while Davis and his crew laughed. When Cocklyn finally arrived, the pyrate fleet attacked six merchant vessels in the harbor, easily taking them with no resistance. The fleet then turned toward the fort. Davis sent a message to the fort's commander, named Plunkett, asking if he had any spare gunpowder, ammunition, or gold he could lend him. Plunkett replied that he had no gold, but he did have plenty of gunpowder and shot to give him. However, that wasn't quite true and the fort soon ran out of powder. After that, the pyrates quickly took the fort.

Bence Island was a slave port and fortification established by the English in 1670.

While looting the fort, Cocklyn eventually came across the fiery Commander Plunkett. Cocklyn held a pistol to his head, cursing him. Commander Plunkett replied with such a string of curse words that soon all the pyrates were laughing, including Cocklyn. Plunkett was released. The next day, three more merchant ships entered the harbor, unaware that it was under the control of the pyrates. These ships were soon taken and one of them, the *Sara*, was kept by Cocklyn as the new replacement for the aging galley, *Mourroon*. During the looting, two of Cocklyn's crew who had been forced into piracy managed to escape. Cocklyn's quartermaster found them and brought them back to be whipped and killed, but Davis didn't approve of that kind of treatment and took the two men aboard his ship for protection. The three captains agreed that it was time to leave the harbor when they spotted yet another galley entering. Deciding that this would make a good prize, all three pyrate vessels sailed up river and out of sight. Then, they waited for nightfall to take it.

Chapter 53
William Snelgrave's Invaluable Account

The large English slave galley sighted by Cocklyn, La Buse, and Davis as it slowly entered the harbor and dropped anchor was named the *Bird*. It was the evening of April 1, 1719 and the ship's captain, William Snelgrave was slightly suspicious. Things just didn't seem right as the night grew darker and he set his watches. He didn't know it, but his ship was about to be taken by pyrates. Most factual accounts of the actions of pyrates came from their victims who gave statements about their capture to the authorities or newspapers after they are released. Their statements were almost always shortened in official reports or newspapers and many of the details were omitted. The authorities were only concerned with the facts and the newspapers didn't have the space to print long stories. The detailed accounts that appeared in most books of the day were generally highly exaggerated and embellished by the authors in order to sell more books. However, this was the exception. Today, we are exceptionally fortunate, because Captain William Snelgrave decided to write a book of his own which gave us tremendous insight into exactly how those pyrates treated him and his crewmen.

Captain William Snelgrave spent about a month as a captive of pyrate captains Cocklyn, Davis, and La Buse. Eventually he was released and returned to England. He later wrote a book entitled, *A New Account of Some Parts of Guinea, and the Slave Trade*, published in 1734, in which he gave us a detailed, first-hand description of his experiences as a pyrate captive. Unlike other publications of the day, Snelgrave's book was straight forward and not prone to exaggerated stories of cruelty. Today, his work gives us an invaluable glimpse into the treatment and motivation of at least a few pyrates. His story is relayed here supported by direct quotes from the aforementioned book.

"The *Bird* lay quietly at anchor just off the coast of Africa the dark evening of April 1, 1719 when suddenly the crew heard the sound of a boat rowing toward them. As the small row boat approached, Captain Snelgrave gave them a hail to ask their purpose. After some unconvincing dialogue, the pyrates opened fired. Not realizing that the pyrates were from the much larger ship anchored nearby, Captain Snelgrave ordered his men to fire back, but they were too afraid. When the pyrate quartermaster boarded, he asked where the captain was. Captain Snelgrave replied, 'I had been so till now.' Upon that he asked me, 'How I dared order my People to fire at their Boat . . .' I answered, 'I thought it my Duty to defend the Ship . . .' "

Later, Captain Snelgrave was in the presence of the boatswain. He wrote:

"Whereupon lifting up his broad Sword, he swore, 'No Quarter should be given to any Captain that offered to defend his Ship.' But Captain Snelgrave quickly ducked out of the way and the boatswain's sword struck the rail and broke. Just then, Captain Snelgrave's crew interceded. He continues, 'Some of my People that were then on the Quarter-deck observing, cried out aloud, "For God's sake, don't kill our Captain, for we never were with a better Man!" This turned Rage of him and two other Pirates on my People, and saved my Life. Then, the quartermaster took me by the hand, and told me, 'My Life was safe providing none of my People complained against me.'

"Captain Snelgrave was taken over to the pyrate ship and brought before Captain Cocklyn who greeted him by saying, 'I am sorry you have met with bad usage after Quarter given, but 'tis Fortune of War sometimes. I expect you will answer truly to all such Questions as I shall ask you: otherwise you shall be cut to pieces; but if you tell the Truth, and your Men make no Complaints against you, you shall be kindly used; and this shall be the best Voyage you ever made in your Life, as you shall find by what shall be given you.' "

Later that evening, Captain Snelgrave was taken to the great cabin on the pyrate ship where, "There was not in the Cabin either Chair, or anything else to sit on; for they always kept a clear Ship ready for an Engagement: so a Carpet was spread on the Deck, upon which we sat down cross-legged. Captain Cocklyn drank my health . . . Then, he drank several other Healths, amongst which was that of the Pretender, by the name of King James the Third, and thereby I found that they were doubly on the side of the Gallows, both as Traitors and Pirates."

This is a remarkable piece of first-hand information that supports the notion that many of the pyrates were indeed Jacobite supporters. Captain Cocklyn actually drank to the health of King James III.

Captain Howell Davis' ship soon joined Captain Cocklyn and Davis met with Captain Snelgrave saying:

> "He was ashamed to hear how I had been used by them. That they should remember, their Reasons for going a pirating were to revenge themselves on base Merchants, and cruel Commanders of Ships. . . . That as for my part, no-one of my People, even those that had entered with them, gave me the least ill Character: But by their respect since shown me, it was plain they loved me. That he indeed had heard the occasion of my ill usage, and of the ill-will some still bore me, was, because I had ordered my People to defend the Ship: Which he blamed them exceeding for, saying, If he had the good fortune to have taken me, and I had defended my Ship against him, he should have doubly valued me for it."

One of Captain Davis' young and inexperienced pyrates came on board the prize ship and found a small chest and opened it. As he was taking out some of the valuables, Cocklyn's quartermaster caught him and asked what he was doing. The young pyrate replied:

> "As they were all Pirates, he thought he did what was right. On that the quartermaster strikes at him with his broad Sword, but the young man running away escaped the Blow, and fled for protection into the great Cabin to his Master Captain Davis. The quartermaster pursues him in a great Passion; and there not being room amongst so many of us, to make a stroke at him, he made a thrust with his Sword, and slit the Ball of one of the young Man's Thumbs, and at the same time Captain Davis upon the back of one of his Hands. Davis, upon that, was all on Fire, and vowed Revenge saying, 'That though this Man had offended, he ought to have been first acquainted with it; for on other Person had a right to punish him in his Presence."

As Davis' crew prepared to board the other pyrate ship and avenge the insult, Captain Cocklyn met Captain Davis and apologized saying:

> "Captain Davis and his Ship's Company, should have their share of Liquors and Necessities on board the Prize: and, That the

Quartermaster, who had wounded you young Man belonging to Davis, should before all his Crew acknowledge his fault, and ask Pardon for the same."

During the looting process, pyrates acted exactly like one would expect. They rifled through everyone's possessions and took everything of value. When alcoholic beverages were found, they were quite often immediately consumed. Captain Snelgrave gave an account of the pyrate's conduct with regard to the consumption of liquor writing:

"It was very surprising to see the Actions of these People. They . . . made such Waste and Destruction, that I am sure a numerous set of such Villains would in a short time, have ruined a great City. They hoisted upon Deck a Great many half-Hogsheads of Claret, and French Brandy; knocked their Heads out, and dipped cans and bowls into then to drink out of: . . . As to bottled Liquor of many sorts, they made such havoc of it, that in a few days they had not one Bottle left: For they would not give themselves the trouble of drawing the Cork out, but nicked the Bottles, as they called it, that is, struck their necks off with a Cutlace; by which means one in three was generally broke: Neither was there any Cask-liquor left in a short time, but a little French Brandy . . . For the Pirates being all in a drunken Fit, which held as long as the Liquor lasted, no care was taken by anyone to prevent this Destruction: Which they repented of when too late."

The pyrates decided to keep the slaver *Bird* and began refitting it as a pyrate ship named the *Windham Galley*. This process involved throwing all the furniture overboard and removing any non-load bearing walls below deck. It also involved putting as many guns on board as possible. On April 20, 1719 the ship was ready and Captain Snelgrave was respectfully invited to the ceremony to which he wrote:

"When I came on board, the Pirate Captains told me, 'It was not out of Disrespect they had sent for me, but to partake of the good Cheer provided on this occasion:' So they desired I would be cheerful, and go with them into the great Cabin. When I came there, Bumpers of Punch were put into our Hands, and on Captain Cocklyn's saying aloud, 'God bless the Windham Galley. We drank our Liquor, broke the Glasses, and the Guns fired."

Several days later, Captain Davis invited Captain Snelgrave to have supper with him on his ship, the *Royal James* and wrote, "Supper was brought about eight a clock in the Evening; and the Musick was ordered to play, amongst which was a Trumpeter, that had been forced to enter out of one of the Prizes." Music was a very important part of pyrate life. Quite often, any musicians found on a prize vessel were forced to join the pyrate crew.

In describing the power of the quartermaster, Captain Snelgrave wrote:

> "I think it necessary to observe in this place, that the Captain of a Pirate Ship, is chiefly chosen to fight the vessels that they may meet with. Besides him, they choose another principal Officer, whom they call quartermaster, who has the general inspection of all affairs, and often controls the Captain's Orders: This person is also said to be the first man in boarding any ship they shall attack; or go in the boat on any desperate enterprise. Besides the captain and the quartermaster, the pirates had all other officers as is usual on board Men of War."

He described an incident in which Captains Cocklyn, Davis, and La Buse, took three fancy dress coats directly from his wardrobe in which he wrote:

> "One day, three Captains coming on board the Prize together, enquired for then, saying, 'They understood by my Book such Clothes were in my Ship.' . . . So they ordered them to be taken out, and immediately put them on. But the longest Coat falling to Cocklyn's share, who was a very short Man, it almost reached as low as his ankles. This very much displeased him, and he would fain have changed with Le Boose (La Buse), or Davis: But they refused, telling him as they were going on Shore amongst the Negro-Ladies, who did not know the white Men's fashions, it was no matter. Moreover, as his Coat was Scarlet embroidered with Silver, they believed he would have the preference of them, whose Coats were not so showy in the opinion of their Mistresses. The Pirate Captains having taken these Clothes without leave from the quartermaster, it gave great Offence to all the Crew; who alleged, 'If they suffered such things, the Captains would in future assume a Power, to take whatever they liked for themselves.' So, upon their return on board next Morning, the Coats were taken from them, and put into the common Chest, to be sold at the Mast."

When the refitting of the *Wyndham Galley* was complete, it now carried 24 guns and was given to La Buse. Cocklyn kept the *Sara* which was stripped below deck and refitted to carry 30 guns and was renamed the *Speakwell*.

His old galley, the *Mourroon*, was given to Captain Snelgrave, who was allowed to sail away with six ship's masters and about 60 other prisoners from the many vessels they had taken in the harbor. Even though the *Mourroon* was leaky and slow, Captain Snelgrave was able to safely sail all the way back to England.

Chapter 54
Partnership Dissolved and Davis' Death

It was early May of 1719 and the Pyrate fleet had left Sierra Leone and was sailing south along the coast of Africa. Howell Davis had been elected commodore of the pyrate fleet of six vessels which was comprised of Davis in the *Royal James*, Cocklyn in the *Speakwell*, La Buse in the *Wyndham Galley*, and accompanied by the *Buck*, the *Two Friends* and the *Guinea Hen*, one of the vessels they had recently taken in the harbor. But there were ill feelings among the captains over a great many issues. The latest was the disagreement they had over the shares given to the crews. Davis divided the total amount evenly, giving every man his fair share. Since Davis had the largest number of crewmen, his ship received the greatest amount of loot. The other captains felt that the loot should have been divided evenly between the three ships, and then subdivided among each member of the crew. This was against the articles, so Davis prevailed. There was also uneasiness between Davis and Cocklyn over the mistreatment of the prisoners and crew. They were different kinds of men and something was about to blow up.

They had planned to capture the four more Royal Africa Company forts located along the Gold Coast, but the temperature was excessively hot and the crew needed to take on fresh water. Davis sent two of his pyrates ashore along with several African natives to get water, but the natives came back alone, saying that the pyrates had run off. Davis was certain they had been killed for their weapons, but he badly needed water, so he sent a larger party ashore under the leadership of his quartermaster, John Taylor. The character of Taylor seems to have been more in line with that of Cocklyn. Taylor began to think Davis was too weak by not treating his captives cruelly. When Taylor got ashore, he decided to find out what had happened to his shipmates by torturing the Africans. He tied them up in pairs and hoisted them above the ground swinging back and forth. His men then used them for target practice, competing in two teams for a bottle of rum. Davis looked on in horror, but could do nothing. Within two days, the crew began to look at Taylor as their leader and voted Davis out of the position of Captain and voted Taylor in. However, the crew recognized the seamanship that Davis had, so they elected him as their quartermaster to replace Taylor.

As soon as John Taylor became captain, he began acting exactly like Cocklyn, bullying his own crew and playing the role of a vindictive brute. It didn't take long for the crew to realize their mistake and Taylor was voted out and Davis was back in as the captain. Walter Kennedy, one of Davis' original crewmembers from Nassau, was elected quartermaster. In a fit of rage, John Taylor and a handful of his supporters left Davis' crew and joined the crew of Captain Cocklyn. After that incident, Davis knew he had to distance himself from the influence of the other two captains, but what excuse could he use for dissolving the partnership? It was the end of May 1719 when the three captains had a meeting to plan where to plunder next. Davis used this opportunity to disagree with the others and suggest they separate. An argument began, but Davis diffused the situation saying, "Since we met in love, let us part in love." With those words, the partnership was over and Howell Davis sailed off with his loyal crew onboard the *Royal James*.

In the speech of the pyrates, to bid someone a "soft farewell" meant that the crew of one vessel quickly sailed away as soon as they got the chance.

Cocklyn and La Buse remained partners and sailed away, Cocklyn as captain of the *Speakwell*, La Buse as captain of the *Wyndham Galley*, and accompanied by the *Two Friends*. However, shortly afterwards, the *Two Friends* "bid them a soft farewell." Perhaps their crew had had enough of Cocklyn's leadership too.

Just after leaving Cocklyn and La Buse, Davis onboard the *Royal James* was cruising off the coast of West Africa when he came across the *Marquis del Campo*, a Dutch merchant ship of 30 guns that had originally been a British ship-o-the-line. The ship was anchored off Cape Three Points on the north side of the Gulf of Guinea in modern Ghana. A ship of that size was a pretty difficult prize to take, it was well-armed and the Dutch had a reputation of not surrendering without a fight. Even so, Davis decided to take her and came in firing a broadside. The Dutch returned fire and the two ships slugged it out, broadside after broadside. The battle lasted from noon to the next morning. Finally, the Dutch ship surrendered. Both crews had many casualties. Unlike some other pyrates who only granted quarter (allowed everyone to live) if the crew surrendered without a fight, Howell Davis believed that even after fighting, once the crew struck their colors, quarter would always be granted. That was even included in Davis'

Ship's Articles. Davis stuck to his convictions and once they surrendered, none of the Dutch prisoners were harmed or mistreated. He even took the Dutch wounded ashore where they could be treated by his surgeon. Davis decided to keep the Dutch ship and renamed it the *Royal Rover*. He gave command of the *Royal James* to his quartermaster, Kennedy. The crew began the process of converting the *Royal Rover* into a pyrate ship, stripping the below decks and refitting the ship with 32 mounted guns and 27 swivel guns. The prize crew remained his prisoners for the time being. Davis' original vessel, the sloop *Buck*, was in such poor shape that it was intentionally sunk. Howell Davis now had two of the most powerful pyrate ships in the African waters, the 32-gun ship, *Royal Rover* and the 26-gun brigantine, *Royal James*.

On June 6, 1719 they entered the harbor of Annambo on the Gold Coast. That was another of the Royal Africa Company's ports and three English slave ships were moored there, the *Morris*, the *Royal Hynde*, and the *Princess of London*. Davis's pyrate vessels raised their black flags and headed toward the merchantmen. The captains of all three ships were ashore and had left only a few mates onboard. All three merchantmen surrendered without resistance. The fort opened fire, but they were hopelessly out of range and quickly ceased firing. Davis was free to loot the prize ships at his leisure. He gave one of the ships, the *Morris*, to the captured Dutch crew and let them go. While looting the *Princess of London*, the third mate and Davis struck up a lengthy conversation. His name was John Roberts and was described as a tall and well-built man with black hair. Like Davis, he too was from Pembrokeshire, Whales. No one knows what Davis and Roberts talked about, perhaps it was their homeland or perhaps it was ship's navigation. Roberts was an expert navigator and knew the waters of Africa well. Davis was very curious to get Roberts' opinion on the winds and other useful information. At any rate, the two seemed to rapidly become friends and when Davis was finished looting Roberts decided to join the pyrate crew, along with 34 other crewmen of the captured ships.

Leaving Annambo on the Gold Coast, Davis sailed south toward the Portuguese port of Principe, taking a few more prizes along the route. They soon noticed that the old *Royal James* was listing and nothing could be done to repair the planking. The *Royal James* was abandoned and the entire company sailed on aboard the *Royal Rover*. In mid-June 1719 Davis arrived at the port of Principe. Repeating his success at Cape Verde and Gambia, Davis told the authorities that he was a British pyrate hunter. They believed him and his crew were granted shore leave in the port. By then, each member of the crew had a very large amount of money, which they readily spent on women and drinks. This was not the usual behavior of underpaid English sailors and the governor became suspicious. As

Davis and part of his crew were ashore, a French merchant ship entered the harbor. Davis's quarter-master, Kennedy, decided that the French vessel was too tempting, so he took a party over to the ship and quickly took it by force. When news reached the governor, Davis had to think fast. The governor was convinced that Davis was a pyrate. Davis told the authorities that the French ship had been trading with pyrates and that his men seized the ship in the name of the King, but the governor wasn't convinced.

Figure 25: *Atlantic and West Africa*

Shortly afterwards, the governor invited Davis and some of his officers to the governor's house for some wine. The date was June 19, 1719. The details are not well documented, but Davis accepted and went ashore with several of his loyal officers. His quartermaster, Kennedy, stayed with the small boat that had brought them ashore and Davis and the others entered the governor's grounds. Suddenly, the crew aboard the *Royal Rover* could hear musket fire coming from the port. Kennedy, still waiting at the boat, was fired upon and rowed back to the ship under fire. The pyrate crew soon realized that while on the grounds of the governor's house, their beloved captain, Howell Davis, had just been killed along with several of his elite group of trusted officers and advisors.

The crew was in an uproar and they wanted revenge, but first, they needed a new captain. As you may recall, Davis' crew had a very unique command structure. His crew was divided into two houses, the House of Lords which was comprised of the captain, the quartermaster, the ship's officers and other crewmembers who had the deep trust of the captain. They had special privileges and made the major decisions for the crew. The other house was the House of Commons which was made up of the rest of the crew. The House of Commons had the authority to overrule the decisions of the House of Lords by calling for a popular vote if the House of Lords made a poor decision.

The decision of who would be the new captain was a very important one. Davis had been captain so long that no one else had ever considered the position. As soon as they began to discuss a successor, arguments among the surviving members of the House of Lords began over who would be chosen. Within minutes, the House of Lords began to fall apart. Eventually they calmed down and came to a very important realization. The most important requirement of a captain was the ability to navigate and none of the current members were accomplished navigators. They came to realize that their strength was in the unity of the House of Lords and the best way to keep the House of Lords united was to select a new captain from outside, from the House of Commons. But that new captain had to be someone who knew how to sail a ship and could also navigate. As the Lords discussed the matter, the best choice became suddenly very clear. In a surprise turn, the crew chose a man who had only been part of their pyrate crew for less than two weeks. He was an expert navigator and the former third mate of the *Princess of London*, John Roberts, a pyrate who became the last great pyrate of the golden age of piracy.

Chapter 55
Roberts Takes Command

For the first time, the pyrate crew of the *Royal Rover* was without their beloved Captain Howell Davis. The only clear choice for a successor was John Roberts, the navigator and former third mate of a prize vessel that they had taken only 13 days earlier. Command of the *Royal Rover* was in the hands of a man that the crew knew almost nothing about, a man who had been a pyrate for only a few days, a man named Roberts.

His original name was John Robert, with no "s" in his last name. He was born in 1682 in Little Newcastle, Pembrokeshire, Wales and went to sea at age 13. His historical record vanished until he was listed as a mate on a Barbados sloop in 1718. He may have served in the Royal Navy during the war, but no record of his service exists. According to the contemporary account of pyrate John Plantain, Robert served as a mate aboard the privateer sloop *Terrible*, out of Rhode Island. Whatever his history, in November of 1718, John Robert, or Roberts as he was then called, was third mate on the galley *Princess of London* sailing from England alongside Captain Snelgrave's galley, *Bird*. When the two galleys reached the African coast, they separated. The *Bird* went to Sierra Leone and was taken by Davis, La Buse, and Cocklyn in April 1719 as described earlier in this book.

After Roberts' ship, the *Princess of London*, had been taken, Davis quickly recognized that Roberts was an expert navigator. As the pyrates looted the ship, Davis and Roberts discussed wind direction, courses, ports, and different types of rigging. They rapidly grew to become friends, although they were opposites in many ways. Davis was short in stature, and a jovial and optimistic extrovert while Roberts was very tall, and somewhat serious natured. They both were naturally gifted leaders, experienced men of the sea, and they were both Welch. By the time Davis asked, "who among you would like to join my pyrate crew," Roberts had already considered his very limited options as a third mate and decided to join. He signed

Robert Jacob

JUNE 1719

Davis is killed and Roberts takes command.

the Ship's Articles and become a pyrate. But just 13 days after his ship was taken and he had joined Davis' crew, Captain Davis was dead and he was elected as the new pyrate captain.

Most biographers wrote that John Roberts changed his name to Bartholomew Roberts. That statement can be traced directly to the "General History of Pyrates" written by Charles Johnson in 1724. A surviving document written by Roberts contained his signature which read, "Batt. Roberts." From that document, it was assumed that "Batt." was short for Bartholomew. If that was true, the nickname of "Black Bart" would naturally follow, although it is believed today that the nickname of Black Bart was given to him by authors well after his death. However, it is far more likely that he never went by the name "Bartholomew" as Charles Johnson assumed incorrectly. Interestingly enough, the name "Batt." may be a nickname for a Welshman, just like "Patti" is often a nickname for an Irishman. If that was the case, his signature may have simply meant Welshman Roberts. In either event, I shall refer him as Roberts or in the same manner he signed his own name, Batt. Roberts.

The first task that Captain Batt. Roberts had to deal with was revenge on Principe. The fort guarding the entrance to the harbor of Principe couldn't fire on them where they were anchored, but it could fire on them as they left. Taking the fort had to come first. He sent quartermaster Walter Kennedy with a landing party of 30 pyrates ashore to take the fort then sailed the *Royal Rover* to a position where it could fire on the fort and support their attack. As the *Royal Rover* pounded the walls, Kennedy and his men attacked from land. The soldiers fled in panic and the fort was taken and totally destroyed. Next came the town. The only safe way to assault the settlement was from the harbor. A landing party would have to travel through the dense jungle to take the town from behind, and possible ambush made that too risky. But the harbor was too shallow for his ship to get into a position where he could fire on the town, so Roberts ordered his crew to build rafts and load them with the guns from the French ship they had previously captured just before Davis was killed. This tactic was very effective, and the town of Principe was completely demolished. The French ship was given back to the French captain and crew, minus the guns of course. Then, Roberts took two Portuguese ships in the harbor and sailed away. Howell Davis had been avenged.

Sailing west along the African coast, Roberts took his first prize at sea as captain of the *Royal Rover* on July 27, 1719. It was the Dutch merchantman, *Experiment*, and Roberts allowed the prize crew to sail away on their ship after the pyrates were finished looting. The next day he took a Portuguese merchantman and two days later, an English ship named the *Temperance*.

With the pyrate fleet of Edward England nearby, Roberts decided they would have a better chance of taking prizes elsewhere and Roberts persuaded the crew to leave the African waters and sail to Brazil. However, trade was very slow in the Brazilian waters and week after week went by with no prize ships to take. The crew began to doubt their decision to make Roberts the captain, so Roberts had to come up with a big score fast.

Roberts Sails to Brazil

In September 1719 Roberts decided to attack the Portuguese treasure fleet at Bahia de Todos os Santos, a very large bay near the city of Salvador, Brazil. When the *Royal Rover* arrived, they discovered that the treasure fleet was comprised of 32 well-armed treasure ships and two Portuguese men-o-war carrying 70 guns each all anchored in the bay. Additionally, the fleet was protected by a large fort with 500 guns that commanded the bay. His crew all believed that this was far too much firepower for them to overcome, but Roberts was the captain and had complete authority. In one of the most daring moves in pyrate history, Roberts decided to attack. His crewmembers were shocked and in total disbelief, but the captain's orders had to be obeyed.

Luckily for the pyrates, there was no moon that night and they were able to approach unseen. While still outside the bay, Roberts captured a small vessel and forced the pilot to guide him into the bay. Once inside the bay, the *Royal Rover* quietly sailed alongside the first ship Roberts spotted. His men quickly and quietly swarmed over the deck and captured the vessel. However, the pyrates didn't plan to loot the vessel, they just wanted the captain to tell them which treasure ship was the richest prize. Taking the Portuguese captain with them as a guide, they sailed for the ship he identified as the richest vessel. It was the 36-gun *Sagrada Familia*. As the *Royal Rover* approached in the dark night, the captain of the *Sagrada Familia* realized they were pyrates and ordered his men to make ready. Just then, Roberts let loose a broadside and threw his grappling hooks over to the Portuguese ship. Within a few moments, the pyrates pulled the two ships close together and quartermaster Kennedy led a boarding party that quickly captured the ship.

Meanwhile, the broadside had alerted the rest of the treasure fleet that a pyrate was in the harbor and all the other ships began to prepare for battle. The guns in the fort opened fire and soon the entire bay lit up with gunfire. Roberts knew that he couldn't stay in the bay, so he tied a towing line to the captured ship *Sagrada Familia* and headed for the open sea with the Portuguese treasure ship in tow. The *Royal Rover* wasn't able to sail at any great speed under those conditions, but it was their only chance. One of

SEPTEMBER 1719

Roberts sails to Brazil and attacks the treasure fleet.

the Portuguese men-o-war made sail and began to close on Roberts' ships, but suddenly turned about and stopped. The captain apparently wanted to wait for the second man o' war to catch up. By the time it did, the *Royal Rover* and the *Sagrada Familia* were out of sight.

Roberts had led his pyrates in a seemingly impossible attack. They had plucked a large treasure ship right out from under the protection of a very large fortress and the rest of a fleet which included two warships. The ship's cargo taken by Roberts was reported in the English newspaper *The Daily Current* in an article dated February 6, 1720 that stated Roberts got 7749 chests of sugar, 128 baskets of sugar in cake, 21751 hides, 92 barrels of honey, 957 quarter chests of sugar, 11238 rolls of tobacco, 205 raw hides, 104 slaves, large quantities of planks and East Indies goods, 759128 octaves if gold dust, and 174,431 gold coins. Other reports include chests of jewels and silver plate, and a diamond studded gold cross made as a presentation gift for the King of Portugal. According to pyrate rules, all valuables were placed in what was called a "common chest" and eventually auctioned off to the crew at "the sale at the mast."

Roberts made the winning bid for the diamond studded gold cross and wore it in every battle from that day on.

The crewmen were badly in need of some fun ashore, so they sailed to Devil's Island off the Guyana coast. In future years, that island would house the infamous French prison of the same name, but in 1719 it was a Spanish port that had plenty of taverns and women for passing sailors. The governor of Devil's Island was delighted to grant the pyrates free reign of the port and to profit from their lavish spending. They stayed there for two weeks. Leaving the *Sagrada Familia* and some of his pyrates in port, Roberts went back to sea in the *Royal Rover* to look for more prizes. In October 1719 he was sailing near the River Suriname on the north coast of Brazil when he easily took a 12-gun sloop from Rhode Island that was under the command of Captain Crane. Roberts kept the sloop and renamed it the *Fortune* and transferred the valuable cargo over to the *Royal Rover*.

During the looting, Captain Crane told Roberts about a larger brig from Rhode Island that was due to arrive at any day and Roberts decided to take that prize too. Soon, his lookout spotted a mast on the horizon and Roberts prepared to attack. However, the risk of losing the *Royal Rover* with all that valuable cargo aboard was too great and the heavy cargo onboard made the *Royal Rover* too slow to chase a prize vessel. So, Roberts decided to use his newly captured sloop, the *Fortune*, and he ordered quartermaster Kennedy to return to Devil's Island in the *Royal Rover* and to rejoin the *Sagrada Familia* and the rest of his crew. To make the *Fortune* even lighter and faster, Roberts had all of the provisions onboard transferred to the *Royal Rover* before it left. Roberts must have figured on getting new provisions from this prize vessel once it was taken. As the *Royal Rover* sailed out of view, the sloop *Fortune* with Roberts and 40 of his best men, including the rest of the House of Lords, sailed after the mysterious ship on the horizon.

Suddenly, the wind stopped and the *Fortune* helplessly bobbed up and down on the calm sea, unable to move. Roberts and his crew watched the prize vessel on the horizon sail on until it was out of sight. The *Fortune* was all alone, drifting helplessly on a windless sea. After eight days, his men began to die from hunger and thirst. Roberts ordered Christopher Moody and a few others to take his longboat and row to the *Royal Rover* for help. Within a few days, Moody managed to row to Devil's Island but the *Royal Rover* and the *Sagrada Familia* were gone. When Moody and his men returned a few days later, they reported that Kennedy had taken the two vessels and vanished. Roberts attributed his actions to Irish treachery and disliked everything Irish after that day.

In reality, Kennedy did not desert. Back on Devil's Island, they waited for Roberts, but when he didn't show up after 11 days, Kennedy and the pyrate crew assumed that Roberts had been sunk or captured. Kennedy was elected captain by the crew and he let all his prisoners sail away on the *Sagrada Familia* under the command of Captain Crane, who made it safely to the English colony on Antigua. Captain Kennedy sailed away on the *Royal Rover* just before the longboat piloted by Christopher Moody arrived in port. Kennedy took a few more prizes in the Caribbean, but they had so much loot, that Kennedy and many of the crew decided to retire from piracy and settle down ashore. Kennedy charted a course for Ireland, but he was such a bad navigator that he wrecked the *Royal Rover* on the Scotland coast. Most of his crew were caught and executed. Kennedy managed to escape and finally made it to Ireland where he bought and managed a brothel in Deptford. However, he was eventually arrested for burglary and while in prison, he was recognized as a pyrate and hanged.

One of the ships that Kennedy took before returning to Ireland was the *West River Merchant*, bound for Virginia. Eight pyrates who wished to retire with their loot were allowed to leave the pyrate crew. They coerced the captain of the *West River Merchant* to take them to Hampton, Virginia. Arriving in February 1720, the wealthy pyrates headed directly for the taverns in the town of Hampton and began a lavish lifestyle. Their boldness, appearance, and wealth quickly attracted the attention of the authorities, primarily because they used gold to pay for things at a time when most Virginians traded tobacco as currency. Other ports may have welcomed wealthy men of questionable background, but not Virginian ports. Governor Spotswood had a policy of no tolerance when it came to pyrates. Suspected of being pyrates, six of the eight pyrates were arrested. They were tried in Hampton and executed.

Still adrift 90 miles off shore, Roberts and his small crew tore out planking from the sloop and made a raft, which they used to row ashore and get fresh water. Eventually the wind freshened and the sloop *Fortune* managed to sail to a small island where the sloop was repaired. It was there on that small island that Roberts and his crew decided to draw up a new set of articles, the ones that Charles Johnson would reproduce in his book "The General History of Pyrates," four years later.

New officers were elected and the crew voted Christopher Moody as the new sailing master and Thomas Anstis the new quartermaster. Jones and Dennis were re-elected as the boatswain and gunner respectively. Roberts was starting all over. He had nothing except his small sloop and 40 pyrates. Roberts did manage to keep his diamond studded golden Portuguese cross, but all the rest of the crew's loot was aboard the *Royal Rover* and now gone. After signing the articles, they sailed toward Barbados.

Chapter 56
The Pyrate Fleet of Edward England

Back in African waters, Edward England was having great success aboard his ship, the *Royal James*. In the spring of 1719 while Davis, Cocklyn and La Buse were looting the galley *Bird* at Sierra Leone, he took up to 20 prizes between the Gambia River and the Cape of Good Hope. He kept two, the *Mercury* and the *Elizabeth and Katherine* renaming them the *Queen Anne's Revenge* and the *Flying King*. This was further evidence that Edward was a Jacobite, or at least pretended to be. The name "Queen Anne's Revenge" as a Jacobite reference was discussed earlier with Blackbeard and the name "Flying King" referred to James the Pretender who was sometimes called the Flying King because he was in exile. The vessels were given to two newly appointed pyrate captains, the *Queen Anne's Revenge* to Captain Lane and the *Flying King* to Captain Simple. Both captains left Edward England and sailed their vessels to the Caribbean.

By the summer of 1719 Edward was sailing north near Cape Coast in present day Ghana. There, he encountered the pyrate ships of Thomas Cocklyn and Olivier Le Vasseur, La Buse. They had recently dissolved their partnership with Howell Davis and were probably unaware that he had just been killed. They were hoping to join with another pyrate captain and build a fleet. Cocklyn was still commanding the 30-gun *Speakwell* and La Buse was commanding the 24-gun *Wyndham Galley*, which he renamed the *Duke of Ormond*.

This is yet another indicator that these pyrates were Jacobites. The Duke of Ormond was a famous Irish general and statesman who rose to great power under Queen Anne's reign. During the War of the Spanish Succession he quickly rose through the ranks as one of England's most effective senior

SUMMER 1719

Edward England sails off Africa.

officers. In 1711 he replaced the Duke of Marlborough and was promoted to Captain General of all British forces and in 1713 was made the Lord Lieutenant of Norfolk. Under Queen Anne, he was among the most respected and powerful men in the British government. However, when King George I assumed the throne, the Duke of Ormond was stripped of all his titles and positions simply because he was a member of the Tory party. He returned to his native Ireland as a member of the Privy Council of the Irish Parliament. But like so many others, in 1715 he was accused of treason as a Jacobite supporter. His property was confiscated and the Duke of Ormond fled to Spain. In 1719, while Edward was sailing the waters off West Africa, the Duke of Ormond was planning a Spanish invasion of England designed to put James Edward Stuart on the throne.

Edward, Cocklyn, and La Buse signed articles with Edward England, who was elected the commodore of a small fleet. However, it's about that time when all references to Captain Cocklyn cease. Perhaps he was killed or perhaps he was simply voted out of office, but Thomas Cocklyn and his pyrate galley *Speakwell* aren't mentioned in any further contemporary accounts. However, one member of Cocklyn's crew was mentioned. He was John Taylor, Davis' quartermaster who had Davis voted out of office and became captain of Davis' ship, then joined Cocklyn's crew after Davis was voted back in. For some reason, as Cocklyn faded into the darkness of the unknown, John Taylor joined Edward England's crew and became the quartermaster. This was a move that Edward would soon deeply regret.

Together, the fleet took a few merchantmen off Cape Coast including the galley *Peterborough* and the ship *Victory*. After looting the *Victory*, the ship was allowed to sail on, but Edward kept the galley *Peterborough*. This is a bit confusing, but Edward renamed the *Peterborough* the *Victory*. The new pyrate galley *Victory* was fitted out for 30 guns and given to John Taylor to command. Edward's fleet now consisted of between three and six vessels. It is certain that Edward commanded the *Royal James*, La Buse commanded the *Duke of Ormond*, and Taylor had the *Victory*, but at some point, the *Speakwell*, the *Queen Anne's Revenge*, and the *Flying King* left the fleet. The exact date is uncertain. Regardless of the exact size, Edward's fleet sailed 100 miles east to the Portuguese fort at Ouidah where they took the English ship *Heroine*, two Portuguese ships, and one French vessel. Badly in need of careening, the fleet chose an isolated spot along the African coastline and remained there for several months. According to Charles Johnson, the crews "lived there wantonly for several Weeks, making free with Negro Women." By the end of 1719 they decided to sail around the Cape of Good Hope and try their luck on the Indian Ocean.

It was now January 1720 and Edward and his fleet stopped briefly at Madagascar. Around the Malabar Coast of India, the pyrate fleet took several Indian vessels and then, Edward England finally got another chance to upgrade to a bigger ship. They spotted a Dutch ship of 34 guns, which they easily took. Edward kept the ship and renamed it the *Fancy* and the *Royal James* was given to the prize crew. La Buse also got a chance to upgrade. He took a 28-gun Indian Merchantman which he kept and renamed it the *India Queen*. Shortly after that, La Buse wrecked his ship on Mayotte Island which is halfway between the northern tip of Madagascar and the African coast. While La Buse and some of his crew were making repairs, other members of his crew used canoes to paddle out to join Edward England's ship. It was August 1720 and Edward England aboard the *Fancy* and John Taylor aboard the *Victory* were sailing alone.

Edward spotted three large merchant ships while sailing for Johanna Island near Madagascar. That was precisely the prize vessels the pyrates had searched for since they entered the Indian Ocean. Those three merchant ships probably belonged to the East India Trading Company and the pyrates pursued. Upon sighting the pyrates, the three ships quickly scattered and sailed away under as much sail as they could bear. Edward's two vessels chose just one ship to follow, the English East Indiaman, *Cassandra*, commanded by Captain James Macrae. As the two pyrate vessels closed the distance, the *Cassandra* suddenly turned about and with all gun ports open, sailed directly toward the two pyrate vessels. Shots rang out from all three vessels and a three-hour battle ensued that consisted of one classic broadside after another. Apparently close to shore, both the *Cassandra* and the *Fancy* ran aground, which made the battle even more intense. Imagine two motionless ships relentlessly pounding away at each other with broadsides. Eventually, Captain Macrae ordered his men to jump ship and make for the island. Edward's crew took the *Cassandra* and her cargo worth £75,000. The *Cassandra's* crew had suffered 37 casualties while Edward's crew lost more than 90.

Ten days later, Captain Macrae and his 47 surviving crewmen came out of hiding and surrendered to Captain Taylor of the *Victory*. Taylor and most of the crew wanted to kill the English crew for what they had done, but the kindhearted Edward interceded. After getting his entire crew drunk, Edward persuaded Taylor and the rest of his crew to allow them to escape. Macrae and his survivors were given the badly damaged *Fancy* and allowed to sail away. But after sobering up a bit, Edward's crew regretted their decision and John Taylor led a mutiny against Captain England. The crew voted Taylor as their new captain and Edward England and the three loyal crewmembers who didn't vote for Taylor were marooned on Mauritius Island, a large and almost uninhabited island about 450 miles east of Madagascar. They eventually managed to build a small boat and sailed to Saint Augustine's Bay on Madagascar. Unable to get any kind of work, they were forced to beg for food. Edward England died a few months later of unknown causes.

Chapter 57
Taylor and La Buse

After marooning Edward England, Captain John Taylor was finally in command of a vessel of his own, the *Cassandra*. At the same time John Roberts was trying to rebuild a crew back in the waters near Barbados, Taylor began his career as a captain roaming the waters of the Indian Ocean accompanied by the *Victory* as his consort. The two pyrate vessels had moderate success, taking Indian, Arab, and English prizes. Arriving at the Dutch trading port of Cochin near the west southern tip of India in December 1720, Taylor paid the Dutch governor an enormous sum to allow his pyrates to carouse in port for a month. They had plenty of loot and the Dutch were delighted to help them spend it. By now, his ships were in need of another careening, so Taylor sailed to Mauritius Island, a small French island about 600 miles east of Madagascar.

Meanwhile, La Buse patched up the *India Queen*, which was wrecked on Mayotte Island, and managed to make it to Mauritius Island. Taylor and La Buse joined forces again, but La Buse's ship was too badly damaged to continue on, so Taylor gave him command of the *Victory*. By April 1721 the two pyrate vessels had arrived at the port of Saint-Denis on Bourbon Island, which was renamed Reunion Island in 1793. About the same time the pyrates arrives in port, a large Portuguese galleon limped into port. That vessel was either named *Nostra Senhora de Cabo* or *La Vierge du Cap* (accounts as to the galleon's actual name differ). The galleon had recently been severely damaged in a storm and was forced to throw all of the deck guns overboard in order to keep from capsizing. While the damaged galleon awaited repairs, the pyrates easily captured it as a prize. Aboard they found diamonds which were valued at over £500,000 and other goods worth over £375,000. The *Victory* was burned and Captain La Buse kept the galleon as his new ship, renaming it the *Victory*. They returned to Madagascar and divided over a million pounds worth of loot

Bourbon Island lies between Mauritius Island and Madagascar.

between their 240 crewmembers. It was said that each man received at least 42 diamonds.

The two pyrates were still partners in 1722 when they plundered the Dutch East India Company's fort at Delagoa, which is now called Maputo Bay on the east coast of Africa in modern Mozambique. But by the end of 1722 the two pyrates finally decided to retire. Captain Taylor sailed for the Caribbean on board the *Cassandra* and persuaded the Governor of Portobelo to grant a pardon for him and his 140-man crew in exchange for the *Cassandra*. John Taylor retired to Panama as a wealthy man. Some sources say that he became a captain in the Panamanian Navy, but that event was not well documented.

Olivier Le Vasseur La Buse wasn't quite so lucky. He attempted to retire on the islet of Bel Ombre near Mahe in the Seychelles, which is a small group of islands in the middle of the Indian Ocean, about 800 miles north east of Madagascar. The French administration insisted that he give them his entire treasure. He turned them down and continued piracy on a small scale in the Indian Ocean until he was finally caught in 1730. By that time, he had accumulated an enormous amount of loot which seemed to have disappeared. Apparently, he buried his treasure as insurance against arrest. He believed that he could bargain for his freedom by offering a portion of his treasure to some local governor, but that plan wouldn't work if his treasure was already in the hands of the authorities. The plan still didn't work. He was executed on Reunion Island on July 7, 1730. As he stood on the scaffold, La Buse threw a coded message into the crowd saying, "Find my treasure, he who can." Many have tried to decode his message including a former British Army Cryptographer in 1948. So far, only 107 pieces of eight, two shoe buckles and a boatswain's whistle have been recovered from Astove Island in the Seychelles island group.

Chapter 58
Roberts Starts Over Again

Back to the waters of Barbados and Martinique, Roberts was starting over again. He spotted a prize vessel on January 10, 1720 peacefully anchored at Laquary Roads near Trinidad. It was the six-gun sloop *Philippa*, commanded by Captain Daniel Greaves. Roberts anchored nearby and waited for night. Quartermaster Anstis led a small party of pyrates over to the Philippa in a canoe. Several of the Philippa's crew began to fire pistols at the pyrates, but Anstis warned them to stop or they would be killed. They were so frightened of the pyrates that they allowed Anstis and his few men to take the sloop without further resistance. Over the next several weeks, Roberts took three more vessels, but they were all small prizes. By now, he had a pyrate crew of 70 counting the 30 men who recently joined his crew from some of prize vessels he had taken. But the *Fortune* was a small sloop of 12 guns. Roberts desperately needed a bigger ship. Without one, he would just be another second-rate pyrate.

JANUARY 1720

Roberts in the Caribbean

As Roberts searched the sea for a bigger vessel, he spotted another sloop and sailed after it. As he closed on the sloop, he saw that the sloop had a black pyrate flag too. It was the *Sea King* commanded by Montigny la Palisse and the two pyrates signed articles and became partners.

JANUARY 1720

Meanwhile, on February 19, 1720, the same day Roberts and Palisse joined forces, the merchants on Barbados sent a petition to Governor Lowther demanding action. Part of the petition read:

Roberts and la Palisse become partners.

"A certain pyrate sloop carrying 12 guns and manned with 70 men hath lately taken several vessels to windward of this island and still lyeth there to intercept their trade."

Governor Lowther commissioned Captain Owen Rogers of the 16-gun galley *Summersett* and Captain Daniel Greaves of the six-gun sloop *Philippa* to stop Roberts. The *Philippa* was the same sloop so easily taken by

Roberts back on January 10, 1720. They sailed from port on February 22, 1720. Four days later, they encountered a French merchant ship that had recently been chased by Roberts and Palisse but managed to escape. The captain warned Rogers and Greaves that Roberts had a partner. Greaves was very apprehensive at taking on two pyrate vessels, but before he could do anything about the situation, Roberts and Palisse were upon them.

Rogers and Greaves fled from the two pyrate sloops in order to make the pyrates think they were merely merchant vessels trying to escape, but it was only a trap. Roger's plan was to keep the *Philippa* sailing on the port side of his sloop, the *Summersett* and allow Roberts to catch him on his starboard side. Once Roberts' sloop fired its first broadside, the *Summersett* would sail ahead and expose the pyrate vessel to the guns of the *Philippa*, then circle around and catch the pyrate sloop in a crossfire. The *Fortune* caught up to the Summersett and came along her starboard side as planned. The crew of the *Summersett* heard Roberts' musicians playing on the quarterdeck as the two vessels prepared for battle. The *Fortune* let loose a broadside into the Summersett's starboard side and Rogers ordered the *Summersett* to sail forward according to plan. The *Philippa* was now in position to fire, but the cowardly Captain Greaves didn't give the order and his guns remained silent. He had recently been a prisoner of Roberts and knew that he would be killed if Roberts captured him again. Roberts swung the *Fortune* around and crossed the *Summersett's* stern. By then, the *Fortune* was towing a long boat filled with pyrates. Roberts' plan was to keep the *Summersett's* crew pinned down with fire from the stern while his pyrates in the long boat boarded from the side. But as the *Fortune* approached, the *Summersett* opened up with a fierce broadside and musket fire from a very large crew. With his sloop severely damaged, Roberts realized that this was no merchant vessel, but a ship of war in disguise.

Just as the *Summersett* maneuvered to finish off the *Fortune* with another broadside, Captain Greaves hesitantly decided to join the fight and clumsily sailed the *Philippa* directly between the other two vessels. Unable to shoot at the *Fortune* without also hitting the *Philippa*, Captain Rogers held his fire. Roberts quickly realized that this was his only chance for escape. Putting on full sail, Roberts slipped away from the powerful guns of the *Summersett*. However, the *Summersett* gave chase and fired its bow guns, hitting the Fortune several more times as it closed the distance. Roberts was in a desperate situation. His new partner, Captain la Palisse, decided that the battle was not his kind of party and sailed away, ending the short partnership. Additionally, the *Summersett* was faster and was rapidly closing on him. Roberts ordered everything to be thrown overboard to lighten his sloop and increase his speed. That included most of the guns. It worked and the *Fortune* slowly pulled away, eventually losing sight of the *Summersett* as night fell.

Half of his crewmen were dead and his sloop had been shot to pieces. Roberts managed to sail his badly damaged sloop to the Island of Dominica, just north of the Large French colony on Martinique. He knew that his stay had to be a short one as the island belonged to the French and he would be arrested if found. While Roberts was making repairs, the French discovered his sloop and sent two warships to destroy him, but Roberts was somehow warned and managed to sail his badly damaged sloop away just before the French warships arrived. The *Fortune* managed to make it to Carriacou Island, which lies 20 miles north of Grenada. They stayed there a few weeks eating tortoises and repairing the Fortune.

Those last incidents began a downward spiral in the psychology of Roberts. Several months earlier, he had begun his pyrate career as captain of the *Royal Rover* and followed the example of Howell Davis who always treated captives exceptionally well and respected and consulted his House of Lords for advice. But after Kennedy's perceived desertion, Roberts slowly began to distance himself from his House of Lords and sought their advice less and less. Then, after the attacks from the governors of Barbados and Martinique, Roberts began to seek vengeance. He slowly turned into a ruthless and bloodthirsty autocrat who demanded total obedience from not only his captives, but from his own crew as well. He began to treat captives very harshly, often whipping or torturing the captains and some of the officers, even to the point of death. He encouraged his pyrates to be especially destructive when looting, destroying everything on a prize vessel that they didn't take, and often sinking the vessels out of spite.

Before, Roberts had always claimed he never forced unwilling men to join his pyrates, but more and more Roberts began to force large numbers of captured crewmen to join his pyrates, whipping and sometimes killing them if they attempted to escape. There is no telling what his House of Lords thought, most of them had been with Davis from the start and probably disapproved of the changes, but there was nothing they could do. With each victory, Roberts became more established and idolized in the eyes of many of his crew. That emboldened Roberts and made him far more aggressive in his actions toward both crew and captives alike. It was soon evident to his lords that to speak against Captain Roberts would be asking for marooning.

Roberts had taken on the full role of the typical Hollywood image of a pyrate captain. He was overbearing, cruel, and ruthless. He was also flamboyantly dressed in the finest bright scarlet damask coat with matching

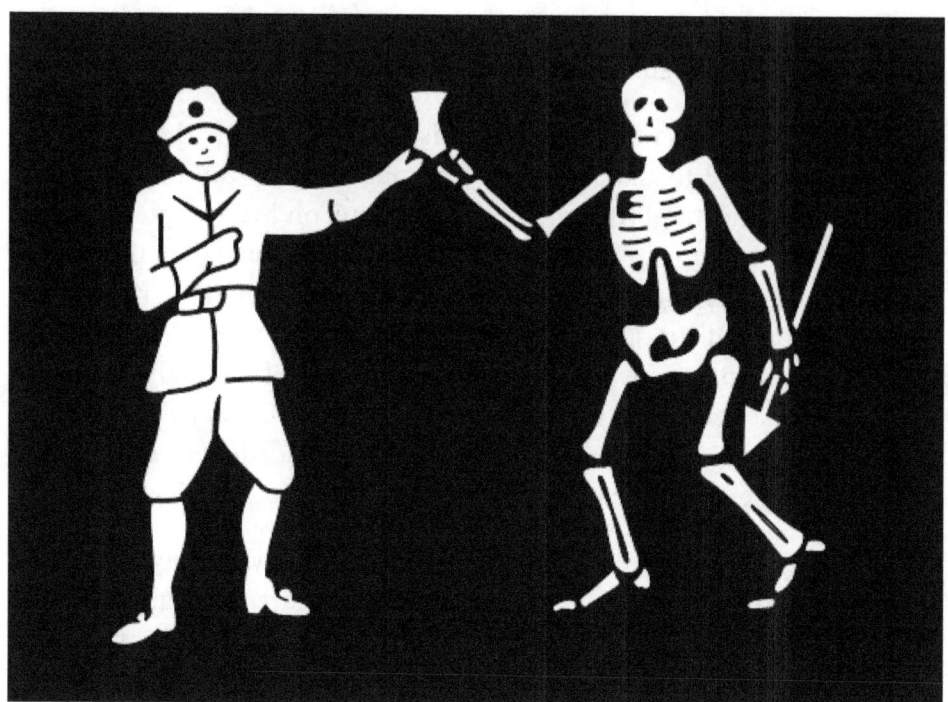

Figure 26: *Roberts, First Flag*

Figure 27: *Roberts, Second Flag*

breeches, ruffled shirt, finely powered wig, a crimson plumed hat, and always wore the diamond studded golden Portuguese cross hanging around his neck on a massive gold chain. He strutted about the quarterdeck with a gold toothpick in his mouth. He also drank a great deal of tea. His motto was "A merry life and a short one."

Roberts even had a series of totally unique and flamboyant flags, two of which are shown here. In the first, Roberts and a skeleton are holding an hourglass and in the second, Roberts, wearing his large hat and holding a flaming sword, stands next to a skeleton.

Roberts was a very different kind of pyrate in many ways. He never drank alcohol. He didn't prevent his men from drinking; he just chose not to ever drink it himself. He was a deeply religious man and always observed the Sabbath. He never pursued women. Some authors have alleged that he may have preferred men, but there is no documentation that he had any sexual desires whatsoever. Personally, he was of a serious nature and always in control of his actions. When going into battle or meeting with captains, he wore a bandolier with two pistols attached. Everyone aboard a pyrate vessel was exceptionally well-armed when going into battle, but with his jewelry and flamboyant dress, Captain Roberts made it a point to stand out among the rest. Additionally, Roberts would always have his musicians performing on the quarterdeck as the pyrates went into action. Potential victims often first became alerted to their doom by hearing the sound of music on Roberts' ship. That of course would soon be followed by the raising of the black flag and a shot across the bow.

JUNE 1720

Roberts takes prizes off Newfoundland.

Roberts was now the most famous pyrate in the world. His daring and destructive attacks on English and French shipping coupled with his mistreatment of his captives made it imperative that Roberts and his pyrates be stopped. Literally everyone was out to kill him. In June 1720 the British Royal Navy stationed 11 warships of various sizes in the Caribbean and along the coast up to New England. Those ships were HMS *Mary, Adventure, Mermaid, Happy, Milford, Rose, Shark, Rye, Flamborough, Phenix*, and the *Squirrel*. That strong naval presence made the Caribbean too risky. In a brilliant move, Roberts decided to hunt for prizes in waters that had never seen pyrates before, the fishing fleets of the Newfoundland Banks.

Roberts took over a dozen vessels on his way up the North American coast, reaching Newfoundland in mid-June 1720. Roberts, aboard the still damaged *Fortune* and 70 pyrates, attacked the small harbor of Ferryland. Burning the largest ship as a warning; his pyrates terrorized the town. The port of Trepassey was next and on June 21, 1720, Roberts' reputation was so intimidating that no one resisted him in any way. Roberts found 22 vessels anchored in port, but they had all been abandoned by their terrified crews. The vessels and the entire town were his for the taking. As the looting on the vessels progressed, Roberts allowed up to 50 pyrates at a time to go ashore to loot the town, drink in the taverns, and enjoy the prostitutes. They totally dominated the community, did what they pleased, and no one lifted a finger to stop them.

St. Mary's, Newfoundland was an important fishing port first known by the English in 1597—Originally French, it became an English colony in 1713.

Keeping a 16-gun brig which replaced his damaged sloop, Roberts called his crew back from the town and fired his guns at the wooden buildings along the docks and burned every vessel in the harbor, despite the total cooperation of the captains and townsfolk. Sailing to St. Mary's harbor in July 1720 Roberts repeated his actions, destroying every vessel after looting. After leaving St. Mary's Roberts took a French flotilla of six ships with no resistance. He abandoned the brig that he had taken only a few days earlier at Trepassey and kept the best one, a 28-gun brigantine, for his new pyrate vessel. Roberts named his new vessel the *Good Fortune*. That larger vessel was the most powerful pyrate ship in the Atlantic. After taking four more French vessels, Roberts spotted a familiar sloop, the *Sea King*. To the surprise of Roberts and his crew, their short time partner, Captain Montigny la Palisse, had followed Roberts to Newfoundland after abandoning them in the battle off Barbados.

Roberts must have been in a good mood because he decided to overlook la Palisse's earlier cowardice and once again sign articles as partners. Together, they took the Boston sloop *Samuel* on July 13, 1720. The *Boston News Letter* reported the incident and described the pyrates' behavior as like a "parcel of furies, breaking open every bale and packing-case." In only one month, Roberts had taken over 60 merchant vessels, 150 boats, and three ports, and had become the number one threat in the Atlantic. The British warships in the Caribbean were sent to Newfoundland to stop him, but they were too late. While the British ships were sailing north to find Roberts, he was sailing south, back to the Caribbean.

AUGUST 1720

Roberts back in the Caribbean.

On his way back to the Caribbean, Roberts aboard his 28-gun brigantine *Good Fortune* and la Palisse aboard his six-gun sloop *Sea King* took two more vessels off the Virginia Capes and one off Carolina. By September 1720 the pyrates had reached the tiny island of Deseada, off Guadeloupe in the Lesser Antilles, where they careened their vessels. While there, Roberts renamed his vessels; brigantine *Good Fortune* was renamed the *Royal Fortune* and the six-gun sloop *Sea King* was renamed the *Good Fortune*. Roberts continued to reuse those two names for the rest of his short life. During the careening, three members of his crew who had been forced to join, tried to escape, but they were quickly captured and were severely whipped. Afterwards, a pyrate council was held and two of them were pardoned, but the third was marooned with a flask of water, a musket with one ball of shot and a small amount of powder as a warning to the others. Roberts' next target was the British port on St. Kitts.

At sea again, Roberts and la Palisse took several more vessels before they arrived at Basseterre Harbor, St. Kitts, on September 26, 1720. As Roberts sailed into the harbor, his musicians played and his black flag flew. The guns from the four forts were positioned poorly, so the governor decided not to fire on Roberts. The pyrates easily took five vessels anchored in the harbor in one day. During the night, the guns of the forts were repositioned to where they could offer more effective fire and as dawn broke the guns opened up. With shot ripping through the sails of the two pyrate vessels, Roberts and la Palisse hastily made sail and fled. But Roberts couldn't let the Governor think he was afraid, so he sent him a letter saying, "Had you come off as you ought to a done, and drank a glass of wine with me and my company, I should not have harmed the least vessel in your harbour. Further, it is not your gunns you fired that affrighted me or hindered our coming on shore, but the wind . . ."

Roberts' next port of call was the tiny French colony on St. Barthelemy. The governor was known to be pyrate-friendly and always encouraged pyrates to sell goods and spend their money in his port. Roberts was welcomed as a hero by the governor and in return, Roberts gave him a gold chain worth a years' salary. His pyrates were welcomed throughout the colony and stayed for three weeks, partying in the town, spending their money, drinking in the taverns and enjoying the company of the women. Back in action again, Roberts and la Palisse took 14 English and French vessels near the Virgin Islands between October 23 and 26, 1720. One of them was a 22-gun brig taken off Tortula. Roberts kept the brig which became his second *Royal Fortune* and he allowed the prize crew to sail off aboard his old and leaky brigantine. He also kept one sloop to act as a store vessel.

Arriving at the harbor of St. Lucia, Roberts and la Palisse encountered a 30-gun Dutch brigantine at anchor. Roberts raised his black flag, but the ship refused to surrender and a four-hour battle commenced. The *Royal Fortune* kept the Dutch brigantine occupied with broadside after broadside while the *Good Fortune* and the other sloop attacked the Dutch brigantine's stern. Eventually, Roberts' pyrates overwhelmed the Dutch crew and the survivors were all brutally killed. However, Roberts' *Royal Fortune* was so badly damaged that he decided to keep the Dutch brigantine, naming it the third *Royal Fortune*. It was fitted out with 44 guns, which included four 12-pound cannons and twelve 8-pound demi-culverins. Roberts now had a fleet of four vessels, his 44-gun brigantine, *Royal Fortune*, the 22-gun Tortula brig he now used as a store ship, la Palisse's six-gun sloop, *Good Fortune*, and the store sloop.

In November and December 1720, they took more prizes in the waters near Dominica, a large island north of Martinique. Then, they decided to return to Africa. Abandoning the Tortula brig and the store sloop, they sailed to Bermuda to catch the trade winds that blew east. But Roberts' notoriety as the most famous pyrate of the day was about to take a back seat. As he sailed for Africa, a story came out in the press that was so sensational that it eclipsed all other reports on pyrate activity. It was the story of two female pyrates, Anne Bonny and Mary Read.

Chapter 59

Calico Jack Rackham, Anne Bonny, and Mary Read

Newspapers exploded with sensational and tantalizing stories of two female pyrates who had been serving aboard a pyrate ship with a crew of 13 men. Nothing like that had ever happened before. Just think of it, two females living in sin among a crew of male pyrates! Newsworthy opportunities like that just didn't get any better for an 18th century journalist. The story had everything, crime, sex, excitement, adventure, and scandal. Every newspaper throughout Western Europe and the North American Colonies ran the story. Anne Bonny and Mary Read were the most famous women of their time.

It was October 1720 and Captain Calico Jack Rackham and his crew were pyrating off the Jamaica coastline in their small and unimpressive sloop named the *Vanity*. Rackham already had a well-established reputation as a pyrate captain and Governor Woodes Rogers had recently issued a warrant for his arrest. Pyrate hunter Jonathan Barnet sighted the *Vanity* laying quietly at anchor off the north coast of Jamaica. As Barnet's men boarded the small sloop, only two members of Rackham's crewmen offered any resistance. Well-armed and dressed like men, Anne Bonny and Mary Read waged a fierce battle against the boarders, shooting pistols, wielding cutlasses, and spewing all sorts of profanity as they fought. Apparently, the rest of the pyrates were either too drunk or too scared to offer any resistance. Bonny and Read were finally subdued and the entire pyrate crew was taken back to Jamaica to stand trial for piracy.

The news spread quickly. As far as scandalous stories about sex and violence go, a story about female pyrates was about as good as any newspaper could hope for. Just the idea must have shocked, thrilled, and excited readers throughout the western world. Think of what modern tabloids would do with a story like this today. It would run for weeks. Additionally, in the best traditions of tabloid journalism, the missing facts would be filled in with all sorts of sordid details that were invented by the highly creative editorial staff. That was especially true in the early 18th century where exaggeration and embellishment by the press were the order of the day. But what is the truth? Were these women real? Where did they come from? Why did they become pyrates? They certainly were real; they were captured by Jonathan Barnet in October 1720 and brought back to Port Royal for trial. But who these women were before they became pyrates and how they came to be a part of Rackham's crew is far more speculative. Three hundred years later, is it possible to separate the truth from the myth?

Figure 28: *Rackham's Flag*

Literally everything we know about lives of Anne Bonny and Mary Read before October 1720 comes from only one source. You guessed it, Charles Johnson's *General History of Pyrates*. If we assume that the facts about Anne Bonny, Mary Read, and Jack Rackham are as embellished, sensationalized, and even fictionalized as we have seen with other pyrates in that book, then we must realize that we really know nothing about them for certain. So far, researchers have not been able to find a single document, record, or even contemporary account that mentions anything about the lives of Anne Bonny or Mary Read before September 1720. Over the centuries, the life stories of these two very real women have been told and retold hundreds of times by authors who have contributed to the invention of their mythical pasts. Their true stories remain cloaked in mystery. Charles Johnson's book remains the one and only source of their earlier lives. His version might be completely true, or it might be partially true, or it might be a complete fabrication. However, there is no doubt that Jack Rackham played a vital role in the lives of Anne Bonny and Mary Read.

Calico Jack Rackham got his colorful name because he supposedly preferred to wear cotton clothes. Don't we all when traveling in the Caribbean? In 1720 the word "calico" didn't refer to the same brightly colored cloth it does today. In the early 18th century, most of the cotton found in the colonies was imported directly from Calicut, India by the famous English East India Company or indirectly through French merchants. Because it came from Calicut, all cotton, even plain white cotton, was commonly known as calico. As you may recall, Rackham was a member of Charles Vane's crew and was with Vane when he shot his way out of Nassau in 1718. Soon afterwards, Jack Rackham was promoted to quartermaster on Vane's sloop and in late August and early September 1718 Rackham was with Vane when they took between eight and twelve vessels at the entrance of the Charles Town Harbor. You might remember that one of the ships Vane took was a 12-gun brigantine from Africa that was carrying 90 slaves. He renamed it the *Ranger* and Rackham was the quartermaster. Calico Jack Rackham was also present when Vane's crew and Blackbeard's crew met for a pyrate Banyan on Ocracoke Island, North Carolina in October 1718. Vane's brigantine *Ranger* and a consort sloop were operating in the Windward Passage between Cuba and Florida on November 24, 1718 when Jack Rackham led the mutiny that removed Vane from the position of Captain. Vane and a few of his loyal crewmembers were permitted to leave and Calico Jack Rackham was elected the new captain.

Rackham enjoyed moderate success taking small prizes close to the Jamaican shoreline. In December 1718 he took his first rich prize, the merchant ship *Kingston*. The problem was that he captured the prize within sight of the Port Royal Harbor. This infuriated the local merchants who hired several pyrate hunters to track Rackham down. In February 1720 the pyrate hunters finally found Rackham's brigantine *Ranger* off Isla de los Pinos, just south of Cuba. The *Ranger* was lying at anchor along the recently captured prize ship *Kingston* while Rackham and his entire crew were asleep on the beach in tents that were made from old sailcloth. As the pyrate hunters approached the vessels, Rackham and his crew became alerted and scrambled into the jungle and eventually escaped on foot. Rackham obtained a small boat somewhere on the island and sailed away with six of his crewmen.

For the next three months, Rackham stayed at sea, traveling around Cuba and eventually making his way to Nassau. According to tradition, his flag displayed a skull with crossed swords. Calico Jack Rackham must have been an exceptionally persuasive talker because he managed to convince Governor Woodes Rogers that he had been forced into piracy by Charles Vane and Rogers granted Rackham and his crew the King's Pardon.

The Myth of Anne Bonny

According to the stories which followed the accounts written by Charles Johnson, Anne Bonny was born in Kinsale, Ireland in the county of Cork just before 1700. She was the illegitimate daughter of a prominent lawyer named William Cormac and his housemaid. Due to the scandal of the relationship, the father, the maid, and Anne left Ireland and settled in Charles Town, South Carolina. William Cormac eventually became a wealthy plantation owner, but his family life soon turned to tragedy. At age 13, his daughter, Anne, stabbed a servant girl with a table knife. Then, a few years later, she married an apparently unimpressive sailor named James Bonny.

The two newlyweds wound up in Nassau just as Governor Woodes Rogers was issuing pardons and stamping out piracy. James Bonny assisted Rogers by informing him about the activities of those who remained pyrates while Anne's love interests wandered. In the late spring of 1719, the very handsome and dashing Calico Jack Rackham arrived in port soon after he had escaped capture off the coast of Cuba. The two of them fell in love. When the husband protested the relationship, Rackham offered to pay James Bonny what was called a divorce for purchase, but the stubborn and money conscious Anne wouldn't allow it. The two of them stole a sloop and headed out to sea. For Rackham, it was his chance to return to piracy and for Anne it was the beginning of an adventure. Their sloop was renamed the *Vanity* and Captain Rackham began recruiting a crew directly from other pyrate vessels at sea. At first, Anne attempted to disguise herself as a man, but soon gave up the pretense. Eventually Anne became pregnant with Jack's child and had to give up pyrating just long enough to give birth somewhere in Cuba. She left her child with her Cuban friends and returned to sea as a pyrate.

The Myth of Mary Read

According to the stories which followed the accounts written by Charles Johnson, Mary was from Portsmouth, England and was born around 1690. Her father was a sailor who was lost at sea. With the family funds running out, Mary's mother went to her mother-in-law for financial assistance. Mary's mother figured there was a better chance of getting support if she had a son, so she dressed Mary as a boy and they maintained the deception even after the mother-in-law's death. As a teenager, Mary sought adventure. Keeping the male disguise, she joined the Royal Navy and served aboard a man o' war. Fearing her true identity would be discovered, she changed jobs often.

Mary left the navy and enlisted first in an infantry regiment and then in a cavalry regiment in Flanders. Mary eventually fell in love with a soldier who knew her true gender and they were married. Mary began dressing in woman's clothing for the first time in many years, but when her husband died, she returned to her old lifestyle. Mary signed on as a sailor onboard a Dutch merchant ship which brought her to the Caribbean. The ship was attacked by English pyrates and Mary joined their crew, keeping her true gender a secret. After Governor Rogers offered the King's Pardon, Mary and the pyrate crew that she had joined decided to accept the pardon and become privateers. It was 1719 and there was a war on with Spain. Mary was sailing in this capacity when the vessel she was on was overtaken by Captain Jack Rackham, looking to recruit pyrates for his crew. Mary figured that the opportunity for wealth was greater as a pyrate, so she joined Rackham's crew, still maintaining her disguise.

In the beginning, Anne Bonny was the only one onboard who realized that Mary was indeed a woman. They became very close friends. Most stories go a lot further than that and claim that they were actually lovers. This is where the story really gets exciting. In many versions, Rackham entered the ship's cabin and found Anne and Mary in the midst of making love. Still thinking Mary to be a man, Rackham became enraged and commenced to attack Mary. Standing between the two, Anne quickly revealed the true nature of Mary's sex, which rapidly changed the dynamics of the entire situation. Afterwards, Anne and Jack maintained their love relationship, Anne and Mary maintained their love relationship, and it seems that Mary began a love relationship with one of the male crewmembers, to whom she revealed her true gender. One can easily understand how a tale like this generated a lot of interest when it was released in print. This was the sex story of the century.

Back to the Facts

Exactly how and when Anne Bonny and Mary Read came to be onboard Jack Rackham's sloop is unknown and will probably always remain a mystery. We know that Rackham was in Nassau in the spring of 1720 after he and six of his crew escaped the Isla de los Pinos. We also know that neither Anne Bonny nor Mary Read were with Rackham before this. Perhaps Anne Bonny did meet Rackham in Nassau exactly as told. It seems likely. In any event, on August 22, 1720 Jack Rackham returned to piracy and stole a sloop named the *William* which he renamed the *Vanity*. In early September

1720 near Harbor Island, Bahamas, he took several small prizes, mostly fishing vessels, and increased the size of his crew by recruiting directly from other pyrate vessels he encountered. With a full crew, he returned to his old stomping grounds, **or should I say stomping waters,** near the shores of Cuba and Jamaica. News of Rackham's piracy reached Nassau later that month and Governor Woodes Rogers nullified the King's Pardon he had recently given to Rackham. Rogers then issued a warrant for his arrest which wasn't actually published until October 1720. Over in Jamaica, Governor Nicholas Lawes sent pyrate hunter Jonathan Barnet in a well-armed sloop to seek out and capture Rackham and his crew.

Meanwhile, Rackham was cruising off Hispaniola on October 1, 1720 when his crew fired warning shots at two passing merchantmen. The ships surrendered and the pyrates boarded. Anne Bonny and Mary Read were mentioned for the first time in the accounts later given to the authorities by the victims. The women were described as screaming like banshees and frightening all the members of the prize crew. A short time later, while cruising the waters off the north coastline of Jamaica, Rackham's sloop stopped a canoe near the shore. The canoe had only one occupant, a woman named Dorothy Thomas. In her testimony at the trial of Rackham's crew, she stated:

The word "Machet" refers to a machete meaning cutlass and "murther" means murder.

> ". . . the Two Women were on the Board the said Sloop, and wore Men's Jackets, and long Trousers, and Handkerchiefs tied about their Heads; and that each of them had a Machet and a Pistol in their Hands and cursed and swore at the men to murther (me)."

Then on October 19, 1720 Rackham and his crew took a schooner captained by Thomas Spenlow near Port Maria Bay on the northern coast of Jamaica. According to Spenlow's testimony, the women were the first to board and continued to intimidate and terrorize the members of the prize crew as they went about taking clothing and anything else they desired.

Sailing west along the north coast of Jamaica, Rackham reached Dry Harbor Bay on October 20, 1720 where he hailed the merchant sloop *Mary*, commanded by Thomas Dillon. Upon seeing Rackham's sloop *Vanity*, most of the crewmen jumped overboard and swam ashore. Several warning shots were fired, and Captain Dillon surrendered. The Mary was robbed of about £300 in cargo. At the trial of Anne Bonny and Mary Read, part of Dillon's testimony reads "Anne Bonny had a Gun in her Hand, That they were both very profligate, cursing and swearing much, and very ready and willing to do most any Thing on Board."

Early on the evening of October 22, 1720, the *Vanity* lay at anchor in Dry Harbor Bay. As their sloop gently tugged at the anchor cable, the pyrates were below deck, playing cards and drinking rum. At about 10 o'clock that night, Anne and Mary were on deck when they sighted another sloop headed directly toward them. The two women shouted out a warning and Rackham and a few others scrambled up the ladder to the main deck while the rest of the pyrate crewmen remained passed out below. It was the well-armed sloop commanded by pyrate hunter Jonathan Barnet. As Barnet approached, he gave them a hail, asking their identity. Rackham replied, "John Rackham from Cuba." Barnet ordered them to surrender peacefully and Rackham answered by firing a swivel gun. Barnet's sloop returned fire and the male members of Rackham's crew, who were on the main deck, all dove for cover.

Realizing that he had no chance, Rackham asked for quarter and Barnet granted it. As Barnet's sloop came along side and his men boarded the *Vanity*, the two women pyrates suddenly sprang into action. According to Barnet's report, ". . .the women screamed, fighting like hellcats as they shot their pistols and swung their cutlasses, refusing to give up peacefully." On the other hand, Captain Rackham and his male crewmembers gave up without resistance. Eventually, the two women were subdued and Rackham and his pyrate crew were taken to St. Jago de la Vega, (old Spanish Town) Jamaica where they were imprisoned.

Governor Nicholas Lawes personally presided over the trial that was held on the 16 and 17 of November 1720. Two of the pyrates, John Besneck and Peter Cornelian, claimed they had been forced into piracy and testified against Rackham and his crew. When it came to Anne Bonny and Mary Read, Besneck and Cornelian both stated that the women were always the first to board a prize and that they wore men's clothing while fighting but women's clothing at other times. Captain Jack Rackham, quartermaster Richard Corner, and sailing master George Fetherston were hanged at Gallows Point on November 18, 1720. James Dobbin, John Davies, John Howell, Patrick Carty, Thomas Earl, Noah Harwood and two others were hanged over the next two days. Rackham's body was placed on display as a warning, hung in a gibbet on a sandbar at the entrance of Port Royal Harbor. Today, this tiny strip of sand is known as Rackham's Cay.

In a surprising finish, both Anne Bonny and Mary Read revealed that they were pregnant and "plead their bellies" at their trial ten days after Rackham's execution. They were found guilty of piracy but couldn't be executed until after the birth of their children since executing a pregnant woman would be executing the child too. Charles Johnson wrote that Mary Read died in prison. According to the Parish records for Saint Catherine, Jamaica,

1720

Calico Jack Rackham, Mary Read, and Anne Bonny are captured.

1718-1722

Sir Nicholas Lawes, Governor of Jamaica

Mary Read died on April 28, 1721 and was buried in the church graveyard. This would have been near the time she was due to go into labor. Pyrates weren't normally buried on sacred ground and the fact that she was buried by the church causes one to speculate that she may have died with her unborn child still inside of her. The church would have wanted to bury the child on sacred ground and if the child was still inside of Mary, they would have to be buried together.

But Anne Bonny faded into the dark vale of mystery. So far, no official record of her execution or release has been found. Furthermore, her name doesn't appear in any record or account after her capture. There are two basic versions told by historians who speculate on Anne Bonny's life after prison. Once version tells us that her father paid to have her released and that she remarried and lived into her 80s. The other version has her returning to piracy. Since factual documentation of either of these claims have yet to be discovered, we may never know the real truth.

As for the sexually charged relationships that transpired between Anne Bonny, Mary Read, and Jack Rackham aboard the sloop *Vanity*, we may also never know the truth. There are no surviving eyewitness accounts. How and when Anne Bonny and Mary Read came to be on Jack Rackham's sloop is unknown, but it is an absolute fact that Anne Bonny and Mary Read were on board the *Vanity*, dressed as men and fiercely fighting to prevent capture when they were arrested by Jonathan Barnet in October 1720. Additionally, it is a fact that Anne Bonny and Mary Read were both several months pregnant at the time of their trial. Perhaps the details of this tantalizing story happened exactly the way Charles Johnson told it and perhaps only some of the details are true. In any event, it remains one of the greatest pyrate legends from the golden age of piracy.

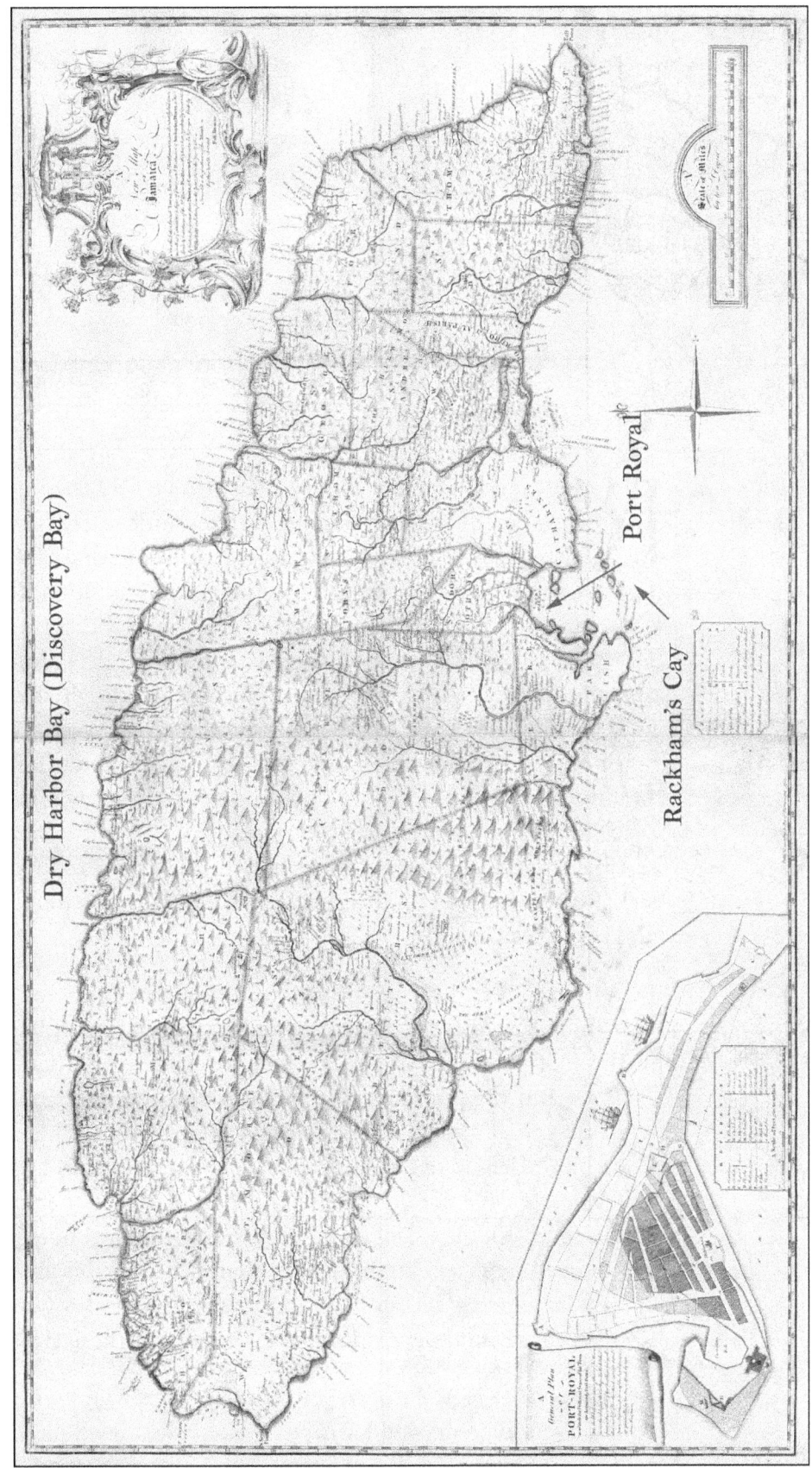

Figure 29: *Jamaica in 1720*

Chapter 60
Roberts Vows Revenge

Roberts and la Palisse aboard their two vessels, the *Royal Fortune* and *Good Fortune*, reached Cape Verde Islands safely, but there were two Portuguese men-o-war, one of 40 guns and one of 80 guns, waiting in the harbor. La Palisse immediately ordered his sloop, *Good Fortune* to come about and flee as he had done before, but Roberts prepared to attack. However, the winds were blowing in the wrong direction and the *Royal Fortune* became caught in the strong easterly winds which carried the brigantine all the way back to the Americas. The long voyage was unexpected and Roberts didn't have enough food or water onboard. His crew had to ration water severely, taking only one swallow a day. The *Royal Fortune* reached Surinam by the end of December 1720, but Roberts' crew was in terrible condition. Many of them had died of thirst and many others were sick. Roberts pushed on to Tobago where he was able to fill his water casks and re-provision.

Roberts blamed his misfortune on the governors of Barbados and Martinique. They were the ones who had forced him out of the Caribbean in the first place. As you recall, the governor of Barbados had sent the *Philippa* and the *Summersett* after him and the governor of Martinique had pursued his men when he attempted to repair his badly damaged sloop on the Island of Dominica. He vowed revenge on both and designed a new pyrate flag; one that showed his hatred for the men of Barbados and Martinique. The flag has his full figure (hat and all) holding a sword and standing with his feet on two skulls. Beneath the skulls are the letters ABH and AMH which stands for A Barbadian's Head and A Martinican's Head. Roberts clearly had developed a deep hatred for these two colonies.

By January 13, 1721 Roberts had met up once again with his partner, la Palisse. Near Pigeon Island, a mile off St. Lucia, they took the Rhode Island brig *Sea King*, under the command of Captain Norton. They also took another small sloop. They kept the brig and gave it to la Palisse as the new *Good Fortune* and la Palisse burned his old sloop. Between St. Lucia and Dominica, they took several more vessels including another Dutch brigantine, the *El Puerto del Principe*, which they kept. Roberts now had his brigantine, *Royal Fortune*, la Palisse's brig *Good Fortune*, the Dutch brigantine, *El Puerto del Principe*, and two other sloops which he used as supply vessels. Roberts then careened on Mona Island, just off Puerto Rico. While socializing on the beach, Roberts realized that he had a storage problem. He had taken too much loot. The gold and jewels he could get rid of anywhere, but the bulkier cargo could only be sold in a port, and Roberts was far too famous to enter any port in the Americas. Captain Norton, who was still a prisoner, convinced Roberts to allow him to take the cargo in the *El Puerto del Principe* and sell it for Roberts at his home port in Rhode Island. Since Norton was well-known there, it wouldn't look suspicious. Norton promised Roberts that he would later rendezvous with him off South Carolina to give him his share of the profits. Roberts reluctantly agreed.

By February 1721 Roberts' pyrate fleet was back in the waters of Guadeloupe where they took more prizes. Christian Tranquebar, the captain of a Danish ship that Roberts took, reported that the crew of the *Royal Fortune* consisted of 180 white pyrates and 48 Creole Blacks. On 18 February 1721, they entered the harbor at St. Lucia where they spotted another Dutch brig of 22 guns. As a general rule, Dutch crews didn't surrender and on that

Figure 30: *Roberts ABH AMH Flag*

occasion, the Dutch crew remained true to form. A long gun battle ensued that resulted in the killing of the entire Dutch crew. Roberts now had a fleet of five vessels, the 44-gun brigantine *Royal Fortune*, la Palisse's brig *Good Fortune*, two store sloops, and the 22-gun Dutch brig. In another bold move, Roberts took the recently captured Dutch brig and sailed into the bay of St. Luce on the south end of Martinique, flying Dutch colors. Roberts kept his other vessels far out of sight. The local merchants assumed that this Dutch ship was an unlicensed slaver and saw the opportunity to make some quick profits. Fourteen local merchant vessels filled with gold approached Roberts' decoy Dutch brig, and they were all easily captured. Their crewmen were whipped, and some were even killed by suspending them from yardarms and using them for target practice. Thirteen of the vessels were burned, one was sent with a warning to the governor not to interfere.

March 1721

Thomas Anstis became a pirate captain.

In March 1721 Roberts was joined by his other vessels. He gave command of the Dutch brig to his quartermaster, Thomas Anstis, who was one of Howell Davis' original members of the House of Lords. Roberts assigned Simpson as the new quartermaster aboard the *Royal Fortune*. The old House of Lords was almost totally out of power. Simpson was a bully and enjoyed mistreating the crew and Roberts was becoming more arrogant and unapproachable. When a pyrate returning from shore with fresh water dropped the cask, Roberts swore at the man. When the crewman swore back, Roberts drew his pistol and shot him dead. Lord Jones, one of the original members of Howell Davis' House of Lords protested and Roberts drew his sword to kill him too. But Jones lashed back with a knife and thrusted it deep into Roberts. The pyrate council ordered Jones to be whipped by every member of the crew. This shocked the old members of the House of Lords. Many of Roberts' crewmembers were becoming anxious and there was great unrest among them.

With his fleet of three vessels, he took more prizes off Antigua then sailed to the Carolinas to meet Norton, but Norton never showed up. La Palisse and his crew became tired of waiting and left the partnership to return to the Caribbean. Roberts was glad to see him go. La Palisse had deserted him twice in battle and was untrustworthy. Anstis' Dutch brig was renamed the *Good Fortune*. Thinking he had been betrayed by Norton, Roberts grew furious. Actually, Norton had been arrested in New England. According to the plan, Norton arranged a secret meeting place to sell Roberts' stolen goods to the local merchants, but so many came that the authorities became suspicious and impounded the ship.

Roberts and Anstis returned to the Leeward Islands and on April 9, 1721 they took the *Jeremiah and Ann*, then saw a French man o' war of 32 guns approaching on the horizon. Roberts must have thought that the large ship would make an excellent pyrate ship, so he sailed toward it. The French ship didn't have their watch set properly and Roberts and Anstis were able to approach the ship with no warning given to the crew. When the French ship realized they were about to be attacked, they surrendered without resistance. That was Roberts' lucky day. One of the passengers on the ship was the French governor of Martinique, the man who Roberts had vowed to kill. True to his word, he hung the governor from the yardarm. Roberts kept the 32-gun ship and renamed it the *Sea King*.

Roberts and his pyrates continued to have the same problem. Their vessels were loaded with plunder, but they had nowhere to trade their goods or spend their money. Roberts' fierce rampage throughout the Caribbean and along the North American coast had caused every port to be on the lookout. Many ports even built fortifications specially designed to protect themselves just against Roberts. Governor Spotswood of Virginia constructed 54 gun batteries in the Virginia ports alone. Merchant shipping throughout the Caribbean and along the North American coast almost ceased for fear of Roberts. The entire economy of the American colonies was in peril. Roberts was enemy number one throughout the French, Dutch, and British empires and every warship in the Atlantic was looking for him. He was now being called "The Great Pyrate Roberts." He was so feared that Captain Witney of the *Rose* refused to go after Roberts alone. Nevertheless, Roberts knew it was only a matter time before he would be caught if he stayed in the Caribbean. Additionally, there was no place left for his crew to enjoy their riches. It was the end of April 1721 and the pyrates decided to return to Africa where pyrate friendly ports still existed.

As they departed for Africa, Thomas Anstis and some of the original House of Lords finally had enough and gave Roberts a "soft farewell" and sailed away on the *Good Fortune* during the night. Anstis remained a small time pyrate sailing the Caribbean over the next two years until April 1723 when his crew mutinied and killed him. While sailing across the Atlantic, Roberts and his two vessels, the 44-gun brigantine *Royal Fortune* and the 32-gun ship *Sea King*, took a Dutch merchantman, two snows, and a galley. Reaching the Cape Verde Islands in May 1721, Roberts abandoned the leaking 44-gun *Royal Fortune* and took command of the *Sea King*. He increased the number of guns to 40 and renamed it the *Royal Fortune*. That was the fourth time his used that name for his prime vessel and he was once again back to only one vessel.

Chapter 61
The Last Great Pyrate

JUNE 1721

Roberts takes prizes off Africa.

Roberts sailed east from Cape Verde and reached the Senegal coast in June 1721 where he allowed two French vessels to pursue him. They were the 10-gun *St. Anges* and the 16-gun *Comte de Toulouse*. Those vessels had been assigned to guard the coast against illegal traders and they mistook Roberts for an unauthorized Dutch merchant vessel. Roberts allowed them to catch him, and then raised his black flag and turned toward the French vessels. Both captains immediately surrendered. Roberts kept both renaming them the *Ranger* and *Little Ranger*. On June 12, 1721 Roberts and his three vessels sailed to Sierra Leone and entered the Sierra Leone River and Tagrin Bay to attack the Royal African Company's fort on Bence Island, just as Howell Davis had done two years earlier. The members of Roberts' crew who had served with Davis remembered the attack well. Before taking the fort, his vessels were badly in need of careening and refitting, so Roberts took a merchant ship while entering the bay, then careened and rebuilt his vessels in one of the many hidden bays along the mouth of the river. When Roberts' three vessels were ready for action, he approached the Bence Island Fort just as Howell Davis did.

Roberts sent a message to Governor Plunkett and demanded gold dust, powder, and shot, but Pluckett gave Roberts the same reply that he had given Davis, saying that he wouldn't give him any gold, but he had plenty of shot if Roberts would come for it. Roberts attacked with his three vessels and after four hours of gunfire, the fort ran out of ammunition. Roberts took the fort and had Governor Plunkett brought before him. Just as Plunkett had done before when he was captured by Davis and Cocklyn, he let loose with such a hail of highly imaginative and unending insults that the crew broke out in laughter. Eventually, even the serious and stoic Roberts began to laugh. Roberts let him go after cleaning out the store houses.

Throughout the rest of June and July 1721 Roberts' crew partied ashore in local native villages and at taverns and brothels that belonged to more than 30 pyrate-friendly traders who lived along the entrance of the Sierra Leone River. The most famous of these traders was John Leadstone, nicknamed Old Crackers. He was an ex-pyrate who operated a pyrate trading post and brothel which had a reputation of always having the best women that could be found. He signaled pyrate vessels with a salute from a brass cannon as they anchored at his dock. Another of these trading posts was at the Rio Pungo and was operated by a hermit named Benjamin Gunn. This name was used by Robert Louis Stevenson in his classic novel "Treasure Island." While relaxing in port, Roberts was told of two Royal Navy 3rd raters operating in the area. They were the 50-gun HMS *Swallow*, commanded by Captain Chaloner Ogle and the 50-gun HMS *Weymouth*, commanded by Captain Mungo Herdman. Both ships had been searching specifically for Roberts and had visited Sierra Leone just two months before Roberts arrived. Roberts knew he needed to be careful.

Sailing south along the coast of West Africa, on August 8, 1721 the pyrate fleet took the slave frigate *Onslow* near Point Sestos, Liberia, with cargo worth over £9,000. While the looting was going on, Elizabeth Trengrove, a woman who was traveling to meet her husband, was raped three times by quartermaster Simpson. This was a serious breach of the Ship's Articles, yet nothing was done. Roberts had lost control of his crew and could only remain their captain as long as he acted as psychotic as they did. They kept the *Onslow* as Robert's fifth and final *Royal Fortune*, mounting 40 guns. The old *Royal Fortune* was given to the prize crew. Continuing east across the Gulf of Guinea, Roberts reached the Calabar River in modern Nigeria on October 1, 1721. Roberts intended to careen his vessels there because the Calabar River has a very wide entrance with hundreds of secluded estuaries that seemed to offer a perfect location to avoid the Royal Navy. Additionally, the slave trading port of Old Calabar, which was about 30 miles up the river, offered the potential for more prizes. Upon entering the river, he found two slave galleys at anchor and took them both, forcing the musicians to remain with him. Roberts found dispatches on one of the vessels telling him HMS *Swallow* and HMS *Weymouth* were at Principe, a little over 300 miles to the south. After looting the two galleys,

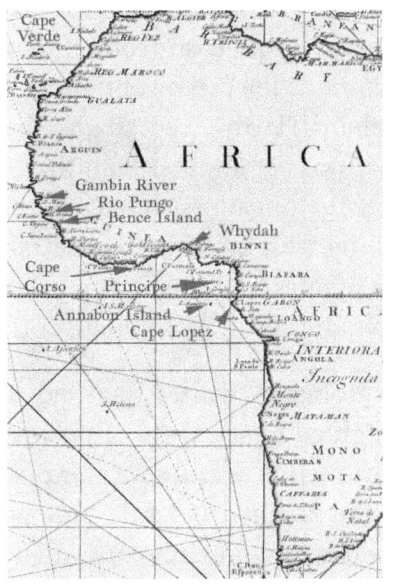

Figure 31: *West African Trading Posts*

Roberts pushed up the river and out of sight of the Royal Navy, but constant attacks from the local natives made that spot impossible, so Roberts decided to careen elsewhere.

Roberts sailed his three vessels 400 miles south to careen at Cape Lopez in modern-day Gabon, even though his course took him dangerously close to the Island of Principe where the royal navy ships were anchored. Arriving undetected, Roberts sent parties ashore to look for a good spot to careen, but one of his pyrates deserted. His name was John Jessup and he had been a shipmate of Roberts on the *Princess of London* before they became pyrates. But over the years, Jessup had become a severe alcoholic, remaining drunk throughout the entire day. His fellow pyrates had lost confidence in him and he worried they would eventually maroon him. After this desertion, Roberts feared others would also desert, so he decided to careen on a secluded island that guaranteed no escape. Roberts sailed to the southwest and reached Annabon Island, a tiny and isolated island a little over 200 miles off shore. Jessup was subsequently captured by a Dutch merchant ship and was taken to the *Swallow* at Principe. Captain Ogle realized the value in having one of Roberts' crewmembers as a prisoner as Jessup could provide invaluable information about Roberts. He was put in chains and after minimal questioning, Jessup told Captain Ogle exactly where Roberts was. On October 20, 1721 the *Swallow* left Principe under full sail.

Back in action, Roberts had three vessels, the 40-gun ship, *Royal Fortune*, the *Ranger*, and the *Little Ranger*. Roberts took the Dutch galley *Greyhound* on December 14, 1721 near Cape Lopez then sailed west back across the Gulf of Guinea to the French Ivory Coast. On January 2, 1722, the three pyrate vessels took the *Elizabeth* off the port of Jacquesville, modern Cote d'Ivoire. While looting the *Elizabeth*, they spotted another prize, the *Hannibal*, and easily took it. Finding almost nothing of value onboard the *Hannibal*, the crew went into a fit of rage and totally trashed the ship. Lord Richard Hardy even struck the captain with his sword and killed him. That was yet another sign that Roberts' crew was out of control. Captives were no longer respected, and brutality was now their standard treatment. Sailing west again along the modern coast of Ghana, on January 4, 1722 the pyrates took two more prizes. Then, on January 6, 1722 they took the slave ship *King Solomon* just off the ancient port town of Beyin.

As Roberts' pyrates boarded, they were greeted by one man who was delighted to see them. That was Peter de Vine, one of the *King Solomon*'s crew members and a former pyrate who had once sailed with Stede Bonnet on the *Revenge*. Peter de Vine willingly joined Roberts' crew. The next day, Roberts and his fleet continued west and anchored off Cape Corso Castle, modern Cape Coast, Ghana. That port was the principal British center of administration for all of West Africa.

Just one day behind, HMS *Swallow* arrived at Beyin only to find the *King Solomon* plundered and Roberts gone. The *Swallow* was scheduled to rendezvous with the *King Solomon* to take on fresh supplies. When Captain Ogle found out that he had just missed Roberts, he knew he was very close, and guessed that Roberts would next head for the port of Whydah, which was the richest port in West Africa. He was correct. On January 11, 1722 Roberts sailed into the port of Whydah with black flag flying and musicians playing. The twelve slave ships anchored in the harbor immediately struck colors. Roberts demanded eight pounds of gold dust be paid by each in exchange for allowing the ships to go free. Eleven of the captains agreed and paid the ransom. Roberts actually gave each of them a receipt. That was also the document that Roberts signed his name as Batt. Roberts:

Whydah is the English spelling for the port city of Ouidah, located in modern Benin at the north end of the Gulf of Guinea.

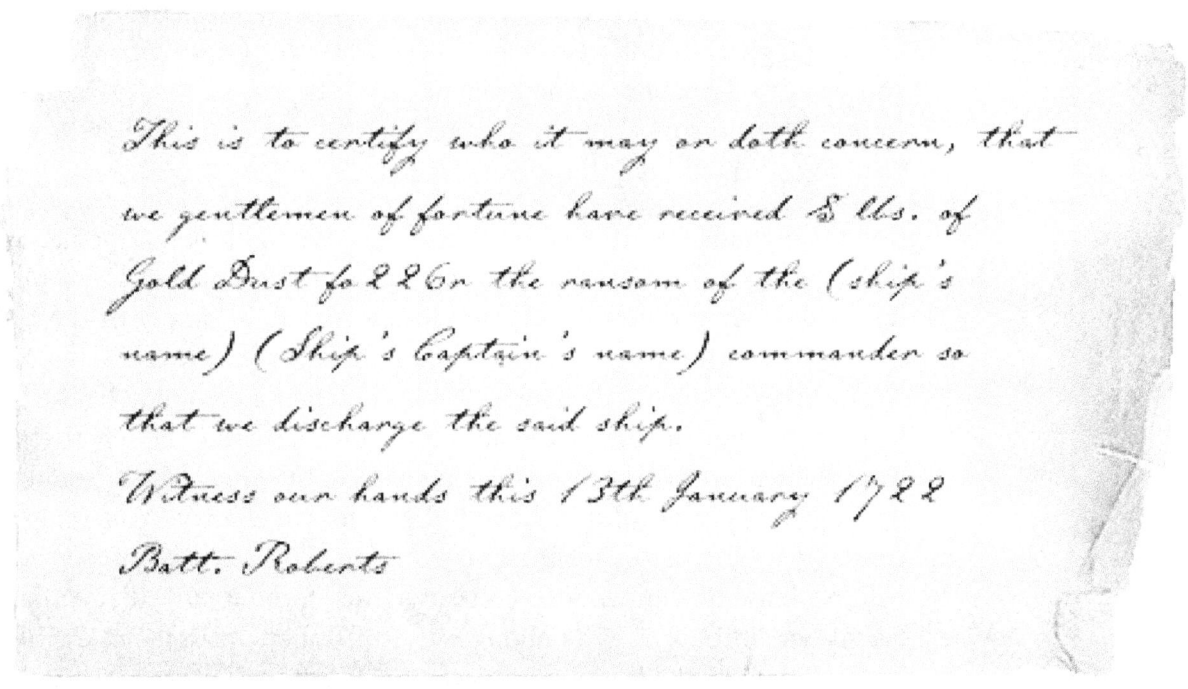

However, the captain of the *Porcupine* refused, and Roberts ordered the slaves freed and the ship burned, but his crew decided it was easier just to burn the ship without taking the trouble to unshackle the slaves. Horrified, Roberts watched the slave ship burn with the screaming slaves still onboard. Then, some of Roberts' crew decided to keep one of the ships that had paid the ransom, the French slaver, *Comte de Thoulouze*. That shouldn't be confused with the other vessel by the same name that Roberts took earlier at Senegal and kept as the *Ranger*. Continuing his vessel naming theme, the *Comte de Thoulouze* was renamed the *Great Ranger* and the old *Ranger* was abandoned. On board, Roberts found documents that informed him that the *Swallow* was nearby, so on January 13, 1722 Roberts decided to leave the port rather than risk being caught. Additionally, he needed to careen and refit the new *Great Ranger* as a pyrate vessel. Roberts gave command of the *Great Ranger* to James Skyrme and the three pyrate vessels sailed out of the port, two days ahead of the *Swallow's* arrival.

As Roberts sailed out of the port of Whydah, he encountered the sloop *Wida* which was entering the port. He couldn't resist such an easy prize and quickly took the sloop. Roberts kept all the crewmembers as prisoners, fearing they would tell the captain of the *Swallow* which direction the pyrate fleet sailed. After a quick looting, the sloop was burned and sunk. On January 15, 1722 the *Swallow* arrived at the port of Whydah and Captain Ogle was immediately told of Roberts' latest outrages. He knew that Roberts' vessels were loaded down with plunder, making them heavy and unlikely to out-sail his warship. He also knew that Roberts would have to refit and rebuild his latest capture into a pyrate vessel. Jessup told Captain Ogle that Roberts preferred the waters of Cape Lopez to careen and went to Annabon Island after he had escaped, so that's where Ogle went next. And sure enough, Annabon Island was exactly where Roberts went to careen and refit the *Great Ranger*.

Roberts' pyrates weren't the brave and effective fighters that he had several years ago. The majority of his crewmen had been forced into piracy unwillingly and couldn't really be trusted in a fight. Many of the other willing pyrates were fairly new and had little or no battle experience. Most of the old pyrates from the Howell Davis days had died or had left Roberts a long time ago. The others remaining with Roberts were now perpetually drunk. There was constant quarreling among the crew which resulted in dueling and fighting while ashore. Roberts' loss of effective leadership and control over his men had finally resulted in a pyrate crew of psychotics with no sense of teamwork or cohesion. The *Swallow* arrived at Annabon Island on February 5, 1722 and saw two of Roberts' vessels on the beach lying on their sides. The smaller *Little Ranger* was still at sea on guard, but only had ten guns and would offer little protection for the pyrates against the *Swallow*.

Captain Ogle observed Roberts' vessels on the beach and knew he had them. But as he tacked in to avoid the shallows, the wind suddenly changed and forced the *Swallow* back out to sea. Roberts was watching the ship's approach from a cliff and mistook the *Swallow* for a merchant ship that spotted the pyrates and decided to flee. The *Royal Fortune* was being worked on and would need more time to become operational, but the *Great Ranger* had just been pulled up on shore and could be put back into the water quickly, so Roberts ordered James Skyrme to have the vessel hauled back into the sea to pursue the prize. In no time, the *Great Ranger* was ready for action and sailed off with 73 pyrates aboard as well as 23 slaves and 16 French prisoners. Perhaps Roberts didn't want the slaves and prisoners in the way as he made the *Royal Fortune* ready for action.

Captain Ogle couldn't believe his luck as he saw the *Great Ranger* approaching alone. He had the opportunity to pick them off one at a time. Ogle pretended to be sailing as fast as possible but was actually holding back, allowing the *Great Ranger* to catch up. Captain Ogle's timing was perfect. The *Great Ranger* came along side of the *Swallow* just as the two vessels were both out of sight from Roberts on the island, a distance of about three miles at sea. As the *Great Ranger* prepared to fire, the gun ports of the *Swallow* flew open and blasted the pyrate vessel with devastating firepower. The *Great Ranger* returned fire but did little damage to the *Swallow*. After several broadsides, the men of the *Swallow* prepared to board. A long time before, Roberts' crew had vowed not to be taken alive and one of the pyrates went below to blow up the ship. Below deck, the gunpowder was lit and the huge explosion consumed the vessel. But as the smoke cleared, the ship still remained afloat. Within minutes, the *Great Ranger* was securely in British hands, ten pyrates had been killed and many others had been wounded. There were 102 men captured alive, including the slaves and French prisoners who were held onboard. The British suffered no casualties. Captain Ogle managed to quickly repair the *Great Ranger* and placed the surviving pyrates on board in chains. Captain Ogle didn't want pyrate prisoners onboard the *Swallow* when he went after the great pyrate Roberts. Ogle sent the *Great Ranger* back to Principe with a small British crew, the pyrate captives, the slaves, and the French Prisoners.

Pink—A three masted vessel with a narrow overhanging stern

Meanwhile, Roberts had managed to get the *Royal Fortune* back in action, but there was no sign of the *Great Ranger*. Roberts assumed that James Skyrme had taken the ship they had pursued and were plundering his prize at sea. On February 9, 1722 the pink *Neptune* just happened to sail past Roberts and attract his attention. That would be an easy prize to take while they waited for Skyrme to return. After taking the *Neptune* Roberts placed all the rest of his prisoners from the *Wida* onboard and told them he would allow them to sail free once he was finished looting the small vessel.

FEBRUARY 1722

Roberts is killed off the coast of Africa.

The next morning as Captain Ogle approached again, he couldn't believe his good luck. He saw the *Royal Fortune* at anchor with the pink *Neptune* anchored beside. He realized that the pyrates had taken another prize and that they would all be either occupied with looting or drunk after an evening of celebrating. In that particular case, it was the latter. Every one of Roberts' crewmen were just about passed out except the always sober Captain Roberts.

It was the morning of February 10, 1722 and Roberts curiously spotted the ship in the distance. As Roberts watched, one of his pyrates who had previously been a sailor on the *Swallow* and recognized the ship told Roberts exactly what ship was rapidly sailing directly toward him. Roberts realized that this was the ship that the *Great Ranger* sailed after and that his friends were either dead or captured. Roberts immediately prepared to get under way. He ordered all pyrates aboard the *Royal Fortune* and abandoned the *Little Ranger* which supposedly had the bulk of his treasure. But the only way out into the open ocean was right past the *Swallow*. It was 11 o'clock in the morning when the two ships passed each other at a distance of just 20 yards. The *Swallow* opened up with a broadside. The 32 pounders of the *Swallow* ripped into the hull of the *Royal Fortune* and into the rigging. The *Royal Fortune's* mizzen top fell, slowing the ship. Then, the inexperienced helmsman of the *Royal Fortune* panicked and turned directly into the wind which stopped the *Royal Fortune* dead in the water. That gave the *Swallow* time to circle about and get directly behind the *Royal Fortune's* stern. Meanwhile, Roberts managed to get his vessel back into the wind, but still couldn't move because the *Swallow* had cut off the wind source. Captain Roberts stood defiantly on the quarterdeck wearing his customary red outfit with diamond studded cross as the *Swallow* rapidly approached and the *Royal Fortune* had no wind to maneuver.

Just as the *Swallow* reached the stern of the pyrate vessel, it veered off slightly and came along side again and fired another broadside. More shot ripped into the *Royal Fortune* and grapeshot tore through Roberts' throat. The great pyrate Roberts fell dead across one of the deck guns. In accordance with his previous instructions, his crew threw his body overboard. Constant fire from the *Swallow's* swivel guns and small arms fire kept the pyrates pinned down. Only a very few pyrates fired back, most of them just laid on deck getting drunk while the *Swallow* raked the deck. After two hours of continuous fire from *Swallow* with no return fire from the *Royal Fortune*, Lord Magness requested quarter. Amazingly in all that fire, only three pyrates were killed, including Roberts. The British again suffered no casualties. Of the 152 pyrates captured on the *Royal Fortune*, 52 were black Africans, perhaps from the Kru tribe, which were from Sierra Leone and renowned as excellent sailors.

On February 12, 1722 Captain Ogle sailed back to Annabon Island where the *Little Ranger* was anchored, but to everyone's surprise, the vessel was empty. All the chests had been broken open. Not a single gold coin was to be found anywhere. That gave rise to the many stories that Roberts had buried his treasure sometime before. Also, the 300 pounds of gold dust worth about £14,000 that was still onboard the *Royal Fortune* when it was captured seemed to have mysteriously disappeared. Many accused Captain Ogle of taking it, but there was no proof.

HMS *Swallow* returned to the British administrative authorities at Cape Corso Castle with all the prisoners. Of the 254 men who were captured, 19 died before trial and the 70 black pirates were all sold as slaves. Of those who were tried, one was pardoned and 20 testified against Roberts and received lighter sentences of seven years Indentured Servitude. However, 74 were acquitted, including 16 French prisoners who were being held on Roberts' vessel, the *Great Rover*. The rest consisted of all the musicians and the recent additions to the crew who convinced the court that they were forced to join. One of the pyrates who was found guilty died in prison before his execution and 52 others were executed in April 1722 at Cape Corso Castle. The remaining 17 pyrates were sent back to Marshalsea prison in England.

Roberts' three vessels, the *Royal Fortune*, the *Great Ranger*, and the *Little Ranger* were kept as British prizes and Captain Ogle sailed them to Port Royal, Jamaica, arriving on August 14, 1722. Just two weeks after reaching port, a hurricane struck and the *Royal Fortune* and the *Little Ranger* were blown across the harbor and lost on the rocks. The *Great Ranger* survived but was heavily damaged. After repairs, Ogle sold the vessel but it apparently sank shortly afterwards, as it appears on a 1724 Royal Navy chart as a sunken navigational hazard. In recent years, archaeologists have recovered many artifacts from the wreck.

Captain Chaloner Ogle left Jamaica for London on January 1, 1723. With the highly publicized capture and trial of Roberts' crew and the sensationalized death of Roberts himself, Ogle became a national hero. He was given £ 3,144 as his share of the prize money and was knighted for his actions in April of 1723. To this day, he remains the only Naval Officer who was knighted for a single deed. As for Captain Roberts, during his 2½-year career as a pyrate captain, the great pyrate Roberts had taken over 500 prizes and booty worth well over one hundred million pounds sterling. Roberts was the last of the great pyrates of the golden age of piracy. With his death, the "Golden Age of Piracy" came to a close.

Chapter 62
Summing Up the Pyrates 1714–1722

The last era of the golden age of piracy began with the close of the War for the Spanish Succession, which devastated the economy of most European nations. It also left hundreds of privateers out of work on both sides. Many of those privateers turned to piracy, some only taking prizes that belonged to their former enemies, others taking prizes from all nations.

Two major events occurred that set the stage for the Era of the Pyrates. The first was the 1715 civil war in Great Britain over the rightful king, George of Hanover or James Edward Stuart. After Queen Anne died, the last of the Stuart rulers in England, George I became king and a civil war erupted. Many thought the rightful king was James Edward Stuart, the son of the deposed King James II. He was living in exile in France and was often called the "The Pretender," the "Old Pretender," and "The Pretender Across the Sea." Supporters of James were called Jacobites. The Jacobite revolution divided the English nobility as well as the commoners. There is no way of telling exactly how much impact this event had on the English pyrates of the time. For some individuals, it had an enormous impact, giving them a political purpose and justifying their actions.

Most historians and people in general think of all pyrates in simple terms as people who simply wanted to rob others at sea for profit. But for many of the pyrates shortly after 1715, there was a clear political motivation for piracy. Were many pyrates actually Jacobite supporters? I think the answer is yes. It began with Governor Hamilton of Jamaica building Nassau as a pyrate base to help fund the Jacobite revolt. While in prison in Charles Town, one of Bonnet's fellow prisoners recalled hearing Bonnet's men drinking to the health of the "Old Pretender" and wishing to see him King of Great Britain someday. Additionally, Bonnet and his partner Blackbeard named two of their vessels after Stuarts. The *Queen Anne's Revenge* in reference to Queen Anne, was the last of the Stuart monarchs in England and the half-sister to James Edward Stuart. Naming his ship as he did could only mean that he intended to have revenge for her against King George I. Later, their sloop was renamed the *Royal James* in direct reference to James Edward Stuart, the actual reason for the Jacobite revolution in the first place

Charles Vane was a Jacobite too. He refused the King's Pardon and shot his way out of Nassau when it would have been far easier for him to take the pardon and simply continue pirating. Vane also wrote a letter to Admiral George Cammock, a strong Jacobite who left the royal navy when George I was crowned. In that letter Vane stated that that if France pledges allegiance to James, then Cammock should come to Nassau to lead a fleet of pyrate ships against the forces of King George I.

Howell Davis and his partners Olivier Le Vasseur (La Buse) and Thomas Cocklyn were also Jacobites. Davis also named his vessel the *Royal James* and his partner, La Buse, named one of his vessels the *Duke of Ormond* in honor of another English military leader and Jacobite who fled England after George I was crowned. However, the most convincing evidence comes from the firsthand account of Captain Snelgrave who was a captive of the pyrates and wrote:

> "Captain Cocklyn drank my health . . . Then, he drank several other Healths, amongst which was that of the Pretender, by the name of King James the Third, and thereby I found that they were doubly on the side of the Gallows, both as Traitors and Pirates. However, if any of those pyrates were true Jacobites, none of their loot ever found its way to the revolution. They kept it all for themselves."

Perhaps they intended to contribute to the cause later or perhaps it was simply a matter of justifying their actions against English ships. We shall never know the truth, but the evidence is exceptionally intriguing.

The other event was the sinking of the Spanish treasure fleet that provided the financial basis for the establishment Nassau, a pyrate base of operations located in the heart of the Caribbean trade routes. Nassau was virtually the nesting center where many English pyrates got their start. The sinking of the Spanish treasure fleet also caused hundreds of fortune hunters to flock to the Caribbean, only to find nothing. The combination of those two events, the civil war in Britain and the large number of British colonists swarming to the wreck of the Spanish treasure fleet, gave rise to

British domination of pyrates during that period. Many English, Irish, and Scottish citizens turned to piracy as a means to fund the revolution or at least to strike back at the English government that had put George on the throne. And many more English colonists, who found nothing when they arrived at the treasure fleet wreck site chose piracy as their only recourse.

Nassau started off as a modest privateer port but rapidly grew into the largest pyrate port since Tortuga, only to be converted into the royal seat of the English government virtually overnight. And in the Caribbean, the ex-buccaneer port of Port Royal became a place where pyrates were tried and executed. Charles Vane and Calico Jack Rackham were executed there in 1720. In 1722 Gallows Point welcomed forty-one pyrates to their death in only one month. By 1720 all the pyrate-friendly ports along the east coast of North America literally slammed their doors on pyrates.

Privateering was all but gone in the second decade of the 18th century. The major European governments realized that it was necessary to maintain large standing navies as a vital means to protect their trade and colonies—not to mention their home ports. Privateers were unreliable and hard to control. They just weren't getting the same quality of privateers as in Henry Morgan's day. The only war was the one between Great Britain and Spain that was declared in December 1718. Unlike the wars of the past, privateering in this war was very limited. There was only a handful of actual privateer operations.

Only one expedition to the Pacific was financed during the war. This was arranged by a group of merchants from Great Britain. That expedition had two ships, the *Success* with 32 guns under the command of John Clipperton and the *Speedwell* with 24 guns under the command of George Shelvocke. Captain John Clipperton had served in the Royal Navy and along with part of his crew, had accompanied William Dampier on his 1704 expedition. George Shelvocke had also been a Lieutenant in the Royal Navy and served under Admiral Benbow in the last war. However, when that war ended in 1713, he was released from duty with no pension.

By 1719 both captains were in great need of funds and employment. The captains received their letters of marque and sailed from London in February 1719. Soon after reaching the Pacific, they began taking many Spanish prizes. However, everything was not well with the crew. The two captains continually quarreled and eventually the two ships split up. Clipperton's crew began to die from scurvy and eventually wound up in China where his crew deserted. He managed to barter passage back to England on a Dutch ship, but died the day after his return.

The *Speedwell* sailed on until May 25, 1720, when it wrecked on Juan Fernandez Island, the same island that Alexander Selkirk was stranded on 14 years earlier which inspired the novel Robinson Crusoe. After being marooned for 5 months, the crew managed to rebuild a small pinnace and soon afterwards, managed to capture a Spanish ship which was renamed the *Happy Return*. They continued taking Spanish prizes along the South American coast and then sailed to Macao. Upon his return to England, Shelvocke was arrested for piracy. His backers suspected that he had kept a large portion of their share for himself and his crew. If he had, there was insufficient evidence and he was acquitted. Following the success of William Dampier and many others, he decided to write a bestselling book too, *A Voyage Round the World By Way of The Great South Sea* published in 1723. He died at age 67 a fairly wealthy man. One of the events in this book tells of his second mate shooting a black albatross. This inspired the Samuel Taylor Coleridge's poem, "The Rhyme of the Ancient Mariner".

Spanish privateers were also active in the war, but their operations were also limited. The English colonies on the Atlantic coast were always worried about Spanish attacks, but the citizens of Virginia became less worried as the years passed without an incident. That is, until 1718. The closest Spanish city to Virginia was St. Augustine, Florida and Spanish privateers began launching privateer operations from St. Augustine shortly after the war began. Two Spanish captains, Don Benitos and Don Pedros, raided the waters near the two capes of the Chesapeake Bay countless times in the first year of the war, but in April 1720, one Spanish sloop pursued a fleeing vessel right into Hampton Roads. Other vessels sailed up the Chesapeake Bay to the waters near Yorktown, Virginia. A report made in July 1720 described 70 captured English sailors who were put ashore on the York River. Later, the bodies of 18 sailors washed up along the Eastern Shore with some of them tied together back to back. One sailor was even found with his hands tied behind his back and his big toes tied together. This latest attack was most shocking because it occurred in April 1720 after the end of the war on February 17, 1720. Governor Spotswood of Virginia protested in writing and sent his protest aboard a Royal Navy sloop to the Spanish governor at St. Augustine to deliver it. There was no response. Apparently, the Spanish also had difficulty in controlling their privateers.

One point of interest that seems to be unique to this time period is the demographics of pyrates. Historian David Cordingly did a study of known pyrates in the Caribbean between 1715 and 1724 and discovered that 35% were English, 25% were from English America, 20% were from the West Indies (mostly the British colonies of Jamaica and Barbados), 10% were Scottish, 8% were Welch, and the remaining 2% of the population of pyrates were from all the other countries combined. However, that did not take into account the large number of pyrates who were former black slaves from Africa. Slave ships were prime targets for pyrates because they made such good pyrate ships. They were fast, big, and came equipped with lots of sleeping space, necessary for large pyrate crews. Once a slaver was taken, something had to be done with all the slaves who were chained below decks. Sometimes the pyrates sold them as slaves ashore, but it was not uncommon for pyrate crews to offer employment to the slaves as pyrates. Considering the alternative, many of the slaves accepted the offer. It was infinitely better than a life of slavery.

Sam Bellamy, Blackbeard, and Batt Roberts all took slave ships and converted them into pyrate ships, retaining large numbers of African slaves as crewmembers. But slaves could also join pyrate crews from other types of captured prize vessels. Slaves often traveled with their owners and sometimes pyrates would offer slaves the same chance to join their crew as the crewmen of a captured vessel. And pyrates were generally equal opportunity employers, giving their black crewmembers equal shares and offering them the same leadership opportunities as any other crewmember. Sam Bellamy's quartermaster was African American. As you may recall, of the 19 pyrates that fought with Blackbeard at his final battle at Ocracoke, five were African American. These pyrates had been Blackbeard's most trusted friends and were with him to the end. It is estimated that between 20% and 40% of all "British" pyrate crews at the end of the "Golden Age of Piracy" could have actually been former black slaves from Africa.

English pyrates dominated this era far more than in the past and patriotism seemed dead among most of them. English merchant vessels were being attacked at much higher rates throughout the Caribbean and along the coasts of North America and West Africa by pyrates who were predominately English. Even major English sea ports were being attacked and blockaded by these English pyrates. Certainly, English ports and shipping had been attacked many times in the past by the Spanish, the French, and the Dutch, but they had never before been attacked by English pyrates, at least not to that extent. Blackbeard attacked and blockaded ships outside the port of Philadelphia and Charles Town and Charles Vane attacked and blockaded shipping out of Charles Town too. Later, the Great Pyrate Roberts destroyed English ports in Newfoundland and West Africa. Perhaps the struggle over the rightful King of Great Britain played a significant role. I think that it did. At the very least it may have caused some pyrates to feel betrayed by their government and therefore no longer obligated to remain loyal.

Dynamic personalities among pyrates also marked this era. Between 1717 and 1722 pyrates seemed to be far more flamboyant and exaggerated than at any other time. Pyrates used their reputation to help intimidate their prey. Each pyrate captain had his own personalized black pirate flag so that prize ships could identify them. The pirates also dressed to impress and to help intimidate the prize crews. That gave them a psychological advantage over their captives during the looting which encouraged their cooperation. The terrifying image of Blackbeard with burning matches in his thick and tangled beard is a perfect example and the Great Pyrate Roberts, who dressed in the most extravagant clothing with gold chains about his neck, is another. The shocking news of female pyrates Anne Bonny and Mary Read also defined this era as unique to the others. There certainly had been female pyrates before and after, but these two were the first to be sensationalized in news stories and books. They captured the imagination of millions of readers throughout all the nations of Western Europe and their American colonies.

The media frenzy over pyrates also played a gigantic role in the shaping of the "Era of the Pyrates." There had been books about pyrates before, but now everyone was reading them, and more were being written every year. Newspapers were covering stories of pyrate attacks for the first time ever, primarily because there were very few newspapers before the early 18th century. Songs about pyrates dominated the taverns and ballrooms and the theater erupted with plays and productions based on pyrate themes. It was like the gangster craze in the 1930s where gangster themed stories dominated the media in movies, radio shows, novels, and comic books, and newspapers. This media frenzy helped stylize those pyrates into the characters we think of today. In many cases, the media wasn't too far off the mark. Among those publications was a book that has dominated pyrate historian's beliefs for almost 300 years, Captain Charles Johnson's *General History of Pyrates*. But as we have seen, that work was more fiction than fact, and severely affected the accuracy of many supposedly historical works to this very day.

The attention the media gave to pyrates in the early 18th century also had a significant impact on public opinion. In past years, many colonists viewed pyrates as bringers of exotic goods and lavish spenders of money. Pyrates were good for local economies. The fact that they took these goods through piracy didn't seem to matter. They were thought of almost like we think of Robin Hood. But the stories that were written during this era turned public opinion against the pyrates. Now they were then looked upon as evil and cruel criminals. That made it easier for officials to pass and enforce anti-piracy laws which kept local merchants from doing business with pyrates. However, it was the deeds of the most successful pyrate captain of the era that really put an end to piracy. The great pyrate Roberts raised the stakes.

Before Roberts, pyrates were merely a nuisance. They disrupted merchant shipping, but the stolen goods eventually wound up in the hands of colonial merchants. To many colonists, pyrates were even good for business. Also, the pyrates seldom actually killed anyone. The authorities were certainly out to stop them, but on a relatively small scale. The great powers of Europe had more important things to focus on. Roberts changed this. After 1720 his crew lost touch with reality. They tortured and killed their captives and totally destroyed many prize vessels. Roberts and his men also destroyed entire ports, one after another. This threw the entire shipping industry into a panic. Roberts moved piracy from a local problem to an international one. As a result of Roberts' attacks, almost all ports throughout the world rejected pyrate trade.

With the highly publicized capture of the great pyrate Roberts' crew and the sensationalized death of Roberts himself, the "Golden Age of Piracy" came to a close. There were still plenty of pyrates sailing the waters of the world, but on a smaller scale and certainly none who would have such an impact as Roberts did on culture, politics, and world events. Over the next several years, pyrates downsized tremendously. They had to in order to maintain a low profile and avoid the authorities. Nevertheless, the real pyrates of the golden age didn't die, at least not in legend. For millions of pyrate enthusiasts, children, book readers, and movie goers, the pyrates of the "Golden Age of Piracy" are just as alive as they ever were.

PART II:
A PIRATE'S LIFE

> The Pirate Captains having taken these Clothes without leave from the Quarter-master, it gave great Offence to all the Crew ... So, upon their return on board next Morning, the Coats were taken from them, and put into the common Chest, to be sold at the Mast.

Chapter 63
The Pirate's Code

This next portion of the book will deal more with how pirates lived and what they owned and used, rather than historical events. Of course, it will be necessary to reference historical events from time to time in order to explain or document a particular aspect of their lives. For me, this is the most important part of understanding the golden age of piracy. It delves deeper into the everyday lifestyles of those men and women. It adds detail and perspective to the historical events. And just like the real history compared to fictional history, much of what has been written and believed about the daily lives of pirates is incorrect.

One of the most romantic aspects about the Brethren of the Coast is their code—the pirate's code. In reality, the pirates of the golden age didn't really have one specific code that everyone lived by. That is one of those pirate myths from literature. However, pirates and privateers certainly did have rules; otherwise there would have been no discipline on board. The buccaneers of the 17th century sometimes called those rules "The Chasse-Partie" or "Charter Party," "The Custom of the Coast," or "The Jamaica Discipline." They were also known as "Ship's Articles" and generally included rules on personal conduct as well as payment amounts for the crew and officers. For rules of conduct, the consequences for breaking the rules were often included in the articles. For example, "If any Man shall offer to run away, or keep any Secret from the Company, he shall be marooned with one Bottle of Powder, one Bottle of Water, one small Arm, and Shot."

It is important to note that these articles varied greatly between crews depending upon the personalities of the individuals involved. Also, it is important to note that for privateers, the nature and scope of those articles could be quite different from pirates with regard to leadership. For reasons that we shall discuss later, privateer vessels, especially in the 17th century, operated closer to royal naval vessels, with their captains

In the 17th and early 18th centuries, mirrors had religious significance similar to holding a bible.

The Chasse Partie are thought to have been standard among many buccaneers in the 17th century.

in complete command, while pirate vessels generally tended to be a bit more democratic. But other than the leadership structure and rules of discipline, privateer and pirate crews operated under very similar articles and had very similar personal lifestyles onboard ship. Some individuals, like Benjamin Hornigold, even shifted back and forth between privateer and pirate depending upon the current state of war among the various European nations.

Actual Ship's Articles seldom survived because a pirate crew would destroy them just before their ship was captured. Ship's Articles made terrific evidence for the prosecution in a trial. From accounts of surviving pirates, the signing of ship's articles was normally a very solemn occasion and may have included a certain degree of ceremony. Some crews signed while holding a bible and others signed while looking into a mirror. One very interesting point about rules was that they generally told you what people were doing before the rules were written. Otherwise, why would they have written the rules? For example, it's pretty certain that pirates gambled onboard ship which led to trouble, hence the rule against gambling. Most modern documentation of these articles comes from "The General History of Pyrates" by Charles Johnson, who claimed to have firsthand knowledge of these articles by speaking with some of the captured crew of Captain Roberts. At any rate, their themes are common enough that the articles published in *The General History of Pyrates* are probably fairly close to the real thing. Alexander O. Exquemelin's 1678 book entitled *De Americaensche Zee-Roovers* (The American Sea Rovers) gives us an indication of the Ship's Articles which he calls the Chasse Partie (Charter Party) that the buccaneers on Tortuga may have used. He describes them in paragraph format, not as a list of articles, but for ease of reading, I have written them in a form similar to the articles described by Johnson.

Chasse Partie of Buccaneers

I.

Providing we capture a prize, for of all the amounts will be deducted from the whole capital as follows. The hunter's pay is 200 pieces of eight, the carpenter, for his work in repairing and fitting out the ship, will be paid 100 or 150 pieces of eight. The surgeon will receive 200 or 250 pieces of eight for his medical supplies, according to the size of the ship.

II.

For the loss of a right arm, 600 pieces of eight or six slaves; for a left arm, 500 pieces of eight or five slaves; a leg, 400 or four slaves; an eye, 100 or one slave, and the same award for the loss of a finger. If a man lost the use of an arm, he would get as much as if it had been cut off, and a severe internal injury which meant the victim had to have a pipe inserted in his body would earn 500 pieces of eight or five slaves in recompense.

III.

After these amounts have been paid, the rest of the prize will be divided into portions as men on the ship. The captain draws four or five men's portions for the use of his ship and two portions for himself. The rest of the men share uniformly and the boys get half a man's share.

IV.

When a ship has been captured, the men decide whether the captain should keep it or not: if the prize is better than our ship own vessel, we will take it and set fire to the other.

V.

When a ship is robbed, nobody must plunder and keep his loot to himself. Everything taken—money, jewels, precious stones and goods—must be shared among all, without any man enjoying a Penny more than his fair share.

VI.

To prevent deceit, before the booty is distributed, everyone will swear an oath on the Bible that he has not kept for himself so much as the value of a six Pence, whether in silk, linen, wool, gold, silver, jewels, clothes, or shot, from all the capture. And should any man be found to have made a false oath, he will be banished from the rovers and never more be allowed in our company.

VII.

If a man has nothing, we shall let him have what he needs on credit until such time as he can pay us back.

VIII.

If anyone has a quarrel and kills his opponent treacherously, he will be set against a tree and shot dead by the one whom he chooses. But if he has killed his opponent like an honourable man—that is, giving him time to load his musket, and not shooting him in the back, we shall let him go free.

IX.

When a ship is captured, we shall set the prisoners on shore as soon as possible, apart from two or three whom we shall keep to do the cooking and other work. These men shall be released after two years.

Below are the Ship's Articles for Samuel Bellamy, Bartholomew Roberts, John Philips, and George Lowther exactly as they appear in *The General History of Pyrates* without the additional commentary by the author, Charles Johnson.

Articles of Captain Samuel Bellamy

I.

Every Man Sworn by Book and Mirror to be true to these Articles and to his Ship Mates, is to have a Vote in Matters of Importance. He who is not Sworn shall not Vote.

Black Sam Bellamy began as a pirate in March 1716 and died when his ship, the Whydah, sank off Cape Codd in April 1717.

II

Every Man to have Equal Right to ye Provisions of Liquors at anytime and to use them at Pleasure unless Scarcity makes a Restriction necessary for ye Good of All.

III

Every Man to be called fairly a Board Prizes in turn by the List of ye Company. Every Boarder is to have a Suit of Clothes from ye Prize.

IV

The Captain and Officers are to be chosen on Commencement of a Voyage, and on any other Occasion as ye Company shall deem fit.

V

The Power of ye Captain is Supream in Chance of Battle. He may beat, cut, or shoot any who dares Deny his Command on such Occasions. In all other Matters whatsoever he is to be Governed by the Will of ye Company.

VI

Every Man shall obey Civil Command.

VII

He who first sees a Sail, shall have ye best Pistol, or Small Arm, from a Board her.

VIII

Ye Quarter-master shall be first a Board any Prize. He is to separate for ye Company's Use what he sees fit and shall have Trust of ye Common Stock and Treasury until it be Shared. He shall Keep a Book shewing each Man's Share, and each Man may draw from ye Common Stock and Treasury against his Share upon Request.

IX

Any Man who should Defraud ye Company, or another, to be Vallew of a Dollar, he shall suffer Punishment as ye Company deeme fit.

X

Each Man to keep his Musket, Pistol, and Cutlass cleane and fit for Service, upon Inspection by ye Quarter-master.

XI

No Prudent Woman, or Boy, is to be brought a Board. No Married Man is to be forced to serve our Company.

XII

Good Quarters to be Granted when Called for.

XIII

Any Man who Deserts ye Company, keeps any Secret, or Deserts his Station in Time of Battle, shall be punished by Death, Marooning, or Whipping, as ye Company shall deeme fit and Just.

XIIII

Not a Word shall be Written by any Man unless it be nailed Publickly to ye Mast.

Articles of Captain Bartholomew Roberts

I.

Every man has a vote in affairs of moment; has equal Title to the fresh Provisions, or strong Liquors, at any Time seized, and use them at pleasure, unless a scarcity (no uncommon Thing among them) makes it necessary, for the good of all, to vote a Retrenchment.

II.

Every man to be called fairly in turn, by List, on Board of Prizes, because, (over and above their proper Share) they were on these Occasions allowed a Shift of Clothes: But if they defrauded the Company to the Value of a Dollar in plate, jewels, or Money, Marooning was their Punishment. If the Robbery was only between one another, they contented themselves with slitting the Ears and Nose of him that was Guilty, and set him on

John Roberts, AKA Bartholomew Roberts, began as a pirate in June 1719 and was killed in April 1722 off the west coast of Africa.

Shore, not in an uninhabited Place, but somewhere, where he was sure to encounter Hardships.

III.

No Person to Game at Cards or Dice for Money.

IV.

The Lights and Candles to be put out at eight o' Clock at Night: if any of the Crew, after that Hour, still remained inclined for Drinking, they were to do it on the open Deck.

V.

To keep their Piece, Pistols, and Cutlass clean and fit for Service.

VI.

No Boy or Woman to be allowed amongst them. If any Man were to be found seducing any of the latter Sex, and carried her to Sea, disguised, he was to suffer Death.

VII.

To Desert the Ship or their Quarters in Battle, was punished with Death or Marooning.

VIII.

No striking one another on Board, but every Man's Quarrels to be ended on Shore, at Sword and Pistol.

IX.

No Man to talk of breaking up their Way of Living, till each had shared A 1000 L. If in order to this, any Man should lose a Limb, or become a Cripple in their Service, he was to have 800 Dollars, out of the public Stock, and for lesser Hurts, proportionately.

X.

The Captain and Quartermaster to receive two Shares of a Prize; the Master, Boatswain, and Gunner, one Share and a half, and other Officers, one and Quarter.

XI.

The Musicians to have Rest on the Sabbath Day, but the other six Days and Nights, none without special Favour.

Articles of Captain John Phillips

I.

Every Man Shall obey civil Command; the Captain shall have one full Share and a half of all Prizes; the Master, Carpenter, Boatswain, and Gunner shall have one Share and quarter.

II.

If any Man shall offer to run away, or keep any Secret from the Company, he shall be maroon'd, with one Bottle of Powder, one Bottle of Water, one small Arm, and Shot.

III.

If any Man shall steal any Thing in the Company, or game, to the Value of a Piece of Eight, he shall be maroon'd or shot.

IV.

If any time we shall meet another Marooner [that is, Pyrate] that Man that shall sign his Articles without the Consent of our Company, shall suffer such Punishment as the Captain and Company shall think fit.

V.

That Man that shall strike another whilst these Articles are in force, shall receive Moses' Law (that is, 40 Stripes lacking one) on the bare Back.

VI.

That Man that shall snap his Arms, or smoke Tobacco in the Hold, without a Cap to his Pipe, or carry a Candle lighted without a Lanthorn, shall suffer the same Punishment as in the former Article.

John Phillips began as a pirate as part or Thomas Anstis' crew in April 1721 and later became captain. He was killed when some of his prisoners joined with his crew and mutinied in June 1724 off Nova Scotia.

VII.

That Man that shall not keep his Arms clean, fit for an Engagement, or neglect his Business, shall be cut off from his Share, and suffer such other Punishment as the Captain and the Company shall think fit.

VIII.

If any Man shall lose a Joint in time of an Engagement, shall have 400 pieces of eight; if a Limb, 800.

IX.

If at any time you meet with a prudent Woman, that Man that offers to meddle with her, without her Consent, shall suffer present Death.

Articles of Captain George Lowther

I.

The Captain is to have two full Shares; the Master is to have one Share and one Half; The Doctor, Mate, Gunner, and Boatswain, one Share and one Quarter.

George Lowther began as a pirate in 1721 and committed suicide to avoid capture by the British authorities in 1722 on Blanquilla Island off Venezuela.

II.

He that shall be found Guilty of taking up any unlawful Weapon on Board the Privateer, or any Prize, by us taken, so as to strike or abuse one another, in any regard, shall suffer what Punishment the Captain and the Majority of the Company shall think fit.

III.

He that shall be found Guilty of Cowardice, in the Time of Engagements, shall suffer what Punishment the Captain and the Majority of the Company shall think fit.

IV.

If any Gold, Jewels, Silver, &c. be found on Board of any Prize or Prizes to the Value of a Piece of Eight, and the Finder do not deliver it to the Quarter-master, in the space of 24 Hours, shall suffer what Punishment the Captain and the Majority shall think fit.

V.

He that is found Guilty of Gaming, or Defrauding another to the Value of a Shilling, shall suffer what Punishment the Captain and the Majority of the Company shall think fit.

VI.

He that shall have the Misfortune to lose a Limb in Time of Engagement, shall have the Sum of one hundred and fifty Pounds Sterling, and remain aboard as long as he shall think fit.

VII.

Good Quarters to be given when call'd for.

VIII.

He that sees a Sail first, shall have the best Pistol, or Small-Arm, on Board her.

There is one documented case when the Ship's Articles actually survived the capture of the crew. Pirate Captain John Gow, a little-known pirate originally from the Orkney Islands on northern Scotland, was captured in 1729 off the coast of Scotland near Edinburgh. When he was taken, an original copy of his articles written in his own hand was recovered.

Articles of Captain John Gow

I.

John Gow began as a pirate in 1724 and operated in European waters.

He was captured by the British authorities in the Orkney Islands and executed in February 1725.

That every man shall obey his commander in all respects, as if the ship was his own, and as if he received monthly wages.

II.

That no man shall give, or dispose of, the ship's provisions; but every one shall have an equal share.

III.

That no man shall open, or declare to any person or persons, who they are, or what designs they are upon; and any persons so offending shall be punished with immediate death.

IV.

That no man shall go on shore till the ship is off the ground, and in readiness to put to sea.

V.

That every man shall keep his watch night and day; and at the hour of eight in the evening every one shall retire from gaming and drinking, in order to attend his respective station.

VI.

Every person who shall offend against any of these articles shall be punished with death, or in such other manner as the ship's company shall think proper.

> **"** No man will be a sailor who has contrivance enough to get himself into a jail. For being in a ship is being in jail with a chance of being drowned. A man in jail has more room, better food, and commonly better company. **"**
> —*Dr Johnson*

Chapter 64
The Captain's Authority

One always thinks of the authority of a ship's captain to be all powerful and unquestioned. Everything the captain says or wants is immediately carried out by the crew either out of loyalty or fear. But this is not always the case with pirates and privateers. In fact, the authority of the captain differed quite a bit between the two classifications and even from one vessel to another. These two classifications are privateers and pirates.

For privateers, privateer captains had letters of marque which gave them the authority to attack enemy shipping. Those letters of marque were normally issued to the individual, not the crew. Therefore, the crew could only sail under those letters as long as that individual remained the captain. There was no voting involved or even the possibility of replacing the captain by other means. The captain was the captain and that was that. This was especially true in the late 17th century with government appointed privateers like Christopher Myngs and Henry Morgan. If the captain was killed, the second in command may have been able to carry on under the letters of marque, but there would have been a thorough investigation upon return to the home port. If it was discovered that the captain was murdered by the crew, they would all have been arrested and tried for mutiny and piracy. Additionally, privateers often were financially backed by individual businessmen or a business company. The man they selected as captain was in complete command as the only authority. Woodes Rogers' funding for his 1707 expedition around the world was provided by Thomas Dover, president of the Bristol Company Voyage Council and, interestingly enough, happen to be Woodes Rogers' father-in-law.

For the privateer crews of these captains who were appointed by either government officials of financial backers, the rules of conduct weren't much different from those of the Royal Navy. Due to the volunteer nature

Privateers operate legally and were generally supported by the laws of the government that issued the letters of marque.

of the crew, however, punishment for an offense may not have been as strict or harsh as in the Royal Navy, but the captain's authority was unquestioned in all matters. No one would have ever questioned any order given by Henry Morgan. Just like a merchant vessel or royal naval vessel, a privateer captain generally would have his own cabin and his ship's officers would have birthing spaces apart from the common crew. That was certainly true of Captain Kidd, Captain Morgan, and Captain Rogers. If the crew was dissatisfied with their captain, their only choice was to mutiny and turn to piracy. That was exactly what the privateer crew of the privateer ship named the Charles II did in 1694 when they mutinied against Captain Gibson, set him ashore, and elected Henry Every as their new pirate captain.

However, some governors issued letters of marque indiscriminately without too much attention given to the person named on those letters. When England ceased issuing letters of marque in the 1670s the French governor on Tortuga, who wasn't so particular, issued letters of marque to any English pirate that wanted them. The pirate crews who managed to obtain letters of marque, quite often, continued to operate exactly as they had. Also, as privateering was downscaled in the 18th century, many smaller independent privateers operated under democratic processes, elected leaders, and obtained letters of marque from local Caribbean governors.

Pirates operated illegally and only obeyed the laws that their crews agreed upon.

For Pirates, rules were far different than the rules for privateers. Each crew was different, of course, but generally during the golden age of piracy, captains were elected by the vote of the entire crew and could be voted out of command at any time. When Charles Vane showed good judgment in not attacking a much larger French warship, his crew took it as cowardice and voted him out of office. When Ben Hornigold refused to attack British shipping, his crew voted him out of office. A captain remained so only with the will of the crew. To be elected, an individual generally had to be a good sailor and a skilled navigator, as navigation was usually one of the captain's responsibilities. Therefore, only experienced sailors generally became captains. When Howell Davis was killed, Roberts was elected as captain, even though he had only been with the crew for a short time. It was most likely because he was an experienced sailor and could navigate. There were other requirements for a captain to have as well. Bravery, good judgment, and charisma were essential qualities.

Generally, for pirates, the captain's authority was only supreme during battle. The quartermaster ran the ship right up to the time when a prize vessel was sighted, at which time, the captain took over as the absolute authority and remained in total control until the fight was over. That concept was essential for success in any battle. There can only be one person making real-time command decisions during a fight, if not; the action soon degenerates into chaos and defeat. A great example of this can be read in the Ship's Articles of Sam Bellamy.

> "The Power of ye Captain is Supream in Chance of Battle. He may beat, cut, or shoot any who dares Deny his Command on such Occasions. In all other Matters whatsoever he is to be Governed by the Will of ye Company."

Of course, the captain played a vital role in all the key decisions made aboard ship. As the navigator, the captain's advice was crucial to all decisions made concerning ship movements and ports of call. Also, it was the captain who usually made all negotiations ashore, arranging for the refitting of the vessel and selling stolen goods.

The one thing a captain wouldn't normally do was to treat a member of the crew harshly without the rest of the crew's approval. The old stereotype of the tyrannical pirate captain who was feared by the entire crew was generally not true. A cruel captain or one who cheated the crew would soon be marooned. Many pirates began as sailors on merchant vessels where tyrannical behavior among merchant captains was common. Pirates normally took great care to ensure their crewmembers didn't suffer any of the injustices they had suffered at the hands of sea captains when they were law abiding seamen. To help with this democratic process, captains had no special privileges except during time of battle. Captains of pirate vessels had no separate quarters and berthed with the rest of the crew.

The power of the pirate quartermaster was unique. In many ways, the quartermaster was the real power on the vessel. That was also an elected position and quartermasters had to have great skill and experience as a sailor. As mentioned before, right up until a prize ship was sighted, the quartermaster ran the ship. If a member of the crew needed to be disciplined, it was the quartermaster who usually dealt out the punishment. The relationship between the quartermaster and the captain must have been an interesting one. He was completely obedient to the captain during time of battle and generally respectful to the captain at other times, but between battles, the captain also had to be obedient to the quartermaster. For that reason, it always worked out best when the captain and quartermaster were good friends.

The quartermaster's duties and responsibilities are described in many accounts and Ship's Articles such as the Ship's Articles of Sam Bellamy as published in the *General History of Pyrates* which states:

In modern terms, a quartermaster is a position in the navy usually associated with the helmsman. In the 18th century, it was a leadership position for the senior enlisted man and referred to master of the quarter deck, which was the part of the vessel where the captain navigated, gave orders, and supervised the steering of the vessel.

"Ye Quarter-master shall be first a Board any Prize. He is to separate for ye Company's Use what he sees fit and shall have Trust of ye Common Stock and Treasury until it be Shared. He shall Keep a Book shewing each Man's Share, and each Man may draw from ye Common Stock and Treasury against his Share upon Request."

Another example comes to us from Captain William Snelgrave in his book, A New Account of Some Parts of Guinea, and the Slave Trade, published in 1734. Captain Snelgrave was taken captive by Captain Cocklyn and Captain Davis off the north coast of Africa in 1719.

"I think it necessary to observe in this place, that the Captain of a Pirate Ship, is chiefly chosen to fight the vessels that may meet with. Besides him, they choose another principal Officer, whom they call Quartermaster, who has the general inspection of all affairs, and often controls the Captain's Orders: This person is also said to be the first man in boarding any ship they shall attack; or go in the boat on any desperate enterprise. Besides the captain and the Quarter-master, the pirates had all other officers as is usual on board Men of War."

There was a documented account also written by Captain Snelgrave where three pirate captains, Cocklyn, Davis, and Le Vasseur, took three fancy dress coats directly from Captain Snelgrave's wardrobe and wore them ashore to impress the local ladies. That was a serious breach of the Ship's Articles, for all valuable clothing was to be turned over to the quartermaster along with everything else to be added to the common chest as property of the ship's company. The crew complained to the quartermaster saying, "If they suffered such things, the Captains would in future assume a Power, to take whatever they liked for themselves." As soon as the captains returned to the ship, the quartermaster made them give the coats back and probably warned the captains of what might happen if this behavior occurred again.

Howell Davis's command structure was one of the rarest and most unique pirate command structures of any pirate crew. He ran his ship more like a government rather than a simple democracy. Decisions were seldom reached by a vote of the crew, instead, they were voted on by a small group called the "House of Lords." That group included the captain and quartermaster as well as all the ship's officers, like the master gunner and the sailing master, and a close circle of trusted friends. Among many traditional crews, the captains had no special privileges or authority except during time of battle. Not on Davis' ship. The members of the House of Lords had special privileges far beyond the rest of the crew. They could walk on the quarterdeck any time they pleased, which was off limits for the others. They also could speak directly with the captain anytime they chose. Here

I will reiterate these strict codes from a previous chapter. When addressing them, crew and lords alike would use the title of "Lord." For example, "Good day me Lord Williams" or "What does Your Lordship think?" The members of the House of Lords were the ones who accompanied the Captain on all shore parties to conduct business.

In important matters, it was the House of Lords who decided, not the entire crew. The rest of the crew members belonged to the "House of Commons" and didn't make decisions for the ship's operations. However, if the House of Commons felt that the House of Lords had made a poor decision, the House of Commons could call for a popular vote of the entire crew. For example, in the section of this book dealing with Howell Davis, I have described how John Taylor, the quartermaster and a member of the House of Lords, took over as captain by a vote from the House of Commons and the entire crew.

Chapter 65
Tools of the Trade—Sailing Vessels

There were many types of vessels used during the golden age of piracy. Within the Caribbean and coastal North America, sloops were the number one choice for local commerce. That made economic sense. Sloops were fast and easy to sail. They also only required a crew of about six, which made them relatively inexpensive to operate. The biggest drawback to sloops was the small amount of cargo space. The larger the vessel, the larger the operating cost, so larger vessels were used to carry large and profitable cargo, especially across oceans. In researching the various types of sailing vessels, the modern reader will encounter some difficulty. That's because some of the names for certain vessels changed between the 17th and 18th centuries and also between nations. For example, to the English of the 17th century, a pinnace was a small rowboat that would be carried onboard a larger vessel. By the 18th century, the English referred to a small one-masted vessel as a pinnace. To the Dutch of the 17th century, a pinnace was a small three-masted ship but by the 18th century, the Dutch referred to a small single-masted square-rigged vessel as a pinnace. There is also confusion concerning vessels called brigantines. In the 17th century, some sources refer to any vessel with two masts as a brigantine, while by the 18th century, brigantines were defined more precisely. When reading any contemporary reference to specific vessels, it's safer to remember that the source may not be referring to the same precise type of vessel that is defined in modern sources.

As to the preference of pirates, it varied greatly depending upon the pirate. Some pirates preferred smaller vessels such as sloops. They required less work, were less expensive to operate, and required fewer crewmen which meant larger shares per man. Also, due to their shallower draft, they could go places where larger vessels couldn't. Big ships need ports with deep

Square Rigged—A vessel with traditional square sails that are generally perpendicular to the keel of the vessel.

Rigged Fore and Aft—Usually triangular sails which are set along the keel.

Sloops—Approximately 70 feet in length with a single mast.

Lateen Sails—Lateen sails were originally invented and commonly used by the Romans. They became popular again in Europe in the 15th century through contact with Arab sailors. They are triangular sails set on long yard arms are rigged fore and aft.

Gaff Rig—A four-sided sail rigged fore and aft and fastened at all four points with to a large spar connected to the center of the mast and hoisted up with lines connected to the top of the mast.

Two-Masted—Two-masted vessels could either be square-rigged or rigged fore and aft and include brigantines, snows, brigs, and barque longues.

water and large docks, but small vessels could put into coves and out of the way ports that were difficult or impossible to navigate with a big ship. Another advantage of smaller vessels was the ease and time it took to careen them. Hauling a big ship onto the beach could be very difficult. On the other hand, as we have seen, many pirates wanted big ships for their fleet. First of all, big vessels carry more guns and more pirates, making them far more intimidating. Also, they can carry far more booty in their holds. The fact is that all the most successful pirates eventually had big ships. Blackbeard, Roberts, Davis, Bellamy, Kidd, Every, and of course, Morgan all had big ships. However, unless they happened to be exceptionally lucky, most pirates normally started out using a sloop.

Single-masted vessels were known as sloops. The sloop was originally designed by the Dutch and combined a European hull with a lateen sail, making the vessel very maneuverable and able to sail almost directly into the wind. Sloops were also fast and very easy to handle, which made them ideal for use by local merchants as well as by pirates. Sloops were single-masted vessels with a fore and aft gaff rigged mainsail, very long bowsprits which carried several jib sails, and often had a square topsail. They ranged in size from 50 to 70 feet in length, could mount between 6 and 14 guns, and could carry a crew of up to 80 men, if they didn't mind being crowded a bit. Sloops drew about 8 feet of water, could sail about 12 knots, and came in a variety of designs. Each nation had their own variation of sloops, but in the Caribbean, two specific English designs seemed to dominate the waters, the Bermuda sloop and the Jamaica Sloop. Bermuda sloops were developed at the English colony of Bermuda in the early 17th century. They were very seaworthy and could easily make an ocean voyage. The Jamaican sloops developed on Jamaica during the time of Henry Morgan, in the 1660s. They had a narrower beam which made them faster and more maneuverable than other sloops, but that also meant a smaller cargo hold.

Two-masted vessels included brigantines, snows, brigs, & barque longues. The brigantine seemed to be the pirate captain's choice for a mid-size vessel. Originally of 15th century Mediterranean design, they were larger than sloops, had two masts, and ranged in size between 90–110 feet in keel length. With a good amount of cargo space, they could mount between 14 and 22 guns plus whatever swivel guns could be mounted on the rails and could carry a crew of 200. The masts could be rigged in a variety of ways, to include square rigged, fore and aft gaff rigged, top gallant sails and royals, and any combination thereof. That ability to alter rigging made them able to use the power of the wind to its maximum capacity and made the brigantine the fastest and most maneuverable vessel of the day. Additionally, they carried oars, sometimes called sweeps, which could be quickly run out for rowing. With the added advantage of oars, a brigantine could pursue a prize vessel in light wind or even directly into the wind. In the 17th and early 18th centuries, it was not unusual for warships and privateer vessels to carry oars. Famous pirate brigantines were Charles Vane's *Ranger*, Howell Davis' *Royal James*, and John Roberts' *Good Fortune*.

The snow was a squared rigged merchant vessel and was generally considered the largest of all the two-masted vessels. This is one of those confusing vessel types. In the 17th century, brigantines that happened to be running with square rigging were often called snows and sometimes snows were called brigantines. Another square-rigged two-masted merchant vessel was the brig. Mounting between 20 and 30 guns and with a length of between 110 to 120 feet, the brig was generally considered to be a smaller version of the snow or a larger version of the brigantine, but during the golden age there was little consistency in identifying all three types. Whether it was the hull size or the rigging that made the determination as to what type of vessel it was seems to have been up to the individual. When one reads a contemporary account that mentions a 28-gun brigantine, that vessel might actually be a brig.

The barque longue is a 17th century vessel primarily used by the French for exploration. It's a sleek vessel with a long and narrow open deck and a sharp bow. It also had a full deck of oars. It was a direct descendent from the Viking long boats and somewhat resembles them except for the European designed quarterdeck at the aft of the vessel. Barque longue means long boat in French. Most barque longues had two masts, but smaller one-masted versions and larger three-masted versions also existed. The masts were square rigged, like their Viking ancestors. Even though these vessels were primarily used for exploring, they also made great pirate vessels. They were very swift under sail or oar and highly maneuverable. However, their narrow deck and oars didn't allow for much armament to be mounted, so their prizes tended to be vessels that couldn't offer much resistance. In the early buccaneer days, the barque longue was used by both French and Dutch buccaneers sailing out of Tortuga. Two barque longues accompanied the pirate fleet that William Dampier sailed with in 1681.

Three-Masted—
Pinks barks, flutes, and ships had three masts.

Three-masted vessels included pinks, barks, Dutch pinnaces, and flutes. In the 17th and 18th centuries, vessels with one or two masts were not commonly referred to as ships; only three-masted vessels that were fully-rigged were called ships. Fully-rigged meant that they had square sails on the fore mast and the main mast and the mizzen mast (the mast behind the main mast) had a fore and aft gaff rigged sail called a spanker. This spanker helped the ship maneuver. Ships came in a great variety and ranged in size from 100 feet up to almost 200 feet in length. The *Mayflower*, the vessel that carried the Pilgrims to Massachusetts, was a ship. The "Pink" was a type of ship with a narrow overhanging stern. In the 17th century, the Dutch had a small three-masted ship design they called a "Dutch pinnace." However, by the 18th century, the Dutch used the term "pinnace" to refer to a smaller one-masted vessel.

Ships that didn't fit into a specialized category were called "Barks." Merchant ships, regardless of actual design or type, were called "Merchantmen" and carried both cargo and passengers. The most valuable cargo came from the Indian Ocean, and about a dozen European nations had well-established companies that specialized in trading with India and the many islands located in the Indian Ocean. Those companies were called East India Companies and merchant ships that belonging to those companies were called "East Indiamen." They were the largest of all merchantmen because of the large and exceptionally valuable cargo they brought back to Europe. Due to the threat of pirates, they were also the best armed of all merchantmen, mounting between 32 and 60 guns.

Galleys used oars for propulsion in addition to sails.

The "Dutch Flute" was a 17th and early 18th century merchant ship with shorter masts and no top gallants or mizzen tops. That modification made handling easier with a small crew. Flutes also had flat bottoms which allowed them to sail in shallower harbors. The broad beams and a somewhat rounded stern of the Dutch flute increased the amount of cargo space dramatically to an impressive 300 tons of capacity for a ship that was only about 80 feet in length. They usually mounted up to 32 guns for protection. Easy to sail, the flute was among the most valued cargo vessels of the day, but it was not a fighting ship. Slow and not very maneuverable in tight spaces, it was rare for any pirate to use one for a pirate ship. The French privateer, Rene Duguay-Trouin, commanded the 32-gun flute for three months. Unable to take any prizes with it he then got rid of it. Blackbeard's ship, the *Queen Anne's Revenge* was said to have been a Dutch flute by several of the captives who made reports to the authorities after their release. However, that is very unlikely. When Blackbeard took the *Concorde*, which became the *Queen Anne's Revenge*, it was being used to transport slaves from Africa to Martinique. Slaves didn't survive long voyages, so any vessel used to carry slaves across the Atlantic had to be fast. Dutch flutes were just too slow for the slave trade. The *Queen Anne's Revenge* was most likely a regular merchant ship with an enlarged stern. A modification like that would have increased the cargo capacity and may have resembled the rounded stern of a flute to those that saw Blackbeard's ship firsthand.

Galleys have a history that goes back thousands of years and they were still commonly seen on the oceans in the 17th and 18th centuries. They had fine lines and were the fastest large vessels of their day. Captain Kidd's vessel, *Adventure*, was a galley and of the nine vessels that sailed with Woodes Rogers, five were galleys. The advantage that galleys had over other vessels was that they could either use oars for propulsion or rely upon the wind. Where it is true that many vessels in the 17th and 18th centuries came equipped with oars, which could be used occasionally in poor wind conditions, those vessels weren't designed to use oars as their main propulsion, whereas galleys were. Additionally, galleys came with up to four masts, allowing them to use both wind and oars in combination for propulsion. That gave them their great speed. Oar ports on galleys were sometimes on the upper deck, sometimes on the lower deck, and occasionally, between decks. The main drawback to using a galley was that it took a very large crew to work the oars.

The largest types of galleys ever constructed were called the galleasses and were primarily used by the Spanish as warships in the late 16th century. Those massive four-masted battle ships had three oar decks and carried hundreds of soldiers. The Spanish Armada of 1588 included many galleasses. By the 17th century galleys were primarily being used as merchant vessels. Those galleys remained very similar in design to their ancestors, rigged fore and aft with one, two, or three masts supporting one large lateen sail each. That design was called "galley built." Beginning in the late 17th century and continuing throughout the 18th century, some galleys were constructed that more closely resembled ships, with three masts that were square-rigged and carried mizzen top gallants and spritsails. Those galleys were called "frigate built." Galleys made great slave ships because they were very fast and could continue on course across the Atlantic when the wind was light or even when there was no wind at all. They also made terrific pirate ships. At 500 tons, the *Charles Galley* was a galley built for war and could travel at three knots with three men apiece rowing at 42 oars. Captain Kidd's ship, the *Adventure*, was a frigate-built galley, one of the first ones made. Regnier Tongrelow used a galley as his pirate ship and Sam Bellamy's pirate ship *Whydah* was a frigate-built galley, just to name a few.

Spanish galleons were large merchant ships common between the 16th and 18th centuries. With three or four masts, the fore mast and the main mast were rigged with square sails with the mizzen mast and aft mast rigged with lateen sails and a small square sail on a high-rising bowsprit. Galleons were also used by the Portuguese. The cargo capacity for smaller galleons was between 500 and 1000 tons, but the larger Manila Galleons, which were used to bring valuable cargo across the Pacific, could reach

Spanish Galleons date to the early 16th century and were used by Magellan during his round the world trip 1519–1522.

Each nation had their own system of rating their warships, but the English were the most well defined.

up to 2000 tons of cargo capacity. The Spanish treasure fleets were made up almost entirely of galleons. They were very sluggish and not capable of sailing anywhere near (into) the wind. They had to sail in the same general direction that the wind was blowing. For that reason, galleons had to follow known trade winds which made their courses predictable. Pirates who wanted to take a galleon only had to wait along one of those trade winds until the galleon was sighted. However, even though galleons were slow and not very maneuverable, they were exceptionally well-armed with anywhere from 30 to 60 guns. Any pirate who took on a galleon could expect broadside-after-broadside before the galleon surrendered—many times it was the pirate vessel that gave up first and sailed away. Woodes Rogers did exactly that when he encountered the Manila Galleon, the *Nuestra Senora de Begona*, in 1710.

Sailing ships built for war first appeared in the 1530s and by 1660 a standard categorization had developed within the English Royal Navy to rate the size of each warship. At first the rating was based upon the number of men in the crew, but eventually it was changed to the number of guns that the ship mounted. However, after 1660 warships were built in larger and larger designs, causing the rating system to constantly change. For example, originally a first-rated ship had 55 guns, but by 1667 that size of ship had changed to a fourth-rated ship while first-rated ships were much larger. During that same time period, sixth-rated vessels went from 4 to 18 guns to 20 to 28 guns. This continued throughout the 17th and 18th centuries making it very difficult to apply the contemporary rating of a ship to later rating systems. The English standardized rating system of 1667 established a first-rated ship as mounting between 90 and 100 guns, a second-rated ship as mounting 80 to 90 guns, and a third-rated ship as mounting 50 to 80 guns. Any ship in those top three rates was called a Ship-O-the-Line. The British ship that captured Captain Roberts' crew in 1722 was HMS *Swallow*, a third-rater of 50 guns. The fourth-rated vessels mounted between 30 and 48 guns and the fifth-rated vessels mounted between 20 and 28 guns. The smallest sixth-rated vessels mounted between 4 and 18 guns and were either sloops or brigantines, but after 1714 any ship with fewer than 20 guns wasn't rated at all.

First-rate Ships-O-the-Line had three continuous decks of guns as well as smaller weapons on the quarterdeck, the forecastle, and the poop deck. Second- and third-rated Ships-O-the-Line had two continuous decks of guns. Those vessels were state of the art battleships. Beginning in 1700 the English began producing warships with three masts that were a bit smaller and faster than the big Ships-O-the-Line. Those sleek ships were fifth-raters called frigates and had three masts with a raised forecastle and quarterdeck. Those frigates were ideal pirate hunters, fast, maneuverable, and well-enough armed to take on the bigger pirate vessels. The Royal Navy also used naval sloops. Very similar to the Bermuda sloop with a sharp bow for speed, those fighting vessel were 65 feet long, well-armed with 12 nine-pound guns, and carried a crew of 70 men. All naval sloops were equipped with oars to continue in light wind or to pursue an enemy directly into the wind. Those war sloops, classified as sixth-raters, were specifically designed for pirate hunting.

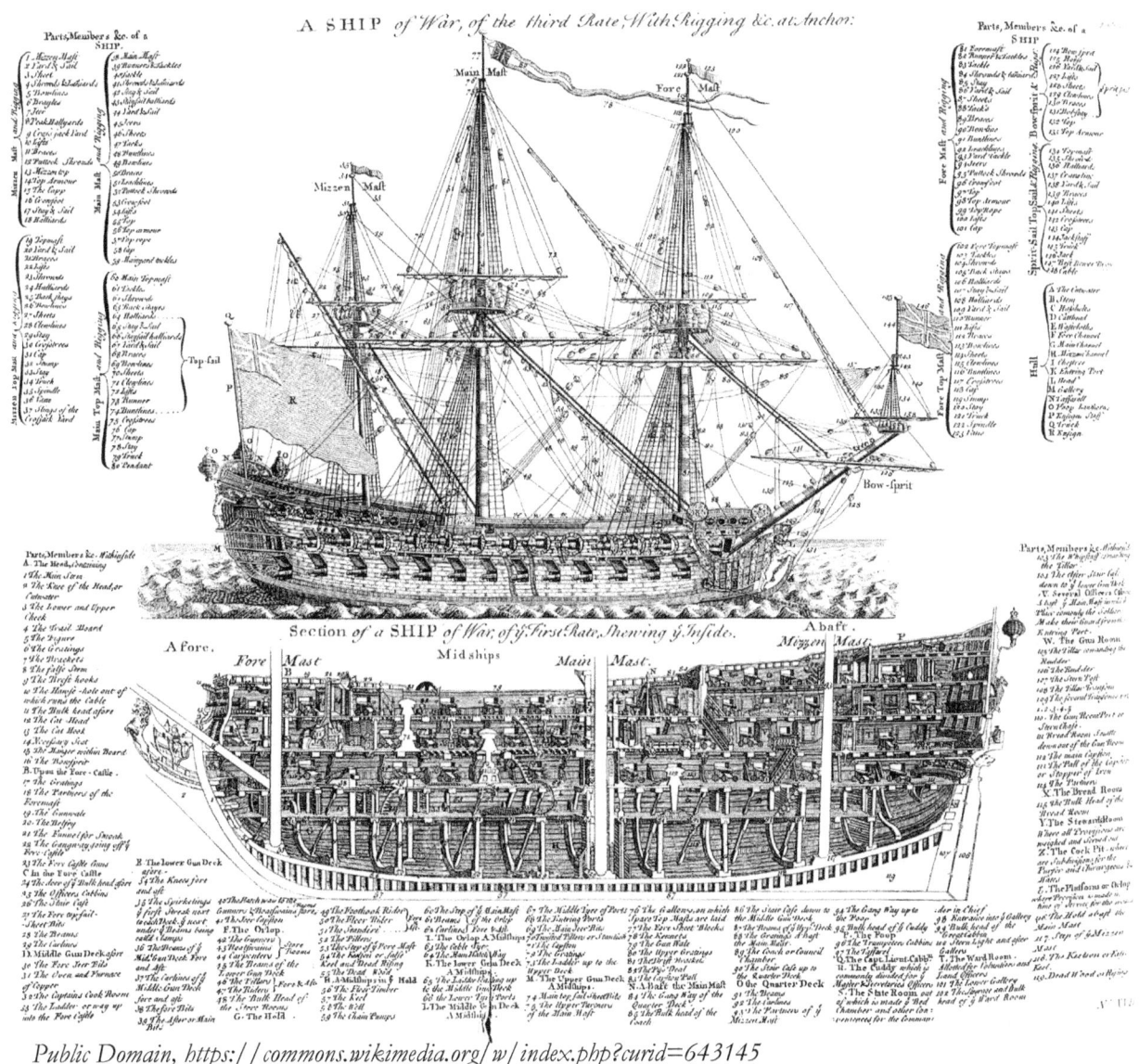

Public Domain, https://commons.wikimedia.org/w/index.php?curid=643145

Figure 32: *A Ship of War, of the third-rate, With Rigging etc. at Anchor, from the 1728 Cyclopaedia, Volume 2.*

Small boats were very important. Among the English, a "pinnace" was a far different type of vessel than what the Dutch called a pinnace. In the 17th century, the English used the term pinnace to refer to any small boat that serviced larger ones, like the longboat carried onboard larger vessels. By the 18th century the term pinnace was used to describe small coastal trading vessels with oars and one mast that could carry between 10 and 60 tons of cargo or hold up to 60 men. Another common small vessel used for coastal travel or trading was the periauger. Those shallow drafted, flat bottomed vessels often had two masts and were also equipped with oars. They carried up to 10 passengers and were primarily used for river travel.

Chapter 66
Tools of the Trade—Guns

This section deals with guns. Not muskets or pistols, I mean "guns," as in the guns on a vessel. In the modern world, we refer to all firearms as guns, but in strict military terms, a gun is a large mounted weapon that is most often fired from a ship. Many modern people refer to guns as cannons, but as you will soon see, this is incorrect. By 1600 the design of artillery had been perfected to the point where guns of all the European powers were effective and reliable. Naval artillery quite often had an effective range of 2,000 yards, although most battles at sea were fought within 1,000 yards and sometimes even within 50 feet. Throughout the 17th century the English made small improvements to the casting process as well as breech and chamber designs, but the general overall appearance of guns changed very little from 1620 until the end of the 18th century. A gun made in 1650 may look exactly like a gun made in 1750, except for the makers' mark, which often included the date of manufacture.

Guns were made of either cast iron or brass. Actually, there were no guns made of real brass, because brass wasn't strong enough to withstand firing. In reality, the guns that were called "brass guns" were actually made of bronze. I shall also refer to them as brass guns for the rest of this book. For larger sized guns, brass was far more desirable for naval use because brass guns were lighter than iron guns, but there were still a lot of iron guns used at sea. In modern times guns are named by their caliber, which is the diameter of the barrel measured in inches, but in the 17th century guns were characterized by the weight of the shot they fired and sometimes by their barrel lengths as well. Each of those categories of guns were then given names. For example, a gun was called a "saker" if it fired a 6-pound shot and had a barrel length of between 8 and 9.5 feet. The caliber of the barrel really didn't matter for classification purposes and often differed a little within the same category from one gun to another. In England, those names and standards were in common use for quite some time and firmly

The *Mary Rose,* which sank in 1545, carried a variety of Cannons, Demicannons, Culverins and other guns.

became established in 1637 by the Surveyor of Ordinance, who was a member of the English Board of Ordnance. Even though each European nation had its own standardized system of categorizing and naming guns they were remarkably similar to each other. The English culverin is similar in size to the Spanish culebrina. The following chart shows the English and Spanish categories; however, the chart is very general and there were many exceptions and variations.

Weight of Shot	Barrel Specifications	English Name	Spanish Name
0.3 pounds		Robinet	
0.5 pounds		Serpentine	Esmeril
1-2 pounds		Falconet	Falconete
3-4 pounds	Length 30"-32"	Falcon	Falcon
5.2 pounds	Length 7'	Minion	
6 pounds	Length 8'-9.5'	Saker	Media Sacre
7-10 pounds			Sacre
8 pounds		Demiculverin	
8-10 pounds	with a shorter barrel		Moyana
10-18 pounds			Media Culebrina
9-12 pounds	with a shorter barrel		Quarto Canon
11 pounds	with a shorter barrel	Bastard Culverin	
14 pounds		Basilisk	
14-22 pounds			Tercio de Culebrina
18-20 pounds		Culverin	Culebrina
24 pounds	with a shorter barrel		Medio Canon
24-40 pounds			Culibrina Real
26 pounds			Pedrero
32 pounds	Length 8'-9'	Demicannon	Canon de Abitar
40 pounds			Doble Culibrina
42 pounds		Bastard Cannon	
48 pounds	with a shorter barrel		Doble Canon
60 pounds		Cannon	Canon de Bateria
74 pounds		Cannon Royal	
80 pounds		Basilico	
90 pounds		Lonbarda	

Carriage guns were designed for naval use. Most guns were mounted on a carriage of some sort so they could be rolled inside the vessel to reload or to close the hatches of the gun ports. Guns that fired a 32-pound shot were the largest used aboard ship during the 17th and 18th centuries by all nations. Larger guns like cannons were just too big and heavy. Even so, guns like the demicannon, or canon de abitar in Spanish, were only found on the bigger warships. The largest guns found on sloops would have been those firing 12-pound shots or less. The bastard culverin, firing an 11-pound shot, was preferred for use on the upper decks of large ships and on all smaller vessels. It had a shorter barrel which made it not only lighter, but also easier to load onboard ship.

Drake guns were also preferred by the English Navy. The drake gun was one with a specially designed powder chamber which tapered toward the breech. That made the wall of the breech thicker, which meant that the rest of the barrel could be made thinner and still withstand the pressure of firing. A thinner barrel was much lighter in weight and more practical for shipboard use. This drake chamber design was available on all guns between minions and demicannons. All of the guns firing 4-pound shot or larger would have been mounted on a naval carriage. That was essential for reloading. Other innovations to the casting procedures and metal alloys used in production were introduced by the English in the mid-17th century, making the English guns the finest in the world.

In 1718 Albert Borgard was appointed by King George I of Great Britain as the Assistant Surveyor of Ordnance. He standardized the weights of the shots at 4, 6, 9, 12, 18, 24, and 32 pounds and abolished the system of using names and established a standardized system which named the guns simply by the weight of their shot. The saker became known as a 6 pounder and so on. The English naval gun known as the "long nine" was well-named. It was a 9 pounder with a longer barrel length to give it greater accuracy at longer ranges. However, that gun wasn't introduced until the mid-18th century, well past the golden age of piracy.

Swivel guns were small-sized guns that could be mounted anywhere. The gun itself was mounted on a swivel, or yoke, which had a long spike that went through the hole drilled in a supporting wood surface. Normally, aboard ship they were mounted along the rails and used to fire anti-personnel grape shot to either repel boarders or to rake the deck of a ship that was about to be boarded. They were capable of firing a small solid shot into an enemy vessel if necessary. Typical barrel lengths for swivel guns were slightly less than three feet, although some pieces had much longer barrels. The gun itself usually had a long handle at the rear, which was used to aim. Swivel guns in the late 17th and early 18th centuries could either be of a regular muzzle loading design, like a very small cannon, or breech loading. Muzzle loaders included the robinet, serpentine, esmeril, and falconet. Sometimes even a falcon was used as a swivel gun, although it could also be mounted on a carriage.

Breech loading swivel guns had been common since the 16th century and would have been mounted on vessels throughout the world by all nations. Breech loading swivel guns were much easier to reload during battle. There were several different types of breech loaders which were called bases, sling pieces, port pieces, and murderers. The bases and sling pieces all had a muzzle diameter of between one and two inches. The bases had fairly long barrels when compared to other swivel guns ranging anywhere from three to five feet in length. The sling pieces had barrels of average lengths, two to three feet long. Port pieces had larger muzzles, between three and three and a half inches wide, with a barrel length between two and three feet. The murderer was an English weapon with a very thick barrel that could hold a great deal of grapeshot. It also had an unusual looking grip that almost resembles modern machine guns. Murderers were found aboard the wreck of the Mary Rose which sank in 1545. By the 1630s they were considered obsolete by the English government and given to colonists as surplus weapons. Murderers virtually disappeared, just about everywhere, by the late 17th century.

Firing steps

Swab wet

Swab dry

Charge with powder

Prick

Load shot

Run out

Prime

Fire

Loading and firing at sea could be tricky. Guns below decks were protected from the sea with hatches that securely closed. When the vessel prepared for battle the hatches were opened and the guns were "run out." That meant that the guns were rolled forward so that the muzzle of the barrel extended beyond the bulkhead. That took the entire gun crew heaving on the gun tackles. All guns, except some small swivel guns, were muzzle loaders and had to be pulled back enough for the crew to gain access to the muzzle in order to reload. It took four to six men on a gun crew to effectively load and fire a gun in battle. Merchant vessels with smaller crews wouldn't be able to effectively sail the vessel and fire their guns at the same time. That put them at a great disadvantage when being attacked by a pirate vessel with a large crew. Ships with large crews, like pirate vessels and naval warships, didn't have that problem.

Before loading, a wet swab was pushed down the barrel to clean out the interior and extinguish any burning embers from the previous firing. Without doing that, a hot barrel would ignite the powder charge as it was rammed down the barrel causing injury or death to the loader. Another swab would then be rammed down the barrel to dry it out. A measured amount of gunpowder would be rammed down next. The gunpowder could be poured in loose but most often it was already packed in a cloth or parchment cartridge. Once the powder was properly seated in the powder chamber, the cartridge would have to be punctured by inserting a metal "pricker" through the touch hole. The shot was loaded next by ramming it down the barrel until it seated. Normally some cloth or paper wadding was rammed down along with the shot to prevent it from rolling out.

Sometimes "hot shot" was loaded and fired. That was a solid shot that had been heated red hot and used to set the enemy vessel on fire. Loading hot shot was very tricky, because the heat of the hot iron could cause the gun to go off prematurely during loading. If hot shot was to be loaded, a wooden plug was rammed down after the powder to keep the shot from setting it off. The hot shot was of a smaller caliber, so it could be rolled down the barrel without ramming. Of course, firing the gun almost immediately after loading was important. You didn't want that hot shot to be in there too long.

If the gun was to be fired immediately, its carriage was run out. The touch hole in the rear of the gun went directly into the breech. When it was time to fire, finer grained gunpowder called "priming powder" would be poured into the touch hole as a primer. In the 17th and early 18th century, a wooden staff holding a length of smoldering match at the end called a "linstock" was used to touch off the gun. Improved ignition devices weren't invented until 1745. Firing was always tricky. It had to be timed with the roll of the vessel in order to hit the target. Additionally, since there was a slight delay from the time the linstock was applied and when the gun actually fired, the gunner had to anticipate a little bit. Once fired, the whole process began over again, but with a very hot barrel that could cause severe burns to the loader. Obviously, the gunpowder used to fire the guns had to be kept in a safe place below the gun deck. Quite often, boys between the ages of 10 and 14, sometimes called "powder monkeys" were used to carry powder from the powder magazine to the gun crews during battle. However, children would have been exceptionally rare on pirate vessels. Between engagements, pirates often kept their guns loaded and ready for action. Guns recovered from several pirate ship wrecks were found to have been left loaded.

Shot fired from the guns came in several varieties. In a naval action, there are several choices of "shot" one can use in the guns. Since guns can't easily be unloaded, captains had to plan the attack well in advance and make sure the guns were loaded with the proper kind of shot for the intended attack. A solid shot is just what it sounds. It is a solid round ball of iron ideal for breaking through the bulkhead and blowing a hole in the side of the enemy vessel. In a broadside, if solid shot was used, the shots that hit the gun deck could destroy the enemy's guns and gun crews. If the shots hit near the waterline, the enemy vessel could sink. Pirates seldom used solid shot when attacking prizes as they didn't really want to sink the vessels. However, they may have loaded a few guns with solid shot just in case the prize ship fought back and they had to try to take out their guns.

> Aiming was difficult—your vessel was moving forward and rolling up and down while the enemy's vessel was also moving and rolling. If the target was the masts, the gunners would wait for the uproll to fire and if they wished to aim for the hull, they would wait for the downroll. Hitting the target depended on a great deal of luck as well as skill.

> Solid shot to breech the hull
> Bar shot to break a mast
> Chain shot to destroy rigging
> Grape shot to kill people

Bar shot is like a cannon ball cut in two with a solid bar between each half. Bar shot is designed to cut a ship's mast in two, keeping the ship from maneuvering or escaping. If a mast is broken at the base and falls over into the sea, not only does the vessel lose sailing power, the mast dragging in the water stops the vessel. Chain shot is like a hollow cannon ball cut in half with a chain connecting the two halves. When fired, the halves separate and spin. This is ideal for ripping through the rigging and sails, thus keeping the ship from maneuvering or escaping. The advantage of chain shot is that it rips the sails and stops the vessel without necessarily destroying the mast. This is very advantageous if your intention is to keep the vessel and sail away on it with minimal repairs.

Grape shot is like a shotgun. The gunner loads the gun with powder then pours nails, glass, rocks, and just about anything else that is available down the barrel. When fired, it won't do much damage to a vessel, but it will kill crewmembers. Grape shot was most often used in the swivel guns mounted on the rails. Most of the time, a few volleys of grape shot from the swivel guns would clear the enemy deck of personnel.

Of course, pirates would have kept whatever guns they took from a prize vessel. Most merchant vessels of the day didn't carry guns that fired shot larger than 12 pounds, so minions (4 pounders), sakers (6 pounders), demiculverins (9 pounders), and bastard culverins (11 pounders) would have made up the bulk of the mounted carriage guns in the pirate arsenal. Swivel guns would have been placed just about anywhere on the vessel in order to reinforce their firepower and most likely these guns would have outnumbered the carriage guns aboard any pirate vessel. Some of the smaller pirate sloops may have only had swivel guns aboard. One reason why the descriptions of the amount of guns on various pirate ships differ so often was that sometimes the swivel guns were added to the total and sometimes they weren't. A ship carrying 20 carriage guns could also have 20 swivel guns mounted about the deck. In some cases, those vessels could be described as having 40 guns, but officially by naval classification, the swivel guns don't count and they would be described as having only 20 guns.

Chapter 67
Tools of the Trade—Firelocks

All weapons that use a lock mechanism to ignite the gunpowder are called firelocks. That term was used in the verbal military commands shouted during the manual of arms until the mid-19th century. For example, "Shoulder your firelock." The first types were harquebuses and matchlocks, which operated identically in terms of technology and mechanism. The only difference seems to be in the caliber of the barrel, the harquebus being a smaller caliber and the matchlock being a larger caliber. To load and fire, a charge of black powder and lead ball, called a shot, is rammed down a smooth bore barrel to the chamber at the base. Then, a small charge of black powder is poured into a priming pan—also called a flash pan—which is attached to the outside of the barrel with a small "touch hole" leading through the barrel to the black powder and shot which rests inside the chamber. The priming pan is covered to prevent accidental discharge or loss of powder. Next to the pan is a lever holding a slow burning match, which is actually a thin piece of hemp or flax treated with potassium nitrate to make it smolder for a long time. When the shooter wants to shoot, the priming pan must first be uncovered manually. When the trigger is pulled, the lever moves the burning match down and the glowing end makes contact with the exposed black powder in the pan. The powder lights and ignites the powder in the chamber through the touch hole and the weapon shoots the lead ball at the target.

The harquebus was developed in the very early 15th century and was used by armies all over Europe by 1450, but the smaller caliber barrel and shot, between 45 cal. and 55 cal., didn't fire a ball that could effectively penetrate thicker armor, so a larger version that could was developed by the late 16th century. With a barrel and shot size of between 60 cal. and 80 cal., this matchlock weapon was known in military terms as a "musket." The term "musket" continued to be used to specify a caliber size of between 60 cal. and 80 cal. throughout the 17th, 18th, and 19th centuries. In the first half to

Lock mechanism is a steel plate on one side of the weapon that holds the cock (hammer) and a spring which makes the cock fly forward when released. The cock is released when the trigger is pulled.

the 17th century, only elite soldiers were issued muskets and were therefore called Musketeers. The famous "Three Musketeers" were fictional characters, but they belonged to a unit that was historically factual. Civilian versions of those muskets were simply called matchlocks. Technically, a matchlock is the lock mechanism itself, so a harquebus is actually a matchlock too.

The matchlock is a very reliable weapon when handled properly but has limited accuracy. Like all other muskets regardless of lock type, the accuracy lies in the barrel, not the lock. In order for the lead ball to easily fit down the barrel, the caliber of the ball is always a little smaller than the caliber of the barrel. For example, a 69-caliber barrel takes a 63-caliber ball. This difference greatly reduces accuracy and makes any musket deadly accurate to only about 50 or 60 yards. The further the target is beyond 60 yards, the more the shooter's luck plays into hitting it. The great disadvantage with the matchlock is the burning match itself. The wick-like match didn't stay lit for very long. In battle, a musketeer had to take a few minutes to light his match before he was ready to fight the enemy. Even then, a strong wind could cause the match to go out and if there was even the slightest drizzle or rain, the weapon became useless. There also could be some delay between pulling the trigger and when the match actually caused the powder in the pan to go off. All these reasons caused gun makers to seek another kind of lock mechanism.

Wheel locks first appeared in 1480 in Italy and were further developed in Germany around 1517. They were used by the wealthy all over Europe by the 1520s and remained fashionable until the late 17th century. A wheel lock is a highly innovative and complex lock mechanism with levers and springs that timed a roughened metal spinning wheel with the strike of the flint held by a clamp on a hammer upon the pull of the trigger. This results in a spark which ignites the powder in the pan. The concept is similar to modern cigarette lighters. This solved the problems with the burning match but the process of making a wheel lock was very expensive. The wheel lock mechanism required fine precision workmanship to make, like the inside of a pocket watch. Most wheel locks were more like works of art, with very ornate and finely crafted locks and barrels and stocks covered with fine scroll work. Only noblemen and the very rich could afford them. Since matchlock pistols were very impractical, the new wheel locks now made the first pistols a reality. This led to the only military application of the wheel lock pistols used by cavalry officers. As for pirates using wheel locks, it was possible that a few wheel locks may have been taken by some pirates operating at the beginning of the golden age of piracy, but that would have been exceptionally rare.

1450–1550 Harquebus

1520–early 18th century Matchlock

1480–late 17th century Wheel locks

Because wheel locks were primarily used for hunting, many wheel locks had rifled barrels. Rifling can be dated as far back as 1494 and is a barrel design in which the gunsmith puts spiral groves down the inside of the barrel. The projectile must fit tightly into the barrel for the rifling to work, so the caliber of the shot must exactly match the caliber of the barrel. This makes an airtight seal that doesn't allow the rapidly expanding gasses from the ignited black powder to escape past the projectile. The groves put a spin on the projectile and the extra power from the tight seal makes the shot go much straighter for a longer distance. Depending upon the skill of the shooter, rifles of that time period can be accurate up to 200 yards. However, there is a great deal of added stress to the metal of the barrel created from this tight seal of the projectile, so the thickness of rifled barrels had to be more than twice the thickness of a smooth bore. This made large rifled barrels too heavy to be practical, so rifles of the day were only made in relatively small calibers, normally between 30 and 50 caliber, and their barrels tended to be rather short in length. Longer rifled barrels weren't typically seen until the 1770s when gunsmiths began gradually reducing the thickness of the barrel toward the muzzle to lighten them.

Rifled barrels were exceptionally expensive and took a long time to produce, which made them impractical for use on matchlocks. Additionally, there could be a delay of up to one second between when the shooter pulled the trigger and when the matchlock actually fired. This delay severely affected one's aim and nullified the advantage of the rifled barrel. Rifles were also impractical for any sort of military application due to the combination of the expense, the light caliber round, and the short barrel length, which was too short to effectively use with a bayonet. Rifles weren't used as military weapons until the mid-18th century, when specialized rifle units began to appear. As newer types of locks were invented, they were immediately applied to rifles, but even so, rifles were produced locally and seldom carried aboard ship. Through most of the golden age of piracy, the rifle was strictly used for hunting ashore. It would have been possible for a pirate to come across a rifle occasionally, but that would have been exceptionally rare.

Igniting the powder in the flash pan was always the issue. The slow burning match worked, but it took time to properly prepare and could go out in wind or rain. The wheel lock worked well to ignite the power in the flash pan, nevertheless, it was too expensive to produce. In the mid-16th century, a new type of lock mechanism was developed that revolutionized weaponry. The concept behind that lock mechanism was simple. The barrel with chamber, touch hole, and flash pan remained exactly the same as with the matchlock; however, the lock mechanism had a hammer, called a "cock" with a clamp on one end which securely holds a piece of flint. Under

Rifling may have been first invented by Gaspard Kollner if Vienna, but some believe that the grooves were straight. Spiral grooves were introduced by Augustus Kotter of Nuremburg in 1520.

The first successful rifled musket used by infantry was the 1853 Enfield.

great tension from a spring, the cock is pulled back until a sear catches a notch and holds the cock in place. When the trigger is pulled, the cock is released, hurling forward and causing the flint to strike a small steel striker called a frizzen. This makes a spark which ignites the powder in the flash pan. The problem was that the powder in the pan must remain covered somehow until the trigger is pulled to keep it from falling out or blowing away in the wind.

1550–1650

Snaphance

The first successful flintlock type mechanism was the snaphance, which was introduced by the Dutch about 1550. It is a very complicated design in which the frizzen and pan cover are made in separate pieces. When the trigger is pulled, the hammer holding the flint strikes the frizzen while the pan cover is moved back by a separate internal mechanism.

1620–1840

Flintlock

The snaphance rapidly gained great popularity all throughout Europe and was used on pistols, muskets, and rifles. Again, due to the expense, matchlock muskets were still the weapon of choice for most military units and common people, but the snaphance pistol was a separate matter. Many military officers and pirates carried snaphance pistols in the late 16th and early 17th centuries. But by 1640 and the beginning of the golden age of piracy, the snaphance was rapidly being replaced by newer designs. By about 1670 the snaphance had vanished in Western Europe and in the colonies of North America. Curiously enough, the snaphance continued to be used in Italy until the mid-18th century and in Afghanistan and North Africa, snaphance rifles were still being used at the beginning of World War I.

The real flintlock is actually simpler than the snaphance, with fewer parts. There are three basic designs, the English lock, the French lock, and the Spanish lock, which all appeared about 1620. In all three, the frizzen is actually part of the pan cover which is held tightly over the flash pan by a tension spring on the outside of the lock. Just like the snaphance, when the trigger is pulled, the cock flies forward and the flint strikes the frizzen producing a spark while at the same instant it pushes the frizzen back to uncover the powder in the pan and fire the weapon. The difference is in spring design and in safety. The cock has to be pulled back to the firing position in order to allow the frizzen to close and cover the powder in the flash pan. As with any firearm, some type of safety device has to be employed to prevent the weapon from firing accidentally. The solution is to hold the cock securely in position far enough back to allow the closing of the frizzen while at the same time prevent the cock from flying forward, even if the trigger is pulled. This position is called "half cock" because the cock is literally locked in position about half way back. When the shooter is ready to shoot, the cock is pulled back to the full position called "full cock."

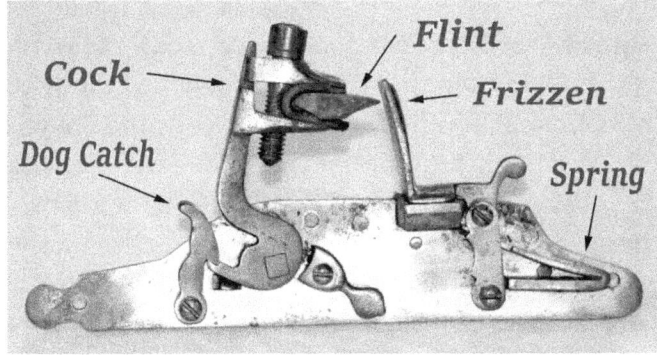

Figure 33: *Doglock with Frizzen Closed*

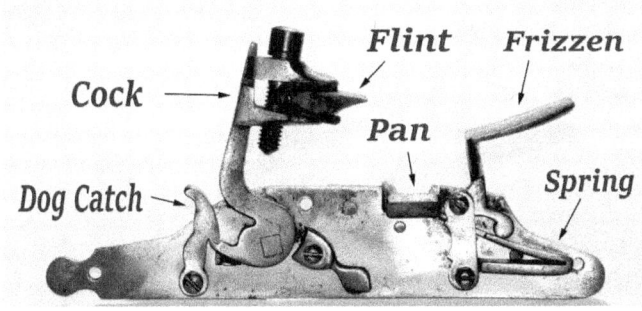

Figure 34: *Doglock with Frizzen Open*

The "English Lock" or the "Doglock" was first developed around 1620 and secured the cock in a locked half cock position prior to firing by using a small safety catch called a "dog catch" on the outside of the lock. The shooter would release this dog catch just before firing to take the weapon off "safe." Early dog lock muskets most commonly had a flared butt stock resembling a fish tail, an octagonal barrel, and no side plate. Frizzens were square and the lock plate itself was flat. Butt plates were flat and nailed to the stock and all metal parts, or "furniture" were made of iron. The barrels were a combination of octagonal and round. Doglocks quickly became the standard lock used on all pistols and military muskets in England. They were used on rifles as well, replacing the wheel lock completely. English civilians and colonists also began using doglocks in the 1630s and the

Loading steps for a flintlock

1. Half cock (pull the cock back half way)
2. Prime the pan with powder
3. Close frizzen
4. Cast about - place the butt on the ground with the barrel up
5. Charge powder
    a. if using paper cartridges:
        i. tear open cartridge
        ii. pour the powder down the barrel
    b. Place paper in the barrel
        i. if loading from a measure:
        ii. pour powder down barrel
6. Load ball (if using a cartridge, the ball will be in the paper)
7. Draw rammer and ram down the charge
8. Return rammer
9. Cast about and bring the weapon to firing position
10. Take aim
11. Full cock (pull cock all the way back)
12. Fire

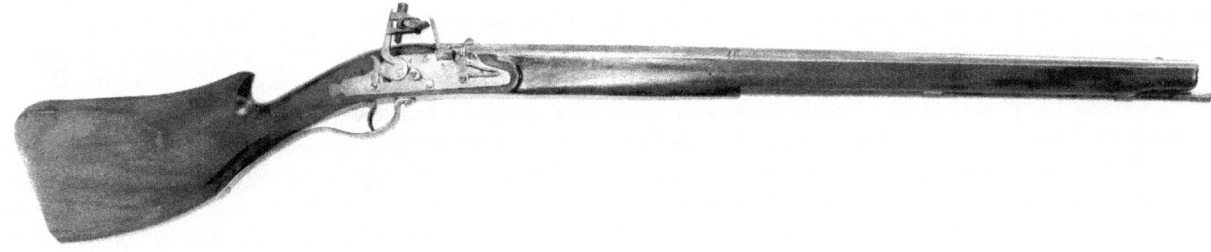

Figure 35: *1670 Doglock Musket*

matchlock was gradually replaced by the doglock throughout England and all the English colonies by 1680.

Ornately designed Scottish metal pistols with doglocks were made from the 1600s to the mid-18th century. Doglocks remained the primary English lock type until about 1710 and were still used in the colonies as late as the mid-1760s. For English pirates of the golden age, the doglock would have been the most common type of firelock for all muskets. Pistols were another matter. Doglock pistols would have been commonly used in the mid-17th century, but by the late 17th century doglock pistols were not the preferred pistol among pirates. Another design was rapidly replacing the doglock everywhere.

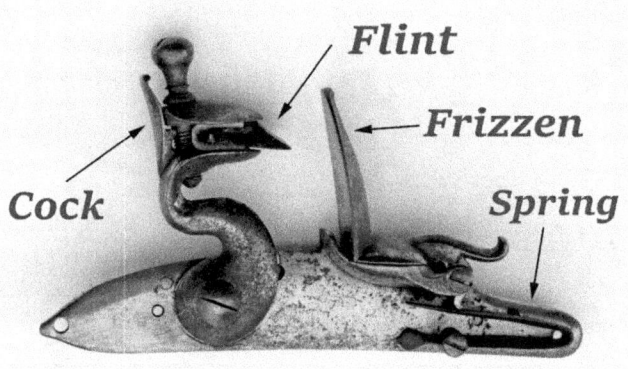

Figure 36: *Flintlock with Frizzen Closed*

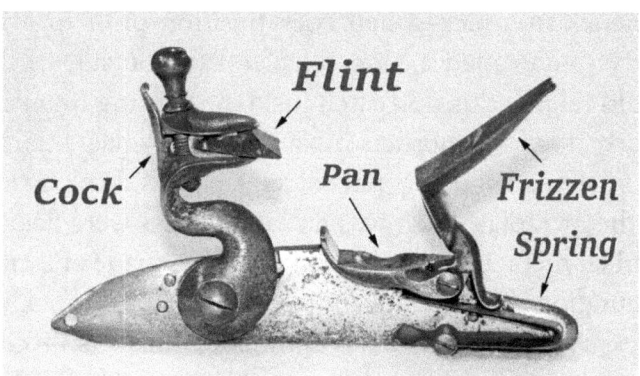

Figure 37: *Flintlock with Frizzen Open*

What modern people call a true "flintlock" was developed in France between 1600 and 1610 and was known as the "French Lock" in the 17th century. It was similar to the English lock but it used a vertical sear and a second notch cut into the tumbler of the cock within the lock mechanism itself which allowed the shooter to keep the cock in the safe locked position called "halfcocked." This development was far more reliable and easier to use than the doglock because the firelock was taken off "safe" simply by pulling the cock all the way back to full cock. Between 1610 and 1640 the flintlock was primarily used only in France, but after 1640 there is evidence that the French lock had gained popularity and was widely used throughout Europe, except for England and Spain. By the 1680s flintlocks were the primary military weapons of French and Dutch armies, completely replacing matchlocks. French lock pistols even began to circulate throughout the English colonies. By the late 17th century gun dealers in Port Royal, Jamaica were selling true flintlock pistols at a remarkably high rate as all records indicate. Those flintlock pistols were state of the art and were coveted by anyone who could afford them. That certainly included pirates. Also, after about 1650 French and Dutch vessels would have carried flintlocks of all types and English pirates could have traded for flintlocks or taken them by force.

1620-1840

Spanish patilla lock

Because of the poor quality of flint available in Spain, the Spanish had to design their own unique type of flintlock which they officially called a patilla lock, but the English, French, and Dutch called it the Spanish lock. It was in full use on muskets and pistols in Spain by 1620. The poor quality of flint required a lock with an exceptionally strong spring in order to get a hard enough strike to make a spark. The only way they could make a stronger spring was to make it larger. The spring of the patilla lock was too large to fit inside the wooden stock, so the entire spring mechanism was located on the outside of the lock plate. A small sear protrudes through the lock to hold the cock at the half cock position. The clamp of the cock is unusually large which allows the clamp to securely hold large and irregular pieces of flint. It also has a distinctive ring on top of the screw to help the shooter tightened the clamp. The frizzen is designed with a squared top. The Spanish seldom used any other type of firelock because their flints wouldn't work in them. This design, necessary for use with poorer quality of flints, was popular throughout the Mediterranean. Today, this type of lock is called a miquelet lock. However, that term was not applied until the Napoleonic wars of the early 19th century. The Spanish mounted fusiliers were known as the "Miquelets" and were armed with patilla lock weapons. British troops who were assisting them fight Napoleon began referring to their type of weapons as miquelet locks and the nickname caught on among the British. At no time during the golden age of piracy would anyone have referred to the patilla lock in that manner. The patilla lock continued in common use in Spain until 1825.

By 1650 the matchlock was totally outdated by the mainstream military units of Europe. However, many reserve units and military garrisons in the New World were issued the old surplus matchlocks. Throughout the 17th century colonists in the New World would have had a mix of matchlocks and more modern firelocks. The Spanish continued to arm their troops in the New World with matchlocks throughout the 17th century and even as late as 1720.

When Henry Morgan attacked the Spanish at Panama City in 1670 he had doglock muskets but the Spanish defenders only had matchlocks. Within the civilian population, many of those military surplus matchlocks were sold at cheap prices to commoners who couldn't afford guns in the past. Matchlocks may have been used by those who couldn't afford newer firelocks until the mid-18th century. Metal parts were reused over and over again, and many matchlocks could have been made over to become flintlocks at some point in time. Buccaneers of the mid-17th century used matchlocks almost exclusively. Between 1650 and 1690 matchlocks were gradually replaced by doglocks and flintlocks. Because pirates had access to all the newest technology through the rich prizes they took, matchlocks may have been discarded as newer ones were taken. However, matchlocks were recovered from the wreck of the Whydah, Sam Bellamy's pirate ship which sank in 1717, so we know that at least a few pirates continued to use matchlocks right up to the end of the golden age of piracy.

1690 was a turning point for military tactics and the development of flintlocks. By then the armies of Europe depended upon firelocks as their main battle force. Throughout most of the 17th century generals still considered swords and pikes as the main attack weapons and musketeers only played a supporting role, but with the new improvements in flintlock technology that tactic had changed. The pike was replaced by soldiers with muskets and bayonets. France was using flintlock muskets in all their regiments and their Marines carried a naval version with a shorter barrel. The French were far ahead of the English with their true flintlock muskets and socket bayonets. The Dutch were too, but the new King of England, William III, was also the King of Holland and Dutch military flintlocks were imported to England in limited quantities. In England doglocks were produced with a stock resembling the Dutch military flintlocks. That set the stage for the development of the Queen Anne muskets.

During the War of the Spanish Succession England was lagging far behind with firelock technology. The first upgrade was in 1707 when Great Britain, as it was then known, introduced its first official flintlock military musket with a completely round barrel. The doglock was out and a new flintlock with the goose neck cock was the prime weapon. The entire stock and barrel were painted black in many cases and the barrels were allowed to rust which was called "browning." In 1710 Queen Anne ordered a new design for British firelocks. The result was the Queen Anne musket and pistol. On the musket the lock was flat with a rounded frizzen. The butt plate was still flat and nailed to the stock, like older models, but the trigger

Flintlocks become useless if the powder in the pan becomes damp. This can easily happen at sea with spray coming over the rails. Matchlocks may have proven to be more reliable at sea as the burning match generally stays lit and the powder in the pan remains safely covered until ready to fire.

guard was curved for the first time. The stock had graceful lines, similar to the future Brown Bess, and the 46-inch barrel was stocked all the way to the end of the muzzle, requiring a plug bayonet. In 1714 improvements to the Queen Anne musket include a banana style rounded lock, side plate, and cast butt plate. Versions with a 40-inch barrel were used for naval and light infantry. However, doglocks were still being used. England still had thousands of doglocks in their warehouses, so they slapped them on cheaper versions of the Queen Anne musket and sent to the colonies. However, it is very doubtful that any pirates in the early 1700s ever had military flintlock muskets. They were only issued to soldiers and marines and weren't carried onboard merchant vessels. The only way a pirate could get one was to take a warship of the royal navy or to capture a military post, which was highly unlikely.

BLUNDERBUSSES

Used from the 1600s on, were common weapons used by law enforcement.

Blunderbusses are a combination of pistol and musket with a shoulder stock and a very wide barrel that fires nails, glass, rocks, or anything else you wanted to shoot. They are close range weapons designed for home defense and police actions much like shotguns are used today. Production of blunderbusses began in the mid-1600s with both doglock and flintlock versions. Made in many styles, they could have a flat iron or brass butt plate. The barrel could be made of brass or steel and have either a round or mixed octagonal to round barrel that could have been either flared or straight at the muzzle. In Great Britain the new style Queen Anne locks were used on blunderbusses after 1714. Blunderbusses were used just about everywhere and would be readily available to pirates. Further, a blunderbuss is an excellent choice for the close fighting of a boarding action and would have been a favorite among pirate crewmen right from the start.

Pistols

Pistols were produced along with muskets in all types of locks since the early 1500s. Early pistols were primarily marketed to the rich and were often extremely ornate. Most pistols of the late 17th and early 18th centuries were long and sleek, with a graceful bend in the stock to form the grip. Dutch pistols often had octagonal barrels at the breech and octagonal rammer pipes. Locks were flat; butt caps were molded brass, often beautifully carved. In the mid-17th century, the English made some rather heavy and bulky doglock pistols to be used by cavalry troops called "Dragoons." They were almost small muskets with barrels between 12 and 14 inches and in larger calibers between 56- and 68-caliber. That was necessary to fire longer distances in battle. To the end of the 19th century large pistols designed for use by cavalry were called dragoon pistols. Pirates would have used any variety of pistols. If it existed at the time, they could have had it.

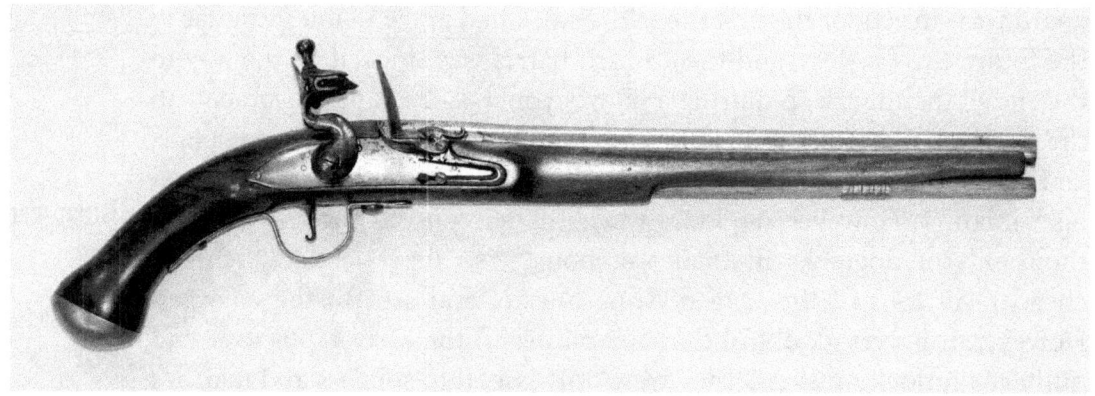

Figure 38: *1685 Flintlock Pistol*

One unique design in pistols was the Scottish metal pistol made since the mid-1600s. These smaller caliber pistols had doglocks and were actually made entirely of metal. The stock would have been either brass or steel and the end of the grip often had an unusual double butting. Frequently ornately decorated, they were fashionable among the Scottish nobility and gentry who seldom left Scotland. A few of those pistols may have found their way into the hands of a pirate, but they would have been rare in the Caribbean. Those pistols became illegal after the Battle of Culloden in 1745. Even so, Scottish military regiments serving in the British army continued to issue brass stocked pistols to their officers into the 19th century. Those later versions weren't as ornately decorated and had flintlocks instead of doglocks. Pirates certainly wouldn't have had the later versions; they weren't around until the 1750s.

> The Battle of Culloden in 1745 was the last battle of the third Jacobite revolution.

The Queen Anne pistol is among the favorite pistols for those portraying pirates in living history demonstrations. Actually, this is an excellent choice for pirates recreating the end of the golden age. Those pistols were made readily available to merchants as well as soldiers and would be onboard many English prize vessels.

The Queen Anne pistol is unique in that it has no stock on the barrel and no ramrod. That's because the barrel actually screwed off to load the powder charge and ball. When a projectile and powder are rammed down a barrel, they often don't seat properly, which affects range and accuracy. Screwing off the barrel allows the loader to manually seat the powder and projectile perfectly. Very few pistols were equipped with such a feature. It seemed like a good idea at the beginning but really didn't improve the firing all that much and touching a hot barrel to reload was impossible. All in all, it was a fine pistol for only one shot and would have been used by pirates any time after 1710. One curious note, however, is that modern reproductions of the Queen Anne pistol are made with the barrel molded to the rest of the pistol. They don't unscrew, so they must be loaded in the conventional manner.

Weapons of the American Revolutionary War aren't accurate. Since I am writing this book partly to assist those who wish to accurately portray pirates as living history interpreters, I must comment on the use of reproduction weapons from the Revolutionary War, 1775–1783. They are easy to obtain but totally wrong for the historical accuracy of the golden age of piracy. It's like using a modern M-16 when portraying a World War I soldier. The most common of all these weapons is the Brown Bess musket. I have spoken to some modern living history interpreters portraying pirates who say that the Brown Bess was introduced in 1721, just at the end of the golden age, and that it so closely resembles the Queen Anne musket, that no one will notice. This is not exactly true. Yes, the first prototype of the Brown Bess was introduced in 1721, but that version was vastly different from the model used in 1775. The 1721 Brown Bess had a round 46-inch barrel and a lock that was somewhat banana-shaped, like the Queen Anne. It also had iron furniture, no nose cap, and the ramrods were made of wood. That prototype was made in extremely limited numbers. The next version came in 1728 with brass furniture and the familiar swell in the stock just behind the tail pipe. However, the "true" first model long-land pattern didn't appear until 1733 and still had a long way to go to get to the 1768 model used during the Revolutionary War. Even if a modern pirate living history interpreter wants to pretend it's a Queen Anne musket, it's still incorrect for pirates. As stated above, those muskets were state of the art military weapons only issued to British soldiers serving in Europe. Pirates would rarely, if ever, have had access to them.

Pistols are another concern. After 1720, the elegant and graceful shape of pistols began to disappear. Stocks were heavier and more curved as they formed the grip. The weight of pistols increased while their overall length diminished. Grips also tended to become shorter. Even on dragoon models, the barrel lengths were shortened from the standard 12 to 14-inch established in 1710 to a noticeably shorter 9-inch barrel length by 1759. By the 1760s. The shape of the grip was moving toward a steeper angle from the barrel with all models. As the 19th century approached, the grip was almost at a right angle. Unfortunately, this is the type of reproduction pistol that one most often sees. They are "Rev War" pistols, not at all representative of the golden age of piracy.

Accoutrements are exceptionally important. No matter what type of firelock you carried or when you lived, you had to carry your bullets and black powder in something. The first method used was the bandolier, which is a thick leather belt worn over one shoulder with about 12 wooden

Most weapons commonly used by regular soldiers during the American Revolutionary War were made after 1762.

containers tied to it. Each container was filled with powder and one shot and could easily be opened to load the musket. The wooden containers were nicknamed apostles because there were 12 of them. Bandoliers were used right from the first and continued until the 1690s when all military tactics changed and soldiers needed more ammunition. In France, England, and the Dutch Republic, cartridge boxes began to be used, but the Spanish seem to have preferred the bandolier method. Pirates and other naval forces continued to use apostles on bandoliers well into the 18th century as apostles were fairly water proof and better suited to use on the Spanish Main. Powder flasks changed little from 1550 to 1700. They were generally triangular in shape. But the innovations of the 1690s saw the powder flask replaced by powder horns that were easier to use. Pre-rolled paper cartridges holding both powder and shot were used throughout the 17th and 18th centuries, but cartridge boxes really didn't come into use until the 1690s.

Cartridge Boxes

Cartridge boxes worn on the belt are known as "Belly Boxes" and were widely used throughout Europe by 1700. They were basic leather boxes with a flap. Some were dyed black, some brown, and some left natural in color. Some were small and square in appearance and others were more rectangular. Their design changed very little throughout the 18th century, so a "Rev War" belly box would be identical to one carried in 1715. Most pirates would have worn cartridge boxes while engaging the enemy. There are numerous contemporary accounts of pirates wearing cartridge boxes. It was even reported that during the battle of Ocracoke, Lt Maynard's sword was deflected by Blackbeard's cartridge box as Maynard made his thrust. Contemporary prints of Charles Vane, Bartholomew Roberts, and Blackbeard all show them wearing belly boxes.

Chapter 68
Tools of the Trade – Edge Weapons

There is no doubt that edge weapons were heavily relied upon as one of the pirates' main weapons. The stereotypical image of a pirate, always with some type of sword or cutlass by his side is actually correct. Every contemporary description of pirates mentions their edge weapons. Let's first, get the terminology correct. Modern people tend to generalize, referring to all large edge weapons as swords. They also categorize cutlasses as smaller swords with large brass knuckle guards specifically used by sailors or pirates. However, during the golden age of piracy, that was not the case. All edge weapons were classified as either swords or cutlasses. Swords had long straight blades that were double edged, in other words, sharpened on both sides. Cutlasses were any edge weapons with shorter blades, either straight or curved, that were sharpened on one edge only. That included a great variety of edge weapons that eventually evolved into specific types, such as the cavalry sabre. The cutlass' association as purely a naval weapon didn't come about until the 1740s.

In the Middle Ages, swords were primarily designed to strike not thrust at the enemy. They were fairly large, many requiring both hands to wield them. Beginning in the early 15th century as full body armor became common, the need for a thin thrusting sword developed to get in between the plates of armor. The weapon that developed was the rapier. With the rapier came a new type of fighting. Hacking away at the enemy was no longer effective and the art of fencing soon developed. By the turn of the 16th century, Italian fencing masters were renowned throughout Europe. The first published fencing book was *Opera Nova de Achille Marozzo Bolognese, Mastro Generale de L'Arte de l'Arm*, which translates as "a New Work in the Art of Arms by Achille Marozzo, the Fencing Master of Bolognese." That book had lots of woodcut illustrations on various positions and was

Early books on fencing date from 1536.

published in 1536. Next came *Trattato de Scienza d' Arme e un Dialogo in Detta Material* or "Treaty on the Science of Arms" by Camillo Agrippa, published in 1553. Agrippa gave advice on dueling with sword and dagger as well as wrestling holds against a dagger if you are unarmed. A great many more people were experienced in the art of fencing than one might think. In the late 17th century, the French privateer Rene Duguay-Trouin actually hired a fencing master to stay onboard with his crew and train them in the use of fencing. Dueling was a common way to settle an argument among gentlemen, noblemen, and military officers. As we can deduce for the Pirates' Articles, a great many pirates dueled as well. And dueling wasn't entirely restricted to men. In the 1670s a Parris born actress named La Maupin was taught fencing by her lover, a fencing master named Sesane. She killed three men in a duel after quarreling with them in a bar.

Modern people often think of fencing in terms of the late 18th and 19th centuries, when few people carried swords and fencing seemed to be reserved for military officers and noblemen. But that wasn't true during the 17th and early 18th centuries. Most people, even commoners, carried an edge weapon of some kind, and knowing how to use it was vital for self-protection. It's kind of like the old American Wild West. In the frontier states of North America in the late 19th century it was very common to see side arms being worn by just about everyone and most of them were fairly proficient with their use. There were experts of course, the proverbial gunfighters for example, but even store keepers and cowboys could hit a troublesome coyote or rattlesnake. By the early 20th century that had changed and it was uncommon to see people wearing side arms. In Europe and the colonies of the Americas in the 17th century noblemen and military officers all would have worn some type of sword, most likely a rapier before 1680 and a small sword after. Many commoners would have carried some sort of cutlass or large knife for protection while hunting or against robbers. This would have been even more prevalent in the colonies where it was normal for commoners to hunt for survival.

Rapiers

The rapier developed by 1490 as a slender and more manageable version of the one-handed fighting sword of the late 15th century. By 1520 the rapier was well-established as the weapon of choice with a slender 45" long double-edged blade that was diamond shaped for strength. By the middle of 15th century hilts with knuckle guards and forefinger rings were added and by 1575 the swept hilt rapier was fully developed and popular. That was the most popular sword among the rich and at court. The cup hilt rapier developed around 1610 and was common by 1620. That is the type of sword most associated with the Three Musketeers.

Spanish Bilbos, 1690

Rapiers were commonly used in the Thirty Years' War. Another type of cup hilt rapier was the Pappenheimer type around 1620. That type was very popular in England through the 1680s. Many rapiers of that period were too finely made for use in combat and were "simply another form of jewelry to be worn against dark costume." A study of portraits indicates that rapiers were worn with daggers until 1635. Cup hilt rapiers reached its apogee in Spain and were worn in Spain until the end of the 18th century. A crude version of the cup hilt rapier was cheaply made for use by the military. This sword was called the "Spanish Bilbo" and had a plain solid shell guard. The Bilbo became standard military issue among Spanish officers in the late 17th century and throughout the entire 18th century. They were still in use during the Napoleonic wars. Buccaneers of the mid to late 17th century would have used rapiers of all types. They certainly would be readily available and preferable to those that knew the art of fencing. By the end of the 17th century Spanish Bilbos flooded the Caribbean and several noted authors commented that the Spanish Bilbo was a favorite among the Caribbean pirates. William Dampier noted that after being shipwrecked Captain Shelvocke traded a silver ladle for a dozen Spanish rapiers.

After about 1680 the rapier was being replaced by the small sword, which became the dominant sword used by gentlemen and military officers alike for the next 100 years. With the refinement of fencing techniques and dueling becoming common, a more effective weapon was needed and by 1660 the small sword was in full use. After 1700 most rapiers would have been remade into small swords or even something else and it would have been very uncommon for a pirate of that era to have a rapier. Small swords really weren't that small, they were just smaller than rapiers. With a straight double-edged blade that was about 36 inches, it was easier to wield. This made the small sword ideal for fencing. The hilt had a double shelled shape and included a knucklebow. By 1680 small swords became the most fashionable type of sword for both civilian and military use. Military versions

SMALL SWORDS, 1680

They really weren't that small, they were just smaller than rapiers. They were the most commonly used sword throughout the 18th century.

of small swords from 1680–1700 were very plain with cast brass hilts. Contemporary prints from the first half of the 18th century which are still in existence show civilians, both upper and middle class, wearing small swords in taverns, at dances, and just about everywhere. There is one print that dates to 1710 that shows a man wearing a small sword in a dress maker's shop while purchasing a hoop for a woman's dress, presumably his wife. Small swords would have begun to replace rapiers onboard pirate vessels in the late 17th century and definitely would have been used by pirates all through the 18th century. Contemporary drawings of many pirates, like the prints of Edward England and Bartholomew Roberts, show many of them wearing small swords. Once again, Sam Bellamy's 1717 pirate ship Whydah provides us with valuable information about the weapons pirates used as many small sword hilts were recovered at the wreck site.

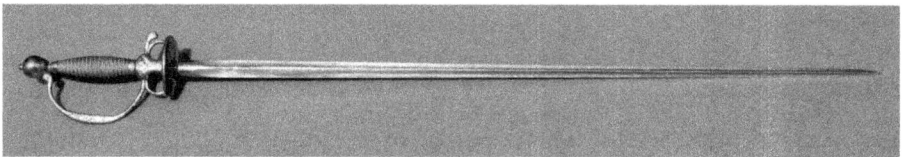

Figure 39: *1680 Small Sword*

Broadswords, 1600

When rapiers became the most common sword carried in Europe in the early 16th century, the broadsword didn't disappear, it just continued to develop. The double-edged blade remained fairly unchanged. At a length of between 31 to 40 inches, it was thick and heavy. Not practical for dueling, it was still a great weapon to use for hacking at the enemy, which made it an ideal cavalry weapon. The improvement to the broadsword was in the design of the hilt. In the early 1500s the hilt developed into a basket hilt to give the hand better protection. Basket hilt broadswords became very popular in Scotland and England and many were taken to America by English troops. Basket hilts from the 17th century have been found by archaeologists at Jamestown, Virginia, the English capital in North America from 1607 to 1698. Broadswords with pierced steel hilts were widely used by English cavalry and were commonly used during the English Civil War. In the 1650s a variation with a long single edged blade for cutting and thrusting was developed especially for cavalry use. Since the English soldiers who conquered and settled Jamaica in 1655 were straight from the English Civil War, the weapons they brought to the Caribbean would have included a great many basket hilt broadswords. Of the buccaneers who accompanied Henry Morgan, many would have carried broadswords. Scottish basket hilt broadswords were numerous and the primary sword carried by Scotsmen throughout the 18th century. Many Scotsmen fled to

America in 1715 after the second Jacobite uprising and they would have brought the basket hilt broadswords with them. The *Boston News Letter* reported that Blackbeard was killed by a sailor of the Royal Navy with a basket hilt broadsword.

Short, curved, heavy, single edged weapons were common among Turkish armies fighting in Eastern Europe. European armies fighting the Turks copied this design from the early 17th century on. They were used extensively in the Thirty Years' War, especially by troops with muskets who needed a secondary defense weapon. As stated above, during the time of the golden age of piracy, a cutlass was a generic term that described any single edged weapon with a shorter blade; the most common of these were called hangers.

Scottish basket hilt broadswords are called claymores.

Cutlasses

Early hangers had curved blades like the Turkish weapons they copied, but by the mid-17th and 18th centuries, the blades were mostly straight or had only a very slight curve. A few hangers had small saw edges on back of the blade, but this was very rare. The hilts came in a very large variety of shapes and styles. Some hangers had a curved crossguard without knucklebow like the hanger shown in the illustration of Blackbeard in Charles Johnson's 1724 publication. Some hangers even had basket hilts and may have actually been broadswords that had their blades reduced in size. Fighting with a hanger was a little different than fencing with a rapier or small sword. Generally, the hanger was a weapon designed for hacking and thrusting, but a certain amount of fencing wasn't out of the question. Hangers were extensively carried throughout Europe in the 17th century by civilians on a day to day basis as shown by newspaper ads of the 1670s referencing lost hangers which were stolen or left behind in taverns. By 1700 hangers were being issued to English infantry troops and were by far the most common edge weapon carried on vessels. That English pattern had a brass heart shaped guard with a curved knucklebow. Hangers of any

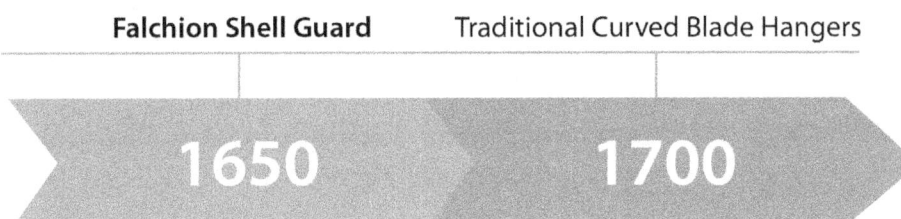

and all types would have been the predominant edge weapon carried by pirates of the 18th century.

Falchion

A falchion is a single edged weapon with a heavy, short, curved blade resembling a machete. It is sometimes called a back sword. Falchions came in a large variety of styles and hilts. Some were made with basket hilts, some with a simple recurved crossguard, and even others with a large scallop shell guard. They differ from hangers only by the thickness of the blade. Falchions were popular on shipboard in the second half of the 17th century and were used extensively by the Venetian fleet. In 1676 a falchion with a shell guard was taken from a Turkish admiral by Count Adler and given to King Christian V of Denmark. Also, the famous buccaneer Rock Brasiliano is shown holding a shell guard falchion in an illustration in the 1684 publication, *Buccaneers of America*. In the first half of the 18th century the falchion's machete like blade became thinner, more closely resembling the blade of a hanger. Sometimes the tip of the blade was a little wider than the blade at the forte to give the weapon more weight when hacking at an opponent. In the early 1700s the term "cutlass" was used to refer to hangers and a variety of other smaller single edged weapons, but by the 1740s the term cutlass became associated exclusively with this thick bladed and curved weapon that developed from the falchion and used primarily on vessels at sea. In 1750; the "naval cutlass" was a weapon unto itself and was specifically designed and issued to sailors of the British Royal Navy.

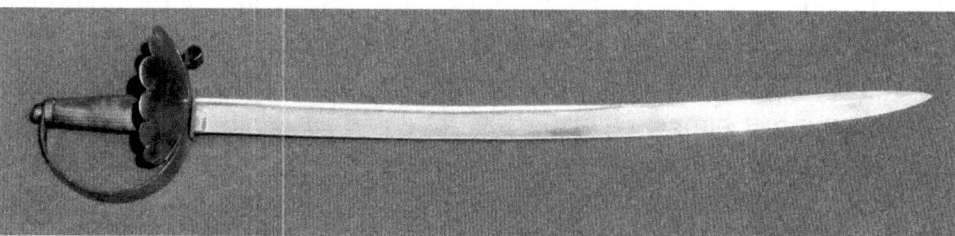

Figure 40: *Late 17th Century Shell Guard Cutlass*

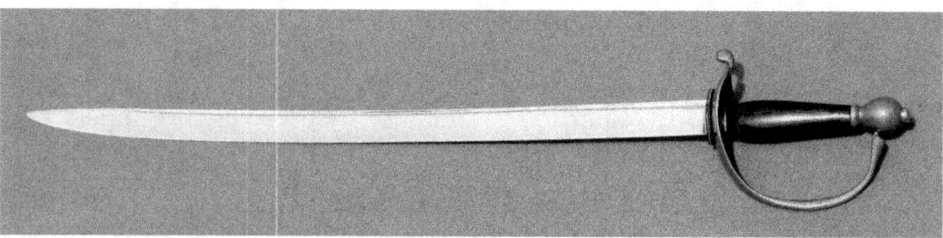

Figure 41: *Early 18th Century English Hanger*

Oriental Edge Weapons could have been used. Since pirates took prizes from all over the world, it isn't inconceivable that a few may have kept edge weapons from captured prizes belonging to Arabs or Indian Moghuls. Pirates raided in the Philippines as well as Sumatra. There are thousands of varieties of edge weapons from the Pacific and Indian Oceans as well as the West Coast of Africa that could have been used by pirates.

As with firelocks, many modern living history portrayers who want to recreate pirates from the golden age choose to use weapons that were developed far past the 1720s. Because the small sword continued to develop throughout the 18th century, many small swords are not correct for the golden age of piracy. The two main changes were to the knucklebow and the blade. Knucklebows were straight along the bottom from 1660 until the mid-1720s when they became more rounded. Also, earlier small swords that are correct for the golden age of piracy have evenly shaped blades, but throughout the 1700s the blades changed to be used solely for thrusting, with a sharp taper making them narrower toward the tip, although they remained wide at the forte for strength while parrying. That type of small sword, similar to the one carried by George Washington, would be wrong for the time period.

Later Period Edge Weapons

Just like small swords, hangers continued to be made throughout the 18th century. After the 1730s hangers were generally cheaper in construction with cheaply fashioned iron or cast brass hilts and wood grips. By 1742 cheaply made military hangers with all cast brass grips and hilts were being issued to infantry troops of most European countries. Also, military hangers of this later period quite often had an asymmetrical bar type hilt, covering the right side of the hand only, which allowed the hanger to be comfortably worn on a belt along with a bayonet. That type of hilt didn't exist before about 1750. Those types of hangers are not correct for the golden age. The traditional naval cutlass is also incorrect. In the 1730s what most people think of the naval cutlass gradually developed from the falchion. The guards were very cheaply made and were simply part of the knucklebow, either swelling to a diamond shape or made completely round. The diamond shape eventually became the officially issued naval cutlass of the U. S. and British navies of the late 18th century. However, the most historically inaccurate edge weapon for the golden age is the brass hilted naval cutlass sold by many modern vendors. That weapon has a thick blade, like the original falchion, but a large brass knuckle guard that covers three quarters of the hand. That cutlass is actually a reproduction of the 1860 U. S. model Naval Cutlass used during the American Civil War.

The 1860 U. S. Naval Cutlass is among the most commonly carried weapon by modern pirate reenactors and enthusiasts.

Baldrics were commonly used by pirates. A pirate wearing a thick leather baldric holding an edge weapon is the classical image one thinks of. That image is absolutely correct. A baldric is a leather sash that goes over one shoulder and holds a sword or hanger on the side of the user opposite to their dominant hand. For example, right-handed users will wear their weapons on their left sides. Throughout the 17th century, and in the first half of the 18th century, wearing a baldric as a means to carry one's weapon was common among military officers, soldiers of fortune, gentlemen, and pirates alike. A 1672 print from *les Travaux de Mars* shows three buccaneers, two carrying matchlocks and one with a pike, and all three are wearing bandoliers with powder apostles, and baldrics holding small swords. Furthermore, almost every contemporary print of pirates from the early 18th century shows them wearing baldrics. Some fancier baldrics were covered with finely decorated cloth or trimmed with gold bradding. Just about any type of design was used. Swords were also worn on belts; it was totally a matter of personal preference. Snelgrave's 1719 eyewitness account describes one pirate as "*a tall man, with four Pistols in his Girdle and a broad Sword in his hand.*" The "girdle" means a belt. Both are correct for the time period, but just after the golden age ended, the use of baldrics to carry swords began to go out of fashion and was all but gone by 1750, except in a few remote places like Scotland.

Knives

Of course, every pirate would have a knife as would most sailors. There are far too many varieties of knives to go into any great detail here. Basically, any type of knife, dirk, stiletto, or dagger that existed during the golden age may have been used by a pirate. Nevertheless, there is one particular kind of knife that was unique to seamen and common among sailors in the late 17th and 18th centuries. Since pirates had to sail their vessels too when they weren't taking vessels or in port, they had to do all the things aboard ship that other sailors did. What makes this knife unique is the design of the blade. Most knives have one edge that is straight and one curved. The curved edge is normally the one that is sharpened. On nautical knives, it's the straight edge that is sharpened while the curved edge has a flat surface. This specific design is very effective in cutting lines or ropes, which is a primary task of all sailors. Kind of like a paper cutter, the sailor can apply pressure on the flat edge and slice the rope.

Chapter 69
Tools of the Trade—Navigation

Very few pirates knew how to navigate at sea. First, they had to be able to read and do mathematics, which eliminated most of them right off the bat. Those who could read and calculate still had to learn how to use the navigational tools, read charts, and plot courses. Any pirate who learned to navigate would be assured a position among the leadership of the vessel, and probably even be elected captain. When Captain Davis was killed one of the reasons that John Roberts was elected captain, even after only being aboard a short while, was that he could navigate.

By the 17th century nautical navigation had been perfected to the point where a skilled navigator could accurately plot the ship's position anywhere in the world. One of the most important navigational tools is the magnetic box compass. Invented in China over 2,000 years ago. The magnetic box compass was introduced to European navigators in the 12th century and every vessel would have had one by the 16th century. The compass is divided into four quadrants and each quadrant is divided into eight points, for a total of 32 points. Each point had a name based upon direction. Beginning with due north and moving toward the east, the points would be north (N), north by east (NbE), north north east (NNE), north east by north (NEbN), north east (NE), north east by east (NEbE), east north east (ENE), east by north (EbN), and finally east (E). North would be the first point and east would be the ninth. Following this same pattern, all 32 points can be named with due south as point 17 and due west as point 25.

Every sailor would know these points and would use them to identify landmarks and other ships. For example, "I spotted a ship two points off the starboard bow." For the sake of this example, let's assume that the sailor's own ship was traveling north east (NE). Two points off the starboard bow would be two points to the right, meaning that the sailor spotted the other ship in the compass direction of east north east (ENE). The ship's compass was located where the helmsman could easily read it in order for him to keep the vessel on course.

Chip Log

To measure the speed of the vessel, a chip log was used. Introduced in the late 16th century, a chip log was a quarter circle of wood attached to a long rope or line on a reel with knots tied every 47 feet 3 inches. The chip log was tossed overboard and as the vessel sailed along, the chip log trailed behind and the knots were counted as the line unreeled. This would be timed with a 14 second or 28 second hour glass. If one knot went out in 28 seconds, the ship was going 1 nautical mile per hour, or one "naught." If three knots were counted in 28 seconds, the ship was traveling at three naughts.

Latitude could be accurately determined using the stars, but longitude requires knowing precisely how far you traveled and what the exact time is. This explains why maps of the period look as if they are stretched out (correct latitudes but incorrect longitudes).

All movement such as course and speed of the vessel would have to be accurately recorded on a traverse board. This is a wooden board with a compass rose showing all the points of the compass. There is a complicated series of holes drilled into the compass as well as another set of holes arranged in rows at the bottom. A set of pegs are attached to the board with strings. By placing these pegs in the proper holes every half hour, the navigator can keep track of the ship's movements. Placing the pegs in the proper holes was the responsibility of any sailor assigned to that watch. The navigator would check the traverse board every four hours and make notes in a logbook.

Even with accurate information recorded on the traverse board, the ship's position had to be checked often. Due to the rotation of the earth, longitude can only be accurately measured if the navigator knows the exact time. Since accurate chronometers weren't invented until the 19th century, a navigator in the golden age could only estimate the longitude based upon the information recorded off the traverse board. Latitude was another issue. The navigator could accurately determine how far north or south a ship was by measuring the angle of the sun or North Star above the horizon. This was called celestial navigation and the first instrument used to measure the ship's position relevant to the North Star was the quadrant. First invented around 1460 the quadrant was a quarter circle of wood with degreed marked along the edge. A line with a plumb was attached to get an accurate reading of the angle of the North Star. The astrolabe was an improved version of the quadrant. Introduced in 1481, it was a metal disc with moveable arms and sights.

Cross Staff

Another device was the cross staff. Invented in 1515, this is a wooded staff with a sliding crosspiece. The navigator aims the staff at the sun and moves the cross piece until one end lines up with the horizon. This gives the navigator the angle and therefore the exact position north and south. The problem with the cross staff is that the navigator has to look directly into the sun. John Davis improved the cross staff in 1594 and published his invention in the "Seaman's Secrets" published in 1595. His invention is called the back staff and works on the same principle except the navigator is facing away from the sun and watching its shadow. More modern navigational tools weren't developed until after the golden age of piracy. The octant wasn't used until 1731 and the sextant wasn't invented until 1757.

Chapter 70
The Black Flag of Death's Head

For centuries, flags have been used by the militarily on land and by merchant and naval vessels at sea to signal many things. Flags are still used in the exact same manner today. For example, everyone knows that a white flag means surrender. A yellow flag means sickness, whether on a ship at sea, in a town or port, or on a wagon train heading across the Rocky Mountains. Black flags mean death. In the 17th century, Europe was engaged in the largest and most brutal war it had known, the Thirty Years' War. Sometimes, armies would attack with no offer of quarter. In other words, no prisoners were taken, everyone would be killed. Normally, the weaker side would be given two options before the attack, they could either surrender unconditionally without a fight or engage in battle and the possibility of death with no quarter given if they lost. This was a commonly used tactic. The red flag was the European signal which meant surrender now or receive no quarter.

In the 17th century Caribbean privateers would always prefer to take a prize vessel without a fight. Since many of those privateers were ex-soldiers straight from the Thirty Years' War, it was not surprising that they generally hoisted a red flag when attacking a prize ship in order to entice the crew into surrender. To put it simply, a red flag meant "Heave to and surrender now or we shall kill everyone on board." In reality, privateers seldom killed anyone, even if they resisted, but the threat was still there all the same. At some point, a French privateer, who shall remain unknown to history, began calling the red flag the "Joli Rouge," which is French for "Happy Red." A French captain might have ordered, "Hoist the happy red if you please." Of course, he would have said that in French. The name caught on and soon the English were calling it the "Jolly Roger."

But this was still just a plain red flag with no other markings, identical to the red flags used by all European armies and navies. They were not unique

MEANINGS OF FLAGS

White Flag—Surrender

Red Flag—Prepare for Battle or No Quarter Given

Black Flag—Death

Yellow Flag—Sickness or Quarantine

to privateers or pirates at all until Henry Every came along. No one can be certain, but it is believed that Henry Every wanted to distinguish himself and added a white skull and cross bones to his red flag in 1694. His partner, Thomas Tew added a white arm wielding a sword to his red flag. At some point, the red colored background of those flags was changed to black, meaning the flag of death. Perhaps Every thought black was more menacing. Or, perhaps Every thought that since they weren't actually going to kill everyone after capture, even if they resisted, the significance of the red flag was inappropriate. This is of course guesswork. Henry Every's flag was the first true pirate flag and his partner, Thomas Tew, had the second.

Figure 42: *Henry Every Flag*

Figure 43: *Thomas Tew Flag*

The trend rapidly caught on and by the early 1700s just about all pirates had their own unique flags, as if to distinguish themselves from anyone else. Those flags were black with white patterns of bones, skulls, swords, or many other more horrifying symbols.

Why would a pirate want to distinguish himself? The answer is to establish a reputation. A pirate with a fierce reputation had a much easier time getting prize ships to surrender peacefully than some unknown pirate that nobody feared. It's the same in any business today. People buy products from well-known companies with big reputations; they seldom try new products from some unknown company. That analogy is a bit strange, but very sound. Consider the black flag as effective marketing.

There are many references in the historic record of pirates flying their own unique flags, quite often referred to as "Death's Head." The *Boston News-Letter* dated June 9 to June 16, 1718 describes Blackbeard's capture of the *Protestant Caesar* and mentions that the flags he used were "Black Flags and Deaths Heads in them and . . . Bloody Flags." The "Black Flag and Deaths Heads" refers to some sort of typical pirate flag. and the "Bloody Flags" refers to a plain red flag, which was used by all pirates in the seventeenth century as the signal for no quarter given. The term "black flag with deaths head" is in reference to some sort of skull and crossbones, with the bones placed either beneath the skull or behind it. The sight of such flags struck fear into the hearts of the passengers and crew of a potential prize vessel and generally resulted in a quick surrender.

Another account in The *Boston News-Letter,* issued in August of 1717, reads, ". . . the Snow Restoration . . . was taken by 2 Pirate Sloops . . .who had in his Flag a Death's Head and an Hour Glass, the other. . .who had in his Flag a Dart and Bleeding Heart . . ." This specific flag is collaborated in a report dated January 3, 1718 made by Captain Jean Dubois, whose ship was attacked and taken by two pirate sloops. Dubois wrote that the pirate sloops "hoisted each of them a black flag with a figure of death holding in one hand a dart and in the other an hourglass at the top of their great mast with another flag of the same color having a figure of a man who holds another under his feet that crosses his throat." The examples shown here are believed to have been the flags used by the pyrates named. In some cases, the flags shown are based upon the historical record, while in other cases, the flags shown seem to have been attributed to the pirates sometime in the late 20th century.

A Pirate's Life in the Golden Age of Piracy

Figure 44: *Rackham's Flag*

Figure 45: *Edward England Flag*

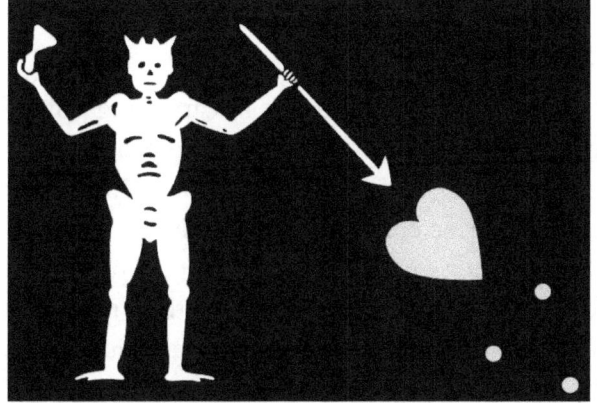

Figure 46: *Blackbeard's Flag*

Figure 47: *Stede Bonnet Flag*

Figure 48: *Roberts, First Flag*

Figure 49: *Kennedy Flag*

Chapter 71
Tactics

Pirates used an almost endless variety of methods in capturing potential prize vessels. Intimidation played a large role in the process. The most successful pirates hardly ever had to actually fight anyone, they relied on intimidation to scare the prize crew into submission. The crews of merchant vessels tended to be rather small. They were out for profit and didn't want to pay wages for anyone they didn't need, so they generally only carried enough men onboard to operate the vessel. That could be as few as six crewmen for a sloop. Even large merchant ships only needed about 25 crewmen to properly handle the ship and they often only carried that many crewmen. Even if the merchant ship had guns onboard, a crew of that size wouldn't be able to sail the ship and fire the guns at the same time. Other merchant ships and slave ships carried bigger crews, especially if they were sailing in waters frequented by pirates. Captain Snelgrave's English slave galley, *Bird*, carried 16 guns and a crew of 45. Not that it did him any good, at the first sign of pirates, his entire crew surrendered.

As for the pirates, even small pirate sloops carried a pirate crew of 70 as we have seen in the first description of Edward Teach, "a sloop 6 gunns and about 70 men." The larger vessels carried well over 300 pirates. That gave them the tremendous advantage of numbers. The overwhelming numbers usually convinced the captains of merchant vessels that their crews would have no chance in a fight, so they generally surrendered immediately. To help with the intimidation, pirates looked as fierce as possible, with lots of weapons about their bodies. They also dressed to impress. Blackbeard put slow burning matches in his beard, giving him a mysterious and terrifying look. Black Bart Roberts always dressed in the fanciest and most elaborate clothing available, giving him a dominating and commanding presence.

Amphibious warfare was perfected by the Vikings in the 9th century.

Deception also played a role in pirate tactics. If a pirate didn't have the numerical advantage, they had to trick the prize crew into thinking they did. Howell Davis forced the prize crew of one ship to act like pirates in order to fool the captain and crew of a second prize ship into thinking the pirates had two vessels. Also, deception was vital in helping the pirate vessels get close to the prize vessels. A pirate vessel had to be close enough for the prize crew to see everyone on board in order for the intimidation part to work. And sometimes deception was used to capture a prize vessel's captain. Blackbeard pretended to be a merchant vessel and invited the captain of another merchant vessel onboard for a chat. No doubt he intended to hold him hostage and take the other ship, but unfortunately someone in Blackbeard's crew left his pirate flag flying, and the merchant captain saw it before he boarded.

Land Attacks

As we have seen from the histories of Christopher Myngs and his protégé Henry Morgan, the English buccaneers introduced a new type of privateer tactic in the Caribbean. From 1657 to 1670 the buccaneers from Port Royal practiced amphibious warfare, attacking Spanish cities from the land. Others copied those tactics throughout the rest of the 17th century, but none were as successful as Henry Morgan. After 1660 most buccaneer crews were primarily made up of ex-soldiers from Europe who were well-trained in European siege tactics. The sailors and landsmen who accompanied them were easily trained in tactics and the proper use of weapons. The large buccaneer raids were always commanded by one captain who would recruit other captains and crews prior to the raid and stop on some secluded island to plan and coordinate the assault. At that meeting contracts would be drawn up to outline the operations as well as sub contracts to specify all divisions of spoils. Captains would vote on the details of the contract and even the target. That worked well, unless the buccaneers were working with regular naval forces as in the 1697 raid on Cartagena, which resulted in the buccaneers not receiving the share they expected.

Buccaneer attacks of cities and ports during that period followed an established pattern. The ships would be anchored nearby and the buccaneers would proceed to the city, either marching overland in military formations with cavalry in support or they would advance up river in small boats. Most of the time the buccaneer force that attempted an attacked of a city consisted of between 500 and 1,500 men. To give them as much advantage as possible, the attacks were timed so that the buccaneers usually arrived at dawn and on either a Sunday or a festival day. Often, the buccaneers would first send a ransom demand to the government, threatening to destroy a city if payment wasn't made. If the government refused to pay the ransom the troops would assault the city in formations and fire in well-disciplined ranks following well-established 17th century military protocol for an assault of a fortified position.

In the assault of Panama in 1670 Exquemelin describes Henry Morgan's buccaneers advancing "with drums beating and colors flying" resembling a body of regular European troops rather than a group of pirates. They fired their weapons in ranks with concentrated fire on specific enemy positions. Buccaneers carried as many weapons as they could. In 1683 Grammont ordered his buccaneers to bring as many firearms as they could carry on their attack on Vera Cruz. "They went into the attack with 3 or more muskets, pistols, or blunderbusses each." They fired in ranks by volley. The Spanish were continually defeated by buccaneers due to lack of training and insufficient numbers. By the 18th century large land attacks were history. The privateers and pirates of the 18th century primarily took prizes at sea. There were still a few pirates who attacked and captured ports, like Howell Davis and Batt. Roberts, but they took those ports through deception followed by swift landing party raids or through intimidation. The large privateer infantry raids of the 17th century disappeared by 1700.

Firing in volley (all soldiers firing at once on command) was the most effective use for muskets in battle. Hundreds of bullets hurling into the enemy's line all at once had a tremendous effect.

Sea Attacks

Taking a vessel was a different matter. It was simple for pirates on shore to take a vessel tied to the dock. Many pirates found themselves ashore with no vessel. Perhaps they were just getting started or perhaps they lost their vessel at sea. In some cases, pirates crossed the Isthmus of Panama on foot and planned on taking a vessel on the Pacific side. Or, they may have just seen a vessel in port that they wanted. While in port most vessels only kept a few crewmembers onboard to watch the vessel. All the pirates had to do was to board the vessel and overpower the crewmembers, then set out to sea. Pirates could also board a vessel under false pretenses, pretending to be merchants wanting to do business. Once alone with the captain in his cabin, the pirates could pull out their weapons and take him hostage, then take the entire ship. If the ship was anchored off shore, pirates could anchor nearby and wait for nightfall. Under the cover of darkness, they could row over to the ship in small boats, climb over the rails, and take the prize completely unaware. Captain Thomas Cocklyn used that tactic to take the English slave galley, *Bird*, off the north coast of Africa in April 1719. But taking vessels that were under sail at sea required special tactics.

To take a vessel at sea the pirate vessel would first have to get close enough to the prize vessel to threaten a boarding action. For those unfamiliar with the term, "boarding action," this is when the crew of one vessel jumps over onto the second vessel. Pirates would always want to conceal their true identity as long as possible and get as close as they could before the prize vessel realized what was about to happen. Sometimes that was accomplished by simply flying a flag that was friendly to the potential prize vessel. In all actuality, the royal navies of all the European nations routinely used this tactic to approach an enemy vessel. In the 17th and 18th centuries, it wasn't considered dishonest at all.

Just before they opened fire, they would raise their own flag. Firing on an enemy without your own flag flying was considered disreputable. For pirates, at some point, the prize vessel would inevitably discover the true purpose of the pirates and begin to "make a run" or sail away as fast as possible. At this point, the "Jolly Roger" would go up as a warning for the vessel to "heave to" and stop or risk total destruction. Raising the flag clearly signaled the intent of the pirates to take the vessel. Sometimes this was enough and the vessel would submit.

To overtake a vessel at sea, it was always best to have the "weather gage." This is a nautical term that means your vessel is up wind of the other vessel. As the pursuing vessel with the weather gage comes close to a second, the first vessel blocks the wind and the second vessel literally has the wind taken out of her sails. The vessel loses some speed and even maneuverability. At this point, the vessel with the weather gage has total control over the engagement. The captain can choose to maneuver to fire a broadside or can easily come along side or even pass the second vessel.

If the potential prize vessel decided to try to outrun a pursuing pirate vessel, the pirates would have to catch the prize before they could board. If the vessels were in range, a few warning shots fired across the bow of a fleeing vessel sometimes made the victims change their minds and give up. But if the prize vessel was still running, the pirates would have to rapidly close the distance between the two vessels. Speed was vital to pirate vessels which is why they are lightened significantly by removing the superstructure. While being chased the prize vessel would attempt to out sail the pirates and keep the weather gage while the pirates were doing the exact same thing. This chase could last anywhere from a few minutes to a few days depending on the distance between the two vessels and the difference between their speeds. In any case, the faster vessel usually won.

The last chance for the prize vessel to surrender without a fight was when the pirate vessel came near enough for the pirates to begin their boarding action. That was the moment of truth. A well-armed pirate vessel with lots of pirates on board waving weapons was a terrifying sight and most prize vessels would submit to capture by that time. But if the prize vessel still intended to fight, they would fire their guns in a broadside. If the

WEATHER GAGE

The vessel that has the weather gage has an enormous advantage over the other vessel because the vessel with the weather gage controls the positioning of the vessels and can shoot when and where they choose.

prize vessel had big enough guns to shoot through the pirate vessel's bulkheads, they might shoot for the waterline and attempt to sink the pirates. If not, they would shoot for the masts and rigging in hopes of disabling the pirates and getting away. The pirates would naturally have to return broadsides until the prize surrendered. Pirates had to be careful not to sink the prize vessel with their return fire. The safest way to fire at a prize vessel without danger of sinking it is to shoot at the masts and rigging with bar shot or chain shot in order to disable the vessel or shoot at the crew with grape shot on deck. An example of a prize crew fighting a pirate vessel with broadsides can be found in the chapter on Edward England. If the prize crew refused to surrender and continued to fight, the pirates would have to eventually begin boarding action or break contact.

Boarders Away

In order to begin a boarding action, the two vessels first had to be very close. This was usually accomplished either by using grappling hooks and ropes to pull the two vessels together or by simply ramming the second vessel. Once the two vessels were side by side, the attacking crew would attempt to "clear the deck," which means to kill as many people on the upper deck as possible. Small arms and small caliber swivel guns firing grape shot were most commonly used. Sometimes men were positioned up in the rigging to shoot down at the men below. They also threw grenades. Grenades were common during that era and were used by most pirates during boarding action. Grenades exploding on the deck of a vessel caused many casualties and created a great deal of confusion—which is exactly what the boarders wanted. We must remember that the defenders were normally using the same weapons and tactics in their defense. After a few volleys of small arms fire and a few grenades had been tossed, the attackers would swiftly move onto the defending vessel by jumping between the two vessels or by swinging over using lines from the rigging. If the prize vessel's crew felt that they were stronger than the pirates, they may have actually boarded the pirate vessel first. This was exceptionally rare, but it did happen. Once the boarding action began, the battle shifted to hand-to-hand combat.

If the attackers had pistols, they would carry them during boarding and fire them at close range as soon as they reached the other vessel. Once fired, they would often be tossed aside so they could draw an edge weapon. Why would the pistols be tossed away? Pistols of the 17th and 18th century couldn't be reloaded during hand-to-hand combat due to the length of time it took and in the fast-moving environment of hand-to-hand fighting. However, since one might not have the time to place a pair of pistols back through a belt or sash during battle, the question remains, what became of the pistols when they threw them away? Sam Bellamy's crew solved that problem. It is very interesting to note that some of the pistols recovered on the wreck of the *Whydah* off Cape Cod had silk ribbons tied between them. This indicates that the pirates could have worn pistols around their necks, allowing them to drop their pistols after firing without losing them. Sometimes, pirates did have time to put their pistols back in their belts or on the bandoliers. Captain Snelgrave's 1719 eyewitness account describes one pirate who attempted to kill him after his ship was captured saying, ". . . his Pistols, that hung from his Girdle, were all discharged; otherwise he doubtless would have shot me." Once the pistols were fired, some sort of edge weapon would be drawn.

Cutlasses were by far the most common weapon used by pirates and privateers of the golden age. As discussed earlier, the term "cutlass" during that era referred to any blade that was sharpened on one side only. Cutlasses are very effective at slashing and hacking, which makes them ideal weapons for those who are unskilled at fencing. New pirates with little or no experience in a fight could be given a cutlass and sent into battle with some reasonable expectation of success, especially against other inexperienced sailors of a prize crew. However, a cutlass was also an effective thrusting weapon in the hands of experienced and skill swordsmen. In a duel, a cutlass could be used exactly like a sword and just about as effectively when fighting an opponent with another cutlass. Additionally, the shorter blades made them highly effective in the close quarters of battle on the cramped deck of a vessel or in the confided space below deck. Knives were seldom used as primary weapons but would have always been carried as a back-up, in case a pirate dropped or broke his primary weapon. Also, fighting with a cutlass in one hand and a knife in the other was very effective in such close quarters.

Swords were also common among pirates. During that time period, the term "sword" referred to a long edge weapon with a straight blade that was sharpened on both edges. The most common types were rapiers and small swords. At least one 17th century privateer captain understood the value of using swords. His name was Duguay-Trouin and he hired a fencing master to remain on board and give fencing lessons to his crew. He even kept a case of swords on deck for his men to practice with. In order to be successful fighting with a sword, you must thrust or strike you opponent in one of two ways; either maintain control of your opponent's blade until you have an opportunity to make a thrust or strike or make your thrust or strike when your opponent is moving his arm back to strike at you. Keep in mind that your opponent will be trying to do the same thing. Maintaining your distance is the safest defense. Once your attacker is "within the blade" you are vulnerable. The idea is to control your opponent's blade and stay out of reach until you have the opportunity to thrust or strike. When fighting in close quarters, like the space below the deck of a ship, keeping a safe distance is difficult. However, if one is very skilled using a sword, fighting in close quarters can be done to a limited extent. On the other hand, due to the direct thrust of a sword in the hands of an expert and the longer reach of the blade, a sword can be far more effective than a cutlass in a duel. Throughout the golden age the use of a cutlass or a sword was a personal choice made by the individual based upon personal skill and availability and pirates and privateers used them both.

A boarding pike was a long pole, anywhere between 5 and 10 feet, with a point and hook or ax at the end. They were very useful at hooking the other vessel and pulling it closer in order to board, then using it like a spear to attack an opponent. A boarding ax was just what it sounds like, an ax, usually with a point, that one used to hack and thrust. In the second edition of Charles Johnson's *General History of Pyrates*, the illustration of Anne Bonny shows her with a boarding ax. It is a very intimidating looking weapon and is very effective in close quarters fighting. There isn't much technique to the use of an ax when compared to a sword or cutlass, so this made it an excellent weapon for the inexperienced pirate.

Chapter 72
Treatment of Captives

How captives were treated after the vessel or port was taken was a vital part of the overall tactics pirates and privateers used. The easiest way to take a vessel is for that vessel to surrender. Generally speaking, if the crew and passengers of a potential prize vessel feared for their lives if they resisted but had some assurance of being released unharmed if they surrendered, the chances of them surrendering was high.

Of course, there was no one way in which captives were treated, it was highly individualized and differed with each captain, crew, and situation depending upon their motivations and political goals. But during time of war, privateer crews sailing legally under letters of marque were far more likely to treat their prisoners harshly, especially if there was deep hatred for the enemy. During the 1660s, French privateer François L'Olonnais often killed his Spanish prisoners in extremely harsh ways. Any Spanish government official who fell into his hands was hanged after being tortured. The Spanish privateers who raided the Chesapeake Bay in 1720 threw some of their English captive overboard with their hands and feet tied.

Pirates generally treated captives very well. Killing or even mistreating a prize crew was bad for business. It was always preferable to take a prize vessel easily, with no long pursuit or violent boarding action. Pirates wanted their potential prize crews to surrender quickly and submit to being sacked. That was far more likely if the prize crew felt that they had the possibility of surviving the pirate attack without physical injury. Once a prize crew surrendered, the pirates would board the vessel looking as fierce as possible, with as many weapons as they could carry. Most of the time they would act bold and aggressive, perhaps shouting at the captives, pushing them about, threatening them with death, and anything else necessary in order to completely subdue their captives. But at other times, they went about their looting in a professional and non-threatening manner as long as the crew was well behaved and stayed out of their way. Edward England was said to treat all his captives exceptionally well, even when they attempted to run or fight. Only a few pirates were actually cruel to their captives, like Thomas Cocklyn, who was known for forcing members of the prize vessel to join his crew, often whipping them into submission. Overall it seems that the captains who treated their captives well far outweighed those who were cruel.

Treatment of the prize ship's captain also differed depending on the pirate crew and their motivations. Some pirates, like Blackbeard, actually treated the captains rather well. Once the prize vessel was secured (in complete control of the pirates) a few of the prize vessels officers, such as the captain, quartermaster, or sailing master, would be taken onboard the pirate vessel as hostages while their vessel was being looted. Blackbeard would sit and drink with his captives, perhaps even play some sort of game with them like cards or dice. It was far easier for the captains to accept their situation when they were drunk, and that made looting go smoothly.

Thomas Cocklyn on the other hand was known for torturing captains to make sure they revealed all their hidden loot. He would hang them by the neck until unconscious, then revive them and continue again and again until they talked or died. On the average, most captains were well treated along with their crew. However, pirates who had previously served under tyrannical captains before becoming pirates asked the prize crew if their captain was a good man or a tyrant. This was the merchant crew's chance to get even with an unreasonable captain. If the prize crew vouched for the good character of the captain, he was treated well and released, if not, he was killed. And speaking of bad merchant captains, there was an example when Edward England's pirates captured the slave ship *Cadogan*, off Africa in 1718. By coincidence, the captain happened to have been the former captain of some of the pirate crew and, apparently, he had treated them badly and cheated them out of some of their pay. After he was recognized by the pirates, he was tortured and killed.

The Great Allen was one of the first vessels taken by the Queen Anne's Revenge in 1717.

If the prize vessel chose to run or even fight, the threat was that the crew would be treated harshly or even killed. That usually didn't happen, but they may have been treated differently when finally caught. Of course, that also depended upon the extent of their resistance and the disposition of the crew. The *Great Allen* attempted to escape capture from Blackbeard in the Caribbean in late 1717. When finally captured, the captain was whipped until he revealed where he had hidden the gold and silver and then the *Great Allen* was burned and sunk. Even so, the crew including the captain was safely put ashore. When Captain James Macrae of the *Cassandra* turned about and engaged the Edward England's two pyrate vessels, a three-hour battle began that resulted in 37 casualties on board the *Cassandra* and more than 90 casualties to the pirates. England's crew wanted vengeance, but Captain England decided to allow the prize crew to escape unharmed in one of the two older pirate ships. Edward's crew soon regretted their captain's decision and voted Edward England out of office and marooned him on a deserted island.

When Captain Snelgrave ordered his crew to fight back against the crew of Captain Cocklyn, the pirates tried to kill him, but after his crew pleaded with the pirates to spare their captain, he was released unharmed. On the other hand, a Dutch ship fought Howell Davis' ship in a battle that lasted over 18 hours. After the Dutch crew finally surrendered Davis allowed them to go unharmed. It was even in Howell Davis' articles that once the crew struck their colors, quarter would always be given.

> A half hogshead is approximately 32 gallons.

During the looting process, pirates probably acted exactly like one would expect. They rifled through everyone's possessions and took everything of value. When alcoholic beverages were found they were quite often immediately consumed. Captain Snelgrave, who was captured by Howell Davis, wrote about their conduct with regard to his liquor. Captain Snelgrave also wrote:

> "It was very surprising to see the Actions of these People. They . . . made such Waste and Destruction, that I am sure a numerous set of such Villains would in a short time, have ruined a great City. They hoisted upon Deck a Great many half-Hogsheads of Claret, and French Brandy; knocked their Heads out, and dipped cans and bowls into them to drink out of: . . . As to bottled Liquor of many sorts, they made such havoc of it, that in a few days they had not one Bottle left: For they would not give themselves the trouble of drawing the Cork out, but nicked the Bottles, as they called it, that is, struck their necks off with a Cutlace; by which means one in three was generally broke: Neither was there any Cask-liquor left in a short time, but a little French Brandy."

In general, women were rarely onboard vessels, except as passengers. Occasionally wives and prostitutes would be onboard merchant vessels, but mostly only when the vessel was in port. However, there is an account of a merchant Captain named Beare whose wife would accompany him onboard dressed as a man. Contrary to many books and Hollywood films, women passengers were almost never mistreated. That was evidenced by the Ship's Articles that promised death or marooning to anyone who molested a woman against her will. Captain Snelgrave also wrote, "It is a

Rule amongst the Pirates, not to allow Women on board their Ships, when in Harbour. And if they should take a Prize at sea that has any Women on board, no one dares, on pain of death to force them against their inclinations. This being a good political Rule to prevent disturbances amongst them, it is strictly observed." Mistreatment of women in contemporary documentation was very rare. The most notable account was the occasion when one of Captain Roberts' crew forcibly raped a woman captive after capturing the *Onslow*. Elizabeth Trengrove was traveling to meet her husband when the vessel was taken. She was raped three times by quartermaster Simpson.

After the looting was complete it is extremely well-documented that almost every pirate crew recruited new members from the prize crew. Anyone who wanted to join was welcomed. That was often true for slave ships as well. Some pirates like Sam Bellamy and Batt. Roberts took slave ships and welcomed the African slaves found onboard to join their crew as pirates. Those that did were given total equality to the English pirates, equal shares, and equal opportunities for promotion. For crew members of prize vessels that possessed a special talent, like carpenters, or musicians, becoming a member of the pirate crew sometimes wasn't an option. If a pirate crew needed those talented individuals, they were forced to join. They were always treated the same as everyone else, but it was understood by everyone that they were there against their will. If the crew was captured, those individuals would claim that they were forced to join, and in most cases they were generally acquitted. It's surprising how many ship's carpenters a captured pirate crew would suddenly have when appearing before a magistrate. The two musicians, David Cordingly and James White, who were captured among Robert's crew both claimed at their trial that they were forced to join the pirates and to play music for the crew. They were both acquitted.

Chapter 73
Pirate Booty

Pirate booty comes in many forms. First, there was actual money; silver coins like Spanish pieces of eight, English schillings and crowns, Dutch thollars, and gold coins like Spanish doubloons and English gunnies. Coins could be easily divided up according to shares and given to the crew as soon as they sobered up. Even gold dust could be weighed and evenly distributed according to shares. Then, there were jewels and pearls which could either be sold for money ashore or distributed to the crew based upon their estimated value. However, valuable bulk cargo taken from a prize, like sugar, cotton, silk, logwood, tar, and chocolate would have to have been sold at a friendly port with the profit shares going to the crew afterwards. If the cargo was too large to be transferred aboard the pirate vessel, the pirates often chose to simply keep the merchant ship as their own and either put the captured crew ashore or let them take the old pirate vessel. In many cases, it certainly was far easier to transfer valuables and personal possessions of the pirates to a new ship than to transfer large cargo and everything else of value from a captured ship to a smaller sloop. That left all the personal items found on board, like clothing, watches, weapons, and other items that a pirate may fancy.

Each crew had their own particular rules for how to dispose of these personal items which were occasionally written in the Ship's Articles. For some crews, everything had to be turned into the quartermaster to be placed in the Common Chest. After the looting was finished and the monetary shares were divided, the personal items in the Common Chest were either distributed evenly or auctioned off to the highest bidder in what was called "the sale before the mast."

Captain Snelgrave gave an account of how his pocket watch was taken by the quartermaster of Captain Cocklyn's crew in 1719.

SALE BEFORE THE MAST

An auction of stolen goods to all pirates onboard.

"When it was delivered to the Quartermaster, he held it up by the Chain, and presently laid it down upon the Deck, giving it a kick with his Foot, saying 'It was a pretty Foot-ball': On which, one of the Pirates caught it up, saying, 'He would put it in the common Chest to be sold at the Mast."

Captain Howell Davis later bought the pocket watch for 100 pounds sterling at the sale before the mast. The price had been bid up by a rival crewmember who didn't like Davis. When it was found out that the watch wasn't real gold, some of the pirates wanted to whip Snelgrave for dishonesty by representing his watch was gold, but Davis thought the whole incident was rather amusing.

Among some other pirate crews, only personal valuables worth over one dollar—or a piece of eight—had to be turned in and other personal items like clothing belonged to the pirate who first found them. Robert's second article states:

"Every man to be called fairly in turn, by List, on Board of Prizes, because, (over and above their proper Share) they were on these Occasions allowed a Shift of Clothes."

Every weapon found onboard a prize ship would of course find its way into the possession of one of the crewmembers. How that was done is not clear and probably differed greatly from crew to crew. However, there is a clue in the articles of Captain George Lowther. Number eight states, "He that sees a Sail first, shall have the best Pistol, or Small-Arm, on Board her."

Whether personal items were turned in for later division to the crew or kept by an individual at the time of capture, every pirate and privateer crewmember would have had access to a great variety of clothing, jewelry, tableware, and other items taken from their prize ships. Based upon the Ship's Articles and contemporary accounts, the captain had no special privileges with regard to obtaining personal items. Pirate captains acquired clothing and weapons in the same manner as any crewmember. When it came to fashion and dress, the lowest member of the crew might have a fancier coat than the quartermaster or captain. Contemporary descriptions of pirates often comment on their eclectic mix of clothing and styles. Literally anything that existed at the time could have belonged to a pirate. In other words, if a certain type of pocket watch existed in 1720 a pirate may have come across one on a prize ship and kept it.

Chapter 74
Coin of the Realm

Obtaining coins was what piracy was all about. During the golden age of piracy, most of the coins that circulated in the Caribbean and colonial North America were Spanish. There are several reasons for this. First of all, the Spanish totally dominated all colonization in the New World for over 150 years before the first English, Dutch, or French colonies got really going. Even afterwards, Spanish cities and commerce far exceeded the combined commerce of the other colonists throughout most of the golden age. The second reason was that the Spanish were minting coins in Mexico, Peru, Columbia, and a few other locations, while colonists from other nations had to rely upon coins being imported to the New World from their mother countries. But perhaps the most important reason why Spanish coins were so abundant among colonists of other nations was piracy. The Spanish were the main targets of the buccaneers throughout the 17th century. All of that captured Spanish money was brought back to English, French, and Dutch settlements to be spent. Henry Morgan alone brought in millions of pieces of eight to the English colony of Jamaica. From there, those coins would have been spent in other colonies throughout the New World.

1536

The Spanish begin minting coins in Mexico.

Getting English coins was a problem for the English colonists. Even though the English settled North America from the Carolinas to Newfoundland as well as Jamaica and Barbados, relatively few English coins were available for use in the colonies. That's because the English government had placed a restriction of the importation of coins to the colonies. No coins were permitted to be minted in the English colonies and large quantities of coins were prohibited from being imported to the colonies by bankers or merchants. English coins in small amounts were allowed to be taken to the colonies by settlers, but no official importation of English coins was allowed. The English crown apparently didn't want large quantities of coins in the hands of the colonists; they wanted to keep the colonies on the barter system. Perhaps that was their way of preventing the colonists from becoming too powerful. Also, they believed that the colonies should be sending their wealth back to England, not the other way around.

Occasionally a few local coins were minted in revolt of the prohibition. In 1652 and again in 1662, Massachusetts minted a series of coins in denominations of twopence, threepence, sixpence, and schillings, all with the symbol of a tree on one side. In Maryland in 1659 coins in denominations of fourpence, sixpence, and schillings were minted under Lord Baltimore. In 1670 New Jersey minted some small value coins. Also, a few other colonies issued tin or brass tokens from time to time. However, those coins did not meet the demand of the people. Other governments had no such prohibitions and coins from French and Dutch settlements began to circulate in the New World but in much smaller amounts than did the Spanish coins. Eventually, the Spanish real became the primary currency used throughout the colonies of all nations. By 1680 Spanish coins were so prevalent in the English colonies that when colonists protested the prohibition to the crown the English government countered by pointing out that the colonists already had wide use of Spanish dollars. But the English colonists in North America still needed more. They were desperate for coinage of any kind and pirates brought them Spanish coins. Perhaps that's why they had such a tolerance for pirates in the late 17th century.

Pieces of Eight

Among the most famous coins is the Spanish pieces of eight. The basic unit of Spanish coins was the real which weighed about 3.3 grams of silver. Coins were minted in values of one real, two reales, four reales, and eight reales. The eight real coin was officially called a peso. The English called those coins "pieces of eight" because they were worth 8 reales. Other Spanish names for these coins are a pataca for the eight real coin, toston for the four real coin, and peseta for the two real coin. Those coins were minted in the New World. Sometimes they were minted in an irregular and rough shape called a "cob" which was short for the Spanish term "cabo de barra" which means from the bar. Cobs were mostly minted in denominations of two or four reales. Those coins can be easily dated by the design on the coin.

From 1536 to 1572 the coins had a shield on one side and two pillars without waves on the other. From 1550 to 1734 coins had a shield on one side with a cross in a flower design on the other. Cobb type coins were made from 1651 to 1773 and have a cross on one side with a kind of tic tac toe design with pillars and waves on the other side. Milled coins are pressed in a mint and are similar to modern coins in basic appearance. From

English colonial coins were generally forbidden.

1732 to 1772 the milled coins had a shield on one side and two pillars with a double globe on the other. A milled coin with a bust on one side and a shield with two pillars on the other were minted between 1771 to 1821. Two coins were being circulated in the Caribbean by the Dutch that would influence the name of the Spanish piece of eight. The first was the German thaler. That was the main coin used by the Holy Roman Empire and most German speaking nations throughout Europe and was worth slightly more than an eight real or "piece of eight." The other was the lleeuwendaalder (Lion Dollar) which was a Dutch coin introduced by 1606 to compete with the Spanish piece of eight and was precisely the same value. Those coins were brought to the Caribbean in the mid-17th century by Dutch merchants and circulated by the Dutch colonists and buccaneers. After 1688, when King William of the Dutch Republic also became King of England, trade between the English colonies and the Dutch colonies greatly increased and German thalers and Dutch daalders became far more prevalent throughout the English colonies. It was about that time that the English colonists began calling the Spanish eight real coin the Spanish "dollar." This was of course a deviation of either the word thaler or the word daalder. In 1776, the United States silver dollar was fashioned after the coin that the American colonists called the Spanish dollar. During the late 17th and 18th centuries it was common to make change by simply cutting a Spanish dollar with a knife into halves, quarters, and eighths, just like a pizza. A piece that was an eighth of the complete coin was called a bit. Therefore, two bits would be equal to a quarter piece. That terminology still exists in the United States, as the slang for a quarter is "two bits." Remember the jingle "Shave and a haircut, two bits."

Doubloons

Golden doubloons were also famous coins. The Spanish also minted gold coins in Mexico, Columbia, and Peru. They were called escudos and came in denominations of one escudo, two escudos, four escudos, and eight escudos coins, just like their reales. Those coins were not milled; they were minted entirely by hand. Perfectly round coins were virtually impossible to make. The gold was melted down and poured into thin strips, then pressed until they met the desired thickness. Coin-shaped pieces were then cut from the strips of metal to create what are known today as "blanks." The blanks were pressed against an engraved coin die and struck repeatedly until the design of the die was embedded in the soft metal. After the coins were weighed, excess metal was trimmed away by hand. The value of those gold coins was 16 times the value of their silver counterparts. Therefore, a one escudo coin was worth double the value of a single eight real coin known as a "piece of eight." That eventually led to those coins being called doubloons, meaning double value coins.

Gold doubloons were extremely valuable and denominations of more than two escudos were fairly rare unless they were part of a treasure fleet. In researching various sources there seems to be some disagreement over the exact demonization of Escudos that was actually called a "doubloon." Most sources say that the two escudos coin, also known as the pistole, was the actual denomination called a doubloon. Other sources contend that the eight escudo coin was the real doubloon. It also makes sense that the doubloon was what the one escudo coin was called because it was actually double in value to the commonly used Spanish dollar, the famous "piece of eight." Since the word "doubloon" was English slang and never part of any official document there is no way of knowing for certain which one is correct. Perhaps they all are depending upon who you were talking to. It is also possible that any Spanish gold coin could have been called a doubloon by the pirates of the golden age. After all, it was a slang word used by pirates.

English Coins

Unlike Spanish coins and denominations, English coins are quite complex. There were many types of coins that were minted and issued in England from the 11th century to the 18th century. **For the purposes of this book, I will limit the discussion to only those English coins that were in use during the golden age of piracy.** English coins always had a bust of the ruling monarch on one side which helps identify the date of issue if the numbers are difficult to read. That practice was put on hold, of course, during the Commonwealth period, 1649 to 1660, when England was ruled by Parliament but returned with the restoration of Charles II. Money was money, and during the Commonwealth coins with images of monarchs were still accepted, just like Commonwealth coins were still good after the restoration. The primary denomination of all English coins was the penny, called the pence. Issued from the 8th century on, pennies were very small silver coins. By the 17th century the value of the penny, or pence, had diminished and the actual silver penny was seldom used because it was just too small to be practical. Copper pennies didn't appear until 1797 which makes pennies inaccurate for the golden age. The farthing is worth a fourth of a penny and actually comes from the word "fourthling." Tin coated bronze farthings were issued in 1613 and copper farthings were issued in 1624. They were discontinued during the Commonwealth years but returned in 1672. Beginning in 1684 farthings were made of tin, but copper farthings made a resurgence in 1692 and continued to be issued throughout the 18th century. Halfpence coins, worth one half a penny, were first issued in 1672. They were made of copper until 1685 when the halfpence was changed to tin with a copper plug, but the full copper halfpence returned in 1692.

The silver twopence, sometimes called the half grot, was worth two pennies and was first issued in 1351. They continued to be issued in silver until 1797 when they were issued in copper. Silver threepence coins were first issued in 1551 and continued throughout the 18th century. Silver grots worth four pennies were first issued in 1279 and continued through the 18th century. Sixpence coins, equal to six pennies, were always marked with a VI, the Roman numeral for six. They were first issued in 1551 and continued throughout the 18th century except for a short gap of 1688 to 1694.

Shillings were among the most popular and well-known of all English coins. Worth 12 pennies, the word "schilling" comes from the Anglo-Saxon denomination called the scylling, even though no actual coins in this denomination were ever made. Originally worth five pennies, King William I fixed the value at 12 pennies in the 11th century, a value that continued until 1971. The first actual shillings were first issued in 1502 and were called testoons. They weren't called shillings until 1548. They are marked with an XII, the Roman numeral for 12. Production was fairly limited until the Commonwealth (1650) when production took off and the schilling became the standard money of account in England. The relative value of the shilling during the late 17th and early 18th centuries can be compared to modern currency by what one could buy with a shilling at the time. A shilling would buy a decent meal, a bottle or rum, or a night's stay in a local tavern; you would have to share a bed of course. That would make it roughly equivalent to $20-$30 in modern currency. A shilling was also called a "Bob" in British slang, which may have come from Sir Robert Walpole, the first Prime Minister of Brittan. Sir Robert was elected to parliament in 1701 and in 1708 became Secretary of War. He played a pivotal role in developing the military throughout the reign of Queen Anne and the War of the Spanish Succession. During that time, the tradition of giving a shilling to each new army recruit began. Perhaps those shillings were called "Bobs" in honor of the man who built the army. No one knows for certain.

Equal to 30 pennies, the half-crown was first issued as a small gold coin in 1526, but due to its small size it was changed to a silver coin 1551. During the reigns of Queen Elizabeth I and James I, the coins switched back and forth from gold to silver, but eventually the silver version prevailed and half-crowns were in regular issue until 1751. The crown was worth 60 pennies, or five shillings and was first minted in 1526. Like the half-crown, it began as a gold coin then changed to silver in 1551. The 1551 crown has the distinction of being the first English coin to show the date of minting in Arabic numerals. The crown went back and forth between gold and silver until 1662 when the gold versions finally ceased. The silver crown is fairly large, which meant that the portrait of the king could be made in detail. That made these coins very popular with the English monarchs after the commonwealth dissolved. Crowns continued to be issued until 1751.

Equal to 20 schillings, or 240 pennies, this denomination has had many names throughout the years, which only adds to the confusion. The denomination began as a sovereign and has been called a gold pound, a unite, a laurel, a silver pound, and a guinea, but they are all basically the same thing and have the same value. Gold sovereigns were first minted in 1489, at slightly higher value than 20 schillings. In 1544 the weight of the coin was reduced to equal 20 schillings and was issued until 1553. Between 1592 and 1602 the coin was issued as a gold pound. Between 1603 and 1642 the coin went back and forth from being called a Unite, a Laurel, and a Sovereign. Then, in 1642 the gold sovereign disappeared and the very large silver pound took its place. In 1663 the silver pound went out of production and the gold guinea took its place. Actually, the coin was officially called a broad, but because the gold that was used to mint the coins came from West African, most people called them guineas. At that time, Africa was called Guinea by the English. Golden guineas were issued through the 18th century. The value of 20 schillings, or one guinea, is what is meant when one says a "pound" or uses the term "pound sterling." Therefore, £2,000 would be 2,000 guineas or 40,000 schillings.

French Coins

French coins are far lesser known. Small amounts of French coins would have first come to the Caribbean with the early French Huguenots who settled on Hispaniola and became the first buccaneers. Later, French settlements on Martinique would have brought more French currency. Even more French currency came to the Caribbean directly from the French government when they funded early fortifications on Tortuga and later developed the French colony of San Domingue. The standard French denomination was the livre, which was first introduced by Charlemagne in the 8th century. They were small gold coins until 1380 when they began to be issued in silver. In the 14th century the livre was unofficially called the Franc and it still carries that name today. By the 17th century the value of one livre was equal to 18 English pennies or a schilling and sixpence. Smaller denomination coins called the sou (sometimes spelled sol) and deniers were minted in copper after 1574.

In 1640 King Louis XIII of France established the monitory system that would be used until 1795. He began by copying the Spanish pistole (two escudos gold coin) and naming it after himself, the gold Louis d' Or. Its value was set at ten livres. The ecu came in gold versions worth five livre and silver versions worth three livre. The original silver one livre coin, called the silver franc, was still around which was further divided by the copper coins. There are 20 sou in one franc and 12 deniers in one sou. When compared to English coins, the sou is slightly less in value to the penny.

Dutch Coins

Dutch coins would have been far more prevalent in the world of buccaneers than one might expect. First of all, many of the original buccaneers came from Dutch settlements in the Caribbean, and they would have brought their coins with them. Secondly, there were three Anglo-Dutch wars in the second half of the 17th century, where English privateers from the Caribbean routinely attacked Dutch ports and vessels. In 1665 the English took possession of the Dutch colonies in North America, renaming them New York and Pennsylvania. The Dutch coins that were in those colonies were eventually distributed throughout the English colonies in North America. Then, in 1689, the King of the Dutch Republic also became the King of England and trade between the two nations took off with a great deal of coins exchanging hands in the process. Finally, the Dutch were all over the Indian Ocean trading in India, just like the English. There is no way of telling how many Dutch coins that pirates like Thomas Tew brought back to North America from the Madagascar waters.

The Netherlands was under Spanish or French control for over one hundred years before they finally became an independent nation in the late 16th century. Consequently, their currency system was a mess. But by the early 17th century, the Dutch were fast on their way to becoming the greatest maritime trading nation in the world. That greatly influenced their monetary system. With international commerce, there were always difficulties converting the currency of the buyers to the currency of the sellers. At the very least, it made the bookkeeping difficult. The Dutch took steps to solve that. They devised a unique monetary system that imitated the well-accepted coin values of all their international business partners and minted coins that matched the values.

The Dutch weren't the first to think of an international denomination. In 1140 Roger II of Sicily introduced the gold ducat which was an international trade coin designed to help standardize trade in the European market. By the end of the 12th century the Venetians were using a standardized silver ducat. And by 1566 the value of the ducat became standardized throughout Italy, Eastern Europe, Scandinavia, the Holy Roman Empire, Austria, the Byzantine Empire, Russia, Poland, and the Netherlands. It was kind of like the modern euro.

The basic denominational measure for all Dutch coins was the stuiver—similar to the penny in England. The stuiver was a small silver coin worth just slightly more than the English penny. Smaller denominations of Dutch coins were minted in copper. Their value compared to one stuiver was 16 penning, 12 denien, 8 duiten, or 2 groot. The pound hollands was a silver coin equal to 15 stuivers. In 1680 the Dutch resurrected the silver guilder and set the value 20 stuivers. That coin remained in use until 1999. They also resurrected the silver florin set at 28 stuivers.

To improve trade with the Spanish, the Dutch introduced the schelling, which was a silver coin equal to six stuivers and exactly matched the value of the Spanish real. Therefore, eight schellings, or 48 stuivers, were equal to one Spanish piece of eight. Also, precisely equal to the Spanish piece of eight was the leeuwendaalder (Lion Dollar) at 27.68 grams of silver. Introduced by 1606, the leeuwendaalder Daalder became the most commonly used coin by the Dutch in trade throughout the Caribbean. To improve trade with England, the Dutch introduced the silver Ducaton, in 1659 which was equal to 60 stuivers and very closely matched the value of the English crown.

The silver rijksdaalder was worth 50 stuivers and matched the value of the silver ducat which made it useful in the Eastern European market where silver ducats were commonly used. It was also equal to the German thaler used throughout the Holy Roman Empire.

The Flemish pound was equal to six guilders or 20 schellings (120 stuivers). And finally, at 3.5 grams of gold, the most valuable Dutch coin was the gold ducat, which was worth two silver ducats. It was also worth just slightly more than a Spanish escudo which weighed 3.3 grams of gold. In addition to Dutch coins minted in Europe, the Dutch East India Company or Vereenigde Oost-Indische Compagnie (VOC), minted thousands of their own coins in copper, brass, silver, and gold. Those coins were minted in many VOC posts throughout the Indian Ocean and the western Pacific and were all marked with a distinctive "VOC" on one side.

Chapter 75
Buried Treasure

It has long been believed that pirates buried their treasure on remote islands and beaches throughout the world. But did they really bury their treasure? Most historians and authors of books on pirate history say no, except for Captain William Kidd. No one can dispute that he buried treasure on Garner's Island in New York because the authorities were able to recover loot worth £20,000 before his trial and execution. Additionally, over the next several months, Kidd continually talked about the treasure that he buried in the "Indies" which can only mean an island in the Indian Ocean. And two of his crewmen, Churchill and Howe, were eventually released and returned to America where they uncovered their buried share of the treasure valued at £1500, and £700 respectively. Nevertheless, most historians say that this was the exception to the rule and that the belief that pirates buried treasure is merely legend perpetuated by novels such as Robert Louis Stevenson's *Treasure Island*, and Hollywood films.

Because there is no documented evidence to prove that pirates frequently buried their treasure historians make that claim. However, it is my opinion that a great many more pirates buried their treasure than those historians are aware of. Burying "treasure" continues today and much of it is never recovered for a multitude of reasons. Logically, there would be very little documentation about buried treasure.

Most accounts of pirate activity and behavior came from one of two sources. The first was from the statements of the prisoners who were held aboard their vessel while it was being looted. It is very unlikely that any pirate would discuss where he had buried his treasure with one of his captives. The other source came from the testimony from witnesses and the accused during trials. Again, for a pirate to admit he had buried treasure would be admitting his guilt. Since I believe most pirates successfully recovered their buried treasure, there wouldn't

be a lot of treasure left around for people to find in the decades after the pirates were gone. We have to use a bit of logic and deductive reason to understand why a pirate would consider burying treasure in the first place.

Far from Home

If a pirate was operating in waters far away from home, especially in waters where there were no friendly ports to sell their loot or spend their money, they would have to bury part of their treasure in order to continue operating. As the pirates took more and more prizes, eventually their cargo holds would become full. They would have to make a choice; either return home immediately with what they had, dump their loot overboard to make room for more, or bury their loot on a deserted island to make room for more. That last choice seems far more likely.

Put yourself in their place. You are a pirate captain operating in the Pacific Ocean off the coast of Peru in the late 17th century and you only have one or two small vessels under your command. Your cargo holds are completely full with silks, cottons, and other valuables that will bring enormous profits back in Carolina or Virginia. You can't take any more prizes because there is no room to add any more loot. Also, your vessels are slow because they are weighted down with your plunder. But things are going well and you want to take even more prizes. It would be very easy to stop at a remote island and conceal your treasure, then continue operations.

When you finally had enough loot to return home, you would simply begin to keep all the ships that you took to use as treasure transports. Then, you would sail back to the island with the buried treasure, load up all the cargo, and sail around the Horn of South America, back to a friendly port where your loot could be sold. According to some contemporary accounts, that is precisely what Captain Davis did in July 1684 when he sailed to Cocos Island off Costa Rica and buried a large amount of treasure. Every successful pirate who operated in the Pacific or Indian Oceans would have been faced with the challenge of what to do with all the treasure. **I'm convinced that many chose to bury part of their loot and returned to claim it before they returned home.**

Avoiding the Customs Inspector

Another reason for burying treasure was to avoid arrest when entering a port that wasn't tolerant of pirates and their ways. By the early 18th century many ports were closed to pirates and the authorities would arrest anyone suspected of piracy on the spot. Pirates who visited those ports had to be very careful to conceal anything that would alert the authorities to their true identity. However, pirates needed to visit those ports to either sell some of their cargo or take on supplies. In any case, entering such a port would have to be done very discreetly without looking suspicious.

Perhaps the pirates would sail into port aboard a small, innocent looking craft, or perhaps they would row ashore on a deserted part of the countryside. But what about all the loot the pirate had? If a pirate planned on sailing into port aboard an innocent looking vessel, an inspection from the local customs officials was very likely. Smuggling was always a concern for local officials and routine inspections of vessels was fairly normal. A pirate wouldn't risk having any treasure onboard that would alert the officials, so the pirate would have to bury the treasure nearby and go back for it later. If everything went well, the pirates would successfully recover their buried treasure and no one would ever know they buried it. That's exactly what pirate captain John Quelch and his crew did in 1704. After taking an estimated £10,000 in sugar, hides, cloth, gold dust, and coins, they stopped on Star Island, just off the New Hampshire coast on their way back to Marblehead, Massachusetts. Most of the crew was arrested and some were hanged, so they never had the opportunity to go back for it. Over 100 years later, gold coins from that period were found hidden in a stone wall on the island.

Or, perhaps a few pirates would first quietly row ashore in a small boat with their treasure aboard, bury it somewhere, then row back to their ship for a safe arrival in port a day or two later. The treasure could be quietly recovered as soon as the authorities weren't watching. I believe that's exactly what John Hinson, Lionel Delawafer, Edward Davis, and Peter Cloise (Davis' slave) were doing one dark night in 1688 when they were caught by HMS *Deptford* in Lynnhaven Bay, just off the Virginia shoreline of what would later be known as Virginia Beach. The four men were all known pirates and were in a small row boat carrying chests filled with gold coins and silver plate valued somewhere between £5,000 and £6,000. As you may recall, this is the same Captain Davis who led the pirate fleet that William Dampier sailed with and the same Davis that supposedly buried some of his treasure on Cocos Island off Costa Rica four years earlier.

Cheating on the King's Share

We didn't take quite as much as expected was a tale that privateers could tell their backers if they had hidden some of it on the way home. Another reason for burying treasure was to avoid large payments to partners or the government. Every privateer sailing under letters of marque owed a percentage of the loot they took to the government official that issued those letters. And you can believe that government inspectors were waiting at the docks when privateer vessels arrived, just to make sure the government got its fair share. After all, they were high stakes tax collectors. Privateers who were exceptionally loyal to their king or the governor who issued their letters of marque would be delighted to pay their percentage of the total spoils, but let's look at this sensibly. How many businessmen in the 21st century look for loopholes to avoid paying high taxes? The answer is quite a lot. The same thing would apply to privateers. But with government inspectors waiting at the docks, the only way for them to avoid paying a large share would be to bury some of their loot on an island before they arrived back in their home port. Upon arrival, they might say something to the officials like, "We didn't take quite as much as we expected. Perhaps we'll be more successful next time." After the official prize loot was tallied and divided among the government and the privateer crew, the privateers could quietly sail back and recover the rest of the loot, tax free.

There are a few cases that might illustrate this point. Olivier Le Vasseur "La Buse" was a very successful French pirate operating at the end of the golden age of piracy. He attempted to retire on the Island of Bel Ombre, in the Seychelles Islands, which are a small group of islands in the middle of the Indian Ocean, about 800 miles north east of Madagascar. The French administration insisted that he give them his entire treasure. He turned them down and continued piracy on a small scale in the Indian Ocean, burying much of his treasure rather than allow the local government to seize it as he put into port.

By 1730, he had accumulated an enormous amount of loot, which all seemed to disappear when he was caught. He was executed on Reunion Island on July 7, 1730. As he stood on the scaffold, La Buse threw a coded message into the crowd saying, "Find my treasure, he who can." Many have tried to decode his message including a former British Army cryptographer in 1948. As reported in an earlier chapter, so far, only 107 pieces of eight, two shoe buckles and a boatswain's whistle have been recovered from Astove Island in the Seychelles island group.

There is one case that is well-documented. This, of course, is the famous accounting of Captain William Kidd. As mentioned earlier in the chapter about Captain Kidd, he buried £20,000 of treasure on Garner's Island in New York before his arrested and attempted to use this treasure as a bargaining chip to obtain a release. Kidd also claimed to have buried treasure on Block Island, New York and Long Island, New York before he was arrested. Later on, two of his crewmen who were released returned to America where they uncovered more of Kidd's buried treasure valued at £1,500, and £700 respectively. In addition, Kidd talked about the treasure that he buried in the "*Indies*" which can only mean an island in the Indian

Ocean. Kidd didn't believe he would be arrested at the time he buried this treasure so why would he bury treasure before returning to his financial backers? I believe that he didn't want to divide the entire amount with the government.

Before he left the waters of Madagascar, Captain Kidd spent seven months at St. Mary's pirate base, often mysteriously sailing off to the China Sea. It is widely believed that Kidd began thinning out his enormous treasure before he even began his return trip to New York. By his own admission, he buried part of it somewhere in the Indies. That, of course, was the East Indies, the islands in the China Sea. You may remember that between 1929 and 1934 four treasure maps were found and sold to a rich pirate enthusiast living in London named Palmer. Of the four maps, two may be authentic. The first three of these maps were found by the London antique dealer, Hill Carter who sold them to Palmer.

According to one theory, the first authentic map was found by Carter in 1929 in a secret compartment of a small chest that Carter purchased from a woman named Pamela Hardy. Apparently, the chest came into her family when the great grandson of Kidd's boatswain from the *Adventure Galley* sold the chest to Palmer's great grand uncle. Carter copied the map twice and hid the forgeries in an 18th century bureau and the Hardy chest which he sold to Palmer. Later on, Carter hid the genuine map in the false bottom of another small chest he got from a man named Dan Morgan who claimed to be a descendent of one of Captain Kidd's jailors at Newgate Prison. He claimed that his ancestor was given the chest from Kidd himself.

The second genuine map looks very much like the first. It was also found in the false bottom of a small chest with the inscription "**William and Sarah Kidd ~ Their Box ~ 1699.**" The box was also purchased by Palmer and has a traceable history back to a man who lived in America in the early 18th century.

The maps were supposedly tested and found to be authentic, but the report and all other proof have disappeared. The maps went into private ownership after Palmer died and remain unavailable to examination or even viewing.

The South China Sea is the body of water with Vietnam to the west, China to the north, the Philippines to the east and Borneo to the south. Some researchers believe the island where Kidd buried his treasure is the island of Hon Tre Lon in the territorial waters of Vietnam, others believe it might be buried in the Nicobar Islands, but they are in the Indian Ocean, not the South China Sea.

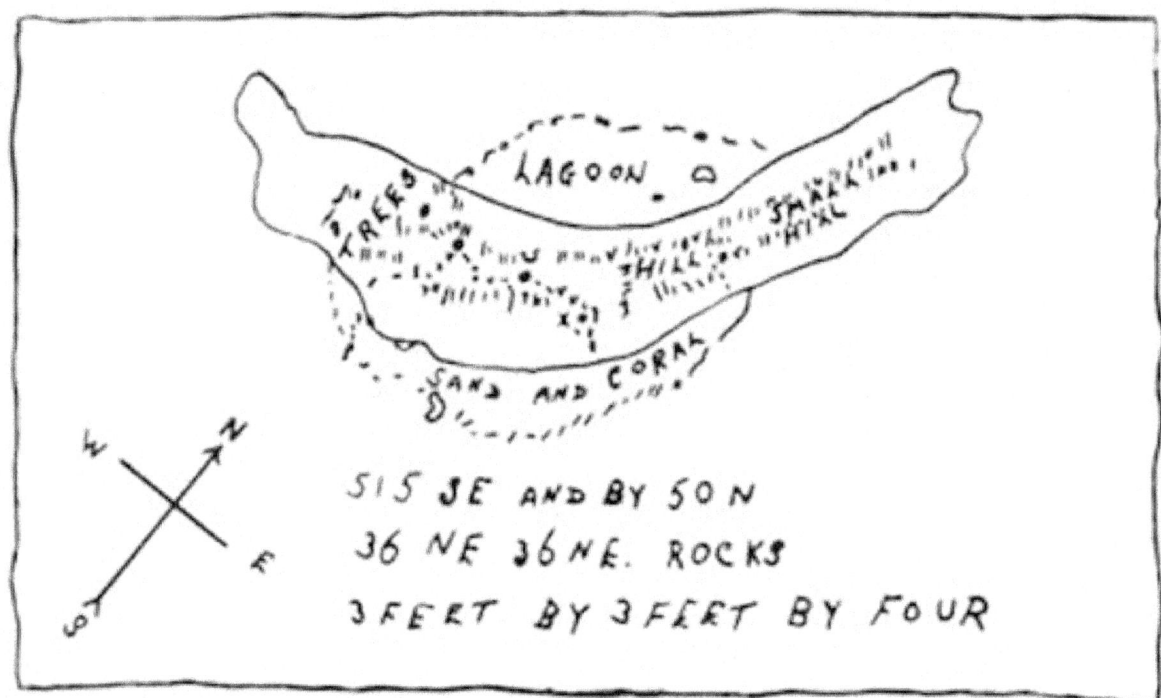

Figure 50: *Captain Kidd's First Map*

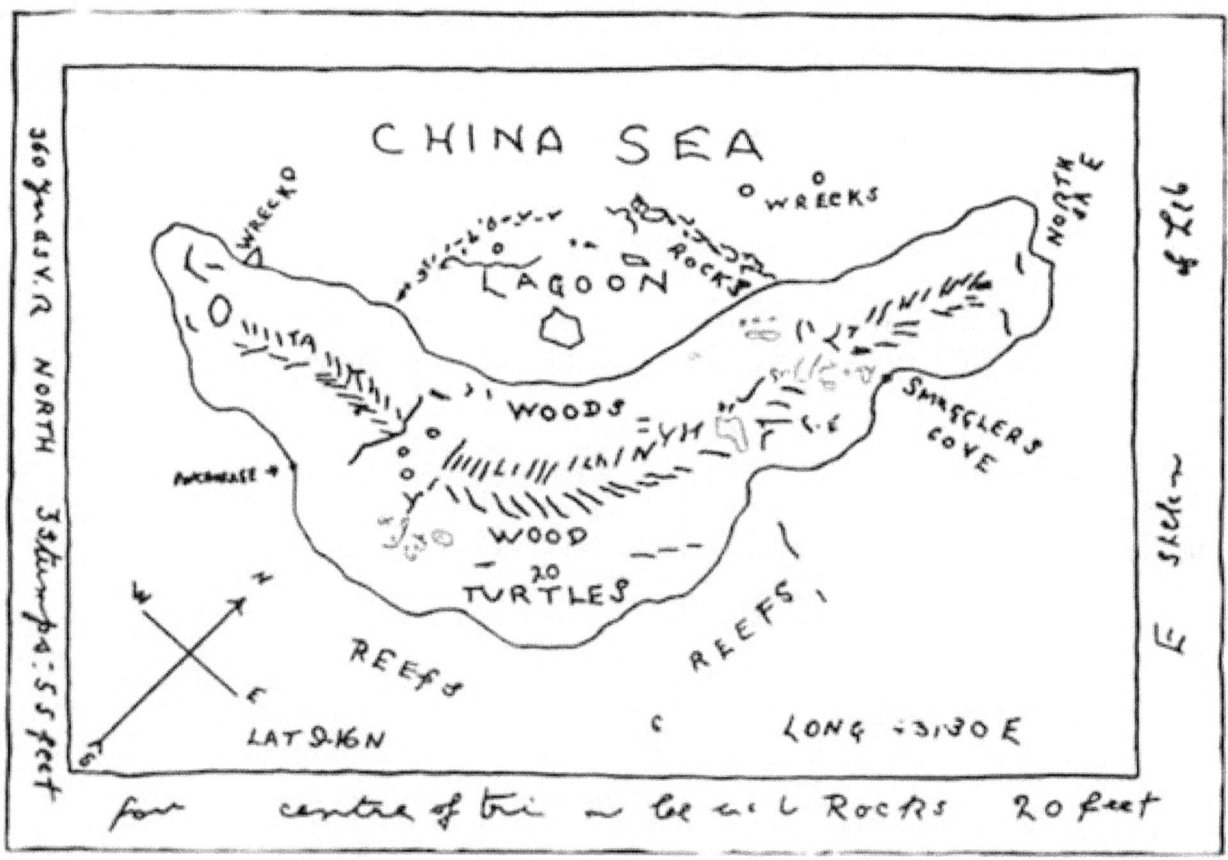

Figure 51: *Captain Kidd's Second Map*

Chapter 76
Daily Life, How They Lived

Pirates were generally treated very well by their captains and officers between engagements. A happy crew is a crew that doesn't mutiny. Harsh discipline such as whipping or marooning had to be done with the majority of the crew's consent. Consumption of large amounts of alcoholic beverages was the norm and kept the crew happy. Reading the various Ships' Articles helps us understand how crews lived.

Maintenance

Daily routine would, of course, involve the crew doing everything expected of a sailor in order to maintain and sail their vessel. However, pirates didn't really have to keep their vessel in tip top shape—at least above the waterline. They were continually taking new vessels, so keeping their vessel in peak condition was a waste of time. Life expectancy for a pirate vessel ranged from a month to a year before it was "traded" for a better one. But below the waterline was a different matter. The hull of a ship below the waterline must have attention every few months. Barnacles, seaweed, and many other marine growth begin to cover the hull, causing the vessel to become slow and unresponsive. That was a very bad thing for a pirate vessel that must be fast and maneuverable in order to overtake prizes and escape bad situations. Also, teredo worms destroyed the planking, causing the vessel to leak and eventually even sink.

Teredo worms are actually a species of saltwater clam.

Cleaning and repairing the hull of a vessel involves careening. This is a process where a vessel is pulled completely out of the water up onto a beach and the hull is scraped of all the barnacles and other growth, then treated with sulfur to kill anything left in the wood. The damaged planks are replaced, and the entire hull is covered with a protective coat of tallow to help waterproof the hull.

While the vessel was on the beach, the pirates would sleep ashore in tents made of old sails. With large crews, it was possible for a tent city to arise on the beach with rain flies covering their eating area. It would be impossible to stay on a vessel that is lying on its side, and the smell of dead barnacles is seriously awful, even for pirates, so the crew probably preferred to camp away from the vessel. That was a dangerous time for pirates. They were pretty much helpless if found by government authorities or unfriendly pirates. If they spotted an unfriendly vessel in the distance, they may (depending on the tide) be able to get their vessel back in the water in time to escape, but if they were caught by surprise, the only thing they could do was to run further inland. Therefore, pirates usually looked for secluded, out of the way, places to careen their vessels. While on the beach, the crewmembers not involved in the careening would take on fresh water and food. If the locals were friendly, they would trade for food and anything else they needed.

Cleaning their weapons was also a vital activity between engagements. According to Exquemelin, "The buccaneer's main exercises are target shooting and keeping their guns clean." Dirty guns won't fire and a rusty sword gives the prize crew the impression the pirate is an amateur. Many of the Ship's Articles address this issue, Captain John Phillips seventh article states, "That Man that shall not keep his Arms clean, fit for an Engagement, or neglect his Business, shall be cut off from his Share, and suffer such other Punishment as the Captain and the Company shall think fit." And Captain Roberts' fifth article states, "To keep their Piece, Pistols, and Cutlass clean and fit for Service." Like most professional soldiers, their weapons would have been kept as serviceable as possible. Rusty swords were for amateurs. Also, the ship's guns would have required a great deal of cleaning and maintenance.

Music

Entertainment was also an important part of pirate life. Singing songs was always a favorite pastime. For that reason, musicians were highly valued. When Captain Roberts' crew was captured by the Royal Navy, two of them were found to be musicians, David Cordingly and James White. Cordingly was a fiddle player. At their trial, those musicians claimed they were forced to join the pirates and to play music for the crew's entertainment and during battle. Other forms of entertainment could include putting on plays. Sam Bellamy's crew was performing "The Royal Pirate," a pirate themed play, on the main deck of the *Whydah*, when a member of the crew who was below decks sleeping off a hangover awoke and came on deck only to see his friend about to be hung. Not realizing that this was just part of the play, he threw a grenade into the crowd. The grenade was meant to save his friend, but instead, it killed several members of the crew—and totally ruined the performance.

Singing songs was a big part of daily life for everyone. Roving musicians would frequent local taverns whose customers would normally join in with the singing. All sailors sang songs aboard ship and those that had instruments played them. It was the same with pirates. It is well documented that Batt. Roberts highly valued musicians and forced them into joining his crew at every opportunity. Roberts even insisted that they play music from the quarterdeck during his attacks. The type of music those musicians played would have been any song that was popular in the day. In other words, sailors and pirates of the 17th and 18th centuries would have played or sung the same songs that were sung in the taverns throughout Europe and the colonies. There were very few songs that were unique to pirates, or even sailors for that matter. That includes "Sea Chanteys."

People have been singing work songs since well before recorded history. Many cultures developed some sort of chant when engaged in team labor, like pulling a heavy load with a rope. This normally involved a call and response, with one individual calling out some sort of chant and the workers responding together in tempo. This sort of chant or singing helps keep the team coordinated and performing at the same time. If you have 50 men pulling a barge up a river or raising a large block of stone to build a temple, their efforts must be coordinated to be effective. Some of those chants were simple repetitive rhythms, but others actually developed into a song-like structure. That is the history of the sea chantey, which is derived from the word chant, and sometimes spelled "sea shanty." Crews aboard ships had to raise anchors, hoist sails, load cargo, and operate pumps. All this involved team effort like pulling a rope or turning a capstan. However, most of the songs we call "sea chanteys" in modern times didn't come into existence until the 19th century.

St James of Compostella was a common pilgrimage spot in the northwest of Spain.

Songs

The earliest reference to a song being sung by sailors while hauling on a rope or line was in an English manuscript which dates to 1400 and chronicles the passage of a ship loaded with pilgrims to the port of St. James of Compostella. In 1493 a Dominican friar named Felix Fabri traveled to Palestine aboard a Venetian galley and wrote, ". . . there are others who are called mariners who sing when work is going on, because work at sea is very heavy, and is only carried on by a concert between one who sings out orders and the laborers who sing in response."

The earliest actual chantey described with all the words was called "Hou pulpela Boulena" and was mentioned in a book titled *Compliment of*

Scotland written in 1549. The crew chanted that song while hauling up the anchor. Of course, there is no way of knowing if any specific melody was used during the chant or if the words were merely spoken in rhythm. The oldest actual chanteys or sea songs with lyrics and music are "Whiskey Johnny" and "Haul on the Bowline" which both come from England and can be documented to the early 1540s during the reign of Henry VIII as he was building the English navy.

However, other than those two, there is very little evidence that any other sort of sea chanteys existed among English sailors in the 17th or early 18th centuries. As for the other maritime nations like France, Spain, and the Dutch, traditional sea chanteys aren't mentioned at all in any documentation or writings. One source noted that French sailors did use a simple chant such as "One, two, three... pull" but nothing that we would describe as a sea chantey.

Unfortunately for all those who wish to accurately portray a pirate from the golden age, all the most well-known sea chanteys are inaccurate for the time period. They didn't come into existence until the 19th century. Even the famous chantey "What Do You Do with a Drunken Sailor" didn't appear until the mid to late-18th century— well past the golden age of piracy. This also includes two of the most famous of all sea chanteys, "New York Girls" and "Haul Away Joe" which both date to the 1830s or 1840s. Pirates must have used some type of chantey, but only "Whiskey Johnny" and "Haul on the Bowline" can be documented to the golden age of piracy and are the only two choices that are correct to the time. Even so, chanties

Whiskey Johnny

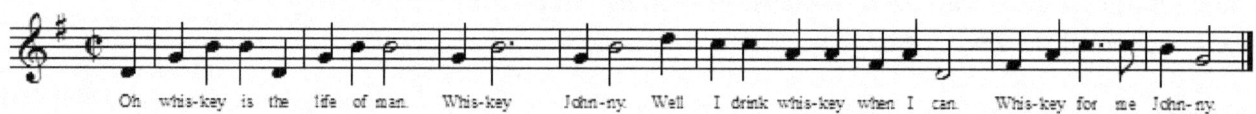

Figure 52: *Whiskey Johnny*

Haul on the Bowline

Figure 53: *Haul on the Bowline*

were never sung for entertainment, they were strictly work chants. Even in the 19th century sea chanties were seldom sung for entertainment. That didn't occur until the folk song craze of the 20th century.

Even if sea chanteys weren't sung at social events, there were lots of popular songs from this era that sailors did sing. One of the most popular songs associated with sailors and pirates was "A-Rovin" which first appeared in a play published in 1630. That song is still very popular today and is often heard as source music in movies and television productions about sailors and pirates. Surprisingly enough, the modern version is virtually unchanged from the original 1630 version.

"Lilliburlero" was another very popular English song which dates to at least the early 17th century and was sung during the English Civil War. The melody of that song was used as a basis for several other songs like "Nottingham Ale" and "The Farmer's Cursed Wife." There were no copyright laws and any song could be used in any manner the singers chose. Actually, it was quite common for sailors to take the melody of a song and change the lyrics to fit their own particular circumstances.

This sort of thing is obviously still done today, especially among high school and college students.

Some examples of popular songs are "Back and Sides Go Bare" which is a drinking song that first appeared in print in 1562, "The Foggy Foggy Dew" which dates back to 1690, and "Jones' Ale" which was first printed in 1595. "The Golden Vanity" first appeared in 1635 as "Sir Walter Raleigh Sailing in the Lowlands" and "The Jolly Miller" first appears on a flyleaf in 1716. These are only a few songs of the day. A terrific source for English songs from this period can be found in Thomas D'Urfey's "Wit and Mirth—Pills to Purge Melancholy"[1] which was a series of editions containing popular songs that were published continually between 1660 and 1720. Another is the 1695 publication, "The Dancing Master" by John Playford. In addition to English songs, a great many colonists in the New World came from Scotland and Ireland; therefore, many popular songs sung in taverns, homes, and aboard ship came from Irish and Scottish traditions.

In reality, many of the songs commonly sung by modern living historians portraying pirates of the golden age are actually from a much later time period. Some examples are "Blow the Man Down" which dates no earlier than 1860, "Fathom the Bowl" published in 1891, "The Mermaid" by Francis Child (1825–1896) published in the 19th century, "Mingulay Boat Song" by Hugh Robertson and published in 1938, "Wild Rover" which was first printed in 1845 but was probably written around 1829 in Scotland,

---

1 Download available at www.RobertJacobAuthor.com

1623-1687

John Playford was a London bookseller, publisher, and composer.

1653-1723

Thomas D'Urfey was an English writer of plays and poetry, composer, and popular standup comic.

"Spanish Ladies" composed in 1796, and "Ring the Bell Watchman" ("Strike the Bell") by Henry C. Work which wasn't written until 1865.

Violins, Early 16th Century

What are songs without instruments to accompany them? There were many instruments available to the musicians at court, but what instruments would sailors and pirates of the golden age have played? Violins certainly would have been among the most popular. They were easy to carry and extremely common among the lower classes. One can't imagine Scottish and Irish folk music without violins. It was the same in the 17th century. The violins of the era looked exactly like modern violins except they didn't have chin rests. For travelers, a miniature violin with a narrower body was quite popular during the 17th and 18th centuries. These smaller versions would have been ideal for sailors and pirates living in the cramped quarters aboard ship.

There were a great many other string instruments available during the golden age, but not the guitar. The ancestor of the guitar was known as the vihuela in Spain and the viola in Italy. It was also the ancestor of the modern viola. The vihuela could be played with either a bow or by strumming. By the mid-16th century, the vihuela had increased in size and had six double strings called courses. Each course consisted of two strings tuned to the same pitch. Musicians would call that tuning in unison. The player would have to push down both strings together. It was during that time that the vihuela began to develop into several different instruments, including the guitar and the lute.

Baroque Guitars, Early 17th Century

The guitar-shaped instrument first appeared in Italy and Spain at the beginning of the 17th century. Known as the "Baroque Guitar," it had five courses, or sets of double strings. Very popular in Italy, the baroque guitar was also popular in Spain and Portugal, although to a lesser extent. However, those guitars were normally played by court musicians and nobility. The guitar wasn't a common instrument among tavern musicians or sailors until much later. Guitars also became very popular in Germany in the early 17th century. Among some of the earliest German guitars still in existence is one made by Jacobus Stadler in 1624. Guitars began appearing in France in the late 17th century as part of the court orchestras and were usually decorated with paintings. By the early 18th century, the five courses were replaced with single strings. Modern looking six string guitars didn't appear until the mid-18th century and weren't popular among the common folk until the early 19th century.

Lutes, Late 16th Century

The lute developed at the end of the Renaissance—in the late 16th century. It is a strummed or plucked instrument with a uniquely shaped body. It resembles a large tear drop, flat on the playing side and fully rounded and fluted on the back, similar to a piece of fruit cut in half. This type of back is often called a bowled back. Originally, the lute had between 11 and 13 courses of strings with the neck normally bending back at a right angle. This instrument was somewhat challenging to play and was not commonly found in taverns. However, a hybrid of the lute and the guitar began to appear around the end of the 17th century when lute makers began putting a guitar-like neck with six single strings on the body of a lute. That instrument is easier to play than a lute and is played exactly like the modern guitar. For this reason, the lute guitar quickly became very popular among tavern musicians and could be found aboard ships. The lute guitar wasn't as popular in Spain or France; however, it dominated the taverns of England and the English colonies from the late 17th century all the way to the early 19th century. There are dozens of 18th century English prints that show tavern musicians playing lute guitars. The popularity and ease of playing the lute guitar would have made it the stringed instrument of choice for English pirates.

Mandolins, 17th Century

The mandolin first developed as a small lute in the mid-16th century and retained the bowl shaped back. By the 17th century it was called the mandora in Spain, the mandore in France, and the mandola in Italy. A variation called the cittern developed in England with a flat back instead of the bowled back. Originally those instruments all had six courses of strings, but versions with only six single strings began appearing around 1650 as the double stringed versions began to die out. In the late 17th century, a smaller version, which retained the six courses, developed in Italy and was called the mandolina. It was this smaller instrument that eventually developed into the modern mandolin. However, was rarely found outside of Italy until the mid-18th century. All of the other variations were played by tavern musicians and may have been carried aboard vessels by sailors and pirates, especially the six stringed versions from the later 17th century.

Recorders and Whistles, 15th Century

The wooden recorder would have been available but not as popular as the whistle. The recorder took a lot more practicing to play well. The most common wind instrument among the lower classes was the whistle. It would also have been a favorite among sailors and pirates. Easy to play and very convenient to carry, whistles have been in existence for thousands of years. Sometimes called fipple flutes, in the 17th century they were often called flageolets. The whistle was generally made of wood, bone, clay, or brass. There is a whistle made of the tibia of a goat in the Museum of London. There are also examples of brass whistles in Scotland that date to the 15th century. In modern times, these whistles are generally made of tin and are called either tin whistles or penny whistles. Unfortunately, for those wishing to accurately portray pirates of the golden age, whistles made of tin weren't yet in existence. The manufacturing of tinplate in Britain didn't begin until the early 18th century and really didn't get going until the 1740s. Tin products like cups first appeared around the mid-18th century. Whistles made of tin weren't produced until the late 18th century and weren't mass produced and marketed until the mid-19th century.

Of course, there were many other instruments of all types that existed in the 17th and 18th centuries, like the Greek bouzouki, but it would have been exceptionally rare to come across any of them outside their native countries, and it would be very unlikely to find one in the hands of a pirate. Some popular instruments that definitely did not exist during the golden age were the harmonica, which was invented in Germany in 1822, the concertina, which was invented in England in 1829, and the banjo, which developed in the United States in the early 19th century.

Gaming

Gaming was also very popular. Some crews didn't allow gambling for money. Nevertheless, playing games or even gambling for trivial things was an established way of life. Drinking games were of course common. One popular game was known as deception dice or sometimes pirate's dice. This is the game of liar's dice that the pirates play in the second installment of Disney's "Pirates of the Caribbean" films. That game originated in South America and dates back to at least the 16th century. It was called, Cachito, Perudo, or Dadinho by the Spanish. Card games included Alouette, a trick-taking game for two or four players, La Bete, a 17th century trick-taking game for anywhere from two to ten players, Bone-Ace, an early 17th century relative of blackjack, Bryncir, a 16th century Welsh game for five people and a whole lot of cards, Cacho, a poker-like Spanish game which was dated to 1691, Flor, another Spanish game from 1610, Picket, one of the older documented card games, and Cribbage, first played in the 16th century. Board games include Backgammon, Nine Men's Morris, The Fox and the Hounds, Goose, Alquerques, the ancestor of Checkers, and the same game of Chess that we play today. The rules to all these games can be found at www.robertjacobauthor.com.

Chapter 77
Talk Like a Pirate

When someone is asked to talk like a pirate, the first thing that comes to mind is "Ahrrrrrrrrrrrr!" This comes completely from the highly imaginative and brilliant characterization of Long John Silver by the actor Robert Newton, who portrayed this character in the 1950s for the movies *Treasure Island* and *Long John Silver*, and then in the subsequent television series by the same name. He also portrayed Blackbeard in a film named *Blackbeard the Pirate*. No other reference to pirates ever saying "Ahrrrrr" exists before that. In developing the character, Robert Newton chose to use a Bristol accent. That made sense. Bristol was one of the largest seaports in England during the early 18th century and many pirates began their careers as sailors from Bristol. But how did Robert Newton know what a Bristol accent was like? Well, Robert Newton was originally from Shaftesbury, Dorset, which is just 35 miles south of Bristol in the United Kingdom.

1905-1956

Robert Newton, English actor

What exactly is the word "Ahrrrrrr" supposed to mean? It is very common among people from some English and Scottish regions to say the word "aye" often when speaking. Technically it means "yes" but it is used colloquially to convey understanding. During the course of a normal conversation, the word "aye" comes up a lot. *Follow me on this.* When a young boy asks a question, an affirmative answer might be "Yes, lad." If the person is a sailor who uses the word "mate" or "matey" to mean "friend," the answer would then be "Yes, matey." If the sailor is from one of those regions that uses the word "aye" the answer would be "Aye, matey."

Alright, we now understand the use of the word "aye" but how does that become "ahrrrrrrr"? There are several regions of the English-speaking world where the vowel "A" is sometimes pronounced as an "R." I grew up in such a region of western Pennsylvania in the United States. In many neighborhoods just south of Pittsburgh, George Washington is pronounced

George "Worshington," and washing your clothes is pronounced "worshing" your clothes. In the North Eastern United States, there is a regional accent that puts and "R" on words like idea. They would say, "That's a good idear." It was perhaps like that in Bristol. "Ahrrrrr" is merely the Bristol accent for the word "Aye" according to the actor Robert Newton. Because of the tremendous popularity of the television series and the magnificent and highly impressionable portrayal of the character of Long John Silver, "Ahrrrrr" is firmly linked to the speech of pirates in the minds of millions of people throughout the world.

In the 16th and 17th centuries there were several terms used as synonyms for pirates. One of the most common was "sea rovers." Going "a-rovin" as in the 1630 song meant to go a-pirating. In the Mediterranean, pirates were called "corsairs." This was one of the terms that the French often used to refer to pirates in the Caribbean as well.

Another term that developed in the early 17th century for pirates was "freebooters." Originally it was a Dutch expression "vryjbuiter" which literally means "freebooter." Some say this was a term originally used to describe smugglers and pirates who would conceal stolen goods in their boots while going through customs. The French translation of this term was "flibustier." By the late 17th century, the English called pirates "filibusters," which was a variation of the French term "flibustier," which was derived from the English word "freebooter," which was a translation of the Dutch word "vryjbuiter." Confusing, isn't it? William Dampier used the word "filibuster" constantly when referring to his buccaneer associates.

The pirates who were originally sailors would have talked like sailors. In other words, they would have used nautical terminology. Many of those nautical expressions and words were still in use by seafaring men in the mid-20th century and some are still used by sailors today. Words like "avast" and "belay" were common words among sailors for hundreds of years. By the way, "avast" means "stop now" and probably comes from the Dutch "houd vast" which means "hold fast." The word "belay" also means stop, but in a far less urgent way.

"Ahoy" is a traditional hailing call used to initiate communication between vessels, kind of like the word "hello" which we used today. Sailors truly had a unique way of speaking and applied nautical terms to everyday speech. For example, instead of saying "Please sit down." They might say "Haul your arss to anchor." However, one famous expression that real sailors and pirates probably didn't ever say was "Shiver me timbers." This expression appears in books, plays, and films, but can't be documented prior to the mid-19th century and was most likely invented by an unidentified author.

Chapter 78
A Square Meal

What every sailor and pirate wanted most was a good square meal. Well, that's probably not exactly true, most would put rum ahead of eating, but a good meal was very important. The term "square meal" comes from the nautical practice of serving meals on square plates that fit into square boxes on the dinner table. That prevented the plate from sliding off the table in rolling seas. It is a misconception that pirate crews functioned on the brink of starvation. It has been suggested by a few authors that pirate captains deliberately kept their crew hungry to increase their desire to take prizes and improve their appetite for combat. This doesn't make sense. Many captains, especially in the 18th century, were elected by the crew and could be voted out of captaincy at any time. Even so, mutiny was always an option for an unhappy crew. I think that if a pirate captain withheld food from his men, the next item on the menu would be his neck.

Food was plentiful to pirates as just about every prize vessel would have food on board. If a pirate crew was lucky enough to take a ship just leaving port, the ship would be loaded with fresh supplies for the long voyage to its destination. If they took a ship that was completing its voyage and was low on food, the next ship they took would hopefully be well-stocked. In the event they were unlucky and didn't find any prizes to take, they could always put into a friendly port. Of course, access to pirate-friendly ports began to diminish after 1718, which was one of the contributing factors to the end of the golden age of piracy. Along the African coast there were still many pirate-friendly ports, even after 1720. Plus, there were thousands of native villages that would trade food and supplies.

There were a few documented cases when pirate crews were starved, but that was always accidental. Stede Bonnet's crew went through a brief period of starvation just after they left Blackbeard in June of 1718 due to their lack of success in finding any prizes. Another time was when Roberts' vessel got caught in the trade winds and blown from Africa back to the Americas. He had just sailed from the Caribbean to the Cape Verde Islands and was just about out of food when he arrived. He was totally unprepared to make the voyage back across the Atlantic and even with severe rationing, many of his crew died of starvation or thirst. But those incidents were very rare. Generally, all pirate and privateer crews were exceptionally well-fed and always had plenty of alcoholic beverages on hand.

The rest of this chapter deals with the food that was available and in common use during the 17th and 18th centuries, most of which would probably be found aboard a pirate vessel.

When discussing food, we must consider two basic types, food on ships and food ashore. Since food spoils, vessels at sea tended to only carry food that could be preserved for the long voyage. However, that doesn't mean that ships never carried fresh vegetables and fruits. Ships making short voyages may have plenty of fresh plants onboard and even ships crossing the ocean may have carried a large variety of fresh food at the beginning of the voyage. Contemporary accounts of the 1715 Spanish treasure fleet describe the decks being covered with stalks of bananas and plantains, sacks of oranges, limes, and coconuts, and a large variety of other fresh fruits and vegetables. Also, pens on the decks held pigs, chickens, goats, cattle, and live sea turtles. However, the traditional English seaman's fair included salted beef, pork and fish served with peas, cheese, oats, and hardtack cakes called "biskets." Documents from the Mayflower's voyage in 1620 describe hardened peas and oats, re-baked wheat flour biscuits, salted meat & fish, cheese & butter, and mustard & vinegar. Cooking ingredients included butter, vegetable oil, vinegar, mustard, and molasses. Beer was the primary drink since well-brewed beer remained fresh for a long time at sea and didn't carry disease like water did. Brandy and wine were also carried in large quantities and, later on, rum was added to the list of preferred alcoholic beverages. Livestock was also often carried on board which included all types of fowls, pigs, lambs, and occasionally even cows. The Spanish had healthier diets including olive oil, olives, fresh fish, vinegar, garlic, onions, dried pasta, rice, cheese, and both fresh and pickled vegetables.

In the Americas and along the East and West African coast, there was a far greater variety of native plants that often replaced the traditional European plants in the diets of the colonists and consequently the seamen. In many cases, those new plants were actually better than the European plants they were accustomed to. Corn, which didn't grow naturally in Europe, quickly became one of the primary food sources of colonists and the seamen that visited them. By the middle of the 17th century, dried corn and corn bread were added to the traditional list. Additionally, when provisioning in the Americas or Africa, vessels would stock up on the types of food that naturally grew there. That included an enormous variety of new kinds of fruits and vegetables.

Pirate fare could have been just about anything. There are some contemporary descriptions of food on pirate vessels from the golden age that helps us understand what they ate. Captain Snelgrave's ship was taken by Howell Davis in 1719 and later writes that the pirates took their geese, turkeys, fowls, and ducks to make a feast. He also mentioned cheese, butter, sugar, Irish beef, and hogsheads of claret and French brandy. Additionally, just about every contemporary source talks about pirates feasting on turtles whenever they were ashore careening their vessels. But the best information we have on pirate cuisine comes from William Dampier's 1697 book *Memoirs of a Buccaneer - New Voyages Round the World*. He was a buccaneer in the Caribbean from 1678–1686 and sailed around the world twice, well documenting every aspect of his voyages. He lists corn, rum with sugar and lime juice, brandy, and rice as provisions on ships. On his trip across the Isthmus of Panama in 1681 Dampier ate fowls, peccary (wild hogs), yams, potatoes, pineapples, and plantains. Dampier also describes a yellow and red plum that is native to the Bay of Campeche and very plentiful in Jamaica. Limes were also grown on Jamaica and were often used in making punch in both the East and West Indies, as well as at sea. Dampier also speaks of drinking hot chocolate about five times a day and mentions taking a Spanish vessel bound for Manila laden with rice, cotton cloth, and corn.

On the East India Companies' post on Santa Helena Island, Dampier describes the settlement as a small English town of 30 houses and a fort where they grow "potatoes, yams, and bananoes" and raise "hogs, bullocks, cock and hens, ducks, geese, and turkeys of which they have plenty and sell at a lower rate to the sailors." Dampier also describes plantains,

"The Spaniards in their towns in America, as at Havana, Cartagena, Portobelo, etc., have their markets full of plantains, it being the common food for poor people: their common price is half a rial, or 3 Pence a dozen. A ripe plantain sliced and dried in the sun may be preserved a great while; and then eat like figs, very sweet and pleasant. This fruit grows all over the West Indies (in the proper climates) at Guinea, and in the East Indies." Dampier also mentions fruits as commonly used ingredients in mixed drinks. He writes, "Their largest plantations have not above 20 or 30 plantain-trees, a bed of yams and potatoes, a bush of Indian pepper, and a small spot of pineapples; which last fruit as a main thing they delight in;

for with these they make a sort of drink which our men call pine-drink, much esteemed by those Miskitos..."

Any food that was available on ship or shore could have made its way into the hold of a pirate vessel. If an English pirate took a Spanish vessel, the menu for that evening would probably be Spanish cuisine. One can't look at an 18th century English cookbook and assume that this was the only fare that English pirates ate. A good example of this is the tomato. For a long time, tomatoes were thought to be poisonous by the English and consequently never used in English recipes. Nevertheless, that was not the case with the Spanish who used lots of tomatoes in many of their recipes and still do today. Another example is the potato, which was seldom used in French or English recipes in the 17th and 18th centuries even though potatoes had already become the mainstay of Irish cuisine and were often used in Portuguese and Spanish recipes.

Chapter 79
Native to the Old World or the New

As European colonists settled America, many of the livestock, plants and spices commonly used in their recipes were brought with them, right from the beginning. Christopher Columbus brought the first European crops to the New World during his second voyage in 1493 which included oranges, lemons, limes, melons, cucumbers, lettuce, and sugarcane. By 1500 the Portuguese were transporting and planting European crops as well as New World crops throughout their entire sphere of influence. They did this so rapidly and efficiently, that within one generation, they had completely changed the diet of many peoples. The crop with the most impact was the peanut which is native to Brazil, but within 20 years became one of the main ingredients in recipes throughout Thailand, Japan, China, and Africa. So rapid was the spread of peanuts that later explorers of the 16th and 17th centuries assumed they were native to Asia and Africa.

By 1517, Portugal had established dozens of trading ports throughout coastal India, Sumatra, Indonesia, Burma, Thailand, and south China.

From the early 17th century, the cuisine of the English, Dutch, and French included lettuce, onions, cucumbers, beets, parsnips, cabbage, cauliflower, watercress, white carrots, asparagus, peas, gourds, salsify, turnips, and leeks. Old World beans included peas, chickpeas, and fava beans. Fruits often mentioned are pears, grapes and raisins, olives, apples, lemons, oranges, raspberries, blackberries, gooseberries, apricots, cherries, prunes, musk melons, dates, and figs. Spices often used included cinnamon, ginger, nutmeg, marjoram, sage, mace, cloves, mint, rosemary, thyme, parsley, pepper, saffron, salt, savory, coriander, and mustard. English, Dutch, and French colonies from Newfoundland to the Caribbean would have grown many if not all of those plants and were available for use depending upon the climate and the season.

The Arab Moors ruled much of Spain from the 8th century to 1492.

Spanish cuisine was very heavily influenced by the Moroccan Arabs and included vegetables like eggplant, spinach, leeks, and cabbage. The Spanish also ate a great deal of rice, pasta, and barley. Fruits also included heavy use of oranges, limes, and lemons as well as pears, cherries, figs, and dates. Olives and grapes were of course a large part of their diet as well. Seasoning with cinnamon, almonds, and saffron was a favorite among the Spanish and used in almost every recipe. Other spices included ginger, cloves, red, black, and white pepper, parsley, horseradish, mustard, onions, coriander, and garlic. Use of vinegar, olive oil, and honey were also common. As the climate of sunny Spain is similar to the Caribbean, many plants would have been introduced to their colonies by the early 16th century. Rice quickly became a mainstay crop.

Lentils and grains such as wheat, barley, oats, and rye all came from Europe. Although oats were only used for livestock feed in most of Europe, oats made into porridge or oatmeal was a favorite food in Scotland. All were brought to the New World by the first settlers except rye, which was rare in the New World until the 19th century. Prior to the early 17th century carrots and beets looked far different than their modern varieties. Carrots were purple, yellow, or white with long roots and were not clearly distinguished from parsnips. Beets were long and thin. Around 1610 the modern looking orange carrot was domesticated by the Dutch and brought to their colonies in the New World. Modern beets developed all over Europe at about the same time.

Radishes were introduced by the Spanish in Mexico about 1500 and in Hispaniola in 1565. The turnip was brought to America by Jacques Cartier, who planted it in Canada in 1541. It was also planted in Virginia by the colonists in 1609 and in Massachusetts in the 1620s. The Indians adopted its culture from the colonists and soon grew it generally. Since colonial times the turnip has been one of the most common garden vegetables in America. Salsify originated in the Eastern Mediterranean and was known as the oyster plant or vegetable oyster. This long, thin root vegetable resembles a carrot in shape and a turnip in taste. Cultivation began in Italy and France in the 16th century and in Britain after that. The English grew salsify in their North American colonies and used it in many of their dishes.

Legumes
Fava Beans

Fava Beans—Old World

Black Eyed Peas—Africa

The only frequently eaten beans native to Europe were the fava beans, called broad beans in English recipes and chickpeas, called garbanzo beans by the Spanish. Both of them quickly faded in popularity in Europe as soon as the huge variety of New World beans were introduced. There was no need to import either fava or garbanzo beans to the New World and their presence in the Caribbean would have been very rare.

Black Eyed Peas

Black eyed peas originated in Africa but soon spread to Europe, where they were known during the classical era, but mostly used as animal fodder. The Spanish took them to America in the 16th century, but they were usually used as food for slaves. Black eyed peas didn't become popular in the southern United States until the early 19th century. Peas were a main staple of the English diet for landsmen and seamen and were introduced to the New World from the first settlements.

Beans—New World

Beans were another crop that revolutionized the European cuisine. Prior to contact with the New World, the only beans native to Europe were fava beans and garbanzo beans. Once Christopher Columbus brought New World beans back to Spain, their cultivation rapidly spread throughout Europe just like Maize. New World beans include lima beans, pinto beans, green beans (string beans) and common beans which come in many varieties such as red beans, white beans, and black beans. Just like maize, beans originated in South and Central America and were cultivated for thousands of years. Their cultivation spread throughout North America as far north as modern-day New England by 200AD.

Common beans were cultivated all over Europe by the mid-16th century. The English called them "kidney beans" to distinguish them from the European broad bean (fava). Lima beans were introduced to Spain after the common bean and was named for Lima, Peru, where they had been a mainstay crop of the Incas. The first known record of lima bean in Europe was around 1591. Beans of all types were commonly grown throughout all the European colonies and would have been carried on all vessels during the golden age of piracy.

Peanuts—Brazil and the Caribbean

Peanuts are native to Brazil and the Caribbean and were first identified in 1502 by Bartolome de las Casas and described in his 1530 book, *Apologetica Historia de las Indias*. He described the natives sowing and harvesting them. The Taino called them mani which is still the Spanish name for peanuts. Gonzalo Fernandez de Ovieda y Valdes arrived on Hispaniola around 1514 and eventually became Governor. In his *Historia General y Natural de las Indias* published in 1535 he writes, "Mani was a common food consumed raw or roasted by Indians on Hispaniola and other Caribbean Islands. True Christians didn't use them unless they were unmarried males, children, slaves, or just common people." In Brazil, peanuts were called Mandubi by the natives. Early on, the Portuguese realized the value of peanuts and transplanted them to all their tropical colonies to include Malaysia, Vietnam, China, Japan, the Philippines, and all along the east and west coast of Africa during the first part of the 16th century. Peanuts became so popular throughout the entire African continent that European naturalists in the 17th century believed the peanut to be native to Africa. Peanuts were used extensively in the slave trade as food for slaves as they were being transported across the Atlantic.

Portuguese sailors also ate lots of peanuts and the Portuguese planted peanuts at all of their refitting stations along the African coast to resupply their ships returning from the Indian Ocean. In 1570 Portuguese naturalist Gabriel Soares de Souza wrote that the natives ate peanuts roasted and cooked in the shell. He also described the Portuguese preparing peanuts in a similar manner to almond confectionery, covered with sugar mixture and confections. By the late 16th century peanuts were being grown in Spain. The first English reference to peanuts came in 1640 by naturalist John Parkinson in his book, *Theater of Plants*. The British botanist Hans Sloane mentioned peanuts being used on slave ships in Jamaica in 1707 but believed peanuts to be native to Africa. By 1712 peanuts were being commercially grown in hothouses throughout England and France.

French cookbooks of the day mentioned boiled peanuts, but peanuts were not cultivated in British colonial America until 1769, and then, they were only used as feed for livestock or food for slaves. Other accounts suggest that peanuts may have been grown in South Carolina a little earlier, as many settlers there formerly lived in the Caribbean where peanuts were grown in abundance. Pirates certainly would have access to lots of peanuts, from slave ships, Portuguese vessels, and from both African and Caribbean ports.

Vegetables
Kale
Kale was also among the first crops the English settlers brought to the New World as well as cabbage, which was first introduced to America in 1541 by Jacques Cartier, who planted it in Canada on his third voyage.

Cauliflower
Cauliflower was popular in Europe and was first introduced in North America in the late 1600s.

Maize (corn)—New World

The most significant New World crop to change the European diet was Maize, commonly called corn. Actually, the word "corn" was a European term that meant grain of any kind. Maize was called "Indian corn" for a while and then finally just corn. Originally from South America, maize was cultivated as a main crop throughout that continent and through Mesoamerica, Mexico, and the Caribbean for 8,000 years. By the third century AD, it had spread throughout the Eastern Woodlands and the Southwest of North America. Maize was first brought to Europe by Christopher Columbus in 1493. By 1500 maize was being grown throughout the Iberian Peninsula and in Italy. In the 16th century Portuguese sailors carried maize to their colonies in East Africa where it rapidly spread throughout North Africa and the Arab world. By the mid-17th century maize was being cultivated all over Europe. English colonists in the late 17th century noted that Native Americans carried sacks of parched cornmeal which lasted for months. This became common among travelers, hunters, soldiers, and sailors of the late 17th century and continued through the 19th century.

Tubers

Yuca Root—Brazil and the Caribbean

Cassava roots were a main staple food for the Mayans and most other native cultures throughout the Caribbean and in Central and South America. Originally from Brazil and introduced into Mesoamerica and the West Indies by 6,600 BC, they are long and tapered with rough brown skin on the outside. Today, they are available in modern grocery stores and are known as yuca roots, pronounced "yooka," as in Yucatan. They shouldn't be confused with the similarly spelled yucca plant. Cassava roots are poor in protein, but rich in starch, which gives the highest yield of energy per cultivated area among all crop plants. The cassava root remains one of the most common foods throughout the Caribbean. During the golden age, they would have been carried locally onboard vessels and probably eaten by all pirates.

Cultivated for over 4,000 years, the potato was one of the main foods of most South America cultures. There were over 200 varieties of potatoes being grown by the Incas when Spanish Conquistador Francisco Pizarro and his men arrived in Peru in 1528. However, the potato of that time looked nothing like the modern potato. It was much smaller and the skin was actually purple in color. It also had a somewhat bitter taste. One can still buy purple potatoes today at selected food stores. Spanish Conquistadors eventually brought the potato back to Spain. In 1573 the first account of the sale of a potato was in Seville. Before the end of the 16th century families of Basque sailors began to cultivate potatoes along the Biscay coast of northern Spain. However, for the rest of the Spanish population the potato was never really appreciated.

The Controversial Potato—Peru

In 1586 the potato was brought to England by Sir Francis Drake and was assumed to be originally from Virginia. Mistakenly called the "Virginia Potato," it was eventually served to Queen Elizabeth, but the cooks didn't realize that they were supposed to prepare the root and instead, gave the Queen a dish of boiled stems and leaves. Unfortunately, potato stems and leaves are somewhat poisonous and the Queen became ill. After the Queen's recovery, the potato was banned in court. This was perhaps the reason why the English didn't adopt the potato into their cuisine until the 19th century. However, the potato flourished in Ireland. In 1589 Sir Walter Raleigh became the first to introduce the potato to the Irish who were at war with England and their food supplies were scarce. By 1663 it was widely accepted in Ireland as a main food source.

In North America, potatoes arrived in the English colonies in 1621 when the Governor of Bermuda, Nathaniel Butler, sent two large cedar chests containing potatoes and other vegetables to Governor Francis Wyatt of Virginia at Jamestown, but the English didn't seem to like potatoes and they weren't grown in North America as a serious food source until the late 18th century.

In Eastern Europe and Germany potatoes were a different story. Cultivation of potatoes began in Eastern Europe in the early 17th century and flourished during the Thirty Years' War (1618 –1648). That's because it was a common practice for armies to burn the crops of their enemies and starve them into submission. However, potato crops survived because the potato remained safely underground during those fires and flourished afterwards. Millions of east Europeans were able to avoid starvation and began using potatoes in almost all of their recipes. That's why the potato is so prominent in many modern recipes of literally all the ethnic groups and nations from that region.

As for use by sailors and pirates, William Dampier mentions potatoes as being used as provisions for sailors of the East India Company on Saint Helena Island in 1685, but he might have been referring to the more common sweet potatoes. The potato wasn't grown in abundance at any of the ports pirates may have visited, so it is unlikely that pirates ate potatoes with any regularity.

Sweet Potatoes—Peru, Mexico, and the Caribbean

The sweet potato is often incorrectly called the yam. Native to West Africa, yams were a mainstay of many African tribes going back thousands of years. Horticulturally, they are totally unrelated to sweet potatoes, but they do have a similar appearance. It is believed that African slaves often called them yams and the name caught on. True African yams were not imported to the New World until modern times. Sweet Potatoes have been cultivated in Peru for about 10,000 years. Prior to the European arrival, cultivation had spread north to Mexico and throughout the Caribbean. Columbus noted that sweet potatoes were being eaten on Hispaniola and went by several local names to include aji, camote, and apichu. But the name that stuck was the batata, which eventually became the potato. Like so many other New World crops, they were brought back to Spain and eventually cultivated throughout most of Europe. In 1593 the Portuguese brought them to Southeast Asia and China.

From Spain, the sweet potato spread to England where they were sometimes called Spanish Potatoes. Spanish potatoes were known in England around the middle of the 16th century. William Harrison mentions them in the 1577 edition of *The Description of England*, but recipes for them do not appear in English cookbooks until the 1580s. It is important to note that in the 16th, 17th, and 18th centuries the English called regular potatoes "Virginia potatoes" while they called sweet potatoes "Spanish Potatoes" or occasionally "Sweet Potatoes." The sweet potato was not known in North America in the 16th century. They were introduced to America north of Mexico by English colonists settling in Virginia. Sweet potatoes were commonly grown from Georgia to Virginia in the 17th and 18th centuries, but due to the climate, they were rare in the northern colonies until the 1830s. Sweet potatoes were exceptionally popular throughout the Caribbean and in the English colonies of Carolina and Virginia. They made an excellent food source aboard ship and pirates from Africa or the Caribbean would have carried them on board.

Melons

Watermelons were brought to America by some of the earliest European colonists, being common in Massachusetts by 1629. The Florida Indians were said to have been growing watermelons by the mid-1600s, and Father Marquette, French explorer of the Mississippi, mentioned them in 1673 as being grown in the interior of the country. Muskmelons and cantaloupes are native to Persia and spread westward over the Mediterranean area in the Middle Ages. Columbus carried their seeds on his second voyage and had them planted on Isabela Island in 1494. Before the end of the 16th century they had been introduced by the Spaniards to many places in North

America. They were grown in the first English colonies of Virginia and Massachusetts and there is a report that muskmelons had been introduced to Bermuda in 1609.

Fruit

Cherries and pears—Asia Minor and China

Plums—Caucasus Mountains

Pomegranate—Middle East

Among the first fruit seeds sent to the Plymouth settlement in Massachusetts by the Massachusetts Bay Colony in 1628 were cherry, peach, plum, filbert, quince, and pomegranate and "according to accounts, they sprung up and flourished." Pears are one of the world's oldest cultivated fruits. By 1640 at least 64 varieties were being cultivated in England and they were certainly brought to the English colonies in the 17th century. Apricots originated on the Russian-Chinese border and were imported along with peaches into Europe through the "Silk Road" that extended camelback trading to the Mideast. Apricot tree seeds are believed to have been brought to English settlements in the 17th century.

Peaches were brought to Virginia in the early 17th century by George Minifie, a horticulturist from England, who planted them at his estate in Virginia. Afterwards, American Indian tribes actually spread the peach tree across the continent by planting seeds as they traveled. Apple trees originated in Kazakhstan and were popular all over Europe for thousands of years. Apple Cider had become a popular beverage in England after the Norman Conquest in 1066. North American apple harvesting began with the settlers at Jamestown in 1607, but they weren't eaten. Traditional apple orchards were first planted near Boston in 1625 by Reverend William Blaxton. Apples don't grow well in the tropics, so pirates sailing the tropical waters would only come across apples if they took a vessel that was traveling from the north.

Peaches—China

Apples—Kazakhstan

Bananas and Plantains—Indonesia

William Dampier mentions plantains as a regular food source in the Caribbean and bananas on St. Helena Island. Originally from Southeast Asia, Indonesia, and New Guinea, the two plants are actually varieties of the same species. Plantains are a bit firmer and lower in sugar content than bananas and are generally cooked. Bananas were introduced in Africa in the 6th century by Arab traders. The Portuguese found bananas already growing in Africa when they began colonization in the 15th century and introduced them to the Caribbean and Brazil in the 16th century.

Plantains were first brought to the Canary Islands by the Portuguese in the 15th century and introduced in the Caribbean 100 years later when they were brought to Santo Domingo in 1516 by a Portuguese Franciscan monk. The name banana seems to be of African origin while plantains may have been named by the Spanish who called them plantanos for their resemblance to the plane tree of Spain. This explains the comments by Dampier. Plantains became a staple food in the Caribbean that were either simply boiled, fried, baked, or added to a soup. Any pirate traveling from the Caribbean may have had a supply of plantains onboard, especially sweetened and dried.

Coconuts—Indian Ocean

Coconuts seem to have been growing in all the tropical regions of the Pacific and Indian Oceans for thousands of years. By the 15th century they had naturally reached the Pacific coast of the Americas, but not the Atlantic coast. The coconut was introduced in the Caribbean by the Portuguese very early in the 16th century. They may have seemed strange to the first Spanish settlers in the New World—but not to the sailors who traveled the Pacific and Indian oceans.

Pineapples—Brazil and the Caribbean

The pineapple is native to southern Brazil and Paraguay. It spread throughout eastern South America and the Caribbean by ancient peoples and was growing in the Bahamas when Columbus first landed in 1492. He even brought a few pineapples back to Europe. When English colonists first saw them in the early 17th century, they thought they resembled pinecones, only larger with a sweet apple like fruit, so the name pineapple seemed a likely choice. The pineapple was a highly coveted item by the royalty of Europe, but no one could get them to grow anywhere except in the Caribbean. Since most pineapples spoiled on the long voyage across the Atlantic, vessels especially designed for speed were commissioned by the kings of Europe to bring fresh pineapples from the Caribbean to the royal courts. King Charles II of England loved pineapples so much that he posed for his royal portrait with a fresh pineapple.

Preserved pineapples lasted much longer and glazed candy pineapple chunks packed in sugar were exported from the Caribbean to wealthy families throughout the English Empire. The English colonies of Carolina, Virginia, and New England were a bit closer and had a better chance of getting fresh pineapples. Even so, they were still very expensive and hard to get. The gift of a pineapple was the ultimate gesture of friendship and consequently, the image of a pineapple became utilized everywhere as a sign of hospitality and welcome. In colonial America, one can see pineapple designs carved over doorways, sculpted on fence posts, drawn on doormats and dishes, just about everywhere. Pirates would have had access to plenty of pineapples while sailing the waters of the Caribbean or on shore, especially in the Bahamas where many pineapples were cultivated for export.

Strawberries

Strawberries grew in both Europe and North America but in totally different varieties. The European variety was cultivated by 1300 but was very tart and was only used as seasoning. Then, in the 1600s, the Virginia strawberry of North America, the one we think of today, was discovered by the first settlers and imported to Europe. However, they weren't really popular until the end of the 18th century.

Tomatoes—Mexico

Tomatoes are native to Mexico and were among the main foods eaten by the Aztecs when the Spanish arrived in 1521. The Spanish quickly distributed tomatoes throughout their colonies in the Caribbean and the Philippines and also brought them back to Spain. Since the Spanish ruled much of Italy in the early 16th century tomatoes were taken there as well. The earliest documentation of the tomato in Europe comes from the Italian botanist, Pietro Andrea Mattioli in 1544 and in 1548 the house steward of Cosimo de' Medichi wrote a note to his secretary informing him that the basket of tomatoes had arrived safely.

However, in Spain and Italy the use of tomatoes in cooking was sparse until the early 1700s and they were eaten by only the very poor and the very rich. This seems to be an odd combination but was apparently due to their eating utensils. The middle class used mostly lead based pewter and the high acid content of tomatoes caused the pewter to break down, thus giving the person lead poisoning. The poor used wooden utensils and the rich used silver. In England, the English botanist John Gerald described tomatoes in 1597 as poisonous. The leaves actually are poisonous, and they resembled nightshade which was used to make poison and was long associated with witchcraft. This, plus the effect tomatoes had on pewter, put a firm belief into the English that tomatoes were evil, or at least, deadly. They were grown ornamentally but almost never eaten. In Mexico and on Spanish controlled Caribbean islands, natives and Spaniards alike safely ate tomatoes, as pewter was rare in that part of the world in the 16th and early 17th centuries. It wasn't until the mid-18th century that tomatoes began to be used as food by the English, at first mixed in stews. English and Dutch pirates of the day would not have eaten tomatoes, even though Spanish pirates probably did.

Avocados—Mexico

Avocados were originally native to México and were a main part of the Aztec diet. They spread to northern South America long before European contact. The Aztecs called them ahuacatl, which means testicle in the Aztec language and was obviously named for the shape. The Spanish pronunciation was avocado. The first mention of them by Europeans came from

---

TOMATOES: ARE THEY POISON?

In England, the English botanist John Gerald described tomatoes in 1597 as poisonous.

During the 17th and 18th centuries, sailors used avocados as a spread over hard-tack and call it "midshipman's butter."

Martin Fernandez de Encisco in his 1518 book, *Suma de Geografía que Trata de Todas las Partidas y Provincias del Mundo*. The Spanish spread avocados all over the Caribbean including their small colony on Jamaica. There were three varieties, the Mexican, West Indian, and Guatemalan, which were catalogued in 1653 by the Spanish padre Bernabe Cobo. The English were introduced to avocados when they took Jamaica in 1655. The first English account of avocados comes from W. Huges during his visit to Jamaica where he writes the avocado is "one of the most rare and pleasant fruits of the island. It nourisheth and strengtheneth the body, corroborating the spirits and procuring lust exceedingly." They are also mentioned by Hans Sloane in his 1696 index of Jamaican plants. During the 17th and 18th centuries sailors used avocados as a spread over hard-tack and eventually called it "midshipman's butter." Ships sailing the Caribbean certainly could have had avocados. This makes avocados a good choice for a pirate meal.

The New World introduced two main spices to the cuisine of the Europeans. Scotch Bonnet is a variety of chili pepper and is considered among the hottest peppers in the world. Native to the Caribbean, it has a distinct flavor and gives Jamaican jerk pork and chicken its unique flavor. The other is allspice, which is also called Jamaica pepper and newspice. Allspice is made from the dried fruit of the pimenta plant, a tree also native to the West Indies, southern Mexico, and Central America. The name "allspice" came from the English, who thought it combined the flavors of their favorite spices, cinnamon, nutmeg, and cloves.

Citrus: South-East Asia, China, India

Orange, lemon, and lime trees were fully cultivated throughout southern Europe by the 15th century and were brought to the Caribbean by Christopher Columbus on his second voyage in 1493 and planted on Hispaniola. By the early 1500s they flourished everywhere in the Caribbean. They seemed to dominate the Caribbean cuisine, especially on Jamaica where they became a large part of Jamaican recipes for both food and alcoholic mixed drinks. At sea, sailors used lime juice to flavor food, to mix with rum and to disguise the bad taste of stale water. Despite stories that the grapefruit was bred in the 18th century, the seeds were actually brought to Barbados and Jamaica from Southeast Asia in the 17th century.

Sweets
Sugar—South-East Asia

The most important crop introduced to the New World was sugarcane. It was the world's most valuable cash crop of the 17th century. Not only was sugarcane used to make sugar, it was also used to make rum. Originally from South East Asia and India, cultivation had reached Persia by the sixth century AD; and from there, sugar spread into the Mediterranean by the expansion of the Arabs. Columbus brought sugar to Hispaniola on his second voyage of 1494 where cultivation as a cash crop helped the colony develop. Before 1500 most sugar production was in Islamic countries in Africa and the sugar sold to Europeans was exceptionally costly. But once the Europeans discovered the New World, there was an alternative source. The climate of the Caribbean was ideal for sugar cultivation and the Europeans could purchase directly from their own colonies without having to pay the "middle man" prices.

Chocolate—Mexico

The cocoa plant was originally from Central America and Mexico. Cocoa beans have been turned into chocolate drink for thousands of years by the native tribes of the region. Chocolate drink was introduced to Europe by Hernando Cortez, who brought it back to Spain after his conquest of the Aztecs in 1528. In 1585 the first regular shipment of cocoa beans arrived in Spain and launched a highly lucrative Spanish trade with chocolate shops springing up all over Spain.

At first, chocolate was exceptionally valuable and a very closely guarded secret among the Spanish, who soon added sugar, vanilla, cinnamon, and pepper to the recipe of the chocolate drink. So closely guarded was the secret of cocoa, that when a 16th century English privateer captured a Spanish vessel loaded with a priceless cargo of cocoa beans, the Englishmen didn't know what the cargo was and burned it. By 1615 the secret had reached France, and by 1650 England. Although chocolate was expensive and normally reserved for the wealthy, chocolate drink was certainly consumed by pirates. William Dampier mentions drinking five or six cups of chocolate every day.

A few important crops were found in both the New and the Old World. The grape vine is native to southern Europe and the Near and Middle East and has been cultivated since about 4,000 BC. However, grapes originated a few places in temperate North America too. When Viking explorers first landed in Newfoundland, they named it Vinland for the grape vines they found. Early English colonists mentioned the bounty of grapes they found in their new home.

The calabash or bottle gourd was also a common food source on both continents. It is now believed that they originated in Africa and were commonly cultivated in Europe and Asia in prehistory and that they were brought to the New World at the end of the ice age by Paleo-Indians. Chestnuts were also native to both the New and Old world. Very popular in Europe and especially England, early colonists were delighted to find chestnut trees growing from Massachusetts to north Florida.

Olive Oil

Olive oil has been a vital commodity all throughout Europe for thousands of years. However, olives only grew in the Mediterranean environment, which meant that olive oil had to be imported in large jars to most of Europe. The first olive seedlings from Spain were planted in Lima, Peru by Antonio de Rivera in 1560. Olive tree cultivation quickly spread along the valleys of South America's dry Pacific coast where the climate was similar to the Mediterranean. Not effectively grown on the east coast of the New World, olive oil still had to be imported in large jars. Large clay jars containing olive oil have been found at shipwrecks dating from the 17th and 18th centuries throughout the east coast of the New World. Interestingly enough, they seem to be identical to olive oil jars removed from wrecks that date to the time of the ancient Greeks.

Late 17th century jars of olive oil have been recovered from ship wrecks off the Virginia coast.

Coffee, Arabia

The exact origin of the coffee bean may be from Ethiopia, and by the 15th century coffee was being grown in the Yemeni district of Arabia. European travelers brought some beans back to Europe and by the 17th century, coffee was in high demand on the European market. Coffee houses sprung up everywhere and became the centers of social activity in the major cities of England, Austria, France, Germany, and Holland. In England, they were called "penny universities" because their patrons could spend one penny for a cup of coffee and then engage in stimulating and enlightening conversation. By the mid-17th century there were over 300 coffee houses in London, many of which attracted like-minded patrons, including merchants, shippers, brokers and artists. Coffee was first brought to the New World by the English, who imported it to the colony of New York in the last 1600s. However, coffee was still rare in the New World during the golden age of piracy, as it was imported but not grown. It wasn't cultivated until 1723 when a young naval officer, Gabriel de Clieu, brought coffee seeds to Martinique.

Spices

Spices are an essential part of many recipes. Some spices grew naturally in Europe while others had to be imported. It is believed that marjoram originally came from the Mediterranean region and was commonly used in Europe to flavor beer as well as food. During the 16th century oregano was used for just about anything. Sage is native in the western and southern Balkans and was another favorite spice that was grown locally. Other locally grown spices in Europe were mint, rosemary, thyme, savory, basil, parsley, cilantro, the seeds called coriander, and saffron.

From ancient times, saffron was widely used throughout the Old World as a yellow die, a flavoring spice, and as a fragrance. It was also the most expensive spice locally grown, because of the labor required to obtain it. Saffron is produced from gathering the pollen of the saffron crocus. Native to the eastern Mediterranean region, the saffron trade in the 13th century was a prime target for pirates. England's King Henry VIII was so fond of saffron, he executed anyone who sold it in a diluted form.

But the most coveted spices all had to be imported at tremendous expense from a group of islands in Indonesia called the Banda Islands. They were also known as the Spice Islands. From ancient times to the 15th century, the only way to import those spices to Europe was through Arab merchants who hiked up the prices as high as they could. The search for a cheaper way to get to the Spice Islands is what prompted the Spanish to finance Christopher Columbus' expedition of 1492.

Nutmeg was a highly prized and costly spice in the European medieval cuisine. It was used for favoring and for medicinal treatments as well as a preservative agent. Other spices that were only cultivated on the Spice Islands were mace, cloves, cinnamon, turmeric, and black pepper. Most of the Spice Island spices weren't cultivated anywhere else until the 19th century.

Ginger, on the other hand, was used in China and India 7,000 years ago and was an important item in the spice trade that stretched overland and by sea from India to the ports of the eastern Mediterranean. The Portuguese took it to Africa in the 15th century and the Spaniards carried it to the New World in the 16th century.

Food Not Available to Pirates During the Golden Age

Not all of the commonly eaten crops of today were regularly eaten during the golden age of piracy, either in Europe or in the New World. Brussels sprouts were first propagated in Brussels sometime between the 17th and 18th century. However, they weren't commonly grown until the 19th century. Celery is a member of the parsley family but was not considered an edible plant until the French began eating it in the 1600s. Celery wasn't commonly grown or eaten until the 19th century. Artichokes were popular among the royalty of Italy and France but not commonly eaten. French immigrants brought artichokes to the United States in 1806 when they settled in the Louisiana Territory. Asparagus was also served in the royal courts of Europe in the 17th century but wasn't available at the local marketplace until the late 18th century. Broccoli was a favorite among Italians. Nevertheless, it wasn't introduced to the rest of Europe until the 18th century and wasn't popular in America until the 1920s.

Okra originated in the Mediterranean and Africa. It was very popular in African recipes and was introduced to the West Indies by African slaves. According to legend, okra was introduced to southeastern North America by the "Casquette Girls" who were 25 young French women who landed at Mobile in 1704 in search of husbands. They brought okra with them that had been obtained from slaves in the West Indies. They used okra to invent "gumbo," which is a soup or stew thickened with okra. Common throughout the southeastern United States in the 19th century, it is doubtful that it would have been eaten by anyone but slaves during the 17th or 18th centuries.

Edible mushrooms weren't used in recipes until the French began using them in the 16th century. Widespread use of mushrooms wasn't popular until the 19th century. Plums may have been one of the first fruits domesticated by humans and were very popular throughout Europe, but the earliest reference to plums in the American colonies came from Prince Nursery of Flushing, New York, that was established in 1737. Pistachio trees have grown in the Middle East for thousands of years and were introduced into Europe at the beginning of the Christian era. However, they weren't brought to the New World until 1853.

Cooking Styles
Boucan
The Tainos were the native people who lived on Cuba, Hispaniola, Jamaica, some of the northern islands of the Lesser Antilles, and the Bahamas. Many references identify them as Arawak, but that is not precise. The Tainos spoke the Arawak language, however, they were actually a sub-tribe of the larger Arawak group. They had a very interesting way of preparing any kind of meat including fish, chicken, beef, and especially pork. In the Arawak language, this cooking method was called "boucan." This cooking method was adopted by the early English and French settlers on the island of Hispaniola, giving rise to their name, "Boucanniors" by the French and "Boucaneers" by the English.

The meat was first seasoned with scotch bonnet and then wrapped in the leaves of the pimenta tree. The next step was to construct a grid of green sticks above a shallow pit which was filled with smoldering hot charcoals from the green wood of the pimenta tree. The wrapped meat was placed above the smoldering fire on the grid. As you may recall, the pimenta tree is the source of allspice. The combination of the pimenta leaf wrapping and the pimenta wood smoke gave the meat a very spicy flavor. Once properly smoked, the meat was removed and cut into strips for easy storage. The Arawak word for this dried meat was "charqui" which was eventually pronounced as "jerky" in English. Boucan meat was hence called "jerked meat." This spicy smoked jerky would keep for months and was ideal for sailors making long sea voyages. The flavor was also far better than the salted meat they got back in Europe. Any vessel sailing the Caribbean would have stocked up on as much jerked meat as they could get.

Onboard

Shipboard cooking was a necessity on all vessels. Just about every vessel had a fireplace on board where a cook could prepare a hot meal. Those fireplaces were rather small when compared to ones ashore. Aboard ship, the fireplace was more like a brick firebox which was constructed on the main deck inside a small structure. It could burn wood, but most of the time ships' cooks used smaller pieces of pre-charred wood, which was easier to store. Most vessels carried a full array of cooking utensils with a variety of pots and pans made of either iron or copper. Still, with only one source of heat, the easiest hot meals to prepare were stews and soups, which were made using one large pot. However, a skilled cook was capable of making just about anything one could make on shore, provided he had the ingredients. Because soups were so common, vessels often carried a sort of dried powdered soup mix, similar to bouillon cubes of today, which would be reconstituted to make the soup stock. The hardtack biscuits were well-named and would normally be dropped into the soup to soften them up and make them easier to eat. Butter would have been available for use in cooking if the vessel had live goats or cattle on board and eggs would have been used if they had live chickens. A large variety of spices would have been carried onboard and used in the preparation of all meals. Allspice was a favorite seasoning in the Caribbean and was almost always present. Another popular seasoning was guinea pepper which was very hot spice originally grown in Africa, but was cultivated in Trinidad by the late 17th century. Guinea peppers were often made into a sauce.

Pirates often careened their vessels on a secluded beach and would have to cook for a very large crew while ashore. For that reason, pirate vessels normally carried plenty of cooking utensils and pots used in the preparation of food in a camp on land. This would of course include iron tripods to hang pots over open fires and iron spits to roast pigs and fowl. Spoons of all sizes were common, either made of iron or wood. Also, large iron two pronged forks were an absolute necessity, normally with a curve on the end of the handle to allow the cook to hang it on a hook. Mortars and pestles were used to crush spices. Small Dutch ovens were also used quite a lot during this period as well as iron and copper pots. Those pots came in many sizes and were basic in shape. However, the very large iron pots with curved sides so often associated with witches, were actually a late 18th century design and not found during the golden age.

Alcohol

By the early 17th century, Europe had a large variety of alcoholic beverages. Wine of all sorts had been around for thousands of years and was well documented on vessels that sailed the oceans during the golden age. Beer had also been around for thousands of years and was plentiful aboard ships during the 17th and 18th centuries. It was safer to drink than water since water carried bacteria. However, beer didn't keep well in tropical climates, so it would have been less common to find beer among pirates sailing the waters of the Indian Ocean, the Caribbean, or along the African coast. However, beer was mentioned as a beverage consumed by Captain Roberts' crew. Distilling whiskey was perfected in Scotland and Ireland prior to the 15th century.

By the mid-16th century whiskey was a well-established drink among the English. The first licensed distillery was the Old Bushmills Distillery in Ireland, established in 1608. Gin was developed by the Dutch in the mid-17th century with about 400 distilleries in Amsterdam alone by 1663. Gin made its way to England in 1688 when the Dutch ruler, William of Orange, became King William III of England. Gin would have been carried on both English and Dutch vessels from the late 17th century on. There is an account of gin being consumed by Captain Roberts' crew.

Rum is the drink most associated with pirates of the golden age. First concocted between 1630 and 1650 by slaves working on the sugar plantations on Barbados, rum was made from molasses, the byproduct of refining sugarcane. Sometime before 1650 the plantation owners began drinking rum and developed methods of concentrating the alcohol by removing the impurities. One visitor to Barbados in 1651 wrote, "The chief fuddling they make in the island is Rumbullion, alias Kill-Divil, and this is made of sugarcanes distilled, a hot, hellish, and terrible liquor." By 1660 rum was being drunk throughout the Caribbean and the colonies of North America. The newly settled English colony of Jamaica was the next location to begin the production of rum. The first rum distillery on the mainland of North America opened on present day Staten Island, New York in 1664, the same year the English took the colony away from the Dutch. In 1667 another distillery opened in Boston and due to their superior metalworking and cooperage skills, New England quickly surpassed the Caribbean in the manufacturing of rum.

Prior to the 1660s the English navy issued French brandy to the sailors aboard Royal Naval vessels, but by the end of the 17th century, the English naval authorities found that rum was far less expensive and much easier to obtain. Rum quickly replaced brandy as the official drink of the navy and was rationed to each man aboard ship. Rum was drunk neat (straight) or mixed with lime juice, as was the common practice on Jamaica. William Dampier even mentions his pirate crew mixing rum, sugar, and lime juice to make punch.

They didn't know it at the time, but drinking lime juice helped prevent scurvy. However, water was a different problem. The water onboard most vessels was filled with microbes and was generally unsafe to drink. That led to dehydration. Around 1740 Royal Navy Admiral Edward Vernon ordered his sailors to drink a mixture of rum, lime juice, and water. The alcohol in the rum made the water a little safer and better tasting. The Admiral's nickname was "Old Grog" because he often wore a coat made of grogram wool. It is believed that this mixture of rum, water, and lime juice was called "Grog" in his honor. The term "Grog" is still used today among naval forces to refer to any sort of rum punch.

Special drink concoctions were very popular. Rum seems to be the ideal beverage for mixing with other beverages and juices, but just like modern times, there were many commonly mixed drinks and a few special ones. Valentine Ashplant, one of Captain Robert's officers, was renowned for making a special drink concocted by mixing beer, sherry, gin, eggs, brown sugar, cinnamon, and nutmeg. Once mixed, it was served heated. Hot buttered rum was also very popular. Mix a liberal amount of rum with cinnamon, brown sugar, cloves, ginger, and nutmeg. Add melted butter, stir well, and serve hot. A "Rummer" was also a common drink, made by mixing rum with brandy and adding apricots, peaches, cherry juice, and lime juice.

Chapter 80
What to Eat With

Many people think of pirates as eating with wooden spoons off of crudely made wooden plates or bowls. That was true for many sailors aboard merchant vessels of the day, but for the most part, that's just not true for pirates. Sailors aboard merchant vessels were treated rather poorly and were underpaid. For the common seaman of the day, wooden tableware was common. However, pirates took what they pleased and would have quickly amassed a large variety of the finest tableware available. Governor Hamilton of Bermuda recounts the testimony of a victim taken by Blackbeard in which he said, "They had a great deal of plate on board, and one very fine cup they told deponent they had taken out of Capt. Taylor, bound from Barbados to Jamaica, whom they very much abused and burnt his ship." Large amounts of fine china dishes and bowls plus pewter tableware were recovered from the wreck of Sam Bellamy's pirate ship, Whydah, which indicates that pirates routinely had things of pretty good quality. Pewter spoons, forks, plates, cups, and porringers would be the most common, as pewter doesn't break. That was important on shipboard. We can't even rule out silver or gold tableware. If it existed at the time, a pirate may have had it.

In the 17th and early 18th centuries, forks came in two varieties. They were either as large as modern forks but with only two prongs or they were smaller than modern salad forks but with four prongs. There are examples of small four-pronged forks recovered from both the 1717 wreck of the Whydah and the 1715 wreck of the Spanish treasure fleet. Table knives had rather large rounded tips which would be used almost like a spoon. Table spoons resemble modern spoons and came in a variety of sizes and shapes. Tableware was most commonly made of pewter, but silver and even gold was used quite often. What really distinguishes the period of each is the design of the handle. That changed from decade to decade along with current fashion trends. The handle of a spoon made in 1680 will look far

Chinese porcelain was imported to Europe through the Portuguese beginning in the early 16th century. Europeans began copying the techniques and producing "China" in Europe in 1712.

different than one made in 1715. The design also changed from nation to nation.

Fine porcelain made in China was imported to Europe and the New World in very large quantities and would have been kept and used by pirates. China porcelain can be found on just about every shipwreck site including the pirate ship Whydah. One might argue that pirates wouldn't have kept anything as valuable as porcelain for their personal use; they would have sold all captured porcelain ashore. That might be true in some cases, but the modest amounts of money they would have made selling stolen porcelain was insignificant to the huge amounts of gold they found. Additionally, they would have spent their time ashore selling any valuable cargo like silk, sugar, and cotton. I believe that most fine tableware would have been kept and used onboard, and in the case of porcelain, used until it broke.

Stoneware

In Europe, stoneware was manufactured from the 12th century on. Early salt-glazed wares have been found at Aachen and Cologne; these grayish, blue, and brown wares were exported in quantity to the Lowlands of Scotland and England. Stoneware was imported to the colonies from the beginning and archaeological evidence shows that every type of stoneware found in England or Holland was being used in America at the same time. Samples uncovered in the Chesapeake region of Virginia that pre-date 1720 include Ashley Ware, Buckley Ware, Tin Glazed Ware, Porcelain, English Brown Ware, Stone Ware, and Delft Ware. All would be available for capture and use by pirates. Border Ware (yellowish with green glaze) was very common from 1600–1660 but not produced afterwards. Pottery with the color of tan and blue (especially with printing on it) was commonly produced after the middle of the 18th century, but not during the golden age.

Glass, tankards, and dishes

When glass is produced naturally it has a dark green tint. Prior to the 1700s, clear glass and glass of other colors were possible, but very rare due to their cost. After about 1690, new processes in manufacturing glass made clear glass affordable, but green glass was still widely produced until about 1720. Clear wine glasses were common among the wealthy and could have been found aboard pirate vessels. Due to the expense of production, common glass bottles were not made of clear glass until the end of the 18th century, so all bottles containing alcohol, or any other substance, would have been green.

The most common drinking vessel was the tankard, usually made of pewter but also made of copper, stoneware, and even leather lined with tar. In the 17th century, tankards were almost always covered with a hinged lid, but by the 18th century most were not. Tin plated cups and dishes weren't common until a little after the golden age. Tin plating was around since 1620, but only in Bohemia. It didn't reach England until the late 17th century. By the mid-18th century tin cups were plentiful, but in the golden age, tin plated products were very rare.

Wooden dishes and spoons were very common from earliest time and they certainly would have been plentiful aboard most vessels during the golden age. They don't break easily and one can hold them with hot food in them. The disadvantage is that the food gets into the porous wood and carries bacteria, which causes the bowls and plates to begin to taste bad after a while. They also tend to crack from the changing moisture. Even so, they would have still been used as serving bowels or plates, even on pirate vessels where the crew had fancy personal tableware.

Chapter 81
Textiles

Prior to 1500 Europe's textiles were mostly wools and linens with a few rare exotic silks that were brought to Europe from China over the Silk Road and cotton that had been imported to Europe in very limited quantities from Egypt. However, with the establishment of regular sea trade between Europe and the Orient in the 16th century, many new types of textiles began appearing in the European markets and in very large quantities. India was the primary manufacturer of many of those textiles. Other sources were China and Arabia. England, France, Spain, Portugal, and the Dutch—all established companies that traded specifically in the Orient, called East India Trading Companies.

Exotic embroideries, painted cottons, and silks that were brought from the Orient by the East India Companies in the early 1600s had become the rage all through Europe by 1660. By 1670 cotton muslins from India were being imported and commonly worn throughout Europe and the American colonies. By 1680 painted calicoes, silk, tick, and taffeta textiles were also being imported in very large quantities. And by 1720 just about *any* natural fabric or mixed weave would be widely available, except in England. This was due to the Calico Act of 1700 which I will discuss a little later.

By the 17th century England was one of the major wool producing nations selling wool fabrics in many grades to include flannel and serge. Kersey is a coarse twill wool cloth used in England for hundreds of years and was the standard material used for military uniforms throughout Europe. It is mentioned in official records as early as 1552. Spanish cloth was a very fine wool manufactured in Spain throughout the 17th and 18th centuries. Spanish cloth was common in England after 1650. Mohair is made from the wool of the Angora goat and was imported into Europe from Turkey as early as 1699. Made from flax, linen is the oldest textile known.

English and Irish linen production was a vital part of the English economy throughout the 17th and 18th centuries.

Indian and Egyptian Imports

The most important textile imported from India in the 17th century was cotton. That was because it had been the most commonly used fabric in India for thousands of years and was exceptionally desirable for sale throughout Europe and their colonies. Cotton was worn in Europe as far back as the Middle Ages, but in very limited quantities because it had to be imported from North Africa. There are four basic varieties the cotton plant, one native to India, one native to Egypt (highly prized for making sails), one native to tropical South America, and one short stapled variety that grew naturally throughout sub-tropic North America, Central America, and the Caribbean. The varieties of cotton native to India, Egypt, and South America all have a long staple or fiber. The seeds have to be removed before cotton can be processed into fabric. The cotton gin is a machine that quickly and efficiently separates the cotton fibers from their seeds. In India and Egypt cotton gins have been in use since the 6th century, which is why cotton was so easy to process in those regions.

Cotton

Cotton fabric was also very common in the New World and was produced by all Native American cultures between the American Southwest, Florida and South America; however, they never developed any sort of cotton gin, so the seeds had to be separated by hand. The Tainos of the Bahamas were wearing crudely processed cotton when Columbus arrived in 1492. Of course, the dominant cultures of Peru all had cotton. Unfortunately for the settlers in North America and the Caribbean, the variety of cotton that grew there had a short staple or fiber, making it difficult to remove the seeds. The Indian and Egyptian cotton gins didn't work on this short-stapled type of cotton. This rendered native cotton from North America impractical for commercial use until 1792 when Eli Whitney developed a special cotton gin designed for the short staple cotton plant.

Indian cotton of every variety was called "calico" because it was exported from the Indian sea port of Calicut. Today, most people think of calico as a brightly printed cotton cloth used for quilting and curtains, but in the 17th and 18th centuries, calico was a generic term which included many grades of cloth that was plain, printed, stained, or dyed material made of cotton, muslin, or chintz. Bengal cloth, sometimes called "Bengal Silk," was a cheap mixed silk-cotton imported from India which was normally striped and was in great demand for its cheapness, rather than its quality, throughout

Europe after 1660. Plain cotton muslin was also imported in large quantities. Alacha was another striped Indian cotton and silk mixture imported after 1660 and often used for petticoats. Painted calicoes were being imported by the 1670s. There is a contemporary reference that painted, flowered, and striped calico was being sold in Salem, Massachusetts in 1677. Chintz is a cotton cloth from India which is painted or printed and sometimes glazed. Guinea cloth was a cheap and brightly colored Indian cotton that was imported by the East India Company after 1680 to the west coast of Africa and the Caribbean for use as clothing for slaves.

Dampier mentions taking a Spanish vessel laden with cotton cloth bound for Manila in 1686. Stained and painted calicoes were mentioned in 1696 as a hindrance to the consumption of English textiles. Atlas was a silk-satin fabric manufactured in India and imported to England in the 1690s. It came plain, striped, or flowered and in a variety of colors. A 1695 New York inventory mentions a chintz petticoat, waistcoat, seven mantels, and a flowered carpet. And there is a New York inventory from 1695 that references nightgowns, neck cloths, aprons, quilted waistcoats, white and flowered petticoats, and curtains all made of calico. And of course, "Calico Jack Rackham" was given his nickname because he always wore brightly colored calico clothes.

Blended Fabrics

Damask is a fabric made of several different fibers, often silk, with a flowered pattern woven into the material. Used by the end of the 17th century, there are records of damask being used in Boston by 1695. Dorea is a striped or checked fabric of mixed silk and cotton muslin from India which was also in use in London by 1695. Taffeta was imported from Bengal throughout the 17th and 18th centuries and includes a wide range of silk and silk/cotton mix fabrics. Many of them were striped or checkered. In 1727 a London merchant ordered Persian Taffetas in white, bright red, gold, bright green, peach bloom, and other colors. They were made in all colors, striped, checkered, flowered, or with patterns. A description of Spanish officers on warships states, "Some officers even wore breeches made of heavy silk taffeta." In England, taffeta colors were commonly red and white or blue and white. They were most often used for petticoats, but by 1711 many other colors were also used.

Textiles were big business. European fabric manufacturers scrambled to come up with copies of Asian fabrics by mixing silk and cotton thread with wool and linen. They produced a large variety of fabrics including taffetas, fustian, damask, cherryderry, dunjars, seersucker, and many others. In France, importation of Asian textiles grew tremendously, and the city of

Lyons became the silk weaving center in France around 1650. In the 1680s cotton woven with brightly colored silk stripes became very popular.

The Dutch took the lead in the mixing of silk, linen, and wool and produced the most coveted textiles of the 17th century. To attempt to get in on the market, England encouraged Dutch fabric weavers to come to England and improve their industry. Many of them did just that—primarily to escape the Spanish occupation of the Netherlands. After that, many fine fabrics of mixed weaves became common in England. In the beginning of the 1670s Lancaster became the European center for cotton and linen weaving. Fustian is a general term used to describe a variety of fabrics made of mixing wool or cotton with linen. Wool-linen mixes have been around in England since 1336. Adding cotton to the mix began in 1674. Samples dating from 1716 were in rich bright colors to include pink, cream, tawny, golden brown, and yellows, just to name a few and in 1676, William Sherwin of London obtained the first English patent for wood block printing. To meet customer demands, he began woodblock printing on fabrics using brilliant colors to replicate the Indian cottons. After 1690 the English were producing flannel.

For the English colonists of the late 17th century, cheaper varieties of Indian cotton were certainly imported to America in large quantities, but most of the more exotic and expensive fabrics remained in England, with only an occasional bolt or two actually reaching the American market. Nevertheless, demand was high among wealthy plantation owners, merchants, politicians, and governors throughout North America and the Caribbean who craved these exotic fabrics for their wives and themselves. The pirates of the Caribbean filled this gap in the market nicely. It seems that the French, Dutch, and Spanish importers weren't as restrictive as the English and all sorts of expensive and high-quality Indian fabrics were imported to their colonies in the Caribbean. That doesn't mean that all these textiles actually made it to their intended destinations, many bolts of Indian fabric wound up in the holds of English pirate vessels and were sold to English merchants in any of the pirate-friendly ports of North America and the Caribbean.

The demand for exotic textiles was one of the primary reasons why there were so many pirate-friendly ports in the late 17th century, ports like New York, Charles Town, South Carolina, and Newport, Rhode Island. The pirates provided the valuable and sought-after Indian textiles to the local merchants who the English importers refused to serve. Thus, lawmakers in the larger ports encouraged the pirate trade for economic reasons.

As for the pirates themselves, just about every fabric was available to them, especially since they took what clothing they wanted from rich passengers aboard their prize vessels. Brightly colored cotton would have been everywhere in the Caribbean by 1660. But at the dawn of the 18th century, changes in England were about to impact the lives of the English colonists in America as well as the pirates.

Calico Act

The Calico Act had a major impact on textiles. Throughout the last quarter of the 17th century, English textile manufacturers protested the stream of Indian fabrics into the English market. England's economy was largely based upon wool and linen and stained and painted calicoes were mentioned in 1696 as a hindrance to the consumption of English textiles. So, in 1700, to prevent the collapse of the English textile industry, England passed the Calico Act, which prohibited the importation, selling, or even wearing of "silks and stuffs mixed with silk of the manufacture of Persia, China, or East India and all calicoes painted, dyed, printed, or stained there." That ban did not include silk or cotton thread to be mixed with linen for the English textile industry, so fabrics like fustian continued in full production.

However, provisions in the Calico Act still allowed all of these banned textiles to continue to be imported by the East India Company as long as the textiles were not sold in England and reshipped to continental Europe or the colonies in North America. That was actually terrific news for the English colonists. Before the Calico Act of 1700 most of the Indian fabrics imported by the English East India Company were sold in England and only a small amount of the fabric made it to the American market, primarily through the efforts of a few pirates. But after 1700, the only way the English East India Company could make a profit on Indian textiles was to sell them in the colonies. Consequently, in the early 1700s Indian fabrics of all types flooded the American market. That drove the price of fabrics down and made Indian textiles a less desirable commodity for pirates to sell. That may have been one of the reasons that pirate-friendly ports began closing their doors to pirates in the beginning of the 18th century. Perhaps Indian textiles played a bigger role than most historians realized. At the very least, the sale of Indian textiles was a contributing factor to the tolerance of pirates in the North American ports of the late 17th century.

Back in England, demand was still high. Spain, France, and Holland had no ban on Indian fabrics and were importing them in great numbers. French manufactures smuggled many of these rich fabrics to England, avoiding the import prohibitions, where they were sold to the wealthy.

Taking advantage of the situation, some English textile manufacturers copied those fabrics and sold them as "French made" to their customers who paid exorbitant prices thinking they were getting authentic contraband French fabric. By all accounts, the Calico Act was about as effective at banning calico in England during the early 1700s as prohibition was at banning alcohol in the United States during the 1920s. In other words, it didn't work. In 1721, a stricter version was issued which had strict fines of £20 for even wearing anything made from cotton. As before, that only applied to the English Isles, not to the English colonies. The Calico Act wasn't repealed until 1774.

As far as American cotton production goes, throughout the Caribbean, Mexico, and the southern part of North America, the variety of cotton that grew naturally was the short staple kind, the variety that the cotton gin didn't process. As mentioned earlier, that made it very difficult to remove the seeds from the cotton fibers and impractical for production into fabric on a large enough scale to make a profit. In the 17th and 18th centuries small amounts of cotton plants were grown locally and spun into crude fabric for poorer individuals like farmers, native Americans, or slaves, who couldn't afford to buy real cotton imports.

South America grew a variety of cotton that could be used with the cotton gin, but the plants grew deep in Spanish territory and in places that were hard to get to, like the jungles of Ecuador. The Spanish didn't pursue cotton production in South America. After all, they were mining huge quantities of gold and silver in the regions that later became the modern countries of Bolivia and Peru. Cotton was produced by native South Americans living in the jungles and pampas.

For those living historians who want to use period correct fabric, it's not enough just to use the correct material. Modern weaving looms are very different from 18th century hand looms. The weave on modern fabrics can be very tight and almost unnoticeable in some cases, whereas hand looms produce a fabric with a definite weave pattern. Many modern looking fabrics, even those that are made from natural materials, will look different if the weave is wrong. The fabric of modern white cotton shirts looks and feels completely different from an authentically made cotton shirt that was produced with a larger weave. Living historians, who are making an outfit and want to look completely accurate for the 17th or 18th centuries, should use material that is not only made of fabric which is accurate to the period, but that looks correct too.

Chapter 82
Fashion

Now that we have a fairly good understanding of the types of material that would have been available during the golden age of piracy, let's take a look at fashion. Just like modern times, fashion and style changed about every 10 years. That was true for the entire 17th and 18th centuries. For example, what was new and highly fashionable in 1660 would have looked old and out of style by the mid-1670s. Additionally, fashion and style were often very different between nations. What was stylish for the Spanish was most likely not considered stylish by the French or English. Nonetheless, nationalistic fashion didn't seem to change with locations. In other words, the colonists always tried to keep up with the mother country. For example, the English settlers on Barbados wore the same styles as those worn back in England.

But would a poorer person have the latest fashion? The answer is yes. Just look at people today. Their clothes may not have been made of the same expensive materials, but they would have been tailored in the latest styles. Another thing to consider is that most lower and middle-class people only had one or two sets of clothes. When you are wearing the same garments every day, they don't last long. Everyone was constantly buying or making new clothes and they would be keeping up with all the latest styles. Even the garments that lasted a bit longer, like coats, were made over into newer styles. There is an example of a waistcoat which is on display in a small museum in Western Pennsylvania that was originally made in 1760 and was continually re-made into the latest styles before it was finally put away in a trunk in 1820. Pirates were no exception to this. When they went ashore they would be dressed in the latest styles, even though those styles may be a mixture of the latest fashion from several different nations.

As we delve into the world of fashion I can only describe a few of the highlights. There are way too many variations to cover everything in this short chapter, but I hope it will convey some idea of what was correct for the period.

Military Styles Affect Fashion

Military tactics changed fashion. Styles between 1650 and 1695 had small changes of course but remained fairly similar in general appearance. This can also be said of the styles between 1695 and 1720. The defining moment that significantly changed European fashion came in the early 1690s when all the European nations significantly changed their military tactics from using pikes as the main assault weapon to using flintlocks. Between 1680 and 1695 each nation slowly changed literally every aspect of military tactics, formations, and discipline in order to effectively utilize this new and highly effective weapon, the flintlock.

To accommodate loading, carrying, and fighting, armies had to design all new clothes. Large cuffs got in the way, so cuff size was reduced. Bulkier loose-fitting coats became slightly tighter fitting to keep the material from getting in the way as well. Pockets were now being used to keep tools and flints, so they developed flaps to prevent accidental loss of their contents. But the most noticeable change to fashion was the tri-cornered hat. Prior to 1690 the brims of all hats were large and round. As we shall see a little later, military necessity prompted the development of the tri-cornered hat.

1706 Naval Contract

In 1706 the English Royal Navy went through a major overhauling and established a set of rules for operations. That included ship building and many other aspects of naval life. It also included a contract for the sale of clothing to their sailors. Prior to 1706 there was absolutely no regulation uniform for sailors, they wore whatever they wanted. The 1706 contract listed items of clothing that could be sold to sailors in the Royal Navy at established prices. The sailors weren't compelled to buy those items, so it really can't be considered uniform regulations in the modern sense, but since most sailors did purchase those items, their appearance began to become a bit more uniform. At any rate, that contract list gives us valuable insight into the type of clothing worn by sailors of the early 18th century. The 1706 contract is as follows:

1. Shrunck Grey Kersey Jackett, lined with Red Cotton, with fifteen Brass Buttons, and two Pockets of Linnen, the Button Holes stiched with Gold Colour Thread, at Ten Shillings and SixPence each

2. Waist Coat of Welsh Red plain unlined, with eighteen Brass Buttons, the holes stiched with Gold Coloured Thread at Five Shillings and SixPence each

3. Striped Ticken Waist Coats of proper lengths, to be one Yard in length at least, with Eighteen Black Buttons, the Holes Stitched with Black Thread lined with White linen and two White Linnen Pockets, at the Rate of Seven Shillings

4. Red Kersey Breeches lined with Linnen, with three Leather Pockets, and thirteen white Tinn Buttons, the Button Holes stitched with white Thread, at the Rate of Five Shillings and SixPence each

5. Striped Shagg Breeches lin'd with Linnen, with three Leather Pockets, and fourteen white Tinn Buttons, the Button Holes stiched with white Thread, at the Rate of Tenn Shillings and SixPence each

6. Striped Ticken Breeches of proper lengthes, lined with white linen, and two linen Pockets, with Sixteen Black Buttons, the Button Holes stiched with Black Thread, at the rate of five Shillings each

7. Shirts of blew and white chequered Linnen, at the Rate of three Shillings and ThreePence each

8. Drawers of blew and white chequered Linnen, at the Rate of Two Shillings and ThreePence each

9. Leather Capps faced with Red Cotton, and lined with Black Linnen, at the Rate of One Shilling and twoPence each

10. Small Leather Capps stich'd with white Thread, at the Rate of EightPence each

11. Grey Woollen Stockings at the Rate of One Shilling and NinePence per Pair

12. Grey Woollen Gloves or Mittens at the Rate of SixPence per pair

13. Double Sold Shoes, round Toes, at the Rate of Four Shillings per pair

14. Brass Buckles with Iron Tongues at the Rate of Three Pence per pair

Coats and Waistcoats

Coats were worn by almost every male during this time period. It was expected. You just weren't dressed without a coat. For farmers, tradesmen, and seamen, it would have been acceptable for them to remove their coats while working, but they wouldn't be seen in town or in a tavern without one. People in the modern day find this difficult to comprehend, but that concept was certainly true of men in the early to mid-20th century. Just look at a photograph of spectators at a major league baseball game in the 1930s and you will see almost everyone wearing a coat and tie. As mentioned above, coats between 1650 and 1695 remained fairly similar, generally speaking, and coats between 1695 and 1720 also remained relatively unchanged.

Coats throughout the entire golden age were cut with no collar and a straight edged front opening extending to about the knee. In the 17th century, coats were a little longer, extending slightly below the knee while later coats were either at the knee or just above. Buttons normally ran the entire length of the coat all the way to the bottom edge. Leaving buttons off the lower half of a coat wasn't done until the 1720s and wasn't standard until 1740, well past the golden age. Double breasted coats in the early 18th century were very rare, but occasionally existed.

Waistcoats were cut very similar to coats except the backs were often made of ticking and were often gathered and laced. They also had buttons running all the way down the front to the bottom edge and were almost always squared at the bottom. Cut away and rounded waistcoats were of a much later design. They were not used until after the 1750s.

After 1700 coats begin to flare out a bit. The back seams opened at the waist with pleats on each side and buttons straight down the back. Coats didn't flare out as much in 1710 but pleats got fuller around 1720. Cuffs were fuller and longer in the 17th century and sometimes folded above the elbow. Cuffs began to get smaller just at the end of the 17th century with the new military styles that resulted from fighting with flintlocks. Sleeve length came to just above the wrist with the cuff extending to just below the elbow. Some cuffs may have had a split in the back and all cuffs had buttons and long button holes. Pockets of the 17th century were usually positioned toward the bottom of the coat with straight openings and no flaps. By the 18th century pockets were placed just below the waist and always had a buttoned flap. During the first 10 years of the 18th century pocket flaps had button holes, but the buttons were ornamental and located below the flap. Functional pocket flaps that actually buttoned became more common as the century went on. Both are correct for 1720. The classic 1724 print of Blackbeard published in Johnson's *General History of Pyrates* is a great example of the typical flared and pleated coat of the early 18th century with pocket flaps and button holes with the buttons sewn below the flap.

Jackets

Jackets were basically short coats often worn by tradesmen and seamen. Many sources mention "short jacketts" including the 1706 Royal Navy Contract. They were cut more like waistcoats with long sleeves. The jacket extended to the top of the leg or sometimes a little lower with buttons on the front extending to the bottom edge just like coats. The sleeve fell to just above the wrist bone allowing the shirt to blossom out below the sleeve. Jacket sleeves didn't have any cuffs. They either had a simple slit at the wrist with three to five buttons, or just a plain sleeve with no cuff. I can find no evidence that the traditional mariners cuff, one with a buttoned scalloped flap, was used during the golden age. That type of cuff probably developed about 1740. Most people think of seamen's jackets as being dark blue, but that idea was influenced by the English Royal Navy's royal blue uniform jacket of 1722. Between 1706 and 1722 the jackets of the Royal Navy were light gray. For pirates, just about any solid color would have been used.

Common fabrics like linen or wool would have been used for jackets, as that was a working man's garment. Linen or cotton was often used for the lining. Buttons were made of plain brass or pewter. Excellent illustrations of those jackets can be seen in the prints in Johnson's *General History of Pyrates*. The 1734 print of Edward Teach and the 1725 print of Anne Bonny clearly illustrate those jackets. No one can say for certain if those historical pirates actually wore jackets like the ones in those prints, but it is certain that someone in the 1720s did. There is a hand painted lady's fan in a museum in Williamsburg, Virginia which dates to 1735 and depicts the English victory over the Spanish at Portobelo. The drawing shows a sailor wearing a short jacket with buttons extending to the bottom edge of the jacket.

Breeches

Breeches have been around since the 12th century and were made of every type of material used for clothing. 17th century breeches were fairly baggy and had a draw string at the knee. In the 18th century breeches were a little tighter but still very roomy. Some still had drawstrings at the knee but others had small buckles. Trousers were made like breeches except that they extended to just above the ankle and seem very short by modern fashion. Trousers didn't appear in common use during the entire 17th century. However, in the early 18th century trousers began to be worn by

English sailors. The log books of ships from other nations have comments that they could identify English ships in the early 1700s by the trousers the crewmen wore. The flies on both breeches and trousers of the period were straight with buttons. Later in the 18th century that type of fly became known as the French Fly to English tailors. That's because the English adopted a flapped fly that buttoned on three sides like the trousers of modern sailors while the French continued to use the straight fly design. This English innovation didn't occur until about 1750, well after the golden age. The 1725 print of Anne Bonny in the Dutch version of Johnson's book effectively illustrates the classic example of the English trouser with a straight fly. Most of the time trousers were made of solid natural fabric, but on the same 1735 drawing on a ladies' fan mentioned above, the sailor is wearing striped trousers with a buttoned fly.

Shirts

Shirts were considered undergarments. They were almost always made of fine linen, cotton, or silk. They were cut from one bolt of cloth, 30–40 inches wide and about 76 inches long, and were folded at the shoulder and stitched along the side. Sleeves with cuffs were then added. There were no seams across the front or back until the 19th century. Shirts changed little from 1600 to 1730 except the sleeves were much fuller prior to about 1700. All shirts had sleeves with gussets and collars. Commoners wore shirts with plain openings; the gentry often wore lace or ruffles at the opening. Cuffs were often ruffled on the shirts of the gentry as almost every contemporary print shows. It's very difficult to do any type of manual work while wearing ruffled sleeves because they get in the way, so wearing a shirt with ruffled sleeves would prove that the wearer was not of the working class. The most common color was white or natural; however, many sources, including the Royal Navy 1706 Contract, state that sailors often wore shirts of blue and white checked linen.

In the late 17th century, the Scotts and Irish often dyed their shirts yellow with saffron. Heavy silk shirts in a variety of solid colors were also documented among the military. It was believed that a bullet would not penetrate silk due to its strength and if shot, the victim could just pull the bullet out of the wound with the shirt intact. Silk actually is very strong and due to the size, shape, and low velocity of the bullets of the day, this just might have been possible, but I'm not going to try it.

Shoes

The open sided shoe was the most popular throughout most of the 1600s. The shoes were held on by a latchet that was commonly tied with hemp twine, leather thongs, or silk ribbons. The shape of the toe went back and forth from rounded to square. In the early 17th century, they were rounded, by 1640 they were squared, and by the 1680s, both were common. Shoes were either open sided or fully enclosed. Open sided was more popular until the 1680s when fully enclosed shoes became far more popular. Open sided shoes were almost nonexistent by 1720.

The shoe buckle was first introduced in Europe in 1660 and became popular outside of Europe soon after. Shoe buckles during the golden age were tiny in comparison to shoe buckles of the later 18th century. They were between ½ to ¾ inches wide. With the introduction of the buckle, the tongue became rather long and remained so until after the golden age. Colors ranged from fawn to dark black, but brown seems to be the most common. Backless leather footwear called mules, which are still in fashion today, were also worn in the late 17th and early 18th centuries.

Archaeologists have recovered shoes from the wreck of the French barque longue, *La Belle*, which sank in 1686 in Matagorda Bay, just south of Galveston, Texas. *La Belle* was part of a French expedition that was searching for the mouth of the Mississippi River in order to establish a new colony. Some of those shoes have squared toes and some have rounded toes. They also had narrow heels similar to modern western boots. Some shoes fastened with a latchet that was inserted into a chape buckle fastener that was attached to the side of the shoe with a stud. Other shoes recovered were simply laced. Shoes have also been recovered from the wreck of the *Whydah* that sank in 1717 that greatly resemble the shoes from the *La Belle*. The latch on the *Whydah* shoe was slightly larger but still under 1-inch. All buckles of that period only have one tang. Buckles with two tangs didn't appear until about 1722.

Sandals are very difficult to document. Original sandals are extremely rare as most didn't survive the centuries. Additionally, sandals in contemporary paintings and prints are extremely rare. There are a few examples, however. Men wearing sandals are depicted in a 1667 painting by Gerbrand van den Eeckhout and a mid-18th century painting by Londonio. Sandals made of rope and leather have existed for thousands of years and were commonly worn in Africa, India, and by Native Americans in the Caribbean during the 18th century. They may have been worn by pirates; there just isn't any hard documentation. They certainly could have been worn by pirates if they wished.

Boots

Nautical boots were also used by sailors, especially those sailing in colder climates. A 1700 painting by a French explorer named DuPlessis shows French sailors wearing over the knee boots while at Tierra Del Fuego, the last stop before rounding Cape Horn at the tip of South America. Additionally, a 1717 illustration of Spanish sailors' clothing shows that knee high sea boots were part of the standard issue. Similar boots were used by the English. Contemporary prints often show fishermen wearing work boots. English nautical boots were made with a simple straight cut that came about half way to the knee.

Over the knee boots have been very popular in European culture since the early Renaissance and worn by anyone who could afford them. In the 1500s boots were slim fitting and extended to mid-thigh. They were sometimes folded below the knee for comfort. Boot straps that tied or buckled around the boot just below the knee were often worn to keep the boots up. The toes were generally rounded. Between 1620 and 1660 fashion dictated that the boots did not rise above the knee. They became much wider at the top and were most commonly worn folded down and scrunched toward the ankles in a rather sloppy looking way. The toes were generally pointed. That is the traditional Three Musketeers style and was worn by everyone in the military, from private to general. They were also worn by well-dressed gentlemen at court.

In the 1690s, the design remained well fitted to the knee with an outward flare out above the fold, but occasionally the top edge of the boot was a few inches higher in the front. Boots altogether fell out of fashion with the rich and famous; however, they were still commonly worn by military officers and enlisted cavalrymen throughout the entire 18th century. They were also common among civilians who rode horses. The early 18th century style military and riding boots looked very similar to the boots of the 16th century except they flared out to become wider at the top. They extended above the knee and were commonly worn so be folded down below the knee for comfort. The toes were generally squared. Those boots are the traditional "bucket boots" one sees so often in pirate media like films and books.

Stockings

Stockings as we know them didn't become popular until the late 17th century. They were knitted in a variety of colors and were usually made of linen, wool, cotton, or silk. In the early 18th century, it was fashionable among gentlemen at court to wear their stockings over top the bottom of the breeches and folded above the knee, although not always.

Sailors often wore gray woolen stockings as referenced in the English 1706 contract. Stockings were often held up by tying a ribbon around the leg below the knee. Thin leather garters were also used. Clocked stockings were stockings with an ornamental design either knitted or embroidered at the ankles. That became popular in the 1680s as boots were going out of fashion. Striped stockings are very controversial among historians. Generally, striped stockings weren't fashionable until the late 18th century and early 19th century, however, many pirates in the media have been depicted wearing striped stockings. That may be correct for the pirates of Jean Laffite's 1814 crew, but what about the golden age? Again, I will reference the 1735 hand painted lady's fan in Williamsburg, Virginia. In that drawing, the Spaniard pleading for his life is clearly wearing striped stockings. It is certain that striped stockings did exist in the 17th and early 18th centuries, but they were probably rare among English sailors and pirates.

Hats and Caps

Typical round hats were an essential part of life in the 17th and 18th centuries, not only for protection from the elements, but as a mandatory part of one's attire. In all the paintings and prints from that period, it is extremely rare to see anyone from any class without a hat of some sort. The most popular were the blocked hats made of wool felt, fur felt, or beaver felt. Round hats date back as far as the 14th century with the majority of production being based in Holland and Spain. Peasant hats didn't change much from 1600 to 1750. They were simple round hats with a smaller brim and a low crown. In the mid-1600s some hats had a high crown with a squared off top. From 1650 to 1690 hats became much larger, with wider brims, but the crown was still rather low. It became fashionable to roll up the back of the brim and to decorate the hat with plumes and feathers. Elaborate lace or plumed trim was often added to the edge of the brim. Round hats made of straw were imported from Italy after the mid-1600s. Less expensive than felt, they offered the common worker and sailor an alternative. A few straw hats belonging to sailors of the early 1700s still exist in museums today. Occasionally, those straw hats were painted black to look like they were made of felt.

Soldiers of the 17th century commonly wore large felt round hats that were generally pinned up on the left side and were often decorated with feathers. The hats were pinned up to allow the soldiers to carry muskets or pikes on their left shoulders without knocking their hats off. That "military look" became popular with the civilian community. As warfare developed and the musket became the dominant weapon on the battlefield, a manual of arms was introduced by each of the European nations to keep the soldiers' movements uniform. By 1690 entire regiments were carrying flintlock muskets while on the march. Anyone who has marched a long distance while carrying a weapon knows that it gets very heavy after a while and has to be shifted from shoulder to shoulder. To solve that problem, precise movements to shift the musket from shoulder to shoulder became a standard part of everyone's manual of arms. However, moving a musket from the left shoulder to the right is somewhat difficult with a round hat, but not when the hat is pinned up on two or three sides. That was the origin of the tri-cornered hat which was actually called the cocked hat. The round hat was pinned with the front point over the left eye and a flat side on both the left and right side. The flat side was enough space to allow the musket to be placed on the left or right shoulder without knocking off the hat. By 1695 all European troops were wearing cocked hats.

As civilian fashion so often copies military necessity, cocked hats became fashionable all over Europe and the colonies by 1700. Cocked hats were often elaborately decorated with feathers and plumes just as in the past century. A type of large bow was often attached to the right side. That was called a "cockade" and was an insignia which represented a military affiliation. In the early 18th century, the cockade was rare on civilian hats. A simple button was most often seen. By the mid-18th century, cockades began to appear on civilian hats and were usually associated with political affiliations. For example, a white cockade signified allegiance to the Jacobite cause in 1745 Scotland and the circular red, white, and blue cockade was used by the rebels during the French revolution of 1789 and later by Napoleon's troops. Seafaring cocked hats were often treated with tar pitch, bees wax, or animal fat to make them more resistant to the weather.

Wool caps were also common among sailors. Pablo E. Perez-Mallaina wrote, "Mariners wore woolen caps called sea caps or bonnets. Even in warm seas, the wind, rain, and long nights on guard made it essential to have adequate protection." The Monmouth cap was first mentioned in history in 1576 and was extremely popular during the 17th and 18th centuries. The original home and name of the cap may have been derived from the Welsh border town of Monmouth. The Monmouth cap is knitted from wool and came in a variety of sizes. Some were bell shaped while others were long with a turned over brim and a tassel at the end, just like modern ski caps. Most had a small loop attached to the brim so it could be hung up on a nail or hook when the sailor was sleeping. In the 17th century they were generally solid colors, mostly red. Striped caps began to appear around 1700. A variation of the Monmouth cap is the thrum cap which has large thrums of yarn attached to the entire hat, giving it a very shaggy appearance. Those thrum caps were very warm and fairly waterproof. If made from black or brown yarn, they resembled bearskin hats and sometimes landsmen thought the sailors were wearing fur hats.

There is an excellent illustration of a thrum cap in one of the depictions of Blackbeard in Charles Johnson's book.

Another style of knitted cap was the "Peter the Great" style, in which the cap was knitted with a brim that went all the way around and resembled a round hat. There were several examples of that type of hat in the Hermitage collection that were worn by Peter the Great when he visited the Dutch and English shipyards in the early 1700s. Those hats became very popular with English and Dutch sailors after that, especially in colder climates.

Belts

Belts weren't generally worn unless the wearer was using it to carry something, such as a sword or knife. They were generally either dyed black or left natural. Based upon the surviving belts and buckles and all of the paintings available, belts of the golden age were usually no more than two inches wide. Thick belts of three and four inches weren't common until the 19th century. Sashes made of all sorts of exotic materials were commonly worn by gentlemen throughout the 17th century, but their use began to diminish in the 18th century. Still, sashes were always available. One question arises when pirates are concerned. Would a pirate wear a sash under a belt, as is so often depicted? I think so.

As a living history interpreter myself, I have portrayed a pirate many times over the years. At first, I always wore a sash under my belt, but when I couldn't find any documentation to prove that pirates wore sashed and belts together, I stopped. That didn't last long. Wearing a heavy belt with pistols, a cartridge box, a knife, and a sword was very uncomfortable without a sash underneath. Also, the belt tended to slip around out of position as I moved. Sometimes the pistols even fell out. Wearing a sash under a belt is not only comfortable but practical. I can say from the standpoint of personal experimentation that it was far more advantageous to wear a sash under a belt.

Pocket Watches

Pocket watches were in use throughout the 17th and 18th centuries, although they were very expensive and only ship's captains and the wealthy could afford them. They were very similar to watches of the 19th century but a little larger. The numbers on the face (1–12) were always in Roman numerals. You will remember when Captain Snelgrave gave an account of how his pocket watch was taken by the quartermaster of Captain Cocklyn's crew in 1719. "When it was delivered to the Quarter-master, he held it up by the

Chain, and presently laid it down upon the Deck, giving it a kick with his Foot, saying 'It was a pretty Foot-ball': On which, one of the Pirates caught it up, saying, He would put it in the common Chest to be sold at the Mast."

Eye Glasses

Eye glasses were exceptionally rare in the late 17th and early 18th centuries, however, a few examples do exist. The lenses were perfectly round and held in a thick frame that did not have ear pieces. The eye glasses were held in place or tied to the head with a silk ribbon. Ear pieces on the sides of eye glasses weren't introduced until about 1750 and oval lenses weren't introduced until 1770. There is a 1721 print showing a pirate wearing eye glasses. The print is of the pirate crew of Thomas Anstis holding a mock trial in Cuba and shows a crewman sitting in a tree is wearing a pair of round glasses typical to the early 18th century. So, it is conceivable that a pirate would have had eye glasses, although I think that this would have been exceptionally rare.

Chapter 83
How Do I Look?

How pirates dressed and what they may have worn has actually been a well debated subject among historians and living history interpreters interested in the golden age of piracy. There is very little to go on. First of all, there are no contemporary drawings or paintings of pirates that were made by artists who actually saw the pirates they portrayed. All of the contemporary prints and illustrations that appear in 17th and 18th century publications were drawn by local artists who were living in the cities where the books were published, not out sailing the waters of the Caribbean. Those artists who drew pirates probably used ordinary seamen as references and simply added weapons and accouterments of the day to suit their imagination. The clothing may be correct to the period, but not necessarily accurate to the individual depicted.

A few well-known historical figures like Henry Morgan had their portraits painted, but in Morgan's case, that portrait was painted when he was the Lieutenant Governor of Jamaica, not when he was a buccaneer. For a true idea of how pirates may have appeared, we must rely on a few contemporary descriptions from eye witnesses and a great deal of "educated guesswork." But before we delve into the world of the pirate, we first must become familiar with what was available at the time. In other words, we must become familiar with the fashion of the 17th and 18th centuries.

There are several publications already mentioned in this book that give us valuable insight into the styles worn by seamen and pirates of the golden age. The 1678 publication, *De Americaensche Zee-Roovers* by Alexander O. Exquemelin and *The General History of Pyrates* written by Charles Johnson in 1724 with later editions containing many more illustrations. In both cases, the illustrations in those books must be taken with a grain of salt. As previously stated, they were drawn by local illustrators living in the cities where the books were published. Those illustrators never actually saw the pirates they drew which means that the pirates depicted in those illustrations weren't necessarily accurate representations of what the real individuals looked like. However, the clothes depicted in those illustrations are usually accurate to the period, at least for sailors. We do know that the illustrations are accurate to the date the book was published. Many illustrators of the 17th and 18th centuries portrayed people in the clothes of the day, not the clothes that they would have worn during their actual lifetimes. For example, the illustration of Henry Morgan in Johnson's book is supposed to show Morgan in 1670; however, Morgan is sporting styles from the 1720s, including a tri-cornered hat, which didn't come into fashion until about 1700.

PRINTS FROM ALEXANDER O EXQUEMELIN'S 1678 PUBLICATION, DE AMERICAENSCHE ZEE-ROOVERS

Figure 54: Bartholomew de Portuguese

Figure 55: Rock Brasilliano

Figure 56: Francois Lolonois

Thus, those prints don't accurately show how pirates dressed. They generally show the captains dressed as gentlemen while the other pirates are dressed like common seamen. Pirates would have a much more eclectic collection of clothes from all nations and social strata. The reason is very simple, and also makes sense. The illustrators were hired to make the book more appealing. They drew upon their imagination and observation of some of the sailors they may have seen around town. The problem is that sailors in London didn't look like the pirates in the Caribbean. Included are some of the prints from these two publications.

Figure 57: *Henry Morgan's Attack on Porto Bello*

Of greatest interest in these prints are the shell guards on their falchions.

The first 1724 edition only had three illustrations and out of those three, only one of them was a portrait.

Figure 58: *Henry Morgan*

Prints from Various Editions of Charles Johnson's General History of Pyrates

Figure 59: *Blackbeard, First Edition 1724*

Figure 60: *Blackbeard, Second Edition 1724*

Figure 61: *Blackbeard 1725 Edition*

Figure 62: *Bartholomew Roberts, Second Edition 1724*

Figure 63: *Anne Bonny and Mary Read, Second Edition 1724*

Figure 64: *Anne Bonny and Mary Read, Dutch Edition 1725*

Blackbeard was chosen to be the only pirate illustrated in that version. The second 1724 edition also had only three illustrations, all portraits. They included a revised Blackbeard, Mary Read and Anne Bonny, and Bartholomew Roberts. A 1725 Dutch edition spiced up the illustrations, showing Mary Read and Anne Bonny in a much more provocative manner. In the 1725 English edition, the three beautifully made illustrations were replaced by a series of cheaply made woodcuts of many of the pirates. Other illustrations appeared in later editions up to 1734. It is interesting to note how dramatically the illustration of Blackbeard changes between 1724 and 1734.

The 1725 Dutch edition of Charles Johnson's *General History of Pyrates* was much more appealing. Dutch publishers had far more freedom than the English. In addition to the sexier appearance and open shirts, they are dressed in men's clothing. Notice the straight button fly on the long strait legged trousers. This illustration is one of the best examples of sailor's trousers known. Also notice the baldrics holding their swords and boarding axes.

SOME EXAMPLES OF THE LESSER QUALITY WOODCUTS FROM THE 1725 EDITION

Figure 66: *Henry Every, 1725 Edition*

Figure 67: *Edward England, 1725 Edition*

Figure 68: *Jack Rackham, 1725 Edition*

Figure 65: *Blackbeard, 1734 Edition*

The most famous illustration of Blackbeard is the one from the 1734 edition. This illustration is another terrific example of straight legged trousers. It also shows a typical seaman's jacket. Notice the infamous burning matches in his beard. They don't appear in earlier illustrations of Blackbeard.

An illustration from one of the later editions of Charles Johnson's book, that is supposed to be of Henry Morgan, is totally wrong for the 1660s. The jacket is of a 1720 style, with simple slit cuffs. The breeches would have been fuller cut. The weapon held over his shoulder looks like a fowling piece from the early 18th century. Moreover, the biggest error is the three-cornered hat, which wasn't worn before the late 1690s. It must be noted that artists often used contemporary styles when illustrating historic figures. It seems that authenticity was not always accurately portrayed. It is interesting to note the Scottish basket hilt sword which is correct for both centuries.

Now that we have a pretty good idea of what landsmen, gentlemen, and regular sailors looked like, and we have seen how pirates were depicted in contemporary prints, let's take a crack at how pirates may have actually dressed.

Figure 69: *Henry Morgan, Charles Johnson Later Edition*

As mentioned before, contemporary images were based upon the speculation of the artists, so I think it is fair to do a little speculating on our own based upon a combination of contemporary accounts, practicality, and human nature. Overall, I think that pirates could have appeared in just about any manner imaginable. The paintings of Howard Pyle are probably fairly accurate. And in many respects, the way pirates are portrayed in film and books are quite often fairly accurate too. They wore a mixture of just about every type of clothing in existence during the time they lived, but with a string of weapons added on. It is certain that they wouldn't have looked like ordinary men—or women.

Early buccaneers

At first, the early buccaneers on Hispaniola would have dressed in buckskins and hunting accoutrement. French clergyman, Abbe Jean Baptiste Du Tetre, stated that they slept beside their smoking fires in an attempt to keep the mosquitoes at bay. He wrote, "You might say that these are the butcher's vilest servants who have been eight days in the slaughterhouse without washing themselves."

By the time they became seagoing buccaneers, they would have looked more like a combination of buck skinners and well-armed sailors. In the 1650s most of the buccaneers were former soldiers and wore many items from their old uniforms. They would have worn an odd mixture of nautical and military attire. By the late 1660s as more and more buccaneers were ex-soldiers, their dress would have been more in line with contemporary military fashion. Of course, the sailors on the vessels would dress like sailors. However, with each raid, the captured clothing would have added to their eclectic appearance. By the 18th century most pirates were former sailors and their clothing would be basically nautical, augmented with whatever they fancied from the garments onboard any captured vessel they took.

Headgear

In the 17th and 18th centuries, it was European tradition for everyone to wear some type of hat. At sea, not only was it customary, but necessary to protect the head from the sun or to keep warm in colder regions. Although there are few 17th or 18th century accounts testifying to the fact that sailors or pirates wore scarfs tied around their heads, it seems very likely that many did. For hundreds of years, wearing head scarfs was very common among the people living on the islands of the Caribbean and Indian Ocean. In fact, it still is today. One of the few contemporary accounts of pirates wearing head scarfs comes from Dorothy Thomas, whose description of Anne Bonny and Mary Read appears earlier in this book. She testified that "the Two Women were on the Board the said Sloop, and wore Men's Jackets, and long Trousers, and Handkerchiefs tied about their Heads; and that each of them had a Machet and a Pistol in their Hands . . ." The important part of her statement is that she specifically mentions "Handkerchiefs tied about their Heads." Brightly colored scarfs of the day were readily available and were made of a large variety of materials including silk. They are easy to wear and don't blow off in the wind, something of importance to a sailor working on deck or even more so in the rigging where there may be no free hand to save a wayward hat from the wind.

Monmouth caps are knitted wool caps very similar to modern ski caps. They were the most common hat worn by sailors throughout the 17th and 18th centuries and came in a variety of styles and shapes. Round hats would also be very common among pirates, although not generally worn by crewmen while working at sea. Most landsmen wore round hats and pirates would have worn them while ashore. Pirate officers may have worn them at sea. They were very comfortable and kept the sun and rain off one's head. Contemporary accounts from the 18th century tell of pirate captains wearing their tri-cornered hats continuously at sea. Captain Roberts wore a lavishly decorated one.

Earrings

Figure 70: *Howell Davis, 1725 Edition*

Figure 71: *Charles Vane, 1725 Edition*

Figure 72: *Bartholomew Roberts, 1725 Edition*

Figure 73: *Stede Bonnet, 1725 Edition*

One of the most controversial issues among those who research pirates of the golden age is the one of earrings. Did pirates actually wear earrings? It certainly wasn't fashionable for men of the 17th and 18th centuries to wear earrings. It is reasonable to ask, "If it wasn't fashionable for men to wear earrings during that era, why would pirates? However, there are a few contemporary accounts that indicated that they did. On November 11, 1615 a land battle between Spanish forces under command of Vizcaino and Dutch pirates under command of Speilbergen occurred at Salagua, Mexico which is near Acapulco. In a letter dated May 25, 1616 Vizcaino describes the pirates as "youths and very gentlemen, some Irish, with great forelocks and earrings." So, it seems that at least some pirates did wear earrings, but why? Apparently, there was an old nautical superstition that wearing earrings increased one's eyesight. Surprisingly, modern acupuncturists believe that piercing the ears actually does improve one's eyesight. Acupuncture was commonly practiced throughout the Orient for thousands of years. That superstition may have come from sailors returning from the Orient in the middle 17th century with earrings they purchased from the locals. Another reason for the wearing of earrings could be that the individuals wanted to prove they had sailed the oceans of the world. Earrings were very fashionable among the local inhabitants throughout India, the China Sea, and West Africa and sailors or pirates traveling those waters could have begun to wear earrings to prove that they were there.

An unlikely reason for the wearing of earrings was for hearing protection. Firing big guns below deck severely hurt one's ears, so sailors packed their ears with wax wadding. Some believe that one reason why pirates wore earrings may have been so the pirates would be able to attach their wadding to their earrings with strings in order to keep their earplugs handy. That might have been true, but it seems to me that if that was ever done, it was because the individuals found a secondary use for their earrings which they already had.

Today, the most commonly believed reason for the wearing of earrings was that pirates wore earrings to pay for their burials. It has been argued that when a pirate died, the gold earrings would be taken by an undertaker as payment for a proper burial. This makes no sense when you think about it. If a pirate died at sea, his earrings were pulled out, his valuables were split among the crew, and his body was buried at sea, which means it was simply thrown overboard. Of course, the captain may have said a few words during the ceremony. If a pirate died ashore, the same thing happened except that his buddies may have taken the time to bury him. If a pirate was hanged or died among enemies, any gold earrings he may have had wouldn't have been used for a funeral. What makes the most common sense is that pirates wore earrings as part of a naval tradition to "prove" that they had sailed in foreign waters—even if they hadn't.

Jewelry

What about other jewelry? Many contemporary accounts of Spanish ship's captains describe pirates wearing a whole array of jewels to include gold chains, buttons encrusted with pearls, diamonds, emerald rings, and so on. But just like today, there were other options for less expensive jewelry. Glass trade beads have been manufactured in Europe for thousands of years. By the 15th century Italy was producing what would be called chevron beads. Since 1500 beads of all sorts were brought to America as trade goods by the millions. They were traded to the natives for gold and fur. Hundreds of glass beads were found around Jamestown, Virginia and other early settlements. Chevron beads and other glass beads were found in great abundance on the wreck of Sam Bellamy's ship, the *Whydah*. Since pirates didn't usually trade with natives, we must conclude that they were wearing them. Also, several coins found on the *Whydah* had a small hole drilled through them so the owner could wear it as a medallion. I believe that the stereotypical look of pirates with earrings, gold chains, glass beads, and coin medallions is fairly accurate.

Tattoos

Some pirates may have also had tattoos. It is well documented that the people of India, the Philippines, and many of the Pacific Islands were tattooing quite extensively for thousands of years. Also, many of the Native American tribes in the Caribbean and even on the mainland were tattooed. That was a common practice as far north as Virginia. In 1585 English explorer and naturalist, John White, visited the area that would later become the Outer Banks of North Carolina and published a series of illustrations of Native Americans detailing their clothing and general appearance. In those remarkably accurate and detailed drawings men and women were regularly tattooed with highly decorative and intricate patterns about their arms and chests. Pirates or seamen in general visiting those locations may have gotten tattooed. They certainly had the opportunity.

I believe that in the 17th and 18th centuries that would not have been as common as it was in later times. It just wasn't part of European culture yet. However, there was one contemporary reference to actual pirates with tattoos during the golden age of piracy. That reference came from our old friend, William Dampier, who wrote that some of the crew made Jerusalem Crosses on their arms by pricking their skin and rubbing pigment in. In the late 18th and 19th centuries, sailors began getting tattooed regularly, but this doesn't seem to be as common during the 17th and early

18th centuries. I believe that tattoos among pirates in the golden age would have been rare.

Boots

Pirates would have worn whatever they had. Many contemporary accounts describe pirates as going barefooted. I'm sure many did in warmer climates, but many more preferred to wear shoes. In the 17th and 18th centuries there was no difference in design between shoes of landsmen or seamen. However, men of the sea occasionally wore nautical boots, especially those sailing in colder climates, like the French sailors depicted in the 1700 painting mentioned earlier.

When it comes to pirates, many pirate historians and researchers completely discount boots as part of the pirate wardrobe. Even though nautical boots were used by many sailors, they wouldn't have been used in the warmer waters that pirates sailed. Not true. First of all, many pirates routinely sailed up the coast of North America. I've lived in Virginia and both North and South Carolina and it gets fairly cold in the winter months, especially at sea. Also, many pirates sailed around Cape Horn, where the temperatures get extremely cold. But what about the traditional pirate "bucket boots" that one commonly sees in movies and costumes? The accuracy of these boots is one of the most controversial debates among those portraying pirates as living history interpreters. Did some pirates wear these large turned down boots?

As mentioned earlier, over the knee boots were often worn folded down below the knee which took on the well-known "bucket boot" look. Boots like those would certainly have been worn by Francis Drake and other pirate captains of the 16th century. Boots were worn by everyone in the military, from private to general and the soldiers fleeing Europe and the Thirty Years' War to become buccaneers would have continued to wear their boots as long as they lasted. In modern times, Henry Morgan has often been depicted as wearing that type of boot. Since he was a European soldier, and wealthy enough to afford anything he wanted, the image of Henry Morgan and his soldier buccaneers marching to Panama wearing boots like that probably is an accurate one.

In Europe, only wealthy people rode horses, but in the colonies, a great many more people rode horses. Middle class merchants and tradesmen often had horses, especially in the English colonies of North America. A large number of boots appear on shipping manifests between England and the colonies. Thousands were shipped to America for sale and every rich passenger traveling to America would have had a pair to wear while riding. Would 18th century pirates wear boots like that? They certainly would have had access to that type of boots. If one thinks logically, any pirate who found a nice pair of boots that fit would have kept them. I think a pirate wearing riding boots in the early 18th century wasn't an unusual sight.

Weapons

Above all, as many contemporary observers noticed, pirates carried weaponry and the accoutrements of war, regardless of any other aspect of their clothing. Weapons were a large part of the pirate image which added to the concept of "bizarria" that men of action had. John F. Watson wrote a book in 1842 entitled *Annals of Philadelphia* where he recounts tales of pirates from oral tradition including how Blackbeard visited his girlfriend who lived in Marcus Hook, only a few miles from Philadelphia. In his book, he described Blackbeard as the tall mariner who was known by Philadelphia's early residence to frequent an inn nearby, always with his sword by his side. But wearing a sword in the late 17th and early 18th century was certainly not unique to pirates; most men during this period wore edge weapons, especially gentlemen. It was almost like wearing revolvers in the American west of the late 19th century.

Hangers, also called cutlasses, were often worn by civilians on a day to day basis. In the European culture of that period, almost every middle or upper-class man wore a sword or cutlass. As mentioned earlier, newspaper ads of the time often included references to lost or stolen hangers—they were fashionable and expensive, similar to the cell phones of today. Thousands of prints and paintings from the time illustrate this. Also, the enormous number of hunting swords, hangers, and small swords still in existence almost 300 years later attest that there were a lot of edge weapons in colonial America in the early 1700s. With the common practice of dueling while ashore, pirates needed to be prepared. Every Ship's Articles mention the practice of settling disputes at sea by dueling ashore. In addition, there was always the possible threat that some out of luck pirate would attack you while staggering from the local tavern and steal what was left of your hard-earned loot. In many cases, protection ashore would be an absolute necessity.

Bizarria

"Bizarria" is a term that was used to describe bold figures of the day. Similar to "Macho" but much more. There is a very interesting description of Spanish officers onboard ships during the 16th century that comes to us from Pablo E. Pered-Mallaina in his book *Spain's Men of the Sea, Daily life on the Indies Fleets in the Sixteenth Century* in which he wrote:

"The captains and military commanders of the royal armadas, apart from wearing typical military apparel, such as sleeveless jackets, broad-brimmed taffeta hats, and leather boots, were distinguished by their bizarria, a term used initially to define persons dressed in colorful clothing.

Because such clothing was a flamboyant affectation of military men, the term ended up signifying the notion of bravura, which was precisely what the soldiers wanted to convey with their attention-getting outfits. It is not rare to find garments inventoried that were silver in color, or tawny, red, violet, or yellow. The generals of armadas and their sons might even sport a whole array of jewels to adorn and distinguish their persons: gold chains, buttons encrusted with pearls, and diamonds, emerald rings, and so on. Masters, pilots, and other important personage often carried articles that brought a certain comfort to their lives. Sleeping clothes, bedding, eating and cooking utensils, and even copper urinals were often carried."

I strongly believe that this concept of "bizarria" existed among all military and naval officers as well as buccaneers and pirates. After all, many of the 17th century buccaneers were former military officers. No matter what era they lived in, pirates would have dressed as flamboyantly as possible, wearing whatever clothing they were able to get their hands on.

Considering the amount of prizes they took, any type of clothing that existed at the time could have and would have been worn by a pirate. But this statement is pretty general. We can break it down a little further. There are three basic types of dress common to all pirates, as well as to all members of any modern military. There is the dress they wear for battle, the dress they wear for everyday work, and the dress they wear when ashore on liberty.

On Ship, in Battle, and On Shore

Much of a pirate's life was spent sailing and cleaning. Vessels obviously had to be sailed, but they also had to be maintained, which meant cleaning and repairing the vessel at sea and careening the vessel ashore. Also, pirates spent a lot of time cleaning their weapons, which included their personal ones as well as all the ship's guns. While at sea or while careening ashore, pirates would obviously be dressed in their older clothes for those types of activities, ones that they wouldn't mind getting dirty or stained. In modern times, everyone has an old set of clothes that they wear to do chores like yard work or house painting. It was the same during the golden age of piracy. Literally every contemporary source that addresses the lives of seamen and pirates agrees that even the lowest sailor on the poorest merchantman had two sets of clothes, one set to work in and one set to be worn ashore. Those work clothes may have started out as shore clothes, but as they began to wear out, the sailors or pirates threw their really bad sets away, rotated their worn sets down, and acquired new sets for wear in port. This makes total sense.

Today, people in the military do the same thing. They all have old sets of uniforms that they wear on working parties and newer sets that they wear while on base or around the headquarters. As the good sets become faded, they are demoted to work sets and new uniforms are purchased. In the English Royal Navy of the 18th century, those older clothes worn by sailors at sea were called "slops." This is where the term "sloppy dresser" comes from.

Not everyone would have been involved in the daily maintenance and physical sailing of the vessel. Ship's officers probably weren't because they were too busy supervising and running the vessel. Privateer vessels were run more like royal naval vessels and the ship's captain and officers were exempt from performing any sort of maintenance. Under sail, their responsibilities would have been in command and control of the crew or navigation of the vessel. Ship's officers generally never wore slops and would have dressed appropriately for an officer of the ship, even under sail. That was traditional for all naval and merchant vessels.

But pirate vessels were often far more democratic. Even so, most pirate captains and officers had similar responsibilities to privateer captains and officers while sailing. Depending upon the crew they may have participated equally in the maintenance of the vessel and the cleaning of the weapons, or they may have retained their status as officers. How they would have dressed would have been a personal choice. We know that Captain Roberts always dressed in his finest red damask coat and clothing, a feathered hat, and a diamond studded cross regardless of what the rest of the ship's crew was doing or wearing. Contemporary descriptions of other pirate captains indicate that they generally dressed up with well-made fancy clothing and plenty of weapons. As for the rest of the crew, they would have worn whatever they wanted. While performing work at sea, they would be in slops of some sort. There are no rules for what slops looked like except that they would have been practical and comfortable to wear while performing their duties.

At the beginning of buccaneer heyday, 1640–1660, the buccaneers could have worn a combination of buck skin and just about anything else. Some were sailors, but many were hunters or farmers who became buccaneers to fight the Spanish and to make a large profit. Their original clothes would have been quickly replaced with finer clothing from their captured prize vessels, with their older clothes becoming slops. Later in the 17th century there would have been a definite difference in the dress between the soldiers and the sailors. As you recall, many of the large buccaneer fleets were comprised mostly of ex-soldiers who did the fighting, with only enough sailors onboard to sail the vessel. The style of "slops" for soldiers would have been comprised of a mixture of old uniforms and regular clothing. Sailors would have dressed in clothing associated with men of the sea. By the 18th century most pirates were sailors before they were pirates, so their slops would have been nautical dress.

At Sea

Short jackets were commonly worn. Coats would have been worn at sea in colder climates. Shirts were the undergarments of the day and were usually patterned the same for poor sailors, soldiers, and wealthy gentlemen alike, except the shirts for gentlemen tended to have ruffles at the collar and very long puffy sleeves. As mentioned earlier, it's very difficult to do any sort of work with sleeves getting in the way; so long puffy sleeves were a sign that the individual didn't do manual labor. Pirates who had fancy shirts with long puffy sleeves wouldn't have worn them while on working parties. Breeches would have been very similar between sailors, soldiers, and landsmen. In the 17th century, they were much fuller and pleated while in the 18th century they were slimmer fitted. Straight legged trousers that go to the ankle were commonly worn by English sailors from the late 17th century on. However, this seems to be exclusive to the English. There was a report made to the English admiralty that the Spanish could identify English vessels by the trousers their crewmen wore.

Ironically, the one type of clothing that sailors and pirates wouldn't have commonly worn was the type of wide legged, knee length, trousers modern people call "slops" and most commonly associate with 18th century sailors. Those trousers are totally impractical for most work at sea. **I personally wore a pair while working aboard a sailing vessel and I soon discovered that the wide legs got caught on just about everything.** At sea, those "slops" would be worn like overalls over top of their regular clothes to keep them from becoming stained. Sailors would have only worn them while performing dirty chores like painting or varnishing. However, those wide legged trousers were often worn by dock workers who loaded and unloaded vessels. Illustrations from the late 18th and early 19th century often incorrectly show sailors wearing these slops. That's because landsmen began incorrectly associating those trousers with sailors because they saw men wearing them while working on the docks and around ships.

In Battle

Pirates would have been armed to the teeth with every weapon they could carry during a boarding action. They would have several pistols, a main edge weapon of some type, and several knives. Intimidation was a vital part of basic pirate tactics and each member of the pirate crew had to look as menacing as possible. Each pirate would have had a sword or cutlass dangling from his belt or baldrics and several knives and pistols tucked in their belts. Contemporary descriptions of pirates all tell of how well-armed they were. Even members of pirate crews who were forced into piracy against their will were required to be exceptionally well-armed during an attack. In Captain Snelgrave's 1719 eyewitness account, he mentions recognizing one of the pirates who took his ship as a sailor he had known years earlier. The sailor told Snelgrave that he had been forced into piracy. Snelgrave describes him as "a tall man, with four Pistols in his Girdle and a broad Sword in his hand."

The pirates maintained that menacing appearance throughout the entire time the prize vessel was being looted, even along after the actual boarding action was finished. Sometimes, it took up to several weeks to effectively loot a vessel. Members of the prize crew who were still onboard were actually hostages and would have been treated as such, even if the pirates were disposed to be polite toward them. Just like a hostage situation today, the hostage takers always show their weapons to continue the intimidation and keep the hostages under control.

Throughout the looting process, pirates would often take personal possessions directly from the captives. Items like clothing, pocket watches, hats, belts, or anything else they fancied were all up for grabs. If the Ship's Articles allowed the pirates to keep personal items, they would have worn them as part of their ongoing intimidation. It would also add to their appearance.

Women Pirates

There is a very interesting description of Anne Bonny and Mary Read that sheds light on how women pirates may have dressed. This information can be found earlier in this book. John Besneck and Peter Cornelian were members of Jack Rackham's pirate crew which included Anne Bonny and Mary Read. At their trial, Besneck and Cornelian gave testimony in which they described the two pirate women's appearance saying that they wore men's clothing while fighting but women's clothing at other times. Another description of these women pirates came from Dorothy Thomas, who was captured by Jack Rackham and his pirates, which included Anne Bonny and Mary Read. Miss Thomas gave testimony at their trial and described the two pirate women stating that "the Two Women were on the Board the said Sloop, and wore Men's Jackets, and long Trousers, and Handkerchiefs tied about their Heads; and that each of them had a Machet and a Pistol in their Hands. . ." Apparently the men who drew the contemporary illustrations of Anne Bonny and Mary Read for *The General History of Pyrates* got it right.

On Liberty—Ashore

What pirates wore and how they looked while on liberty ashore greatly depends upon the port and the circumstances surrounding the pirate's visit. Pirates who visited ports that were not pirate-friendly dressed in a manner that didn't stand out or else they would be arrested. In other words, they dressed in normal clothes just like the locals. The pirates may or may not have been dressed in nautical attire. Pirates had access to lots of clothing from the vessels they captured. They could have dressed like merchants, or even gentlemen.

During the golden age it was very unusual for common sailors to have a lot of money and anyone dressed as a sailor spending lots of money in taverns would have immediately attracted the attention of the authorities. However, some pirates overlooked that and went ashore dressed in common clothes with lots of money anyway. There are many accounts of pirates being arrested while in port and in each case, the authorities identified them as pirates by their lavish spending and/or outlandish behavior. When Blackbeard's quartermaster, William Howard, visited Williamsburg, Virginia in the summer of 1718, he dressed just like everyone else to avoid being arrested, but his lavish spending drew the attention of the authorities and he was eventually arrested on suspicion of piracy.

On the other hand, when a port was under siege or being held for ransom by a pirate vessel or fleet, many pirates often went ashore as part of the looting process. In that case, they dressed in the most intimidating manner possible, even if they just went ashore to have a good time. For example, in 1718 when some of Blackbeard's pirates came ashore in Charles Town during Blackbeard's blockade of the harbor, they were dressed for battle and acted in a very aggressive manner. One eyewitness account described one of Blackbeard's captains, a pirate named Richards, as he and his men came ashore, "Richards and his men were parading themselves up and down the principal streets, and their imprudent behavior aroused the indignation of the people to the highest pitch." They were protected by fear of a bombardment from Blackbeard's ships.

Another example was when Captain Roberts' pirates came ashore at the Newfoundland port of Trepassey. Roberts' reputation was so intimidating that no one resisted him in any way. After taking 22 vessels anchored in port, Roberts allowed up to 50 pirates at a time to go ashore to loot the town, drink in the taverns, and enjoy the prostitutes. They totally dominated the community, did what they pleased, and no one lifted a finger to stop them. In these circumstances, the pirates who went ashore did so as an extension of the intimidation process. They were very well-armed, giving them a fierce and menacing appearance. They also most likely dressed in their finest and fanciest clothing.

The big question is, "How did pirates dress when they were ashore in a friendly port?" Friendly ports included Tortuga, Port Royal from 1660 to 1670, Charles Town and New York in the 1690s, Marcus Hooke, Pennsylvania in the early 18th century, West African ports where they were known and welcomed, and hundreds of other spots where being identified as a pirate didn't result in arrest. In friendly ports, pirates wanted to do everything they could to be recognized as successful pirates. The more successful they looked, the more respect they got from the locals. That was good for business. Pirates wanted to sell their stolen goods and get the absolute top prices and the more respect they got from the locals, the more profits they could make.

Today, businessmen wear expensive suits, carry expensive pens, and have all sorts of high-tech gadgets intended to impress a client. The same principle applied to pirates during the golden age. In 1699 buccaneer Captain John James arrived in Elizabeth City (modern Hampton, Virginia) with his ship *Providence Frigate* of 26 guns. He claimed to have taken several million pounds of treasure at sea and to convince the local merchants of his success, "his men were seen walking the streets with gold chains about their necks" according to a contemporary account. Also, well-dressed pirates received better treatment from the tavern owners and ladies. But it went further than that. It was part of pirate culture.

Most of what people wear is determined by their culture, especially if they are members of an elite group. A prime example of this in modern culture is that of the motorcycle club. Regardless of the specific club affiliation, members of motorcycle clubs are easily recognized by their leather jackets, type of boots, head gear, and lots of other things. Even members of motorcycle clubs who are known to operate outside the law wear their club colors with pride. Pirates ashore would be proud of their affiliation with their captain, their ship, and their reputation and would want everyone to know it. They would wear their best clothes, which would include as many fancy and frilly items as they could get their hands on.

Most round hats and tri-cornered hats were made out of beaver felt and were called beaver hats.

Hats with feathers, jewelry, coats made of fine material, and lots of weapons were all part of that pirate culture. Successful pirates had access to just about everything that existed. One passenger, whose ship had been taken by the pirate Edward Low, listed some of his garments that had been taken in an article published in the *Boston News Letter* in June 1722. These articles included "one scarlet suit of Clothes, one new grey Broad Cloth Coat, 1 Sword with a fine red Velvet Belt . . . one Scarff of Red Persian Silk, fringed with black Silk . . . one Beaver Hat bound with Silver Lace." They sometimes wore a mixture of fine clothing and common seaman's attire. Father Jean Baptist Labat was a French Dominican priest who traveled throughout the West Indies in the late 17th century and kept a journal of his experiences, especially those that concerned buccaneers. He describes buccaneers dressing in fancy clothes taken from prizes. He also describes buccaneers wearing fine striped shirts with ordinary seaman's trousers while going bare foot and wearing fancy wigs and plumed beaver hats on their heads. Labat wrote that "Many filibusters (irregular military adventurers) went ashore dressed in laced justaucorps and plumed hats but no shoes or stockings, or shoes but no stockings, or stockings but no shoes." Buccaneers were often called filibusters; justaucorps were coats commonly worn by just about everyone in Europe and the colonies in the 17th and 18th centuries. There are accounts of pirates wearing fancy coats made of exotic materials, silk shirts, taffeta breeches, and feathered tri-cornered hats to their own executions.

Fancy clothes weren't just for captains; common crewmen wore them too. Every member of the crew had the opportunity to wear the finest clothing taken from a prize. As you may recall, in his 1734 book Captain Snelgrave recounted an incident in which Captains Cocklyn, Davis, and Le Vasseur took three fancy dress coats directly from a captured ship's wardrobe including one made of "Scarlet embroidered with Silver . . ." When the quartermaster found out, he confiscated the coats and returned them to the common chest. He wrote, "The Pirate Captains having taken these Clothes without leave from the Quarter-master, it gave great Offence to all the Crew; who alleged, 'If they suffered such things, the Captains would in future assume a Power, to take whatever they liked for themselves.' So, upon their return on board next Morning, the Coats were taken from them, and put into the common Chest, to be sold at the Mast." This fascinating account told by an eyewitness indicates that those fine clothes were available to every member of the crew, to be purchased out of their share at an auction called the "Sale at the Mast."

GLOSSARY

A

Admiral
naval rank of a commander of a fleet or an officer of very high rank.

Aft
nautical term for the rear of a boat, ship, or any other type of vessel.

Amphibious Assault
an attack on land made from landing soldiers from a ship or vessel.

Anglicans
members of the Church of England, representing a middle ground between Catholicism and Protestantism.

Arawak Language
native American language originally spoken throughout the Caribbean and parts of northern South America.

Astrolabe
metal disc with moveable arms and sights used as a navigational instrument at sea. It was an improved version of the quadrant and was introduced in 1481.

B

Back Staff
late 16th century navigational device used at sea. It was an improved version of the cross staff and works on the same principle except the user looks away from the sun to get a sighting.

Baldric
belt for a sword or other piece of equipment worn over one shoulder and reaching down to the opposite hip.

Barcolongo
large Spanish fishing boat having two or three masts.

Bark
term used in the 18th Century for a nondescript vessel that did not fit any usual categories.

Below Decks
nautical term meaning the inside space of a ship or vessel which is literally below the main deck.

Bermuda Sloop
17th and 18th century single-masted vessel with a triangular sail rigged fore and aft with a square sail above that was designed for trade, measured approximately 70 feet in length, and had a large cargo hold.

Blunderbuss
short-barreled large-bored gun with a flared muzzle.

Boarding Action
when the crew of one vessel jumps over onto the second vessel during an attack.

Boatswain
senior member of the ship's crew who is in charge of operations on the deck.

Booty
valuable stolen goods. Synonyms: loot, plunder, haul, or pillage.

Boucan
Arawak word for the process of smoking meat over a slow burning fire.

Bow
front of a ship, boat, or vessel.

Bowline
knot used to form a fixed loop at the end of a rope but can also mean the anchor line.

Bowsprit
spar extending forward from a ship's bow, to which the forestays are fastened.

Brethren of the Coast
syndicate of pirate captains.

Brig
two-masted vessel with square rigging and an additional gaff sail on the mainmast.

Brigantine
two-masted vessel with a square-rigged foremast and a fore-and-aft-rigged mainmast.

Broadside
the nearly simultaneous firing of all the guns from one side of a warship.

Buccaneer
17th century term meaning a pirate.

C

Calico Acts
a series of English laws passed between 700 and 1721 which banned the import of most cotton textiles into England.

Calvinist Movement
a major branch of the Protestant Reformation that follows the theological teaching of John Calvin.

Captain General of the British Army
military rank for the senior general or the commander in chief of all generals.

Careening
the cleaning and repairing of the hull of a ship or vessel below the water line which requires taking it out of the water.

Carriage Gun
artillery piece that is mounted on a frame with small wheels, allowing the gun to be rolled short distances for loading and aiming.

Chevron Beads
small glass beads usually with stripes worn as inexpensive jewelry.

Chip Log
late 16th century navigational device used at sea to measure the speed of the vessel. It is a quarter circle of wood attached to a long line on a reel with knots tied every 47 feet 3 inches.

Close the Distance
military term meaning to move toward and engage the enemy.

Colonel
military rank below a general for an officer who commands a regiment or a similar sized group of soldiers.

Colors
military term meaning a national flag. To raise the flag is to raise the colors. Colors flying is synonymous with flags waving.

Commissions

instruction, command, or authority given to individuals in writing.

Consort Vessel

small vessel used to carry supplies in support of other vessels.

Cross Staff

early 16th century navigational instrument used to measure the sun's angle and determine the vessel's latitude.

Crossguard

part of the handle of a sword, it is a metal bar placed at a right angle to the blade between the grip and the blade to offer protection to the hand.

D

Damask

reversible fabric made from silk, linen, wool, or cotton usually woven with a single color with a glossy pattern visible on both sides against a duller background.

Dandy

man devoted to style, neatness, and fashion in dress and appearance.

Dunjars

plain woven striped textile popular in early 18th century England.

Dutch East India Company

Dutch maritime trading corporation established 1602 which imported textiles, spices, and other valuable products from locations throughout the Indian Ocean.

Dutch Flute

16th through 18th century Dutch merchant ship with a rounded hull designed to carry large amounts of cargo.

Dutch Pinnace

fast and maneuverable 17th century Dutch ship with square rigging used for trade or as a small warship.

E

Earthworks

an artificial fortification made of soil used for defense.

East Indiaman

any type of merchant vessel that belonged to an East India Company and carried goods between the Indian Ocean and Europe.

East Indies

the lands of India and South East Asia to include Malay Archipelago and Indonesia.

English East India Company
English maritime trading corporation established 1600 which imported textiles, spices, and other valuable products from locations throughout the Indian Ocean.

English Guinea
English gold coin minted between 1663 and 1813 and valued at one pound and one shilling.

English Lock or Doglock
a type of flintlock mechanism commonly used in England during the 17th century that ignites the gun powder in a firearm by striking a piece of flint against a metal frizzen causing a spark and has a small catch designed as a safety device to hold the cock in place.

English Pinnace
English term for a small service boat such as a row boat or long boat.

English Restoration
the restoration of the monarchy in England in 1660 when Parliamentary rule ended and Charles II was crowned king.

F

Falchion
broad, slightly curved sword with the cutting edge on the convex side.

Fence
individual who acts as a middle man between thieves or pirates and the eventual buyers and receives or knowingly buys stolen goods in order to resell them for profit.

Filibuster
17th century English term for pirate.

Fire Ship
any vessel intentionally set on fire and then sailed into an enemy fleet to cause panic.

Firing in Volley
military term meaning for all the soldiers in a designated group or line to fire their weapons at one time.

First Mate
senior member of the ship's crew who second in command to the quarter master.

Flag Ship
vessel used by the commanding officer of a group of naval ships.

Flintlock
type of lock mechanism introduced around 1550 that ignites the gun powder in a firearm by striking a piece of flint against a metal frizzen causing a spark.

Flyboat
Dutch designed small vessel with a flat bottom used as a costal cargo vessel or to service larger ships.

Fore Mast
mast in the front of the vessel usually in front of the main mast.

Forecastle
structure on the front of a ship or vessel usually containing all the ropes that are not in use.

Fowling Piece
smoothbore firearm designed to hunt birds similar to a single barreled shotgun.

French Arcadians
French colonists who settled in Arcadia (at the Gulf of St. Lawrence in Canada) during the 17th century.

French East India Company
French maritime trading corporation established 1664 which imported textiles, spices, and other valuable products from locations throughout the Indian Ocean.

Frigate
three-masted ship designed for war but is smaller in size and armament than a ship-o-the-line.

Fully Rigged
nautical term for a ship with three masts all of with have square sails.

Fusil
light weight and generally shorter flintlock musket generally used by elite soldiers.

Fustian
fabric with a cotton or wool weft and a linen warp.

G

Gaff Rigged
sail configuration plan for a four-sided sail rigged fore and aft and fastened at all four points with to a large spar connected to the center of the mast and hoisted up with lines connected to the top of the mast.

Galley
large vessel with up to three banks of oars that uses oars as its primary propulsion but also has sails.

Gaol
17th and 18th century term for a jail.

General
highest ranking military officer who is above the rank of Colonel and who commands several regiments or has supreme authority in military matters.

Glorious Revolution
revolution by the English Parliament in 1688 to overthrow King James II of England and place William III, Prince of Orange, who was James' nephew and son-in-law, and Mary II, who was James' daughter, on the throne.

Gregorian Calendar
calendar named after Pope Gregory XIII, who introduced it in October 1582 as a refinement of the Julian calendar, although it was not adopted in England until 1752.

Gunner
naval rank for a member of the crew who is an expert with naval ordinance and who is responsible for aiming and firing one or more of the ship's guns during battle.

H

Harbor Pilot
person who is thoroughly familiar with a harbor and guides large vessels into port.

Harquebus
the earliest form of hand held firearm introduced in the mid-15th century with a relatively short barrel of small caliber that uses a match lock mechanism to ignite the gun powder.

Heretic
person holding a different religious belief than yours.

HMS
English nautical abbreviation meaning His/Her Majesty's Ships and precedes the name of all vessels officially listed as part of the Royal Navy.

Huguenots
16th and 17th century French Protestant denomination revived from the Calvinists.

Hull
main body of a ship or other vessel.

Hung from a Gibbet
the common practice of hanging the corps of a pirate or criminal in a metal cage in a public place as a deterrent to others.

Jacobite Revolution
a series of revolutions primarily conducted by the Scottish and Irish people in 1688, 1715, and 1745 to restore James II or his descendants to the throne of England.

Jamaica Sloop
17th and 18th century single-masted vessel with a triangular sail rigged fore and aft with a square sail above that was designed for trade, measured approximately 70 feet in length, but had a narrower construction than other sloops in increase speed.

Jolly Roger
a pirate flag which came from the French term "Jolie Rouge" which means "Happy Red".

Julian Calendar
calendar named after Julius Caesar, who introduced it in 46 BC as a reform of the Roman calendar.

Justaucorps
long, knee-length coat worn by men in the latter half of the 17th and throughout the 18th century.

Kersey
coarse woolen cloth, lighter weight than broadcloth.

Knucklebow
part of the guard attached to the hilt of certain swords which covers the fingers, extending from the cross guard toward the pommel.

Larboard
the port, or left side of a ship, boat, or vessel.

Lateen Sail
large triangular sail originally designed by the Romans that gives a vessel more maneuverability than a square sail.

Leeward Passage
channel between Puerto Rico and the Virgin Islands by which vessels can exit the Caribbean in calmer waters.

Letters of Marque
document issued by an agent of a government giving the holder permission to attack all vessels of nations listed in the document which are deemed as enemies to the issuing government.

Line
nautical term meaning a working rope that is connected to a sail, anchor, or any part of a vessel used to sail it (a rope becomes a line as soon as it is attached to a part of the vessel).

Lock Mechanism
mechanism attached to the side of a firearm which is designed to ignite the gun powder in the barrel when a trigger is pulled.

Lord Protector of the Commonwealth of England
title given to the head of state of England during the time of Parliamentary rule known as the Commonwealth 1649–1660.

M

Main Mast
tallest and most important mast on a ship or vessel.

Main Sail
on vessels rigged fore and aft, it is the largest sail and on vessels that are square rigged, it is the largest and lowest sail on the mast.

Major General
military rank for a general office below the rank of general.

Manila Galleon
Spanish merchant vessel that routinely traveled between the Philippines and the west coast of Mexico, primarily between Manila and Acapulco.

Man-O-War
class of warships in the 17th and 18th centuries that are the largest in size and armament.

Marooned
the act of being set ashore and left alone on a deserted island. Usually done as a punishment for a serious violation of the ship's articles (rules).

Matchlock
larger version of the harquebus, it was introduced around 1520 and is a hand-held firearm that uses a match lock mechanism to ignite the gun powder.

Mate
member of a ship's crew.

Merchantmen
17th and 18th century term for any merchant ship or vessel.

Midshipman
naval rank for an officer cadet or someone who is in training to become a naval officer.

Midshipman's Butter
18th century term for avocados that were usually spread on hard tack.

Militia
military force that is raised from the civilian population to supplement a regular military force.

Miskitos
Native American group indigenous to the Caribbean coast extending from Honduras to Nicaragua.

Mizzen Mast
mast directly behind the main mast.

Mogul
ruler of India or a member of the ruling dynasty of India, the Moguls were a warlike culture that concurred India in 1526 and remained in power until the 19th century.

Mojito
cocktail that consists of rum, sugar, lime juice, soda water, and mint.

N

Navigation Acts
series of English laws issued in the late 17th century that greatly restricted foreign trade, especially in the colonies and required that all foreign goods be shipped to the American colonies through English ports.

Nor'easter
storm or wind blowing from the northeast, usually accompanied by very heavy rain or snow.

O

Ordnance
military and naval term for artillery or guns onboard a ship.

P

Papists
person whose loyalties were to the Pope and the Roman Catholic Church, rather than the Church of England.

Pappenheimer
popular type of rapier that originated in Germany in 1630 and had a two-piece shell guard which provided great protection to the hand of the user.

Pechelingues
16th and 17th century Spanish term for Dutch pirates.

Periauger
shallow draft, often flat-bottomed two-masted sailing vessel, often without a bowsprit, which also carried oars for rowing.

Pewter
metal alloy of tin mixed with copper, antimony, and lead commonly used to make inexpensive table ware and tankards.

Pieces of Eight
term for a Spanish coin valued at eight reales but could also be applied to other Spanish real coins of lesser value.

Pike
very long thrusting spear commonly used by the English military up through the late 17th century and used by pirates during boarding action into the 18th century.

Pink
three-masted, square-rigged sailing vessel, typically with a narrow, overhanging stern.

Pirate Banyan
gathering of pirate crews to socialize and form alliances, usually involving large quantities of food, drink, and general camaraderie.

Porringers
small, shallow bowl with one or two handles, usually made of wood, ceramic, pewter, or silver that was used for a variety of foods.

Port
left side of a ship, boat, or vessel.

Pounds Sterling
denomination of English currency equal to 20 schillings.

Powder Flask
small flask containing gun powder and usually worn on a rope over the shoulder.

Presbyterians
members of the reformed tradition of Protestantism, influenced by the Reformed theology of John Calvin.

Pretender Across the Sea
18th century term for James Edward Stuart, the claimant to the throne of England who was often referred to as the "pretender" and who lived across the sea in France.

Privateers
private person or ship that engages in maritime warfare under a commission also known as letters of marque.

Prize Vessel
any vessel that has been captured by another vessel.

Protestant Reformation
1517–1648, a schism in Western Christianity initiated by Martin Luther and continued by John Calvin and other protestant reformers in 16th century Europe.

Pull Alongside
nautical term meaning to bring two vessels side by side.

Puritans
a member of a group of English Protestants of the late 16th and 17th centuries who regarded the Reformation of the Church of England as incomplete and sought to simplify and regulate forms of worship.

Q

Quadrant
ancient navigational instrument consisting of a graduated quarter circle and a sighting mechanism used for taking angular measurements in order to determine latitude.

Quakers
member of the Religious Society of Friends, a Christian movement founded and devoted to peaceful principles, with a belief in the doctrine of "inner light" and rejection of formal ministry and all set forms of worship.

Quarter
military term meaning mercy shown toward an enemy or opponent, generally used as "No Quarter" or "Quarter Given".

Quarterdeck
raised deck behind the main or mizzen mast of a ship or vessel where navigation is done or where the captain commands the vessel.

Quartermaster
within a naval context of the 17th and 18th centuries, it was the rank of the senior member of the crew (not including the officers) who was responsible for the care and discipline of the rest of the crew.

R

Rapier
sword with a long and narrow straight blade that was popular in the 16th and 17th centuries.

Rating of Ships
classification of warships which indicated size and armament.

Re-provision
when used as a nautical term, it means to take on all manner of supplies on board a vessel.

Rigged Fore and Aft
configuration of sails on a vessel where triangular sails which are set along the keel.

Rigging
the system of ropes, cables, or chains to support a ship's masts (standard rigging) and to control or set the yards and sails (running rigging); and the action of providing a sailing ship with rigging.

Royal African Company
a company established by king Charles II of England in 1660 to trade along the West African coast for gold and slaves.

Royals
small sails flown immediately above the top gallants on square-rigged sailing vessels.

Rudder and Sails
nautical term meaning the navigational charts (rudder) and sails of a vessel, which was used as an expression "to take one's rudder and sails" meaning to keep one ashore.

S

Sailing Master
nautical rank for the officer responsible for setting and adjusting the sails of a ship or vessel.

Sailing Under False Colors
to raise the flag of another nation above one's ship or vessel.

Sale Before the Mast
term used by pirates for the auction of stolen goods for the crew after taking a vessel.

Schooner
two-masted vessel with sails that are rigged fore and aft.

Sea Beggars
17th century Dutch term meaning pirates.

Sea Chanteys

type of work song that was commonly sung aboard a ship or vessel.

Sea Rovers

17th century English term meaning pirates.

Seamen

general term for a person who serves aboard ship as a member of the crew.

Seaworthy

nautical term for a ship or vessel that is in good enough condition to sail on the sea.

Seersucker

thin and puckered cotton fabric that is commonly striped or checked.

Shift

17th and 18th century term for a woman's long shirt resembling a night gown and considered to be an undergarment.

Ship

three-masted vessel that is fully rigged with square sails.

Ship of the Line

largest and most powerful naval warships with either a first, second, or third rating usually carrying at least 80 guns.

Ship's Articles

rules for discipline and conduct agreed upon by the members of a pirate crew which could include anything from division of captured goods to treatment of prisoners.

Shot

military term for any type of projectile fired from a gun.

Sloop

single-masted vessel with a triangular sail rigged fore and aft.

Snaphance

first successful flintlock type mechanism introduced by the Dutch about 1550 with a complicated design in which the frizzen and pan cover are made in separate pieces.

Snow

large, two-masted merchant vessel that is rigged with square sails and can also be constructed with oars (galley-built snow).

South China Sea
body of water with Vietnam to the west, China to the north, the Philippines to the east, and Borneo to the south.

Spanish Bilbo
type of cup hilt rapier commonly issued to Spanish military and naval forces by the Spanish government from the end of the 17th century throughout the entire 18th century.

Spanish Doubloons
17th and 18th century English slag term for an extremely valuable Spanish gold coin.

Spanish Galleon
large Spanish merchant ship commonly used between the 16th and 18th centuries with three or four masts with the fore mast and the main mast rigged with square sails and the mizzen mast and aft mast rigged with lateen sails and a small square sail on a high-rising bowsprit.

Square Rigged
vessel with traditional square sails that are generally perpendicular to the keel of the vessel.

Starboard
right side of a ship, boat, or vessel.

Stern
outer back rear of a ship, boat, or vessel.

Superstructure
any structure or cabin built on or above the main deck of a ship or vessel.

Sweeps
nautical slang term for the long oars used on any vessel.

Swivel Gun
small caliber gun that is mounted with a swivel device on the wall of a fort or on the rail of a vessel that can be easily aimed and fired at close range.

T

Taffeta
an expensive silk fabric with a higher quality weave.

Tainos
Native American group native to the Caribbean Islands.

Tallow
fatty substance made from rendered animal fat and used in making candles, soap, and waterproofing the hulls of vessels.

Top Gallant
square sail immediately above the top sail on a square-rigged vessel.

Top Sail
square sail immediately above the main sail on a square-rigged vessel.

Touch Hole
small hole in the side or top of a gun barrel through which the gun powder inside the barrel is ignited.

Tradesmen
person who works in a trade such as a carpenter, black smith, gun smith, printer, etc.

Treaty of Breda
treaty between the Dutch Republic and England signed in 1667 that ended the Second Anglo-Dutch War that ceded the Dutch colonies in the mid-Atlantic to England.

Treaty of Madrid
treaty between England and Spain signed in 1670 and settled colonial disputes in America and officially ended the fifteen-year long war in the Caribbean that began with England's invasion and colonization of Jamaica.

Treaty of Ratisbon
treaty between Spain and France signed in 1684 that ended the War of the Reunions.

Treaty of Ryswick
treaty between France and the Grand Alliance signed in 1697 that ended the Nine Years War.

Treaty of Tordesillas
treaty between Spain and Portugal signed in 1494 that settled conflicts over lands newly discovered or explored by both Spanish and Portuguese explorers that divided the entire world in two halves, one belonging to Spain and the other belonging to Portugal.

Treaty of Utrecht
treaty signed in 1713 that ended the War of the Spanish Succession.

U

Under Full Sail
nautical term meaning that all the sails are raised in order to sail as fast as possible.

Union Act of 1707
an act officially joining England and Scotland as one nation with one ruler.

V

W

Vice Admiral
rank for a senior naval officer below the rank of admiral.

Weather Gage
nautical term that means your vessel is up wind of the other vessel which gives you far more maneuverability that the vessel downwind.

West Indies
islands in the Caribbean that include the Greater Antilles, the Lesser Antilles, and the Lucayan Archipelago.

Wheel Locks
type of lock mechanism for firing a weapon that ignites the gun powder by creating a spark by touching a flint to a spinning steel wheel that is operated by winding a spring.

Windward Passage
the strait between Cuba and Hispaniola and extending along the Florida coast with consistently favorable winds blowing north by north east that was used as the primary route for vessels leaving the Caribbean.

BIBLIOGRAPHY

American Revolution Org. Clothing of 18th Century England, page one of three, 1700–1735, Easy Productions, retrieved in 2010 from http://www.americanrevolution.org/clothing/clothing2.html, copyright 1996, 2010

Art History Resources. 18th Century Art and Baroque Art, numerous works of art, retrieved from http://witcombe.sbc.edu/ARTH18thcentury.html, no copyright information given.

Art Renewal Center. Search the ARC Museum, numerous works of art, Art Renewal Center, 100 Markley Street, Port Reading, NJ 07064, retrieved from http://www.artrenewal.org, no copyright information given.

Association of Watch and Clock Collectors Inc. Pieces of time, 17th Century Watches & 18th Century Watches, email: info@antique-watch.com, retrieved from http://www.antique-watch.com, no copyright information given.

AvoTerra. Avocado History, retrieved from http://www.indexfresh.com/avocado_history.htm, Index Fresh Inc., 2014.

BLN (Boston News-letter), 1704–1726, Boston, Massachusetts

Baker, David W. Early English Glass Apothecary Vials 16th 17th Centuries, Apothecary Glass, copyright by Angela M. Bowey, retrieved in 2010 from http://www.theglassmuseum.com/Englishvials.html, copyright 1997, 2012.

Baumgarten, Linda. Eighteenth Century Clothing at Williamsburg, The Colonial Williamsburg Foundation, P.O. Box 1776 Williamsburg, VA 23187, 1986.

Beeches of Saint Croix, retrieved in September 2014 from http://www.stcroix-beaches.com/John-Davis.html, no copyright information given.

Bennett, Charles. Laudonniere & Fort Caroline, History and Documents, University of Alabama Press, Box 870380 Tuscaloosa, AL 35487, 2001.

Bevis, Richard W. English Drama: Restoration and Eighteenth Century 1660–1789, Taylor & Francis, 1988.

Blackmore, David. Arms & Armour of the English Civil Wars, Boydell & Brewer, Limited, 1990, 2003.

Blair, Claude. Pollard's History of Firearms, Macmillan; 1st American edition, 1983.

Braun & Schneider. Historic Costume in Pictures, Dover Publications, 31 East 2nd St. Mineola, NY 11501, 1975.

Brears, Peter C. D. Food and Cooking in Seventeenth Century Britain, English Heritage, 1985.

Breverton, Terry. Black Bart Roberts, The Greatest Pirate of Them All, Pelican Publishing Company, Inc., 1000 Burmaster St, Gretna, Louisiana 70053, 2004.

Breverton, Terry. The Pirate Dictionary, Pelican Publishing Company, Inc., 1000 Burmaster St, Gretna, Louisiana 70053, 2004.

Brinckerhoff, Sidney D. & Chamberlain, Pierce A. Spanish Military Weapons in Colonial America 1700–1821, Stackpole Books, Harrisburg, PA, 1972.

Brown, Stephen R. Scurvy, How a Surgeon, a Mariner, and a Gentleman solved the Greatest Medical Mystery of the Age of Sail, Thomas Dunne Books, 175 5th Ave NY, NY 10010, An Imprint of St. Martin's Press, 2003.

Bruyneel, M. Isle of Tortuga, Short History of Tortuga, email: M.Bruyneel@ubvu.vu.nl, retrieved from http://zeerovery.nl/history/index.htm, copyright date not given.

Bull, Stephen. The Furie of the Ordnance, Artillery in the English Civil Wars, Boydell Press, 2008.

Burgess, Robert & Clausen, Carl. Florida's Golden Galleons, The Search for the 1715 Spanish Treasure Fleet, Florida Classics Library, Port Salerno, FL, 1982.

CSPCS (Calendar of State Papers, Colonial Series) America and the West Indies, Preserved in the Public Record Office. Edited by Cecil Headlam. London: Cassell & Co. Ltd., 1930–1933.

Cahoon, Ben. Chronology of Tortuga Governors, World Statesmen.org, retrieved in October 2014 from http://www.worldstatesmen.org/Haiti.htm#Saint-Domingue, copyright date not given.

Coe, Michael D., Connoly, Peter, Harding, Andrew, Harris, Victor, Larocca, Donald J., Richardson, Thom, North, Anthony, Spring, Christopher, and Wilkinson, Frank. Swords and Hilt Weapons, Barns and Noble Books, Imperial Works, Perren St., London, NW5 3ED, 1993.

Chapel, Charles E. The Complete Book of Gun Collecting, Coward-McCann, Inc., Van Rees Press, New York, NY, 1947.

Clayton, Tony. Coins of England and Great Britain, Copyright reserved by the author, Tony Clayton, retrieved from http://www.coins-of-the-uk.co.uk/coins.html#index, this version is number 440 dated 17th April 2014.

Clifford, Barry. Expedition Whydah, Harper Collins Publishers, Inc., 10 East 53rd St. NY, NY 10022, 1999.

Clifford, Barry & Kinkor, Kenneth. The Real Pirates, the Untold Story of the Whydah, National Geographic Society, Library of Congress Cataloging-in-publication 1145 17th St. NW Washington DC 20036-4688, Email: ngbookrights@ngs.org, National Geographic Books Subsidiary Rights, 2007.

Coins and History. French Coins, Monarchial, retrieved in February 2014 from http://www.coinsandhistory.com/countries/French_coins1.html, no copyright information given.

Collins, A. R. PhD. British Canon Design 1600–1800, retrieved in January 2014 from http://arc.id.au/Cannon.html, no copyright information given.

Cordingly, David. Life Among the Pirates, the Romance and the Reality, London, Little, Brown & Co., 1995

Cordingly, David. Pirates, Terror on the High Seas–From the Caribbean to the South China Sea, London, Turner Publishing, 1996

Cordingly, David. Under the Black Flag, The Romance and Reality of Life Among the Pirates, Random House Trade Paperback Edition, 2004

Cordingly, David and Falconer, John. Pirates Fact & Fiction, Collins & Brown Ltd., London, 1992.

Creech, Millicent Ford. Early British Table Silver: A Short History, 581 South Perkins Road, Memphis, TN 38117, Email: mfcreech@bellsouth.net, retrieved in 2010 from http://www.mfordcreech.com/Early_British_Table_Silver_II.htm, no copyright information given.

Cox, Sam. I Say Tomayto, You Say Tomahto, retrieved in September 2013 from http://www.landscapeimagery.com/tomato.html, no copyright information given.

Dampier, William. Memoirs of a Buccaneer, Dampier's New Voyage Round the World, 1697, First published by James Knapton, 1697, Dove reprint of the work originally published in 1927 by Argonaut Press, London, under the title *A New Voyage Round the World* with introduction by Percy G. Addams, Dover Publications, 1968, 2007.

Day, Jean. Blackbeard and the Queen Anne's Revenge, Golden Age Press, 599 Roberts Road, Newport NC 28570, 2007.

Dow, George Francis & Edmonds, John Henry. The Pirates of the New England Coast 1630–1730, unabridged republication first printed by the Marine Research Society, Salem MS, 1923, Dover Publications, NY, 1996.

Du Coeur, Justin. Medieval and Renaissance Games, retrieved in November 2013 from http://www.waks.org/game-hist, no copyright information given.

Duffus, Kevin P. The Last Days of Blackbeard the Pirate, Looking Glass Productions Inc., PO Box 98985 Raleigh, NC 27624, 2008.

Eastman, Tamara J & Bond, Constance. The Pirate Trial of Anne Bonny and Mary Read, Fern Canyon Press, PO Box 1708 Cambria CA 93428, (805) 927-4151, pirates@ferncanyonpress.com, 2000.

English Civil War Society of America (ECWSA). Retrieved from, http://www.ecwsa.org, copyright 1998, 2009.

Erickson, Mark St. John. Governor Risks all in Hampton Roads Pirate Battle, retrieved from http://articles.dailypress.com/2012-05-29/features/dp-nws-pirates-4-20120529_1_mark-g-hanna-hms-shoreham-pirate, merickson@dailypress.com, 757-247-4783, 2012.

Erickson, Mark St. John. Hampton Roads pirates: Black Bart Vows Revenge after Shipmates Hang in Virginia, Virginia Daily Press, May 30, 2012, retrieved from http://articles.dailypress.com/2012-05-30/features/dp-nws-pirates-5-20120530_1_west-indies-black-bart-crew, merickson@dailypress.com, 757-247-4783, 2012.

Esquemeling, John. The Buccaneers of America In the Original English Translation of 1684, First published by W. Crook, London, 1684, Current edition published by Cosimo, Inc., Cosimo P.O. Box 416 Old Chelsea Station, NY, NY 10113, Email: www.cosimobooks.com, 2007.

Exquemelin, Alexander O. De Americaensche Zee Roovers, First published by Jan ten Hoorn, Amsterdam, Holland, 1678, The Buccaneers of America, Dover Publications, 31 East 2nd St. Mineola, NY 11501, translations Copyright 1969 by Alexis Brown, Introduction copyright 1969 by Jack Beeching, this edition, 2000.

Eyeglasses Warehouse. Rare 18th Century Spectacles, Email: information@eyeglasseswarehouse.com, retrieved from http://www.eyeglasseswarehouse.com/18th-century-spectacles.html, no copyright information given.

Filippone, Peggy Trowbridge. Sweet Potato History, retrieved from http://homecooking.about.com/od/foodhistory/a/sweetpothistory.htm, no copyright information given.

Fisher, Peter. The Calico Acts: Why Britain Turned its Back on Cotton, History Theses, University of Puget Sound, p_sher@pugetsound.edu, retrieved from http://soundideas.pugetsound.edu/cgi/viewcontent.cgi?article=1001&context=history_theses, 2012.

Gerhard, Peter. Pirates of New Spain 1575–1742, Dover Publications, 31 East 2nd St. Mineola, NY 11501, 2003.

Gretton, Lel. Old and Interesting, Everyday Domestic Pottery, US & UK Traditions, numerous articles, retrieved from http://www.oldandinteresting.com/pottery-earthenware.aspx, copyright date not given.

Hamer, Frank, The Potter's Dictionary of Materials and Techniques, Watson-Guptill, 1975.

Harmon's Snowshoemen. Benjamin Church's Company 1675–1701, retrieved from http://www.snowshoemen.com, no copyright information given.

Harrison, Michael. The Alderney Elizabethan Wreck. The Alderney Museum, Alderney Museum Trust, High Street, St. Anne, Alderney, Channel Islands, GY9 3TG, or email hugo@alderney-wreck.com, retrieved from http://www.alderneywreck.com, copyright date not given.

Hart, Avril & North, Susan. 17th and 18th Century Fashion in Detail, V & A Publishing, 2009.

Hawkins, Paul. Captain William Kidd, Site design and layout Copyright by Paul Hawkins, pfrh@live.com, retrieved in March, 2014 from http://www.captainkidd.org, 2000, 2009.

Herriot, David. The Information of David Herriot and Ignatius Pell contained the Appendix to: The Tryals of Major Stede Bonnet, and Other Pirates, London, Printed for Benj. Cowse at the Rose and Crown in St. Paul's Church-Yard, 1719.

Heymsfeld, Ralph. Collecting the Coins of France, retrieved in January 2014 from http://www.coinspot.org/france.html, no copyright information given.

Hirschfilder, Gunther & Trummer, Manuel. Food and Drink, retrieved from http://ieg-ego.eu/en/threads/backgrounds/food-and-drink/gunther-hirschfelder-manuel-trummer-food-and-drink. Published, Copyright August 20, 2013.

Hirst, Kris. The Domestication of Cassava, retrieved from http://archaeology.about.com/od/caterms/qt/cassava.htm, About.com, 2014

Historic Florida Militia, Searle's Attack on Saint Augustine, made possible in part by a grant from the St. Johns County Tourism and Development Council, retrieved in September 2014 from http://historic-florida-militia.org/events/annual/searles.

Website by DeeLee Productions, LLC, 2014.

Hughson, Shirley Carter. Blackbeard & The Carolina Pirates 1670–1740, first published in 1894, current edition Port Hampton Press, Port Hampton History Foundation, 115 Harbor Drive, Hampton, VA 23661, 2000.

Hugill, Stan. Shanties from the Seven Seas, Mystic Seaport, 75 Greenmanville Ave., P. O. Box 6000, Mystic CT 06355, 1961, 1994.

Hume, Ivor Noel. Early English Delftware from London and Virginia. Colonial Williamsburg Foundation, 1977.

Hume, Ivor Noel. A Guide to Artifacts of Early America. Alfred A. Knopf Press, New York, 1985.

Jefferson Patterson Park and Museum. Stoneware, Maryland Archaeological Conservation Lab, retrieved from http://www.jefpat.org, copyright 2002, 2008.

Johnson, Charles. A General History of Pyrates, Original edition published in London, 1724, second edition, 1724, third edition 1725, Daniel Defoe, A General History of the Pyrates, edited by Manuel Schonhorn. Dover Publication, Dover Publications Inc. 31 East 2nd St. Mineola, NY 11501, 1999.

Jordan, Louis. A Brief Outline of Dutch History and the Providence of New Netherland, Department of Special Collections, University of Notre Dame, Notre Dame, IN, retrieved in January 2014 from http://www.coins.nd.edu/ColCoin/ColCoinIntros/Netherlands.html, no copyright information given.

Journal of the Royal Artillery, including excerpts from The Art of Gunnery, published in London in 1647 by Nat Nye, Royal Artillery Institution, 1861.

Juniper, Sarah B. Hand Sewn Boots and Shows, 109 Woodmancole, Dursley, Gloucestershire GL11 4AH, United Kingdom, email: sarah@sarahjuniper.co.uk, retrieved from http://www.sarahjuniper.co.uk/index.html, no copyright information given.

Ketchum, William. American Redware, Henry Holt & Co., 1991.

Konstam, Angus. Pirates 1660–1730, Osprey Publishing, Osprey Direct, care of Random House Distribution Center, 400 Hahn Rd, Westminster, MD 21157, 1998.

Konstam, Angus. The Pirate Ship 1660–1730, Osprey Publishing, Osprey Direct, care of Random House Distribution Center, 400 Hahn Rd, Westminster, MD 21157, 2003.

Konstam, Angus with Kean, Roger Michael. Pirates, Praetors of the Seas, Skyhorse Publishing, and Text and Design, Thalamus Publishing, Skyhorse Publishing, 555 8th Ave., Suite 903, NY, NY 10018, 2007.

Konstam, Angus. Blackbeard, America's Most Notorious Pirate, John Wiley and Sons Inc., 111 River St., Hoboken, NJ 07030, 2006.

Konstam, Angus. The History of Pirates, The Lyons Press, PO Box 480, Guilford, CT 06437, 1999, 2002.

Konstam, Angus. Scourge of the Seas, Buccaneers, Pirates, and Privateers, Osprey Publishing, 443 Park Ave South, New York, NY 10016, 2007.

Kupperman, Karen Ordahl, Providence Island, 1630–1641, Cambridge University Press, 1995.

Landstrom, Bjorn. The Ship, An Illustrated History, Doubleday & Company Inc., Garden City, NY, also Produced by Interpublishing AB, Stockholm, 1961.

Laver, James, art by Brook, Iris. English Costumes of the Eighteenth Century, Morrison and Gibb Ltd., London and Edinburgh, S. & C. Black, Ltd., 4, 5 & 6 Soho Square, London, W. 1, 1931.

Lavin, James D. A History of Spanish Firearms, Arco Publishing Co., 1965.

Lee, Robert E. Blackbeard the Pirate, A Reappraisal of His Life and Times, John F. Blair Publisher, 1406 Plaza Drive, Winston-Salem, NC 27103, 1974.

Leigh, Laura. Fine English and Irish Antique Glass, Laura Leigh Antiques, Church Street, Gloucestershire, GL54 1BB, retrieved in 2009 from http://www.laurieleighantiques.com/pages/wineglasses.html, no copyright information given.

Levins, Hoag. Pineapple History, Email: HoagL@earthlink.net, retrieved in 2013 from http://www.levins.com/pineapple.html, copyright 1995, 2009.

Ligon, Richard. The True and Exact History of the Island of Barbadoes 1657, This Edition edited and annotated by J. Edward Hutson, Cole's Printery Ltd., Wildey St. Michael, Barbados, Email: natrust@sunbeach.net, 2000.

Linnane, John BSc, MSc. A History of Irish Cuisine Before and After the Potato,

Email: Jflinnane@dit.ie, retrieved in October 2010 from http://www.ravensgard.org/prdunham/irishfood.html, copyright 2000.

Little, Benerson. The Sea Rover's Practice, Pirate Tactics and Techniques, 1630–1730, Potomac Books Inc., 22841 Quicksilver Drive, Dulles, VA 20166, 2005.

Main Rum Company Limited. History of Rum, email: mainrum@btconnect.com, retrieved from http://www.mainrum.co.uk/historyofrum.htm, copyright date not given.

Manucy, Albert. Artillery Through the Ages, US Government Printing Office, Division of Publications, National Park Service, US Department of the Interior, Washington DC, 20402, 1949, 1985.

Marcus Hook Preservation Society. The Plank House, Marcus Hook Preservation Society, P. O. Box 703, Marcus Hook, PA 19061, retrieved from http://www.marcushookps.org, copyright 2014.

Marine Research Society. The Pirates Own Book, Authentic Narratives of the Most Celebrated Sea Robbers, originally published as Publication Number Four of the Marine Research Society, Salem, Massachusetts in 1924, Dover Publications, Inc., 31 East 2nd St. Mineola, NY 11501, 1993.

Matterer, James L. 17th Century English Recipes, The Accomplish'd Lady's Delight, 1675, retrieved from http://www.godecookery.com/engrec/engrec.html, 1997, 2009.

McCellan, Elizabeth. Historic Dress in America 1607–1800, Philadelphia, G. W. Jacobs & Co., Book contributor: University of California Libraries Collection: cdl; americana, Possible copyright status: NOT IN COPYRIGHT.

McMonnon, Rhondda. 18th Century Clothing & Accoutrements, email: http://www.digits.com, retrieved in 2011 from http://www.18cnewenglandlife.org/index.htm, copyright 1996.

Mesnier, Charles. Excerpt from a letter from Charles Mesnier, Intendant of Martinique, describing the capture of the French slave ship La Concorde, of Nantes. La Concorde was owned by Rene Montaudouin, and commanded by Capt. Pierre Dosset. Aix-en-Provence. Centre des archives d'outre-mer. AN Col C8A 22 (1717) f°447. 10 décembre 1717.

Millar, John Fitzhugh. Buccaneers Davis, Wafer & Hingson, and the Ship Batchelors Delight, William and Mary Alumni Association, One Alumni Drive, Post Office Box 2100, Williamsburg, VA 23187, retrieved in 2012 from https://www.wmalumni.com/?summer10_pirates, no copyright information given.

Montegomery, Florence M. Textiles in America 1650–1870, W. W. Norton and Co., 500 5th Ave., New York, NY 10110, www.wwnorton.com, 2007.

Museum of London. Ceramics and Glass Collection, Museum of London, Mortimer Wheeler House, 46 Eagle Wharf Road, London N1 7ED, retrieved from http://www.museumoflondon.org.uk/ceramics, copyright date not given.

Nassau, Paradise Island Promotion Board. Nassau, Our History, Tourism Internet Marketing by VERB, retrieved from http://www.nassauparadiseisland.com/about-the-island/our-history, copyright 2014.

National Maritime Museum, Collections, retrieved in 2009 from http://www.nmm.ac.uk, Copyright 2012.

Native American Technology and Art. Evolution of Maize Agriculture, retrieved from http://www.nativetech.org/cornhusk/cornhusk.html, Native Tech, 1994.

Nello's Itally, L. L. C. Pomodoro! The Tomato in Italy and my Kitchen, retrieved from http://www.nellositaly.com/the-history-of-the-tomato-in-italy.html, Nello's Italy, P.O. Box 80441, Raleigh, NC, 2014.

Newton, Arthur Percival. The European Nations in the West Indies, 1493–1688, London, Adam & Charles Black, 1966.

North Carolina Maritime Museum. Queen Anne's Revenge, North Carolina Maritime Museum, 315 Front Street, Beaufort, NC 28516, retrieved in 2009 from http://www.ncmaritime.org, copyright 2013.

Perez-Mallaina, Pablo E. Spain's Men of the Sea, Daily life on the Indes Fleets in the Sixteenth Century, Translated by Carla Rahn Phillips, Johns Hopkins University Press, Baltimore,1998.

Peterson, Harold. Arms and Armor in Colonial America 1526–1783, Dover Publications, 2000.

Peterson, Harold. Round Shot and Rammers, South Bend Replicas, INC., 61650 Oak Rd., South Bend, Indiana 46614, 1969.

Phillips, Michael. The Age of Nelson, retrieved in January 2014 from http://www.ageofnelson.org/MichaelPhillips/info.php?ref=5105, copyright 1995, 2007.

Pirate Images, Pirate Maps, email: beej@beej.us, retrieved from http://beej.us/pirates/piratemaps.html, no copyright information given.

Pope, Dudley. Harry Morgan's Way, House of Stratus, Stratus Books Ltd. 21 Beeching Park, Kelly Bray, Cornwall, PL 17 8 QS UK, 1977, 2001.

Porter, David. Eighteenth Century England, Coins, Currency, and Cash in Eighteenth Century England, Money and Denominations, Department of English, University of Michigan, Student Project Showcase, retrieved in February 2014, from http://www.umich.edu/~ece/student_projects/money/denom.html, no copyright information given.

Powell, John T. Military Artifacts from Spanish Florida, 1539–1821, An Internet Museum, retrieved in 2010 from http://www.artifacts.org/default.htm, copyright 1998, 2004.

Quimby, Ian (editor). Ceramics in America, University Press of Virginia, 1972.

Randolph, Anthony G. The Analysis and Conservation of the Belle Footwear Assemblage, A theses submitted to Texas A&M University, 1/ETD-TAMU-2003-THESIS-R378, retrieved from http://repository.tamu.edu/handle/1969, Copyright 2003.

Rice, Prudence. Pottery Analysis, The University of Chicago Press, 1987.

Ringrose, Basil. A Buccaneer's Atlas, A Sea Atlas and Sailing Directions of the Pacific Coast of the Americas, 1682, edited by Derek Howse and Norman J. W. Thrower, University of California Press, 2004.

Ross, Kelly L. PhD. British Coins before the Florin, Compared to French Coins of the Ancien Régime, retrieved in September 2014 from http://www.friesian.com/coins.htm, Copyright 1997, 1999, 2002, 2007, 2009, 2010, 2013.

Ruiz, Bruce C. Panama History of Pirates, retrieved in August 2013 from http://www.bruceruiz.net/PanamaHistory/Pirates/pirates_and_buccaneers.htm , September 19, 2002.

Salinger, Sharon. Taverns and Drinking in Early America, Johns Hopkins University Press, 2715 North Charles St., Baltimore, MD 21218, 2002.

Sedwick, Daniel Frank LLC. The Colonial Coinage of Colonial America, P.O. Box 1964, Winter Park, Florida 32790, Email: office@sedwickcoins.com, retrieved in September 2014 from http://www.sedwickcoins.com/articles/colonialcoinage.htm, copyright 2008.

Seitz, Don Carlos. Under the Black Flag: Exploits of the Most Notorious Pirates, Courier Dover Publications, 2002.

Smith, Andrew F. Peanuts, The Illustrious History of the Goober Pea, University of Illinois Press, 2002.

Smith, Julia. Historic Pottery Reproductions, Our Pottery in Colonial America, email: julia@juliasmith.com, retrieved from http://www.juliasmith.com/historicpottery, no copyright information given.

Smith, Woodruff D. Consumption and the Making of Respectability, 1600–1800, Routledge, 29 West 35th St, New York, NY, 2002.

Spargo, John. Early American Pottery and China. Charles E. Tuttle Company, Rutland, Vermont, 1974.

Squire, Geoffrey. Dress and Society: 1560–1970, New York: The Viking Press, Inc. 1974.

Wright, Irene. Nederlandsche zeevaarders op de eilanden in de caraibische zee en aan de kust van columbia en venezuela gedurende de jaren 1621–1648, Irene A. Wright, translated from Spanish by C.F.A. van Dam, Utrecht, Kemink, 1935.

STAY IN THE KNOW

Be among the first to know about Robert Jacob's appearances and pirate news.

www.RobertJacobAuthor.com

ALSO AVAILABLE FROM AWARD-WINNING, BESTSELLING AUTHOR, ROBERT JACOB

Pirates of the Florida Coast: Truth, Legends, and Myths

ISBN: 978-1-950075-59-1 Hard Cover)
ISBN: 978-1-950075-09-6 (Paperback)
ISBN: 978-1-950075-11-9 (ePub)
ASIN: B09HYMBKQ6

Florida has a long and rich history of pirates plundering its shores, cities, and shipping lanes. Tales of Florida pirates abound from Key West to Pensacola and from Miami to Jacksonville. But how much of it is true? Come aboard and join Robert Jacob on a captivating adventure into the world of pirate lore.

Digging deep into the true history of piracy along the Florida coast, Robert has unearthed a treasure of information that reveals the truths and identifies the myths about Florida Pirates from Sir Francis Drake to José Gaspar. *Pirates of the Florida Coast: Truths, Legends, and Myths* will transport you back to old Florida and paint a vivid picture of piracy throughout the years.

Blackbeard: The Truth Revealed

ISBN: 978-1-957832-39-5 (Hard Cover)
ISBN: 978-1-957832-41-8 (Paperback)
ISBN: 978-1-957832-40-1 (ePub)
ASIN: B0D4WVQFQM

Finally, an accurate, comprehensive, and well-researched book on the world's most famous pirate has been published. *Blackbeard: The Truth Revealed* provides all the known facts and details about Blackbeard as well as discussion on his myths and legends. It's the book that Blackbeard enthusiasts have been waiting for since 1718.

Set sail with Robert Jacob as he unravels the mysteries and uncovers the truth about Blackbeard. Logical explanations, clear commentary, and visual descriptions will organize and clarify potentially confusing facts encountered throughout your literary voyage. Robert will expertly navigate you through the extensive array of records, including authoritative research and original eighteenth-century manuscripts, that corroborate the authenticity of Blackbeard's motivations, actions, and interactions with other pirates.

www.ingramcontent.com/pod-product-compliance
Lightning Source LLC
Chambersburg PA
CBHW080832230426
43665CB00021B/2822